CONTENTS

Publisher's Note ix

Diarist's Note xi

I. 1964 1

Vacation in Jamaica—Utilization of Western coal for energy—Inter-American Development Bank: integration in Latin America—Trip to Colombia—Visits with: Robert Oppenheimer and Edward Murrow—Trip to Iran—White House luncheon for Shah of Iran—University of California (Los Angeles) Commencement and the Shah of Iran—Trip to Colombia-Venezuela border area—Meeting with President Johnson—Visit with President Truman in Independence—Trip to Peru

II. 1965 77

Trip to India—In Iran, attempt on the Shah's life—Development in the Ivory Coast—Indiana University Commencement—Trip to Peru—Latin American integration study—Visits with: George Kennan, John Gunther, and Roger Baldwin

III. 1966 181

Meeting with President Johnson—White House dinner for Prime Minister Gandhi—Peace Corps undertaking—Trip to Colombia

—White House discussions about postwar economic planning in Vietnam—Trip to Colombia and Venezuela—Fairless Lectures at Carnegie Institute of Technology—Agroindustrial pioneering in Khuzistan—Senator Robert Kennedy and Bedford-Stuyvesant project

IV. 1967 339

Trip to Colombia—Washington and preparation for Vietnam undertaking—Trip to Hawaii, Thailand, and Vietnam—Report to President Johnson—Conference at Guam—University of Illinois Commencement—State dinner at White House for Shah of Iran—Trip to Vietnam—Report to President Johnson and the Cabinet—Trip to French Polynesia en route to Australia

Index 537

A section of illustrations follows page 238.

PUBLISHER'S NOTE

When David Lilienthal wrote *This I Do Believe* in 1949, he electrified the country; this short book is a ringing affirmation of faith in the power and dignity of the individual.

In *TVA: Democracy on the March*, published in 1944, Mr. Lilienthal told vividly about his experience, which was to extend from 1933 to 1946, as chief architect and founding Director of the Tennessee Valley Authority, the vast development project which changed the landscape of an area the size of England and Scotland and remade the lives of millions of people. Following this unique achievement, Mr. Lilienthal was appointed the first Chairman of the Atomic Energy Commission, a position he held from 1946 to 1950, the period of America's atomic weapons monopoly, during which a secret struggle for nuclear control took place between civilian and military leadership and the decision was made to produce the H-bomb. When Lilienthal resigned from the Commission, he was "the most controversial figure in Washington since the end of the war," one newspaper wrote.

In February of 1976 David Lilienthal asserted, "We are the greatest underdeveloped country in the world." He meant that the United States has tremendous opportunities for further development—opportunities which have been neglected for decades, such as the chemical conversion of coal to oil. Mr. Lilienthal knows whereof he speaks, for his signal contribution in the last twenty years has been to develop energy—electrical and human—in foreign lands through the Development and Resources Corporation, which he invented, in 1955, as a unique kind of corporate enterprise—a private profit-making business with public service objectives.

In 1964 the first volume of David Lilienthal's *Journals* was published; it was recognized as a major publishing event and, as succeeding volumes appeared, this series was hailed by Allan Nevins as an "unmatched and probably unmatchable record." Volume VI, *Creativity and Conflict*, dealing with the years 1964–1967, covers a wide range of important events and personalities, from atomic hazards to the author's development work in Iran and South Vietnam. Written in an easy, informal diarist's style, the book makes absorbing reading.

DIARIST'S NOTE

The life I lived during the years 1964 through 1967 was an active one. Many of the events I participated in and recorded and reflected upon in these entries were not without significance. But it is the personal narrative of the inner life of one particular man exposed to a broad range of experiences that is the essence of this volume. So the entries, reproduced virtually as written, tell of elation and euphoria, of frustrations and disappointments, of vanity and self-pity, of the ebb and flow of high energy and extreme fatigue. In short, this volume tells the way it was with a man of action who wrote from day to day of what he saw, and was part of, in many parts of the world.

During the years in which these entries were written, the whole world was going through a period of tension and of creativity. This was the setting for my own personal story of intense activity and worldwide travel, interspersed with episodes of peace of spirit, of the joys of human relationships, and observation of nature at its most glorious.

Vignettes of hundreds of particular individuals—people of great and small estate in many countries—are scattered through the entries. There are close-ups of Peruvians, Thais, Colombians; of American Senators and diplomats; of Iranian leaders and villagers; of American and foreign technocrats and international civil servants; and of high-ranking military officers, American and foreign. People on the streets of New York City are here, along with famous scientists (entries shed light on the last days of Robert Oppenheimer) and journalists, publishers, and broadcasters, among them Charles Collingwood, John Oakes, Ed Murrow, and Hugh Downs. There is a detailed account of the meeting with the South Vietnamese leadership in late March, 1967, on the island of Guam, participated in by such Americans as Averell Harriman, Henry Cabot Lodge, Ellsworth Bunker, and General Westmoreland. President Lyndon Johnson is seen in the White House, on "Air Force One" flying the Pacific, and in Guam. Many as-it-happened entries describe my personal and working relations and encounters under a variety of circumstances with a man now in the center of world attention, the Shah of Iran: just after an attempt had been made to assassinate him; in a new agricultural center in once-desert Khuzistan; in a hotel suite in Los Angeles; in the Imperial Palace in Tehran.

Many of these entries of nearly a decade ago are a preview of the present, and a picture of the unfolding future. The major problems that impinge upon the everyday life and concerns of the average citizen in 1976 are foreshadowed in entries in this volume, as seen through my eyes, my bias, and my background of experience. Thus, here the "energy crisis" is portrayed in an earlier guise: the sobering hazards as well as the promise of atomic energy; the potential, as an alternative to imported petroleum, of Rocky Mountain coal and its conversion to liquid and gas fuel. Here is evidence, among nations that supply raw materials, of the gathering clouds of resistance to exploitation of their resources for the benefit of the industrialized countries. A dramatic meeting at the border of Venezuela and Colombia which foreshadowed what has become the Andean Common Market is recounted in these entries. And there are on-the-spot entries from South Vietnam critical of American efforts to solve foreign policy problems by military measures.

Here is evidence as well of the growing—and now almost complete—disillusion with dehumanizing banker-style project-by-project economic "aid" to developing countries, which is in contrast to the humanist integrated methods of the Development and Resources Corporation, the unique institution that I founded in 1955, whose continuing trials and achievements in combining the idealism of public service with the disciplines and constraints of private enterprise are recounted in these entries.

No words are adequate to express my personal as well as professional indebtedness to my wife and partner in most of the activities described in this volume, as well as in those that preceded it, recorded in the first five volumes of these journals. Ours has been for over fifty years both an intimate and supportive relation, which happily continues to this day. It was my wife's monumental task to help me to select the entries to be published (limits of space permitted the publication of only about one-third of the total entries I wrote during the four years of this volume) and to collaborate in preparing the manuscript for the printer. Hers too was the innovative design and execution of the index, a tool without which such a chronological account as this, covering so many subjects and events, would be far less useful.

I wrote the entries in many places and circumstances, all in Gregg shorthand. The transcription of these by my secretary and friend Miss Mildred Baron was a tour de force of skill, stamina, and good humor for which I am grateful and deeply admiring. I also acknowledge with gratitude the many sensitive comments and suggestions of my lifelong friend Beatrice S. Tobey, and the encouragement and guidance of the dean of American publishers, Cass Canfield.

D.E.L.

Princeton
February, 1976

The Journals of David E. Lilienthal

VOLUME VI

CREATIVITY AND CONFLICT

I

1964

Vacation in Jamaica—Utilization of Western coal for energy—Inter-American Development Bank: integration in Latin America—Trip to Colombia—Visits with: Robert Oppenheimer and Edward Murrow—Trip to Iran—White House luncheon for Shah of Iran—University of California (Los Angeles) Commencement and the Shah of Iran—Trip to Colombia-Venezuela border area—Meeting with President Johnson—Visit with President Truman in Independence—Trip to Peru

JANUARY 1, 1964
1:30 A.M.
OCHO RIOS, JAMAICA

Happy New Year! Helen and I are just back from a party at the Spences' lovely island home, "High Hope."

I was struck by the "entrance," in the Spences' great living room, of a tall woman introduced to me as Mrs. Jacobs, wife of a Jamaican physician. She turned out to be the redoubtable Rt. Honorable Beth Jacobs, who had been among the speakers at a recent Planned Parenthood dinner at the Plaza.

I ventured the opinion that the Family Planning "movement" (of which Cass Canfield is the Honorary Chairman) needed to develop more affirmative ways of stating the case. Could increased and improved food production be made part of the concept? Could not the two concepts, population control and limitation *and* greatly increasing food production using methods we now know about—could not these two be joined, married into a *single* program, giving the population control movement a more positive, less fearsome appeal? Could the population control movement also include the movement of populations giving young people in an overcrowded country encouragement and help in settling in a country that *needed* people? For I am clear that overpopulation is *not everywhere* the grave issue it is portrayed to be in the literature of the family planning councils.

Beth Jacobs on this was very forthright. "The trouble is, you see, that the countries that are overpopulated are those of color; and people of color are not wanted in countries that could use them. You speak of a million Indians—where would they go? Not, as you suggest, to Australia; they won't *have* anyone of color."

Later, her determined-looking husband, Dr. Lenworth Jacobs, said: "I went through the experience of being refused admission to hotels and places to eat in America. I learned to hate. And then I met the lady who later, as it happens, became my wife, and I learned to love, and learned that you can't truly love unless you have also known what it is to hate. And now I do not hate, ever."

JANUARY 2, 1964
OCHO RIOS

Dinner with John Humphrey and his wife. He is Secretary General of the Commission on Human Rights of the U.N., a handsome grey-haired man with penetrating blue eyes. He spoke of being in Vietnam with a fact finding commission, looking into charges of violations of the rights of the Buddhists. Then he was sent to Afghanistan—he didn't know why, and neither did the Afghans. On a chance he suggested holding an international conference on Human Rights in Kabul; the idea was cordially received. He had also been to Australia recently, again on Human Rights matters.

I said something about how interesting a life it must be, going about the world on so important an issue. He looked at me sadly and said, "Yes; but it would be good to do something *concrete*."

JANUARY 6, 1964
NEW YORK

About six o'clock a call from Charles Mohr of the *New York Times*. Con Edison has just announced that they have withdrawn their application to build a big nuclear power plant in New York, that instead they will buy water power from Canada. "Since it was your statement of opposition to the plant that started the controversy about its safety, the *Times* would like to have any comment you care to make."

I could only say blandly that I thought their decision was in the interest of the health and safety of the people of Greater New York, and Con Ed was to be congratulated.

Never let it be said that one man's voice is *always* negligible, even against such formidable forces.

As we struggled to get our baggage last night at Kennedy Airport I was struck by the obvious prosperity of the passengers racing to get through customs.

As we left I noticed, for the first time, a carved inscription in the marble of a wall, a quote from Emma Lazarus' great poem about the Statue of Liberty, she who holds aloft so prominently the flame which I see from my office window. "Give me your tired, your poor, your huddled masses," etc., it read. Well, the irony of it, as I looked around at my super-affluent fellow returnees from Jamaica and elsewhere, was too much, and I had to stop and roar with laughter.

JANUARY 7, 1964
NEW YORK

This working day began at a little after 7 A.M.; at 7 P.M. I was still at work, one of my few twelve-hour days lately. What a day: such steady outpouring of energy, of exposition, of attempted, and largely successful, persuasion! In short, our first full-scale meeting with our new D&R [Development and Resources] partners, the Utah Construction group.

Gathered in my office, under a glowing painting, eleven and sometimes more of us explored and explained what D&R has done and, thereby, the range of what it is capable of doing. This was "business" at its most satisfying—to see the respect that men confer on a remarkable achievement in so short a time. But most satisfying of all, these "private enterprise" lads from the West said in a half dozen different ways: your company is unique, there is nothing quite like it. And one of the things that makes it so is the sense of concern for "the public interest." That is a great asset; don't let us of Utah do anything that will spoil that image.

At one point we discussed our ideas of Western coal and the expanding need for electricity in the West. Ed Littlefield, a D&R Director and head of Utah Construction, said: "The conflict between private electric power and public power in the West is so intense, the antagonism to Government having anything to do with power so strong, that one utility executive told me: 'I would not buy one ton of coal from any mining company that sold any coal at all to a public power outfit.'" I said: "That man is on his way out; that isn't a position that is maintainable in the face of the facts of life."

JANUARY 12, 1964
SATURDAY, 10:30 P.M.
PRINCETON

David and I are knocking out the very last of the MS of the second volume of the *Journals*, *The Atomic Energy Years*, and knocking me out in the process.

The process we are going through is sometimes knotty and perplexing: "*What* does that phrase mean, for God's sake; what the hell did I have in mind?" I mutter as I read some vague and perhaps intentionally undecipherable entry made in the "secret" atomic energy days when "security" had become second nature, yet apparently I felt I just *must* write of some experience or episode or I would bust. *Or*, "Why, Dad, did you cut out that little paragraph of satisfaction in getting a lecture 'fee' of $350?" ("It will help," I had written.) "Well," I respond, "it seemed so trivial, in the middle of the death and destruction issues I was dealing with at the time, and of no possible interest to a reader of the *Journals* today." A big grin from David, who has a devastating smile when he turns it on. "Do as you want to, but I thought it was charming, for the very reason that it is so human, to be thinking about little things like that right in the middle of these big public issues. That's part of the point of the *Journals* as a whole; instead of a guy behind a long white beard issuing communiqués, there's a man like the rest of us."

JANUARY 13, 1964
PRINCETON

Luncheon meeting at Lazard last Wednesday noon. André Meyer [the senior partner] looking avuncular and gracious indeed at the head of the long table in the Lazard dining room; I at the other end. In between, twelve men: several from D&R, several from Utah.

We talked about "David's big Western energy idea"; I was glad this came up in André's presence, for the dimensions of the concept are so great that only a big man—and André comes closer to that than any single financial man I know—would respond to it. One of the Utah men remarked that the "assumption" that atomic energy would be the source of electricity for the *full* needs of the West Coast had been pretty well "accepted" by most utility men, but Utah thought differently for a long time; he was interested to find that D&R had the same, or a similar, conviction.

JANUARY 14, 1964
NEW YORK

Talked informally last night on how change comes about, as the guest of a dinner discussion group. These are very intelligent, lively minded intellectuals. None have had the kind of life of action that I have had. They seemed to find especially interesting the specifics, illustrations drawn chiefly from my Persian experience. I emphasized how primitive—almost without change—was the life of the peasants, and yet how they had begun to learn *by doing*, so that there was a complete change in their way of producing the substance of life, food. Every once in a while the verbal *abstractions* which are the stock in trade of my hosts would show how little they could comprehend these specifics.

One member, long committed to the future of nuclear energy, gave it to me straight about how sad my "defection"—criticism of atomic energy—had made the many men "who had been stirred by your great leadership and now found you had deserted them," adding that my criticism of the Con Ed plant for Queens and particularly my American Nuclear Society speech* were acts of treachery.

This is quite a price to pay, for saying your say.

What he said should be taken in some perspective, though: He has a strong professional commitment to nuclear power. Just the same, I should not minimize what he has said. The scientific community, perhaps almost to a man, once looked upon me as their spokesman and defender; now, smarting and furious about what I have said and the debacle of the Con Ed plant, they regard me as a turncoat.

JANUARY 17, 1964
PRINCETON

I have just spent three solid hours with thirteen men who are in "mid-career." Drawn from almost every conceivable branch of the Federal service, they have been given a year at Princeton as Princeton Fellows in Public Affairs to think things over, go to classes, argue and exchange ideas among themselves.

We ranged from my idea of where foreign aid had gotten off the track, to Persia and what my company does there, to AEC and the Con Ed issue, to my criticism of the esoteric "think tank" types.

This session found me bringing to the surface, from the deeps of my subconscious, hunches about what one looks for in a public servant, indeed in any man who bears responsibility for a particular job or a broad function.

* November 19, 1963 (Vol. V, pp. 521, 527).

Can the special quality that sets one man off from another be *taught* in a university? I mean that quality which sets off A as reliable and creative and effective, and B as stodgy, full of words, or steeped in technique and little else?

What is it you want in a man? Technique in personnel management, procurement practices, or fiscal management? This you can acquire by study and training of the kind a university provides. But that isn't the most valuable, the essential quality. What you want is that amorphous thing called "judgment," which is a composite of many things, mostly character, temperament, and morality (in the broad and classic sense). Judgment and "guts," these are the two essential qualities. Can you teach a man "guts" in a classroom or through books?

Perspective, motivation, respect for your function as a member of the Government, these *are* things that can be taught academically, I should think, and they can strengthen the inherent personal qualities which are the components of judgment and guts.

JANUARY 18, 1964
5 P.M.
PRINCETON

Just back from a walk to the rise that overlooks the Institute; the dark curves of the roadway, the etched trees against the soft glow of a winter's twilight sun, all held in a kind of faraway enchantment by the visible air. The almost solid but soft blue light enfolds the purple-white of the everywhere-snow, and it enfolds me too, as I trudge along, overcome by the beauty of it, looking straight into the lowering sun, its brassy glitter and low flame repeated in reflected torches of blazing windows.

There is a spell that winter casts that is unlike any other; the silence that can be seen and, strangely, heard is so real to the sense: the purity of white out of which the dark of trees and shadows flows.

And to think that all this contained and quiet beauty came out of the teeth of the tempest of a few days ago, the earth groaning in ecstasy and screaming and moaning and holding on for dear life as the powdery white took command, whirling and exploding and racing from corner to corner as if pursued by invisible hands in fierce play. Now such peace. Under the white (the sky is still faintly glowing) lies my garden, dormant but not dead, dormant as I am in these interstices of rest and motionless slack tide, when the high energies and the excitement of struggle are still, satisfied and happy—satisfied and happy because soon the struggle will begin again and the excitement and zest return.

Here, like the fallen rain returning once again to the clouds, is another of those majestic cycles of nature, where the end is always a new beginning.

9 P.M.

The wonders of diversity!

How I revel in diversity, and particularly the diversity of the many faces of mankind.

This afternoon I met Lyman Spitzer, astronomer and authority on stellar space and such erudite subjects as the "conductivity of ionized gases," a subject which has produced a new role for the astronomer in the Princeton Forrestal Lab's work on thermonuclear energy. Intense, spare, jerky in physical manner, not a man for a relaxed fishing expedition I would say; but though we conversed hardly at all it fascinated me to be in the same room with such a brain.

JANUARY 21, 1964
NEW YORK

At the Motor Boat Show at the Coliseum: the sailboats all have their sails set—what a beautiful sight—despite being surrounded by big chrome-ishy flashy motor cruisers. Is there *anyone* more snobbish than a small-boat sailor sneering at a big-engined cruiser?

God, the waters will be as full as the streets are now, come another five years of prosperity!

JANUARY 23, 1964
NEW YORK

Ken Galbraith was billed as the speaker at a Planned Parenthood fund raising dinner tonight. I looked forward to hearing Ken; I assumed his speaking style would be as fluent and witty as his writing is.

What a letdown (if "down" can be used for a human being so elongated). For he uh-ed and uh-uh-ed between words, he put his glasses on and took them off in a most distracting and professorial way.

What he said was that India is overpopulated and is becoming more so; that it is time to do something about it. The silver-haired Lady Rama Rau (so handsome in her lovely sari) replied with gentle asperity: India knew it had a problem, that the family planning movement, internationally, *began* in Bombay years ago, and that *everything*, including sterilization and even abortion, was approved policy—but the results were meager so far.

JANUARY 25, 1964
PRINCETON

A most unusual experience Thursday night: seeing a play portraying an event in the real life of a man who was our host at the theatre, then having "supper afterward" (at the Algonquin) with the actor who did the portraying and the "real" man he portrayed. The host was the famous trial lawyer Louis Nizer; the play, *A Case of Libel*; the actor, Van Heflin.

With us at the theatre, and at dinner before, was one of the wonder men of the contemporary theatre, Alan Jay Lerner, who wrote the books and lyrics for *My Fair Lady*, *Gigi*, *Brigadoon*, *Camelot*, etc., and his dazzling young wife, Micheline.

Lerner was taut. Even the curls of his jaunty head seem wound up tight. Made me think of a lightweight boxer in fighting trim. But as the evening wore on, you could almost see the lines of care draw their way across his brow and down his cheeks, his eyes become weary and abstracted. One eye is a bit askew, which adds to a certain look of bewilderment he has.

Friday morning I met around a great round table with some forty men, members or staff of a special committee on "Improvement of Executive Management in the Federal Government."

The most voluble was [former Senator] Bill Benton, who is never at a loss for words. His chief contribution was to say that the ability of an executive in Government to get work done efficiently might well depend on "owning a piece of a powerful Senator." I found this *not* amusing and felt impelled to respond that in public service it was the *constituency*, not the Senator, that counted most; as in business, in the end it is the "customer" who is always right.

Former Defense Secretary McElroy, a handsome huge pink-faced man, made a lot of sense. "You have to learn that efficiency in Government may be a good thing or it may not, but it has little relevance to efficiency *in business*. It takes longer to get things done in Government because you have to explain things to a lot of people and persuade them, and that time is well spent. If, because it takes longer, that is inefficiency, that isn't a very good definition of efficiency as applied to many Government activities."

Jim Webb, head of the Space Agency, as full of propellants as his Titan II rocket and contemptuous of everything about "Government management" that is B.S. (Before Space), roared off his launching pad a couple seats from me in the most original and by all odds most spirited performance of the morning.

He had listened to John Corson describe the "project" for analyzing management among the cadre of 5000 top or middle "executives" who "run" the Federal Government: Personnel management is recruitment, incentives, compensation, etc., the prosaic techniques one must bring to his job.

"I would like to say some things that will be abrasive about my friend John Corson's report," Jim said. "Since the end of World War II everything has changed." Then he lit into a dazzling picture of the Space Agency's executive programs—dazzling because of the super-management concepts, the great amount of dollars he is spending, the range of American industry involved—all in contrast to Corson's more conventional approach to the "improvement" of Government management.

JANUARY 30, 1964
WASHINGTON, D.C.

The way you can tell whether a man has guts—an essential quality of a good public servant—is to see him after he has been exposed to controversy, Congressional attack, Presidential indecision, and newspaper columnist "advice" on just what he should do.

This noon I sat with the towering David Bell, who as head of the Agency for International Development had recently been through the fiery furnace. He passes the test, my test at least.

That same boyish grin, the same sidelong look of concentration on what you are saying, an interest in the future rather than a rubbing of old sores, a bit of irony in his manner but no expressed bitterness. All in all, a fine example of a public servant whose stature and character have been strengthened, not impaired, by a really rough experience.

Bell found my "theme" of the high priority for food very much to his own thinking. This emphasis on food is my latest way of stating the old proposition of "unified" or comprehensive development, as distinguished from the project-by-project or piecemeal method still so dominant, especially in the World Bank staff. And so terribly wrong.

Bell said he had learned while working "in the field" in Pakistan what I mean by the interaction of the components of a food production program, putting the parts together. But raising food is so filled with variables it makes any industrial production management job of fitting things together seem like child's play.

JANUARY 31, 1964
WASHINGTON, D.C.

A beautiful clear mild pre-spring day in Washington. But I do dislike this city. I used to feel that way because it was here that I came, from the Valley, to take a pummeling about TVA appropriations, legislation, etc., or to fight off the tribe of Washington empire builders, kibitzers and the rest who could not see that it was TVA's autonomy and flexibility that made it possible for it to do a job that everybody envied—and, therefore, wanted to mess with.

The hostility or discomfort I feel about Washington continues, a personal alienation toward those sites of centralized political power where institutions are their own self-justification.

This afternoon just before train time, an hour with Felipe Herrera, head of the Inter-American Development Bank [IDB]. A forceful man with a clear head and a passion for his work. Discussed his idea for a joint development undertaking between Venezuela and Colombia; gave me a chance to describe my allergy to having such an undertaking begun by sessions between the National Planning Agencies of the two countries. This national planning phobia in Latin America has led to more yack yack and *less action* than any other single thing, unless it is the temperament that would *rather put something on paper than get it done.*

Lunch with Pierre Moosa, head of the World Bank Division for Africa, which handles forty-two nations, I think he said! Dark and extraordinarily bright, with quick eyes, dark hair, a way of looking at you with heavy eyebrows raised.

We talked first about Guinea. There are a few very capable Guineans, he told me, but the country is going downhill physically. He emphasized "physically." Moosa was housed there in the elegant mansion that was once the residence of the French Governor General. Only two electric bulbs were still burning. When one went out he was sure no one would know how to get another.

Mali, a nation now, has cash on hand of some 30,000 francs, or the equivalent of $116!! And owes God knows how much. That is literally all the cash they have. His comments about West Africa I thought earthy and in considerable contrast to the full page ads (written by U.S. public relations firms for these little lands) that appeared recently in the *New York Times* Africa supplement.

But always Moosa spoke with respect and compassion. Nothing to be discouraged about, said he; it will just take time. And no bitterness about the throwing out of the "colonist" (i.e., the French). "They [Africans] are like the boy who is fed up [he used the Americanism] with home and parental authority. Then he finds when he is left on his own that there are so many things his parents did for him that he doesn't know how to do for himself, and he begins to see what those hated parents did for him."

FEBRUARY 1, 1964
PRINCETON

Being "sorry for yourself" is a disease, one of the sins against the spirit, which ranks in my lexicon beside cynicism and despair.

To be able to identify one's self-pity and get it under control is a form of self-therapy I believe in. No one else can do this for you.

These recriminations arise from a spell of having been sorry for myself yesterday.

Why, I said to myself, should I pour out my energies, suffer frustrations, put up with stuffy people when I don't have to?

Then I begin to apply self-discipline. Look at what D&R has meant to you and to others, to people who need the kind of leadership you can provide. More than that, in D&R you have a *freedom* and a control of your time and interests that you could not get in any other way. Teaching? You know that's not for you. Writing? You can't spend all your time writing; too many years of action have spoiled that as a sole outlet. Travel for travel's sake? Much to be said for this, but you wouldn't care for it as a main occupation.

I know damn well why I want to have a definite task, why I don't want to "take it easy." A sweet old gent I met about the time I left public service expressed the reason about as well as might be for my kind of person. This was Frederick H. Ecker, who spent eighty years with Metropolitan Life and was its Chairman when I met him. Day before yesterday he died at the age of ninety-six; the *Times* quoted him as saying (in 1957):

"I don't think anybody yet has invented a pastime that's as much fun, or keeps you as young, as a good job . . . I would be willing to endure quite a bit of leisure, if I had to, for the pleasure of working. If I had really retired at seventy I probably wouldn't be here now, and I certainly would have missed a lot of fun."

If a man who spends his life running an *insurance* company can call that a "good job" and a lot of fun, think how I should feel about my job—and the freedom and variety it gives me—as head of D&R.

FEBRUARY 4, 1964
1:30 P.M.
AN HOUR OUT OF BOGOTÁ, COLOMBIA

The Andes! A great snow-crowned head, held so proudly above the great range that borders the coast of Colombia.

Colombia: what a cloud of memories this invokes; the day in 1954 Helen and I first saw the shocking, filthy, but vital port city of Buenaventura from the deck of our Grace liner, the long, racking drive through the Andes from Cali to Bogotá, the wait for hours while a slide was removed so we and a hundred cars behind us could get through.†

† See *Journals*, Vol. III, *The Venturesome Years*, p. 480.

FEBRUARY 5, 1964
HOTEL TEQUENDAMA
BOGOTÁ, COLOMBIA

I have rarely seen such a change in a man! When Alberto Lleras strode into the neat little living room of his home late yesterday afternoon, greeting me with a firm handshake, I only barely recognized in this stooped, hollow-cheeked, harassed-looking man the vigorous Presidente I remembered from a long and memorable lunch in the gloomy palace on my last visit here, in December, 1961.‡

He *had* in fact been ill. "Everything seemed to go wrong," he confided. "The coronaries, the sinuses, everything all at once. The strain of twenty-four hours of work a day, always the phone to the ear [he demonstrated], to hear the always bad news." It had been too much.

I mentioned the name of his cousin, Carlos Lleras, who was such a help in the CVC [Cauca Valley Corporation] fight in the Colombian Senate years ago. "He will certainly be the next President of Colombia. And he will be the best President Colombia has ever had." This was said in a matter of fact way—after all, Alberto Lleras is regarded as the best President *any* Latin country has had, in recent memory at least—and then he went on to explain: "Carlos is creative. It was he who created most of the institutions in this country that have great meaning today: the Institute to provide housing—that was twenty-five years ago; the land reform policy and Institute—INCORA;§ the agricultural research institute going on alongside the Rockefeller Foundation here near Bogotá. He had the chief hand in writing a report for the UN on river basin development."

NOON

Carlos Lleras Restrepo, "the next President of Colombia," turned out to be an exceptionally short man with that rare thing among unusually short men, a serene countenance as well as a quiet sureness and understanding.

We met him in the study of his home at about 11 A.M. He reminded me that he had met me years ago. ("You are not a foreigner in Colombia, you must know.") I asked him how he appraised Colombia's chief problems; its strengths, compared with most other South American countries, were widely known.

Foreign exchange—the constant, nagging problem of not enough foreign exchange—was certainly at the head of his list. Food for

‡ See *Journals*, Vol. V, *The Harvest Years*, pp. 286–289.
§ Instituto Colombiano de la Reforma Agraria.

domestic use? "This is no problem"—a dismissal I find less than persuasive, since it affects political stability, health and vigor, etc. But in addition to many other things he is an economist, and in Latin American countries foreign exchange is the beginning and the end of every analysis of a country. It is because he believes certain agricultural products can provide foreign exchange, or can avoid the use of foreign exchange, that he regards the INCORA agricultural program as so vital.

This man is different from any political leader I have found in Latin America. The amused, shrewd look in his eye, the lack of *any* gestures at all, to say nothing of the vehement ones so common to Latins. No rhetoric at all. A composed, warm man.

Bogotá. A city of over a million; sophisticated; expensive underpasses, apartment buildings and office buildings rising on every hand. Yet on the sidewalk, a pathetic pair of cows with their two feeble calves; and on the patch of green, steep as a cliff, to the right of the bull ring, horses grazing and little peasant boys driving more cows along worn paths to the wide concrete street that leads up the mountain.

FEBRUARY 7, 1964
10 A.M.
ABOARD BRANIFF AIRWAYS, HEADED FOR KENNEDY AIRPORT

Enrique Penalosa[a] (at the Bogotá airport): "It is very difficult to get the Parliament [his word] to appropriate money for agricultural development. But if you call it 'land reform'—ah, that is an attractiveness, from the po-o-litikal point of view."

I found this far from self-explanatory. If the "Parliament" doesn't find it politically attractive to spend money on agriculture, why should "land reform" for the benefit of the peasants have any political appeal?

"Ah—the reason: In the cities the unions are of the Liberal Party. The unions in the cities favor land reform. Besides, many of the members of the unions have come from the country, hundreds of thousands of them. In the *country* they are conservatives, but—and this is always true and not easy to explain—when they come to the cities, Conservative peasants become Liberal Party members.

"The peasants break no windows, form no mobs, as the workmen in the cities do, because they are all separated. But for land reform the union Liberals will make a big fuss and fight the enemies of land reform, and they are very powerful."

A tide of antagonism has risen to a new height here against what is considered by Colombians as the World Bank staff's "dictation" and

[a] Managing Director, INCORA.

bullying. I was struck by the way in which the Colombians I saw, the intelligent, perceptive people, have come to realize how much power these staff men, who *represent no one* (in a democratic sense), have assumed over the lives of Colombians. Said a leading citizen of Cali: "A man came to Cali, spent a day, and said, 'No jet airport for you. We say you don't need it.' Not that the Bank had considered financing the airport, but it is part of Colombia's national spending program which the staff man disapproved. Then he got back on the plane and returned to Washington." Should Cali force the issue, this man threatened that the entire loan program to Colombia would be limited or cancelled.

An even more extreme example, and one that will bear watching: the insistence of the Bank's engineers that no power development in any region go forward except after the Bank has decided that it is the best and most economical approach. If the power to *run* the electrical energy development of Colombia is in the hands of a body, the World Bank, which is not accountable to the American Congress or any other public body, such control smacks of World Government by the "financial elite." What an issue this is going to be one of these days!

FEBRUARY 8, 1964
SATURDAY, 4 P.M.
PRINCETON

There it is, big as life; the *Journals* seem *real* for the first time:

The Journals of David E. Lilienthal
Volume I
The TVA Years
1939–1945

In type: sample pages.

FEBRUARY 9, 1964
PRINCETON

Where do you get your energy? You're just back from a hard and engrossing trip to South America and back in a few days.

From your ancestors? From the joy and delight you get in living, from a conviction that what you do comes to something worthwhile? And not the least, to a growing sense of the enchanting beauty of this world?

When I finally gave up the effort to sleep at about 5:45 A.M., I looked out upon a scene of pure magic: the tall locust trees, their arms entwined against a luminous blue sky, the dying moon delicate and slender as a young girl seen through the lattice of the leafless trees; then the first diffusion of orange light, the coming of another day.

And below, "my" garden (Helen's and mine, of course, but this morning it seems mine), the dark clumps of the candytuft that soon —perhaps in April—will be white, the pansy volunteers not complaining about the cold and probably harboring buds, stunted but undaunted ones that will bloom at the first February thaw (what plucky things they are).

The things of this earth *are* beautiful; does this account for this *strange* gift of energy?

Even more to the point, does this "energy" come from the people who love me? The word "love" covers all kinds of affirmative human feeling by one being toward another: respect, affection, compassion, admiration for one's shortcomings as well as his strong points, passion, delight in another's presence and his sense of fun and perception—it's a big word, love.

FEBRUARY 13, 1964
NEW YORK

Last night I think I discovered why I am having such difficulty in preparing a statement about Development and Resources Corporation, to be used in what most companies would refer to as a brochure.

The difficulty is not in the writing. The difficulty is that two conflicting concepts of D&R are chasing each other around in my head. Is D&R to be distinctive because of the *motivations* that have driven me most of my life? Or do we make those motivations secondary and think of this organization as just another (though in some ways superior) management or technical organization looking for jobs to do because they keep us busy and keep up our revenues?

Is D&R to be directed by the same basically idealistic motivation that has kept me going for twenty years in public life and made it possible for us to do the fantastically successful Iran job? Or is it going to follow a more conventional impulse simply to get clients and customers, competing with those who do not have my background of wanting to make some lasting contribution to the lives of people? Will it create patterns and concepts of development both overseas and in the United States of the kind I believe in down to my heel taps?

At the beginning of D&R, Dr. Albert Hettinger (Hett) was one of our Lazard Directors. He is a legend on Wall Street—and a scholar to boot—and is supposed to be the greatest authority on investment on the Street. He made one perceptive contribution to D&R, in the form of a remark to Gordon Clapp and me: "You fellows stand for idealism. If this company can maintain its idealism, you will have no competition."

Development and Resources presents a distinctive picture not so much because of *what* it has done or what it is, but because of *why* it is and why it came into being.

I must remember that years ago Overseas Consultants, Inc., went to Persia to make a plan for that country, spent a mint of money, accumulated a ten-foot shelf of reports—and nothing happened because there wasn't a drop of anything but cynicism about Iran in that whole operation. And yet they were a technically competent group.

I must remember the increases in food and forage production in Khuzistan that have already been achieved, the establishment of a going concern *of Iranians* in KWPA [Khuzistan Water and Power Authority], the improvement in the agricultural skills of the peasants, the beginning of a public health program in a foul sink of trachoma, bilharzia, malaria, etc. The survival of this work in the midst of land reform revolution is in marked contrast to the failure in West Pakistan, where conditions are more favorable physically, and where every foreign aid outfit in the world has been pouring in people and money.

West Pakistan has had foundation people, Harvard professors, AID people, World Bank staffers, British aid experts; it has had a stable government under a military dictatorship; it has had the Indian Civil Service; it has had the longest continuous period of irrigation expertise probably in the world. And yet the other night at the Coffee House Club, Professor Daniel Bell, the sociologist, leaned across the table, said he had been in Pakistan as a consultant and observer, and asked: "Why is it you make so much progress in Iran and there has been no progress to speak of in West Pakistan?"

There are reasons for these things. We should not begin to ape those who have idealism of a vague, academic, social-worker kind but only flabby managerial muscles; or those "consultants" whose preoccupation is getting a contract regardless and treating their volume of revenue as their prime measure of success.

When I describe the "why" of D&R, I am referring to its basic purpose of public service, a purpose not inconsistent with being a private company operated for a profit, nor inconsistent with doing a tough-minded, careful, efficient job.

To stick to such purposes will require guts, the rarest commodity, I am beginning to think, among men these days. It is a quality of independence that has put us in the bad books of some bureaucratic minded staff people.

In the end I have never known that kind of independence to fail to win respect and usually to prevail. Prevail or not, it is the only way

I can live and, I think, the only way in which D&R can make the kind of mark that is worth the effort.

FEBRUARY 16, 1964
PRINCETON

Last evening Helen and I saw our first basketball game since we were in college, the winter of 1919! Princeton has a galumphing genius, name of Bill Bradley,* but except for his exploits throwing baskets while being covered, the game didn't have a modern touch—except for one amusing episode.

A scramble in mid-court; time out; a Harvard player rubbing his eye, looking dazed, then looking down at the floor as if to recover himself from a biff. Then *everyone* was on hands and knees, looking all over the shining wooden court, players, officials, even one old boy, a spectator. The player had lost one of his contact lenses and the game couldn't go on till this thing was found—which it was, with great shouts of triumph from the crowd. Well, that was the contemporary touch; the rest seemed like basketball of yore, Hoosier style.

1 P.M.

A walk through the Institute woods with General Edward S. Greenbaum. No one ever looked *less* like an "Eddie," yet that's what everyone calls him. What a stalwart he is. Years older than I, with a great record as a public servant and lawyer, arguing landmark libel suits, representing the *New York Times* in the Supreme Court; as sage and solid a man as I believe I have ever known.

FEBRUARY 17, 1964
NEW YORK

A dispatch from Tehran: Abolhassan Ebtehaj completely "cleared" of charges that while head of Plan Organization without legal approvals he had engaged D&R (usually described as "Lilienthal and Clapp") to develop the Khuzistan Region and had provided us with large sums of money which had not been accounted for. While agents of the Justice Ministry were trying, vainly, to substantiate these charges, Mr. Ebtehaj was confined to jail for months.†

* Since graduation, and a degree from Oxford, he has played professional basketball with the New York Knickerbockers.

† See *Journals*, Vol. V, *The Harvest Years*, pp. 276–277, 290–291, 314–315.

FEBRUARY 18, 1964
NEW YORK

Tom Mead back from Conakry, in Guinea, West Africa. He, Walt Seymour, and several other D&R men have been out there working on a report for our first "private" client, Harvey Aluminum, which has acquired a bauxite concession. The Guinea Government wants a picture of *general* development of the country.

A delightful story about old man Harvey, an emigrant from Lithuania, now seventy-five and apparently still ruling the roost of a family business he built up more or less singlehandedly. In discussions with him one of our men said: "Well, we could take that up tomorrow." Harvey's son said: "But tomorrow's Saturday." The old boy said: "*I'll* be here; never mind whether it is Saturday. This fellow [pointing to his son, the President] has a rich father, but *I* haven't, so I work on Saturday, too."

FEBRUARY 23, 1964
PRINCETON

A long letter from Ed Littlefield about my Western Energy idea. It seems that what I thought of two and a half years ago—that coal would be a prime source of energy for the development of California, with production in a *huge* power plant near the Rocky Mountain coal fields‡—Stone & Webster is now getting worked up about. Whether or not we are the ones who will carry out this important idea, it is a comfort to find this confirmation of its soundness.

If our Utah partners will throw their resources and ideas into such a venture without waiting until it has been *proven* by figures, this may be one of those large enterprises that justifies my continuing to work so hard. If they are too timid and slow, we may miss the boat, as Lazard missed the boat years ago when I proposed a big investment§ in pine, in the South, for paper making. Later Bowater Paper Company moved in and made a great success of it.

Bankers are indispensable for some purposes, but so often they seem to have a built-in feeling that saying "No" is an act of statesmanship.

FEBRUARY 24, 1964
NEW YORK

"If our agricultural chemicals don't contribute something durable in a country—we're talking about Iran, but any country—that benefits the people of that country, then our tenure there won't, in the long run,

‡ *Journals*, Vol. V, *The Harvest Years*, pp. 341–342.
§ *Journals*, Vol. III, *The Venturesome Years*, p. 57.

be very solid, and if it isn't good for that country in the long run, it won't be profitable for Socony Mobil."

The speaker was P. V. Keyser, Jr., an Executive Vice President and a Director of Socony Mobil, a distinguished looking man, full head of grey hair, which doesn't necessarily mean he isn't a handsome stuffed shirt. The occasion: a luncheon meeting set up by John Fennebresque, President of the company's new chemical division.

Is it possible that what I have been saying about business for so long is becoming true: that businessmen of the generation of these men, mostly in their forties, are actually aware that only by keeping the public interest in the forefront can their business prosper? I'd like to believe this; today's experience, taken literally, or even with a considerable amount of skepticism tends to confirm it.

To help weld the private interest of business and the public interest has been a dream of mine for a long, long time. In the TVA I first made this a kind of evangelical doctrine; I wrote about it in a chapter of the TVA book,[a] in 1943: "The Decisions of Businessmen." What I preached as a *purpose* of TVA, this bringing together of public and private interest, may become one of the great functions of D&R.

FEBRUARY 28, 1964
NEW YORK

F. B. Korsmeyer, Manager of Overseas Development for Socony Mobil, came in yesterday afternoon. Gave me a chance to improvise further about how an important American company could do things in a country such as Iran. Building a country (in my opinion) means food production as a preliminary to and part of erecting fertilizer plants, rather than the usual formula of "selling" a country such a plant and then ducking out. To work this out will require an invention on my part, a device, an administrative mechanism, in which both Iranians and outside foreign technical talent are joined.

But it will have to be something never yet seen; for a conventional joint venture between foreigners and Iranians (or whomever) won't accomplish what I have in mind or what I think is needed for the next important chapter in development in such countries—or for the next step in internationalization, for that matter.

FEBRUARY 29, 1964
PRINCETON

Brother Ted here for the afternoon; visiting his daughter, Elise Copeland, in Philadelphia.

[a] David E. Lilienthal, *TVA: Democracy on the March*, Harper & Row, 1944 (Rev. 1953).

What a noble man is this younger brother; how gay and sweet, at sixty-two how extraordinarily young! Life has not been easy for him, he's had a succession of illnesses. But where is that hangdog expression, the pulled down mouth, the dulled eye that one sees in so many, many men and women? Not in Ted. His natural optimism and joy in life show in everything about him, his posture, his walk, his delightful laugh. We had many a noisy laugh during the sunny afternoon, looking out of our living room on the purity of a snow covered garden.

A man who at sixteen or sixty-two can give others joy by his own goodness, there is a man who has realized his potentials. That is Ted.

MARCH 6, 1964
NEW YORK

I have just heard what is surely a classic description of the effect on public affairs of the limits of human energy. At lunch, Dr. Alberto Lleras spoke of Thomas Mann, Johnson's new Assistant Secretary of State for Latin American Affairs.

As Lleras described Mann, there emerged, with each stroke of the word-drawing, the picture of a harassed, "very tired" man who was "clever, bright, intelligent," but trying to do a job impossible for any one man. (Washington is full of such impossible jobs and such overtaxed men.)

Mann began, Lleras said, with the handicap of being pictured in the press as a "close friend of Lyndon Johnson" and as a hardheaded, two-fisted man who would pound the table and treat the Latin American countries with toughness. Actually, Lleras said, Mann is a quiet-spoken State Department professional. He was picked by Acheson, who insisted that *one* man should be given the sole authority for Latin America and then be left alone to do the job, as had been the case with [Assistant Secretary] Eddie Miller. But that isn't the way it works today. Now there's the Alliance for Progress with its big promises and its big problems—which Miller and Acheson didn't have. Now, too, there is Cuba, which stirs up the whole picture.

"It simply isn't working. Mann has too much to do. He must meet all twenty of the ambassadors from the Latin American countries; he must take *each* of them, when they have problems, with him to see Secretary Rusk; then he must take them—each one—to the President. It is quite impossible. I see nothing very encouraging for Latin America or the United States coming out of Mann, though he himself is a clever man."

MARCH 9, 1964
PRINCETON

After a heavy week of work; determined to make this a day to catch up by doing nothing.

But how does one stop the machine that whirs in my mind? As Dr. Atchley says, "Your turn-off mechanism doesn't work too well." So, long phone calls, new ideas (or what goes for ideas in their early stages). I reconcile myself to this difficulty of "turning it off" by the dubious consolation: think how awful it would be if you had nothing to turn off; if "it" were always turned off.

MARCH 12, 1964
NEW YORK

Have just come from a feast. Two hours with Charley Wyzanski. I had almost forgotten the delight in listening to a great conversationalist. The Judge, physically diminutive, was towering in the power and range of his mind and his interests.

He remarked that I was the only man he knew who had been elected to the faculty by the Harvard Corporation and had declined. "David, do you ever regret that decision?" I answered quite honestly that I didn't regret it. It was not the place for a man of my background, or of my temperament.

The Judge told me that during the time he was in Washington in the early New Deal years (he was Solicitor of the Labor Department at age twenty-seven) he wrote his mother every day. He puffed at his pipe. "Those letters," he said, "were the kind of reports that a 'junior' would be expected to make after a conference; they were more than letters to one's mother."

In those letters he reflected the astonishment a kid felt at being in the middle of such big events, though, he added modestly (not perhaps accurately), "my own part in them was very junior indeed."

Wyzanski understands better than anyone I know why it is so natural for me to "write myself out" in my journals at times of stress and intellectual excitement during certain periods of my work.

MARCH 13, 1964
PRINCETON

Snow patches still white along the edges of the herbaceous borders. But the earth is mellow and warming; the yellow crocus discs that I put into the soil last fall now have thrust their darts upward and crocus gold spills out of the dark earth into the sunlight, the cool brave sunlight of an "in-between day," between winter and spring. I couldn't resist; I got my spade, opened a pit in the crumbly stuff, dug out a sprawling candytuft plant and moved it from the middle of the south border to a place in the front. I delight in this process and almost hate to wash my hands when I come in.

MARCH 14, 1964
PRINCETON

Kitty and Robert Oppenheimer here for a drink and a visit this afternoon, the first time they have been in this house together, though we have lived next door seven years now. She burns with an intensity of feeling one rarely sees, mostly with a deep resentment against all those who had any part in the torture Robert had to undergo. I remarked that the last time I had seen them they were basking in the glow of the Presidential smile.* Kitty's dark eyes smouldered in the half light of the porch: "That was awful; there were some awful things about it." Robert, his head bowed in that kindly, almost rabbinical posture I have seen so often when Kitty was blazing and saying violent things: "There were some very sweet things said," he murmured, so low I could hardly hear him.

I told Robert I had persevered in trying to get declassified the memorandum I wrote about the National Security Subcommittee meeting on the H-bomb, just before we reported to the President. It had taken ten years to get it, but I wanted it badly for it said some things that should have been said in the public record at the time of Robert's in camera "trial." He sucked at his pipe (he seems to have given up cigarettes) and a flash of anger came into his eyes: "Yes; when I testified that Dr. Teller and Dr. Stanislaw Ulam had done a great technical job in solving the problem of the H-bomb, in the transcript someone had stricken out Ulam's name and left only Teller's. Can you imagine!" So the wounds are still sore.†

"It is eighteen years," he said, "almost exactly, since you and I first met, since we began work on that report. It has stood up very well, I think, don't you? It is something we need not be ashamed of!" (He was referring, of course, to the Board of Consultants' "plan" for the international control of the bomb.‡)

* Oppenheimer was given the Fermi Award on December 1, 1963. See *Journals*, Vol. V, *The Harvest Years*, pp. 529–530.

† See "The Debate over the Hydrogen Bomb," by Herbert York, *Scientific American*, October, 1975, pp. 106, 111.

‡ See *Journals*, Vol. II, *The Atomic Energy Years*, Acheson-Lilienthal Report.

General Greenbaum and Dotsie were here too. What a delight she is, so handsome and cheerful despite the handicap of being barely able to hear unless one is talking directly to her. Reminds me of a comment of Robert Kennedy on the Jack Paar show last night; he was "on" to promote the Kennedy Library at Harvard. In answer to a question from Paar, Kennedy said his brother, the President, was in pain half of his adult life and throughout his Presidency. "He never spoke of it; I never remember him speaking of it. He never once complained. He never thought that God was treating him badly. The only way I could tell that he was in great pain was that he would be somewhat grey in color and there would be lines around his eyes and mouth."

"What would you say your brother did for his country?" Paar asked. Said Robert:

"He made the country feel young again." How wonderfully put, and how true.

MARCH 15, 1964
NEW YORK

That gleaming half circle out there in the darkness, twisting, turning motes floating across its face, is the Wollman Skating Rink in the midst of Central Park. From my room on the sixteenth floor cliff of the Plaza Hotel I see not New York City but something a child's imagination has dreamed up.

And outside: clop, clop, the sound like no other in the world, the hollow, comforting roundish sound of a horse's hooves, before the old carriages that rest their ratty-ness before the Plaza. A good going-to-sleep sound.

MARCH 16, 1964
NEW YORK

The headline opposite the editorial page of the *Times*: James Nicely Dead at Sixty-four.

It did shake me; I'm still not only sad but uneasy. Jim was the very picture of success: the head of my Law School class, Justice Holmes' secretary, a favorite of John W. Davis—but deeply disappointed that Guaranty [Trust] had passed over him for the Presidency.

Now he is dead. Are *you* bearing down too hard? What about these eighteen-hour days, these seven-day weeks? You're enjoying them, but does this make sense?

Is there some sensible and workable middle ground (workable for me, with my restless energy)? Perhaps I am "taking care of myself" (to use that terrible phrase) better than I realize, for my life is *full* to overflowing, I get great joy and a minimum of frustration from what I do, both in business and in my "personal" life.

So again this journal is the means by which I "talk myself" out of baseless fears or the doldrums.

MARCH 20, 1964
NEW YORK

How does one distinguish between what is *change* and what is just a paper-thin *verbiage* that makes things look new and changed when actually it is only the surface that is different?

How does a man of my background, experience, and responsibility make others feel the effect of change, of what I might call a different *style* of living? How can I guard against the third-hand word-ish people who portray this as a changed world without really understanding it, or being able to dig deeply enough, *out of their own experience*, to know what is really happening in the world?

The gimmick hunters: how do we distinguish them from the innovators, the creative people?

Artists—writers, musicians, and particularly painters and sculptors—have had this to contend with in recent years in an almost exaggerated form. The mood today of the patrons of art is the reverse of other times: they want something that looks wild and different and is therefore "great" because so much at odds with what is accepted.

Artists who create only *novelty*, which is now "the thing," are not saying what is inside them, but what they believe will appeal to others. They express *not* something *they themselves have experienced* firsthand, but rather a sympathetic picture of this "new world" that they hear about secondhand from the facile men of the big magazines and the TV program people.

When I last saw my cousin Beatrice Tobey I could see that as a painter she is struggling with this same problem: trying to find a way of expressing on canvas the "impact" of a world that has no longer the sweetness of Renoir, nor the repose of Rembrandt, nor even the kaleidoscopic energy of Pollock.

We are all caught up in the same kind of wrestling match with the admittedly great transitions going on about us; those who feel they simply *must* express that changed style are the lucky ones. But it is tough.

MARCH 22, 1964
PRINCETON

"The first day of spring," so it sez. Opened our eyes this morning to the dazzle of a mid-winter overcoat of snow, the kind that clings and drapes, bows down the pines and laurel, turns the dogwood into cotton candy.

Friday night I sat in the grandeur of Madison Hall on the Princeton campus, among some serious faces gathered for one of those never-ending "conferences." This one concerned "doing something" about the Appalachian region, a region that was poor and stranded when I went to TVA more than thirty years ago, and has gained no ground since.

President Kennedy, seeing real rural poverty for the first time, I rather think, when he campaigned in West Virginia, created the President's Appalachian Commission, headed by Franklin D. Roosevelt, Jr. Their Report (i.e., statement of a program) was to be presented to President Johnson on Thursday and released to coincide with the Princeton Conference. Somebody "leaked" the recommendations to the *New York Times*. This happens so often I'm surprised anyone bothers to get mad about it any more, but, so I was told, Johnson got mad and, to discipline the leakers, refused to keep his appointment with F.D.R., Jr. So the Report wasn't released.

After a dinner of what were surely plastic African lobster tails, that great mountain of a man, F.D.R.'s second son, arose to speak. His opening remarks turned on my presence, and it was the kind of "tribute" that unnerved me: F.D.R.'s son talking about the great regional achievement, TVA, for which, so he said, I was responsible.

But it is apparent that any effort to use some of the basic lessons that the TVA demonstrated about how to get a region back on its feet simply will not be attempted.

A smiling young man, about thirty-five, John Sweeney, said, half-apologetically: "I have been quoting that part of your book§ where you say that the thing that prevents a genuine regional development is the old-line bureaus in Washington. Whatever we propose for Appalachia brings on an argument with the bureaus, not because it will or will not benefit the people in that region—that seems the last thing in their minds—but because it will invade their *jurisdiction*." He threw up his hands, as apparently they all have.

APRIL 5, 1964
PRINCETON

As Ebtehaj came into my office Friday, I thought to myself, "This man has a smile as warm and sparkling as ever I've seen on a man's face. His whole body is smiling, not just his face."

"The way things have been done in the Khuzistan is the only way

§ *TVA: Democracy on the March.*

to develop an underdeveloped country." He laid this down as an immutable law, not just one for the Medes and Persians.

He reminisced about my first trip out there with Gordon Clapp, when Ebtehaj was head of the Plan Organization. "We sat down together after your five-day trip to the Khuzistan and in a couple of hours we had an agreement, an agreement unique in history. When our meetings were over, Hector Prud'homme—he was head of my Technical Bureau then, you'll remember—said to me: 'Mr. Ebtehaj, in an hour or so you entered into a *most* important transaction, involving great consequences and commitments; how can you possibly do that in so short a time?' And I answered: 'Why waste time? The resources are there; these two are the best men in the world to develop them; so not an hour, not a day should be wasted. It's as simple as that.' "

APRIL 8, 1964
FLYING THE ATLANTIC, TWA, TO ROME

An opening—a thematic chord—for a book on change came to me over the ocean. Change is the most heartening fact of life. "Tomorrow will be not like today, not like yesterday. Next week, next year, next decade—each will be different."

Change, the battlecry of the hopeful, buoyant human spirit, the theme that gives life its zest, as certainty makes it dull. Change is a phenomenon not fully appreciated, studied, or relished.

And then: Change can be *made to happen.* Man can *make* change happen.

You can measure a man by this yardstick: Does he relish change, look forward to it with a kind of joy? If so, this is the token of his greatness, of his humanness, of his love of life and his belief in life.

Do the times welcome change, do the times proclaim an *affirmation* that change is synonymous with the most creative thing in life? If they do, then it is a *good* time to be alive.

Look ahead with joy to the morrow—and with the fortitude that says: whatever comes, I am ready; and after tomorrow is another tomorrow.

APRIL 9, 1964
THE ATHENS AIRPORT

"Do Monsieur and Madame wish to stay aboard?" Incredible, but yes, Monsieur and Madame do. The Greek cleaning women who come aboard, are they the women for whom the lecherous gods' mouths watered? Surely not.

And those promontories, as we dropped lower and lower, with the deep blue sea fringing them, a sturdy wind blowing up the delicate lacing of whitecaps—were those, and the islands beyond, really the inspiration for such great poetry? On the airfield a long sleek blue ship, more graceful than anything a Phoenician ship designer dreamed of, a Boeing 707—and high on the tail fin the Star of David.

You must live in the present, in this maelstrom of needle-nosed U.S. jets flashing by like dazzling kingfishers, of Greeks still plying their second best and second oldest profession ("Antiques, Madame?"), and the flow of undersized, eager-eyed men and women "returning"—by air—to the Promised Land of Israel nearby. "What have they been promised?" I didn't stop to ask them.

Don't let them fool you, friend. The scholars tell us that all that matters are the thoughts of the men who talked and wrote and sang here ages ago, here where today overhead sprinklers are keeping the golf fairways of the Olympic Country Club playable. Let the professors talk, and listen attentively. But to understand the only life *you* will live, you had better understand what goes on today, here and now.

APRIL 11, 1964
4 A.M.
AT G-11, GHOLESTAN VILLAGE, NEAR AHWAZ

This time tomorrow morning—about 6 A.M.—the air will be full of parachuting Americans, dropping from the sky with heavy machinery, etc., for an "attack" on the Pahlavi dam and its "defense." "Operation Delawar" it is called, a drop of men and arms sent directly from their bases in Kentucky and Florida. This is a major military maneuver, made jointly with Iran.

Alexander "took" this part of Persia, but compared to this big drop he did it the hard way. This scarred and open land of the Mesopotamian plain has seen many a warrior and many a movement of men at arms, but never one like this.

APRIL 12, 1964
ANDIMESHK, IN THE HOME OF "MAC" MCCULLOCH OF D&R

Yesterday morning at Ahwaz, as we set out for "The Dam," the dust storm was so dense that all around us people seemed to be swimming in an amber sea, the sunlight warming a dust so heavy you could hardly see across the street.

What a noble sight! How moving it was to stand at the base of the dam, in the canyon's heart, and look up at that cathedral-like mass above.

It actually happened: all the economists and nay-sayers to the contrary, there it is. It is the *reality* of something actually having happened in this country, something that you can see. No amount of skeptical "it will never happen" psychology can dismiss *this* reality that is giving a sense of confidence to an often tortured land.

APRIL 13, 1964
ANDIMESHK

Without advance word yesterday the Shah and I had a relaxed visit about the Pilot Irrigation Project, *not* in the Palace, but standing in the machinery yard at our headquarters at Kutyan, me in dusty pants and the plum colored shirt I love so, Helen also dusty in what I call her "Girls' Reform School matron dress."

For two years I have been saying to the Shah at every opportunity that he should see what is going on in what I regard as the most important part of this whole Khuzistan development, not excepting the great dam. Then, at the best possible time, here he comes, when "our" irrigated wheat and barley are beautiful, while other regions show the glum results of wheat in a very dry year. After having gone along the very route and through the very villages I had visited a couple of hours before, the Shah stepped out of his car to greet me with a light in his eye. Nothing I have said, with my unrestrained enthusiasm, about the world-wide significance of this development in the "pilot area" could have been more excited than what he said to me. "Now I see, Mr. Lilienthal," he said (among many other things equally gratifying), "why you spoke as you did about this work; now I see why you have been willing to put so much of your heart [his expression!] into the Khuzistan these last eight years."

The Shah slowly walked around the yard, looking at farm machinery (he was greatly taken with a drill that plants seed and fertilizer in the same operation). He shook hands with me as he got back into his car, and said in his informal way, "See you Tuesday." Which he did—but at the glittering Palace.

APRIL 16, 1964
TEHRAN

I looked down the long luncheon table at the American Ambassador's◖ residence—twenty-six people—and groaned: a complete waste of time. The French, the Spanish, the Chinese, etc., ambassadors and their wives. Diplomatic people seem to me almost functionless, cable and telephone from their capitals being used so readily.

But it was by no means a "complete waste of time" after all, because Ghirshman, the great French archeologist, was there. For thirty-four years, digging around Susa has been his life. I had guessed from

◖ Julius Holmes.

his reputation that he would be a thin, irritable, dyspeptic Frenchman. Instead, he turned out to look like Santa Claus sans whiskers. A mane of white hair, pink cheeks, a vivid blue perky bowtie with blazing white polka dots. Helen sat next to him; it was worth the trip to see their heads together, the dedicated amateur archeologist and the master.

APRIL 18, 1964
PAN AMERICAN 118 LEAVING BEIRUT

Hassan Ali Mansour, the new Prime Minister, whom I visited yesterday morning, is the greatest possible contrast to his predecessor, Amini, whom I visited in that blond office on Pasteur Avenue, across from the Palace.

Young—perhaps forty. His hair flows back from an elliptical-shaped forehead—everything flows back as if he were under water, his hair, his brow, even his ears.

His quarterback, compact-looking private secretary said that they have been working every day and long into the night. Both he and the Prime Minister looked it, too. Everything relating to Tehran, for example, comes to the Prime Minister; we met the Mayor and head of the Tehran police outside the office.

Mansour is one of that group of younger men who are now running the country—or trying to. Others include Reza Ansari, who accompanied me, Mehdi Samii, head of the Central Bank, and Khodadad Farmanfarmaian, deputy governor of the Central Bank.

I'm trying to put off the journal writing for this remarkable week until we are on the boat and I am beginning to unwind (I hope). But I can't hold back any longer recording the sense of achievement I feel with what I have been able to do since we reached Persia.

For so long I have looked to the time when the discussions here would be affirmative, positive, and forward-looking, not nagging and pettifogging about figures, tables of the budget, crabbing. None of that on this trip really. When I think of all the Gloomy Guses I have had to live with these past years—disaster ahead, long faces—Gordon, Nate [Greene], even John Oliver and Ed Murrow (his sour film about Iran: *The Brittle Regime*), it is a wonder I don't crow louder over what we have prevailed over, emotionally as well as substantively.

I remember one of those critical worry sessions when I told a meeting of our staff at Ahwaz: "Let's divide the job. You do the work, and let me do the worrying."

"Your Arabic script goes the wrong way," says Helen, watching my Gregg shorthand.

The most important thing about this trip, in the context of eight years of talks, is, I think, that the Shah has invited—yes, requested—me to communicate my views *directly to him* from time to time.

APRIL 21, 1964
ABOARD THE LEONARDO DA VINCI
TWO HOURS EAST OF GIBRALTAR

An emotional pain is an affirmation. I mean that classic "hurting" that flows from the emotions of injured pride, of longing, of loneliness. One first encounters this sometimes exquisite ache as a child, and we call it "being homesick." But this hurt of the emotions is not a sickness. It is so often a sign of being alive and functioning, responding to the fullness of life, the reaching toward something so often beyond grasp—but the *reaching* goes on, and in that lies the affirmation. Those who are human vegetables, or who have given up reaching, do not have that kind of pain.

APRIL 25, 1964
AT SEA, ABOARD THE LEONARDO DA VINCI
TWO DAYS OUT OF NEW YORK

It is now about two and a half weeks since Helen and I began our trip. Unbelievable that I had only a week in Persia. As I mull it over, what impressions stand out most clearly?

First, I think, comes the warm sense of how much better things are for the people in those miserable villages in Khuzistan in the Gebli area, now known as the Dez Pilot Irrigation area. And second, how wonderful to see the dream I have had of making the desert green again actually happen. Driving a Land-Rover along new and dusty roads, on either side dark green bands of glorious wheat and barley (headed out and soon to be threshed), berseem clover, horse beans, alfalfa, and the green sprouts of early cucumbers and squash. Elsewhere the dry farming grain looks parched and puny, but this area, where irrigation has barely begun, appears so fruitful. On the desert, no rain for weeks and weeks.

Going into the many homes in the villages I visited was a revelation, compared to similar visits during the past five years. The "village leaders" insured a welcome; but no one could mistake the difference—the "change," to use the term that has occupied my thoughts so much lately. The floors of the huts are pounded and hard: earth, yes, but not, as before, dust (and mud in the wet season). A pallet was all the furnishing in one of the best of these village huts, but the floor was clean, whitewashed too, and had been sprayed with insecticide.

There were sick children, of course. Many of the brilliantly beautiful young Arab girls had sore eyes, the dust storms (according to Dr. Gremliza*) having aggravated the symptoms of trachoma. But the donkeys and the occasional horse were fat with clover; clover was piled in the courtyard, and always pointed to proudly by the man whose home we visited.

The results of our work here *are* reaching the people I want all this to reach: the men and women and children who have been lost and forgotten for centuries. They act differently, even from a year or so ago. Time was when the village women would run and hide; you could see their heads peeking shyly at the strange visitors from around the corner of a house. *This time they stayed*, with the men, in the courtyard, or even in the houses, as we came along. And they spoke: "Shalom," to a male outsider! Two old gals (probably forty, but looked seventy) held their hands out to shake as we crossed the doorsills of their homes.

So this is the thing that comes first to mind: this *is* getting to the people. The Shah said he had stopped his car to talk to some of the peasants: these included some I had visited with earlier the same day. They thought what was happening here was fine. Then he questioned them more closely and repeated to me what they had said. One man who was connected with a bank in Dezful told the Shah that the peasants were now *selling* some of their forage, raising more than their animals needed. Some villagers were even opening bank accounts. This impressed the Shah—and me. It is an echo of the early impact of TVA on the isolated hill farmers of East Tennessee.

The next thing in importance, as I "mull over" that week, is the change in my relations with the Shah.

When we (Reza Ansari and I) had our audience on Tuesday, the Shah was still glowing about his trip to the Dez agricultural area. (He had talked to everyone about it, judging from the comments of the Prime Minister and others.) We must go ahead, must expand the area, must use the "most advanced technical methods," he said. In slow, solemnly articulate speech, he spoke again, as at Kutyan, about the world-wide significance of what he saw going on in the Khuzistan.

I kept silent; then I asked if I had his permission to say some things about the future, with complete candor. I spoke of the dangers and obstacles that confront a successful undertaking: the complacency, the loss of momentum and sense of urgency that fire a challenging, untried venture.

When I finished, the Shah asked me to put my views and recommendations along this line into a letter *directly to him*. I underline this

* Dr. F. G. L. Gremliza, D&R's Director of Village Health and Sanitation.

because having direct access to a ruler, rather than always dealing through someone else, and being invited to "tell me what you think," is an enormous advantage.

I sat down that afternoon and drafted the letter. Then I took it up with Ansari, who suggested I include some reference to the importance of keeping KWPA autonomous. This of course I was glad to do, as I believe it so completely. Portions of the letter as I transmitted it to His Majesty are here quoted:

> *April 15, 1964*
>
> YOUR MAJESTY:
>
> In the audience granted to me yesterday Your Majesty requested that I put in writing a statement of my views and recommendations. Those deal primarily with ways and means of averting or overcoming *dangers and obstacles* to continued and accelerated momentum forward of the national program for development of the Khuzistan region. . . .
>
> Your Majesty stated at our first meeting eight years ago, and yesterday and at other times has reaffirmed, this proposition: That the program for development of the rich physical resources and the human resources of Khuzistan is an undertaking of vital importance to all Iran, and that it therefore is to have high priority in the interests of the whole Iranian nation, her people and her future . . . that the stakes in this program for development, for all Iran, are so high and the opportunities so special and unique that a different kind of organization and different methods of operation were required. The good results attained so far are in my judgment largely attributable to the autonomy and flexibility accorded this unique organizational structure.
>
> I believe it would be highly relevant and important at this time to give clear reaffirmation to some basic principles on which the Khuzistan program was founded. . . .
>
> One such principle is that this Khuzistan program can most effectively and efficiently be carried out on the basis of an integrated long-range plan which . . . recognizes the crucial interrelationship among the various parts of this development program. . . .
>
> A . . . key principle has been that this integrated Khuzistan development program can most effectively and efficiently be administered by an autonomous and accountable regional governmental authority such as KWPA—an agency . . . coordinated with other governmental operations by means which do not destroy its capacity for effective action. . . .
>
> Underlying this . . . principle [of regionalism] is the fact that this program for integrated development . . . calls for unified management of various interrelated efforts and activities . . . not only water, land and its use for agricultural production,

generation and distribution of electric power, but also such matters as industrial development, health and education which are directly related to achievement of the program's fundamental objectives. Certainly KWPA, in its activities in these various fields, should continue to cooperate, as it is now doing, with other governmental agencies concerned with those fields on a nation-wide basis; but to subordinate KWPA to any such agency in activities vital to the success of the Khuzistan program could only, I am convinced, seriously impede the accomplishment of Your Majesty's objectives for that program.

Respectfully and sincerely yours,
DAVID E. LILIENTHAL
Chairman of the Board of Directors

Another strong impression: D&R and our Iranian colleagues in the Khuzistan have managed to become a *single entity.* A great achievement, a sense of one-ness among these people, who are perhaps two-thirds Iranians and the other Westerners, "our people." Whether it can ever be done anywhere else I don't know, but in this one place the *unifying effect of a common job* has smashed the "foreigner enclave" business to bits, socially and in every other way. This is a story that puts great heart in me.

It was at a D&R social gathering for us at Dezful, of perhaps one hundred and fifty people, men and their wives, that the reality of this struck me hardest. I could sense how little difference it made who was American and who Iranian. The eagerness with which young Iranian engineers or agriculturalists would form a semicircle around me and talk and answer questions, along with an American or two, all chiming in, agreeing, not agreeing, giving "for examples." The same thing was true, perhaps even to a stronger degree, in my day or so in the field with the "village leaders," young Iranians and their American supervisors, D&R men.

I mentioned this to Dr. Ahmadi.† He went even further in saying that there was simply no longer a line between Americans and Iranians. This, he said, had *never* happened in his country before. The reason for this contrast to the "foreign enclave" tradition in an overseas land is due to our success in training, proving that what we most want is that Iranians increasingly *do* have actual responsibilities.

Responsibility is the key to training; to train people as if that were an end in itself is pretty much a waste of time. But training deserves the name when it is carried on in such a way that a man takes responsibility for *doing* something: throwing a switch, signing a voucher, working out an alternative system of spare parts—big or little though the job may be.

† A graduate of the Cornell University College of Agriculture, then Deputy Managing Director of KWPA, and later Deputy Minister of Agriculture.

APRIL 28, 1964
NEW YORK

The frosting *on the frosting* of the cake of the Persian expedition (not even Herodotus or Darryl Zanuck could write a script like this): I have just had word that I am to receive an honorary degree from the University of California at Los Angeles at Commencement time, while the Shah delivers the Address and also receives the University's degree.

MAY 2, 1964
PRINCETON

Yesterday, Friday, a meeting of the Twentieth Century Fund Board. A remarkable group of men, as able and as diverse as you will find in a long day.

Ken Galbraith in his most useful role: the provoker, the dissenter. No, we shouldn't buy bonds for the Fund's portfolio; stick to common stock. He discounted Adolf Berle's intimation that a depression was possible.

When we discussed poverty and unemployment—and who doesn't these days?—Ken said:

"This is a problem not of unemployment or poverty but of the *whole* economy."

Then he spoke about how many of our own population were "functionally illiterate," stressing the fact that unless people are literate (I thought he meant could read and write; maybe I misunderstood) there was no hope for their employment.

"Since education is a problem of the economy," he said, "keep the economists out of this with their Keynesian gimmicks."

For a long time I have been in favor of keeping the economists out, but I was astounded to hear this from our most fluent *economist.* I cautioned about going all out for "education" as a *cure*: "I would add to Ken's 'keep the economists out,' 'keep the educators out,'" I said. "My experience in the TVA and in Persia makes clear that literacy and ability to acquire skills aren't synonymous."

Said Ken: "I couldn't disagree with you more. You mean they can become good farmers [that is what I had said about Iran]—can be trained without being able to read?"

"Exactly," sez I.

"Don't believe it," said Ken.

MAY 5, 1964
PRINCETON

One more spring. The flowering crab out there glows in this early morning light; our garden rises from the sweet brown earth, vigorous and lusty, as if for months it had not been dead, but asleep, under the snow and through the cold. And as the sun was at a slant last evening, an orchard oriole in the great apple tree across our neighbors' fence, a golden star, sang; and on the topmost branch of a still bare locust tree, a cardinal burnished by the sun filled the whole of the sky with a peal of sound.

How many more springs? What does it matter? This one I have.

MAY 16, 1964
PRINCETON

The Director of the National University Extension Association, Bower Aly, has written the Princeton Press further about his ambition to get my "Change" book, in a paperback edition, in the hands of 10,000 high school students. He says, to Hubel of the Press: "I would be especially pleased to be able to distribute Mr. Lilienthal's book . . . because he sheds about the only ray of light in all the encircling gloom of the publications concerning weapons control. I should like for the young people . . . to be able to hold on to some kind of lifeline toward the future."

Have just been pawing through a couple of drawers in my highboy. Astounded by the meaningless accumulation of this and that; oddments no longer used, even their original function a mystery. What a pile of useless debris—yet all of it once meant something.

It is not only outworn things one accumulates; one collects ideas as well. Those that no longer have present meaning I *try* honestly to dispose of. This sometimes riles people, leads them to call me a turncoat, etc.

But emotional accumulations; these I am reluctant to jettison. Why?

Wouldn't it be a healthy thing for a person to "clean house," to throw away everything, objects, ideas, sentiments, attachments, every ten years, say, and start afresh?

MAY 17, 1964
PRINCETON

The theme of the Two Functions of Man (the man of action and the analytical man) continues to interest me as a kind of shorthand to underline how I feel about the trend toward empty studies and surveys and "facts" for their own sake. These are far removed from the reality of the true "function" of contemplation, reflection, poetry, vision—a function unlike that of the doers, but a virile and fruitful one.

MAY 18, 1964
PRINCETON

Luncheon today with Mehdi Samii. A gentle, soft-spoken, youngish man, with the warm bright hazel eyes so common among true Iranian aristocrats. Samii is short, with a very erect carriage, a man of clarity of thought and expression who cuts across the jargon of economists and bankers. I thought to myself: this man is as capable as any central banker I have ever known, including McChesney Martin when he was first Chairman of the Governors of our Federal Reserve.

Samii told of having visited the World Bank; there has been a great change there, much more sympathy and understanding, a new readiness to help rather than to "lecture." But AID is another story.

Amused by the irony of it, but not outwardly indignant, he said: "The AID people find our balance of payments picture is not bad; indeed, it is rather good. So, says AID, since your balance of payments situation is good you don't need any help; our criterion is that we help only those whose balance is *bad.*"

I reminded him of General Marshall's story of the Minister of an underdeveloped country seeking economic aid. Asked Marshall: "And how many Communists do you have in your country?" "Communists! Why we have none, ours is a democratic, freedom-loving people." "In that case," said Marshall with a grin, "I can't give you any help. Go back and get some Communists and then I can give you aid."

MAY 22, 1964
PRINCETON

"Combative": I guess the word fits me. Maybe "belligerent" isn't too strong. The anomaly is that most people, I think, noting my demeanor in ordinary matters, would classify me as almost "meaching": low voice; "unruffled," the newspaper men used to say in their stories about Congressional hearings in which I was under fire.

Bob Moses gets a great deal done in New York State because he *is* combative, makes people scared as hell to tangle with him, uses tough adjectives to describe those who don't act as he thinks they should, in the interest of the historic work on which he has set his redoubtable heart and great skills.

On Moses it looks good. But on me? I doubt it. Why should I feel so half-apologetic for wanting to lace out at people who either are ignorant of what D&R does or show lack of sensitivity to the obligations one bears to a partner?

MAY 24, 1964
PRINCETON

The annual Lilienthal garden party yesterday had everything; the herbaceous garden itself was glowing under the flood of sunlight, and Helen and I were glowing too—with a slight blush—from the compliments, oh's and ah's poured on by the guests. Then six of us had supper together in the moonlight, under the old apple tree.

Robert Goheen‡ looked more than ever like a college valedictorian, a handsome and assured fellow in his white jacket. "Yes, I'm holding my breath that we get through the next week or so without the annual spring outbreak of student exuberance." His wife, Peggy, a lovely young woman as keen as a razor's edge, is now foreman of a grand jury. "She will learn a lot about some shocking things," commented Bob Meyner.

Robert Oppenheimer just back from a hectic visit to Berkeley—and, I gather, Los Alamos. He looks waxen with fatigue; I have rarely seen a man shrink, physically, the way it seems to me he has. He never has looked robust, not ever, but somehow I had an uneasy feeling about the look in his eyes. My imagination probably.

Harry Smyth, one of the bravest of the brave, seeming to warm up to me a bit after a period when I am sure he thought I had gone off the deep end with my skepticism about the peaceful uses of the atom. I confess that having these old scientific friends provoked with me isn't a happy situation.

Years ago my life as Chairman of AEC was beset by the damnedest furor over the "disappearance" of seven grams of enriched uranium at Argonne Lab.§ (It later was found in a bottle in a "garbage disposal" can.) Senator Hickenlooper howled and the Commission top echelon of scientists and managers had to go through days of angry public hearings. Seven *grams*.

This morning's *Times* has the news that the AEC "lost" 2.2 *pounds*, a kilo, of plutonium, worth a million dollars, about the most poisonous substance man has ever devised. That amount is about what the core of the first plutonium bomb weighed. The story was that the kilo was to provide the power for a satellite device that didn't work properly. All this was explained by saying that it was the result of "a human error"—a beautifully ironic expression in this age when science never makes a

‡ President of Princeton University.
§ See *Journals*, Vol. II, *The Atomic Energy Years*, p. 531.

mistake, only human beings, as if reliance upon a system where such consequences can come from one "human error" makes an error sit better.

MAY 27, 1964
NEW YORK

Nehru dead.

India will never be quite the same, nor East Asia for that matter. But this would be true even if Nehru had lived for another ten years.¶

The great foundation of Nehru's political philosophy, and, therefore, of the policy of India after "independence," was his fixed idea of the brotherhood between India and China.* That foundation not only collapsed, it was shattered overnight. And with that collapse other things began changing, *fast*, chiefly the increased and overwhelming power of the big Ogre-Bear, the Soviet Union.

How wonderful it is that life can be so fluid, that nothing is irrevocably fixed. Nehru is dead, and that is a fact beyond change. But India will find new leadership and a new role in the world.

This afternoon Helen and I went to the Van Gogh exhibition at the Guggenheim. The early drawings and paintings were interesting because so pale and conventional, but few of those vivid, electric paintings one associates with Van Gogh were included. Then to the Jewish Museum at 92nd Street. A most moving sculpture, out of doors, in iron or perhaps bronze: "The Procession." Inside, most of the interesting things—to me—were from Mesopotamia, half of them Persian, including three old Torah cases in silver, the tops of which were in the shape of a *Moslem mosque*, the bulb shape that is so beautiful—but hardly Jewish, I thought.

MAY 28, 1964
NEW YORK

I got to the Council on Foreign Relations early yesterday, after walking breezily up Park Avenue. The only other man there introduced himself as an officer of Liberia Mining Co., Ltd. Joe Johnson† was in the library puffing on his pipe, and the two men got to talking. Suddenly this bombshell: "We of Liberia Mining were glad to see the African American Institute take on X (whose name I don't remember) and get

¶ The Lilienthals were house guests of Nehru in February, 1951, as recounted in *Journals*, Vol. III, *The Venturesome Years*, pp. 89–115.

* See *Journals*, Vol. III, *The Venturesome Years*, pp. 94, 95, for Nehru's statement on historic ties between India and China.

† Joseph E. Johnson, President, Carnegie Endowment for International Peace.

a new spurt of energy. Of course, it was a lot easier when the CIA provided the money to get it going and operating; money came easy then."

Joe Johnson obviously was as much hit over the head by this casual disclosure as I was and turned a little grey. The man from Liberia, sitting on a table swinging his elegantly tailored legs, noted the chill that came over the room and said, "Of course, we were sworn to secrecy about the CIA, but now they are out of it; there is no secrecy about it any more." Still Joe Johnson looked troubled. I kept my mouth shut, but I couldn't help wondering how many of these fine civilizing institutes got their start in the same way, in secrecy and with public funds.

Ironically, the next man to enter the library was Allen Dulles.‡ Except for brother Foster, Allen is the most self-assured man I have ever known. Needless to say, we did not further pursue the CIA's part in financing these "cover" institute enterprises. It is now the morning after and I am still shocked. Am I just too soft for this world, or is this really another piece of our imitating practices that we are fighting to uproot when they occur in other countries? Has the British Intelligence done this sort of thing for generations? It is the secret façade, the deep-lying hypocrisy, that heats me up.

JUNE 4, 1964
5:30 P.M.
NEW YORK

I have before me a paper place mat—the kind that is so often put before each guest at "business" lunches. This affair was held in the Ford Foundation offices on Madison Avenue. All over the embossed 18″ x 18″ paper are my scribbles, in shorthand mostly, made during the first discussion of whether a Committee on a Dialogue between Latin and North American "leaders" should be formed. The Ford Foundation has endorsed the idea; but it originated, I would guess, with [former Colombian President] Lleras, who presided.

One of the participants was the former President of Venezuela, Betancourt. His face in repose is like a beetle; then he begins to speak and the eyes back of the heavy glasses brighten, he grins, chuckles, and he becomes the kind of man who can succeed a military dictator, stand up to Communist street riots, talk straight-talk to the overweening Americanos.

Betancourt appealed to me very much. There are things that could be *done*, he said, about the population crisis (growing more grave all the time), about education, about "the influence of the military, in-

† Director of the Central Intelligence Agency, 1953–61.

cluding the U.S. Pentagon" (he looked grim at this point); discussions *between governments* simply didn't get to the heart of things.

What kinds of people should be invited to such a conference? I was dubious about Jim Perkins' [President of Cornell] strongly voiced opinion that the participants should be those who could speak for "the power structure." (That is a typical "foundation" type term: power structure.) Well, if one set of power structures simply meets with another power structure, will that produce ideas? The *whole point* about Latin America is that their power structures are determined to keep things as they are, whereas the rest of the people, particularly the young people, are determined on change.

JUNE 5, 1964
WASHINGTON, D.C.

In the receiving line at the White House luncheon for the Shah, the President seemed huge and overwhelming alongside the slender, shorter Shah. Johnson greeted me as "Dave" and began to hand me over —as is the custom—to his guest, His Imperial Majesty. The Shah's face brightened; he threw his arms wide, his eyebrows raised: "Oh, we are old friends." I said it was good to be able to welcome him to *my* country, after he had made me feel at home so often in his. The Empress was about the only woman wearing a hat, a high-crowned yellow felt, setting off her dark impassive beauty.

The First Lady's comment to me was in her usual friendly way: "Mr. Lilienthal, when we were in Iran all we heard about was the wonderful things you have been doing for that country. You should feel very proud and happy about it, as we do."

The President rose to make a little speech and drink a toast to the Shah, according to the ritual. The handsome young King arose from his golden chair beside the First Lady and began his response in a thin but elegant voice. Just then this big hunk of man who is the center of power in the world leaned far to one side in *his* big gold chair so he could get at the handkerchief in his hip pocket, got it out, wrapped it around a good sized nose, and blew; blew a lusty tug-boat kind of snort.

I liked that touch. This natural, human, unrefeened country-man; when he needed to blow his nose, he didn't do it in any Brahmin way.

[Senator] Mike Monroney and Ellen drove Helen and me back to the hotel. Monroney said that when Franklin Roosevelt, Jr., had asked John Kennedy, after he was President, why he didn't *talk* to people and go to the country with fireside talks so that the mail would roll in for him, too, Kennedy had answered that he was uneasy about doing this, that he felt unsure of himself. "He could write beautiful prose, like that beautiful stuff of Adlai's," Mike said, "but it didn't sound as if he *cared. This* fellow [meaning Johnson] cares like everything. He was even dickering with me [at the lunch for the Shah] about two votes he needs to get a bill out of a committee. 'And I want that bill out by Monday, d'hear.' "

Said Ellen: "He called Mike on the phone at night, he's on the phone all the time pushing and shoving for the things he wants."

JUNE 6, 1964
DULLES AIRPORT
WASHINGTON, D.C.

At the National Gallery's exhibition of 7000 years of Iranian art, Helen and I encountered old friends, Al Friendly and his buoyant, beautiful wife, Jean.

Al has an almost unique eye for the personalities that are more than half the story of the unfolding of "events" in Washington. Unlike some columnists (or three times a week pundits, if you prefer), he has been a reporter in the literal sense. Now, as Managing Editor of the *Washington Post*, i.e., general manager on the news and editorial side of the most influential paper in any *capital* city, he has an *operating* man's insights. This is an important distinction. I mean the distinction between the day to day operator's responsibilities for a reporting instrument (a newspaper) and those of an "essayist" at however high a level, say, a Lippmann or a Reston, who are somewhere in between the pundit and the reporter.

Al's comments always stir me, particularly since they are said with a little boy's sidelong crooked grin, a lighting up of the eye, and a half snort.

About President Johnson, says Al: "He's terrific. But nothing will satisfy him except that *everyone* votes for him. Everyone. Businessmen, every one of them." That's why there is a good chance, Al intimates, that it will be McNamara for Vice President. L.B.J. never overlooks any criticism; "he had us of the *Post* over for a luncheon and went over and over some statement we had made in an editorial—what was it about? Trade? I've forgotten—but he was determined to show us we were wrong. Maybe we were, but what I mean is the *Post* is strong for him, but we have to be for *everything* he does or he is upset."

JUNE 10, 1964
LOS ANGELES

A Churchill anecdote reported this morning, apropos the death of Lord Beaverbrook, fits into the impending flood of Lilienthalia, now that the first volumes of my *Journals* are about to appear.

Churchill to Beaverbrook: "What are you doing?" "Writing," said Beaverbrook.

"What do you write about?"

"Me," says Beaverbrook.

"A good subject," says Churchill. "I have been writing about me for fifty years and with excellent results."

How "excellent" the results, time and the critics of my *Journals* will tell; but writing about me for fifty years is about the story of the *Journals*.

Have just received a black covered pamphlet entitled "Cue Book" for the forty-fifth annual Commencement of the University of California, Los Angeles. Page 33 reads:

"(Mr. Lilienthal will come forward, removing and holding his mortarboard, followed by Chancellor Murphy as his sponsor, and will take his place near the President, etc. Chancellor Murphy: 'Mr. President, I present David Eli Lilienthal.')" And so on.

"(After the words of the citation come to a close Chancellor Murphy will place the hood over Mr. Lilienthal's shoulders, opening out the folds so the University colors are visible. . . .)" And so on.

Don't leave anything to chance these days.

JUNE 11, 1964
7 P.M.
HOTEL BEL AIR

A morning full of tension, and of satisfaction and pride, at the UCLA Commencement exercises. The tension because of the fear of some kind of violence from a "demonstration" against the Shah, topped by a Wild West performance of a police helicopter "dog-fighting" a small plane bearing an anti-Shah streamer flying over the Commencement throng, the throwing out of the stands of men with anti-Shah banners, the State Police patrolling the rooftops with carbines in hand, the Empress sitting in the audience, her long, slim legs crossed. Her worried look most of us on the platform shared.

I have just come from a visit with the Shah at the Ambassador Hotel. A very satisfactory one. He was warm, clear-eyed, no mark of fatigue or irritation.

The Shah's demeanor was quite different from what I can remember in any of the many meetings I have had with him, perhaps because of the excitement of the day, the heavy security guards, the banners of the pickets, the long session with the hundreds of Iranian students—I don't know. But his eyes were wide open, the conscious inner restraint or control, the half-open eyes so characteristic of him, were gone. His eyes actually were very deeply dark and a-glitter, the pupils dilated. He had a vigor and quickness of comment that I have never seen in our meetings in the Palace or at his Residence.

Of the most substantive importance was the Shah's vehement statement in opening our talk. We must without a day's delay begin the Second Phase of Khuzistan, the next dam. He informed me that he had given directions that the full additional 125,000 hectares should be developed. I reminded him that this entails approval by the Plan Organization of the KWPA program and budget for the balance of the Third Plan, which Plan Organization has been continuing to study since I saw him in April. Whether he will "follow through" on this, I don't know; but I have learned that this man has an amazing ability to grasp and remember operational details.

The Shah recited the names of the Senators who had lunched with him in Washington, and was only hesitant about one "who is particularly interested in agriculture." "Senator Aiken?" I asked. Yes, that was his name. (Could I recite the names of an equivalent number of Iranians I had never before met, on the basis of a couple of hours' lunch? No.)

"I told your people [this is the way he usually introduces what he has to say to me about meetings with anyone in our Government] that Khuzistan is the key to Iran's present and future, that it must be held at all costs. I know that if Russia goes across our border, with her it is war, all-out war. But Khuzistan they would like to take by brushfire war." (I put in, "and infiltration.") He continued, "Beneath the earth is the oil, in vast quantities, and upon the surface of the earth, the soil to feed the whole of Iran. Khuzistan is the key to Iran, and therefore to the whole Middle East, and to Africa as well."

I told the Shah of the twenty-two young Iranians who now operate the Pahlavi powerhouse; that none of them had *seen* a control room before they began their training; that in eighteen months the Canadian Hydro team we brought in to train them had turned them into responsible operators; that we had had similar experience in the seasoning of men on line crews.

At first he looked at me quizzically, but intently. He has a flattering way of listening *hard* when something really interests him, his head cocked to one side, leaning forward a bit. But there are many other times when it is different. When he is listening patiently to set speeches (in Persian, of course) at such ceremonials as the dedication of the dam on the Dez, he gazes off into space, as if praying that the speech won't be too long. Or when he stops at decorated archways on the road, as I have so often seen him do, and the local sheiks sweat over their scripts in the hot sun, and sweat too because of the excitement of this great chance to tell their story to the Shahinshah, then too he looks really bored.

"I know," he said, looking away from me, "that you don't need to do this work in Iran. You do it because you are dedicated to that work and have been most of your life. I know that."

Well, thought I, we have come a long way since Gordon Clapp and I wrote our first sketch of the future possibilities of a region that I knew damn well—and so did Gordon—was proffered to us because it was a "hot potato," and one the FAO had written off as no-count.

I phoned the substance of this talk to John Oliver; also His Majesty's comments about a national electrification program, along with my expression of reluctance to undertake such a project without knowing how big a job it was. "It is *before* I get into things that I stop and calculate; after I'm in I want to throw everything I have into making it work."

JUNE 12, 1964
10:00 A.M.
HOTEL BEL AIR

Yesterday morning, at 9:30, I was dutifully standing in front of this hotel when Dr. Clark Kerr, the President of this enormous "multiversity," as he has dubbed the University of California, drove up with his wife, to take me to the "robing room."

Kerr has penetrating eyes behind rather strong rimless glasses. "What you said in your Princeton Lectures a year and a half ago, *events* [he bore down on this word, giving me an almost stern look] have proven, and continue to confirm each day. Your book§ I think was one of the best things that has been said in recent years, the insight into how things get done."

As we walked together to the Chancellor's beautiful residence, he turned and said: "As a labor mediator, which was my principal work, I have always believed in not reaching for too big bites of a problem, so what you said about the 'manageable job' fitted into my own experience of life."

JUNE 14, 1964
SUNDAY, 12:30 A.M.
CUCUTA, COLOMBIA

The day began eighteen hours ago, and I have been at it hard ever since: flying over much of eastern Colombia, listening to speeches and having them made at me, driving on winding mountain roads like crazy, getting no food until we had been standing up for hours. One night without going to bed at all. God, what a day. I'll do this sort of endurance contest once too often one of these days.

§ *Change, Hope, and the Bomb,* Princeton University Press, 1963.

5 P.M.
ABOARD AVIANCA HEADED NONSTOP FOR NEW YORK,
WHERE I'LL BE IN FOUR HOURS.

Is it possible that at noon today I was sitting in a circle of men in the "breezeway" of a crude shelter on the banks of the Zulia River, a primitive place in the Colombian way-back country, the Andes rising on every side? We had just come across this rapid stream in a dugout piloted by two "ignorant" (that is, illiterate) hill men; but about how to get that little dugout across the stream and back they knew more than all the rest of us "literate" characters put together.

On the whole these last two days in Colombia have been a good experience. The qualification is required by honesty. That I had some low moments is an understatement. For example, last night about 10:30, with practically nothing to eat since breakfast, and on the go the whole time, I would have given all of South America back to the Conquistadores, gladly.

But what now crowds to the fore of my mind—being an absolutely hopeless optimist and in love with life—are scenes of the kind that do not happen often to any man.

Four hundred people—Governors, Bishops, and the upper crust rank and file of the Border Area of two countries—gathered in Cucuta, jabbered, ate lunch together, and then got into cars to drive perhaps thirty miles for this ceremony, the signing of an agreement between the power companies of Cucuta in Colombia and San Cristobal in nearby Venezuela.

This was to be the first step in the "integration" of these two countries, then of the Andean◖ countries, and then, even more remote and still more hopefully, of the whole of Latin America—a Latin American Common Market.

But instead of having speeches by dignitaries of the two countries —and the signing of the compact—in the plaza or at the hotel, there was a gesture of the Latin American sense of history, a romantic, symbolic gesture. We all went to the partially ruined but wonderfully inspiring and beautiful remains of a colonial church. It had been wrecked by an earthquake, but it was the church in which Simon Bolivar had signed an important declaration in the early 19th century, affecting La Gran Colombia, or what is now the two countries of Colombia and Venezuela.

My eye was more taken with the local amateur brass band—my

◖ In 1969 an Andean Group was formed at Cartegena consisting of Colombia, Chile, Bolivia, Ecuador; by 1972 Venezuela had become a part-member of the Group; by 1975 the members are functioning actively on economic integration small-town background, no doubt—than with the beautiful setting. But it was magnificent: a white arch, with columns on either side. It was within and behind this arch that the altar stood when Bolivar orated and signed that historic document. Above the arch the church tower rose intact; and as the afternoon changed into evening the lights on this tower, and the shadows cast by the great royal palms that surround the church, gave this work of the Spanish conquerors a beauty that, ironically, the free men who followed them have never equalled.

At the site of the former altar sat the dignitaries, among them Felipe Herrera, a good public servant and an extraordinarily good orator, and the Colombian Minister of Agriculture, Virgilio Barco. Cucuta is Barco's "home town"; from here he went to MIT to study for four years under Walt Rostow and other figures in the great world.

Barco was in the midst of an impassioned speech about the historic nature of the occasion when I suddenly heard him begin to talk about "doktor" Lilienthal, who is "simbólico" of integration, etc. It was a bit startling to hear myself spoken of in these terms in the backcountry of South America, in a place hallowed by Bolivar, when only two days before I heard comparable words about me from the Shahinshah of Persia.

The past two days have had a measure of natural beauty, magnificent monumental beauty, that the episodes about "development" tend to obscure. The Andes! Cordillera Oriental. They reach for the sky, and the sky should be proud that they do. The soft purple delicacy, which I remember so well as marking the Great Smokies, that these great works of God have, particularly at a great distance. Seeing them from a few thousand or even a few hundred feet as we flew in the Piper, or sitting on the bank of a stream, or driving: here is a bonanza of joy of the senses that all the gloomy—and perhaps accurate—forebodings of intelligent economists cannot fog over. These mountains—green now in the spring—are one of the great gifts God has given to man. The Conquistadores and the economists of the AID or "Harvard Group" missions, or the solemn Colombians determined to improve their country, have long since ceased to *see* these encircling arms of our Maker. But I find them there all the time. Lift thine eyes unto the hills.

A line from a review by Alan Pryce-Jones of a book by Ernest Hemingway, *A Moveable Feast:*

". . . joy to read. . . . He is at his best in evocation of being young and in love."

Why is there always this synonymity between love and youth? Don't people know that love takes more, far more than youth can possibly have to offer? Youth has not yet lived; it is only those who have lived, fully, who can understand what love is all about, the focus, the intensification of the experience of a man and a race. The laser intensifies light—a form of energy. Love intensifies and focuses the whole range of living. It is the sum total of youth *plus* that journey through the valleys and to the mountain peaks, the blood and tears and triumphs and disillusion and fulfillment that are life at its best.

JUNE 16, 1964
5 P.M.
ABOARD THE PENNSYLVANIA AT WASHINGTON

Jack Valenti met me at the door of the Cabinet Room, a short compact dark-haired fellow with a harried look and pronounced hollows under his dark eyes. He opened the door to the President's office, ushered me through with a little bow and called out, "Mr. Lilienthal, Mr. President." From across the room came a soft voice: "Be with you in a second, Dave." Crouching forward in his chair, talking into a phone, was the President. Valenti asked me to sit down on a divan near the door to the Cabinet Room, but somehow that seemed wrong, so I stood. The President swung across from his desk with his almost shambling gait, his trousers loose and baggy. His way of walking, half pigeon-toed, half shuffling, reminds me of how some of my amused friends describe my own style of walking, down to the extra material in my pants, ready-made for a large-waisted man.

A big hand, roughened by shaking hands with a million people. In a soft, almost inaudible voice he said the usual courteous things: he was glad to see me, appreciated my coming in. He pointed to the sofa and settled himself in a huge padded rocker, a symphony in ugly brown cloth, hoisting his feet onto a matching brown foot-rest dingus tilted at an angle.

At close range—he pulled his chair right to my elbow—he looked extremely healthy.

I expected him to do most of the talking, but instead, he paid me the highest of all courtesies, acting as if everything I said either on my own or in response to his laconic questions or comments was of great interest to him. None of the kind of big-shot appearance of thinking about something else, despite the fact that the troubles in Southeast Asia—Laos at present—are growing to a severe climax (Valenti reminded him that the NSC [National Security Council] was gathering and would be ready for their meeting with the President in fifteen minutes).

"The Shah thinks a lot of you and what you are doing; when he was here the other day he made it mighty strong. I guess he is doing a good job and means business about land reform and developing that—what's the name—that region you are doing over for him. What do you do, advise, draw up plans, and that sort of thing?"

I told him the project was going well; that the Shah was making a strong effort on land reform; that he thought of Khuzistan as a great national asset and wanted to speed up its development; that we had received real cooperation, that the Iranians were now running a big part of the job after we had got it started.

I made some reference to the "sensitive" kind of area Khuzistan is, with Arab pressure from Iraq right along the border. "I don't say that Khuzistan is like South Vietnam, but there is this resemblance: what we have been doing is giving the peasants—they use that word though I prefer farmer—a stake in the country. Now they feel that they are being thought about and things are happening *for* them. There is an effort by Iraq to infiltrate the region—a good part of which is made up of Arab-speaking Iranians. Poor and neglected as it was, the constructive things now going on in Khuzistan just could make it less likely that some day soldiers will have to be sent there."

"Using troops is the very last thing we want to do," Johnson said, putting his head back and looking at me through the lower part of his glasses.

As I got up to go—he was paying no attention to Valenti standing there waiting anxiously—he looked at his hands and in a simple quiet way said: "Dave, what is going on in Iran is about the best thing going on anywhere in the world."

As he strode to the door and to the responsibilities of a sinkhole kind of "war" in Laos, just before an election here, he said over his shoulder: "Get me my NSC minutes." He looked at me hard, his head cocked. I hadn't seen such close, intense listening in that room, ever. I said I was seeing Walt Rostow in the afternoon. "A good man," he commented.

JUNE 17, 1964
PRINCETON

When I reached home last evening, David 3d, tall and graceful as a reed, rushed at me, arms outstretched, with the warmth and outgivingness that make him a very exceptional boy. What a handsome fellow he is, with his blond thatch, his mischievous grin, his outpouring of love.

To wander with your own grandson and namesake through the dappled woods in the late afternoon, he ahead of you, bouncing and running, then walking alongside to tell me *his* technique with his father. "I just hinted and hinted, just once in a while, and then Dad said to me: 'I'm going to Princeton to work with *my* father; would you like to go along?' That's what I had been hinting for a long time, so I acted surprised and said, 'Yes, I would like that.' "

A big to-do today over a World Bank staffer's letter to the Plan Organization, uncovered yesterday by John Oliver, which raised all kinds of picayune questions about the Greater Dez program. The letter dealt with Khuzistan as if the loan involved a mortgage on a little retail store instead of being an important asset of a country and a big factor in its future and that of the free world. The letter will fit beautifully into that archive of evidence of how petty some men are who deal with great and vital issues. I am making a collection of these and someday may put the mosaic together for the world to see. The notion that we are ready for World Government when there aren't even enough people with a decent sense of vision and responsibility to operate a lending institution!!

JUNE 19, 1964
NEW YORK

Tuesday morning I saw Senator Fulbright in his office for a half hour or so. With a characteristic twinkle and that delightful drawl he told me of the luncheon meeting with the Shah, attended by a group of Senators.

"The Shah spoke of that region you have been working in with great enthusiasm; biggest thing in his country, going well, results very satisfactory, going to expand it—well, you know all about that. Then he talked about you strong."

The Senator went on to say that he was expecting a call any minute for a Southern caucus committee on the Civil Rights Bill, headed by Senator "Dick" Russell.

I broke in to say that Senator Russell was a noble man; I was sorry, personally, to see how painful it was for him to lose his long fight against civil rights legislation, however mistaken.

The Senator agreed about Russell as a man. "But I try to persuade Dick that when seventy-seven Senators voted for cloture we had lost, and that to go on offering amendments after amendments made no sense. But Dick keeps using dramatic phrases right out of the Civil War and the Confederacy. 'Drain the cup of hemlock.' 'The honor of the South is in our hands.' That sort of thing. John Sparkman and I don't agree with him, but we're the only ones in our caucus who see it that way, so it goes on and on.

"You are seeing Johnson, I understand." "Yes, in about fifteen minutes." Bill lowered his head, looked at the floor, shook his head slowly: "A remarkable man."

ON THE "4 O'CLOCK" AT PENN STATION

Tearing down that dignified monument of another day, Penn Station, is a painful thing to see. Noble columns, great space, the memory of late afternoon sun through the upper windows. Now, hard hats and drills all around, the air filled with the dust of a once handsome ornament which, apparently, this poverty stricken metropolis can no longer afford.

JUNE 24, 1964
NEW YORK

It takes a deep and intense emotion to give one second sight, that capacity to see beneath the surface, to see people, on the street or the subway, for example, not as blurs or daubs, flat and non-dimensional, but as infinitely interesting, each completely and utterly special, unique.

When I look at the faces of those who no longer *see*, truly see, the world about them, I know that I am looking at people who are no longer capable—were they ever?—of feeling intensely, capable of that love which marks the person fully alive.

JUNE 29, 1964
NEW YORK

Don Straus, prominent in the Planned Parenthood–World Federation, asked me last week to include my name as one of the signers of a full-page ad in the *Times* this Sunday: the bite of the ad is to "persuade" politicians that birth control is no longer a sensitive policy issue, and that a program of providing "services" to people who want to have less than a baby a year can be a proper and safe subject for government.

All OK; but there was a paragraph headed "What about the Catholics?" which went on to say that birth control was no longer a religious issue.

I told Don I didn't want to sign the ad; I thought that the *facts* had produced such a good effect on everyone, including Catholics, in the last two years that the less said about "the Catholics" the better at this time—lest it seem that such outside pounding and not the facts was producing the change. I also said I thought making birth control an issue at the conventions and in the campaign would be a serious mistake. This is a long-range program, involving sensitive *personal* questions, and it would not be helped by being thrown into a political cockpit.

JUNE 30, 1964
NEW YORK

A fine glow of elation as I opened the *Times* in the taxi at 7:30 this morning: a big picture of the [Dez] Pahlavi Dam, Development and Resources mentioned by name, and an eloquent story about great engineering works, treating dams as a manifestation of contemporary life; this apropos the opening last night of the Modern Museum's engineering exhibition.

This afternoon I visited the show. The working model of the Dam stood at the gateway to the exhibit, beautifully lighted so that it could almost be an abstract sculpture, graceful, enigmatic, and strangely *light*, almost floating.

JULY 3, 1964
6:30 A.M.
PENN STATION

Mid-Manhattan in the early hours is a different city from Manhattan at 8:50 A.M., when the commuters pour onto the sidewalks from Darien, Westport, etc.

The streets at 6 A.M. are almost empty of people and cars. But there are the garbage trucks. To most of us the garbage trucks are a *sound*, a nuisance disturbing our postdawn sleep with the grinding rattle of the cans and noise of the trucks. But to a good many men—I saw them at work this morning—they are not merely a noise; they are troughs into which smelly garbage is poured, like the pig troughs back in the days when I knew farms.

JULY 9, 1964
MARTHA'S VINEYARD

Received and savored my beloved physician Dana Atchley's Commencement address at Washington University. A scientist who knows how important, how vital, is imagination. Atchley quotes Francis Bacon: "The office of medicine is to tune this curious harp of man's body and reduce it to harmony." Then: "This poetic concept of the physician displays the fundamental insight that poetry achieves . . . as it holds the mirror to human affairs." The speech explains why I have found in this man such riches of understanding, reassurance, and self-education. A gentle reminder: *"Patient, heal thyself"* (to modify the older "physician, heal thyself").

Then Atchley quotes Montaigne: ". . . there is nothing so beautiful and legitimate as to play the man well and properly, no knowledge so hard to acquire as the knowledge of how to live this life well and naturally; and the most barbarous of maladies is to despise our being. . . ."

JULY 11, 1964
MARTHA'S VINEYARD

Thoughts on returning from a wild, exciting sail yesterday—single hand as usual, in a thirty-mile northeaster.

My little open boat is brave, but so puny; the sea so beautiful, so furious, so angry at our pretensions. Riding through the lashing, hissing violence—and bringing the little craft home, grinning and shouting as one dark cascade after another snaps at us, hurls buckets of water over my head, down the sleeves of my jacket.

I shouldn't do such things, I know, but there is such delight in fighting something so much bigger and more powerful than oneself.

"What are you trying to prove?" I am continually asked. Well, the evasive answer is: "Prove? Nothing. What do you mean, prove?" The more honest answer, I suppose, is: I'm proving I am a man unafraid. That sounds overdramatic and certainly not "sensible." But behind all my alleged "judgment" and common sense lie thousands of years of man's inheritance that make it deeply important to "prove" that one is unafraid; or, if afraid, to plow ahead, with the relish and gusto that distinguish a full-brown male from one of the increasingly numerous intermediates.

JULY 12, 1964
MARTHA'S VINEYARD

A warm and most dignified letter of appreciation from Abdol Reza Ansari refers to my account of my "audience" with the Shah in Los Angeles, adding that the approvals I urged upon His Imperial Majesty are substantially in hand. Then come some sentences which sound almost like the kind you issue for a guy's memorial service: "The credit for the success of our programme is largely due to your foresight and untiring efforts. . . . It [Khuzistan program] will stand as a tribute to the statesmanship and perseverance of a great American."

But Reza has been through another tough period, particularly tough for so sensitive and highly tuned a patriot. Although he had been given assurance that KWPA would not be affected by the establishment of the new Ministry of Water and Power, the night before the Shah left for the U.S. KWPA was "attached" to that Ministry. Reza reports to John Oliver that he therefore informed the Prime Minister that he had resigned. The Prime Minister refused to accept the resignation, assuring Reza personally that nothing would "happen" to KWPA. Now the Shah has named Reza Governor General of Khuzistan, as a mark of recognition, and to help overcome his unhappiness about being made part of the Ministry, if that is what it amounts to.

If the Minister were a Persian-style ego-ridden Harold Ickes, surrounded as Harold was by apple polishers, I would say this action about KWPA was disastrous and should be fought tooth and nail; but surely this action isn't, and need never become, disastrous. Making Reza Governor as well as Managing Director of KWPA would seem a typically circuitous, Rooseveltian way of dealing with a combined administrative and personality issue.

JULY 16, 1964
MARTHA'S VINEYARD

What was out of the question in the minds of the political wiseacres six months ago became harsh reality last night: Barry Goldwater was nominated, by a reorganized Republican Party which is hard as nails and contemptuous of almost everything we have learned since the end of the War—or thought we had learned.

I wonder whether ever again, in my lifetime at least, the Western countries, and those parts of Asia friendly to the West, will be willing to follow our lead, as they did for the first ten years after the War, almost without question.

JULY 20, 1964
HOTEL BILTMORE
NEW YORK

The nomination of Goldwater—a good bit of which we watched on a portable TV—was a disturbing experience. It is easy to view with alarm anything the opposition does; but this was more than a rehash of the "this is the last chance for freedom" kind of rhetoric we have been hearing since Willkie's foray of 1940.

No, there was an *unhealthy* note, at times hysterical here. The jeering and howling down of Nelson Rockefeller was something hard to believe, so wild and unrestrained and lacking in fairness to an opponent. That word "opponent" seems strange, considering that this man was the front-runner for the nomination, the Republican Governor of a great state. Yet "opponent" was the mildest word that came to mind as we watched that performance.

The theory that Goldwater *could* win by appealing to whites against blacks, not only in the South but particularly in the Northern states, seemed farfetched, despite the relatively strong showing that Governor Wallace of Alabama made in some of the Northern primaries. And then I return to New York City the night a pitched battle is going on in Harlem between Negroes and the police. True, Harlem is an extreme case, but it is these extreme cases that create pictures of *fear* in people's minds, pictures that politicians are eager to make use of, and do. Indeed, that is part of the profession and practice of politics.

The news today about Nate Greene is sad: another stroke. That this sometimes mischievous, sometimes waspish, always intelligent little man, my private conscience as I called him, should be doomed to months of disability of the worst kind: how utterly heartrending. And added to the script of tragedy, poignant and frustrating, his young wife Rosalinda to have a baby within the next two weeks or so.

This hotel is filled with middle-aged, successful business and professional men from all over the country, decked out since dawn in green satin bloomers and the rest of the Shriner regalia. But except for setting off explosives (for noise) in the corridor here, and playing on their glockenspiels and other instruments, it is certainly a harmless way of having fun, if fun it is. Male fellowship takes many forms, and this is one of them.

I wish someone would do a detailed story of a Shriner national convention. Who are these usually sedate men—that is, sedate back home? What do they get out of these activities?

It is Americana I'd like to see documented, sympathetically but factually.

JULY 24, 1964
WOODS HOLE, MASS.
ON THE STEAMER FOR THE VINEYARD

An intensely interesting talk with Don Straus as he drove me from Boston to Woods Hole.

I had had considerable skepticism about the urgency of birth control, or population control (the better term in the U.S.). I had limited my comments about the importance of the issue to countries like India. So I asked him to give his concept of the linkage between our serious problems in the U.S.—unemployment, race-relations, urbanism, etc.—and population growth.

What followed was one of those refreshing experiences (as we drove along the sea marshes) that comes when you re-examine an idea, separate it into parts, test it and put it together again, in the company of a fairminded, objective, and extraordinarily well motivated man like Don.

Don convinced me that in the U.S. as well as in the underdeveloped and poor countries, limitation on the rate of population growth is intimately related to the ability to cope with many other national problems.

It troubles him that large segments of the business community feel that *their* interest lies in continued population growth; retailers, real estate men, the automobile industry—all those businesses that prosper, or think they do, in direct relation to the number of people who are their customers. It will be a tough job to persuade them that this isn't true.

JULY 25, 1964
MARTHA'S VINEYARD

Don Straus believes that the next year or two may be decisive in getting a strong population control "movement" established and effective. There have been important confabs at the Vatican. So sure is he that the Pope will take a favorable position on the relationship between the "pill" and the Catholic approved "rhythm" method of birth control that he showed me a press release he has already prepared against the good prospect of a very early announcement from the Vatican.

Don has the kind of temperament so priceless in today's emotion-charged atmosphere. He *cares* deeply about the population issue; yet he *works* hard at trying to understand the religious and even the subtle theological doctrines which the Catholic Church must square, somehow, with the realities of the desperate need for a stabilized population. He reads Catholic theological magazines and papers and talks to priests in his efforts to understand how they think and feel, rather than condemn their views as hindering the prevention of a population catastrophe—which he believes will be on us within a generation.

I told him one of his chief problems was the competition of other issues for highest priority, the chief one being the race violence issue in the U.S. Just a moment ago came the alarming and to me surprising news that a race riot broke out in Rochester in upper New York State, of all places, smashing up a large part of the business section of the city. What *is* this?

JULY 30, 1964
MARTHA'S VINEYARD

Last night, with a sweet and gentle fog outside, this pleasant living room was boiling with emotion as Peggy [David's wife] relived for us her experience in Williamston, N.C., where she and four women friends "tested" local denial of civil rights and were arrested and jailed.

She was a moving, almost heroic figure: looking much too young to be the mother of a sixteen-year-old, but exhibiting the intensity of feeling of one who is just learning of the depth of the differences in the outlooks of human beings, of man's capacity for disdain and cold hatred, of her own capacity for bitterness and revulsion at how other people treat their fellow men. I wanted to protect her from feeling hatred and contempt for "that sheriff" and "those vicious teenagers" in Williamston who cursed her or were enraged by what she said or did. You reach out this way to your own children, to "protect" them, but you know that they must learn by their *own* experience. If they aren't equipped to avoid the *self-consuming* fires of hate or oversensitivity, there is nothing much you can do about it.

John Oakes, also a guest last night, has almost white hair, in a crew cut; he is slender and athletic looking, though since he is thirty years out of Princeton, he is no longer as much the young man as his eager, intensely interested demeanor suggests. Speaking from the pulpit of the Great Voice of American Journalism, the *New York Times* editorial page, which he heads, he is the sophisticated Opinion Formers' opinion former.

Yesterday he was not the city man, but a passionate lover of the out-of-doors. At luncheon he spoke to me of the crime it would be if this unique island suffered the fate of much of Cape Cod—honky-tonk, overcrowding, etc. There must be some ingenious way to prevent this from happening to the Vineyard.

The crucial factor, of course, is that the year-round residents are the only ones who have votes here and are therefore the only ones who could enact zoning restriction, if zoning is the answer. *Their* interest is in increasing taxable property, which means further development of the island, including the spots of rare and perishable beauty. "Summer" residents who are property owners, having no vote, can't directly influence what happens; they can "protest" but in a town meeting they are ineffective. A national park doesn't seem possible; a state park, as an alternative to zoning, seems even more difficult to get through.

As we were leaving the Nat Eliases', where we were lunching, Oakes saw half a dozen trout lilies (a wild, flaming lily) on the mantelpiece. He stopped short as if he had seen the ghost of his grandfather sitting there. "Who picked those?" he demanded. Nat, taken aback, said he had; weren't they pretty? Oakes, apologizing only formally for criticizing his host in his own home, proceeded to read Nat a lecture on the sin of picking these lilies; if picked, the root dies! Refreshing, seeing this intense interest in the natural world from a man who lives in a

New York City apartment and whose life is spent largely in setting down words on broad and cosmic issues for all the world to ponder.

Here Helen is completely content and happy. No life of leisure: she does a good-sized laundry, including the ironing, sweeps, and cooks the meals and washes dishes; she even disposes of the garbage. She goes into town several times a week, returning with sacks and sacks of groceries.

Helen really loves this place, "Topside," most of all, I think, because here she can see the sky in all its moods and fancies. Not the sliver of sky one sees from the usual house, for our big room here has windows that seem almost to touch the very sky.

Here the sky—and, as yesterday, the sweet coverlet of the fog—dominates. It is the sky, and the green that lies in all directions unmarred by any sign of man, that is the reason for our being, the center of life, *not* what goes on inside the house or even inside my head.

AUGUST 4, 1964
MARTHA'S VINEYARD

It has become fashionable of late to speak of the "deep discontent" in America. This is an old and sure-fire theme for commentators, Communists, novelists, and dramatists.

Public figures have picked up this note too. President Johnson the other day—a sanguine man if ever there was one—himself said that Americans are the best fed, the best this and the best that—naturally—and then went on to add, "*but* Americans are discontent."

Of course we are. That is the very mark of a restless, vital, imaginative, dynamic, volatile, interested, and thoroughly alive human being—and the same can be said of a people. The people who are forever "content" are those who are stagnating, resigned, dull, nostalgic, with no real *vitality*.

Is it necessary to remind ourselves that there was no "content" in the men who crossed the Appalachians, who headed for the Missouri and the West? Is it necessary to recall that this very nation derives its peculiar and distinctive vitality from discontent, the discontent that has brought us new blood from all over Europe, particularly in the last seventy-five years?

AUGUST 12, 1964
MARTHA'S VINEYARD

A terrible confrontation between our professions and our conduct goes on this summer all over America.

Tonight on this island there are parents whose children are spending the summer on the voter registration drive in Mississippi, at the risk of their lives (recalling the horrible fate of the three young men destroyed near Philadelphia, Mississippi, not more than a month or so ago). So not only our Peggy and her "cell mates" but a great many comfortable people and their children are really doing something; my money contributions are as nothing, a kind of buying myself off the way well-to-do men paid for their replacements during the draft in the Civil War.

How much "good" all this does is hard to say. But it is *real*, it is concrete and specific, it makes a few black people know that there are some people who are thinking of them in their really tough time.

This doesn't "solve the Negro Problem," shake the bastions of hatred, or bring on a New Day of Love and Understanding. But the power of an honest act of human consideration, however limited, is never wholly wasted.

AUGUST 22, 1964
MARTHA'S VINEYARD

Elizabeth Janeway, the novelist, and her business-journalist husband, Eliot, here to dinner last night. Also David and Peggy.

Mrs. Janeway seated under a light in our big friendly unfinished living room was anything but the picture of one of America's leading writers of fiction and criticism. Small, she has none of the brittle aggressiveness one associates with the female author. Her reading glasses perched way down on her nose, she got out her knitting and seemed to yield the arena to her expansive husband. Perhaps a good division of functions. When some remark interested her, she would peer over the top of her glasses quizzically or with a chuckle, and then resume her knitting.

To get the conversation away from the staple item: Goldwater ("As of tonight, Johnson couldn't win," Eliot pontificated), I tried to turn the talk to fiction, having two novelists in the room. I asked each of them, she and David, how their stories evolved in their imaginations.

David said his began with a plot or situation idea, and the characters grew out of that; Mrs. Janeway said almost the reverse, that people came to her mind who got in some kind of "fix," and it was their characters that created the narrative, the plot, rather than the plot calling for a cast of characters. The thing she felt she must try to avoid is "making up"—to use a phrase she said she got from the *Journals* of Virginia Woolf. I asked her to explain, since I thought fiction was entirely "making things up."

"When I find the people work themselves out of—or into—situations that grow out of the kind of people they are, that's good. But sometimes I try to help them out by 'making up' and that is bad."

It's another world, is all I can say. *My* characters do the darnedest, most unlikely things, but they are real people who do what they do—make up or not—and that's all there is to it. It may not be according to the rules or the art of fiction for a Wall Street prodigy—Jim Forrestal—to become Secretary of Defense in a Democratic administration, to be harassed and harrowed, and to jump out of the sixteenth floor at the Naval Hospital—but that is what in fact that particular "character" in my career's story did.

SEPTEMBER 2, 1964
MARTHA'S VINEYARD

Last night at the Jerry Wiesners' Ed Murrow's smile was warm, his handclasp strong, that light in his eye the same as when he was in the midst of the almost violently active life he loves so well. I was so relieved that outwardly, at least, his terrible ordeal of cancer, of facing death and wrestling with inactivity, hadn't marked him more than it had: one shoulder noticeably drooped; he was somewhat thinner; that was about all.

He spoke with such pride of the "quality" of the men in public service, in government, telling me how he had laid into Bill Paley, General Sarnoff, and Frank Stanton when they commiserated with him about having to work with third rate people in the United States Information Service, which he headed: "I said you gentlemen think I know something about this broadcasting business, at least you paid me a considerable amount of money on that basis. I tell you [here he turned on me fiercely, with that old familiar glare], I tell you that I could build a broadcasting outfit with the men in this Agency that would beat anything you have."

Janet Murrow, too, spoke quietly to me after dinner of how much he enjoyed his work in Washington, how important it was that he be there "for the Agency . . . and for the country." Then the merest suggestion of a sigh: "But, there it is."

What troubled me was how long it would be before this rare man, who almost single-handed had felled McCarthy when he was riding high, would *want* to do hard things again. This *desire* is so often the first casualty of such a grave illness as he has been through; and with it, the depression induced by radiation treatment, deprivation of accustomed excitement, etc. To have that desire to do hard but satisfying work for which you are destined *and* not have the stamina it takes is frustrating enough; every one of us who are drivers of ourselves knows about this in periods of minor and reversible illness. But when that impairment is deeper still, what then?

But after another year of recuperation, Ed may not only desire but be able physically—and psychically—to give the world again the gifts that are so uniquely his, not the least of which is just plain guts.

Like many passionately devoted Kennedy men (and Stevenson people), he isn't aroused by Johnson. The "lift" isn't there, and the skill in compromise is called "opportunism."

A long discussion, after dinner, about Eisenhower, little of it admiring. Someone attributed his vacillation about Joe McCarthy to his hope that his brother Milton would be a candidate and his waiting for that to develop. Louis Cowan (a long time CBS "colleague" of Ed's) said: "To think that it took a man from the broadcasting industry to start McCarthy's disintegration. Think what we might have avoided—in our China policy, in the near destruction of our State Department—if Eisenhower had used his leadership and enormous popularity to eliminate McCarthy, and not left that to a man in the broadcasting industry." (He was referring, of course, to Ed's famous TV program about McCarthy.)

With the recollection of the Philadelphia riots still disturbing me, I thought this was a good opportunity to talk about "moral leadership" in the Presidency. I suggested that President Johnson must exercise the leadership implicit in being President at a time of crisis to slow down this rioting and looting. He doesn't seem to be able to do so by military means: troops, etc. So he will have to try another tack.

Now all this country sees of the Philadelphia disturbances are night shots of Negroes looting and policemen striking them or putting them into paddy wagons. The President is followed everywhere he goes by the TV cameras. If he went into one of these storm centers, the country could follow him, literally, with their eyes. Johnson has shown a fearlessness in going out among friendly crowds who want to touch his hand. Could he somehow use this half-worship of the Presidency to do something to turn the country's mind into useful directions about these disgraceful pillages? The power of the President's "moral leadership" would be magnified a thousandfold.

First thing this morning I sat down and wrote a note to Ed Murrow, telling him how "heartening to see you again at close range, once more to hear . . . the rumble of your voice and those six-inch uppercut phrases of a man with conviction. Of all the men who have commanded the ear and eye and heart of their fellows with the coming of electronic communication, you are the only one who still has the direction, the freshness, the individualness that you learned in the North Carolina woods, and in the hardboiled idealism of your youth. No one and nothing has ever really scared you and never will."

SEPTEMBER 5, 1964
MARTHA'S VINEYARD

"The amount of it is," I read in *Walden*, "if a man is alive, there is always *danger* that he may die, though the danger must be allowed to be less in proportion as he is dead-and alive to begin with. A man sits as many risks as he runs."

So much for risk-taking.

SEPTEMBER 6, 1964
MARTHA'S VINEYARD

Sailed *Lili-put* to Oak Bluffs, then across the Sound almost to Falmouth Harbor, with Leona Baumgartner. We talked for a couple hours about AID. She seems set to leave her post as Deputy in AID right after the election; a pity, for she has been able to make that abstract-economist ridden agency see that *people*, individuals, are the subject matter of that program and not just an afterthought, something incidental to Gross National Product rate of increase or part of the mumbo jumbo of Hollis Chenery's* esoteric "linear programming."

Leona's place in American medical administration is unique. So I was astounded—I managed to keep hold of the main sheet and hang on to the tiller, but barely—when she said, "Dave, American medical service is badly, hopelessly organized." "But I read and hear of great technical steps forward," I protested. "What do you mean?" "I mean that getting medical service *to the people who need it* is utterly chaotic and inefficient." She looked so distressed. This is apparently something about which she has been thinking hard—and suffering about—for a long time.

The triumphant cadence and excitement of Beethoven's Ninth roar and pulsate and throb through this unfinished pine room; the stars look in through room-high windows, and beyond the darkness of the woods the lights of New Bedford sparkle. What a dramatic setting for this majestic music.

To "conduct" music is to guide and lead many instruments so that they are one. "Administration" of men is something else. In a great orchestra ninety men subordinate themselves willingly and happily to the lead of one man, their director. But in the leadership of men it is *not* subordination one seeks but an opening of the *separate* and *individual* talents and ideas of those you lead. More difficult, but more genuinely creative for that reason.

* Harvard Professor currently (1975) chief advisor to the President of the World Bank.

SEPTEMBER 7, 1964
MARTHA'S VINEYARD

To a roaring rolling South Beach (at Katama) this morning with David, Peggy, and the younger kids. Little three-year-old Margaret is a sprite, a charmer, with her tiny pug nose and gay laughter. She can be so solemn too; and her technique with her grandfather may be obvious but it certainly melts me into a little puddle of goo. Sidling up to me, a sidelong glance: "You are my friend," she says.

SEPTEMBER 22, 1964
PRINCETON

Call from E. P. Hoyt, Editor of the *Denver Post.* That wonderful, gravelly voice, a sound like a cement mixer with pebbles being tossed around in it. Told me he had just received first returns on a "scientific" poll they have been taking in Colorado for sixteen years; it has "never missed." Shows Johnson 60%. "That surprised hell out of me. Story going around that a lot of people don't want to say they are for Johnson. Not according to our poll. And he *is* a good President; known him for a long time, knew he was a good politician. Saw him couple times last week; he remembers his old friends. He *listens.* Said to me: 'Ep, what am I doin' wrong?' That's something new in a President."

OCTOBER 8, 1964
PRINCETON

As I looked out on the audience (perhaps five hundred people) at the political dinner in Newark, on behalf of Johnson's candidacy, and saw Helen, I was reminded of how many times we have gone through the same working "routine": I try out a speech on her the afternoon before; then she sits there in the audience listening as if it were all new to her; this has been going on since our college days!

Ben Shahn, a great artist, was one of the "figures"—as well as one of the promoters—of the Newark Democratic dinner last night. Shahn is in appearance a plump blob-like man with a Chinese half-smile. Never did a man *look* less like what he is: an artist with a searing sense of the injustice of man to man, a creative man who has had an influence on a whole generation of artists, an artist with a set of ideas about the world, not only about the techniques and pretensions of artists.

At the same meeting, got great joy out of the singing of Pete Seeger, who ruffled a big guitar while he sang folk songs. Tall, slender, his head tilted back when he talks to you as it is when he is belting out a song, he spoke most interestingly about his singing trips around the world—India, Nairobi, etc. Television, he said, breaks down the barriers between people far better than any other medium, much better than radio. He is convinced of its cultural importance as a way of promoting international understanding.

OCTOBER 9, 1964
CLEVELAND, OHIO

Is there any business in this world that isn't interesting when you can see it through the eyes of those who are living it, who give themselves to it? *And* if you yourself have your eyes and heart open?

Tonight I spoke here to the American Booksellers' regional meeting. Before I was called on I sat between Howard Klein (who has a chain of fourteen bookshops here) and Ann Udin, a diminutive woman with a full charge of TNT as her propellant, who runs Higbee's, a famous bookstore here.

I asked them about the book business *as a business*; and sat in a cross fire of exciting ideas about what it is that sells books ("exposure, and more exposure," said Miss Udin). They both agreed that TV hasn't kept people from reading; on the contrary, it sells books. Young people are reading more than ever.

OCTOBER 12, 1964
KANSAS CITY

On the bulletin board of the Muehlebach Hotel: Meeting of the American Association of Retired Persons. By God, we *organize retirement*, just as we organize the work from which we retire. Twenty years from now organized retirement (like organized Serenity, like organized Solitude) may seem so clearly a necessity that if I were still around I would wonder why in the hell I thought that bulletin board announcement was worth putting down on paper.

A strange sensation: the intervening years rolled back, and there I was, sitting at the corner of President Truman's desk, basking in that warm confidence he placed in me from the very start. Yet that was more than fourteen years ago, and the place then was Washington, not, as now, Independence, Missouri.

President Truman made me feel that he was happy to see me. To me he was not a memento, a relic of another period of my life, but the living reincarnation of the most troubled, harassed, and satisfying years I have lived.

My knees fairly trembled when I was taken to see the replica of

Truman's White House office; there was that little straight chair at the corner of the big desk where I had sat through so many personally trying times.

The President said he and David Noyes, once his White House Assistant, now his aide at the Truman Library, had been talking about me not long ago. "I said to Dave Noyes here that when a man has the stuff, when he can take the gaff and survives such a trial as you did, then your place in history is assured; and it is," Mr. Truman said with that clipped way of talking I remember so well.

He moves much less certainly, with much less of the vigorous military jauntiness of yore (he is now eighty), but except for that I thought he was the Truman of old.

His extraordinary humility in the middle of the trappings of glory is still his chief characteristic. "I hadn't much brains, but I *listened* to fellows who were superbrains," is the way he puts it. I responded that he had what is most important of all, an intuitive sense of what was right and of how to do it, plus guts.

I reminded President Truman of the day when, under terrible attack, I sat at the corner of his desk in his White House office and said: "Mr. President, if these attacks on me are causing you embarrassment, as they must, I will resign any time you want, right now if you wish." Like a wise parent he said, "Now, Dave, stop that kind of talk. You start brooding over all this political fracas and you will go the way Jim Forrestal did." Which stopped me right then. Today President Truman added: "Poor Jim, he just went all to pieces. [Noyes broke in to say something about the day he had cried before the President.] I sometimes think," Truman continued, "that I was the cause of his death."

OCTOBER 13, 1964
HOTEL MUEHLEBACH, KANSAS CITY

Doesn't look as if our beloved country will starve for lack of food. (She *can* starve for lack of vision.) This famous hotel is overflowing with boys, Future Farmers of America, from all over the land; and noisy though they are at times, at night they are a wonderful looking lot. They wear blue jackets, in the current American way, "identified" on the backs of the jackets, in gold letters, by the states and areas (little towns, I expect) from which they come. Utah-Teton, Idaho-Spanish Forks, Virginia-Brookville, etc. They are all sizes from huge to enormous; all kinds of voices (chiefly Southwest or South). They probably know more about the practical art of raising good cattle than all the agricultural stations and extension agents in the country. I would like to turn some of these boys loose in some of our undertakings, particularly in Latin America.

A great to-do in the press and TV; the Russians have a three-man spaceship lobbing around the earth every ninety minutes. If the Russians had half-way met their people's needs for food, *that* would be something to hosanna about, and conceivably to concern us. If they had been able to produce these young, stalwart Future Farmers, and what they produce in the way of food, this would be far more important to my mind than spectaculars in space.

10:30 P.M.

Back from a wonderful day at the University of Kansas. Just what I had hoped for when I made up my mind weeks ago that, as a healthy change from so much overseas work, I see something of my own country and particularly its young people.

Francis Heller, Acting Dean of Liberal Arts, turned out to be a companionable and knowledgeable guide. He arranged for me to visit around a table with twenty-five undergraduates. Getting them to talk to me about what is in their minds I knew wouldn't be easy; but I found them candid and articulate. Almost to a man or woman, they said they are "worried" about the effect of "specialization" upon the wholeness of their life. Here in college they are taught the Ralph Barton Perry liberal arts philosophy of freedom to choose. They see, or fear, that whether they go to professional school or into business—or whatever—they will be in a constantly narrowing groove, and this frightens and bewilders them. These are not eastern seaboard urban sophisticates but small town Middle Westerners.

The very fact that this troubles them is the best assurance that they will be able to work their way out of the pincers of the narrow life they fear.

As I left, the Chancellor took me to the window and pointed out Baumgartner Road, named for my dear old friend, Leona's father; "and his ashes are beneath that tree along the side of the road; that was his own request." I was terribly moved by this.

On our way to Lawrence we stopped at Tom and Rita Benton's home, a roomy place set about with trees. We had some trouble finding it, until I noticed a doughty looking little man with a copious waterfall of grey hair swept back on his perky head, standing behind a gate, with the bemused look of a retired sea captain wondering how in hell it was that he was digging in a garden after all those years of commanding a ship at sea. A skipper off the quarterdeck. It was Tom, of course. And yet Tom is anything but a retired and lost man; he continues to paint; he showed me a big painting of what he called a modern bacchanal: a group of young people on the Vineyard dancing the twist.

OCTOBER 14, 1964
11:30 P.M.
BROWN PALACE HOTEL
DENVER, COLORADO

Ep Hoyt just phoned. Bad news: Lyndon's assistant Walter Jenkins, Colonel in the Air Force, was picked up October 7 on a morals charge.

Ep had me to lunch with his staff this noon; then I spent a couple hours with Bert Hanna, an excellent reporter, outlining my idea about Western coal and America's energy needs—hard, concentrated work and no idea how it will come out.† Then Ep and I walked over to the State House to listen to Goldwater speak to a rally of a few thousand people: not impressive. After dinner with the Hoyts and their remarkable four boys (champion skaters among other things) and listening to Mrs. Hoyt talk with intensity and knowledge about geology, we watched Barry on TV here—most of the speech devoted to "crime." He probably had heard about this Jenkins thing.

OCTOBER 15, 1964
DENVER

Ep called: The Affair Jenkins looks very bad; the White House wants to talk to Ep in an hour; what should the President *do*? The whole country is buzzing and much of it is troubled. A man who has been Johnson's confidant for twenty years or so, and friend of the family, full of top level "secrets." In a political setting it is a sad break. The fact that a man has a trusted confidant who is not sexually normal, in the eyes of many these days, certainly reflects on his judgment about picking people.

In a tough fight you can always expect the unexpected. That young graduate student, a young Communist,‡ we selected for an AEC unclassified scholarship at Chapel Hill strictly on his merits as a scientist caused me more criticism than all the substantive issues I had to face. But I didn't back away from it. Senator LaFollette, the elder, once won a campaign against an incumbent Governor on the main issue that the Governor had shipped his family cow to Madison on a railroad free pass! The illustrations of such minor derelictions becoming major issues are numerous.

† The interview, "A Plan to Tap Resources of the Rockies," appeared in the *Denver Post*, November 17, 1964.

‡ See *Journals*, Vol. II, *The Atomic Energy Years*, pp. 531 ff.

OCTOBER 17, 1964
CHICAGO

The announcement of the Chinese A-bomb and the flood of stories about Khrushchev's replacement have drawn some—not all—of the fire from the tragic business about Jenkins.

OCTOBER 23, 1964
NEW YORK

"Sex and the *Single* Woman" and other sides of single life have been given a lot of verbal bestseller attention recently; by the time these journal entries are read this part of the contemporary scene may be forgotten completely.

But what about the married *man*, anything but single, adrift in a strange city—or a familiar one? This is the lot of more and more men in this business-oriented society that sends men scrambling around the country on business.

Well, *my* experience is that a lone man in New York City has become a leper, a pariah, a source of the worst form of contempt: he isn't really there.

Item by way of illustration:

Wednesday night I was at loose ends, didn't feel like going back to my hotel room to read—as ordinarily I do. Where to eat? Like a dope, I wandered into Sardi's alone.

The man at the door looked at me as if I had a communicable disease. "Alone?" Yes, I admitted, humiliated. He turned away from me to more interesting prospects—it was early, no crowd, the downstairs dining room half empty. This made me mad. "I came here to get a meal; are you in the business?" I asked. The Eminence gave me a look of scorn at this sarcasm, and turned back to some expense account quartet. If I had appeared in shorts I couldn't have been treated with more eyebrow lifting. "Alone!" "Hm."

OCTOBER 26, 1964
HARKNESS PAVILION, PRESBYTERIAN MEDICAL CENTER
NEW YORK

If I were going to have my entire insides removed tomorrow morning and replaced with plastic (and therefore improved) organs, there couldn't be a more impressive scientific parade through this unhospitable-looking room: the blank-faced young women with their syringes, after my blood (and getting it; filling a dozen little bottles with the dark brown stuff); the tall Ivy Leagueish young surgeon with a blue-eyed smile a yard wide, right out of a TV soap opera series; the anesthetist, so professional with his questions, so careful in answers to my questions. Then three different nurses in figure-fitting uniforms of a kind I don't remember nurses used to wear—or am I more observant now? Then Dr. Atchley looking quite unhappy. A urologist will be along later, and an orthopedist, and of course the "help": the gals in blue and grey, with the dinner tray and the mop for the floor. All for what I thought (mistakenly) would be a simple surgical repair of a hernia.

OCTOBER 29, 1964
HARKNESS PAVILION

I had forgotten how long the nights can be, when you are a voluntary prisoner of that benevolent dictatorship known as a modern hospital.

OCTOBER 30, 1964
HARKNESS PAVILION

A call from Helen, about 5 P.M. "Nate Greene died this afternoon."

No matter how little a man has left to live for, and Nate, paralyzed and in the prison of speechlessness, had less than most, dying is so irrevocable that it is always sad. Nate had a strange, unusual philosophy of life. Up from the streets of Brooklyn to a most distinguished record as a legal scholar, right hand of Felix Frankfurter during the New Deal, the theme of his life was not to *commit* himself to anything. I underline "commit." He had opinions, sharp, waspish, and barbed, but there was never any commitment. To me, being committed to life has been second nature. This man of great talent puzzled me all the more, for I liked everything about him *except* this unwillingness to give himself to living for something. It wasn't long after he began law practice that he had periodic episodes of retiring—first, I think, to Taos in New Mexico; then he would go back to practicing until he had some money and then *withdraw* again.

And yet this man, so utterly different from me, helped me mightily when I came to New York. I relied on his judgment because, although he was *part* of the financial establishment, he became a kind of father confessor; he had some part in keeping me from being so dazzled by business and Wall Street that I soon recovered my perspective—I probably never really lost it—and came through what might have been a sickening letdown.

Everyone is fed up with the presidential campaign; everyone will be relieved when it is over. Walter Lippmann, in a column [my secretary] Miss Baron showed me today, said it was about the foulest "in memory"—and his memory goes back even farther than mine. If this *isn't* the low point in all our history, I don't want to see a lower depth.

OCTOBER 31, 1964
HARKNESS PAVILION

Is there a more magnificent and all-encompassing picture of New York, the City of Cities, than one gets from the south precipice of this great hospital? A burnished, slowly-dying autumnal sunset to the west. The dazzling lights come on along the Drive. The peaks of Manhattan's own special cathedral-like spires thrust against the fading sky off to the south, each outline familiar to me now that I am no longer (except in a self-derisive way of talking) a country boy.

Dana [Atchley] in, on his "rounds." He's reading the *Journals* and my references to Dr. Harcourt A. Morgan. I had forgotten that H. A. had been Dana's teacher, in more ways than one, when Dana was at the University of Tennessee. "That remarkable man took me, the son of a Baptist minister, and opened my mind to evolution, to the sense of science," Dana reminded me. It was H.A. who awakened me to that great concept he called our "Common Mooring," the unity of man and Nature.

NOVEMBER 3, 1964
HARKNESS PAVILION

Election day; by 10 o'clock tonight some of the questions about America's future will have been decided. Some only. An election like this can determine a major turn in the road, but the important reaches between the signposts are always in the lap of the gods.

NOVEMBER 4, 1964
PRINCETON

By 8:30 last evening there was little doubt about the outcome of the election, a Johnson landslide.

NOVEMBER 16, 1964
NEW YORK

Long talk this afternoon with that personification of good judgment and good sense, now my counsel, Joseph Flom. How steady a man, how warm beneath that external gravity!

After discussing my finances and tax problems, we talked, with pain in our voices, about our so recently departed friend and my advisor, Nate Greene.

What was Nate's special contribution? It isn't that Nate argued the pros and cons of a problem with you; nor did he take one position and press it on you. And yet he influenced people of all kinds to an extraordinary degree.

Nate made you objective *about yourself.*

NOVEMBER 17, 1964
NEW YORK

Anyone who insists that I am hopelessly impatient, that I blow my top at the sight of little organizational termites and lesser insects nibbling away in papers, papers, papers and thereby keeping full-grown men from getting a job done—these folks don't give me credit for the way I have suffered and cursed without blowing AID out of the water over their quibbles about overhead allocations in D&R's Ivory Coast Southwestern project.

A large gathering in my office this afternoon promises to be the beginning of something useful at last.

The Ivorian Minister of Finance and Plan, M. Saller, a sharp, benign, and businesslike man, led the "delegation," which included eight or nine people representing the Ivory Coast. We should hear from Washington by Friday, Minister Saller told us, whether AID is in agreement. And then to go to work on what could be an exceptionally interesting and rewarding task, "planning" and developing a completely unsettled region of Africa, starting with the slate clean.

NOVEMBER 18, 1964
NEW YORK

It takes a lot of living thoroughly to comprehend that one hour is not the same as another, equal though they are on the clock. The quality, the intensity, the meaning of one hour, thoroughly lived, with all the perceptions and senses one has, may make that hour worth a lifetime of tepid, unlived hours.

The *Journal* reviews continue to roll in; today, one that pleased me inordinately, in the *Washington Post*, by Mike Amrine. He said I had done something toward restoring the lost art of journal writing.

NOVEMBER 26, 1964
(THANKSGIVING DAY)
PRINCETON

Burnett and Mead have again been called to Washington, *not* to witness the signing of the Ivory Coast contract with Minister Saller (*they* and we have been in agreement lo these many months), but for more haggling about this minor term and that. Gordon said long ago that it was impossible for an outfit like ours, which wants to get things done, to work under AID financed contracts, because most of the time and energy would go not into the work, but in argufying and paper-pushing exercises to satisfy the fearful bookkeeper minds that, for the most part, man many of the contracting functions of our Government.

NOVEMBER 29, 1964
PRINCETON

While on a walk to the Institute woods with Eddie Greenbaum this morning we met a Princeton physicist, for years a neighbor of Einstein. Later Eddie, his eyes twinkling, told me a wonderful story about Einstein, which is also a story about Einstein's layman common sense vis-à-vis the expert. The physicist, it seems, had some anatomical trouble involving the midriff; a flock of doctors prescribed a complicated brace that would fit around his waist. He complained that the darn thing would keep slipping down, so that in the middle of lectures he would have to hitch it up—a nuisance. The man's wife confided his predicament to Einstein, for his judgment as a great mind. Einstein said he would think about it; the next day he left his solution in a one-word written message: "Unterhosen"—long underwear. Laughing merrily, Eddie said: "And it *worked*!"

NOVEMBER 30, 1964
PRINCETON

Sat on that "dais" of the Waldorf ballroom, where I have been so many times before, as part of the "wax works," this time as a speaker. A Book and Author Luncheon, put on by the *Herald Tribune*.

A fascinating talk with Irita Van Doren before the meeting began —she was Chairman, but is now retired as head of the book review she conducted for so many years. I knew how close she and Willkie were in the years when he and I were tangling over TVA, and up through his nomination for the Presidency. Or perhaps I should say Wendell told me, rather explicitly, how close. But this was the first time Irita had ever done more than mention his name. I spoke of his book, *One World*. This reference set Irita off, in a charming, understated way. "Wendell used to stop at my place on his way to the office in the morning; he would pace back and forth, dictating to me. I didn't write shorthand, but I'd scribble as hard as I could and then read it back to him, and we'd make changes here and there until it suited him." She smiled so sweetly, her eyes bright and merry. That picture of the devotion and dependence of this fragile, literary lady on that big, strapping, bellicose man, viewed now, twenty years later, I found touching and beautiful.

DECEMBER 7, 1964
FLYING AIR FRANCE, OVER THE BORDER
OF ECUADOR AND PERU

The lines of a perfect cone, reaching upward to a point, the lines as sharp and clear as a notation in a geometry textbook, and at the apex a lazy drift of smoke: one of the great active volcanic peaks of Ecuador, seen from 35,000 feet.

DECEMBER 8, 1964
GRAN HOTEL BOLIVAR
LIMA, PERU

When we came into the Josephconradian tropical port of Buenaventura [Colombia] twelve years ago, greeted by an eager, handsome group of Vallecaucanians—Cauca Valley young leaders—we were building on the reputation made in the far distant Tennessee Valley. This time, in Peru, it is more the CVC (Cauca Valley Corporation) that provides my credentials for getting something going. The stalwart men from Piura in northern Peru who nudged President Belaunde into inviting us here have already visited back and forth (Bernardo Garces [of CVC] coming to Piura, they traveling to CVC).

In the late afternoon to the office of the Instituto de Planification, headed by Carlos Pestana. He represents the President as our host here. A trim, taut, slight, handsome young man of about thirty-five, with the quick movements of a bird, and a mind as alert and quick as his movements.

TVA is a living reality to such a man as this, and the CVC stands as a demonstration of what can be *done*; whereas for so long "planification" alone has been the rage. He asked: "How long did it take to prepare The Plan for TVA?" I tried to explain—as I did in my TVA book more than twenty years ago—that we *started* before anything but a broad concept was completed, and revised and modified as we went along. He looked puzzled.

DECEMBER 9, 1964
PIURA, PERU

A big delegation of earnest, no-nonsense men at the airport here, after our three and a half hour flight from Lima. At the two stops, Trujillo and Chiclayo, great stores of sacked flour, sugar, steel pipes, brooms, canned goods, etc., were ready for flying over the Andes (18,000 feet) to the interior. The inland town of Tarapoto is the busiest airport in Peru (though the town is small) because *everything* is brought by air. No roads whatever; none. Twenty-five head of cattle carried in a single plane, for instance. We used to say, "You must crawl before you walk." Across the Andes, they fly before they use the wheel, or even the burro.

DECEMBER 10, 1964
PIURA, PERU

This morning I wandered off around the town, on my own, something in which I delight, and from which I learn more (by going into the stores, the warehouses, the bank lobbies) than from figures. Por ejemplo: this is a trading center of people who have cash and who spend it, largely on expensive, imported goods—cloth, canned food (mountains of cans of evaporated milk)—and articles connected with farming—insecticides and devices for spraying it. Great energy everywhere.

DECEMBER 13, 1964
LIMA

The President of the Republic has sent word that he will see us Tuesday morning. So my mind is full of the question: Can the region of Piura become a Peruvian TVA, or more aptly, does it have the ingredients of a Peruvian CVC? The Piurians are certain of this; Bernardo Garces thought so, after his visit here.

DECEMBER 14, 1964
LIMA

Can there be anything more engrossing than the way an idea is born, unfolds, develops, droops, burgeons, stumbles, changes, crystallizes, becomes something in the world of action? Not even the "way of a man with a maid," said to be mysterious and unpredictable, is more fascinating than this.

This rumination grows out of our week here. What can I do, through D&R, to accelerate and strengthen the efforts of those, a tiny group of people in Peru, who are fired with a determination to make things better in this country? In my day and night absorption in such a question during this past week, my ideas have gone through a process of growth, rejection, testing, variation—an intensely wearying but on the whole satisfying and happy kind of experience for me, and for some lively-minded Peruvians, even if, as is likely, no contractual engagement for D&R ensues.§

DECEMBER 15, 1964
LIMA

The picture, as we have it so far in Peru, is a classic one: a proliferation of "feasibility studies" (this is the latest jargon) and "experts" falling all over each other's feet, experts on animal husbandry, salinity, public administration, etc., etc., most of this paid for by the AID program. But after the studies have been made, what then? Who has responsibility for doing something about them? A maze of expertise, disjointed, needing to be pulled together into a program of action.

What a paradox! So unplanned a country as the U.S. insisting through its AID program (and the World Bank in part) on *"a national plan"* before providing funds to such a country as Peru. Hence studies all over the place, providing plans that have no legs to travel on. By "legs" I mean no modern managerial mechanism by which to get something done. A further paradox: in a country that can't afford to wait, this preoccupation with planning (in itself good enough) has bred the idea that until A Plan is *completed*, nothing in the way of action can be *started.*

In the TVA we were hard at work doing things three years before our "Unified Plan for the Development of the Valley" was ready; likewise in Persia and in the Cauca Valley, things were started while the planning process went forward.

At 11:30 this morning the conference with the President, a private meeting on which we had counted so much, was called off. Two hours later I was at the Palace, standing in the huge drawing room while the President, surrounded by most of his Cabinet and others of the younger leaders of the country, made me a Comendador de la Orden del Sol del Peru.

President Belaunde's speech in conferring the Order had me choked up: in a country I had never visited before, and have no connection with, he said this was Peru's way (he speaks beautiful English) of recognizing my work "through the TVA not only for my own country but for people all over the world."

§ In fact, none did.

DECEMBER 27, 1964
GUADELOUPE, FRENCH WEST INDIES

During the next few days in this relaxed setting I want to record in a connected way the "case history" of a by no means atypical effort toward regional development—in the Piura region of northern Peru.

The story is a rough prototype of scores of such development efforts all over the world, marked as it is by the impact of ideas and their evolution, and the equally important imprint of strong individuals.

Whether in the event a particular development effort succeeds—as in fact it did in the Cauca Valley of Colombia (the CVC) or the Khuzistan region of Iran (the KWPA)—or dies aborning, as it may in the Piura region, such a case as Piura seems worth recording in some depth. It is not an abstract exercise, but a story of passionately held ideas and of particular people, of how the ideas and people sorted themselves out, were evaluated and modified, and of the concrete actual barriers confronted on the way.

Diarist's Note

The case of Piura, as Lilienthal recorded it in three lengthy and detailed entries on December 27, 28, and 30, throws light on the realities of the development process.

These entries are to be found, just as they were written, in the Papers of David E. Lilienthal in the Firestone Library at Princeton University. They have not, however, been reproduced here in the published version of the Journals *largely for reasons of their length. But they do provide that "amount of detail without which the tale lacks body and validity," as Lilienthal notes. The entries in their entirety give a picture of the cast of characters—local leaders, landowners, foreign bureaucrats—and the conflicting human motives to be found in many if not most development issues. This* interaction *of a specific physical setting, of individuals, and of ideas, whether in Latin America or elsewhere, is relevant not only to students of the technical aspects of the "development process," but more particularly to observers of human nature and the life style of bureaucracy.*

II

1965

Trip to India—In Iran, attempt on the Shah's life—Development in the Ivory Coast—Indiana University Commencement—Trip to Peru—Latin American integration study—Visits with: George Kennan, John Gunther, and Roger Baldwin

JANUARY 10, 1965
PRINCETON

This has been a memorable week, but for an ugly reason. During the last several days I gave way to a fury of frustration as I haven't done in a long, long time. The cause: *still* no end in sight to the petty, aimless debate which has been going on for four months with the contract and audit people at AID over minuscule details of the projected contract for our development of the Southwest Ivory Coast.

I *know* better; this takes a toll of me, and I shouldn't permit it to happen. But I am—let's face it, as the kids say these days—I am an impatient man; my impatience has produced some results in my public work that would not have been produced by a more patient man. It is not easy to turn this impatience off just because your head tells you it does no good to your peace of mind.

On a day of soft snowfall transforming the landscape into serenity, I should draw on some of that peace, or I'll not be of much use to others; I'll be of no use to the President and the people of the Ivory Coast who have been waiting three years for us to start out there on a solid regional development they want and for which we are and have been ready to go. I'll be of no use to those who look to me, on a wider horizon than I would have believed was the case, for leadership. A frustrated, angry man has limited value to anyone. Particularly to himself.

A call on André Meyer. He said he had kept in touch with D&R through Jack Franklin [a Lazard D&R director]; that he had said to Franklin what he had always said to me about D&R: that anything I wanted to do, he favored; if I wanted Lazard to step out as a stockholder, they would, or they would increase their participation.

He was greatly provoked by a memorandum a D&R senior staff man had written, a thinking aloud kind of rumination about how, out of our now plentiful retained earnings, D&R could pay off our outside stockholders and have the working staff go it alone. Writing such a memorandum without consulting our partners—this is the sort of thing André is very sensitive about, and I agree. "If you have a partner you don't speculate in that way about how to get rid of him," he said. I listened for a few minutes and then I said, "André, if you want to talk about what is past, you certainly have that right; I have told Franklin I don't want Lazard out of D&R. What *I* want to talk about is the *future*."

He grinned; said I had the floor.

"Ten years ago—almost exactly—you and I developed the idea for a company that would represent the kind of things I stand for—public development along TVA lines—and that you stand for—forward-looking finance. We were thinking about what lay ahead, and the kind of services and company which would meet the future, unlike most of the other bankers on Wall Street, who were whining about the good old past. What attracted me to you then, and still does, is that though you are a great figure in international finance, you see the job as one of adapting finance and banking to the facts *as they are*, rather than complaining because the world has changed. Together we created D&R, a corporation we thought would supply the needs of the future, in this combination of public and private experience and expertise. It was something unique and distinctive then, and it still is now.

"I want to go ahead and make D&R live up to the hopes and expectations we had then. On the public side it has done a notable job; the work in Iran is historic, has benefited a great number of people and is something to be proud of. I am proud of it, and I think you are. In the private sector, true, we haven't yet accomplished anything as a company. Perhaps we never will. Perhaps having D&R participate—as you have invited us to do—in the Ivory Coast Bank will provide a way toward that private sector activity that so far—the fault or shortcoming is probably mine—we haven't achieved. But I want to continue the alliance. Let's not talk about breaking up a partnership that made D&R's beginning possible and to which Lazard has contributed not only that opportunity for it to come into being in the first place, but has made such other contributions as bringing to us the Ivory Coast people and the Sofina people, with their water improvement idea."

By this time he was André at his best, his eyes alight.

I lit into the AID people for their piddling with the new contract and quarreling about an overhead allocation as if accounting would develop the great southwestern part of the Ivory Coast.

He was amused at my vehemence and some of the words I used to describe the midget minds I find so criminal in public affairs. "Now, David," he said, sliding down on his spine in that $14 straight wooden chair he sits in for his sciatica. "Now, David, you find that kind of pettiness and long winded negotiation over *nothing* between private corporations. I have it on my plate *all* the time."

To have had the great business genius, himself impatient, at times irascible, calming down Dave Lilienthal gives me a picture, as I look back on it a couple days later, of how unreasonably fired up and mad I was.

JANUARY 11, 1965
PRINCETON

My self-esteem (euphemism for just plain old-fashioned vanity) has taken a terrific wallop these past couple days. I honestly thought I was old iron-pants, the man who had limitless energy and endurance and could expend emotional reserves and nervous energy without any sense of rationing. For months and months I have acted that way. Well, this last brutal week, beginning when I arrived at the office Monday (after four hours' sleep) and ending as I looked through a carload of mail on the train home from Washington Friday night—that, or the *reaction* to that puerile demonstration of overextended adrenaline—has certainly given me a more realistic picture of myself. Will I profit by the lesson? All I can say for sure is that I never have before.

In any event, I have promised the good angel who watches over me that I'll stay home tomorrow, as well as today.

Have been walking in the crisp and tonic air that a great snowfall brings—we have about eight inches of the stuff, quite Currier and Ives all about. But the cursed head keeps racing along with ideas. It is all right, really, when ideas keep churning about when I should be thinking of *nothing* at all; but when worries are mixed in that brew I know I am walking on the thin ice of overtiredness, with her children irascibility and half-fear hanging at her damned skirts.

Lying on the floor before a sputtering fire, I "come to," feeling virtuous about taking the time to soothe overstrained nerves, and then sit up and let out a bellow of laughter. My idea of a rest: to spend the entire morning on the phone, energetically laying plans for the Facile Vita, the easy life, by starting a whole new series of things D&R and I should be doing.

JANUARY 12, 1965
PRINCETON

I talked to Dana Atchley about my state of shakiness, the wear and tear of last week's energy explosion, sustained right through the week. It had mystified me, but I knew enough to stay home for a couple days.

He said, "Your passionate intensity is what communicates itself to others; it's one of your prime assets. The other side of the shield is impatience, and that is wearing. You are just fatigued; when you are rested—and you come back fast, you always have—all this will change; and you know it."

JANUARY 16, 1965
PRINCETON

Have just come in from a tramp (or trudge) in a wild northerly snowstorm. The landscape a white-on-white: today's white on last weekend's still-white. How could anyone live without the chance occasionally to throw himself against such a blast of nature (it is about 10° above) and the erasure of everything with which one is familiar by this swirling, twisting grace that is a great snowstorm? As a steady and unvarying diet you can *have* the palm trees—and even the bikinis, I guess, though this is a closer question.

As a final flourish I drew a huge fox-and-geese on the smooth, clean blackboard that is our "back yard"—and with a rush there came back the many times Nancy and I performed this ritual in Palos Park,◖ when she was not forty but four. What a darling she was, with her bonnet framing those round, rosy cheeks, and her so-very-blue eyes so merry. And then, with a stick, I had to draw Jerry the Jiraffe and others of our invention on the snow.

The exuberance I have just felt—and partly recorded—isn't wholly due to snow. Last evening a call from John Oliver, in Washington: After two more days of struggle about the overhead allocation that has been holding up the Ivory Coast Southwestern development project, an agreement has been reached on a formula suggested by Edmond Hutchinson, Regional Director for Africa—a simple and completely satisfactory answer to a disgraceful stalemate. This may, at long last, open the door to other useful programs in West Africa that could have some of the historic significance of the Cauca enterprise in Latin America.

◖ We were living in Palos Park, a Chicago suburb.

JANUARY 17, 1965
PRINCETON

Just back from a dinner and meeting of the Executive Committee of Education and World Affairs, consisting of John Hannah, President of Michigan State, Herman Wells of Indiana University, and Bob Goheen of Princeton: as able three men in every category of human judgment and sensibility as one is likely to find in one room.

I have found it interesting to be on that board because it gave me a chance to see something of the way the "higher education" administrators' minds work.

Herman had just returned from spending some time this week at Berkeley, and Bob had spent the morning in Washington with Clark Kerr, President of the University of California at Berkeley. So they talked about the strange things going on on that campus. The climax, they seemed to think, was the action of the Senate of the Faculty, on Friday I believe, in passing the following resolution: that the students who lost time fighting the University rulings on political activity on the campus, putting on demonstrations against the University position, etc., should not be required to take their examinations now, but should be given time to catch up and take the exams later.

This quietly outraged Wells, Hannah, and Goheen. Said Hannah: "That's a serious step along the road to turning control of the University over to students, the sad story of Latin American higher education." But they all agreed that the Chancellor of UC (who has just given up his post) had made some blunders in dealing with the students; his rules were contrary to the students' constitutional rights as citizens, and arresting students in a mob was a great mistake.

An intensely interesting discussion, for me who knows so little about that whole important area of life, though I do know a good deal about, and feel strongly about, preserving people's right to grumble or even to demonstrate. I said to them: "But isn't there a good side to all this, too? Doesn't it show a kind of vitality, a striving to be individuals?"

Bob Goheen's face sobered, then lighted up; he squinted in that way he has that is very affirmative: "There *is* a good side to it. These students are not conformists, not lethargic about political matters as was the student generation before them." Hannah, as we sat down to dinner, added: "This is the best generation of students I have ever known, far better than in my time or later."

Good, balanced men, these university heads.

JANUARY 18, 1965
NEW YORK

Bad or troublesome news comes, like starlings, in flocks—but so, apparently, does good news. The good news couldn't have been timed better, since I could report it to André Meyer at our meeting, set some days ago for eleven this morning. To wit: a two-year extension of the Iran contract is on its way, by simple letter agreement, without the cliff-hanging and emotional wear and tear of earlier years; the Ivory Coast Southwest development argument about overhead seems settled not only decently, but with no blood spilled—on the contrary, with AID apparently thinking the better of us now that we are no longer abiding in the lower depths where only accountants and such dwell.

I wanted to outline to André my thoughts about "the second decade" of D&R.

The first decade was spent establishing an organization and a record of achievement as a distinctive kind of organization for development: an action rather than a "report and survey" organization. That record is a good one.

But, I said, simply to repeat oneself and do nothing more is neither stimulating nor fertile; I would like the second decade to show the beginnings of different kinds of usefulness as well as to expand and refine the techniques and the record of the first.

Coal and water: here are two areas where, in the U.S., there will be a revolution in the next ten years involving huge expenditures of public and private funds. More than two years ago we anticipated this and began to acquire knowledge and some sense of direction about these fields to add to what, through the TVA years, we had already accumulated.

In the West, we said, the Rocky Mountain area probably had the greatest reserves of coal to be found anywhere, and it was our hunch that the technology of transport of coal and power would make it economic for the wildly burgeoning West Coast's need for electricity to be supplied largely by that Rocky Mountain fuel; these resources were not too far from the Coast, given the changes that were on their way in coal handling (i.e., mining), transport, large (but *very* large) mine-mouth power plants, etc.

Our first idea was that coal would be a good investment and that we should prepare ourselves to provide services in the tying together of power systems through the West based in part on this great newly available energy supply in the Rockies.

In the past week I have been thinking along a complementary line.

An "explosion" in the increased mining and use of coal was due in the Rockies, where the use heretofore has been almost negligible. (Utah's two and a half million ton mine on the Navajo reservation is now the largest coal mine in the whole West, although only a year or so old.)

But such an expansion of coal mining and transport and use for electricity as I envision will mean an expansion in the *components* of such a change: coal handling equipment, drilling equipment, all the things up and down the line that it takes in the way of equipment for such a major change. Small manufacturers of such components in the West will have a great growth opportunity; larger ones will grow rapidly. They should be good investments; there should be good opportunities to buy into such companies against the growth that is almost inevitable.

Much the same kind of thing applies to water improvement, anti-pollution activities, augmenting water supply, sewerage, filtering, etc. For suddenly the country has faced the fact that a major effort is required to increase and upgrade the water supply. If one adds up the *public* expenditures likely in the next decade, it could be in the billions, most of it going into private equipment and service activities. D&R is somewhat ahead of the game in our thinking on this, we believe, and if we had gone ahead to organize that company with Belgium's Sofina instead of waiting until we were sure we had clients, we could be taking advantage of all the public interest since engendered.

Of course, it was the opportunity to buy into companies that lighted André's eyes. Have we had help from Lazard's research department about this, and if not, why? I didn't try to explain that research analysts who don't know the operative, graphic, concrete facts and dynamics of an *industry* can only look backward, hardly ahead. I'll try to establish that *we* can do this.

It is quite a bit to bite off—or bite *into* is a better way of putting it—as a start toward a new D&R.

JANUARY 20, 1965
NEW YORK

A cable from D&R's John Burnett in Iran: "Highest" (our obvious cable code for the Shah) wants to include funds in the budget for the design, etc., of another major dam in the Khuzistan, one we identified on the Karun River as Karun #2. The cable was to get assurance from us that, in the face of strong competition from others to do the job, we are ready to do it with full vigor. Of course we are; I'd feel pretty let down if someone else was selected, and I have written the Shah to that effect today.

From about 12:30 until after 5:30 P.M., Joe Flom and I (eating absurdly untasty sandwiches at my desk) went over my personal affairs and two of D&R's big ideas that are puzzling. Puzzling because we don't have anyone (beginning with me) in our company who has a *promoter's* skill. I am a salesman up to a point, but none of us thinks in those concrete terms that distinguish the enthusiast, propagandist, and idea man —I think I answer those descriptions—from the fellow who has the twist of the wrist that can persuade people with venture capital to put it into the early stages of a venture, at the exploration stage. And that is where both our water improvement scheme and the Western coal notions are.

In his quiet way, this relatively young man *has* the touch. He knows so many cases of people who have put up a million dollars or more before anything was forthcoming, before one had even come to grips with the raising of substantial sums for the substantive project. One example is the Tennessee Gas Transmission empire, now a reality, but only after years of fighting to establish that the idea was marketable, followed by the long process of getting official approvals, getting a financial group together, hearings to get certificates, etc.

JANUARY 21, 1965
NEW YORK

Who should come into the little German restaurant at Hanover Square this noon, alone, but Jim Szold,* who then joined John Oliver and me.

What a delightful fellow: so full of verve and a kind of skepticism that belies (or does it?) a deep-seated sense of responsibility to others that one *must* call idealism, in a big banker or anyone else. The glow in his eyes when he told me, on my asking about his daughter, that her husband had quit the law (settling claims didn't seem enough for a life) and has joined the Peace Corps.

"Someplace in *The Journals of David E. Lilienthal*"—he grinned—"which I have read from beginning to end, there is recounted a conversation with Jim Szold, back when you first came to Wall Street. I had asked you what you were doing in Wall Street, and you answered: to make money. I asked: 'What for?' Now that you *have* made money, how would you answer the question: What for?"

I had no very good answer; I dodged it by muttering something about the "challenge," like the reason for climbing Everest. But I did remark that after I had made enough by my standards ("by any standards," he broke in) I find myself back doing the kind of things that meant most to me when I was a public servant, without money.

* James Szold, partner in the banking house of Lehman Brothers.

And now it is India.

A call from Nick Farr at AID; the new Mission Director for India, John Lewis, wants to get something done about agriculture "that is not engineering-dominated"; from D.E.L.'s writings and convictions, he must be the man to get it done. Will you send someone to India—soon—to look at the Indian Punjab, etc., and use the methods used in Iran?

JANUARY 23, 1965
PRINCETON

A long phone talk with David. His writing goes well: sold two stories to *Cosmopolitan* and to *Playboy*; the movie option on *Seconds* was "picked up," which makes it "more likely," he says, that the film will be made this year.

Most of our talk was about Development and Resources, in which he continues to take a strong interest, partly perhaps because it seems to provide such a good outlet for my "driving impulse," partly because of his inherent interest in it himself.

I again raised the question of "capitalizing," by brochure or public relations advice, on the resurgence in the company's prospective activities of the past two weeks, and on my own pressing on such broad-as-the-sky ideas as the Western energy and water concepts and the way in which explicit interest in regional development for Peru and India has perked up.

"Think of the amount of time and energy you would spend educating someone from a big public relations or advertising agency in what D&R is about," David said, "where its new business might come from, etc. I would think you could use that time and energy much better in other ways. Because, Dad, it isn't 'new business' you are after, in the ordinary sense that an ad agency or public relations man would understand. You aren't so much interested in new business—just *any* new business—as in more opportunities to *put your ideas to work.* The way that will happen isn't by a brochure—oh, a simple statement of what you do just to answer questions—that perhaps—but by actually having more opportunities for doing things *your way.*

"The most effective 'advertising' will be done by the people who know what you are doing—the André Meyers, the Marriner Eccleses,† and so on. Events—the things you *do* in Iran, the Ivory Coast, in Colombia—those are the things that make for added opportunities to do more and different things; you really aren't interested, are you, in 'new business' in any of the usual senses of the term?

"Is there any reason why you can't go to a country where you

† Marriner S. Eccles, former member of the Board of Governors of the Federal Reserve System.

haven't been invited, to observe and study what is going on? A good many of the people responsible for development in some of these countries are oppressed and confused and need help, but until you show up, as a non-business observer, they don't know what you can do. They need ideas, as well as people to do things, and your visits could do that; you shouldn't tie everything to 'new business' in the sense that an engineering firm sends salesmen around.

"Aren't there two separate ideas: first, to get your ideas around, those such as 'The Road to Change'‡ ideas that have gotten such a remarkable reception, and second, to find new business? The first is the more important to you; the second is a completely separate thing, and should be kept separate."

JANUARY 25, 1965
PRINCETON

One recurring comment that comes to me about the *Journals* is this: "How could you find time and energy not only to do the things you do, but at the end of the day to write about them?" To which is often added: "You must have your life very well *organized*."

Well, I don't see the slightest evidence of organization about my work habits. No one could be less organized than I am. I work at a sharp clip, particularly when I am in my office. I get quite a lot done, somehow. I encourage other people to do things, reviewing what they do and letting them do things differently than I myself would. But anyone who likes to do a dozen different things at one time as I do surely can't be called well organized.

I do have a great deal of energy; I run through this energy with no visible method of conversation or discrimination between the important and the merely interesting; when the pool of energy has been used up I dawdle and doze, or garden, or idle until, applying the accelerator of adrenaline or excitement that is in me, I can again expend a lot of energy.

A pity, I suppose, that I don't have something like Justice Brandeis' "organization." But then he was a man more nearly ruled by a great intellect than I am, by many miles. My emotions govern me. I don't discount this. Some of the finest flowers of creativity spring more from the heart than the cool head. Still, this is not the path to an "organized" life. When one's driving forces are feelings, when emotions play about one as erratically as the sun darting in and out of the clouds, how can there be (should there be?) a neat agenda or schedule for one's energies?

Brandeis and some of his generation had a far higher attraction

‡ Lilienthal, adapted from the 1964 Hillman Lecture, Columbia University.

to "scientific management" than I do. "Efficiency" as something measurable by a stop watch or by the techniques of the economist has a *limited* role, as I see the problem of human effort. My chapter on "The Release of Human Energies" in the TVA book back in 1944 comes closer to my notion of what "efficiency" really is.

Just back from a couple enjoyable hours with Alpheus Mason, of the Woodrow Wilson School, the biographer of Brandeis. An easy, relaxed man of my age (though looking ten years younger, I thought).

At one point Mason turned to me and said, rather sharply and intently: "I'd like your reaction to this question that has been troubling me—all of us, I guess, who are involved in the new [Princeton] Graduate School for Public Service. The question is: Do you think that you can *teach* men to become good public servants?"

My answer was hardly an answer: I said I thought it was worth a try. The difficulty is that the essence of a good public servant is the way he carries *responsibility*, and how can you teach that? How can an *observer*—that is, a student with no responsibility—get the feel of how you carry responsibility for public acts? But *parts* of it could be taught; public servants who have that experience should write about it, at the time, as I did in the *Journals*.

Mason spoke of the use of the *Journals* as teaching materials: Their virtue is that they are informal, not set down in a textbook fashion that scares students off.

"The incident in the *Journals* that made the biggest impression on me—remember I'm a *historian*—had nothing to do with public events. It was the way you told the story of a crisis with your young son, when you thought he hated you, and how this completely devastated you—for a time. Well, I had much the same thing happen to me, and when I read that, I thought I knew you better than through anything else in the *Journals*."§

Odd, isn't it, how recording events that had nothing to do with my *work* appeals to so many serious people?

"Nothing to do with my work." Perhaps it had everything to do with it, for such side glances at the inner man explain why the outer man acts as he does, makes the kind of decisions he does—in short, functions in the world of action.

Continuing the reading of Samuels' biography of Henry Adams, *The Major Phase*.

Such consistent, half-hysterical, learned, professional pessimism fascinates and intrigues me. I should like someday to try my hand at an

§ *Journals*, Vol. I, *The TVA Years*, p. 89.

essay: "The Anatomy of Pessimism." Adams and his kooky brother Brooks were deep-dyed pessimists because their *function* was dwindling. Their forebears, revolutionaries; they, men without (as Brooks says somewhere) "a daily occupation like the rest of mankind." I'd better continue to have a "daily occupation"; it is the road to health, or at least a detour around such abysmal and thoroughgoing, fully "reasoned" and irrational pessimism.

10 P.M.

Mystical? Very well. But I am convinced after these past days of brooding about what I envision as "The American Renaissance" that we, the present generation of Americans, are the custodians of as great a destiny as man ever looked upon, a destiny of the spirit so shining and splendid as to shame every early period of our history—yes, of any period of which I know anything. The foundation stones of our structure are not—as was the case in Greece—slavery for many, but freedom for few.

In Peru, at Cuzco, Helen pointed out to me the great Inca stoneworks; upon that foundation the Catholics of Spain had built a church. An earthquake not so long ago brought down in ruins the church of Spain but left untouched the great Inca foundation of the Temple of the Sun. I see the foundations of a belief in individuals as standing untouched, and upon that foundation we can build a great City of Man.

FEBRUARY 13, 1965
PRINCETON

I keep coming back from time to time to the puzzle: why am I, so mercurial of nature, in the end always so consistently, stubbornly, and completely an optimist? The word "optimist" has been cheapened, but the concept of faith in life, in its glowing potentials—no bandying of the word "optimist" by smoothies can lower or make this common and vulgar.

But why is it that one who his whole life has been looking for injustices to fight and for indignities suffered by others that he feels he must rectify—why should such a person look with such full-blooded joy and confidence upon a world that has shown him its ugliest face—two wars, many cruelties, stupidities without number?

Why?

Henry Adams is once more a partial answer—in reverse, or by light of contrast. Instead of *living* life, he became lost in *observing* it—and so never really lived.

At the very beginning of his *Education* he said that he, Adams, "never got to the point of playing the game at all; he lost himself in the study of it, watching the errors of the players. . . ."

The deep satisfaction I get out of life has come to me—despite being by nature too vulnerable to the pain of battle—because I *did* play the game. I have been a man with a job to do—a succession of jobs, of course—and the errors I have been absorbed in are not the errors of others but my own, connected with my own responsibility for doing.

11:30 P.M.

As our dinner guests stepped out into the cold, Helen Meyner, looking at the heavens, exclaimed, "Oh, what a great ring around the moon; I've never seen such a large one." Robert Oppenheimer, his porkpie brown hat in his hand, puffed at his pipe and said calmly: "It's standard; the size is determined by the angle of the crystals." So now we know that the ring about a misty moon is determined not by magic or elves, as I had thought, but by the angle of the crystals.

The amusing thing about Robert's chilling remark is that of all the people I know, his imagery in speaking is the most poetic. In talking about France tonight, for example, with Joe Johnson, Robert's use of beautiful literary figures to express a conviction about political and economic conditions in France was remarkable, remarkable even to one like myself who has listened with awe to his command of expression, the sentences paced and cadenced, built on the frame of a great command of the language.

"I understand," Robert said, "that NBC had a documentary about the [atomic] test in New Mexico and that after it was over, and successful, Sir James Chadwick [the British scientist] is said to have turned to me and said, 'And now we're *all* sons of bitches.'" Robert's comment was "and I guess that is just about right."

FEBRUARY 17, 1965
NEW YORK

The other day, at the birthday celebration for Adolf Berle, a tall figure unfolded right next to me, got to his feet, peered at us like some water-walking shore bird, and then Newbold Morris (Commissioner of Parks) began: "It seems to me that all I do these days is go to funerals."

I avoid funerals; but I have come to that "time of life" when I *could* spend much of my time in that probably compassionate but, to me, sterile avocation—I mean, shouldn't we try to see more people while they are alive?

These early morning reflections result from reading that Paul Miller died yesterday, age sixty-five. This news brings back many memories, almost all of a long time ago indeed; of the Harvard Law School, where he reached the summit of his entire life, as one of the men on the team that "won" the Ames moot-court competition; of Washington during the pre-New Deal days, where he was one of Solicitor General Robert Taft's bright boys and, I recall, spent much of my time discussing with me how he could best cash in professionally on his brief public service.

Paul was the archetype of a familiar style: the handsome, bright, socially ambitious boy from the sticks [East Chicago, Indiana] who planted himself most successfully in a Wall Street law firm and never let it cross his mind that when he came to die at sixty-five he might have asked the question: now just what has it all been about?

A warm, personally attractive man, a lawyer's lawyer. But an early death like Paul's seems more tragic than that of Gordon, who had something creative to show for his life's efforts.

FEBRUARY 18, 1965
11 P.M.
STATLER HOTEL, BOSTON

When I said in my Stephen Wise Lecture at Brandeis University this evening that optimism isn't a popular note, particularly among students and intellectuals, I certainly spoke true. Dr. Clarence Berger, Dean of University Planning and Development who introduced me, also commented on my talk before the "question" period; how unconventional it was, he said, to talk optimistically to a student audience. Not only unconventional; distasteful to the young. The older people liked the cheerful note, the young were unconvinced.

FEBRUARY 20, 1965
PRINCETON

A taxi ride from the offices of Arthur D. Little, Inc., to the Logan Airport yesterday served to remind me of what I so often forget: that the elegant sector of a great city gives the falsest kind of impression of what the city truly is. I had forgotten that Boston is *not* Copley Plaza and Beacon Hill alone. Yesterday's ride through Chelsea and the edge-of-the-port area of Boston made me realize, and with a vengeance, how wrong I was. Junkyards, cobbled filthy streets, acres of baled waste paper, the most hideous two-story "apartment" houses, women scurrying by with peasant scarves over peasant heads—this is Boston, too. I must not forget it in the transformation now going on in the downtown area: great high buildings (the Prudential Center) and a brand new expressway that hurtles more cars into the heart of Boston than the little 17th century streets can carry. The old city is coming alive and being polished; but all around are the Chelseas.

As we left the offices of Arthur D. Little yesterday, I was struck by a remark of its physicist president, Howard McMahon; two puffs of white hair beside a bald head, flanking a quizzical face, like a lean Ben-Gurion.

Apropos my proposal that Arthur D. Little should take on the job of a serious attack on the atomic waste problem, so far neglected by the cocky young men of the AEC, he responded: "It isn't a problem that has much intellectual or scientific appeal to technical men." I knew this; it has a great deal to do with the fact that the awesome danger of atomic wastes is about as far from being satisfactorily solved as it was fifteen years ago.

FEBRUARY 23, 1965
PRINCETON

I am trying to face up to the task of deciding about the exclusions and clarification of the material in the 1950 *Journals* which will open Volume III. How much like a surgical operation *on one's self* this can be. To express the often inexpressible is difficult enough; even more difficult is to *leave the record stand* as I have done in the published *Journals*. There in print one faces up in public to exposing one's emotions or stupidities or near-misses or grossness.

In Edith Hamilton's *The Roman Way* she compares the Cicero of his great orations and public declarations with the Cicero of his private letters to his friend Atticus. "That [the orations, etc.] is the façade, stately, imposing; and if it were not for his letters that is all we should see, as it is all we see of the heroes of history everywhere." But in his letters to Atticus "he was content to appear just what he was." So he makes fun of his oratorical effects (what I have called "the ham" in me). Wrote Cicero: "All that purple patch I so often use to decorate my speeches—the passage about fire and sword . . . Ye Gods, how I showed off!"

Another comment that is apropos is in John Hersey's *The Wall*. Hersey describes the notes of his narrator, Levinson: "Levinson never had time to go back over what he had written and revise it. In fact he chose not to." He wrote that "the principal value of these jottings for later use will be as a guide to the reactions of the moment, and I cannot help it if they remind and embarrass me." Hersey continues: "We can be glad of this rule for it gives us an opportunity to see the shifting opinions, the inconsistencies, the resourceful self-delusions of a man in vital difficulties."

With Governor Meyner this morning, at his invitation, to meet with the Meadowlands Commission, of which he is Chairman. Their job is to try to report on how the Meadows, the large area of dismal waste swampland in New Jersey across the river from Manhattan, can be put to use, developed, reclaimed, etc.

The Commission asked Bechtel Corporation to present a proposal; this they did, in the usual beautiful leather binding with incised gold letters. The Proposal recited all the surveys and studies that have been made of this problem—one hundred fourteen in all—and, *of course*, proposed that they make still *another* report!

With my views about survey-itis, no mystery about what *I* felt: the Commission should find out what is causing this continuous record of no-action and get at that cause. I found the skepticism more than shared by these men on the Commission—laymen, prominent citizens.

I hope the Commission will report the need for a single state agency, established by a law that sets out the framework of policy—and with authority to *do* something. Apparently I'm not the only one who is fed up with the habit, all through business as well as government, to propose one report or study or survey after another, in order, as one of the Commission said, *not* to have to make a difficult decision about *doing* something.

7:25 P.M.

Felix Frankfurter, who seemed to those who knew him to be the fountain of life that would flow on forever, is dead.

At the end of a telecast, the voice of Walter Cronkite: Justice Frankfurter just died of a heart attack.

A part of my youth has died in a Washington hospital today. My mind will tell me—but not now—that this man lived a long and happy, a buoyant life, full of great achievement, and leaves an imprint on lives and thought that will go on and on. But that is no help, that solace, in the irrevocable moment of finality.

A cable from John Oliver: the Minister of Water and Power, H. E. Mansur Rouhani, agrees with Ansari that D&R shall be the "engineer" to design and supervise two dams, one on the Karun River and the other on the Marun, the construction of which had been approved by the Government. [The proposed dam on the Karun River was originally described as Karun #2 in D&R's Unified Development Plan of March, 1959, but was later known as the Reza Shah Kabir Dam.]

This could be a turning point indeed. As Ansari said, in a very cordial personal letter to me this morning, he looks forward to seeing me soon on the occasion of the "new chapter in the history of the

Khuzistan program." [D&R's proposal was not accepted; the dam was designed by Harza Engineering Corporation.]

"Great-Grandfather, what was it like to live in that great big fast-as-lightning modern city of New York in 1965?" Well, it is elegant Bentleys turning the corner into Wall Street from Broadway at Trinity Church, and chinchilla chilly dames waiting for their cars before the Regency Hotel.

But not entirely. For today, down on lower Hudson Street, what should come right through a red traffic light but a dray, a dray pulled by a horse with blinders. Ice formed around his nostrils as he blew frosty air into the gloom of that cobbled street.

In New York in February, 1965, it was like that on Hudson Street on lower Manhattan Island.

FEBRUARY 24, 1965
NEW YORK

I am always impressed with the scientific mind's desperate need to reduce the components of a problem to numbers, or to an analogy to the more mechanistic flavor of science. Henry Adams, a historian (that is, a "social scientist"), tried to formulate a *universal* hypothesis about the affairs of men by applying what Lord Kelvin had summed up in his doctrines of the science of thermodynamics, the dynamics of energy or heat. Adams' theorem turned out to be nonsense, though very elaborate nonsense.

Now the physical scientists are paying the social scientists back by applying systems analysis and computer thinking to human affairs, such as the raising of food production in West Pakistan.

A group of twenty experts, an MIT-Harvard group headed by Professor Roger Revelle, goes to the Punjab to look at waterlogging, the steady death of Pakistan land through salinity. It is charmingly naïve and refreshing to watch a scientific mind try to find some way to put the elements of such a problem into *numbers* that can be made into a "model." Truly they have concocted a beautiful model, but it tells no more than what actual experience in dealing with the land and its people on it can tell.

One must go at such a problem as waterlogging (salinity poisoning of land) by recognizing that not salt in the soil alone but the *whole unified fabric of life* is the problem, with the development of people the heart and core of its solution. All this elaborate statistical analysis stops where the man whose job it is to get something done *begins*: how do you get the *people on the land* to put into practice what many of them already know, or what in any case is known by men who have been working at these problems long and hard, not on paper but on the land and with the people?

It isn't—as I once thought—that the use of systems analysis is something to be opposed; *any* way of describing a problem and its components is probably useful. But this isn't what is most needed, these fine analyses; they divert attention and energy away from the problem of action.

The Revelle Commission analysis left the problem where they had found it. Each year more and more land of Pakistan is being ill-used and destroyed by salinity by the very men who must depend upon it for their bread; and this despite hundreds of millions of dollars for canals and other engineering works.

FEBRUARY 28, 1965
PRINCETON

It must be three years ago or more that I came up with the idea that coal, particularly in the West, would be a resource (chiefly for electric energy) that would give Development and Resources an important thinking and catalyzing function here in the U.S. We did a good job of looking into the question of whether there existed coal in large enough amounts and under conditions where mining could be economical. We hired a bright young rolling stone, John Allen, a metallurgist by profession and a poet by inclination. He tramped over areas of the Rockies where geologic survey crews apparently hadn't trod. He recommended, and we agreed, to hire the Colorado School of Mines Research Foundation to prepare a report—which confirmed the presence of enormous quantities of good coal. Walt Seymour, with an assist from our wise friend Ed Morehouse, did a number of spot studies. All these added up to confirm the major thesis: coal from the Rockies could help supply the prodigious needs of California for electric energy. We applied for coal exploration permits on the Kaiparowits Plateau in Utah, and some of these were granted.

Then what? How to put this concept in such shape that D&R would have a part in this potentially huge development in an area of American life that has been my business for so long, i.e., energy?

Last July I decided that one way to find out whether there was any place for us in this dynamic new energy development was to speak out about it, in the Western mountain area that stood most to benefit by this revolutionary change in source of energy on a very large scale. The upshot was a full-page interview with me in the *Denver Post*.

But nothing happened; we were ahead of our time. But the time *will* come when Kaiparowits Plateau and other mountain coal will fuel the West Coast's needs.

MARCH 1, 1965
PRINCETON

The classic case of how *not* to bring change is that of the Helmand Valley of Afghanistan: A hundred million dollars paid to a big construction company (Export-Import Bank financed, I believe) to build a beautiful pair of dams, canals, etc. Thirteen years go by; nothing happens for the people on the land, not even a knowledge of which land has a chance of being productive and by what means. The place crawling with "study" groups at public expense; a couple hundred Afghan extension-type workers; the Robert Nathan firm teaching them "planning" at Kabul, and more recently a contract to J. G. White for some similar purpose.

The Afghans are becoming restless; small wonder. They *have* established a Helmand Valley Authority, thinking, I suppose, poor dears, that that meant they had a TVA and things would be OK.

The Deputy AID Mission Director for Afghanistan yelled for us; Leo Anderson and John Burnett spent five hours with him and others of the Washington staff on Saturday and reported to me this morning. We always seem to get the things that other people have botched up, e.g., the Overseas Consultants with their huge expenditures in Iran just before we went there, and similarly the FAO folly in Khuzistan—a report concluding that Khuzistan could never amount to anything.

MARCH 2, 1965
NEW YORK

David and I sat in my room and talked for a couple hours about things very close to our hearts. I felt the need to talk to him about what goes on inside a fellow, another human being, rather than the father-to-son business. I never thought this would ever be possible for me—to discard almost every vestige of the father-role; I needed to get things of the deepest kind out of my system, and he sensed I think that the man who sat slumped in a chair before him was in need of someone to "communicate" with, not just someone to chatter with about grandchildren. It was a memorable experience for me—perhaps for him.

David left home when he was just sixteen, so his impressions of his parents were all formed before that age. It was startling to learn how acutely he sensed the imponderable, subtle things in that home; for example, that his parents never believed in too much talk about emotional problems—a matter of long accepted principle. The young *sense* these things, and at almost forty they still remember—and understand the implications.

Even Henry Adams, that overcultivated brain, could express so simply the need that everyone has to be "emotionally dependent" on someone. The phrase was David's last night; I said, sotto, "That is one term; a better one is love." And then we talked about "remoteness," and "self-sufficiency." He concluded, with a look of disdain: "Self-sufficiency—that is . . ." I finished the sentence in the slang (of yesterday) ". . . for the birds."

That young man *understands* more about the soul and the spirit and the springs of the inner man than I did, surely at his age or many years after. No wonder he is an artist and a good writer. I grew up according to *patterns* established by the world around me; he seems to have seen through these, but probably at the price of great anguish.

MARCH 9, 1965
NEW YORK

This morning at breakfast, in the aseptic hotel coffee shop, sat next to a perky little man with the empty-happy face of the teacher's pet boy in your high school class—unmarked by *anything*, though he must have been sixty, judging by his white hair. Across the table the girl he married in some little town while very young, she now a shapeless mound, so much bulge across the shoulders that her neck seemed to be sinking into the green waves of her dress. She eyes the menu severely. He had already ordered, brightly, with that cheeriness before coffee that is so abhorrent. Says she, over the top of the menu, "Which Kiwanis group was it you are going to today?" "In Greenwich Village," said he.

I was so startled at this bit of the small town life I know so well there in the heart of Manhattan. I was enchanted. The day had started well.

MARCH 11, 1965
ABOARD PAN AM HEADED FOR ROME,
EN ROUTE TO NEW DELHI

The outline of the Vineyard far far below, the triangular outline familiar as the palm of my hand, the peak at the top, the long flat line below. The indentation of the harbor where my *Lili-put* rides in the summer; my son and Peggy and the children are down there. And I'm off for what promises to be a rich experience, an adventure—if I don't take it too tensely. Enjoy, my right shoulder-perched angel tells me.

Monday afternoon I crossed the street to Two Broadway, a building as enameled and synthetic as a brand-new set of false teeth, swooped up to the tenth floor and slithered through glass doors to the executive offices of American Electric Power Co. My mission: to talk to a chief officer, Phil Sporn, about joining the D&R Board.

I seated myself in the spacious reception room to await word that the truly distinguished gent would see me, and was nearly knocked over by a stainless steel truck filled to overflowing with garbage—topping the mess, an old fashioned type garbage can on its side, oozing food remains. The motive power of this vehicle was a short, sturdy character in a filthy busboy uniform, grunting and pushing. I was so amused by this picture that I started to whoop. The grey-haired receptionist muttered something about an executive dining room on that floor, adding, "Mr. Sporn will see you right away; follow that corridor and turn right." "Will the garbage wagon know the way?" asked I, still snorting.

Executives have to eat, and executives who eat leave garbage.

Yesterday noon a session with André, bringing him up to date, in a sketchy way, about the major developments in D&R.

André was in high fettle, bouncing into the office like a boy, his eyes agleam, slouching into a chair, listening intently to the story about the prospect of two dams in Iran and the political implications of the Nasser-Iraqi drive on the Khuzistan. He was obviously intrigued by the progress I think I've made recently on the Western coal idea, assuring me that he would be interested in putting some money in it—as always with the banker's qualifying words about seeing more details, although he was for it "in principle," all said with the old glass-eyed caution, born of experience, but with a light in his eyes of genuine enthusiasm in seeing an idea begin to take shape, and compared with many of the things he does, *big* shape.

Then a phone call from Leslie Gould of the *Herald Tribune* about a "deal" which Lazard was negotiating. I was struck with the great change in André, actually taking a call from a newspaper reporter, talking frankly with him, assuring him that *if* a paper was signed—and it might be in a day or two—"you would be the first to know," the quid pro quo being that Gould let the story remain unpublished for a day. All of this showed a pro's handling of the press, whereas ten years ago I remember how difficult it was for André to understand that putting out a press release with the story as *he* wanted it didn't at all mean it would be handled that way. The process of André's American sophistication is pretty well complete, I would say.

These business transactions give him real delight—even the headaches—but I had never seen this so clearly demonstrated before—his chuckles of pleasure, sitting at the center of the exercise of power, with all its excitement and intellectual enjoyment. The fact that there would be considerable money made—or lost—out of the transaction, or that the deal itself really had only limited importance to the world, made no difference, of course.

This morning's *Herald Tribune* has the story, though the Lazard name is hidden (the newspapermen are playing the game) by being called "a prominent Wall Street investment banking house."

I hadn't seen this deal process, performed by one of the very best professionals, at so close a range for a long time, and I found it strangely interesting, even though it did mean that my own matters, which I thought more important, had been set aside.

Perhaps the Peru caper is not quite dead after all. Word from the World Bank: could Renato Rossi, the Big Bull of San Lorenzo, and the Bank's loan officer come to see us? Yesterday Bank officials were in our offices most of the day. It is evident that they think well of our idea of a region-wide enterprise, more extensive than any we have suggested, to include both their sad-sack scheme, San Lorenzo, Piura, *and* some of the eastern region cattle-raising land, beyond the coastal range.

This comes during the week *Time* has on its cover a handsome picture of the extraordinarily handsome President Belaunde, and inside a most favorable story about him. In the story is a comment on survey-itis that sounds like Dave Lilienthal, and this is how it reads: "Peru is being studied to death," Belaunde recently told U.S. officials. "We have pre-surveys, pre-pre-surveys, pre-investment surveys, pre-pre-investment surveys. Committees of experts study us. Everybody studies us, and in spite of all these studies, Peru is moving ahead."

I would like to send a copy of this statement to the whole galaxy of those who would rather write a report than *do* a damn thing about anything.

MARCH 12, 1965
3 A.M.
HOTEL HASSLER
ROME

Until you have moved through the streets and among the truncated columns and monuments of Rome at 3 A.M. you haven't seen Rome or *felt* Rome, or heard Rome, either. And with a low-hanging, dying orange moon to boot.

At that hour those cursed Fiats stand motionless like sleeping cattle, not as in the daytime hooting and squawking and swishing around corners so that all one saw of Rome were those metal insects of hell. It was wonderful: silenzio.

What do they do with themselves, the well-to-do retired older people? I never go on a trip that I am not depressed by this question. For a while I thought these couples were just one further demonstration of the way marriages become utterly meaningless after their *function* (children, bringing them up—or down) is over. Well, the picture of people (no older than I, I suppose) who are so bored with each other that it is painful *is* a commentary on more than marriage; as *individuals* they are out in the cold. At the next table here at the Hassler a woman with a horrible voice kept talking for fifteen minutes about one silly thing: she was *sure* that the dining room had been longer when she was here before. Her husband, who should never have been allowed to "retire," says sadly, "I am tired right now, and we've only had two days of the trip." The prospect of going on to Venice brought from her the comment: "I suppose I'll like it when I get there, maybe, but I would like to be home right now." "So would I," says he.

MARCH 13, 1965
LEONARDO DA VINCI AIRPORT
ROME

The card in the taxi I took out to the airport posts the Tariffa in three languages. The English version covers all contingencies:

Dogs (except lap dogs) (not obligatory)	30 L.
Lap dogs (obligatory)	Free of charge

AIRBORNE, APPROACHING BRINDISI

The thought of agreeing to go halfway round the world, to New Delhi, to co-lead a discussion of "administrative science" (their expression, not mine), embarrassed me; the agenda included sophisticated statements by the new religionists of management, the systems analysis boys, and their beautiful magic lute, the computer. (Most people will do *anything* to keep from sweating out the difficulties of actually making decisions, of running things, and a mysterious and expensive machine, the computer, is the latest diversionary device.)

What in the hell could I say useful to Indian civil servants? The young President of IBM World Trade Corporation assured me of what I already sensed, that in a highly departmentalized organization fragmented by bureaucratic barbwire, the computer was of no use. And in India, fragmentation reaches a new high; unwillingness to make decisions is chronic.

If I stick to what I know, some of it may rub off. All this fancy "management science" computer technology becomes just wind if it isn't put to use by the farmers on the land or the industrial engineers or businessmen who design equipment to make that technology of use.

MARCH 14, 1965
CLARIDGES
NEW DELHI

The desperate and dramatic state of the area on which this country depends for food makes it clear that what has been done, and the way it has been done in the past, just won't do for the future. This realization in itself is a step toward doing *something* that breaks the circle of repetition. But it will take more than a "realization" to get the bureaucrats to accept the organizational ideas I have developed. (Based on the concept of a *unified* attack on the food problem, my proposals would modify the absolute "sovereignty" of each of the various ministries.) In a bureaucracy-ridden atmosphere (Washington *or* Delhi) this is the last thing that will be embraced willingly. And yet it was accepted on our recommendation for the Damodar Valley,* years ago. Perhaps that was due to Nehru's experimental, searching mind—something quite different from the usual British or Indian Civil Service mentality, in my experience.

MARCH 16, 1965
NEW DELHI

Since I arrived there haven't been really absorbing things going on: a meeting with the fussy over-his-head Minister of Irrigation and Power (Dr. K. L. Rao) late yesterday afternoon, in the burning red catacombs the British left as their contribution to "Indian" official architecture. Or a meeting with John Lewis, AID Director, and his staff yesterday morning. Lewis is a flurried young man, an economist more at home in dealing with economic concepts than with people and bureaucracy. Or listening to a steady stream of boiler-plate official State Department optimism about India from the attractive Ambassador, Chester Bowles, last evening as we sat on the terrace of his modest home.

I feel let down, wondering whether I am not repeating myself in such a trip as this. And if there is anything my restless nature rebels against it is going the same path twice.

MARCH 17, 1965
NEW DELHI

Yesterday, after a meeting with ministers and the Planning Commission, we were driven to a 14th century Mogul university for a "pic-

* *Journals*, Vol. III, *The Venturesome Years*, pp. 113, 114. For an account of this enterprise by its first General Manager, see Sudhir Sen's *A Richer Harvest*, pp. 89 et seq.

nic," the product of Mrs. Bowles' imagination and energy. A stage had been set before the door of a Mogul tomb, and on it an Indian dancing troupe performed some delicious dance figures. I can still hear the tinkle of the little bells on the feet of the dancers; the utter grace of one of the young women dancers still stirs me—exquisite in its controlled pattern.

But what was pure magic was the setting for this "picnic" attended by much of the diplomatic corps and most of the younger people of the U.S. Embassy staff. The grounds of the university are dotted with small, separate stoneworks, like great mushrooms with curved tops and slender supporting pillars. They stretch out from the main building and tomb, over what was once a small body of water—the Persian liking for rectangles of water—now empty of either water or the houris one imagines must have disported themselves in such a setting. The moon was full. From every surrounding wall and shelf and crevice candles burned, thousands of candles.

NOON

Is the foundation of all wisdom about "public affairs"—"administration," "public policy"—the character and emotional make-up of a *particular*, *separate* human being? Are there then no "general principles," no unifying system of thought that will apply to whatever individuals are temporarily visited with authority or influence on decisions? Is decision-making as anarchistic as all that? Is it true after all—as I wrote so many, many years ago in my callow youth in *The Outlook**—that this is a "government of *men*, not of laws"?

More and more in my experience in countries that are new to me I find I am forced to this most unlawyer-like, most unjudicial position, in spite of my desire to believe that there is a universal principle to tie to.

The seven deadly sins (or strengths?) of humankind—blinding pride, personal vanity, driving ambition, jealousy, greed for power, etc. —more and more these limitations and their counterbalancing positive human qualities seem to be the terms in which I size up what is called a technical or administrative or public policy picture.

Does this make it impossible to predict, to forecast, *to plan*?

It does appear clearly that what is decisive is the various ministers —the cast of characters—who affect the lives and the amount of food and shelter of hundreds of millions of unseen people. Should I mourn that this narrow view is true? Should I rejoice? I'm not sure. I would rejoice if I were to discover the truth of my long-held hunch that the

* "Oklahoma, a Test of Our Theory of Constitutional Government," *The Outlook*, CXXXV (October 10, 1923), 216–217.

best plan is *to have no detailed plan*, that it is the infinite varieties of human personalities who have their hand on the tiller at a given moment that determine whether things go well or badly—or in any event, *where* they go.

These reflections grow out of the past two days in India, and particularly a dramatic confrontation late last evening at the official residence of the Minister of Agriculture, Subramaniam.

The issue: how to increase the production of food in a country that is always on the edge of famine and has been for centuries. (There would be a famine now except for the millions of tons of American surplus wheat.)

How to get maximum food production turns on the question we "foreign experts" were brought here to consider: is the water brought to the land through extensive physical structures of storage dams and canals being put to the best possible use *on the land* by the farmers? Are measures that have a chance of succeeding being taken to stop the growing blight and creeping cancer of salinity and waterlogging (monsoon water not being absorbed by the soil and so preventing the growing of crops)? Are effective steps being taken so flood waters that destroy crops—and people—are being "managed" to minimize this heartbreaking loss?

This is the issue: life and death for hundreds of millions of ragged, undernourished human beings. It is no abstract issue for report writers or computer technologists.

The poor devils on the land and in the villages (though we are told repeatedly that this Republic is a "democracy") have precious little to say about the basic decisions concerning food—or hunger. They can riot and raise hell, as they do from time to time when food scarcities or elevated prices stir them, but on the positive side, there's damn little they can do.

Who are these few men who make the belly decisions? How do they think and feel—and being Indians they *feel*, and can and do articulate abstractions in a way that is overwhelming, and to this somewhat more pragmatic Westerner, sometimes a bit repulsive.

Sitting in the driver's seat is the Minister for Irrigation and Power, K. L. Rao. The Minister is an extremely tense little man, thin, sorrowful, harassed, pulled and hauled, an engineer of the old irrigation school, Indian Civil Service style, than which there is no more conventional kind of engineer. (For generations throughout the period of British storage reservoirs, to get water to more and more acres and people, has been the Indian answer to the food needs of the country.)

He was deeply offended by a report by the AID Mission, just published, in which three American irrigation engineers had criticized his

Ministry, saying that further irrigation expenditures should halt until there had been a reappraisal of the methods. "This report has done damage to *my* Ministry," Rao said, to introduce our conference, attended of course by his chief technical people.

But on prodding he admitted that increasingly land was being lost by salt and waterlogging. He conceded that the purpose of irrigation was to increase food production (this was considered a great concession). It is an ironic caricature of the bureaucratic mind which regards the maintenance of its bureau as the end—"my ministry," not my country, or the people who depend on us for water and food, but *my* ministry—that phrase tells a lot, all over the world, from Ickes on. . . .

At the meeting last night the most impressive man was Minister of Agriculture Subramaniam. Small in stature, in gleaming white Congress dress, the blackest of hair and eyes, quite young, of an inquiring mind, ready to do battle with the man he regards as his natural antagonist, Minister K. L. Rao.

Subramaniam led off: Mr. Lilienthal and his organization and its accomplishments were well known. It was thought they could help on some of the problems of irrigation, ground water, and organization, providing an "integrated approach" to the water management problems of the Northwest region.

I was invited to say something. I led off by saying that India's technical competence in irrigation was extensive. It was not, I thought, sensible to consider a re-examination of the way irrigation and power *engineering* was being carried on. India, thanks to the British, had a corps of well trained and experienced engineers.

But the interrelation between the work of the engineers and the *use* of that water for crops—well, here was an area where we of D&R had experience that might be useful.

Despite my effort to be tactful, Rao went into a frenzied outburst. He must be "frank"; he would oppose any idea of looking at what had been done in his Ministry, anything that would suggest to the Indian people that *his* engineers did not have the answers, that the program attacking salinity, waterlogging, etc., wasn't completely correct. It was a classic performance of the bureaucrat at his worst from the sensitive and unsure man.

Subramaniam began to spit back, complaining about the way irrigation engineering had impeded agriculture, citing this case and that. It was a spat, a furious one for a while.

Then the Vice Chairman of Planning, Ashok Mehta, tried to smooth feathers. He reminded the distraught Rao that it was not the irrigation engineering that might be the subject of our advice, but its organizational relationship to agriculture. V.K.R.V. Rao perked up. Wasn't it the *economics of water management* that was the issue, not the engineering? I said I thought the term helped. Gradually things settled down.

All this time the bug-eyed "audience" of a couple dozen high staff, plus an amused Ford Foundation veteran in India, Doug Ensminger, listened and enjoyed the spectacle.

My temper is easily stirred; but when others lose theirs, I seem to become more and more calm and less prickly. I let the storm play itself out. The thought occurred to me once more that it is easier to write a book or a report on the "way out" for India than to confront a clash of personalities—which is what always lies at the bottom of these issues, I fear.

MARCH 18, 1965
ON THE FRONTIER MAIL,
FROM DELHI TO AMRITSAR

"I just don't believe it," I kept muttering as I walked through the railroad station; Kipling has described it, but I still don't believe it. Those great white turbans rising like the erupting top of a cake; tiny five-year-olds carrying naked two-year-olds on their hips.

MARCH 19, 1965
AT THE "REST HOUSE"
NANGAL DAM, PUNJAB

What sights I saw yesterday, from the time we climbed off the train at Amritsar in the early morning, through the long day until late at night! Our car, one of a caravan of four, found its way to this ugly island settlement that once housed the "government officials" for the Nangal-Bhakra Dam—and every step of the way I was struck by the *vitality* of the Punjabis (which really means the Sikhs). This exceptional breed of men is only a fraction of the population—would it be as much as one third?—but they are indeed the leaven that leavens the hell out of the passive, under-energized types that I have seen all through the north of India.

What a handsome, *male* breed they are. The head engineer who greeted us at the train was full of the graces of virility: no muscle man he, but the fire in his eye, his erect carriage—and of course, the beard that made him look like the commander in the field of some ancient conquering force! Hindus there were throughout the day, of course. For example, Mr. Uppal, head of the research institute at Amritsar, full of talk-talk about the smallest details of his sprawling hydraulic and soils laboratory. Hindus in the towns along the way. But even they were infected (compared with Delhi, say) with the self-assurance and the upstanding (literally) figure and fire of these Sikhs, with arrogance very close to the surface. By God, these are men, chock full of the sperm of life and showing it in their every gesture of militancy, self-reliance, and initiative.

The classic appearance of these turbaned Punjabis is so well known, from pictures and movies, that when you see them in the villages and towns, or even in a laboratory, you have to remind yourself that this isn't a movie set. We hardly saw a person who wasn't *doing* something. No languishing, no sitting looking off into space or dozing. In two small towns along the way, I yelled for the driver to stop so I could better see a group of men swarming over sheet iron as they made farm machinery by hand (no machine tools, and no mere assembly of parts from Moline), small threshers for wheat, dozens of them standing outside a crude machine shop.

When I contrast the vitality and ingenuity of these Punjabis with some of the overtrained, overintellectualized American "helpers" we send out there, I groan.

The crops in the fields we saw in our almost three hundred mile drive were luxuriant, almost without exception. The quality of wheat of these parts was exceptionally good, though last year the crop was poor; this year it will be great. This puts the light in the eyes of these farmers, and of the merchants in the towns who supply them—and probably rob them.

MARCH 21, 1965
NEW DELHI

Back again. Dust in every crack and crevice, and very short of sleep, jostled until my backbone rattled like a pair of castanets, but having had an intense course of education on India today, out in the boondocks.

Such a panorama. The elephantine hugeness of the completed Bhakra Dam, which Helen and I saw fourteen years ago starting on its long, long construction period. A jolly visit in a tiny Punjabi village; drinking sugar cane juice and lemon under a tree on a friendly Sikh's farm; an elaborate feast under a gay pavilion; and a solemn conference with officials of Punjabi Institute at the show-off new capital at Chandigarh, designed by Le Corbusier.

For the first time since I can remember, I lost my temper in public on this trip. The trigger was a complacent, self-satisfied Chief Engineer. He blandly said—as did the Minister of Irrigation the other day, in an excited, tense, defensive way—that everything was going fine and nothing needed to be done. I was tired, and pretty fed up anyway, and somehow this was too much. In a voice that—halfway through—

actually trembled (I can't remember that happening to me before in all the provocations and heckling on a Congressional witness stand), I told him and the other officials that this was fine; that I was delighted that the stories we had been told in America about food shortages in India were in error, that America had been sending them shiploads of wheat under a misapprehension; that when I returned I would talk to my friends in the Congress and explain that the Indian officials had told me that they could raise enough food, that their program was in fine shape. I was mad.

If by changing their archaic management methods and providing real assistance to "cultivators" they can double or treble production, as has been the case in Iran, then the U.S. with its vast grain gifts is simply making it easier for India to continue to be unwilling to do sensible things about its agriculture.

Agriculture, not engineering, is the orphan child in this country; until that is changed, nothing can be expected.

MARCH 22, 1965
CLARIDGES
NEW DELHI

Sitting here feverishly writing notes for a "public lecture" I'm due to give at 6:30. And while I think of what to say about "modern management," I see the bullock carts and the latest Italian sports cars go by!!

MARCH 23, 1965
NEW DELHI

An hour with Minister Subramaniam at his official residence (dark knowing eyes, the kind of eyes behind which one senses centuries of the struggle for survival against nature and man, prejudices and mysticism). Ashok Mehta, a smouldering kind of man, eyes half closed, an iron-grey beard covering most of his face, reminding me of Civil War generals in the Brady photographs, very deliberate and low-voiced. "Prof" Thacker, also of the National Planning Commission, in a coffee colored costume, buttoned high at the neck in the fashions of men of a certain official distinction, troubled looking, his academic, abstract proclivities confronted with a *practical* problem which he wishes would go away so he could continue to deal in general "thinking," a gentle and extraordinarily respectful man.

They want my "analyses." I spoke of three areas where things could be improved, one gap which must be improved, essentially transforming the Agricultural Ministry from an advisory organization into an "action oriented" one helping the farmers *on the land.*

10 P.M.

Bone tired. But still going.

Leo and Esther Anderson and I had supper in my enormous suite: three bowls of tomato soup. To serve same, four servants, as follows: the room bearer; two waiters, the foregoing with cockades; and a steward, in black, denoting his elevated rank. For three bowls of Campbell's tomato soup.

MARCH 24, 1965
NEW DELHI

Met with Doug Ensminger today. I assumed he would say: Oh, yes, all your ideas as you explained them to the sessions of ministers and associated staff have been tried before; or, We are already doing all those things. Not at all. "This is the time, and you are the people who may turn this thing around and put India on the road to food sufficiency." To our skepticism about timing he said over and over again what he said after the first ministers' meeting: "This is the *time*."

MARCH 25, 1965
NEW DELHI

Since his belligerent explosion at our first meeting of ministers, Dr. K. L. Rao has become very friendly; asked us to breakfast at his house with his family: his square-faced, bright-eyed wife, a lovely gazelle of a sixteen-year-old daughter, her long black queue of hair floating as she dashed away to school, a huge, very dark-skinned son of about nineteen, and a sweet-faced, gentle "old" man, a historian, he explained. We ate things we knew would be heard from later (and they were), but Leo and I were so charmed by the close family circle into which this fighting cock had admitted us that we couldn't think of turning down the urgings of Madame that we try this and that—food from the South.

Leo Anderson turned to the son, who was as self-possessed as anyone you ever saw, and asked: "So you are taking your math exams today. Are you going to be an engineer too?" "No; I'm interested in space."

That says it. With agriculture still in the most primitive state—even the mold board steel plow still a rarity—and bullock carts in the streets of this capital, the young man wants to go off into space. (Yesterday the Russians announced that an astronaut had dangled along outside a space capsule, on a tether.)

9 P.M.

My morning meeting with Rao, Subramaniam, Lewis, and Thacker brought agreement by the Indians on the program Leo and I had pounded out of many hours of talking—and out of our long-time predisposition *to start* by *doing* rather than by writing reports.

MARCH 26, 1965
NEW DELHI

Our sessions with the AID people all morning, and again this afternoon, have not been too productive of either understanding of what we are proposing or agreement with it. They started with a certain hypothesis of what seemed to me an academic kind, whereas our proposal calls for tangling, out in the boondocks, with the toughest kinds of problems. Naturally AID is reluctant to take responsibility for our kind of action program. Whether anything will come of the trip for D&R or India—at the moment it seems unlikely—it has been a great experience being plumb up against a whole set of realities, some physical, mostly human, and I wouldn't have missed it for the world.

The doctor who saw me this afternoon just called with pleasant news: the clinic found a few amoebic "eggs" (cysts) in the specimen but he is confident he can kill the dratted things. Greetings from Mother India!

MARCH 27, 1965
NEW DELHI

Surely no one can move through the byways of Old Delhi as we did this afternoon without a sense of pain that so many of his fellow men should live so close to the edge, indeed many of them over the edge, of utter bestiality and suffering. And yet nothing brings home to me a more profound sense of awe that human beings are made of such enduring stuff that they not only persist but show such vitality and dignity in the face of the horrors of the life so many of these poor devils face each day.

MARCH 28, 1965
FLYING ACROSS PAKISTAN, FROM NEW DELHI,
HEADED FOR TEHRAN

Looking down on the broad Rajasthan Canal—four hundred fifty miles of beautiful digging—my partner in D&R, Leo Anderson, a farmer first and foremost, grimaced and said: "They dig the canals and send the water into them and then say to the water: 'Good luck, pal.' "

That phrase tells the lesson, to us, of this trip to a land so hungry and so short of food that the U.S. pours millions and millions of tons of wheat, shipload after shipload, into it. Beautiful canals and dams, but *what happens to the water when it gets to the land*? They—the old-fashioned engineering mentality—couldn't care less about *applying on the land* what the agriculturalists know should and could be done for the land, what they write about in their never-ending flood of "reports and reports and reports"—which remain just that: reports.

We proposed substantially what we have done in the Khuzistan—on-the-farm assistance to the cultivator—which is what distinguished our work in the Tennessee Valley, too.

At our last meeting with the ministers Thursday morning, Leo explained what we proposed—strengthening of agricultural *on-site* help ("strengthening," he says; thus far it is only advisory, which is nothing to a hard-pressed farmer; like giving him a pamphlet). Subramaniam agreed; Dr. Rao was still uneasy after the last AID survey team had so vigorously criticized "my Ministry," but he finally went along. Lewis was asked by Subramaniam if he would "get a piece of paper for us by April 1st, next Thursday." He agreed.

In the morning Lewis had questions—good ones—but found the approach stimulating and challenging. During the noon recess his timid advisors had him pretty well talked out of it. When we reconvened at 2:30 P.M. at Lewis' home, he said he had "had a double take." I could see that the action aspect of the program, actually going to bat with the food problem where it exists, *not in New Delhi* but out in the country, seemed just too much for AID to handle.

So, led by his advisors, we went back to their "original concept" of a useful but de-sexed regional report, making an effort to make the Minister of Irrigation and the Minister of Agriculture "cooperate" *in the capital.*

MARCH 30, 1965
TEHRAN

In only two weeks I saw more of the reality of the "top" of India than I ever did before—despite the fact that we had once stayed with Nehru and his family. And I saw more, far more, of the degradation and resignation and hopelessness than any "tourist" would see, because I *felt* for these people; even more I felt how horribly inadequate the people at the "top" are for their needs—and how even less adequate we, or any Americans, are for the needs of India.

MARCH 30, 1965
ABADAN, IRAN

As our DC-6 landed at Abadan, the fences dividing the airport from the field were one mass of human beings, almost all of them in the dress of the desert—flowing robes, burnooses, turbans, faces unused to the unrelenting electric lights. And an undercurrent of almost hysterical excitement. What in the hell *is* this?

These, it turns out, were Muslims from all Persia and nearby countries who were waiting to board our plane—for Mecca. The ambition of all devout Muslims is to go to Mecca and earn the honored title of Hajji. With them, their relatives, friends, neighbors, and just plain enthusiasts, such as would see a small-town Indiana basketball team off to the state tournament.

How good it seemed to be back in Iran. What a constantly changing place—brighter, livelier, cleaner, and more hopeful each year.

APRIL 1, 1965
AHWAZ (AT GHOLESTAN)

A wild wind has churned the placid, almost motionless Karun River out yonder into whitecaps; in the city of Ahwaz, from which I have just come, a blinding dust storm.

I wonder if I have ever seen quite such a rapid and complete change in a town as the transformation that has come over Ahwaz, this provincial capital in the midst of a flat, hot, and remote area.

When Helen and I first set eyes on the town nine years ago, it was an overgrown village. On the main street, an old man in turban and flowing garments, plumped on a little donkey, was almost obscured by a huge sheep he was carrying in his arms; the shops along the street were mere ugly yellow brick openings.

Even from last year I notice a great change. The main street has a covered arcade, with Persian pointed arch-shaped openings, over the stores, little machine shops, carpenter establishments, etc. And the industrial activity that has grown up, in the way of small machine shops and repair shops, gives a busyness and workmanlike tone to this town so recently dormant (if not decaying).

No change is more obvious than that in the Governor's Palace, and in the man who now occupies it, Reza Ansari, who is also still Managing Director of the Khuzistan Water and Power Authority as well as Governor General of the province. That Palace, which I have visited often during these past years, had been so ugly and depressing. Now the reception room is a shining white and gold, the furniture tasteful. And Reza himself is the very picture of the new Persia—gone the windy or empty men (with one recent exception) of a generation that stood for nothing except inaction and resignation.

At the end of the long roadway leading to the Governor's Palace I saw a compact figure, Reza, walking and awaiting me. "This is my only time for exercise," he said. So we walked around and around the two-way drive for perhaps fifteen minutes, while he told me of the "problem" side of his work (and therefore ours); the "good" side is great: the enthusiastic reaction of a whole delegation of members of the Majlis and the King's brother. The security officer attending the Majlis group summed it up, after a visit (of twenty-five cars full) to the entire project, the dam, the pilot project, etc., in these words: "Such a change in the spirit of the people here; they are now so hopeful and full of doing things, for themselves."

Reza was troubled, however, by the issue that arose when a Ministry of Water and Power was created, part of a move to make the Plan Organization wholly planning and to transfer its operational duties to ministries.

Reza had been assured that the inclusion of KWPA in the Ministry was a purely formal thing; there would be no attempt to run KWPA from the Ministry, but just to "coordinate." In fact, he says, a little group of "small men" in the Ministry are beginning to peck away at the most successful—almost the only completely successful—example of doing things Iran has seen (except for the National Iranian Oil Co.) since the building of the railroad from Tehran south.

APRIL 2, 1965
AHWAZ (GHOLESTAN)

Our Muslim neighbors here on the banks of the Karun are doing this morning what they have done, I surmise, for centuries on this Friday that closes their New Year holiday: standing or squatting outside their homes all day "to let the evil spirits" leave their homes; they won't return indoors until sundown, picnicking gaily in the meantime.

And not only the orthodox, but even the Westernized and sophisticated Iranians do the same.

6:30 P.M.
ANDIMESHK GUEST HOUSE

"My eyes have seen the glory" this day, the glory of what faith in men can accomplish, the result of knowledge of the ways of Nature and hard work and perseverance—but most of all the faith that indeed moves mountains and makes two blades grow where none grew before.

That sounds solemn, I must say. But I feel moved, deeply moved, by what I have seen this afternoon. This wasteland growing crops of unbelievable vigor, the wheat so strong and green, the broad beans tall as young trees, the flax and berseem clover, and Anderson going with me through the fields explaining and expounding with extraordinary clarity, like farmers I have known before—Dr. "H. A." of TVA, for example. In an office or hotel room I find Leo almost incoherent; in the *fields*, with his feet in the rows, he is clear and eloquent in a simple way.

But most of all I was moved by the majesty of the great dam. The air today was pellucid, the sky a dome of blazing azure, the shadow on the canyon walls soft, with the light cover of spring's green. It is only at this time of year that there is this touch of green. And pounding through the flood spillways a foaming, struggling Niagara of water, energy incarnate.

I was proud.

10 P.M.

A "party" for me tonight for all the people—Iranian and "expatriate" —working in agriculture, engineering, health, education, and administration, and their wives; there must have been two hundred standing in a semicircle around me. What I said with feeling evoked feeling among them.

My contribution is a limited one, but this is it: providing perspective in which people see their daily work fitting into some bigger pattern, and exciting them with the feeling that what they do has historic vitality.

Coming to this remote place from the "outside world" adds to the weight of one's words and presence, and now the prestige that comes with having succeeded in doing what you set out to do adds an authority and quality that no amount of managerial skill alone could give.

From the compound next door, in this little dusty town, I can hear the monotonous, repetitious whine of some musical instrument and the thud of a drum (bum bum—bum*bam*bum, it goes), the accompaniment to an extraordinary dance which I walked out to see this afternoon before dinner; now the night is filled with the same music and dancing. A circle, now in firelight; two men in Western dress, coatless but wearing vests, each with a long stick, whirling, occasionally lashing at each other. It is a tribal dance of one of the Bakhtiari subtribes. Quite graceful and intense, despite the lack of interesting, colorful dress; probably these two young men were dancing the very same dance their forebears danced, with hardly a change—except in their clothes. The women standing about the circle wear about as bedraggled a costume as I have seen; a pity they don't use the high color of the Rajasthan women or others in India.

The boom boom and the whine and a metallic sky pierced by shiny stars make a fitting end to a remarkable day.

APRIL 3, 1965
AHWAZ

To the west an ugly sky, now red, now death-black, shutting out the sun, and five minutes later the whole world of sand seemed to be flung at our car on the last leg of our drive back from Andimeshk late yesterday afternoon. Then for almost an hour—it seemed longer by far—we could not see ahead, but crawled along peering into this fury to try to find the middle line of the road, hoping that the big bruisers of trucks—dangerous on a clear night—wouldn't bash us as they roared out of the black. One bus, abandoned, lay way off the road; two trucks had overturned, one lying on its side, unable to right itself, like a beached hippopotamus.

One of the strange things was the explicit sensation, yes, conviction, that we were actually moving not forward but *backward*. I figured it out later: the sand was moving past us, covering the road, at such a density and velocity that it created this illusion. A weird feeling, that complete loss of optical perspective.

We made it, with no casualties. I kept thinking: this is an experience with a dash of danger and mystery.

How adolescent can you get?

APRIL 7, 1965
TEHRAN

Ebtehaj whirled me around corners and we charged up to the gates of his magnificent new residence at the foot of the mountain in Shimran. As I extricated myself from his Alfa-Romeo sports car, along this winding street of palaces came a camel train, led by a frowsy camel driver complete with little brown beanie and six-day beard. The seven beasts squnched along past the cream colored, glamorous automobile. Where they came from or where they were going even Ebtehaj couldn't guess, though he said that for many years this now fanciest of residential areas was crossed by a caravan route. What made this apparition even more remarkable—like a cooked-up story from Hadji Baba or O. Henry or Damon Runyon—is that one rarely sees a camel anywhere on the streets of Tehran anymore (though they were quite common when we first came here).

At lunch Ebtehaj and I reminisced, like a couple old GAR veterans, about the early days (in 1956) when the Khuzistan program was only a wish in his mind and an inchoate idea in mine.

I enjoyed most of all having my "memory refreshed" about a long session on the day of our arrival in 1956, a meeting that Ebtehaj said had been one of the most depressing in his experience. He related how he had arranged to have all the "experts" of the Plan Organization, the FAO, etc., meet around a table with us. He had not told us that it was the Khuzistan that he had invited us to Iran to advise him about. One by one, these experts who had looked over the soils and water of Khuzistan gave their grim and despairing appraisal: the land was salted, the water itself was too salt laden for irrigation, the heat was too intense in summer for the raising of crops, etc., etc. As this went on, Ebtehaj said, "I became more and more disconsolate: I've brought Mr. Lilienthal over here, on my responsibility, to develop the Khuzistan and here they say it is impossible."

I remember that session well for one thing in particular: I cross-examined these doleful men and found out how little practical experience they had, and when they said the food of Iran would have to be raised somewhere else in the country, I asked if they saw any *other* area, in a single reach, as large and with as much water available—five snow-fed rivers. How did they explain the historical fact that this very region had been in ancient times a flourishing center of food raising? The answers were mumbles. I went to Ebtehaj's office afterward and said I simply couldn't believe this story; would he arrange for us to go take a look at the region? Two days later he did.

This noon I called on the Minister of Court, H. E. Nakhai. Knowing he is a scholar, I talked to this very un-Persian looking man about his poetry, which he writes both in English "quatrains" and in Persian. I was so obviously entranced—in fact, open-mouthed—at the color of his speech and the breadth of his interests that he warmed up and talked to me for an hour.

The Persian language, he said, has always been a "poor" language, as contrasted with Arabic, which is very rich. But the Persian tongue also has many Greek words—he said five thousand, which I find hard to credit—and the way Greek made such an impression on Farsi is a story quite new to me.

About two thousand years ago Greek scholars left, or were driven out of, Greece and were given refuge in Persia, Nakhai said. They established themselves in as many as fifty different places, perhaps seventy-five in a group, throughout Iran, and were here for almost a hundred years. They brought with them a bent for philosophy and mathematics, which Iran needed. But the Persian language did not have words adequate for such concepts, so Greek words were introduced into Farsi and are still there.

When the Queen of England visited Iran a few years back, Nakhai was Ambassador in London and accompanied the royal party. One night they were visiting, in Tehran, with His Majesty. "I said to His

Majesty, did he know that Iran had once come to the rescue of England?" His Majesty became quite excited; no, how could that be? "Don't be excited," I said. "It was quite indirect, and I will tell you how it was. The Roman legions were defeated in Persia by our King Shapur and almost the whole of their army was driven by us into the Black Sea and drowned. This so weakened the Roman reserves that they were forced to withdraw their occupying forces from Britain so that is the way Iran saved Britain from the Romans." A good tale, told with great relish and humor.

APRIL 8, 1965
TEHRAN

Have I been giving too much emphasis, in thinking about D&R, to the necessity for its continuity? I'm afraid so. Why should I care whether D&R goes on indefinitely after I leave it?

When I get home (would that it were tomorrow—I'm wearing down, emotionally, with this long absence) I can discuss organization without the distraction or preoccupation with continuity, in the sense of finding someone who could present a face to the world of the kind I have, someone representing in his person the public and developmental concept I stand for. D&R after D.E.L. will be different: start with that premise. It will build on the foundation I laid, but it will be different, better or not, but certainly different.

Today a meeting with Rouhani, whose approval of the $200,000,000 dam undertaking will be required. I refused to dicker over fees. I laid it on the line. I will stake my reputation on the *quality* of our work. A top priority with D&R is the basic *safety of the structures*—this on the basis of our past record in Iran and in the TVA—and this preoccupation with *safety* understandably increases our estimate of costs. If some other firm will do it for less, that is for Iran to decide.

This sounds cockier and more belligerent than in fact what I said added up to, for I put it on the basis of the degree and extent and cost of exploration of foundations and construction supervision we give such a job.

The Minister is about forty, stocky, very Persian in appearance and manner, and speaks excellent English. Rouhani argued that the percentage figure, representing our compensation for the design and supervision of construction, was much higher than that a competing firm had charged for another dam now being built near Tehran. This was because they used European technical men who receive less salary than Americans, etc.

I followed with a blunt and plain statement. We had proved by our action in the past nine years that we had put our heart into the work for Iran, that what we said we would do, we did; that others had seen the Khuzistan and despaired of it, that an engineer from a well-known firm had flown over the Dez site and his notes said it wasn't much of a site; that others might build these structures for less of a percentage as compensation, but the actual cost to Iran would be greater unless the quality and engineering integrity we had shown was part of the work; that we believed in close supervision of construction, which raised the cost of supervision but lowered the total cost and *increased the factor of safety;* and that building a dam is a great and grave responsibility (I reminded them of recent dam failures).

When I finished there wasn't a sound, not a word said.

We parted with Rouhani renewing his expressions of good will and the hope that I would be in Iran for many years. [In the event, our proposal was not accepted and another firm, Harza, selected.]

At lunch, Ansari and I discussed his idea that KWPA be reconstituted into a genuine multipurpose development agency and taken completely out of any *single* ministry. I plan to make a strong case for this at my audience Saturday, unless circumstances warn me that this would be a fatal time for such a broad subject.

APRIL 10, 1965
TEHRAN

Audience with His Imperial Majesty the Shah, 12:30 to 1:10, at the Marble Palace.

Past the basketball player size guards at the Palace gate, handed from one group of Army officers to another, they chatting gaily in the warm sunshine of the first springlike day since I have been here, down past the garden where I stopped, transfixed (to the puzzlement of my officer "guide") by a huge Judas tree in magnificent flower; around two sides of the gleaming Marble Palace; again passed from one smiling, bowing servitor to another, and finally into a huge room outside the Shah's "office." I sank down in an overly overstuffed chair. Then, not being quite able to stand the tennis court size tapestry of fat dumpling maidens bathing, with dogs and fawn and forests and Cupid and his arrows off to the side, I stood up to look through the window at the splendor of an early Persian garden.

I wasn't alone long. Three breasts filled with medals walked in, chattering French, two of them adjusting dangling gold swords at their sides; I made out that they were French naval officers. They were soon joined by a Court official in tailcoat and striped pants, and three even more resplendent military men, one bald eagle (or condor, more like it) with a vermilion sash fully six inches wide draped diagonally across his front, all of them with more gold braid than I knew existed.

I was so amused to watch these birds of paradise lifting each other's medals or decorations, discussing them, polishing the handles of their swords with the white gloves they carried in their hands.

Soon Tailcoat took them in hand. I gathered that someone, perhaps Red Sash, was getting a decoration—though where he could wear it with all his present decorations I couldn't figure out. In they went, all talking at once; then silence as they disappeared into the royal chamber.

I was alone again and glanced at a bespectacled, bald-headed man, sad looking, across the way. What a dun English sparrow among tropical birds of glorious hue he seemed—I was looking at myself in a full length mirror; I needed at least a yellow turban or a sports jacket after that display.

At 12:30 on the dot a tall young man appeared, bowed, and opened a door across the reception chamber, and I walked in to see the Shah walking to greet me. I thought he looked quite tired, his color greyer than usual, his demeanor more muted as he motioned me to a divan next to his chair. But his warmth returned as I began to respond to his question about the Khuzistan, and he himself spoke with feeling and at times almost animation, although in a voice thinner than at any time I could remember. What was said I will write about tomorrow on the plane.

After about thirty or thirty-five minutes, the ground having been covered, he began to rise and I said my goodbyes. "You will be back again, I hope, in a few months?"

The audience was over. He walked slowly with me to the door, opened it for me (only afterward did I consider this not quite the thing), and I went out.

I wandered out to find only a wisp of a worn old man who handed me my hat and my heavy coat, which I put over my arm. The escort I had coming in was entirely absent; I looked lost, and was. The old man pointed to a corridor beyond which was a door to the garden. I didn't even wonder, then, why I wasn't escorted, or taken through the huge foyer through which I had entered. I pushed on the high double door; it wouldn't budge. Locked. I noticed an ordinary key in the lock by the handle, and not wanting to go wandering about, I turned the bright steel or chrome key, opened the door, and stepped out into a walk along the side of the Palace, again admiring the flowers and the brilliant sun, still carrying my overcoat across my arm, hat in hand. I wasn't sure in which *direction* to go to find the gate, so I stood there, looking one way and another. At a corner of the Palace, perhaps fifty feet away, was a lone soldier, submachine gun in the crook of his arm, looking away from the direction I was coming. I walked up to him, he motioned "that-a-way," and, still unescorted and unchallenged, I went past the back of the Palace toward the gate. Again I stopped a moment to gape at the lavender cloud, the great Judas tree afloating; then a crunching sound back of me, and I stepped out of the walk to let a squad of soldiers, bayonets fixed, march by, the platoon guide hump-humping the count. No one paid the least attention to this obvious foreigner ambling along, a heavy coat over his arm. And nothing about it seemed strange to me. I went through the big iron gate; the blue-coated "doorman" standing between the huge guards in their two sentry boxes recognized me, motioned for my car, opened the door for me, and away I went.

I set down all this detail (it is now 11 P.M., and I have just come from a dinner party of excited people at Ebtehaj's) because at a little after six I learned from Ansari that about two hours before I entered the Palace there had been at attempt on the Shah's life there in the garden I so admired; a guard—or a man dressed as a guard—had tried to shoot the Shah, and had been shot and killed by a guardsman.

The official paper *Ettela'at*, from which a somber Ansari read the account—a brief story—said that two guards had become involved in a fight in which one had shot the other. No indication of where this had occurred. Ansari said: "It was an attempt on the Shah's life."

This was the first I had heard of it.

No wonder the Shah looked worn and grey. The remarkable thing is that the audience was held at all. But the most astounding thing—and the reason for my relating in such detail how I got out of the Palace—is that a stranger, carrying a coat under which he might have hidden a submachine gun or pistol, came out of a locked door of the Palace unescorted and wandered around the very grounds where this violence had taken place only a couple hours before, without anyone paying the slightest attention or challenging him. Indeed, now that I think of it, it is surprising that no one shot *me*, in the state of excitement that must have existed at an hour when Iran might have been plunged into something like chaos.

APRIL 11, 1965
FLYING BOAC TO LONDON

I shall try to record yesterday's audience as it happened, rather than in the afterlight of what I later learned.

He heard, the Shah said, raising his eyebrows behind his very heavy dark glasses, that I had been in the Khuzistan a week or more. This year, for the first time in five years, there should be a good crop; how did I find things?

I was bullish, of course. I reminded him of the dire, sour predictions of the "experts" nine years ago (almost to the day)—"Has it actually been nine years?" he asked—so I knew he was listening, not always the case with men with much on their minds, even as you and I.

I described the crops that I had seen on the trial farm, or in the pilot area. I said there were broad beans three meters high, the stalks "as big around as"—I pulled back my sleeve and pointed to my wrist, then I changed it to—"a young willow tree trunk." "The farmers are making money," I continued, "one of them enough to buy his wife an electric sewing machine, which means there is now electricity in the village." "And his wife will have plenty of sewing to do," the Shah put in. I bubbled about how well that soil and the training our Iranian area leaders have given the cultivators have worked out—and that this is just the beginning.

"One day," he said, quite solemnly, and without the kind of ebullience he showed at Kutyan last year, or at Los Angeles in June, "one day people will see that the land of the Khuzistan is more valuable even than the oil," the very analogy I used to make but without much response. I spoke glowingly of the purity of the water of the five rivers, probably the best water—i.e., with the lowest salt content—of any in the world being used for irrigation; the water in the All-American canal in California being *three* times as salt-laden.

After more of this, on both sides, he looked far away and said: "Our country has money now; we should go right ahead with other projects in the Khuzistan—on the Marun and the Karun." He opened his hands, palms up, in the slow Persian gesture: "Why not?"

This gave me the opening I sought to get down to cases about the two new dams. I reminded him—as if he, who has a memory like a data processing machine, needed reminding—of our talk in Los Angeles, when he directed that I put my organization at once to getting ready for "another dam." This we had done; there had been long discussions with Ansari; he had been rather tough with us, on our compensation almost to the limit, but we had reached an agreement this week, and it was "workable." We are ready to begin core drilling and bulldozing a first access road near Bebehan "just as soon as Your Majesty gives the word."

He seemed puzzled; I went on to say that the project, it appeared, required not only the agreement of Ansari but the "concurrence" of the Minister of Water and Power; Rouhani had not concurred, but wanted reductions in the estimated costs of our services.

(We are crossing the Red Sea, near Aqaba; my ancestors are reputed to have accomplished this with the help of the Lord, and an assist by Moses; BOAC has done it with more éclat, but our crossing will not live in "history" as did that of the Children of Israel. What a wriggling, snake-like aspect the dry beds of the "torrents" make from this height. . . . And now the mighty Nile.)

To return to the Shah:

I launched into the reasons why "I will not take responsibility for cutting corners on the quality of engineering, though others may, because a dam is not like a factory: if it isn't most carefully designed by the best people, and the construction intimately supervised, a failure could occur," citing the recent disaster in Chile and the great troubles the Indians have had and are having with the gates of the spill tunnel at Bhakra Dam. He listened intently, as indeed he does to anything about India, when I compared India's stagnation in food production with the upswing in Khuzistan.

The Shah looked troubled at the prospect of the failure of a dam through shortcuts in exploration and supervision and "economy"; I pressed the point saying that we had assembled the same "team" of Bill Voorduin and the other senior men who did such a good job on Dez (I quickly changed this to Pahlavi) and that I could give him my personal assurance that nothing would be spared to make these projects not only on time and economical, but *safe*.

Ansari had asked me to have this audience, alone, so the Shah could have "your judgment" about the unnecessary harassment and loss of time in having the Ministry review his actions where substantial sums were involved, or in the offering of rates for industry. Ansari's suggestion was that we follow the earlier recommendation about treating Khuzistan as a special and unique case by setting it up outside any one (or more) ministry. The Shah said he couldn't understand why Ansari thought he needed anything more. "He has the authority as Managing Director; I have made him Governor to be responsible for all activities of every kind—health, education, roads and the rest, in the Ostand; besides [and here he looked hard at me] he is my personal . . . [he hesitated for the word] adjutant. So if he has any problems he has complete access to me to have them resolved."

I told him something of my trip to India and of their food problems; how they were were losing land to salt and waterlogging, were building a four hundred and fifty mile canal into the Rajasthan desert, for example, without having given adequate attention to *how* the water would be used by the farmers, as Iran is doing so famously in the Khuzistan. "Yes," he said sadly, "but why doesn't the West understand these comparisons; why is it you never hear of them?"

And then he pounced on the "political dangers" to the Khuzistan (meaning from Iraq and the Nasserites); this with alarm, almost, and high feeling. I recited something about my recent flight over that desolate swamp area lying on the border of Iran and Iraq, with no roads, no nothing, yet there are many substantial villages, and probably 100,000 Iranians, Arab-speaking and vulnerable to subversion because of their poverty and deprivation. Instead of offering a billion dollars—as President Johnson did recently†—to provide a reason for Southeast Asia to eschew Communism, why not throw billions into Iran, and particularly Khuzistan, to give these people on Iran's western border near Iraq every good reason for devotion to their own country in the event of any interference from the outside?

He nodded sadly. "But I fear your Government does not understand this. Not yet, and perhaps never."

APRIL 17, 1965
PRINCETON

The first days of gardening come again. After five weeks as a wayfarer, never touching the soil, actually or symbolically, what a joy to break the earth with a spade, to feel it crumble in my fingers, the tilth particularly friendly because I "made" that soil, over the years, with precious compost and the cookery of a gardener who puts in this and that—"just enough"—as a chef would stir ingredients to make a luscious dish for the table.

It was only a few hours after I was once more back in the States that, in dinner jacket and with a somewhat blurred vision—lack of sleep—we went to the Freedom Award dinner honoring Harry Truman. He seemed somewhat more shaky in walking than when I saw him last October in his home in Independence, but the earthy tang that is his was just as full flavored as ever.

Dean Acheson made the chief address, a witty and barbed exposition of the foreign policy lines of the Truman Administration. He appeared to emphasize, more perhaps than was seemly, that everything Truman did was right.

Dean writes and thinks with great clarity; but as a speaker there is a singsong about his delivery, and to those who don't know his warmth and humor as I do, his demeanor does give the impression of arrogance.

Chief Justice Warren made a strong speech, surprisingly frank about the kind of issues the Court has been passing on recently. I spoke to him briefly before the meeting, and from my seat on the dais I was struck by how extraordinarily little he has changed since I first dealt

† In a speech at Johns Hopkins, April 7, 1965.

with him years ago, when he was Governor of California: still youthful and vigorous in his movements, his face forceful, a great warm smile, complete self-possession.

APRIL 20, 1965
NEW YORK

In the mid-afternoon persuaded Beatrice to give me a Bee-guided tour of the new and enlarged Metropolitan Museum—and it was a memorable experience. Great skylights in the new wing give everything a special luminosity. Presently exhibiting some magnificent Chinese figures of heroic size, the kinds of objects that in a dark and fusty "museum" would look like nothing in particular; but in the lavish setting of the Met's expanded home they are breathtaking.

A remarkable exhibition of American paintings—also a few pieces of now quaint sculpture of a Victorian flavor. In the welter of abstract, and then Pop, and now Op art, I had almost forgotten how delightful and pleasing such paintings that were essentially illustrations could be; e.g., "The Final Moments of John Brown," as near a photograph as one can imagine. The Early American portraiture: how good to see them again, old friends many of them, the stern self-conscious self-righteous faces staring right at you. And Whistler and Sargent: how stylized these paintings of people now seem, and yet I daresay in their day some of them must have seemed rather daring and novel.

But the most telling thing about the Metropolitan is the *use* of it. It was reported that 60,000 people went through it last Sunday, that 30,000 isn't an abnormally large crowd. And the children! Droves of children of all sizes and ages. Beatrice said that when she was an art student years ago, and would go to the Met as part of the Art Students League curriculum, the place would be virtually empty. "But now you wouldn't see this many people in an art museum, or as many interested children, anywhere else, even in Paris. And they call us a country of oafs!" Something like this is also going on in Des Moines and St. Louis and even Knoxville. One reads about this renaissance of interest in art all over America, but to see it as I did today is reassuring.

APRIL 21, 1965
NEW YORK

How relaxing and happy a haven for me is the Tobey home on Central Park West, a break in the inexorable pressures of my work in this frenetic city. Barney, the accomplished *New Yorker* cartoonist, living in a world so different from my own; the children—the greatly talented and beautiful Nancy, the ambitious and acute young businessman David; the whole place filled with Beatrice's paintings and with a spirit of laughter and of youth. But best of all, for me, is Beatrice herself: laughing at my solemnities, present and past; her forthrightness and irreverence; those sharp, observant eyes of the true artist. Our common heritage makes her a tangible and very much alive link to my youth and growing-up days, a background that now we alone can fully share.

APRIL 28, 1965
ON THE TRAIN, ABOUT TO PULL OUT OF PENN STATION

As I walked to the subway, the entire front page of the *Post*: Ed Murrow dead at fifty-seven.

How priceless is a man who is a real man—and how irreplaceable. For Ed Murrow was unique in almost every way.

At first, when I saw this "bulletin," a flash of pain, for Ed, for Janet, for the hours we spent together. And then, as I sat here in this crowded car, I thought how Ed must have suffered when he knew that never again could he carry his formidable lance into the battles he so enjoyed, the battles that cowed less hardy men. The bitter frustration that a diseased body should hold him back from the great days we live in.

The pictures of Ed crowd in on me. I *should* rejoice that such a man existed and worked, that his great influence was felt, his voice heard. But the sadness of the finality: that rumbling voice, heard so often, that cock of the head, that lift of the eyebrows, that design of flaming words—never again.

A most un-Bernardo letter from Garces, complaining sadly and in disarray about the adverse action of a Loan Committee within the World Bank, a setback for CVC, and implying that they needed our advice. I say *un*-Bernardo because for years he has felt so confident that he could manage things entirely on his own, in particular matters with the World Bank. I had been reassured by Bernardo's self-confidence, for the Colombians' feeling that they could run their own affairs was my ultimate goal of the whole CVC undertaking.

Garces went on to tell a story so dramatic and horrible, and personally painful, that even Bernardo's habit of muted understatement was overwhelming.

It was about the murder of Harold Eder, one of my first friends in Colombia, largely on whose initiative I was brought to the Cauca Valley more than ten years ago, when the CVC was conceived.

"I am afraid," Bernardo wrote, "I have to give you the very bad news of Harold Eder's death under the most distressing circumstances." He continued:

"It seems that he had received numerous kidnapping threats, a new form of crime which, after considerable progress by the Government in suppressing banditry, has now become prevalent. Although he did not take these threats seriously (or pretended not to), his wife and children lived under great apprehension.

"Twenty days ago they all went to one of their farms, a beautiful place in the part of the Valley that belongs to Cauca State. It is at the foot of the Central Cordillera and has a large acreage of hills and mountains.

"Although everyone, including his farm manager, tried to dissuade him, Harold insisted on riding [by horseback] up to the mountains. About two hours' riding distance from the ranch house his party was set upon by a group of armed men. A detective who was with him was killed, the farm manager was wounded and allowed to go home by the bandits, and Harold was captured.

"The reports were that he had been wounded, though not seriously, and that the kidnappers had made off with him into the mountains. A very intensive search was immediately started. . . . Yesterday afternoon he was found in a shallow grave at a point several hours' distance from where the attack was made. . . .

"You can well imagine what a terrible shock this has been, not only to his friends but to the whole country. . . . Harold was universally admired in Colombia not only for his ability as an organizer and administrator, but even more because he was an apostle of hard work who gave everything of himself all his life, although he had the means to have led a very different existence. He was a leader in giving a fair deal to labour. . . . In a very quiet way, he was a great philanthropist. He refused even to consider going to live abroad or taking any of his wealth out of the country.

"He died in character, refusing to be afraid or to buckle down to interference with his work and his way of life. Just as he was an example during the whole of his life, I think the manner of his death may not be in vain, because the widespread revulsion . . . may move many persons to do their duty and face up to reality."

I remember my first meeting with Harold. An intense, wiry man, of short stature actually, but so full of energy and ablaze with an independent spirit (which contributed to his death, I suppose) that he filled a room. A skeptic, he knew the limitations of the Latin temperament, its ebullience and verbalizing, short sometimes on action, never short on rhetoric and enthusiasm. He knew those limitations, but he had the kind of skepticism which is *not* negative; on the contrary. He was, politically, a Liberal at a time when, in Cali, Liberals and Conservatives were, most of them, unwilling to sit down at the same table or work on the same board. Yet he ignored all this synthetic cleavage, went his way, and was the most influential man in that group of strong figures who enabled me to get the CVC started.

To have Harold Eder show you around Manuelita, his sugar operation—as he did Helen and me on more than one trip—was a great lesson in how a self-sufficient and dedicated man comports himself. In a white cloth hat and cheap white pants, he went around that sugar mill knowing every single detail, what pipes were leaking, what the production figures were last year at this time. Not the great man striding through his factory, but just another workman, a hard working one. He could account for every moment of his time, and he scheduled himself unmercifully—perhaps as a reaction against the common Latin feeling that schedules are things to make but not to pay any attention to thereafter.

I mourn him, and Ed Murrow, and try to remember how lucky I have been to know, almost intimately, the kind of men who make a difference in this world.

APRIL 30, 1965
PRINCETON

The huge coffin moved, as if on the very air, over the line of heads of the congregation, as the organ filled the great arch of the church. The men carrying Ed Murrow's body were not visible, only the great dark coffin, as it moved out of the church into the bright, warm sunlight of a spring day. I was not the only one who couldn't hold back the sobs.

I had almost crept in, avoiding the battery of newspaper cameras lined up at the entrance, and found a place against the wall. I don't like to go to funerals, but this was one that somehow I *had* to attend, even though the high society tone of St. James [in New York] somehow didn't seem like Ed.

So many recollections crowd in on me. But these are not for tonight. Tonight I should remember that for the past eighteen months at least Ed has been terribly unhappy, and during the radium treatments he must have been physically miserable. But most of all, so frustrated that something like a cursed lung—a bit of spongy flesh—could keep him out of some of today's great "stories," the very thing that all those years of pioneering as a reporter had fitted him for.

Ed put his whole heart in what he did, and that is the test of a man.

MAY 5, 1965
NEW YORK

The outcome in Iran—will we be told to go ahead with the Marun/Karun dams?—is still seriously in doubt. A cable from Oliver says that he has discussed it with Asfia, who was "cordial but inconclusive"; John is on his way home. Each of us marched up the hill, and marched right down again. Rouhani's efforts to take over the Khuzistan go on apace. Since the Khuzistan is the only completely successful and vigorous going concern in the development world in Iran, it is understandable that some ministry should seek to annex it. And it is surely understandable that we should have to justify fully our costs and compensation for so large a new undertaking as Marun/Karun. But if the result of these "negotiations" is to suck all the distinctive *regional autonomy* out of Khuzistan—the heart of the whole development—this will be most damaging for Iran.

But we are not at this doleful juncture yet. Engineer Asfia, a truly great man, has been selected by the Shah to report to him on the issue. Oliver has written Asfia a letter which is a masterpiece. It is entirely on the merits, written in clear and strong prose, without the provocative expressions I am afraid I might have included had I written the letter.

A warm and happy note in our work here, a few days ago. Diawara, a tall, distinguished looking Ivorian, was in the office to discuss the Southwest Ivory Coast program. His understanding of our ideas of regional development as *a way of getting things done* was clear. I was delighted with his sense of humor and grace. I was told by Tom Mead that the self-assurance and articulateness he displayed here had not been evident when, in Abidjan, he sat in, as a subordinate, in meetings with Minister Saller and other French technical men.

D&R now has an outpost on the sea at Sassandra, a small town in the western area of the Ivory Coast, manned for us by a few able fellows. D&R can now make real headway for the Ivory Coast in that almost virgin southwestern area.

I like to think about constructive things—even when combined with such headaches as the indecision in Iran. For the air is full—the newspaper and broadcast air at least—with the landing of our Marines in the Dominican Republic and the continuing battles going on in Vietnam, American troops no longer merely "advisors."

President Johnson is showing a *style* that is so different from Kennedy and vastly different from Eisenhower: it resembles the Truman touch of boldness—perhaps because (I assume) he relies so much on Dean Acheson, who provided much of Truman's feel in these foreign crises.

It is always a sign of trouble when a leader loses the support of the intellectuals. (I mean chiefly the academic people, teachers and students, particularly the teachers.) This seems to be happening with Johnson because of Vietnam, and it will probably also happen because of the Dominican affair.

To lose the confidence of the intellectuals doesn't mean a political leader is wrong, God knows. So many intellectuals, not having responsibility, will whipsaw you on any decision that is unpleasant in its immediate consequences. *They* need not choose a course, but only debate its wisdom or high cost or risk: a playing with abstract alternatives. A public official may *not* complain, in public at least, at the irresponsibility of those who do not have to *decide* but only need to weigh "options."

MAY 18, 1965
NEW YORK

I have just been asked, why, when you have a day or two when nothing really presses on you, don't you sit back and drift, reflect, "take those inner resources out of their boxes and see what they amount to" —or just idle? Isn't it more than restlessness, isn't it immature and almost adolescent to feel that you *must* have something new, exciting, and absorbing *all* the time? You know perfectly well how things come in bunches; ease up emotionally, mentally, between those peaks.

The fact is that this insistence that something must be brewing *all* the time makes me difficult to work with—or to live with. It has certainly not made things easier for my business associates; I daresay it is my chief liability at home.

MAY 19, 1965
NEW YORK

When the "social history" of this period is written, I hope the contemporary records are candid and firsthand on the commercialization of young women or girls' distinctive physical characteristics, that is, the ones that set them off sexually.

That is the way the sociologist may put it; a simpler term would be: the business uses of the tease. Nothing new, goodness knows, about exploiting physically attractive females—i.e., attractive or exciting to the male animal. But the widespread commercialization seems distinctive.

A young fellow, Hugh Hefner, in Chicago (the social historians may conclude, thirty years hence), is the Father of the idea of making a great fortune out of a kind of chain-store marketing of the female breast, bottom, and long, sexy legs: this, of course through the Playboy Club and *Playboy* (3,000,000 circulation!), a magazine in the current issue of which, incidentally, my serious-minded, Kafka-like son has an excellent and far from titillating story!

But the swanky Playboy Club phenomenon breeds imitators, for the "lower-middle," as I observed in a very ordinary "Chinese cuisine" joint on 58th Street.

I wish I could find in this proliferation of sybaritic developments some touch of gaiety, or abandon, or even something positively wicked and decadent. I get the impression it is just plain dull, that all this contemporary sexiness is simply a business matter, done in a *grim*, businesslike way.

MAY 21, 1965
PRINCETON

Few indeed are the men whose ideas and styles have had greater influence on great events than George Kennan. Architect of the containment policies of the West vis-à-vis the Soviets; designer of policies for our relations in the Far East; the most eloquent sponsor of the policy of closer ties with the Tito-ish forces in Eastern Europe, which promote independence from Soviet domination on the U.S.S.R. flank; Ambassador and acknowledged "expert" on Russia and Yugoslavia; respected scholar, elected to the Academy of Arts and Letters—what a roster! From this record I assumed, as well I might, that this is a man who understands the world today and can gauge its tomorrow.

We dined with the Kennans at the Oppenheimers' last evening. At the end of three hours of talk, as we walked home, I realized I had still one more confirmation of an important insight a lifetime of experience has given me. It is this: that man's *individual* characteristics, his inborn temperament and outlook, are decisive in *judging* the quality of his judgments about broad public issues.

I was prepared all over again to be overwhelmed with George's scholarship, wide experience in foreign affairs, extensive exposure to international issues. And I came away shaken about his limited understanding of human affairs and of the give-and-take of a democratic society.

This was not just the result of last evening's colloquy. It goes back a good many years, back to the days of my admiring official acquaintance with him when I was involved with atomic energy, in the late forties, and he was Chairman of the State Department Policy Planning Committee, under Acheson. He did a pioneering job. But even then I felt that it was in the field of abstractions, of "logical" thinking, that he excelled.

When less intellectual people—a Senate Committee, for example—stood in the way of agreement with his careful, beautifully architectonic conclusions, he became a frustrated and angry man, outraged by the crude processes of democratic debate and delay, by people less intellectually competent, by "the time wasted" in discussions and Congressional hearings.

In this he was no exception among public officials. But somehow

I felt that his frustration was filled with despair—indeed, he spoke the language of despair. He was more than irritated; he expressed disbelief that *our system* could meet the (to him) obvious needs of international foreign policy if it was necessary to go through this wearying, fruitless process of persuading ill informed and even dopey Senators, or people in the military establishment, or others who did not have the background to understand what to him was clear and the product of close lifetime study. This gigantic intellectual impatience I thought then—in the forties—was merely the result of a weary and highly motivated man's having to make a verbal attack on a roadblock to a particular result. I didn't think it went so far as to be the postulate of broad general conclusions on the fundamental failure of the democratic system, political and economic.

Such a profound disbelief is shared by many of our intellectual elite, a mark, I fear, of abstract thinking.

I certainly grant the usefulness of abstract thinking, "philosophizing" in the raw. But I sense its grave limitations.

Illustrations of this tendency I notice particularly these days in talk about the way in which the U.S. Government lines up with dictatorial elements—usually in reference to the sending of Marines to the Dominican Republic, or to supporting the "oligarchs," i.e., the rich people in Colombia or in the Piura region of Peru. Yet when you examine the Dominican Republic *concretely*, or Colombia or Peru—as I have had opportunity to do—you find that it is these people well-off who are at the moment the ones capable of taking effective affirmative action in the *direction* I would want—i.e., development of natural resources to increase food, improve health, redistribute income, etc. Those you want most to have an opportunity to help themselves do *have* the *latent* ability —I am positive of this, and have much experience to support this conviction. But unless you are prepared *now* to work with the more prosperous and educated people—Bernardo Garces, Moncloa, and Pastoriza, in Colombia, Peru, and the Dominican Republic, for example— who else is there to *start* with?

So the rhetoric about siding with the poor people who need their chance in such countries *is* abstract thinking, so far as getting anything done for those who need it most.

But to return, more specifically, to this extraordinary man, George Kennan, and the way in which it seems to me abstract and personalized thinking and feeling distort the judgment of a gifted man.

The issue: the current distressing series of strikes in public services. George complained about the arbitrariness of the unions' simply stopping public services because they had the power to do so, and to hell with the convenience of the public. On this he became very emphatic, standing up (those famous galluses showing), his mouth drawn down. I listened for nearly an hour before I tried to point out the affirmative and creative *historic function* of unions, including the resort to strikes, in community and industrial life—which had apparently not come fully within George's ken. Was his frustration about strikes of a piece with his resentment about the "irresponsible" and "ignorant" Senate Committees, whose affirmative function in the democratic process had somehow escaped him, escaped him because he was so intent on the rightness of his abstract intellectual analysis of our foreign policies?

Is this part of a personal quality in this distinguished intellectual, akin to that which may have been Woodrow Wilson's undoing—and with it the undoing of his great ideas for a League of Nations?

MAY 23, 1965
PRINCETON

Greatly pleased this morning to hear Kitty Oppenheimer's "Hi" as she came through our house and out into the garden. A really distinguished botanist, with a great love of growing things in her hothouse and garden; it was like having one's handiwork—Helen's and mine—observed by an artist in the ancient magic of garden making.

Sitting under our apple tree, she made one remark about the discussion with George Kennan of the other evening. "You finished the discussion about labor with a sentence I'll not forget: 'The strike is one of the greatest of America's assets.' "

MAY 25, 1965
NEW YORK

I have just read a nine-page, single-spaced letter from D&R's Regional Representative in Iran, Lee St. Lawrence, to our counsel John Burnett dated May 17th, and with it the translation of a lengthy letter from Reza Ansari to the Prime Minister, dated May 8th. Both of these recordings deal with the present struggle going on in Iran over the way in which the Khuzistan program should proceed.

As an example of "as-it-happened" recording of the realities of statecraft in the economic field, of the interplay of political forces, personal ambitions, individual pride and sensitivity, the stature—or lack of it—of people in positions of power, these two documents have more reality to them than any book or stuffy lecture on "economic development" that I can think of offhand.

Such communications as these letters, which go back and forth, are distinctly informal. They are not "position papers"; they are not the product of committees, are not censored or muted for possible political implications, are not full of bureaucratic gobbledygook. Instead they are written in the heat of events, describing the issues as they appear *that day*, not as an afterthought. These communications therefore represent honest, realistic, and authentic records of how men actually feel and function on important issues—and such documentation I find rare.

The issues involved in statecraft—whether it concerns the launching of a military campaign against the Nazis in North Africa, working our way through the tragedy in South Vietnam, or economic development in Iran—simply cannot be seen and understood if they are separated out from certain elementary impulses of the human heart: pride, vanity, and what is sometimes called "face." To attempt to comprehend these human factors without having before one the *particular individuals* involved is to distort one's judgment about methods, techniques, possibilities, impossibilities.

Here then is the basis of my skepticism about the excesses of most economists' approach to public affairs, including economic development, or the even more distorted view that the cult of model making and computer programming provides. For such precisional thinking, in an area where the decisive factors are the temperamental dispositions of particular individuals, is bound to give what Justice Holmes called an "illusion of certainty."

Today we see the near collapse of wholly military methods of increasing our country's influence for good in various parts of the world—methods the British and French found quite adequate throughout the 19th and early 20th centuries. And one finds a strong impulse to swing to an *alternative of military action*. The Khuzistan program, what we did in Colombia, the Indus, and what we are doing in West Africa, are all part of that evolving alternative.

There is now, I hope, a real prospect that economic statesmanship as an alternative, in whole or in part, to military and purely diplomatic measures, may come into its own.

Such may be the most important lesson that I will have learned out of this enterprise begun almost exactly ten years ago.

The translation of Ansari's letter to his Prime Minister contains a clear exposition of principles, as applied to Iran, that we worked at and preached about in TVA years ago. I am amazed at how concepts and ideas refuse to die, if they have life juices in them and their time has come. I feel a little ashamed of myself for my constant railing at the "intellectual" when I have so many demonstrations in my own work in the past thirty years that an idea—which is the stock in trade of an intellectual, isn't it?—has a life of its own, and, therefore, is a highly "practical" thing.

MAY 26, 1965
FLYING ("SHUTTLING") TO WASHINGTON

Yards of newsprint about turmoil and violence—and the U.S. Marines—in the Dominican Republic. At the bottom is lack of food, etc. This sparked the impulse to talk to Bill Fulbright.

Three years ago Fulbright saw that a "spectacular," i.e., a TVA success, in the Caribbean was what was needed. He then nudged Ted Moscoso into asking Clapp and me to take a look at the prospects of such a "demonstration" in a certain valley of that country, the Yaque del Norte—the Cibao.

American diplomatic and "defense" experts are all over the place (amid the Marines) in the Dominican Republic. They will dope out some kind of top government coalition, push through an OAS blessing—and then, *suddenly*, someone bright will look for a political Cloret, a breath sweetener, to remove the bad taste of an expensive military occupation.

We in D&R had proposed for that valley an economic program, one we could do something about, promptly. Will Fulbright want to push this, now, in anticipation of the President's impatient demand for some such gimmick? Should D&R spend more energy and our own money on what will probably again get bogged down in the Washington bureaucratic swamp?

So I visited today with Fulbright, seeking guidance which I didn't get.

"This President, he is a very remarkable man, no doubt about it," Fulbright said. "But you disagree with him just that much [holding the index fingers of his hands almost together] and he is off you, completely."

The smiling, relaxed, and young-looking Chairman of the Committee on Foreign Relations of the U.S. Senate looked rueful for a moment, as if some recollection of a Presidential rebuff had crossed his mind. And no doubt there have been more than one such rebuff or scolding, for Bill Fulbright has been persistent in his criticism of the overemphasis given military missions and advice from military sources—criticism I share, in spades.

"When it comes to domestic things, he is a wizard, he works miracles." Bill grinned that boyish grin of his. "Hell, we have tried for twenty years to get an aid to education bill through, and he gets it through just like that—and through *this* Congress.

"But he is in *real trouble* in Vietnam. And now we are being criticized all over the world for the Marines in the Dominican Republic. He's trying to set it right, bringing in the OAS [Organization of American States], but everyone knows that is just a façade."

I told him the chief purpose of our visit (John Oliver was with me) was to "touch base" on what Gordon and I had been asked to do in the Dominican Republic three years ago. I said I thought the idea of a "demonstration" in the Caribbean had been his idea. He said, no, not exactly.

"We went down there," I said, "at D&R's expense, not our Government's; we found a good opportunity for development and people who could do a good job. But though we spent a good deal of time and money, somehow nothing happened. When I saw all this to-do about Dominica, I thought I ought to give you this background; perhaps the 'brains' will want to do something in the way of development as a demonstration of our good will, and to take something of the curse off the Marine occupation."

You would have thought Bill Fulbright was the head of a little college (as he once was) and not head of the Committee that, in effect and by constitutional tradition, is almost a co-equal of the President in foreign affairs. He made a statement, quite casually, that astounded me: "I don't know anything about what's going on down there, except what I read in the newspapers. I was at a conference in Vienna at the time things broke out and the Marines went in."

I had difficulty in imagining Arthur Vandenberg or Tom Connally or even perhaps Alexander Wylie, his predecessors as Chairman, depending on the newspapers for knowing what goes on in a crucial area of foreign affairs.

"The President is in trouble around the world, no doubt about it. He listens only to military people, I'm afraid.

"Well," he added, as if he had no more responsibility than the next fellow, "he'll figure it out some way, I reckon."

Fulbright doesn't in fact feel as relaxed and almost non-responsible as all that, I'm sure as I can be. But that is the way he appeared on this afternoon visit.

MAY 28, 1965
6:30 A.M.
AT THE REMAINS OF THE PENN STATION

"Dave, I don't know what you are trying to do, and I frankly doubt if you do." The speaker was Ed Littlefield; what it was that I "didn't know" was our idea for Western coal for electricity, the latest effort in which I had just described to our D&R Board meeting late yesterday afternoon.

If Ed had said—as he did, essentially, later in the discussion—that he didn't think we could get a "customer" for the kind of program we are now proposing be supported by coal companies, and business interests in the West generally, I would certainly have shared his misgiving. He is an experienced coal miner; he has a mentality typical of the man who digs into the earth: find the mineral, but at the same time find someone who will buy the stuff at a price.

I got a good deal out of his candid sort of criticism, blunt as it was. The way to clarify a situation in business, he says, is to talk to a prospective customer. He thinks the only possible users of our ideas and perspective regarding energy from coal are the two chief potential users of that coal, PG&E and Southern California Edison. The former has a staff that is obdurately wedded to the idea of nuclear plants; the latter has already decided on a big mine-mouth plant in Nevada.

If Ed is right—neither of us has always been right, even in our own respective fields—then the three years of sweating about Western coal, as far as D&R is concerned, have been wasted, and we have suffered a setback.

If I have been on the wrong track all this time, it is nevertheless useful to learn something from the failure.

One thing I learn is that I am long on seeing ahead, on concepts. André once described me as a poet of business rather than a businessman. There is a spread between having the understanding to see what should be done in the *public* interest, and what will be done in the interest of a particular business having a commodity or service that is *currently* exchangeable for money. This marks the difference between a successful businessman in the limited sense, and some other critter who is neither an academic type nor a great theoretician, but someone in between, a man long on looking ahead but lacking the touch of the day-to-day pedestrian businessman.

JUNE 4, 1965
NEW YORK

Helen and I had dinner last evening with John and Jane Gunther; a vivid, lively evening of talk, no other guests.

They returned only a few days ago from one of their John Bunyan trips of observation—ten Latin American countries in about three months! John looked tired after such an endurance contest. But Jane, more beautiful than ever, in spite of household problems *and* her part in the writing of their travels ahead, looked as fresh as a flower. *And* as sharp and intense about ideas, a probing, questioning mind.

It was a lively, spirited conversation among four people who have seen a good deal of the world at fairly close range and not as tourists or "official" observers. Of all things discussed, the most interesting, to me, was an "admission" by both John and Jane that they saw no evidence of the kind of "Communist" leadership that could spark a serious overthrow of what these countries now have. Said Jane, in that anxious deeply concerned manner she has—nothing casual about her convictions or feelings about poor struggling people, despite the elegance of her appearance—"that is *just* the trouble: there is no strong leadership anywhere, either among the established oligarchy or on the other extremes."

John Gunther is probably the most widely experienced and generally acclaimed observer and recorder of events and men now functioning. There is hardly a great political name he hasn't known and written about, the world over. His judgments about men have been extraordinarily well expressed, and his judgment, almost without exception, has stood the test of time. There are few men about of whom as much could be said. He could, at this stage, assume the mantle of the know-it-all with a good basis for such a superior attitude. He does nothing of the kind, either in what he writes or, more important, in the way he talks to those of us who have far, far less experience, and far less foundation for our notions. Some men never seem to lose the learner's, the student's, the fresh observer's outlook on life and on people. It is this about him that most impressed me this time.

Few men have had more non-fiction books published; "inside" has become a word synonymous with John Gunther. And yet he never seems completely self-confident or at ease about how his writing will go. It is one thing for me to be skeptical about the reception a book I write will have; for John Gunther to reflect this as he did at our dinner meeting tells a great deal about this out-giving, modest man.

JUNE 10, 1965
NEW YORK

A novel experience yesterday—a colloquy *by telephone* between a graduate seminar at the Maxwell School of Citizenship, Syracuse University, and me in my office in New York.

Many of the questions and comments were about my personal characteristics (as inferred from the *Journal* entries). There was even the comment that apparently I enjoyed feminine beauty, judging from the numerous references to pretty girls. Yes, I opined, I did—and still do.

Dr. Edwin A. Bock, head of the seminar, said he noted that other volumes of the *Journals* would be following: did that mean that I would take my place along with Pepys, in a *revealing* diary? Will there be an unexpurgated version? Could be.

This performance was hardly over when I found myself in the middle of highly sophisticated talk—to which I contributed very little—from Marriner Eccles, probably the most important single influence on

American thinking about central banking. In his seventeen years as head of the "Fed" [Federal Reserve Bank] he laid the foundation for present-day American financial policy and practice.

A few days ago his successor as head of the Federal Reserve Board of Governors, Bill Martin, shook Wall Street—and Washington, too—with a mild enough speech about the seriousness of the U.S. balance of payments' chronic state of near-deficit.

What did the shaking—the market took a pasting—were a few paragraphs comparing the stock market boom of today with the period that just preceded the desperate slide of 1929 and the collapse we call the "Great Depression" of the early thirties.

I was provoked with this. I said: "Bill Martin knows the difference between '29 and '65 as well as you do; then why did he make the comparison?" The answer Marriner gave was that Martin wanted to be sure that his basic point wasn't missed: that the stock market was too high, that inflation was a threat; to remind us of '29 was a good way to shake us up.

It certainly did.

Eccles is an exceptional and unique American phenomenon. A hard-line Western Mormon banker and industrialist, out of the craglike traditions of the developing West of the early 20th century, he has no fear whatever of labels or of what other people think of his ideas. When I reminded him that Galbraith recently described him—as of the early thirties—as one of the earliest John Maynard Keynesians, Marriner looked a bit puzzled, and said: "Well, I guess I was practicing Keynesian ideas, but I didn't know it; in fact, I don't read much and had never heard of Keynes until long after. I saw all these factories idle and 40% of our people out of work, and said this is crazy." And then, looking off into space above our luncheon table, "I guess I am a socialist, come right down to it."

There are a lot of socialists—in that sense—about the place, including Wall Street, but how many of them would ever countenance having that tag pinned on them—including me!

If the market is much too high, you would suppose that those who believe that would be selling their stocks. No; Eccles says (and Jack Franklin, a banking convert, nodded agreement vigorously) "the market needs a shaking out." Which means that people who hold stocks need to be induced to sell—by such statements as Martin's—in order to safeguard the market from going too high. Yes, that's it.

"Are you selling?" ask I. "Oh, no," says Eccles. "Not selling stocks I own, nor out of large trusts I'm responsible for."

The shakeout is *for the other fellow*. Now, to be fair, it may be that the other fellow, usually a small investor, holds his stocks at far higher prices than Eccles or the institutions who aren't going to sell, and therefore they don't need "shaking out." But I got the uneasy feeling that the result of the shakeout would be that the wise guys who stand under the tree will then buy the shaken out stock.

JUNE 11, 1965
NEW YORK

Albert Hettinger is conceded to be the wisest man in Wall Street. I spent two hours with him yesterday. He looks exactly the same as when he first took me in hand, when I came to my undefined role at Lazard Frères fourteen years ago. Apple-cheeked is not a cliché, applied to him; it's a literal description of those smooth ruddy cheeks made all the warmer by a crown of white hair.

The purpose of our meeting was to see if Hett thought Helen's and my investment program met my *present* objectives. And what are those objectives?

"The objective" when I first came to Lazard, with almost nothing but hopes, financially speaking, was to so manage my business life that I could increase my capital. Now my objective—at sixty-five—is to take minimal risks, to keep what I have.

"On that basis, I would say that the portfolio here [shaking out the big 'appraisal' sheet] is perfect. It is the kind of balance between equities and bonds I prefer for myself." Hett described our investments as "affluence enough to ensure your independence—and that's the *only importance* money has for a man like yourself—or me."

But for forty-five minutes, before we got down to D.E.L. and H.M.L., Hett gave a remarkable "lecture" about the broad background against which particular investment judgments should be based. I found this fascinating, not because much of it was new or fresh, but for another reason: where else would you find a *scholar* sitting next to the throne of power, in Wall Street, discoursing on the historical background of the money system, of the evolution of paper currency from the year one (in China?) with its constant "deterioration" (the conservative traditional banker, i.e., creditor and lender, shows through when Hett talks, even though he thinks he is wholly objective), going on to the "big event," the recent market-shaking Bill Martin speech of several days ago.

Whether Hett's long-perspective way of looking at "what happens now" produces a better result for Helen and me as investors or not, the appeal to history and long term trends fits my style and gives me the assurance that the smart aleck broker (often just a day to day tipster) certainly doesn't.

What troubles Hett are almost exactly the things that trouble

Martin as a central bank head and that the other day troubled Marriner Eccles: the great expansion in credit, in borrowing, and the sending of American capital abroad for investment in Europe, so Europe in turn could *call on our gold* and put us under pressure with our own capital funds.

On one subject Hett was realistic—in an area I know a good deal more about than he does. That is the strong neo-populist impulses of our President.

President Johnson's father, he said, had seen in his own life as a poor Texas farmer how tight credit can squeeze the little guy. As long as there is any way (short of threatening the dollar) to avoid the kind of discipline Hett and other like-minded men would prefer ("discipline," meaning restricted credit), Johnson will keep credit relatively easy. I could add that not only is this a traditional *Western* viewpoint, part of a fascination with trying to cure things by fiscal gimmicks, but Johnson wants to keep the unprecedented prosperity we have going on and on, which deflation won't provide—quite the contrary.

Hett is a figure one wouldn't actually expect in Wall Street. Only a many sided man like André would rely so heavily on a man who is essentially a scholar and thinker rather than a trader. Yet on particular investment judgments he can be quite wrong, as he freely admits—even insists.

JUNE 12, 1965
PRINCETON

Exceptional people fascinate me—people with some very unusual quality. I lunched with such a man last Tuesday: Phil Sporn.

Looking tired and on a lower key than I have ever seen him, he perked up when he spoke about what D&R is doing "on the most important problem"—the only really basic one—developing resources to improve the lot of people.

"When I go to a country which I haven't visited before—Spain, for example, near Barcelona—I first get some of the basic information: how many hours of labor does a man have to give in order to get a pair of shoes, a shirt, food for a week, and so on. And when I find—as I did in Spain—that many people must give 91% of their working lives just to get food to eat, I don't feel like musing over the tourist attractions.

"No other organization is set up to do something about the dreadful poverty of the people in these less developed countries; if it can be done, you of D&R will have to show the way—and I believe you are. The commercially minded countries are drawing the blood out of these countries instead of adding to their strength. Greed is creating terrible hatred against this country. And the government agencies for aid are so poorly manned, most of them, and so filled with procedures and timidity that we get mighty little out of *that* route."

JUNE 13, 1965
THE UNION BUILDING, INDIANA UNIVERSITY
BLOOMINGTON, INDIANA

The transformation of Indiana that this extraordinary University represents! I am astounded. And in every area: a *great* music department, art, business, etc. Most of it the result of one robust, sturdy "artist" in dealing with people, a man of conviction but not stuffy about it: Herman Wells.

I'm exhausted from driving a rented car (sans brakes) from Cincinnati. But though the four and a half hours of driving along winding roads was most tiring, it gave us an opportunity we'll never have again of seeing the warm beauty of the southern Indiana landscape, including a ride across a primitive ferry at Aurora. And on to Brown County, Abe Martin's town of Bean Blossom.

The Indiana University Commencement exercises, where I received an honorary degree, were very much like all others. The chief rewards of the expedition were in seeing Indiana again, by car, driving to Crawfordsville, going slowly past the little house on E. Jefferson Street where we were married forty-two years ago. At DePauw University, indulged in nostalgia, standing alone, on the platform in empty Meharry Hall. Quite moving to me, looking out on those old pews: it brought back, of course, poignantly, and yet not unhappily, the first times I faced an audience of my young peers, standing up there, alone, a boy of seventeen. It was from that platform, looking into that rising row upon row of seats, that the career that followed was launched.

JUNE 16, 1965
NEW YORK

The door of 28G in the Waldorf Towers opened to my punching the bell, and I was greeted by a plump, round-faced man, his grey hair partly plastered flat, the voice of "Hello, Dave, you haven't changed a bit" reedy and tentative. Don Maxwell it was, whom I remembered only as a skinny, scrawny, stooped son of a Greencastle singing evangelist, now the powerful successor to Colonel Robert McCormick, owner of the *Chicago Tribune*. A member of the *Tribune* Board had repeated to him the story I told at Bloomington about how Don and I—fellow undergraduates then—had been suspended from college because as editors of the *DePauw Daily* we ran an editorial calling the faculty hypocrites in their opposition to "social dancing."

"Don, how does it happen that two fellows who came out of similar environments have been so diametrically opposed in opinion from the very beginning and continue to be? The *Tribune* lambasted the daylights out of me, in TVA, and I returned the compliment when I could about your moss-back editorials. How come?"

He didn't try to explain it other than to say that when he began working for the *Chicago Tribune* (as a lowly reporter), to him "Colonel McCormick was God" (his words). "He was generous to me, I prospered under him, I was close to him in a personal way, and so naturally my ideas became the ideas of the Colonel. Were my views about things affected by the Colonel's views? Of course. What he believed, I believed."

JUNE 18, 1965
NEW YORK

Men who wield power, great power (as Don Maxwell certainly does), fascinate me. But Don is a special case. He did not create this power (the McCormick fortune—the Colonel did that), but inherited it because of his, Don's, merits in the eyes of the Colonel.

Don's humility *about himself*—to me, at least—is quite in contrast with that of most men of power who rose to heights "from a single gallus."

Don and I had been talking about the divergent courses he and I had taken, starting (superficially at least) from a common point in small-town Indiana.

"I'm not well educated," he said, "and I don't read much, never have. When DePauw wanted to give me an honorary degree, a Doctor of Literature, Marge [his DePauw college-classmate wife] said she wouldn't go to the doings. 'You don't know anything about literature; the only things you ever read were the *Henty* books and *Frank Merriwell on a Gunboat*—that sort of stuff.' I'm not smart that way at all. But the Colonel wanted me around; I did the things for him he wanted, smart or not. He didn't like to have *too* smart ones around him, and he wasn't very smart himself about some things. He would say some of the damnedest things, like telling Canada they could come into the Union as one state—made the Canadians mad as hell.

"But he wanted to make a good deal with Canada for her trees [Don didn't say timber], which he needed for newsprint, and this kind of baiting was good for making that kind of deal. He did have a kind of imagination, though. The Colonel was the first man in the newspaper business to see that owning trees was essential for newspapers; he saw that you needed to have your printing plant on water so you could bring in those big tonnages of print, so he built the *Tribune* Tower on the lake, and the other papers like the *News* built theirs back in the heart of Chicago.

"And when he died, who did he name as trustees to run the *Tribune*? Not some lawyers or trust companies or big-shot names, but his three lieutenants, the men who worked with him, and I was one of those three. That's the kind of man he was."

These things Don said squnched down in a soft chair, occasionally taking a sip of whiskey, a thoroughly self-possessed man who had no reason to put on a show for me by pretending that he was Horace Greeley.

"Now my younger brother Phil has been putting on music festivals and such, as promotion for the *Tribune*, and he is far, far better known than I am. Sometimes people come up to him and ask, 'Whatever became of your brother Don?' As we get older we resemble each other more and more, and people will come up to me in some public place, like a restaurant, and ask to shake Phil Maxwell's hand." All of this said with a Hoosier kind of humor that I found delightful. No front, not with me.

But when he answered the phone—a call from a subordinate, I gathered—he barked, his voice dropped an octave, and it might have been Colonel McCormick as I myself remember him.

A cable from Oliver: we had been passed over in Iran for the Marun/Karun dams; the engineering responsibility for the Karun dam—called Karun #2 in our Unified Report of 1959—was awarded to the Harza Company of Chicago, "which had better local connections."

Greatly disappointed about the effect on our ongoing program; but by noon I had myself well in hand.

I reflect on and face up to the rebuff we have had in Persia—a blow to my pride, of course, and more than that—but certain friendly words come back to me: "You know what is *really important*, and what is not." Marun/Karun, even D&R itself, are not "important" in the sense of these words. What *does* matter goes far deeper.

JUNE 20, 1965
"THE TIDES," NEAR IRVINGTON, VA.

Reflections at a "retreat"—a meeting of the Board of Education and World Affairs:

Frank McCullough, distinctive with his shaved and polished head, just in from forty hours of flying, from the Far East, where he directs the *Time-Life* forces. Tired as he was, he was full of concern and half-despair at the *military* measures our country is employing in Vietnam.

McCullough speaks with a bluntness amounting to cocksureness. "That big bomber raid [B-52s] will make us the laughing stock of all

Asia. Tiger with paper teeth; flying all the way from Guam to do absolutely no damage. The Vietnamese say: 'OK, if it is your war, *you* fight it.' We're stuck with it now, and McNamara is so articulate that he overwhelms Johnson; McNamara always has an answer for everything. And these computer strategists are compounding the error—geometrically."

JUNE 22, 1965
NEW YORK

I am once more impressed with the superior caliber and special characteristics of the university presidents on the EWA Board: Goheen of Princeton, Hannah of Michigan State, Wells of Indiana, Vince Barnett of Colgate, Glennan of Case—this is an aggregation of talent, seasoned experience, and a range of responsibility that produces a unique breed.

I find fascinating how these university presidents must—to do their job—present a combination of qualities rarely found in a single individual: a respect for learning and a savvy and a toughness with the highly independent people called "professors," with their built-in resistance to innovation as it affects *them* (i.e., their "tenure") in spite of their intellectual and theoretical commitment to thought and, therefore, to change. And these presidents must be *managers*, too, and be able to dig into a set of figures, or leap at once from a beautiful "project" to meet the businessman's demand: "Cost it for us."

JUNE 26, 1965
SATURDAY NOON (IN THE GARDEN)
PRINCETON

A day of such brilliance of light and blueness of shadow in the garden. And never do I remember such a profusion of birds; bird sounds from morning till dusk; a steady flight to and fro across the rectangle of the garden, from the mulberry tree off into the deep green beyond, a quartet (or more) of orchard orioles, their color as gay and moving as the day lilies now beginning to spot the garden with gold and the warm yellow of Hyperion. But best of all the family of tiny wrens, in their twittering flight, with a doughty, commanding trill that fills the air—and me—with confidence that not everything in this world must yield to size (the huge and cocky blue jay) or flamboyance (the oriole with his gaudy doctor's degree hood down his back).

A letter from Senator Fulbright, dated June 21st.

"I spoke to the President about your experience [in the Dominican Republic] and sent him a copy of the report you left with me. It seems to me that if they would take this approach a little more seriously rather than looking for Communists under every bed, they might make more progress."

JUNE 27, 1965
PRINCETON

I am a "difficult" person, and no mistake. It's not only because I bite off far more than I can chew, and lack a talent for repose or inaction. I characteristically want conflicting or inconsistent things; thus, I hate a change of routine or surroundings, and yet crave excitement and change. What a mess of a man.

How Helen manages to maintain her outward serenity and composure with this kind of immaturity going on about her I'll never know. Yesterday I had an irritable spell while we were deciding which of my things should go to the Vineyard, a routine I despise. I asked her to forgive my fuming. She said: "Your being irritable when you have something to do you don't like is just a safety valve, and if you can't let off steam with me, I don't know where you can. When you get that way—it's not often and you know it—I just let you alone."

And letting me alone is good sense from her point of view, and probably from mine.

Have just read an early novella of Saul Bellow, *Dangling Man*, written in the form of a journal.

The opening paragraphs—which I'm quoting here—shed interesting light on the question of why a man writes a journal that includes his inner reflections.

"There was a time when people were in the habit of addressing themselves frequently and felt no shame of making a record of their inward transactions. But to keep a journal nowadays is considered a kind of self-indulgence, a weakness, and in poor taste. For this is an era of hardboileddom. . . . Do you have an inner life? It is nobody's business but your own. Do you have emotions? Strangle them. . . . Most serious matters are closed to the hardboiled. They are unpracticed in introspection, and therefore badly equipped to deal with opponents whom they cannot shoot like big game or outdo in daring.

"If you have difficulties, grapple with them silently, goes one of their commandments. To hell with that! I intend to talk about mine. . . . It has become necessary for me to keep a journal—that is, to talk to myself—and I do not feel guilty of self-indulgence in the least."

A delightful couple hours at Joe and Kitty Johnson's yesterday afternoon. Their home has great dignity, the Virginia touch in a modern setting. Their guests included a number of academic people, and all of their guests had intellectual or artistic interests.

I am repelled by people who live *too much* in the world of abstractions, who pull away from action. But "action" people can be pretty shallow and uninteresting too, in the world of ideas. To combine a talent for and respect for ideas—to hold the life of ideas as a worthy one and to possess a drive to get things done—this is the great combination, the one that I like to think is the pattern I set for myself.

To miss real greatness by just that much—by the lack of an added ounce of guts, or through timidity, or through fear of "what people will say," or through futile anxiety about inconsequentials, or through an excess of conventionality or caution; to miss greatness not for lack of insight or proven capacity or talent or being born at the wrong time, but for lack of that thin wedge of boldness or that extra feather's weight of energy—there lies the real tragedy.

JUNE 29, 1965
NEW YORK

The time has come for a new relationship of D&R and Khuzistan to be made explicit.

Ever since, on our initiative, we turned over most managerial responsibility to KWPA—it must be almost three years ago—both we and they have been inhabiting a twilight zone: D&R continues to be held accountable for results and schedules and personnel and performance, *but* with the authority we once had to get things done our way and through people we selected having been, at our insistence, progressively and most willingly handed to Iran's KWPA.

The Iranians have wanted it *both* ways, they making the crucial decisions essential to getting things done on time and within estimates, and we taking the blame for things that didn't go as intended or promised.

But it was not only the Iranians who were caught in the toils of this kind of ambiguity and preferred it that way. Our people as well, being accustomed to leadership because of the early history of D&R and Khuzistan when *we were* the *managers*, fretted and fumed and drove themselves crazy when they couldn't perform because the decision-making on those *vital details* which are the mosaic of which management is built was in Iranian hands.

We should write a formal communication calling for a redefinition of our role, a recognition that *they*, the Iranians, are now fully in charge, and that we are no longer the managers we once were, i.e., no longer responsible for making decisions or for results of decisions made —or *not* made—by Iranians, for *delay* is the curse of that country.

All of this could be said quite affirmatively and without rancor. We simply want our arrangement to reflect the facts of the third stage of our activities.

The clearing up of water pollution—and preventing it—is going to be a major undertaking, comparable to the development of the inland waterways themselves. Yet I for one have heard nothing discussed about the institutional framework for this vast undertaking, nor the process and practice of how the cost is to be shared, as between the general taxpayer, the industries who need better water and/or "pollute" the water they use in their necessary industrial operations, and the municipalities that need good water and at the same time are dumping their sewage into the streams which must then be upgraded at the expense of the general taxpayer.

Talked to Anderson today about such a water upgrading idea in the United States. Is it *possible* that his experience in Iran and that of others in the irrigation districts of the West in finding formulae for dividing the cost of providing water for land could be adapted to this tricky problem of allocating the costs of *preventing* pollution of American streams—or the cost of *clearing up* that pollution—among the "malefactors" and the beneficiaries?

JULY 1, 1965
FLYING TO MARTHA'S VINEYARD

The other evening I sat next to Bethuel Webster, a member of the legal Establishment of New York and a Trustee of the Ford Foundation. Mentioned that I had recently been to India about their food program, and spoke in terms of the warmest respect of Doug Ensminger, who has represented the Ford Foundation out there for fifteen years. "Ford's people here in the New York office have been trying for years to *institutionalize* Doug—and I think it is a serious mistake," Beth said.

I knew just what Beth meant. When you find a genius of sorts, with vision and capacity for innovation and for exciting other people, you won't be likely to find in the same man a fellow who fills out the forms or prepares a neat and inflexible program or budget—so let him alone! For God's sake, nourish him and support him with those countless mediocrities who can keep his accounts straight or whatever administrative sandpapering his concept and imaginative activities require—or it is thought they require.

Without knowing, consciously, what I was doing, this is precisely what I did in the very earliest days of TVA with Llewellyn Evans, whom we brought out of the Northwest as Chief Electrical Engineer.

An "odd" man to straight-line administrative carpenters—who frantically recommended a conventional engineer be put in charge of power "to keep things straight." But to the despair of almost everyone, I rejected that advice and took Evans under my protection and gave him my support.

Llewellyn had spirit; cared like mad about getting power to farmers, and was stimulated by his strange new life in the South. He would stop the auto on our busiest trips to go into a cotton field to examine his first cotton boll, or a gin, or a "chopper's" cabin; or he would *personally* see the digging and spacing of pole line holes, or himself get down into a waterwheel pit to see the condition of the turbine blades. But however harumscarum he was, sometimes assigning the same job to two different people, this was a man who should not be "institutionalized," to borrow Beth's wonderfully impersonal phrase.

JULY 2, 1965
MARTHA'S VINEYARD

How good to see Davey. What a handsome, gay, bubbly boy. I measured him today: ten years old next Wednesday, and he is five feet tall! The special appeal Davey has for his grandfather is the old cherished one, the illusion of immortality that other besotted parents and grandparents get from their young—and which carried too far leads to overdependence by the elders and interference in the lives of the younger generation.

I said, on the phone, I understood he was in the Boys' Club Drum and Bugle Corps, and would be in the Fourth of July parade Sunday. "I hear that in the parade you are going to carry the flag." "Yes, I carry the flag." (Long pause.) "*American* flag."

Reading Olive Shreiner's story of *An African Farm* again, the first time in perhaps twenty years. What a strange, stirring epic this is, and written by a girl in her very early twenties.

". . . what a man expends in prayer and ecstasy he cannot have over for acquiring knowledge. You never shed a tear, or create a beautiful image, or quiver with emotion, but you pay for it in the practical, calculating end of your nature. You have just so much force; when the one channel runs over, the other runs dry."

And well worth it, say I. The "practical, calculating end" is well lost. But this doesn't mean one's perception of the astounding wealth of infinite detail that lies about us in the outer world is dulled by the inner life of emotion and feeling.

JULY 9, 1965
MARTHA'S VINEYARD

We in D&R have a non-business trait we never seem to be able to control: we too often forget that we are a private business, competing with other private businesses in the service field. So we spill our guts of our distinctive ideas—our chief stock in trade—as if we were still in the government and our ideas as public servants were requested. Then, so often, some other firm is selected to carry out *our* ideas, under contracts which are sometimes the very kind we should be asked to enter into.

One foot in the public service mentality and one foot in business sometimes produces ambiguous results!

JULY 13, 1965
NEW YORK

André told me yesterday of a call from Roy Ash, President and a principal owner of Litton Industries, an aggressive holding company that has become huge and fabulously prosperous in a short time, having begun, I think, with electronics.

Apparently Ash is exploring the prospect of acquiring, or acquiring an interest in, D&R. André said he would suggest that Ash get in touch with me. John Oliver had already been visited by two vice presidents of Litton, interested in getting their company into the field of "economic development," particularly overseas; "how did D&R go about it; how did we find the people," that kind of nosing around.

I have no desire to pull out—none at all—nor to have to trim our sails to the wishes of stockholders having a quite different motivation than mine. But on the other hand an aggressive group like Litton might give us a lift—a new and challenging direction.

JULY 14, 1965
NEW YORK

In an emotional nothingness these days. With only so much time left to me, with the possibility of a disability one of these days, with my sixty-sixth birthday just behind me, it pains me to let a day go by without the *fullest* enjoyment and participation in it. Life is so precious, New York is such a showplace of the human race, that to be neutral, to walk about without my usual enthusiasm and zest, is a great pity. Perhaps I ask too much of life. *Can* you, ever?

Instead of brooding about it, I should try to remember that it is only human to have emotional dips, even to operate on a low platform for a while. *And* that I am probably tired, more tired than I know. So once again I turn to these shorthand squiggles, trying to get out of my system some fears or self-deprecation or judgments and to bring them to the surface of my consciousness.

Lunched with Don Straus. Don comes out of a professional background of "labor relations"; one of his most treasured experiences was when, as AEC Chairman, I asked him to serve on a "panel" to develop AEC labor policies vis-à-vis its contractors. Now he is head of the American Arbitration Association, and has creative ideas by which segments ("manageable" segments, as I would put it) of disputes can be submitted to some variation of the mediation or arbitration *process*—for it is a process (even a philosophy) rather than a formula.

I spoke of my Peru trip, and of disputes about who should get water in an area where water is essential to life and prosperity. Conflict over water such as the people in northern Peru face is one of the oldest and most difficult and most explosive of issues, sometimes disguised as political or ideological or even religious, but essentially a dispute over who gets the water.

He is working to set up arbitration procedures with countries overseas to help put disputes—he hadn't thought of water particularly—into a setting where the views of the disputants could be expressed and their grievances ventilated until a conclusion emerges "out of the facts themselves," he concluded. "That is what you did, in a pathfinder kind of way, in the Lilienthal Consulting Board in the early days of the atom." And then he said, "You have been engaged in mediation throughout your career."

I reneged; I don't have the temperament to be a mediator. Don answered, "You mean because you have strong feelings about the things you are involved in; but that isn't inconsistent—that passion—with being a mediator in the broad sense I'm using; on the contrary."

JULY 15, 1965
ON THE TRAIN FOR PRINCETON

The "picture" of New York in the mid-sixties ordinarily doesn't include the trooping of people without number into the subway orifice—and then that ride, at the rushest of the rush hour. The near-panic of men and women hitting other human beings with their bodies, the way I was taught to buck a line in football ages ago: not the most uplifting picture of human society. But there are always the considerate, those who apologize for climbing over others, the shy kind of grin that makes you a partner with others who are trying to maintain some kind of dignity in the midst of this cattle-car tumult.

A sad cast over the whole day: the columns and columns about the sudden death of Adlai Stevenson.

He was by no means a dramatic or romantic figure, with that dumpy figure and the hesitating speech. I couldn't agree that he was a good public speaker—it was his great talent for eloquence of *words* that made him a speaker—and that isn't the essence of an orator, but of a great poet, a weaver of words which I thought read far better than they sounded.

JULY 18, 1965
SUNDAY, 4:30 A.M.
HOTEL BOLIVAR
LIMA, PERU

This trip to Peru could verily be called an expedition prompted by duty, rather than a firm expectation that out of it something will "happen" to put D&R in a position to help a regional development in the Piura area.

JULY 19, 1965
LIMA

President Belaunde looked worn and tired. He is preparing for the 28th of July address to the country—a kind of 4th of July occasion—and probably his days and nights are filled with negotiation with the various opposition parties to pull things together "against the Communism menace."

Belaunde said he didn't have any use for what he called *another* "study" in an area—Piura—that was filled with studies and engineering firms. The idea that John presented very well, that an instrumentality was needed to pull the various pieces together into an ongoing regional development, made no impression at all. To get people into the field, where you can *see* that they are building something—that is so difficult, he said, and *why* all the lending agencies make it so difficult is the President's despair. The TVA idea that an organization mechanism is all-important was obviously meaningless to him.

Why don't we consider starting from scratch, in a river valley in the South—he pointed it out to us on his illuminated map—where nothing has been done, and develop that virgin territory rather than work over an area—Piura—that already had been given so much money and attention? "If you were picking a bride," said President Belaunde, a twinkle in his eyes and oozing charm, "would you want someone you would start with afresh, or someone who, like the Piura region, had been worked over by all the college boys?"

As an act of allocation of resources, what Belaunde said is readily understandable.

And yet we are right; our idea is right. All that money and all those projects do need some kind of regional organization to make them really work. But try to tell that to a President who sees that his record depends on how many things are done "in the field," as he puts it.

JULY 20, 1965
LIMA

D&R is having problems, no doubt of it.

But I must remember that this is a business, an enterprise that I created from within my own head and heart, a dream that began with me and within me. This is not something I inherited from my father or grandfather; this is not something that was already going and that I was "hired" to run. This is a child of mine, and whatever happens to D&R happens to a dream I had. If U.S. Steel runs into trouble, or prospers, if Corning or Lazard go up or down under the hand of their present leaders, that is another matter, for Roy Blough and Amory Houghton and André Meyer all succeeded to something begun long before their time. Theirs wasn't the act of creation, they did not have the trials (and satisfactions) of those beginning years.

This happened to me—this being responsible for something I created—twice before, with TVA and AEC. This is a responsibility—to my own dignity—that should not be abandoned lightly. I may *have* to quit—must, someday, of course—but it should not be because momentarily I am bored or discouraged or disappointed by this or that setback normal to any business, however mature or well established.

Mark Childs of the *St. Louis Post Dispatch* on my phone here at the Hotel Bolivar: would I make an effort to get an appointment for him with the President? Yes, of course, I'll get a message to him. Then this bombshell: "Dave, have you heard who President Johnson has appointed to take Adlai's place at the UN? You haven't? You couldn't guess in a thousand years. A thousand years. Arthur Goldberg! They must *both* have lost their minds." Said I: "Johnson is making a place for Abe Fortas on the Court." Mark exclaimed, "Dave, I think you just about guessed it! What kind of a game is this anyway?"

Dinner tonight with the head of the Agricultural Bank, Señor Benavides. Round-faced man of about forty-five, in appearance anything but the scion of a line of Peruvians who in the mid-17th century pushed the Indians off the land he now farms. Spanish grandee of the Peruvian oligarchy (he kidded himself about being one of that "class"). Just returned from a month in Australia, where he sought out and bought $2000 worth of seed, mostly legumes, for pastures. He found, he said with some glee over the irony of it, that these legumes had been discovered in the "jungles of Peru" many years ago by American and Australian agronomists, developed in Australia—and now he brings the legumes back home.

JULY 21, 1965
LIMA

Wanting to get away from the yack yack of trying to get something going in Peru, I went to the Museo National de Antropologia y Arqueologia, out on Plaza Bolivar.

Enjoyed the gold objects from Lambayeque. But as usual it was the living objects in the Museo that fascinated me: hordes of young Peruvians, with their school notebooks, coming by in troops. The alert and handsome faces of so many reflected the very admixture of culture the Museo displays.

The things that excite me as I travel (in my own country or abroad) make quite a list. People first of all. Ports high on the list. How people make their living: markets. The marks of the distant past in *local* museums.

The port of Callao was exciting. Great rusty cargo vessels at the docks, flying many flags. A tangled cluster of short, clumsy ships that looked, across the harbor, like kids' toys: the anchovy fishing fleet, many of them wooden, none more than forty or fifty feet long. The shipbuilding yards with these odd-shaped craft rising, their ribs looking like the bones of a carcass. The old vessels being repaired have that look of decay that makes one think of a Conrad tale or a remote Pacific island.

As we left the wharf area, a ferry put in, and out of it a great stream of dumpy women, Indian looking, carrying empty, colored straw bags. The wives or women of "political" prisoners on a kind of Devil's Island offshore, returning from visiting their menfolk, bringing them the comfort of consort, in the Latin manner of prison life, and food to last till their next visit. Something rather homey about the whole thing, and very unpuritanical. The men were put away, but why make it any worse than it was, I suppose, is the idea.

JULY 23, 1965
FLYING FROM LIMA TO (I HOPE) NEW YORK

"The peepul in Piura, in the north, they very much like Belaunde. *Now*, very much. The Liga will write a good letter to the President. Dos años—two years past, no. Now, sí, the President is good." So Romulo Franco, in the car taking me to the airport this morning.

Franco, the operator for the well-to-do people of that provincial area that produces a large proportion of Peru's land-wealth, then spoke with a restrained eloquence about what the less practical people who observe Peru take many more words to say: "Before Belaunde only the *reech* families are importante; forty families, what they say is what is true. We neeeed the reech, but under Belaunde other people are importante also."

The "ferment of change" that the Peter Druckers and Douglass Caters and Adolf Berles write about is not just an academic notion when a man like Franco, and the provincial rich he represents, finds it possible to say this as his final comment on this trip.

JULY 26, 1965
MARTHA'S VINEYARD

"Achievement." What a fascinating, protean, mysterious concept this is.

Yesterday Helen and I stood in a small circle of people before an old house in nearby West Tisbury while we were reminded of the virtues of Captain Josiah Slocum. The occasion was the "unveiling" of a plaque before this house where Slocum lived, briefly, after his great feat of sailing, alone, around the world in an old thirty-foot sloop. He wasn't going anywhere in particular; he didn't set out to discover anything; he didn't pretend that he was adding to "scientific knowledge," as the modern zealots of space justify their elaborate forays. No, he just set off to sail around the world, singlehanded. This was Slocum's idea of achievement. All the rest of us have our own idea of what achievement consists of.

JULY 27, 1965
MARTHA'S VINEYARD

Conflict and tension *within* a man I have long felt have been the source of creativeness in the individual, and essential to a useful and imaginative and lively way of life.

But a pulling and hauling within one's self is only really a fruitful state *if one is aware* of the strings that pull this way and then in the opposite or a divergent direction.

In short, "know thyself" is still one of the wisest sentences ever written. Not "kid thyself," or "ignore thyself," but *know*. I wonder if a large part of the motivation for writing journals wasn't always a sense that this was necessary, however short of utter and complete candor they often were—and are.

It is easy to understand why in "inventing" D&R ten years ago I should have sought an instrumentality by which I could continue the drive I have always had to help other people strengthen their lives, a frankly and patently idealistic pattern of life.

But I believed that this could be *combined* with business objectives, the making of money by uncovering opportunities for business in the underdeveloped countries in which D&R worked in its idealistic role.

Are these two compatible, or are they so much in conflict that that part of the original D&R design not only did not produce results in this second or business role, but never will? And if this water of idealism and the oil of business cannot mix, doesn't this reflect itself in a pulling and hauling *within me* that serves no good purpose?

If this conflict is indeed one that cannot be resolved, *in the nature of things*, then to recognize this is not to rid myself of a conflict that is "uncomfortable"—since it is only really uncomfortable people who get much done—but it is part of the process of facing up to the facts of a conflict.

The Chairman of the Research and Policy Committee of the Committee for Economic Development, Ted Yntema, has just written me a letter that raises again the question: Why did I want so deeply to have a career in business after twenty years of throwing myself wholeheartedly into service to the public and to an ideal I had carried in my heart since my youth?

Yntema writes his Committee wants me to act as Chairman of a study and report committee on "business structure." This analysis of business structure will take me into the basic question—in my mind at least—of the creative possibility of modern business in America in furthering individualism and the values that in our speeches we extol, but in practice we mostly overlook or ignore.

Today, after a phone call from the President of CED, Al Neal, I accepted the chairmanship. This was on the understanding that the report would not be simply a rehash of stuff about antitrust laws and mergers, but something far broader, something about what this country —and the world—can expect of the American business system.

MIDNIGHT

A fury of the demons of lightning, forking the sky in all directions from this hill, with such power as to shake the very heavens; an accompaniment of celestial kettledrums like a series of sonic booms one can feel as well as hear; and torrents of water thrown against the unprotected tight skin of this little house. Is the explanation for my surge of depressed spirits no more complicated than the supercharged atmosphere released by this sudden tantrum from the skies? Now just the echoes of rumble can be heard, the whimper of rain no longer full of fight. The air cleared, is this self-pitying, self-dramatizing man also to be cleared, with the change in the electricity in the air, the rise of the barometer? Are we human pygmies, who see ourselves the center of the world, in fact the result of forces as readily explainable as these majestic displays of Nature, oblivious to our piddling individual concerns?

AUGUST 1, 1965
MARTHA'S VINEYARD

Yesterday a remarkable sail, long to be remembered and treasured. Not because of a struggle with a twenty-five-knot breeze or a stubborn current. Actually the wind was steady, out of the northwest and only about ten knots. No, memorable because Davey was the skipper, handling *Lili-put*, in the roadstead full of sails, with a composure and confidence quite remarkable for a complete beginner.

Driving him home, I raised the question of his going to a boys' camp here on the island. His parents and all four grandparents want him to, as he knew; his cousins, the Bromberger boys, are going.

"Grandfather, it's like this. I don't like a camp. Someone is always telling you what you have to do, what games or things you have to play. Yes, you're right, some of the things are fun, and most of the boys I'd like. But I'd rather just find someone to play with myself."

I praised him for making up his own mind. I couldn't help thinking that most of these youngsters we see in early July, streaming through Grand Central or Penn Station, in ordered batches on their way to fun at expensive camps, are going there because their parents want to get rid of them more than anything else. And that when I was ten in Valparaiso, if the boys in my neighborhood wanted to go to Sager's Pond or Flint Lake, we "organized" it ourselves, or we stayed around the neighborhood playing "tippy tappy toe" with a ball we made of a Bull Durham sack stuffed hard with grass. No adult herded us off someplace and told us when and what to play, and with whom.

AUGUST 11, 1965
MARTHA'S VINEYARD

Phoned John Macy at the White House yesterday. From being one of AEC's ablest employees, first in Washington while I was there and later at Los Alamos, he has become the most modern and liveliest Chairman of the Civil Service Commission in my memory. This is the first time I have made a suggestion to John (who has become Johnson's talent scout). How much more orderly it is to have a man with the chief personnel responsibility of the Government in charge of looking for new people instead of the random and extracurricular activities of Tom Corcoran and others in the early New Deal days.

President Johnson has a sense of the structure of the Federal service that exceeds that of anyone in the Presidency in my time, and a full appreciation of how important it is to give public service dignity and prestige.

Talking with John Macy, I referred to the President's expressed concern for a new emphasis on health, including medical research, and I quoted his remarks when he signed the new health research bill the other day. Then I suggested that in Leona Baumgartner the country has the most experienced public health administrator, with an extraordinary record in New York City. I said it would be an excellent outlet for her professional talents, her imagination in the field of health, and "particularly helpful now when, almost suddenly, birth control has for the first time an opportunity to move ahead a hundred years in a decade."

I referred to a talk on population problems Leona had given the other night at a church, before a most conservative kind of Vineyard Haven audience. She was not vague—describing the plastic loop, referring to condoms and diaphragms—all in a very dignified, clear fashion. That such things could be talked about was a mark of a change in thinking that should be exploited *administratively*, through efforts to make things happen, rather than by an emotional crusade.

Macy was most cordial; asked me to suggest someone for the post Joe Swidler is leaving as head of the Power Commission; accepted my suggestion that he consult with Dana Atchley, who probably knows more top grade younger physicians than any other man in the country, as students who went through his hands or as practitioners, about the post of Surgeon General; and then said some warm things about the *Journals*, which he "went out and procured" and has read. I reminded him that I published the *Journals* partly because they give a picture of one public servant's life, which might be interesting to young people entering that field.

AUGUST 14, 1965
MARTHA'S VINEYARD

In the calm and the sweet fog that enfolds this beloved hilltop, it is impossible to believe the words that fill the airwaves: primitive carnage in Los Angeles; not just "another race riot," but a return to the jungle, or to Toussaint L'Ouverture in Haiti; burning violence with a hysteria and on a scale such as I don't recall in this country. Actually confronting a whole section of a great city with thousands of troops, and the end not yet.

The irony of this: at the time when a Texan has just forced through Congress the most important addition to the political rights of Negroes since the Emancipation.

AUGUST 18, 1965
MARTHA'S VINEYARD

What is there about life here that makes it so utterly different for me than in any other place?

Here I live with the sky; this is the chief reason. The sky enters this house on all sides, indeed is part of the house itself, and therefore part of me. The whole sky, too, the horizon, the zenith—the whole of it.

AUGUST 20, 1965
MARTHA'S VINEYARD

Rattling open my Friday *Times*, fresh from the mailbox; the entire back page is an ad that is mostly white space; the word "*Seconds*" caught my eye—lo and behold, it *is* promoting the film from David's novel, *Seconds*.

Think what comes out of the imagination—and the sweat and agony too—of a young man who happens to be your son.

In the midst of this exultation about David's "making it," against such enormous odds, comes sorrow and a sweep of memories: Phil LaFollette dead. I have just written Isen [Mrs. LaFollette] of my sorrow, reminding her that it was Phil's faith—*blind* faith, for he had never seen me before—one night in February, 1931, that gave me my chance for public service—the night he asked me at the Mansion in Madison to go on the Railroad Commission although I was then only thirty-one and not even a resident of Wisconsin.

AUGUST 22, 1965
MARTHA'S VINEYARD

Roger Baldwin‡ came in to see us yesterday afternoon. What is it in some men—some very few men—that gives them at eighty all the qualities of vigor, gusto, and good humor that we usually associate with the "prime years"?

Roger is a good citizen. There are men who concern themselves with faraway problems, internationalists and world-law enthusiasts as he is; but those same men wouldn't lift a finger for the problems of their own neighborhood or community. And then there are men who give themselves to the needs of their community, but are provincial and often contemptuous of anything beyond that circle. Roger is as active in community affairs here on this island as anyone who was born and brought up here, and yet he gives himself wholeheartedly to United Nations affairs. This is really being a good citizen.

‡ Roger Baldwin was a founder of the American Civil Liberties Union.

"Dave," he said, "what impressed and puzzled me the most in reading your diaries was where you could find the energy to sit down and write on top of all you are doing. Where did the energy—and the motivation—come from?"

As he pressed this question in that robust, carrying voice of his, he peered at me, an intense, youthful look on his weathered face, a face that has seen so much and learned so much in eighty-two years of life.

I had no answer to his question. Helen, trying to help explain, said that much of the time the entries were written "in transport"—on planes, trains, waiting in railroad stations and airport terminals. This did not satisfy Roger: lots of people have time to write, but when they are on trains or planes they doze or read papers or look at people; "Most people can't write in the middle of a railroad station or an airport waiting room."

Such questions as Roger raised revived another one that has puzzled Helen and me: Why, writing these notes at such length and often with such spirit, did I so often omit entirely what should have been the most interesting things of all—things not only interesting today but obviously interesting at the time of writing—and yet I included other things of far lesser importance?

An example came to hand yesterday, as I was reviewing the entries for May, 1951, the time of an American Assembly Conference at Arden House. The Conference was supposed to consider "political problems of Western Europe." A group of scholars had prepared a lot of homework on that subject for the participants to study before the meeting. At the time the Conference met, however, the exciting thing in the news was the nationalization of oil in Iran, the Mossadeqh eruption. It just happened that in the gathering were a number of the most knowledgeable and most concerned people in the oil industry, largely of course from Texas. What we all wanted to talk about was certainly not Western Europe but the "shocking" events in the Persian Gulf, the seizure of the world's largest oil refinery, the threat to the fuel supply of the Western world, the prospect, as it seemed even to such sophisticated people as Anne O'Hare McCormick of the *New York Times*, that the Soviets might grab off Persian oil, with encouragement of course from the Communist-inclined Mossadeqh. These were the subjects we discussed around the conference table, at meals, in the lounges, discussed and speculated about with a sense of apprehension and with lively and informed judgment.

Yet my journal entries for that meeting made only one passing reference to Persian Gulf oil!

AUGUST 25, 1965
MARTHA'S VINEYARD

Gertrude Luce lives to the east of us, a mile or so, on the other side of Indian Hill. She is a wisp of an old lady, almost ninety. Her husband, long since dead, was a Vineyard farmer-fisherman. Nothing anyone can say will persuade her to leave the little house in which she lives all alone; not even in the winter, when the drifts sometimes pile high. In the winter, so our neighbor Harold Rogers told us last Sunday, she heats her little house by a coal fire. He tried to persuade her to put in electricity for a pump and to install an oil heater. No, she said firmly, *she wouldn't trust a fire she couldn't see.*

Spent much of the day trying to think my way through the challenge Herrera of the Inter-American Development Bank put to D&R last week: how to devise a "strategy for integration" in Latin America, to use his language.

Sitting on a huge boulder on Miss Emma's beach, on the Sound, I tried to divide the subject of strategy into its parts, in what could be an intensely interesting and too often highly verbalized issue: bringing the countries of Latin America closer together economically by fostering multinational economic undertakings or through the process of trade.

Here we live amid treetops. My eye is constantly observing the tips of branches, watching the direction and force of the wind—with earnestness, because the wind has a meaning to me as a sailor. (Not a good sailor, but a devoted one.)

AUGUST 29, 1965
MARTHA'S VINEYARD

My young cousins Nan and David Tobey arrived Friday night. He tall and slender and far more poised than ever. She full of new ideas and a new vocabulary derived largely from a summer in a group of "design" people at the University of Washington, Seattle. Nan has a quick, facile mind. She lives in a world whose *words* sound strange to this ear, but as the explanation of "design" and "communication" and the terms from calculus or psychology tumble out, I recognize that these are actually familiar ideas clothed in new terminology. Part of the *new* aspect of this "design" thinking comes from the impact of the computer. I thought it clear, once more, that though the computer could shake up people's thinking by making available far more information, the thinking process itself remains essentially unchanged, remains the *essential* ingredient.

SEPTEMBER 2, 1965
NEW YORK

A long, long day, this one. But an interesting, a stimulating one.

This roaring city, in the sharp light of an early autumn day, was as beautiful in its way as the sky and water and woods I saw so recently from our Island hilltop.

At about four a very personable man came to see me at the office: Roy Ash, President of Litton Industries. A big, broad-shouldered man, appearing younger than his age. A fine forehead, soft voice, cultivated fluent manner of speaking. Hard to recognize in this very modest-appearing fellow the driving and (some say) ruthless partner of Tex Thornton.

He explained that Litton Industries has begun to venture into the field in which "you here are so well established and have so much experience," that is, economic development, or development of natural resources. They had a contract with the government of Greece to apply "systems analysis management" to the many problems of Greek development, and had thirty-two men representing various specialties (including sociologists) out there; they were beginning to wonder if they were on the right track, and so he just "dropped in" to talk about our experience, etc.

John Rubel, the vice president in charge of Litton's new economic development division, a small, dark, tired, and worried looking man, an expert in missile design, came with Ash. The more he talked about this Greek undertaking, the more I was sure—well, that *we* wouldn't go at it that way, that Ash was troubled about the systems analysis concept of applying theoretical planning to such a country as Greece and was wondering whether they shouldn't drop the whole thing.

I felt repaid for the two friendly hours with Ash by coming to know a new *kind* of business personality, and an amazingly successful one, who doesn't look or sound like any tycoon I've ever seen.

SEPTEMBER 3, 1965
NEW YORK

I saw despair, utter sadness, written on a man's face this morning, in the sunlight of my harbor-view office. S. S. Khera's eyes were deep caverns of darkness, the eyes of an Indian who had lived through the years of the struggle for "independence," then the fifteen years of the new republic, when problems were great but hope was in the air. Today the life seemed suddenly to have burned out; his face was gutted with sorrow not only for India but for the whole continent, for his brothers across the imaginary line in Pakistan.

He views the outbreak of armed conflict between these two countries in the most serious way. But it is not only the black cloud that has driven him to such a state of hopelessness—that simply triggered off a sense of despondency over the quality of present Indian leadership ("I wonder if this would have happened if Jawaharlal were still there?" he mused) and the quagmire of rising population and failure to do things about salinity, waterlogging, food production—the things we went out to India to try to be helpful about.

SEPTEMBER 8, 1965
NEW YORK

A long and, for me, highly "educational" meeting of the Board of Directors of Minerals & Chemicals Philipp Corporation (M&CP), running from 10 A.M. until almost 3 P.M.

The session was presided over by the Chairman, Charles Engelhard, one of the financially most successful American industrialists. Engelhard in his person displays some of the qualities of *intellectual reflex* that mark a man who really *runs* a business enterprise, standing astride it, fully understanding it, rather than the kind of business top executive who is carried along by the momentum of a business (exemplified by the top officers of most of the very big companies).

Engelhard is a man of powerful physique, great shoulders, a head of heroic size capped by grey hair in a close curl; he carries before him a great "corporation," but is such a strong man that his overweight isn't obvious. I was fascinated by the working of his mind when a business issue was presented. You realize this is a man who knows not only figures, but industrial *operations*, at least in the field of metal processing. (His company is chiefly a refiner of rare metals, gold, platinum, etc.)

We had an item on the agenda that didn't appeal to him as an example of good operations. It concerned a subsidiary or division that smelts scrap into bronze ingots chiefly. When he dug into the smooth and fluent (and rehearsed) presentation of the young man in charge of the division you saw the questioning process at its best, a process I have seen before Congressional committees but rarely in business circles. For when the young man dismissed a question by using a big (and to me decisive) word like "inventories," and the figure that went with the term, Engelhard dug into it: how did we know what that inventory represented in real value; tons, yes, but what quality?—that was the question. As he jabbed one needle after another into the big-balloon business terms, I could fairly see the reality: piles of scrap, the furnaces, and the kinds of accounting ambiguities there might be in such a business, where the *units* being dealt with weren't standardized and couldn't be.

I sit through such a session as today's board meeting more interested in the tableau of people acting out their roles, functioning—not the way I do, which makes it even more fascinating. The terrible necessity to subordinate everything to making a profit just isn't in me.

SEPTEMBER 12, 1965
PRINCETON

Yesterday from 8 A.M. until noon and all of the preceding day working hard with a lively group of minds and personalities: the Committee on Selection of the Rockefeller Public Service awards.

We sat in a hollow square in one of the seminar rooms of the magnificent new Yamasaki Woodrow Wilson School Building; on all the tables were huge stacks of files, and there we sat, going through a hundred or more of the records of those among the "career" Federal public servants who had been nominated for what is regarded as the top honor of this kind. Until the last couple hours, just plowing through files, making notes and not saying a word.

As a Committee member I was assigned to the "category" of "the general welfare and natural resources." There were the usual nominees from Interior, Agriculture: the Chief Hydrologist, the Administrator of the Soil Conservation Service, etc.

One name, however, struck me because it wasn't what I could have expected : Huntington Cairns, "Treasurer and General Counsel, National Gallery of Art."

Here, thought I, was that rare opportunity to honor, *as a public servant*, a humanist, a renaissance man of the widest interests, and at the same time to remind the U.S. that *art is a natural resource* as well as forests or rivers.

Several of the members were attracted to Cairns as a candidate, but the idea that he should be selected in the field of "general welfare and natural resources" seemed a bit, as several said, "sentimental." The more I thought about it, however, the better the idea seemed.

The interest of the public in art, *throughout the country*, I said, is one of the most heartening things in the present scene, in new museums in smaller cities, and even in the hanging of superior paintings in business establishments.

The reward for me, as is so often the case, is the satisfaction I get from spending time in a working capacity, i.e., functioning, with good people. The Chairman, Lloyd Berkner,§ a huge solemn man, one of the

§ Chairman of the Board of Trustees and Professor, Southwest Center for Advanced Studies.

outstanding administrators of science this country has produced, orderly, earnest, full of talk about his particular field, the atmosphere. Slender, white-haired, gentle but firm, Dr. Robert Loeb,¶ whose comments about particular scientists who had been "nominated" were always dominated by a measuring of their creativity and originality. Judge William H. Hastie,* with great precision of speech, delicate features, much amused at my tactics of advocacy to persuade the group to do something new in the Cairns case.† Anna Lord Strauss,‡ so distinguished looking, so careful lest we honor Miss Margaret B. Arnstein§ not simply because it would look well to honor a woman because she is a woman ("I am tough on women, as you know"). Jim Mitchell, the former Secretary of Labor, now of the Brookings Institution, a real pro, a delightful grin, who *knew* the files thoroughly, responsive to my comments about getting more mobility into the Federal service. Perhaps most delightful of all, a chance to sit for a day and a half, in business sessions and socially, with one of the most remarkable diplomats of all, Bob Murphy,¶ relaxed, loose-limbed, a devastating smile, but alert to press hard (and successfully) for recognition for Alexis Johnson against the argument that because Ambassador Johnson had been involved as Deputy Ambassador in Vietnam it would be "injudicious" to give him the award.

Murphy's stories out of his vast store of experiences had a touch of humor and a graphic quality that one doesn't associate with diplomats. I thought, as we broke up, that here is a man who sees diplomacy in terms of individuals more than anyone I have ever known.

SEPTEMBER 16, 1965
NEW YORK

"It is not a question of 'should we have a revolution'; the Dominican Republic has had a revolution and we who are the business people, the bankers, the manufacturers, the sugar plantation owners—we the 'oligarchs'—we are for the revolution.

"My brother-in-law, Dr. Garcia-Godoy, and the rest of us have always stayed out of anything that could be called political, but we got into this new government because we believe in this revolution. Ironic that a revolution in charge of people like ourselves is said to be led by Communists."

¶ Director of Medical Service, Presbyterian Hospital, and Professor, College of Physicians and Surgeons.

* Judge, Third U.S. Circuit Court of Appeals.

† Cairns received an award.

‡ Former President, National League of Women Voters, member of various UN committees, civic affairs and women's groups.

§ A distinguished leader in public nursing.

¶ A principal executive of the Corning Glass Group, formerly a distinguished Foreign Service officer and ambassador.

This came hurtling out of the innards of an intense, taut, overly dramatic friend, Tomas Pastoriza, sitting here at my desk a half hour ago.

"The people in the Dominican Republic were ready to fight, and they did fight, these so-called rebels, for this revolution. That there may have been Communists who were also fighting is also probably true. But the image that this new administration of ours is filled with Communists is terribly wrong."

Pastoriza's comments to me today could hardly have been more timely. The *Times* this morning was filled with a speech by Bill Fulbright; what he said fitted in with Pastoriza's comment. The Dominican military intervention, Fulbright said, was based on faulty advice to President Johnson by people who—I paraphrase—see Communists under every banana tree in the Caribbean. The other side of that coin is personified by this bright-eyed, intelligent young man who sat across from me this morning. What the people who advise the President don't see is what Gordon Clapp and I saw:* the great strength of a group of Dominicans who are enlisting in a social revolution without being touched with any leftist ideology, to say nothing of being conspiratorial Communists.

Ever since Joe McCarthy, timid bureaucrats and cloak-and-dagger CIA characters feel they can never go wrong if they find traces of red. Fulbright has put the bee on them for bad advice in what has certainly been an inglorious and unhappy use of arms in the Caribbean.

SEPTEMBER 19, 1965
PRINCETON

Felipe Herrera does not have the advantage that Bolivar had when he became the head and the symbol of unity among the Latins of South America: a military title, a gold-encrusted uniform, a great head of wavy hair. But Herrera, short, bald, without a uniform or a great horse to ride, offers a continuity with Bolivar in being possessed with a great creative idea, one that comes at the right hour, the idea of the economic integration of South America.

Bolivar united the people of Latin America in order to free them from Spanish rule, but he left a continent of many countries, *each independent.* Herrera has set himself the task of bringing these free, independent (and often contending) countries back into some kind of functional or economic unity, which he calls regional integration.

A monumental task.

Now Herrera is trying to interest D&R in standing with him in an

* *Journals,* Vol. V, *The Harvest Years,* pp. 321–326.

advisory role on the strategy of bringing this idea along to fruition, an idea I described to him in this way: "The most creative idea in the past century of Latin American—and hemispheric—history: a mystique of integration that will fire the imagination and the will-to-do of the new generation of Latin America which you exemplify."

We should soon know—perhaps by the end of this coming week—whether we have been selected to act as his advisor on matters of policy in this undertaking.

SEPTEMBER 20, 1965
NEW YORK

To the special exhibit of water colors at the Brooklyn Museum with Beatrice, then walked back across the great bridge. My first time, and it was a great experience. From the footpath, the masonry towers reach up into the sky, and their arches are *Persian*, definitely: the high, narrow jointed arch of Persia. And then the city rises before one—it was hazy, and a gentle softness hung about the city—rectangular blocks of light, murky, like a long sunken ghost ship risen from the dark sea, afloat in mystical nothingness, a city with neither roots nor foundation nor zenith.

SEPTEMBER 22, 1965
NEW YORK

Six obviously affluent "young matrons" from New Rochelle (or wherever in suburbia) bounced in to the long table near mine at the restaurant on 53rd Street where I ate in solitary (and grateful) isolation. The headwaiter, wisecracking, said: "And where are the husbands?" Snorted one of the gals: "Husbands; who needs them?"

OCTOBER 9, 1965
AIRLIE HOUSE
WARRENTON, VIRGINIA

This seminar of the leading Latin American experts—mostly social scientists—was designed to re-establish a "dialogue and communication" (those words certainly get a workout these days) between the State Department and the academic community of the U.S. A good opportunity to meet the men who now run the Alliance for Progress.

My opinion—actually "prejudices"—about social scientists and what they can contribute to public affairs was deep-seated when I came. Nothing that has happened here has greatly diminished that prejudice. If they would just learn to speak plain English! They are much like the rest of us mortals, holding strong emotional views while proclaiming that the role of the social scientist is to be objective, to hold aloof from what "ought" to be done. On such a subject as the Dominican Republic business they are full of dogmatic, passionate opinions. They are like the rest of us *except* that they have a jargon only they can understand.

Was profoundly impressed with Jack Vaughn, the new Assistant Secretary of State for Latin American Affairs. A slight, short man with an alert, lithe figure. (I learned tonight he had been a professional boxer and boxing coach, as I had been in college.) He believes passionately and speaks from the heart—and eloquently—about the role of the U.S. in Latin America. A most remarkable public servant.

OCTOBER 12, 1965
NEW YORK

In the next year can I "make a statement" (as the art critics say about a painter), can I think and write something fresh and of this time, or am I bound to my past achievements? Like water that can rise no higher than its source, are my imagination and mind now limited to what I dreamed and fashioned in my forties and fifties?

A comment about Picasso's paintings of the past two years, he now being in his eighties, brought this to mind. These, I am told, show a vitality and a spring-like freshness.

These thoughts grow out of my debate with myself about undertaking the Fairless Lectures (a new book, actually) and also the "business structure and performance" report for the CED. In both instances, I *don't* want simply to dig into my barrel of older ideas.

Protecting one's past record is one of the most characteristic marks of an old man, whether he is forty-five or seventy-five.

Is there still within me something of that vernal touch? Can I still look to the future without fear or timidity? Do I still retain something of that living glow of tender, almost naïve freshness of spring's first leaves, leaves that are only a promise, and yet also a reassurance of the recurring newness of life, welling up from the brown and seemingly dead earth, the unfolding leaf that nourishes the hopes of men?

OCTOBER 13, 1965
NEW YORK

A man and his grown son: it can be a very special relationship, or it can be a zero.

Have just read in the current *Playboy* a story by my son ("Angel of Mercy"). David has become the Jonathan Swift of the caged Organization Man, the Commuters' Montaigne. He can, in a swift phrase, create a character complete; he catches people completely unguarded and transfixes them by the verbal spears he throws with such apparent ease.

OCTOBER 20, 1965
NEW YORK

A "crusade," with well-to-do ladies leading the phalanxes into battle, is a special kind of phenomenon. The Planned Parenthood "movement" is such a one, judging from the audience of over a thousand I faced last night in the ballroom of the Waldorf.

The theme was a new one to most of the audience: that limitation of population growth is not, as is still assumed, a problem only for the underdeveloped and poor countries. It is an urgent issue for the United States, too, since population growth for the U.S. threatens the quality of American life.†

The people I met—out front, and later in small groups, and at the Don Straus home on 73rd Street—are cultivated, intelligent, good people in every sense. Whether they are so good, and so prosperous and "expert," that they are not likely to find ways of educating the very individuals who need to *do something* about the size of their families—mostly very poor and often very ignorant or uneducated people—seems to me the real question about any crusade of "well-to-do" people.

OCTOBER 27, 1965
NEW YORK

In almost everything Development and Resources does, or holds itself out to do, there is a deep current of public affairs. We are organized as a private corporation; we have monthly financial statements, we are concerned with the same kind of detailed management problems as other companies—personnel, finance, procurement—and with much of the same kind of subject matter as a management or engineering firm has—technical analyses, economic studies, schedules.

But what gives this enterprise its distinctive place and its potential for effecting change for many, many people is that at bottom I look at its work as *a form of public affairs.*

Gordon Clapp and I never had any problem seeing eye to eye on this concept. I don't find it easy to communicate it to some of my present chief associates, however. Immersed as they are in defining proposed "scope of work" contracts, preparing reports, and deciding on technical actions, they tend to look upon public affairs discussions as just "gen-

† D. E. Lilienthal, "300,000,000 Americans Would Be Wrong," *New York Times Magazine*, January 9, 1966.

eralities," or as one blunt-spoken executive said, impatiently, the other day, "frothiness." But I must persist—and get someone in with us who does understand how central public affairs are to the kind of development work we do.

It is this ability to see that public affairs has become an *integral part* of most *ordinary* business of any magnitude that marks the difference between a modern, alive top business executive and the old-fashioned characters who run many, if not most, of the big companies.

A long and fascinating letter this morning (dated September 30, 1965) from Gremliza's Rahimeh Camp in the Khuzistan. He responds to some questions I put to him about where we stand concerning control of the snail disease, bilharzia. Then he goes on to outline his views on a wider problem: the contamination of water through the expanded use of agricultural chemicals as fertilizers. Dr. Gremliza sees that these chemicals are just beginning to be used in the Khuzistan, under conditions where he is in a position to measure the pollutant effect of chemical fertilizer better than almost any place I know.

He says some arresting things: the "water environment" in the village areas he knows so well is as important in effecting bilharzia control as all the other elements—medical, educational, economic, etc.

About parasites in general he writes: "Nature is as much concerned with the welfare of the parasite as with that of men." He sent me a paper, by Dr. Clay Huff of the U.S. Naval Medical Research Institute, discussing "Man Against Malaria"; it makes the point that we are far from having malaria licked, as is so often assumed. We have not yet learned to think like a mosquito, which as far back as the building of the Panama Canal was put as the basic prerequisite for research and control.

Extraordinary man, Gremliza.

OCTOBER 28, 1965
NEW YORK

Dean Acheson quotes Duff Cooper as saying that he counts life in decades; after the third (youth) "then for thirty years a man is middle-aged until he hears the clock strike sixty and knows that old age has begun." (This is in the introduction to Dean's slight book, *Morning and Noon.*)

If my life the past twenty-four hours constitutes old age, all I can say is that it was a pity to waste all that time on middle age.

The newest white hope of the international lending agencies, Brazil, has tossed out any pretense of a legislative form of democracy, the armed forces standing behind the President in his decision to rule by decree.

The largest country in South America has turned back from a promising beginning at legislative processes.

But "democracy" isn't a concept of fixed content everywhere and at every hour.

I am not dismayed. Let's get on with the job.

OCTOBER 29, 1965
4:30 P.M.
ON THE AFTERNOON CONGRESSIONAL
HEADING FOR PRINCETON FROM WASHINGTON

More than two hours with Felipe Herrera, seeking through D&R to help carry forward his dream of "integration" in South America, using the Inter-American Development Bank as the channeling force.

This train opens some of the loveliest vistas in Eastern America: the hazy blue traceries of water-tapestry that indent this shore. More than makes up for the ugliness, of which there is much; not that industrial plants, like the Chrysler assembly we are now passing, are "ugly." The pattern of water tank on long legs, of stacks that have their own symmetry against the sky, the domes of chemical silos, these appeal to me as being as beautiful as the mosques over which Sacheverell Sitwell —and I—emote.

A new kind of "Hemisphere Citizen" will have to emerge, over a long period of time no doubt, before integration becomes more than a technical concept of economists or politicians and approaches the reality which enables a man now to say: "I am a citizen of Indiana, but I am also a citizen of the United States of America."

NOVEMBER 2, 1965
PRINCETON

A great break in our efforts to build a vital agricultural staff: Leo Anderson has agreed to come back into the fold, full time. I was elated.

NOVEMBER 10, 1965
NEW YORK

Last evening I was at tea at the Council on Foreign Relations with a group who had come to hear Felipe Herrera talk about economic integration. It was deep twilight; the scurry homeward was in full swing out on Park Avenue. The lights in the elegant room wavered, came up again, then went out. And stayed out.

The meeting went on by candlelight, enlivened now and then by reports from a young man with a pocket radio—reports no one quite believed. It is not just this block, it is the whole area to the East River; then, *the whole Eastern seaboard.*

Felipe, game and composed, went ahead with his talk, to his great credit—with squat candles spaced around his script, the whole scene in that high-ceilinged room making me think that this is the way the night sessions of the Founding Fathers must have been—or a high-level liberation junta plotting freedom against the Spaniards.

From time to time outside we could see the startling beams of a cruising police car, siren on full blast—and still no lights. At about 10 P.M., the meeting over, Bob Oppenheimer renewed an invitation to take me back to Princeton in his car. With no lights, no taxis, no elevator at the hotel, and I not a little troubled about how Helen was faring, I accepted.

We drove down Broadway, the White Way, completely dark except for the headlights of the cars. What a weird sight; and crowds, great masses of people trying to get home. The radio said there were 800,000 people caught in subways, and the picture of people underground for hours was a sobering one.

How could this happen? A fifteen minute stoppage, yes; but on and on? (Actually, the stoppage lasted twelve hours.)

Such a common experience, shared by millions of people, had an interesting effect on the mood of the city. People shared experiences: "Where were you?" "I was in the subway four hours," etc. Something about many people being in the same boat does something to individuals. I suppose the blitz in London bred something of the same mood—so strange in a great and usually impersonal city.

NOVEMBER 14, 1965
PRINCETON

Yesterday morning an hour's visit with an exceptional young man, Daniel Sachs. A tall man, with a head of dark straight hair, deep brooding eyes, a lithe figure (he was one of Princeton's best running backs five or six years ago). He asked to see me about the best way to get into politics. But I sensed that what he really wanted was a chance to talk out the things that have been going on in his head, rather than expecting (an unreasonable expectation it would be) that I could "advise" him.

An honor graduate of Princeton, a fine athlete, a Rhodes Scholar, and now in his third year at Harvard Law School; that is a combination difficult to match. I particularly liked his interest in local and state government and state and federal government relations—an unusual interest and one to be encouraged as best one can.

These young people I see encourage me greatly by their interest in public life and service. Thursday night (after a hard day in the city) I spent a couple hours here with the mid-career Federal public service group. A set of lively young minds and good spirits, with a diversity of talents and occupations as broad as the whole spectrum of the Federal Government.

NOVEMBER 16, 1965
NEW YORK

As I was slowly working my way through breakfast, and preparing for the assault upon the day, this thought occurred to me about the entrepreneurial life: that it is not confined to business enterprise according to my concept. Entrepreneurship is a quality of life that characterizes almost every *creative* person or institution. Picasso, the early fathers of jazz rhythms, T. S. Eliot, Newton—and so on.

So the entrepreneurial spirit is an element of unity; it gives coherence to all forms of creativity, making blood brothers of businessmen, engineers, poets, musicians, and statesmen.

NOVEMBER 19, 1965
PRINCETON

Walking down Broadway the other night I saw a brooding photo mural high above the lights of Times Square at about 43rd Street: five males in black, dour, young-old faces, with long hair and longer scowls. And beneath this far-out mural, way up there above the garish marquees of the girlie movies of 42nd Street, a legend I copied down, in shorthand, standing against a light pole:

"The sound face and mind of today is more relative to the hope of tomorrow and the reality of destruction than the blind who cannot see their children for fear and division. Something that grew and related. Five reflections of today's children."

And then, in bigger and bolder letters: "The Rolling Stones."

I know that the Rolling Stones are a Beatle-like quintet, but what in the world went into putting that sign, that strange, illiterate, ominous, and rebellious-sounding sign at that particular place, Times Square?

Perhaps my granddaughter Pamela, or one of the long-haired young men in boots I saw on the corner of 43rd Street, could explain it to me.

There is a kind of illiteracy that takes the form of using sophisticated "in" terms, and "related" is one of the favorites among the glibsters these days.

NOVEMBER 20, 1965
PRINCETON

Marver Bernstein, Dean of the Woodrow Wilson School, told me about the visit of President Johnson's remarkable wife, Lady Bird, last Thursday. Came to see the School and to inquire how the School goes about serving as a center for the teaching of politics, preparing people for *elective* office.

Bernstein was impressed—as everyone who sees Lady Bird in action always is, which certainly includes me—with her intelligence, how much she *knows*, how strongly she feels, and how gracious and honestly simple she is.

There is to be still another "center" to house still another President's papers—Johnson's, of course—this time at the University of Texas; it is the educational center in connection with this that she is looking into. Just like her to come with no fanfare, by commercial plane to Philadelphia, then in an ordinary Chevrolet to Princeton.

NOVEMBER 21, 1965
PRINCETON

Henry Wallace's death last week at age seventy-seven saddened me *only* because he still had a devouring appetite for life. There are so few men of any age who have that gift. Among those who once were at the center of things and then are hardly on the stage at all, this rarely happens; sourness, resignation, bitterness, a turning of their back on life—this is the usual thing. When I read a quote in his *Times* obit, from an address to a high school class some time back, I felt a real pang: "I will live to be a hundred," he said, "because I just can't wait until morning each day to see what has happened in my garden"—this was the gist of it.

How many men are there in the whole history of the world who not only made two blades of grass grow where one grew before, but who were part of a change (hybridizing) of an ancient plant, corn, that made the bins of the Middle West fairly creak with overabundance and helped feed the hungry of the world? This was the result of this one gentle man's scientific genius and his drive.

NOVEMBER 23, 1965
NEW YORK

Yesterday in Al Neal of CED I found a kindred spirit: an economist who understands that "economics" explains only a very limited segment of human affairs, that it is a useful technique but not a substitute for a far broader outlook.

As a professional economist dealing constantly with economists, Al has been through the mill I have been through, seeing economics recede in importance as a decider, a formulator of human policies, to the role it *should* have as one of the disciplines upon which we can draw for a technical check on general propositions far broader than economics.

We met for lunch, spent a couple hours or more discussing the "structure and performance of American business" project which I am to head for CED. He will send to the trustees who will serve on my subcommittee a statement I prepared as a basis for discussion with the Committee members at our first meeting together. Here are a few of the salient passages:

"The thesis of my own thinking goes something like this:

"Business has become the central dynamic fact of American life, affecting and shaping not only our 'economic' life, but every other facet of living and thinking and feeling. . . .

"If we try to find measures or criteria of business as an institution, as a going concern in contemporary American life, as one of the *principal means of improving the quality of life in the United States and the world* (or downgrading that quality), of measuring the performance of business in terms of individual living both in a physical and . . . non-physical sense, and of the opportunity for development of the individual, we will, I think, be plowing new ground.

"Take one instance . . . the issue of bigness, size, can be better analyzed and evaluated once we are agreed upon *what it is we expect* of the American business enterprise, in terms not merely of output, but of performance in the lives of employees, of executives, of consumers, etc. If the *consequences* of the American business enterprise in terms of *performance* turn out to be very bad . . . then clearly the structure of American business, in which the units are predominantly huge, would also be bad; and contrariwise, if the performance, carefully measured and critically observed, of business in terms of individual living and the quality of life generally is good, and grows increasingly better, then the question of great size almost answers itself."

NOVEMBER 24, 1965
NEW YORK

The arms competition continues to spiral madly. This morning's *Times* reports on a decision pending to launch an all-out Anti-Missile effort. Whether it is H-bombs or anti-missiles (to cost billions of dollars), the record that is being played by passionate advocates is pretty much the same old record: "We must do it before the Communists do."‡

‡ In December, 1975, the U.S. Defense Department announced that, after very large expenditures, the Anti-Missile program was to be abandoned as a failure.

When I proposed in 1951 that we try to find some better way than starting another round, in that case the H-bomb, I got exactly nowhere. Whether discussions with the Russians at that time would have produced any good results no one will ever know. Probably not. Now a fifteen-man panel headed by Wiesner and Gilpatric comes up with a proposal that before we go into a crash program on another weary round, we try to get an agreement with the Soviets for a three-year moratorium. I can't quite picture this effort having much better luck than our stand in 1950, *except* that this time the issue is brought out into the arena of public discussion, whereas in 1950 those of us who had strong doubts were muzzled by official secrecy while the proponents had no scruples about making a public and emotional issue of it.

There is one brighter light in the sky this time, though: relations with the Soviet Union *are* improving, generally, compared with 1950. But both the Soviets and ourselves are caught in a typhoon of events that seems to make men powerless to do anything to save themselves from a course that is insane for *both.*

NOVEMBER 27, 1965
PRINCETON

Off to the south of us, come night, the sky is lighted as if by a great fire, or a city seen at a distance. And when the clouds hang low, the whole sky seems to rock, to shake, as if a huge stage had been set for Wagnerian music.

The *cause* of this spectacle is an architectural innovation, completed only last spring, at the Institute for Advanced Study, across the common a quarter mile away. The new Institute Library, of which Robert Oppenheimer is so proud, has an oddity in the way of a roof: glass louvres, set at an angle to catch the daylight. And at night, with the electric lights on, of course most of the light goes *upward.*

I thought this night effect was intended, until I had a visit with Robert this noon in his office. I had mentioned how beautiful was the setting about the new library—the lake, the greenery, etc. With a little-boy grin he said: "The library *is* beautiful, and the setting. It is also an illustration of how we don't anticipate the most obvious consequences. This happened to us in a major way with the bomb at Los Alamos. As for the ceiling for the library, we wanted the best light, the light in just the right way. Wallace Harrison,§ who designed the building, was skeptical about whether such a roof could be built, structurally. In the daylight it turned out to be wonderful. But no one, *not one* of us foresaw that not only would light come in, but it would go out—into the sky."

§ A prominent architect.

As an instance of my favorite theme about the limitation of the human capacity to plan and to foresee, this is a classic.

A very good talk with Robert. I told him about the new assignment for Herrera in South America, and he helpfully suggested the names of two Latin Americans he thinks are great men. We talked about Jean Monnet, whose name, of course, I brought up when we talked about a Common Market for South America. What an "action-minded" man he is, we agreed. Robert then added: "Even before 'your Committee' [the AEC] was organized, Monnet asked me whether atomic energy would solve the problems of the reconstruction of Europe. I told him, no." But Monnet went ahead with his ideas about Euratom, despite that advice, and mine, also negative, given later, in Paris. (It is still not much more than a name.)

I mentioned the *New York Times* story about the report on the anti-ballistic missile—ABM—of a few days ago; that a panel headed by Jerry Wiesner had recommended to the President that we not now go full blast into such a program. Robert saw the analogy to the issue he and I confronted together about a crash program for the H-bomb years ago.☾ But there are important differences too, of course. The question here is not whether such a device *can* be built—it would mostly involve the use of "hardware" now on the shelves, whereas no one knew what an H-bomb would be like if it *could* be built. Said Robert, lugubriously, "The pressure to go ahead will be very great, for reasons based on the merits, but also because of the great industrial pressures that will build up, for this means an expenditure of ten billion dollars a year for a number of years."

Wednesday night John Oliver phoned with the most unexpected news: the Peabody Coal people want us to go ahead with the Western energy study and report, and they are prepared to pay the price we put on it.

This particular bee in my bonnet actually goes back at least to 1953 or 1954. The period of idea gestation sometimes makes that of the elephant seem indecently brief.

NOVEMBER 28, 1965
PRINCETON

Secrecy in public affairs: I have thought a great deal about this, have seen at firsthand how it can stultify public policy discussion and lead to irrational witch-hunts—and the rest. I have subscribed to the

☾ *Journals*, Vol. II, *The Atomic Energy Years*, pp. 580–585, 587–591, 613–614, 615, 620–633.

doctrine—I suppose it is fair to call it such—that until the Soviet Union becomes an "open society" there is little hope for peaceful coexistence with them.

But now I wonder if there *is* any secrecy. Not because Russia has changed its ideology or its mystic faith in secrecy (its closed system), but because of technical advances: the inanimate "spy" of the camera, carried in a satellite far above the earth. Even while I was AEC Chairman, an air filter in one of our planes brought us information no spy could have been relied upon to get out of a "closed" Soviet Union, i.e., that the Soviets had detonated an A-bomb of a certain kind. An orbiting object can make every inch of the Soviet Union—and China—as open as you wish, without the intervention of spies, 007s, or any of that kind of dated espionage.

So we had argued vociferously, "Russia *must* open its borders if there is to be peaceful coexistence." I have probably said just that myself, and certainly many responsible people have. But *change* is there, within reach, *not* by "diplomacy" or exhortation or denunciation of secrecy, but through the change that technology and science bring.

What I have just written may not be completely true today; but in five years it will probably be old hat.

DECEMBER 2, 1965
NEW YORK

Those three men sitting over their steaks in a booth across the way: how can you be sure they aren't rehearsing the script of some way-out *satire* on modern jargonese? I kept jotting down some of the phrases. None of it made any sense whatever, neither the jargon nor the earnest forceful conversation.

"Now, Ed, I am primarily action-oriented . . . target groups . . . we have simply got to systematize our system . . . related . . . related . . . feed-back . . . I say where is the pay-off . . . but the thing I keep saying planning is not production . . . agency profile . . . the agency isn't doing what they think they are doing . . . problem oriented . . . the community is just agency-minded. . . ."

And so on.

I have my own troubles with jargon—not always as colorful, but equally thin in meaning. I have a violent aversion to "implement" as a verb, but unhappily it has become a part of the bureaucratic vocabulary. Yesterday, at a staff meeting about a proposal we're making to Ethiopia, I came on the adjective "implementable."

What's the matter with the verbs to act, to do, to carry out?

DECEMBER 5, 1965
PRINCETON

Arthur Schlesinger has been the center of as lively a barrage of brickbats and at the same time of the highest, most extravagant praise as I can recall whirling about the head of a historian. The cause, of course, is his huge book *A Thousand Days*, about President Kennedy as Arthur saw him.

As he sat at the huge round table in the Trustees' room at the Twentieth Century Fund on Friday morning he seemed by all odds the most composed of men.

Arthur looked different. I wondered whether the high praise and the blaze of well-deserved publicity of recent weeks had "changed" him. He looked more mature, less the schoolmaster barely concealing his mild irritation at having to explain things to less complex minds.

Sitting next to him—they made an interesting picture together—was Robert Oppenheimer. Peering intently over his half-glasses, deep furrows in his forehead, Robert listened to Adolf Berle with an almost fierce concentration, as Berle expressed some of those visions of crisis and pending disaster that come so easily to him. God knows, *this* time he may be right, about World War III hovering closer, of the converging of *three* kinds of crises (one of them "nihilism" on the civil rights front)—eloquent but, to me, not persuasive.

Morris Abram spoke about his recent experience at a White House Conference with the six or seven chief Negro leaders—Roy Wilkins, James Farmer—the whole spectrum, or most of it, from the Urban League to the way-out newer revolutionary leaders. What an impressive, strong—and handsome—figure Abram is, what a sense of discipline and control you feel, and yet what profound convictions and passion.

He was aghast at the vast intolerance toward anyone, Negro or long-tested white friend of Negroes, exhibited by some black leaders at that meeting. Those "Not in the Movement" were simply outlawed, no matter how much they had contributed to the great progress that has been made. It was not so much what Abram *said*, but the sense I had of being in the presence of a brave and stalwart man. For it takes courage to stand up, as Morris did, to such a disappointing performance, after having given as much as he has—in Atlanta and since—to the cause of civil rights.

Reminded me of what Alan Paton said when he was asked what would happen to him if the Negroes in South Africa took over. Without a moment's hesitation he, who had fought apartheid, said he would be treated as bitterly as the whites who had been supporters of apartheid. At Freedom House's dinner for Paton I said something less dramatic, but of the same order: that the test of the Negro would be how he treated *other* Negroes.

It takes a strong soul to bear up, to continue to have faith in men, when things are going badly for the underdog—and almost as much strength to persevere in one's faith when the underdog becomes top dog.

DECEMBER 8, 1965
4:45 P.M.
EN ROUTE (VIA AIR SHUTTLE)
WASHINGTON TO NEW YORK

At 3:30 I walked into Hubert Humphrey's office in the Executive Offices—the State War Navy building of years ago—and there followed one of the most delightfully relaxed forty minutes I have had with a "high" public official. I wanted particularly to speak to him about what Felipe Herrera yesterday called our "marriage," i.e., the working together of D&R and his "bank of integration" to push into *action* the great vision of a united Latin America. And on this topic he *listened.* I bore down on the political foundation, as I see it: that this is a Latin American initiative, a Latin American mystique which fired not only the experts, but the public men as well. So we should welcome a chance to support this idea, and "go easy" on the constant talk, on our part, of "reform." But an economic integration if acted on *in concrete cases* inevitably carries with it reform, economic and social.

In his address this noon at the Rockefeller Public Service Awards ceremony, Humphrey had spoken eloquently of the profound satisfaction that comes to those in public service. It is an old theme, and true enough, but with his natural skill as a speaker he made it most inspiring, even to an oldtimer. I picked up this theme in our talk in his great high-ceilinged office, speaking of the satisfactions I found, in private life and with a private company, in providing more food, better conditions of health, and more opportunity for training in the areas where we worked; I wanted to be sure he had *some* idea of what we are doing.

Talking about the satisfaction of doing things for people set him off. Looking around, wild-eyed, at his office, as a lithe wild animal might his well-provisioned but constraining cage, he exploded: "I get so fed up sometimes; I have to make all these banquet speeches, go out and raise money for the party night after night, getting mauled and petted and fussed over and beating my brains out. And every once in a while I say to hell with it, and I go to a small college and see young people. None of them can do me any good, but it just recharges me."

I found, I said, when we first lived in New York that you could be among millions of people yet lose all touch with people. I had tried to find a way of living that would counteract this.

Humphrey broke in, full of ebullience: "That's right. It takes some thinking to figure out how to live so you don't lose touch. Especially in public life. Most especially in a job like this one of mine."

At the talk this noon he said, "When I grouse and grumble about what I have to put up with, with the frustrations and the long hours, my wife says, 'No one from on high called *you*, Hubert,' and that settles me down."

He rushed on: "All this talk about a house for the Vice President—looks like Congress is going to provide for it. But Muriel and I have a house, a little one—no, it's not so little, at that—and I sometimes wish they would stop talking about a government-owned house for us. When I get out to *our* house, I say to myself, this is *mine*, and that feels good."

John and Blanchette Rockefeller, refusing any help from me with their many bundles, asked me, as we were getting off the plane at La Guardia, if they could drive me to my hotel; they are as thoughtful people as any I have ever known.

The ride together gave me a chance to tell John that among the many great achievements to the credit of the Rockefeller Foundation, the Medical School in the University del Valle in Cali must rank very high. John is so amusing when one says something that is right about his philanthropies. He just looks very glum and says not a word. No head ducking, no disavowals, but also no "Aw, shucks, wasn't nothin'." Just looks right at you, very solemn. A delightful human being.

DECEMBER 18, 1965
PRINCETON

Thursday an intensely interesting and gratifying meeting of the M&CP Board, presided over with gravity and a professional touch by our almost storybook Chairman, Charles Engelhard.

I say "professional" because through several hours—it was a long, long meeting—he never wasted a word, never asked a meaningless question. An impressive thing, a "pro" in any field, and not the least in business. Such a man performs at his best when there is a specific question before him. He is not as impressed by figures as a less successful or less experienced man might be. And I noted that on two occasions Engelhard used the term "moral"—"What was the moral position?"

This was no mere general vaporizing. For example, the management came to the Board with a proposal that we buy a certain company, this after several months of negotiation. A statement was to be issued to the public saying that "in principle" the parties had agreed on the transaction, subject to a two-month further investigation which could only be made after their books and operations were fully disclosed. But, said one of the negotiators, "we have an escape clause; if in two months we don't feel like going ahead, we can get out."

"No," said Engelhard, "if you don't now think you want to go ahead, don't issue this statement. The moral position is that we are committed, subject only to finding something in the nature of a misrepresentation, a most unlikely circumstance."

The whole business of announcing a transaction with the idea that one side could back out just didn't appeal to his "moral" sense. I found that this hardboiled man had a better sense of what is "correct," about what is ethical, than many more abstract and philosophical people.

DECEMBER 21, 1965
NEW YORK

Dr. José Cardenas of the Inter-American Development Bank phoned yesterday: the Board of Directors had formally approved the contract with us to further interaction in Latin America.

This assignment can be as important and challenging and imaginative as we make it. It can be a dreary matter of going through and evaluating all the proposals for multinational *physical* works—there is a card file, Walt Seymour tells me, *that* thick—and choosing some of them. *Or* we can see this as a big enterprise—joining a whole continent together by developing its rivers—but *also* one close to the people, who need to have *something happen* that affects their daily lives.

Walter Lippmann, just back from a South American trip, wrote a couple columns last week that report (without directly saying so) the kind of long and magnificent view that I hope we shall get into this integration undertaking—and thereby erase the physical barriers that lie between the countries: the Andes and the jungle.

This is at the heart of our assignment, though it is called by the colorless (in this context) term "investment policy."

The spangled fantasies, the splendor of fairy-tale imaginings of childhood are as nothing compared with the bounding joy of reality, if only there be a heart full of wonder and love, if only eyes look upon the world free of doubt and fear. This boon is given not only to little children; those no longer children can find for themselves a world that is fresh and new. A moment or an hour of such an awareness of the world is worth a decade of ordinariness.

"I thought you had gotten over this sort of thing." Tom Corcoran greeted me sheepishly, I thought, as we shook hands in, of all places,

Sulka's on Fifth Avenue. I was having a big time buying a couple new ties, a wine-red vest, a burnt-red shirt.

Tom hasn't changed in demeanor in all these years since he strutted about the Washington scene as F.D.R.'s left hand. His hair, still wavy and handsome, is now entirely white, but that lopsided grin, his way of tilting his head and looking slantwise out of wise and merry eyes, seem about the same.

DECEMBER 29, 1965
NEW YORK

The angst over "our war" in Vietnam grows apace. Anxiety not only about whether we can "win" (a hope pretty well abandoned), but over the fact that we may have no way of withdrawing even if we wanted to, much less of contriving some kind of face-saving "negotiation" (negotiation being the highest goal one ever notes discussed).

But one would never believe that there was a worry in the world, to judge by the people on the streets and in the restaurants. Parties of papas and mamas with their children, Park Avenue glittering with lighted trees, the great glass eyes of the new buildings staring gaily at this flossy scene of self-satisfied people. Among these, the complacent, is this lone walker in the streets of Babylon.

The angst is spreading. A passionate, beautifully written letter today from Marriner Eccles, enclosing a statement violently opposing the war, on practical as well as moral grounds. At the end he mentions, but only barely, the issue I wish would be explored carefully in public—the alternative to withdrawal. What are the historical precedents for such an admission of failure? What are the most likely guesses of the consequences elsewhere? Just how could it be done without great loss of American and South Vietnamese lives?

III

1966

Meeting with President Johnson—White House dinner for Prime Minister Gandhi—Peace Corps undertaking—Trip to Colombia—White House discussions about post-war economic planning in Vietnam—Trip to Colombia and Venezuela—Fairless Lectures at Carnegie Institute of Technology—Agroindustrial pioneering in Khuzistan—Senator Robert Kennedy and Bedford-Stuyvesant project

JANUARY 1, 1966
PRINCETON

For the first time in ten years, I think, I haven't done a solemn summary of the year that has passed.

Why not? Perhaps it is because I look forward to the mystery of the year *ahead* with such joy and anticipation.

No happier experience for me than to see a man full of enthusiasm and ideas about his work. We had just such a visitor yesterday: Van Morgan, heading TVA's development of a unique recreational area in western Kentucky called "The Land Between the Lakes." A huge area, served by the giant Kentucky Lake and the lake behind the almost completed Barkley Dam on the Cumberland.

Van sat way forward on a chair in our living room, his elbows on his knees, his west Tennessee country man's drawl erased by his excitement about his work. It was a tribute—that enthusiasm and recognition of the new and expanded role of TVA in public recreation

—to the vitality of TVA as an organization, of which he has been a part for more than twenty-five years.

He told me things about the kids who come to these TVA parks and recreation areas that gave me a new look into how different are the urban children (not just big-city, but any urban area) from the small-town and country kids I knew or grew up with. He says these youngsters, and their parents, shy away from even the gentler forms of outdoor "roughing it," very few of them "know what a cow is," except perhaps at a distance, and creepy crawling things in the woods alarm them. A long, long way, these "camps," from the camp I set up at Bass Lake when I was a college student, cooking on an upside down wash boiler or over an open fire, digging a pit as a "bathroom" for the kids I was taking care of. Now, says Van, these kids won't go into the bushes to do the necessary; "unless there is a *door to open* they don't believe it's a place for that performance that is still so natural."

John Lindsay is Mayor of New York, since six o'clock last night, at which time the Transit Workers Union walked off in a strike that could give some idea of how vulnerable the great cities are. If the strike goes on a few days, and then we have our first snow, we can see in miniature what turned Great Britain against labor for a long time following the General Strike of a generation ago.

JANUARY 4, 1966
PRINCETON

Manhattan is an almost strangled place at best; this morning its windpipe is about closed off. The phrase I stuck into my "300,000,000 Americans Would Be Wrong" article (appearing Sunday in the *Times Magazine*), "a bumper-to-bumper way of life," is what has happened to New York, not in the year of our Lord 2000, as I predicted, but in the year of labor leader Mike Quill 1966.

Public indignation is directed against the union and particularly its president, a blustering wild man (he urged New Yorkers to choke the streets with cars!). He may be found in contempt of a court injunction this morning. But courts and their injunctions can't run subway trains and buses. (My earliest convictions as a young man centered about "government by injunction," the Norris-LaGuardia Act, which limited the Federal Courts' issuance of injunctions in labor disputes, so my mind tells me that sending Quill to jail isn't a sensible way of dealing with this chaos, even in the short term.) The frustration of a great city completely hamstrung by what appears to be one man (this is the way it always seems, picking out an individual to hate) makes for bad solutions which are no solutions at all.

Dr. Nathan Feinsinger, head of the mediation panel seeking to help bring on a settlement of the transit collapse, was interviewed on TV a few minutes ago. "Sad" was the word this experienced and wise man used, and sad it is. Sad that a labor leader should be put in jail, as a way of adjusting an inherently difficult economic and human issue. The very fact that Quill is such a bombastic and verbally provocative man is all the more reason why the issues of peaceful adjustment rather than anger or force should become part of this sorry picture.

In the days of my youth, when I was with Donald Richberg* representing the railroad unions, a great national strike had injured the country and the Government had resorted to the courts. Some of the unions espoused the Plumb Plan for Government ownership and operation as the right course. This would have made all railroad employees public employees, and that was thought radical or liberal then. The transit employees in this imbroglio *are* public employees, and under state law public employees may not strike. But making a strike illegal does not settle a labor dispute, as we said so many times in TVA, where we espoused collective bargaining, but opposed prohibition of strikes of public employees and even advised the New York City Corporation Counsel against such a move.

What will insure against occasional mass interruptions of essential public services no one knows, but none of the panaceas—compulsory arbitration, illegality of strike, public ownership—will do it.

Even though the strike causes hardship and financial loss, I still say it is good to live under conditions where men may strike, however arbitrarily. We can recover from the inconvenience and financial losses; we couldn't recover from the effect of tying people to their jobs.

Perhaps this is an outmoded "liberal" idea; perhaps we need some way to prevent these occurrences. But I would like to look at the alternative carefully before I would be convinced.

JANUARY 7, 1966
PRINCETON

Battered, stifled New York is still floundering in the midst of one of the greatest demonstrations of the vulnerability of a great city that one can imagine. It is made all the more dramatic because Quill, the head of the subway unions, and Mayor Lindsay are of two completely different eras.

* Donald R. Richberg was a major figure in the early New Deal, as general counsel and later Chairman of the National Recovery Administration (NRA). In the 1920s he was one of the nation's leading labor lawyers, and he employed me, on my graduation from Harvard Law School in 1923, in his Chicago office.

8:30 P.M.

Dinner with David Tobey. Early in February he begins a new chapter in the career of a new-generation international businessman, after a tough four-year "apprenticeship" in the esoterics of world-wide ore trading, or "marketing," to use the new and deliberately more respected semantics.

Whereas a year ago he was very much discouraged—I listened to his tale of near-despair but had sense enough not to dispute with him—now he breathes the air of adventure that an international business career, or any other, come to think of it, should have about it. He is moved to Tokyo first, then Taiwan, and then for a couple years perhaps to the Philippines, touching on Hong Kong and perhaps Malaysia and Indonesia. Finding and developing business in the ores of Southeast Asia will be his job. What an opportunity! He has had a tough training here in Philipp Brothers, and with his native ability and strong motivation he should give a good account of himself. But what is more important, he should have an interesting time, within and outside his business life.

JANUARY 13, 1966
NEW YORK

Twelve hours ago I turned on the TV: the strike was over, settled sometime after midnight. But its remnants are all about us in this city.

A visit with André Meyer yesterday forenoon, a relaxed exchange between friends.

I said I came to see him not for any particular business problem I had, but just because I enjoyed seeing him now and then. This set the tone of our conversation, from one of tension and a race against the minute hand of the clock to a more normal exchange of views between men who have more in common than I realize, despite such different backgrounds and experience.

Why is it that for so long, for years, almost invariably something in my metabolism reacted sharply when I was with André? A kind of fear, a tension, an apprehension. I have a considerable admiration for his genius in finance and his vast experience and achievements; but an uneasiness would build up in me when I had a meeting with him coming up.

Yesterday none of this at all. Here was a man who had the same need that the rest of us have for friendship, for the appreciation of friends and an interest in him, for himself, rather than for his financial genius.

I spoke about our new contracts. Then I said: "You told me years ago that D&R was not geared to ordinary business, and that has been true."

"But you are not losing money; you are making—what is it?" he asked. I gave him the figure. "But," André said, "it is an achievement; you have built something important. That counts, doesn't it?"

I said almost casually: "The satisfaction I have had out of building this enterprise has been one of the many things you have made possible for me, and as a friend I want to assure you again how deeply I appreciate it. And the same thing is true of the financial independence I have, now that Minerals & Chemicals has gone so remarkably well. You told me years ago that I would be unwise to accept Sarnoff's offer that I take over the color television project in RCA [then in great trouble], that a big company like that would absorb and lose me, and it wouldn't make me financially independent either. You found a little broken down company, Minerals Separation Corporation; all it had was cash of a half million dollars, and we built it up into a big, successful enterprise—and you only had one reason that I can see for taking such an interest in me, and that was a sense of wanting to help a man whose work as a public servant you respected."

He broke in: "About the only satisfaction left for me now is being helpful to people I like. *You* remember what I did." A youthful grin: "But not everyone does remember, I can tell you."

Then we talked about Vietnam. He agrees completely with Marriner Eccles' recent statement against the war, favoring pulling out as best we can. I wasn't convinced we could do that without great loss to us all over the world. "Are there precedents for this?" I asked. He threw back his head, his voice boomed: "Algeria, Algeria. Three generations of French life in that country. A far more difficult case. When you have hurt your finger, why should you go ahead and lose your hand, then your arm, perhaps your whole body?"

I asked him, suddenly: "What is the age of your grandson?" "Nineteen. Why should I see him and others be sent to the jungles of Vietnam? Young men like him, like the young Frenchmen who were lost in Algeria and Indochina, particularly since the Vietnamese—I know about them—don't care whether we are there or not, don't care one bit."

As we walked out, the look of care returned, the kind of look that asks for sympathy and understanding. "We are in so many things here at Lazard, making such progress. Very hard on me. I only sleep five or six hours." He put his thumbs in his vest armholes, joining his fingers before his chest—a characteristic gesture—looked at the floor, then at me. I remarked that he looked very well, which I thought was true. He walked with me out to the elevator, slowly. "There ought to be more time for such talks," he said, and turned to plunge back into the role of the driver of an undertaking he has made one of the great financial institutions of the world.

This visit with André was a revealing experience. "Revealing" in what I saw more clearly than ever before: beneath the mask of harshness he so often wears is a man who needs other people, people he respects, people who treat him as a human being and not just a financial machine.

It was "revealing" too, this half hour, in what it made more clear *about myself*, as I was years ago (not true of the past five or six years).

I too had achievements, honors, "glory" (a term an English reviewer of the *Journals* used about my TVA work), notoriety, a reputation for winning whatever race I set out to run. I too was the "man who had everything" to the outside eye. In fact, however, I was "cold, lonely and afraid," cut off from a closeness to people that my nature craved.

The parallel between André and my own case is startling, considering the vast differences in our background and area of life. But a parallel just the same.

JANUARY 16, 1966
PRINCETON

Around the corner this noon for lunch with Robert and Helen Meyner. Almost four hours of as interesting and varied a group of people as one could wish for, in the setting of their small but exquisitely tasteful house.

Helen Meyner has the warm and easy manner of a cultivated woman, and is so handsome, with features that are so strong and pure, that one thinks he is looking on the head of some great marble sculpture of ancient Greece, yet her coloring one finds only among American women. And such a magnificent voice, clear, strong, but with a gay tinkle in it—and what that voice says makes sense, which is a rare quality at a social gathering when the hostess must keep one part of her mind on seeing that things go properly. Which they did.

Among the guests Chet Huntley (who has a farm near Flemington) and his youthful and pretty wife. The TV picture of Huntley doesn't convey the warmth and friendliness in this man, whose features are probably more familiar to the American people than those of any other human being today. Much taller than I had pictured him—about my height—and quite thoughtful. This latter I was prepared for, because while he was still broadcasting in the West he was known for having *ideas*. A successor to Murrow, or as nearly one as can be to the unique person Ed was, but without giving the impression of being on stage—an actor, even a "ham"—that Ed conveyed and enjoyed and did so well.

Bob Meyner was hearty, which comes naturally to him, and critical of President Johnson's concept of leadership, though approving highly of his State of the Union message. "I spent some time with him yesterday," he said, "and Johnson kept talking about how the polls supported him. I don't think this consensus idea is the right one. Decide what you believe in, what you think needs to be done, and then fight for that—that's my idea of how a political leader should perform." But he said L.B.J. had fully recovered his vigor, though he looks thin and drawn.

JANUARY 17, 1966
NEW YORK

The meeting of the EWA Board, in the Board of Directors' room of the Morgan Guaranty Bank—from 9:30 A.M. until 2 P.M.—was interesting and I had a sense of dealing with real issues. It has taken me a couple of years to comprehend the world in which the "institutions of higher learning" live, which is quite another one than my own—but a good one, I must say, despite the occasional softness of thinking, and the special jargon.

One of the very serious staff members said that the drive for a large amount of money for an Adlai Stevenson Memorial Institute could not wait (the prospect of delay was somehow relevant to the discussion of EWA getting involved); he pressed the point by saying that unless it proceeded very rapidly—a month or less was critical—one of the "distinguished men" who were expected to contribute would probably be dead, "and this could cut the total contribution to the fund by 50%."

I commented that I thought this was probably the "least compassionate remark that I had ever heard in a fund-raising drive, and there was a lot of competition for that dubious honor." Happily, this was taken to be a joke—which was intended—but the episode does throw light on the atmosphere in which the frantic fund-raising drives are conducted. Then when the money is raised they don't know how to use it—witness the Franklin Roosevelt and Eleanor Roosevelt memorial foundations, neither of which measures up to even the slightest of these great figures' accomplishments, which are their true memorial.

JANUARY 23, 1966
PRINCETON

The very first snow of the winter descended during the night; an orchestration of high winds making the great pines outside my bedroom moan and sing, the tall locust trees bend and twist like things alive. Something atavistic perhaps makes me feel secure here in my study, surrounded by my books and my semicircular desk (now returned to me after its absence in Washington).

A happy and varied week. The first full-dress meeting with the men in D&R who have been working in Washington on the first steps of our assignment in the integration of South America. The pace is slow, by my impatient standards; Herrera has not yet made a public statement about our engagement by the Inter-American Development Bank. The practical effect of this delay (it had been planned for January 6th) is that until this is officially announced I can't begin the process of visiting with leaders, particularly in the U.S. Government. But the digging through the files of the Bank, examining proposed multinational undertakings, this does go on, and is useful.

For all of my skepticism about abstractions and generalizations, I back off from the "analysis" of details or specifics unless set in the frame of a whole picture, unless a long-range goal has been set, described, and emotions stirred about it. So, in our staff meeting at 1 Whitehall Street, I heard my voice rise, with some feeling as well as vigor, about the need for some grand and historical setting for all these descriptions of specific projects—a road here, a port there, a beginning on the Parana or Paraguay River.

I spoke of the analogy in American history of the *dream of free land* beyond the Appalachian Mountains, and the effect this produced on the spirit of the men who lived on the Atlantic seaboard; this followed by the effect of a succession of such openings of new land on the migration of hardy souls into the Mississippi Valley, by trail, by canal, by wagon; then later the great trek across the mountains of the West. The opening of virgin land—without roads or waterways to reach them, with hostile Indians, and all the rest of that saga—those lands proved to be the unifying and energizing force for the "economic development" and the "integration" (to use the jargon of today) of the parts of a continent into a single nation. Not industry, but land.

There is land to which the landless who now crowd into the shanty areas of western South America can go: the Selva, the "forest shelf" of the Andes. To open that land to the Indians of the west of South America is physically possible, by highways extending north and south from Colombia, south through Peru and Bolivia, with transverse roads from this north and south backbone road to the west coast. This is the dream of President Belaunde; he had to persuade Walter Lippmann of it; I needed no persuading. An engineering study has already been done (probably a pretty good one). What is lacking isn't money alone. Some kind of historical perspective and analogy is needed to lift it out of the unimaginative, traditional "cost-benefit" view of it as a "project."

Oliver and Burnett discussed with me the proposals Burnett has formulated to be presented to Iran for our continued work in the Khuzistan. Our special position in Khuzistan as the designer and unifying technical force, for the time being, is gone. Accepting this with as good grace as we can—and I find I am philosophical about it now—we decided that rather than withdraw completely, we would make a proposal that we could live with, if accepted. The only thing that interests me personally now is that we should continue in the Greater Dez food production part of the program, which we pioneered and brought so far along. But I find my heart isn't in it, as it was even two years ago.

Sometimes one must recognize that his function is fulfilled, even though far short of the completion of an important task. And is any great task ever "completed"?

An interesting exchange of letters with a great man this week: Dr. I. I. Rabi, Nobel Laureate in Physics and a member of the original AEC General Advisory Committee. I wrote him about his review of a book about the people I called Methodologists in my "300,000,000 Americans" article (and in *Change, Hope, and the Bomb*). He replied that the "professional strategists frighten me." I can't be very much off the beam if Rabi, with his great insight and scientific knowledge, can say almost the identical thing I wrote more than two years ago.

Which reminds me of an episode apropos the entry (or attempted entry) of these "defense analyst" groups into the economic development field. Herman Kahn, the high priest of the Hudson Institute, which I lampooned for their nonsense (as I saw it) in defense analysis, went to Brazil to persuade the Brazilians that the methodology they have nurtured could present a plan for the development of the Amazon Basin. With that *dummheit* about human affairs and feelings that characterizes so many of these people, he rhapsodized about the "internationalization of the Amazon River." Whereupon the proud Brazilians, naturally, told him to stop wasting their time.

Deeply engrossed this week with a four-letter word, as important a word as there is in the world today: *food.*

For years now—indeed since TVA days—increasing food production has been part of my life, in one way or another. I was dismayed, in the early days of D&R, by the secondary (or third) place agriculture was given by the World Bank, AID, and private industry. Suddenly, in the past couple of years, and notably in the past year, all this has changed. Now agriculture, *not* more and more industry, is being thought of as the lever by which "underdeveloped" countries can get their start on the long road. It may not be entirely accurate, but my impression is that some of the great theoreticians among the economists—Walt Rostow, for example—contributed to this notion that industrialization could bring these nations to that fictive juncture called the "take-off" point.

With the opening of an office for our agricultural work near the Davis Campus of the University of California, we may be ready for a four-square drive to work at food production in a way that no other private firm has yet done.

JANUARY 24, 1966
ROOSEVELT HOTEL
NEW YORK

Down the corridor a small blue bicycle; riding it a self-possessed boy, hair cut in bangs, soft, inquiring eyes. He races back to the suite at this end of the fifth floor. Out of the double door of the end suite the tall figure of a man, carrying a suitcase, with him a spirited looking woman. The Mayor and his wife, the boy their youngest.

I am living on the edges of Mayor Lindsay's temporary home.

The bellman had warned me to watch out for a tricycle on my floor, operated hell bent for leather by the Mayor's son, but I thought he was kidding.

Dr. Bhabha, the Mr. Atom of India, dead on the summit of Mt. Blanc; an air crash. Spent an evening with him in Nehru's huge living room back in 1951. A gentle, soft-spoken man, and a great enthusiast about what science, and particularly atomic energy, could do to pull India out of its slough of inertia.

JANUARY 25, 1966
NEW YORK

My day began, at the office, at 7:30 this morning. A long night; couldn't sleep.

But rocky as I felt for a while, it turned out to be a wonderful day. (My definition of a wonderful day is working with ideas, not alone but with a group of active minds concentrating on a central goal.) In this case, it was making important things happen about Western coal. Mullins, President of Peabody Coal, "our client," turned out to be a sturdily built athlete of perhaps forty, very much the modern miner: very big machinery, big ideas, but very close to the needs of today. More imaginative by far I thought than the Utah Construction people.

I listened to the D&R sharpshooters, Roland Kampmeier, Walt Seymour, Joe Swidler, during a long and intense morning. We had before us a huge map of the country, from the Twin Cities to the Coast; on it were marked the coal deposits (in Wyoming, Utah, Colorado, etc.) spotted by the Colorado School of Mines Research Foundation, which we engaged in 1962, soon after this coal-for-energy idea first became such an obsession with me. The talk was very specific: specific areas, specific markets. I enjoyed watching these first-rate minds with such different backgrounds function, smooth, well-organized, no self-deception and no euphoria, carving out the problems that needed answers before we could be sure of the rightness of our premise: a great future for this fabulous source of energy in the Rockies.

At lunch I spoke to Mullins about my work of more than ten years ago in the coal conversion field—making hot char for boilers and fuel oil out of coal.

I said: "The economics of the process ten years ago may have seemed doubtful; but with power stations of the size now in the picture, under our scheme for the West, wouldn't the economics have a different coloration?" His eyes opened wide, under extraordinary eyebrows, bushy, out of place in so young a face. "It probably would. That may be the thing that would put this whole thing way beyond any competition from nuclear power, adding that factor."

Wouldn't it be wonderful if that idea I labored on so hard—with no results—would prove to be decisive as a part of a great development of the West? Exciting prospect.

Mullins was the officer of Peabody who was skeptical about engaging D&R for this "study." Merl Kelce (the Chairman, with whom I had met a couple months ago) on the other hand, was on the bullish side, convinced that something useful to Peabody and the coal industry generally would come out of what we could do—and this on pretty slender evidence, I must admit. His chief reliance was our "reputation," I was told. But today, as we went from one hard-line approach to another, I felt that Mullins was becoming convinced that this was not only an important and interesting venture, but one that would be worth to Peabody what it costs them, and that will be a good deal.

I got something of the measure of the man, I thought, by the way he dismissed the big study by Robert Nathan Associates, paid for by the Department of the Interior. That report is aimed at much the same question D&R had undertaken to examine at its own expense. It would not have been remarkable if Peabody had said: What can D&R add to this huge report? But Mullins dismissed it with a quiet comment: "That report uses a broad brush."

I liked this because what we have set out to do—against the skepticism and even gentle disbelief or ridicule of Ed Littlefield—is consistent with our basic philosophy: no reports for their own sake; *action* is the purpose of a study. And we are going to stick to that conviction here.

We talked today, not about abstractions, but about huge power plants using coal from *particular* reserves in the Rockies region, intended for *specific* "load centers" of use almost from the Mississippi to the Coast, with a transmission network that could affect the future of the West as did the railroads and highways in an earlier time. This was the theme of my almost impromptu interview in the *Denver Post* in November, 1964; that grand design seems more realistic today than it did when it was only an inner hunch plus some of my rhetoric.

Joe Swidler reminded me of something quite moving, as we headed for lunch. Said he: "It was almost exactly thirty-five years ago that I walked into the law office of this young man here [meaning me] and was interviewed for a job." We have been involved with each other's work—and lives too, for we lived as next-door neighbors in Norris—for most of the time since that day. And here we are, working together again. How life does whirl people's lives about!

JANUARY 26, 1966
7:45 A.M.
ROOSEVELT HOTEL
NEW YORK

A little boy running down the carpeted corridor past my room. Then a voice familiar to millions during the recent transit unpleasantness, the choppy Ivy League voice of His Honor the Mayor of the world's greatest city. But the voice is that of papa from down the hall, commanding junior to come along "right *now*," and no nonsense.

JANUARY 27, 1966
NEW YORK

John Oliver back from a quick trip to the Dominican Republic. The AID Director, Alexander Firfer, wants us to respond to their invitation to do an agricultural development job in the Yuna Valley in the northeastern part of the country. If it were not for the torture and frustration in dealing with AID's present contracting procedures and personnel, the public interest in helping to get something actually accomplished in that unhappy place would justify our trying it out—with not a little skepticism about how effective we could be *unless* we were turned loose to get the job done. As it is, I am of two minds, but told Oliver to go ahead on submitting a brief report and see how—and when—AID in Washington responds. Since it took *months* for them to complete a contract providing simply reimbursement of travel expenses just for Oliver and Anderson to take a look, it is hard to believe anything good can come of this.

The World Bank, acting for the UN Special Fund, took over the Yaque del Norte, which Gordon and I saw almost four years ago, and made out a rough plan of action.‡ The French firm the Bank selected was to take two years to complete a feasibility study; it has been two years, and they haven't yet *started* on the study.

Parts of the world may starve, but the red tape artists will continue to thrive.

Yesterday noon went to the Century for lunch. While having a glass of sherry, I recognized a great figure, Dr. Raymond Fosdick, studying a magazine which he held up before him. A copy of the latest *Esquire*; on the cover a gal prominently displaying those parts of her which have long been a preoccupation of the male, but usually a male who hasn't been a scholar, a divine. And who doesn't wear rimless pince-nez glasses, under a white thatch. I thought it was a picture of contemporary life I had not expected I would see in the solemn halls of the Century.

FEBRUARY 3, 1966
NEW YORK

Back after a vigorous day in Washington, trying to explain to the boys at the "upper Washington elevations" my ideas about how we intend going at the food production program.

Dave Bell has great presence, with his tall, very slender, slightly stooped figure. Not the presence of a solemn man, a stern young man as I was when I first assumed great responsibility beyond my years, but with a warm and almost shy one-sided smile. He tilts back his chair (precariously, I thought) and keeps his eye on you in an attitude of full attention.

What Bell wanted most was to talk about India, and my views about what I had found there. I went over the steps: The AID Mission wanted a regional water management study; we didn't see that this, however useful and important, would meet the need for food next year, or the year after.

The heart of what we thought should be done would be to provide technical assistance, Indian and American, directly to the farmers who had the best prospect of increasing their yields. All sorts of objections had been made to this, but of a political character—favoritism, not democratic, etc.

‡ This trip is described in *Journals*, Vol. V, *The Harvest Years*, pp. 320–326.

I said that if we continued to pour grain into India every time they had too much rain (as last year) or not enough (as this year), they would stick to their theoretical principles about equality, and continue to be hungry.

After hearing how little real headway the AID Mission had made in the past year, I said to Bell that we would not make a proposal.

What a contrast between Bell and Walt Rostow, whom I saw in the afternoon, his feet propped up on the radiator, his coat off, on his face the bright light, the shining light, of a quick, a dancingly quick, mind and imagination. Dave speaks slowly, listens carefully, asks questions deliberately; Walt shoots darts of ideas in all directions.

These are men of the very first order of ability and dedication. There is no business empire in the country that wouldn't be hard put to find their equal.

FEBRUARY 6, 1966
PRINCETON

Rostow was all charged up about the Latin American integration. He looked out of the window as he talked, in his staccato way, with a good deal of the economist lingo interspersing the geopolitical phrases. The timing of my call on him could not have been better.

"I talked to the President about all of this yesterday," he said. "He expects this will succeed because you have undertaken it, and will go all the way, when we have your report. In the meantime I have been made responsible for getting all the parts together within this Government—I didn't suggest this, it was his idea. And that I'm doing.

"Matter of fact, I'm leaving late today for Peru, and the other countries affected by the—my Spanish isn't good enough to say Carretera and so on—the road along the margin of the forest. I'll see Belaunde tomorrow. Lippmann's column about opening up the new land with this great road won't stand up to economic analysis, the way he puts it."

He said this disdainfully; which I could understand, since much of Lippmann's comments about Latin America derided U.S. policy, or the lack of it.

Then in his intense and ebullient way he described the four places in South America where he thought the prospects for multinational physical developments were most likely; these happened to be the same ones Seymour and his boys described to us in a staff meeting a few days ago. So far so good.

Then Walt returned to the strong feeling the President had expressed about the importance of the Latin American integration task: "Jack Valenti just called me again about it, speaking for the President.

"What I would like is *your* reaction, Dave," he continued.

I said I thought this was one of the most difficult and at the same time most satisfying chores I've ever had a hand in. The areas he had described may—probably will—be recommended in our report, but it is too early to say. My only reservation at this early point is that it seems important to me to keep this a Latin American initiative, a Latin American venture, and not something out of Washington.

Rostow's face fell (it's a most mobile one, the extraordinarily intelligent eyes reflecting every mood). He said, "The President says he doesn't care about his image in Latin America; let the historians sort that out. He isn't going to splash it out big from the White House. I think he agrees—certainly I do—that it should be kept a Latin American idea and initiative. But he expects to put great energy behind your report when it comes along.

"The TVA mystique is strong in Latin America," he said, "you know that. Your name on that report will carry great weight with them."

I told Walt that the idea of a great highway along the "forest shelf," paralleling the coast but way inland, would open new land. Belaunde, however, seemed to forget—judging from my talks with him—that that new land would not be productive of more food just because it became *accessible*. I tried, I said, to get him to think about food production, and the planning for it, as a necessary part of the first stages of this great undertaking. "But I made no impression whatever," I confessed.

Rostow grinned in the knowing way that shows he is more than a first-rate abstract economist. "Belaunde is a man who loves his country, loves it *physically*. An architect, you know. It may be something to do with the fact that his personal life has been so tragic."

Yesterday the TV was full of Bell's testifying before the Senate Foreign Relations Committee. Much storming about the war in Vietnam—directed to the Director of the AID program! He was cool, candid—an excellent witness. I didn't think the Senators behaved very well—trying to be on both sides (except Wayne Morse!) with equal self-righteousness. I'm sorry now that TV wasn't in general use for news coverage when I had some of my most difficult hearings—it displays the legislative process in a way that makes for a great civics lesson.

When I drew Arthur Schlesinger aside last evening at Joe Johnson's big cocktail party, and told him what an extraordinary book about Kennedy he had written—and why I thought so—at first he looked at me as if surprised and defensive, as if he had expected something quite different from me. But as I went on to tell him of my sense of what *emotional* strength it took to write such a book about a man for whom, as a person, he had such a deep individual commitment, he responded at once. The fixed stare of a celebrity such as he has become left his eyes; he visibly relaxed. Then began an intensely interesting exchange.

"It was, I suppose, a kind of therapy, writing the book so rapidly and so close upon Kennedy's death. I have been criticized for not waiting long years before doing it. But there is some virtue in writing while the impressions are freshest. Of course, some people feel hurt, and they strike back, and some of it hurts, still hurts. But I think it was right, even as a historian it was right."

When I said there had been a real question about the "taste" of my publishing my *Journals* while I was still alive, rather than letting it wait until long, long afterward, he said he was surprised to hear there had been criticism. (Actually, very little, all told.) He said this was absurd; he described my *Journals* as "one of the most important such records of this century"—which coming from him fussed me. I should have encouraged him to say why.

Bill Marvel brought over to where I was standing a lithe, athletic fellow of about fifty, close cropped curly hair, very alive and warm countenance: Sol Linowitz, the spark behind Xerox, which has become one of the great entrepreneurial achievements of the last ten years. Linowitz said, "I remember everything you said at your lecture at Rochester—at the Eastman Theatre—and that must be fifteen years ago. And what you wrote about private business and the public interest even before that. Most everything you said has come about."

I would like to know Linowitz better; he has a fervent feeling for public affairs that isn't common enough among successful businessmen.

FEBRUARY 8, 1966
YOUNG ISLAND
ST. VINCENT, BRITISH WEST INDIES

Ten minutes after I set foot on this idyllic spot—meaning ideal for idling—I charged into the water, swimming about like a water spaniel too long confined in an apartment, then after a while came charging out, shaking the water off and heading for a rum drink.

A slender, grey-haired man came down to the water's edge and gave me a warm handshake: Howard Turner. He recalled that some ten years ago he and I had met when I was looking over the Consolidation Coal Co.'s coal conversion pilot plant near Pittsburgh. As we chatted on the shore he turned to Helen: "I haven't seen your husband for ten years. He looks as young as ever." Said Helen, "He *acts* as young, too." I was pleased, as any vain male *at any age* can be at that kind of sweet talk;

but I thought to myself that as to the acting part, she's right, only more so. For during those days of "adjustment" to private life—venturesome is *now* the word, but worrisome, searching days would be more accurate —I certainly didn't *feel* as buoyant as I do now.

If this place doesn't prove to be just what I have been looking for, for a winter break, I shall be much surprised. Our cottage is new and simple but convenient and attractive; we look back upon a great mound of green mountain, and in the foreground, blue water on which several big yachts sway. The sounds are delightful and soothing: the trade winds rustle the coconut palms and the leaves of banana trees, birds twitter—and in the morning a little Sardinian-type burro, a pet, will come around to add the Latin touch.

FEBRUARY 11, 1966
YOUNG ISLAND

The "yacht" that was to sail us to Bequia in the Grenadine Islands turned out to be an ancient, beat-up, and awkward coastal tramp. Her sails were huge, as they are on local boats in this trade wind area. But unhappily for my sailor sentimentality, a noisy, chattering, smelly engine, midship, went pounding along all the way. The crew of five was very good, and this was fortunate. For we were overtaken on the return by two lusty squalls. During one of these blustery blows and driving rain, the main halyard parted; there was great flapping, two of the boys of the crew, quite dashing in their white pants and very dark skins, scooted up the rigging and made the two parted ends fast; a jib sheet got badly fouled, in the middle of a blow, with the swells quite strong, the bow plunging into the valleys and then rarin' up like a bronco. Still the crewman went out on the bowsprit and did his job. Quite lively.

On the parched island of Bequia we were taken in hand by a pioneer type, a young man who built a solid and unbeautiful little hotel overlooking Friendship Bay; a magnificent postal-card vista, the water of the bay embraced by the green arms of the island—delightful. On one of the chops, as we say on the Vineyard, one could see the establishment that Sir Anthony Eden occupied while he was recuperating. Except for this, no sign of habitation. But as a dour Italian physicist was reported to have said, while others were exclaiming about the Sangre de Cristo Mountains, to be seen from the lodge at Los Alamos, "One could grow quite tired of this view." The same could not be said, I think of Young Island.

I have "promised" that I would work at resting, so I would come back refreshed for the hard (and happy) work ahead. So we have kept pretty much to ourselves, Helen and I; and this isn't difficult. Only eighteen other guests on the entire place. But one personage, the man responsible for this place, is a stimulating and unusual man: John Houser.

For years he planned and developed hotels around the world for Hilton; at Istanbul, at Cairo, and so on. But he is much more than a Hilton executive. A thoughtful and articulate man, quite moved by the needs of St. Vincent and obviously taken by the gentleness and sweetness of these local people, despite his many obstacles in training them to build this place (the workmanship of the wood parts and the stonework are splendid) and the even more exasperating process of training and overseeing the operation.

For two days we have had heavy rains with only intermittent sun. This produces the usual gloom, and self-pity too, in some of the guests. But not us. The barrage of rain last night on the roof of our cottage had the same effect of making one feel secure that the less vehement rains of the Vineyard do on our house on "Topside."

FEBRUARY 13, 1966
YOUNG ISLAND

The slim figure of the Queen came down the gangway from the gaily bedecked Royal Yacht,§ her yellow dress making her seem like a tropical flower among the white-suited guard of honor. The cannon boomed the 21-gun salute, her dark-skinned "subjects" massed along the waterfront cheered, the band marched—and England's most expensive luxury, the Royal Establishment, once more proved that it was worth what it cost. Why, otherwise, should the black faces look so happy and proud? Doubtless the same enraptured looks among the thousands on the shore as on the ones around us on the little ship where we watched all this.

We have seen Queen Elizabeth, seated on her horse at the trooping of the colors in London, amid huge city crowds of British. And the Shah among his subjects in southern Persia, or in the Marble Palace in Tehran. But about this appearance of royalty this morning there was something particularly poignant and dramatic. These people and their present-day governors are descendants of African slaves. Few peoples have suffered more, been put upon more, in the past, by their British (and other white) exploiters. How could a long, long tradition and history of royalty have any place here? Those two laughing young boys paddling out there on a crude canoe have as little in common with England as one could imagine—viewed logically. But logic has little to do with it.

§ Queen Elizabeth and Prince Philip were making a tour of the British West Indies.

It was a gay and happy ceremonial: the great ship that houses the Queen, flying highly colored flags that looked like tropical birds; the grey British battleship alongside, lined with the descendants of a great line of sailors, the best; the flower-covered little launch of Young Island, close in, the awkward but gaily decorated tramp inter-island boats, such as the one that brought us and ten of our fellow tourists and the hotel "help" and a six-piece "bamboo melodeon orchestra." Very happy outing for all.

Time—*the* time of day—means very little to the people of this tropical island, I should say. Yet every last one of them wears a wrist watch—the maids with their little blue caps, the boys who wait on us at table, the members of the bamboo band, the men who are building a new cottage—every single one of them!

The other evening John Houser had a minister of this island, name of Tannis, in to dine with us. Bulky, stolid man of about forty, fine deep measured voice, eyes that showed a startling rim of white when he turned his head to speak to someone around our circle. His story is a familiar one to me: "We need industry." Apparently there is no processing plant of any kind on the island of St. Vincent, though they can raise almost anything. Even the sugar cane goes to Jamaica for milling and refining. No cannery. Could I do something about this?

I was glad to meet so intelligent a man, because I wanted to find out what "technical assistance" means to a colonial power (this one of the few places that is still completely a colony, as I understand). After listening to him respond to my questions about why the British were not the people to help remedy St. Vincent's lack of industry, my guess was that an American firm might have hard sledding in these British possessions. Whatever industry or processing there is will be done either in England or, more likely, in one of the islands, such as Jamaica, where British commercial interests find it most profitable.

An all-out period of do-nothing-ism, such as this blessed holiday has been. Vigorous physical activity—swimming like mad several times a day, calisthenics stepped way up. And by contrast: watching a banana leaf open just outside our cottage; passivity to the nth power.

Our first time off this tiny island: an auto trip to the "Mesopotamia Valley," on St. Vincent. Such verdure! Careful use of very steep slopes, the harmonious pattern of banana groves climbing them. Lovingly tended vegetable patches. We stopped at a banana packing station, saw the "grader"—a bright looking fellow, whose life is just one decision after another: as the farmer puts a stem of bananas on the scale the grader looks it over quickly, rejects it because of some bruise or because the stem is too full, or not full enough for the long journey to some English greengrocers, or accepts it, whacks off the ends, and turns to the next one.

On the windward coast the crop is arrowroot, the landscape is not green, and the life of the people (reflected in their houses and their faces) is much tougher, just as hewing the arrowroot out of the slopes is heavy labor compared to the relatively easy life of the banana and truck crop area. For many years this was sugar cane country and the remnants of old sugar mills are scattered through the hills. But no cane now. Where the workers banded together to get better treatment, the British owners simply shut down, pulled out—and left 1200 people without what little income the sugar had provided. The slaves in St. Vincent had been freed with a single decision, but it is a strange kind of freedom for the man without land or a job.

Wherever you go the winds of competition blow, even on a backward little island in the Caribbean. Sugar makes fortunes, so sugar is grown elsewhere and the world price must somehow be met; arrowroot flour commands a good market, until Brazil begins to grow it at lower cost. The bananas of this exuberantly productive island must compete with those of Honduras and Guatemala and the Dominican Republic—even Somaliland. No matter how idyllic and tranquil a tropical setting appears, Nature so responsive that "anything can grow" and a man need only reach out his hand to be fed by her bounty—in some other part of this sea or some other remote region the wind of competition blows and reaches the simple growers, none of whom will probably ever see any other part of the world than their little valley.

FEBRUARY 17, 1966
YOUNG ISLAND

A beautiful wedding last night; the chief man at the bar and his girl. She in a billowing white wedding dress and full veil, he with a white carnation, necktie. And lady attendants in white gloves and hats. The groom, a smiling, happy, slender young man, explained the marriage: They had been living together for two years and she had had two miscarriages; now they wanted to adopt a baby, and to do this it was necessary to get married. A new twist on an old story.

John Houser is an entrepreneur. But of a style I have never encountered before. A huge man, perhaps fifty, great shoulders, an impressively massive head, the very picture of a restless builder. Yet his eyes reflect a poetic, artistic temperament, as does his speech and, most of all, this transformed island, his handiwork. Long talks with him—and his wife, an energetic woman of a Gaelic temperament—stirred up my preoccupation with the entrepreneurial function and personality. For the only way I can think of this function is in the form and substance of the people who perform it.

John Houser, as much as any one man, made the name Hilton an international symbol of the American luxury hotel in distant places.

But after dealing for years with very big and complex undertakings in foreign countries, he began this tiny ten-room hotel in this little uninhabited island offshore of the little-known British island of St. Vincent, risking his own capital, which he says was limited (probably also that of close friends or relatives). Risky because relatively few people have the desire to isolate themselves as much as they are here, with "nothing much to do." Risky because he is a perfectionist who wants the cottages, the plantings, the operations, to conform to an almost storybook picture of a tropical island—and this takes much effort and money.

What was behind that decision only he knows fully. He volunteered some of the reason he moved from the role of a salaried, enterprising executive of the Hilton complex to this personal risk-taking venture, the classic role of the entrepreneur.

"I made up my mind I would never again be a cog—even a big one—in a big business."

He spoke feelingly (though always with a boyish grin, and not a trace of self-pity) of how lost a man can feel when he has been accustomed to a big staff, and then must be his own staff. "The worst thing, strangely enough, was not to have a secretary."

This sudden change from running a big enterprise to being responsible for a small one, but one in which he had a big stake, of course evoked recollections of what I went through sixteen years ago: one day the head man of an enormous establishment, the Atomic Energy Commission, with a large staff, four secretaries, someone to tend to all the details of daily life—then just a little cubicle of my own (the story is told in the third volume of my *Journals*).

"I brought over 500 men, each day, by rowboat from St. Vincent across that bay. All this stonework, all the planting of the hillside (and done with such style and feeling), these cottages, the plumbing and electrical work—men had to be trained to do it, to supervise others. And I had no big staff to turn this over to."

None of this said with any bragging—though bragging would have been in order, I thought. For it is an extraordinary achievement, without a single flaw in taste, not a false note in the composition of such a place for a certain kind of guest he had in mind when he conceived the place.

Can Young Island be made to carry itself? I don't see how any "financial forecast" made in advance could be more than approximate. So it is one of those dreams, spurred in part by a desire to make a profit, but into which other motives enter.

And the motivations are interesting: "fed up" with a big enterprise, the escape to independence not by dominating a big undertaking but by taking a risk in a small one that is "mine own."

FEBRUARY 19, 1966
YOUNG ISLAND

The vacation, or period of non-activity, is about over; we leave early morning day after tomorrow.

I keep reverting to my mental exploration of the life of the enterpriser. The essence of the function itself, and the distinguishing characteristics of the entrepreneur as a man: Is it economic risk-taking? Is it risk-taking that makes such a man different from other men in the economic world; is it risk-taking that provides the conflict, the tension, the fears—the *drive*, in short, that in turn supplies that quality which when we approve of it we call creativity or innovativeness, and when we don't approve, we call greed, brashness, insensitivity?

All of this speculation I have been going through implies that risk-taking is an *economic* phenomenon, that is, a *business* force.

With my perverse habit of trying to find a universal quality common to all human behavior, I have tried to think of the entrepreneurial life as one that describes the thinking and feeling of a public official (of a certain kind) as well. But risk-taking I kept thinking of as a business thing: the man (or company) might lose its economic shirt, the individual enterpriser would see his capital and effort go down the economic drain.

This morning as I walked the beach (watching a Chesapeake schooner, rake-masted, and a yawl triple roller-reefed heading off into a vigorous breeze), I think I saw for the first time the universal quality of risk-taking, that is, I thought of it as a mark of all human behavior.

The argument is a simple one. It may not be true and it may be banal. It goes something like this:

Risk-taking is in reality not the *taking* of a risk but the *balancing* of risks. This is simply another face to the mental process I find myself reverting to in my business more and more, what I describe as the plus and the minus, meaning that almost every decision in my work involves *some* minus, and the decision process determines whether the pluses outweigh the minuses.

But the balancing of risks—the prospect of profit against the chance of no profit or of loss is not an economic or business process alone: this is what hit me on my beach walk. (Surely this is obvious, but it is a new concept to me.)

Make it very personal: I take large risks that are not economic or managerial (and so does nearly everyone else, I would guess). Risk of scornful disapproval and censure, for example, must be weighed against the satisfaction of wants, even the excitement that such risks involve.

The publication of the *Journals* while I am still around is a valid example of non-economic risk-balancing. Even after the deletion of some highly censorious hotheaded remarks about people I am working with, the pages are full of the drawing of a self-portrait that is far from flattering. In Volume III, my eagerness to make money, my looking up to men whose chief quality is a ruthless drive for money and power, the self-serving passages in which I am trying to sustain my ego after the deflationary process of suddenly leaving the center of authority and prestige—all such things involved me in a decision about the balance of risks. On the plus side there is the satisfaction in the idea that my narrative is worth publishing, and that I will (presumably) be around to hear the reaction to it, much of which is bound to be critical and even shocked—at the high-minded public servant in the earthy business of making, if not exactly "a fast buck," certainly a lot of money in a very short time.

No life worth very much is without risk-taking, risk-balancing.

During this two week holiday I have hardly given my company a moment's thought; this is quite a sharp contrast with my vacation periods on the Vineyard, with the almost daily telephoning, the regular mail from the office, work on writing, and so on.

Only one facet of D&R has gone across the surface of my mind. sorting out priorities among the things we do or are striving to do. The lack of concern about the *relative* importance of one piece of work over another has troubled me.

I can understand why this should be the case. Much of the fault is mine. I run things with a light rein, and do so deliberately. I have always found that an organization develops better that way, particularly in the formative period—and D&R is still in that period.

It is to the development of some way of allocating our brain resources that I should devote myself in the coming months.

This will not be easy. The financial return yardstick for such allocation of energies and attention helps, but it falls far short of providing such definite answers or guidelines as one would find in an ordinary business, such as Mineral & Chemicals Corporation, for example. Our D&R objectives are not very closely related to financial return. The monthly statement provides a kind of discipline but doesn't provide a measure; it doesn't provide an affirmative, goal-setting function.

I have an equally pressing problem of personal priorities, of allocating my individual energies. I function best, I have found, when I have (*a*) many things of *different* kinds on my personal agenda of activities, all demanding attention and energy more or less at the same time; and (*b*) when I have more to do than I can possibly do.

Cutting out things doesn't seem to increase my "efficiency"; quite the contrary. A spell of working at half speed induces the beginning of boredom. Boredom is an illness with me, as with so many other people (many of whom don't understand this until it is too late—the premature retirers, for example).

And since no one is sensitive enough about his own capacities and level of effectiveness and of enjoyment to know exactly where overstimulation and too much to do ends and boredom begins, I am inclined to take a chance on "overdoing" and then find a way—such as on this holiday—of slacking off the overtaut line.

FEBRUARY 22, 1966
AT THE OFFICE
NEW YORK

I am looking out upon what surely must be one of the greatest views in the world: New York harbor at twilight, the western sky aglow as the lights begin to punctuate the growing darkness, the lamp of the Statue of Liberty shining against the darkening sky, plodding cargo vessels leaving a smooth path as they head for the Narrows on the still, metallic surface of the water.

As I went through the papers that had accumulated during our two week holiday, one amused me: a check to the county clerk of Tazewell County, Illinois, for $2.00 for a copy of the record of the birth of a child, name not given, on July 8, 1899: the certified copy of this record was to help qualify the sixty-five year old David Eli for Medicare.

A long road, from Morton, Illinois, in the hot summer of 1899, to this office at the tip of Manhattan Island; a long and full roster of years lie between.

I have enjoyed this day quite alone in this office. The city, downtown, is deserted. This is the way and the time New York is very special to me.

FEBRUARY 24, 1966
NEW YORK

For more than a half hour last evening I "sat at the feet" of the human being in whom is centered the greatest measure of physical force —military power—and the brightest beacon of hope in the world. Literally at his feet, for my seat in the front row of the waxworks, on the dais at the Freedom House annual dinner at the Waldorf, was directly below the President of the U.S. as he delivered what I thought was one of the best speeches of his career. And a foot away from me, the smiling, serene Chief Justice [Warren], a man who has changed the course of freedom in the U.S. more than any other man in our history, not excepting Abraham Lincoln.

The most reassuring effect of watching the President, intently and at such close range, as he spoke, was the appearance he gave of superb health and energy. None of the haggardness of the TV picture of him, none of the anxious, almost fearful look he had when he was living a restricted life following his operation. As a speaker before large audiences—the Waldorf ballroom is not unfamiliar to me, God knows—I know how fatigue or the least uneasiness physically shows through under the brilliant light. At one point he struck an affirmative note of passion and pride, in the face of mounting criticism of his Vietnam policies; that was a new Johnson, so far as I can recall. No consensus seeker in that passage.

Public dinners in this city can be wearisome and repetitious: the flowing testimonials sedulously worked up by professional (i.e., paid) testimonial dinner specialists. The glittering dinner audience made up largely of people who are there because they should be seen. The plaques handed to the protesting honoree.

But this Freedom House dinner was an *event*, a "happening" as the current jargon has it.

Outside, several thousand pickets against the Vietnam war; inside, even in the dinner audience, a protester jumped up the moment the President began his speech, yelling "Peace in Vietnam" and displaying a banner across his shirt front. I was watching the President at close range, and though there was a disturbance (the man was grabbed and hustled out), the President showed not the least sign that he heard what was going on, though most of his audience turned around to look back at the commotion. Then, too, the ballroom was sprinkled with Secret Service men, facing the audience, feet wide apart, each looking stonily and with concentration on a particular spot in the tiers of galleries that looked down on the President as he spoke in the bright TV lights.

The men of contemporary history who were on the dais made this an event too. The Chief Justice and the great bulky Negro who argued before his Court in the pioneering civil rights case, Thurgood Marshall, now Solicitor General of the U.S., Arthur Goldberg, our UN Chief Delegate, looking less pleased with himself than in his usual "image," and such a comedown from his predecessor, Adlai Stevenson, in presence and distinction, looking like a white-haired, bright-boy member of a college debating team. Right back of me, sitting next to the Chief Justice, Senator Robert Kennedy. Chewing at a cigar, looking sullen and cynical as Johnson recited all the answers to his critics (of which Senator Kennedy has recently become one), and "I have heard all this hokum a thousand times" written on his face *until* Johnson quoted from the closing lines of President Kennedy's inaugural address, when the look of the tough guy momentarily left the Senator's face. Justice Tom Clark, whom I hadn't seen for years, still bland, his now white hair like frosting on a face that seemed unmarked and unlived in. John Lindsay, a very handsome figure, applauding politely but seeming a bit lost, the grim, strong face of the transit strike period put away—someone else had the burden of troubles that night.

On one side of me, on the dais, was General Matthew Ridgway, one of the ablest professional soldiers we have produced in years. That he has serious doubts about the military theory we are following in Vietnam was plain enough. I remarked to him that there were always risks in applying too broad analogies between this war and the one he led in Korea. His very erect and noble head bent forward, thoughtfully: "No, this is not like Korea." I didn't ask him in what way—too intimate a question for so casual an occasion—but I would like to know. Across the aisle on the dais, General Lucius Clay, who looked definitely unhappy throughout the Vietnam part of the speech. Perhaps he was trying to figure out how the President's troubles in Asia could help Clay in his considerable job of raising money for the Republican Party. I thought Clay looked remarkably fresh and less saturnine—in appearance, not in manner—than on the night in 1949 when he and I jointly received the Freedom House Award, he just back from his great achievement in Berlin.

On my other side was a remarkable and extraordinarily handsome woman, Mrs. Constance Baker Motley, President of the Borough of Manhattan and just nominated as the first black woman to be named a Federal judge. Made me think of some of the beautiful East Indian women I have admired, except for her size: she is tall, almost an Amazon.

At the reception before the dinner I had a chat with Douglas Dillon. He always wears the look of a man who is troubled, though I have never known of his becoming upset or losing that quality of judgment that has seen us all through tight places. He couldn't understand why the liberals were so antagonistic to the President on Vietnam. I reminded him that something of the same thing occurred when President Truman went to the defense of Greece and Turkey. And that Helen Douglas and Claude Pepper and others said much the same kinds of critical things of Acheson then that other liberals say about

Rusk now. Here, too, I thought to myself later, the analogy is a most imperfect one. Greece and Turkey were closer to our national interests and those of our Atlantic allies.

I had my first opportunity to see, at close range, the latest "aid" to the public speaker, the President's elaborate gadget-filled podium. While I've never used the old fashioned Teleprompter, I have seen it used—quite awkward and obvious, giving the impression of something between a ghost-written speech and an impromptu speech to a live audience.

But this version was done with mirrors. Someone pushes a button and three segments of glass rise up, one before the speaker, one on each side, at an angle, and supposedly not visible—but they are. The President looks at these pieces of glass, and, I assume, reflected in them is the unrolling script, in large type. I saw these rolls earlier, in a cartridge inserted by some minion into the machine. Some day before long we can eliminate the speaker entirely. The ghosts will do the writing, the machine itself will speak. And to think that I once laid my text—or notes—flat on the podium and by merely glancing at words I had sweated out in the writing, would speak so that hardly anyone knew I had a text before me. I don't think I'll change this practice, no matter how many gadgets there are.

But the Teleprompter mirrors were only the beginning of this elaborate Presidential podium. Three separate heights for speakers were provided. For Roscoe Drummond,¶ who stands about five feet tall when he wears his shoes, someone pushed another button, letting down a standing place a foot off the floor, and on top of this a box was placed; on this he and later Leo Cherne* stood to deliver their quite eloquent messages. For Douglas Dillon, a tall man, and for the President, also tall, the box was removed and the mechanical platform came to floor level, all worked by buttons. I was fascinated.

FEBRUARY 26, 1966
PRINCETON

Yesterday headed for the 4 o'clock train through the messed up tunnel of a wrecked Penn Station. Stopped at the familiar counter in the cave beneath what is left of the station to buy some roses to take home. A pale careworn man had just bought some; his beat-up campus style hat (like mine) seemed familiar. George Kennan: "My wife is giving a dinner tonight; thought the roses would be appreciated." This

¶ Columnist and Trustee of Freedom House.

* Chairman of International Rescue Committee and Chairman of the Executive Committee, Freedom House.

with a charming little-boy smile. We walked to the train together, through the maze of scaffolding.

George Kennan, long out of the public service, is now very much in the news, a leading voice in the tide of criticism of American action in Vietnam. His views are again being quoted as the basis for a major change in our foreign policy, as it was in the days when he was Chairman of the Department of State's Policy Planning Council, when he wrote his famous article for *Foreign Affairs* on the "containment" of Soviet Russia, under the transparent cover of "Mr. X."

But instead of being elated, or gratified, that his views have had such an extraordinarily wide hearing, in the press and in long TV exposure during his appearance before the Foreign Relations Committee, he was irritated and hurt, and glad of someone to whom to air his sense of injury. This doesn't make him any different from anyone else who feels the rub of criticism more than the satisfaction of having made a dent on history—as I think in this case he definitely has.

Looking straight ahead, glumly, he said: "Cyrus Sulzberger said some pretty nasty things in his [*New York Times*] column this morning." (I had read this: Kennan an "admitted neoisolationist"; flopped in Moscow; irritated the Yugoslav press, etc.—in other words, Sulzberger was hitting at Kennan as a person rather than sticking with a criticism of his seven hours of testimony.)

George turned to me, a hurt look in his eyes: "I didn't *ask* to appear before the Committee; I was invited to express my views. A private citizen surely can't refuse to express such views as he has!"

This shuffle, through the crazy jam in Penn Station, at the side of a great figure in the development of foreign policy and a noted scholar, coming on the heels of the big demonstration *for* the President last night, struck me as one of those quixotic things that can happen in this country, but which I can't imagine anywhere else.

Much occupied in my mind with the book I hope will emerge from the Fairless Lectures, that is, with the Lectures as stimulus and foundation; a book quite different from anything I have done (including the *Journals*, of course) is something I have my heart set on.

What I want to write is something that grows out of my experience in getting things done, that is, in the role of manager. I would like to redefine and describe the manager, the Managerial Way of Life, the role of the manager—which I now think I can establish is currently a decisive role—in the development of contemporary society and the direction of individual life. Taking the place, perhaps, of the theologian or preacher, the political leader in his older sense, the scientist and technocrat.

Few are the men who have great power over the lives of others and can remain unaffected by that fact. Harry Truman was the greatest example I have known. But George Woods, though different in almost every other way, runs him a close second.

This is what I thought as George ushered us into a tiny office he has in the UN Building Thursday late afternoon. "They didn't tell me you were waiting," he began, giving out with that great warm home-town grin and welcoming glint of the eye that marks him off from any banker I have ever known—and most other men who have had their own way for decades.

I know that Woods has food and fibre—agriculture—much on his mind, and I pressed on that. My chief purpose in seeing him, with John Oliver, was to report on our decision to expand our agricultural services by new personnel and the branch office at Davis, California. Woods' job, as head of the World Bank, is to find capital and lend it for capital works—dams, canals, fertilizer plants. But, I tried to say, the weak link in the chain of increased land productivity is where all the things required for those increases converge, i.e., on the farm, on the farmer's land. It is to help strengthen that link that we are committed in our company.

[The next day I wrote Woods a letter in which I summed up this point; I quote from it here:

"Our experience over a generation indicates that provision of practical know-how, supplied to the farmer *on the land* (not just in the agricultural ministries or extension stations), is still the weakest link in accomplishing increasing productivity. It is a weakness we think we can have a share in strengthening.

"After all, enormous sums have been loaned and expended in the past two decades on structures related to land productivity—dams, tubewells, canals, and the like. Comparable amounts of capital are needed, from private and public sources, for fertilizers, pesticides, credit, machinery, and so forth. But past experience doesn't support the thesis that increased productivity will necessarily follow from such capital outlays.

"My personal observation in India as recently as last spring confirms this. Even the habitually oversanguine official Indian view now agrees. Listen to this, for example, in the *Weekly India News* (Embassy of India, Washington) of February 25th:

" '. . . land utilization efficiency (i.e., increased production per hectare) has not improved significantly, *even where irrigation has been provided.* In other words, full advantage of irrigation facilities is not being taken even in areas where such facilities exist.' "]

Woods is a man of gay spirit. But the frustrations and disappointments show through, which proves that he is human and that he cares deeply, despite the banker nonchalance. For example: I had referred to our engagement by the Inter-American Development Bank to help in multinational integration in Latin America (he had heard this—he keeps up with everything, as far as I can see). He said, "Yes; I am much interested in development on a regional basis; always have been. Got five out of seven countries of Central America almost in agreement on a telecommunications system. We at the Bank supervised, for the UN Special Fund, an expensive study for linking these five countries together. Then all but two dropped out; jealous that it would benefit the others more than it would them." At this, he exhaled in the way I know so well, when one recalls all the effort that can go up the stack when people are intractable and selfish. "Oh, it will come, that particular project; nothing else makes sense. But . . . it . . . is . . . discouraging at times."

MARCH 5, 1966
PRINCETON

Splitting a man into three pieces is a common enough task for a good manager. But when the pieces must be deployed in three different places as far as Bogotá, Colombia; Dezful in Iran; and Davis, California, this calls for most unusual resources of managerial innovation—and some luck—to make it work.

This is just what I had to take responsibility for doing, early this week.

Bob Harkens, a bright eyed, intense star, had just returned, full of fire and enthusiasm, from a week or so in Colombia. He recited to me the progress we have been making in developing several food-raising areas for INCORA. One of these lies south of Cartagena and Barranquilla near the Atlantic coast; one, a new one and large, in the Sinu region in northwest Colombia; another in the upper Cauca Valley. Penalosa wants action and relies on us to provide not just "planning" advice or "engineering," but to give drive to the program, "to tell them what to do," says Harkens.

We promised to have a man full time, resident in Colombia, as a kind of deputy or right hand for Penalosa. He finds Harkens and Anderson the kind of men he respects and needs, in contrast to the vaguer advisor types and the host of "specialists" most outfits send out to these countries.

Harkens wanted to be sent to Colombia to take charge, not because he likes the idea of living in Bogotá, but because his heart is in moving these things along, and these occasional trips are not the way to do it.

But the Greater Dez Irrigation also needs Bob, and badly, for that pioneering program has been lagging. We are committed to have him there.

And our new center for agriculture in Davis, California, will succeed or not depending upon Bob, who is the man who came up with the idea of locating there, knows the people, is a product of California farming.

We must quickly determine which comes first, and I decided that it was Colombia, the *future* prospect of results there, plus my long association with Colombia, plus the fact that we had a client there who had the drive that is so rare, plus the delay in providing the resident promised a year ago (no good man could be found)—put all these together and it spelled giving top priority to Colombia.

Send a message to Penalosa: Harkens will be resident there, beginning *at once*, until we can find a suitable replacement. Then make the other places where Bob is needed fit into that decision: forays to Iran at a critical time, the same with Davis; use Anderson as an alter ego for Bob when a piece of him is in Iran or Davis.

I have so often seen men in a management post frozen by just such a "dilemma," as they call it. But dilemmas are what management is made up of, all the time. The scholar can describe dilemmas, but the manager must put an end to them, but quick. This he does by choosing, acting. This ends the "dilemma." Later he may *unmake* it, by still another choice, another decision, and thereby make it necessary to make still another choice. With a good manager, "dilemmas" should not last long.

Inaction or too great *anticipation* of all the possible difficulties arising out of a choice is the chief curse of the mediocre manager.

Peace, in this room, with the flutter of an open fire; and outside fog, after the first spring rain. Peace, we two, years of living together behind us, playing our regular postprandial game of scribbage—a silly child's game of making words out of white dice, each marked with a letter. A silly game, but a peace-inducing one, as if this mattered, this game. But for the moment it *does*, and that is the definition of a good, relaxing game, isn't it? Peace, and the years of somehow, with almost no effort, agreeing about most everything, little and big. Peace, with the memory of our great son's visit last week, but saying little about family things, just taking that all sweetly for granted, as the framework, the foundation of a long life together, where little needs to be spoken or even strongly felt.

MARCH 6, 1966
PRINCETON

Senator Fulbright has now, I believe, reached full stature as a statesman. The Johnson Administration will have to take this man's views and influence into account; he can't be taken into camp by being nasty to him, by flattering him (this is yet to come), or by snubbing his Committee.

Bill has decided that, come what may, he is going to see that the Vietnam war is the legitimate subject of public inquiry and discussion. I say this because of what I have just seen on Channel 7, the *Issues and Answers* program, in which he appeared a few minutes ago. He announced, with a look of grim resolve such as I have never seen on his face before—and I know that face pretty well after all these years—that he is going to conduct hearings on Red China. He referred to the "taboo" that has surrounded any discussion of China. He is going to break that taboo, or the taboo will break him. I think he knows that he has cast down the most chilling of all gauntlets, for a public man: to examine what is going on in China, and our China policy, rather than accepting the long-held idea that they are bad people, and that is that.

He has the McNamara-Rusk position on Vietnam backed into a corner, I thought as I heard him today. Depending on the military views of Generals Ridgway and [James] Gavin, he says *not* that we should withdraw from Vietnam, but that we should make an asset of our staying; an asset in the sense that for us to establish an impregnable defensive military position in Vietnam, but one that does not carry the war to the Viet Cong, will ultimately bring them to a negotiating state of mind, because we will conserve our resources rather than exhaust them in the kind of straight-out military campaign we are now engaged in.

Pulling out—this was an alternative that weakened the opponents of the war; but staying, yet not trying to "win," and doing so with highly respectable military opinion, is painting the President into a corner. Johnson isn't the sort who will gladly be put into that kind of corner, with the pressure against more men and more money and more casualties producing a political hazard of considerable dimensions.

This may be the turning point.

MARCH 7, 1966
NEW YORK

The Flower Show this year was notable for great "settings": whole gardens transforming the Coliseum; a pine tree that must have been seventy-five feet tall as the center of the Sterling Forest exhibit. Orchids, wild flowers (think of transplanting a wild moccasin plant forced into bloom?), rhodos to make your mouth water (including my new acquisition, Scintillation) and a vast rose garden in full bloom.

But the most fascinating thing about the show was not the flowers but the people. Mostly women, middle aged and some definitely "elderly," with that Garden Club look, and *not* a New York City crowd—all the towns for a hundred miles around were represented by their most earnest ladies. There were men, of course, but most of them seemed to be there in tow of determined women, and most of them were taking pictures; the still ruddy and active retired types with photo gadgets dripping from them. Taking up photo-ing as a therapeutic retirement hobby is the impression I got. But what a wonderful country it is when so many people take the raising of flowers so seriously, not to say solemnly.

MARCH 8, 1966
NEW YORK

A panorama of how it is to live in the U.S.A. in the sixties is quite incomplete without illustrations of how utterly changed is the idea of sex. And the public discussion of it. This has been most noticeable in two areas. The first of these is birth control. I've noted this more than once in these *Journals*. The other, less soberly put, is in journalistic statements, "exposé" in tone, about the new outlook on sex among the younger people, particularly those in college.

This morning's *Times* reports another important change: the beginning of a defensive attitude among adults, parents particularly, about tut-tutting over freer sex conduct of the younger generation. A speaker denounced this older-people alarm about the younger ones as hypocrisy—and nothing puts people on the defensive more than an attack on the sincerity of their moralizing.

The next step—perhaps it has already happened—is free and frank discussion of the change in ideas of sex relations among the older generation. That will pretty well complete the cycle.

Victorian England's upper crust was, so we are told, verbally most stern about sex, while in conduct not only "free" but pretty casual. If "appearances" (as Lord David Cecil uses the term) were preserved, men and women of that class could do almost anything, and did. Remove the curtain of appearances—as we seem to be headed for in the sixties—and you do have a kind of revolution not only in views of "sexual conduct" (meaning sexual intercourse, naturally) but in standards of honesty, candor, and sincerity. And *that* would be a landmark.

An invigorating meeting with Robert Goldmann, economic editor of *Vision*, a monthly magazine for Latin America. My reputation in Latin America, I could see, made him self-conscious at first; but he was soon over that, and proved to be an articulate fellow with a sense of humor. I boomed about how short of our pretensions about economic development were our North American capabilities and performance, whereas our rhetoric too often made it appear that if the recipient countries would just act sensibly (our kind of "sense"), things would move quite swiftly toward "development." Nonsense, I said.

The main subject under discussion—with Leo Anderson stating much of the case—centered around whether we should propose to the Peace Corps (on their invitation) an arrangement for providing them with an agricultural or rural living program, something toward which they are reaching, because the need is so great. I was puzzled about why the AID organization wasn't doing this. Ervin Peterson explained this by saying that AID was organized on the basis of projects, where the services of sophisticated experts, such as to be found in the extension services, were useful. The Peace Corps, however, would direct its total help—by practical demonstration—toward individual primitive farmers. Here, he thought, was the place to begin in the underdeveloped countries; and of course this is precisely our philosophy, which he stated as well as I have heard it, in human as well as agricultural terms.

Leo came in to see me in the late afternoon. He would like to see the new center of agricultural development at Davis given a name that would tell what it is about. Would I object if it were called—as he thought it should be—the Lilienthal Center for Agricultural and Human Development? I didn't hesitate in saying that wouldn't do, much as I appreciated that thought. I wanted this enterprise to have continuity; since I wouldn't be around indefinitely, I thought it would be a mistake (and, I thought to myself, bad taste) to name it after me. I know that this is the mode, naming power stations and research centers for living people (Sarnoff Research Center, etc.), but I thought it unwise. And embarrassing, frankly.

MARCH 9, 1966
NEW YORK

As I got out of the Lexington Avenue subway at Bowling Green my eye was caught by a cascade of brown, glistening hair, shoulder length, pointed shoes, a heavy cordovan. A male. This sounds like what the solemn reviewer of my *Journals* would call trivia. But, this isn't trivia, it is the rolling wave among the young to show that they are *different*.

I mentioned this to Beatrice: I asked her to take a walk along Madison Avenue, to a number of galleries. "As an observer of the U.S. in the middle sixties," she said, "*don't dismiss* the way these beats behave just because, like myself, you find them sometimes annoying and worse. Something is happening in the subterranean streams of American life, and this kind of effort to call attention to youth is *not* dismissible.

"So with the draft card burning—absurd and illogical. I don't agree *at all*. But if one is trying to make a record of what it is like in the mid-sixties, these are things that should be included in a description, a catalogue, of how it is. And the same thing with those rectangles of nothing but white we saw at that gallery, nothing but a rectangle of white in a frame. Art! No more art than the piles of junk we saw in another gallery. But these things can't be overlooked or dismissed if it is the future you are interested in—and you always have been trying to look ten or twenty years ahead."

MARCH 11, 1966
AT THE WASHINGTON AIRPORT

The big, bulging, jovial Captain of the Guard at the West Gate of the White House asked, "And have you some identification?" Then, looking at a bank card I showed him: "Why, Mr. Lilienthal, I hardly knew you with a hat on; go right in. Well, well, after all these years, Mr. Lilienthal."

The lounge looked like nothing I had seen before in what used to be a serene, almost bare room, with the huge Philippine round table (whatever happened to it, I wonder?) and the furniture: green pseudo leather, like the lounge in the Elks Club in some small Midwestern town.

Doug Cater† looked fresh and relaxed for a fellow about to fly to Saigon in the morning—and looking forward to it—for an eight day work session.

He asked what I could provide the President "in the way of talking points" when Mrs. Gandhi arrived for an official visit. I talked a lot—too much—about the gap between fertilizer and water, *and the farmer*.

Thinking about it on this noisy airplane, these thoughts occur to me:

1. India needs a new and different agency to get emergency food production going. Mrs. Gandhi, in her inaugural, said she was ready to introduce new managerial techniques; let's call her on that.

2. AID isn't up to this job. So let's match her new emergency instrument with something outside AID, concentrating on one thing and one thing only: aid and instruction to the farmer on the land.

† A special assistant to President Johnson.

Joe Volpe had a visit the other day with John Steelman, once Truman's Assistant at the White House, who asked, "Do you ever see Dave Lilienthal? Well, when you do, you tell him I said hello, and tell him this story, don't think he ever heard it. Fellow came in to see the President, complaining about Dave, what a terrible fellow he was—you'd know his name if I told you. Then later Dave saw the President and when he went out the door of his office, the President called me in and said: 'There goes the best public servant in this government; after listening to that other s.o.b. and his stuff about Dave, I think even more of him. And don't let that other s.o.b. through that door again.' "

MARCH 13, 1966
PRINCETON

The meeting at Barnard yesterday morning—a panel on economic development—sponsored by the "Reform Democrats" and Congressman Bill Fitts Ryan, was fun for me—and I showed it I guess.

I had expected to develop a debate of sorts with Bob Nathan [a leading economist] by the provocative things I said about planning; but he turned them aside by agreeing. So the point about the emptiness of that kind of planning was lost.

Why am I so belligerent, aching for a fight? Is it tilting at windmills? I asked Helen this morning. She thought it was the crusader impulse. Don Quixote was dealing with fantasies, I with real issues and real fights.

At the Barnard meeting I urged the need for completely new tools of management in the AID program, ironically quoting a statement by Madame Gandhi, who will have mighty little luck in her own country giving substance to her recent statement.

I read Madame Gandhi's statement (I got it from a letter of Doug Ensminger's, the Ford Foundation man in India). "In economic development," she said in her Republic Day speech, "there is a disconcerting gap between intention and action. To bridge this gap we should boldly adopt whatever far-reaching changes in administration may be found necessary. We must introduce new organizational patterns and modern tools and techniques of management and administration. We should instill into governmental machinery greater efficiency and a sense of urgency. . . ."

A good platform for India, surely; but what about the U.S.?

In response to a question from the floor at Barnard about increased food production, I gave my philosophy about "starting from where we are" with primitive farmers, rather than giving them the sophisticated methods from our U.S. land grant colleges that AID usually finances. This is the theme of our discussions with the Peace Corps, who want to begin that kind of an agricultural program.

If we don't begin where we are, *now*, when the dark cloud of hunger threatens so many millions of people, if our present agencies continue their present course, then said I, "the Peace Corps will do it"—which brought applause from the audience, and a glower from the young stand-in for Lincoln Gordon, the new Assistant Secretary for Latin American affairs.

I hope that remark about the Peace Corps gets back to Washington. It may antagonize AID. We may, as a result, never get another contract from them. If the agonies of delay we have been through with *past* contracts is a measure of the future, we'd be better off if we never did business with them again. Leave that to those who do nothing but prepare reports and have none of my impatience for results. D&R will manage somehow.

But antagonizing the sources of your business isn't orthodox practice, and perhaps I'm going at the problem of changing things in the wrong way.

10 P.M.

Archie MacLeish, brown from the sun of Antigua, looking smaller than I remembered him, walked to the podium in 10 McCosh and held a packed house in the hollow of his hand for an hour and more. What a magnificent head. As he looked upward, the softness of his light voice belying the intensity within, I knew this was more than an ordinary poet: *he* has wrestled with God as did the Job of his play *J.B.*, the subject of his lecture.

I had hoped Archie would apply the theme of *J.B.* to the current cry of this wonderful young generation: that they find no *meaning* to life. The meaning of life is the truth about life; and the truth, so Yeats and MacLeish, and Job too, advise, is not for our eyes, any more than justice is our right. If we love life and live it fully and exuberantly, taking what life gives and in spite of sorrows and defeats go on loving it, then we live the truth, and that is as near to knowing the "meaning" as is vouchsafed man.

I think this is what Job says to a generation who are frustrated because they see no meaning. Search they should, but find ultimate meaning they will not.

MARCH 14, 1966
8 P.M.
NEW YORK

My day of work began twelve hours ago, riding in a car with Bill Marvel, heading for New York, and a meeting of EWA [Education and World Affairs]. The object: "spreading the educational process internationally."

Watching a master of chairmanship functioning through several hours, one sees what the physicists call elegance when they speak of a splendid solution of a difficult problem or a superb experimental proof of an abstraction. And elegant is what Ed Mason's [of Harvard] performance was today, as Chairman of the EWA committee on policies; elegance in the sense of symmetry and "collected" movement (a horseman's term).

Though it required close thinking, it was definitely pleasurable for me. One by one, we went through questions, with the Chairman always prodding but never pressuring, shaping and summarizing as we went along, but never deciding for the rest. Mason, big hulk of a man, with a huge Gibraltar of a head, and torso to match, is an extraordinarily wise man.

The hours from 11 to 3 went swiftly and not solemnly. Doug Knight, President of Duke, was witty and at times gay, with a light in his eyes that tells of the native capacity behind that slight figure and relative youth. Herman Wells spoke of being in Cairo two days ago, and of other long trips, all with relish. His pride in one of his "boys," Congressman John Brademas of South Bend, who will pilot the President's international education bill through the House, exhibited that same quiet, unexpressed satisfaction that—well, that I feel about David's achievements.

This is 1966 in the banking "business" too: in the spacious ground floor of the Manhattan Savings Bank across the street, a woman playing a grand piano! Part of the "feel that you are at home in our bank" thing. But from the Grecian-pillared bank Hank Loring's father ran, on the square in Valparaiso [Indiana] ("the Bank that *looks* like a bank" was their tag line, meaning it looks forbidding and austere and will look after your nickels) to the "you have a *friend* at Chase Manhattan," to the all-glass front of the bank on 43rd Street, well, the grand piano playing at midday was a logical extension. Discotheque girls in cages, as on 8th Avenue, are next.

I think I'll keep my money in a corner of the mattress.

MARCH 19, 1966
10 A.M.
PRINCETON

Felipe Herrera and his attractive wife were our guests here just before dinner last evening. He was to speak to the Latin American Affairs conference sponsored by Whig-Clio of Princeton.

Rarely have I known a public servant with so many of the talents of an economic statesman—and such a statesman is what the times demand, particularly in the southern part of our hemisphere. He has such warmth, always interested in whomever he is talking with. When he talks to an audience, as he did for an hour and a half to an almost full house in 10 McCosh last night, his natural eloquence and conviction, and artistry with words, in a language other than the one he was brought up in, give one the feeling: here is the very picture of a democratic leader, who knows what he is talking about, wants action, yet can speak in the words of vision, humor, and vividness.

I am about to take off to participate in a panel of economic integration as part of this morning's conference.

8:30 P.M.

Five minutes before the panel was to begin, the apple-cheeked student "in charge" of the Latin American conference came up to me in the grand foyer of the Woodrow Wilson School: "I'm embarrassed to ask you, but I forgot that we have no moderator for this panel: will you act as chairman and moderator?"

I did, and I enjoyed looking up into the amphitheatre of young and intense faces—plus a few men of earlier vintage—and leading the other panel members, articulate and impressive fellows, through two hours of lively discussion.

Someone asked the speaker, Herrera, if it wasn't true that the wealthy landlords would take the wealth that was produced in South America and, instead of putting it back into the land, send it to Swiss banks; and that they and their sons lived lavishly? "Some did," said Felipe. "Even in the U.S. there are 'playboys.' But mostly the young men are interested in technical and managerial careers and work hard, as they do here. There was a time when the chief interest was in being lawyers and poets; the shift has been rapid and noticeable."

I remarked that listening to the vision and eloquence of Herrera, a banker, I was reminded of the saying that it would be a happy day when philosophers were kings and kings philosophers; to this it should be added that it is a happy day when a banker is also a poet. There is hardly a Latin who isn't underneath the skin (sometimes a pretty tough one) a poet.

At dinner time I answered the phone; a voice said: "This is John; John Rockefeller. Do you have a minute?"

Purpose of his call: the population cause needs new ideas badly. Would I join a group he is calling together April 15th? He feels I could stimulate such new ideas "though I realize it isn't quite in your line, as an operator in international matters; but your article in the *New York Times Magazine* was so good, and your concern about food fits into a new initiative about population." I said I would, and was pleased that my name was in his mind.

But mostly I was touched, and strengthened in my basic faith—in the goodness and, indeed, the purity of human beings—that a man who could so well rest on his oars should be spending time phoning people, phoning me of all people, of a Saturday evening about an issue so impersonal as the rising tide of population, an issue impersonal to his own concerns, but desperately personal to his sense of responsibility and humaneness.

MARCH 21, 1966
NEW YORK

Sitting across a luncheon table from Jim Geraghty, you would never guess the role he has played in American life. For this soft-spoken, physically slight man with the inquisitive face has created a new style of contemporary satire in the cartoon-plus-gaglines he has approved, stimulated, *or* turned down for the pages of *The New Yorker*. By comic style I emphasize *style*: a new manner of seeing ourselves, kidding our foibles. This is not really satire or ridicule; he is no graphic Swift nor Voltaire nor Mark Twain. The humor is not the uproarish kind, on the whole. "Comic" here takes on a different meaning, but in the classic sense it comes as close as any word to describe what he has created.

MARCH 22, 1966
NEW YORK

A glorious Colombia day! Early this morning an exciting visit with Enrique Penalosa, one of the truly great public servants of Latin America by any measure. He brought word of the success of Carlos Lleras' party in the Congressional election Sunday. This means that the father of land reform and of INCORA will certainly be President of the Republic by next fall, and a new, dynamic chapter in Colombian history, Enrique is confident, will then begin—indeed it has already begun, now that any uncertainty about the new regime is settled.

I sent a handwritten message to Lleras, and agreed to Enrique's eager invitation to visit Colombia in late April or early May. It will be a great day, that, for I have left my mark on Colombia, strange as it seems to me, and a new cycle can now begin.

The Atlantico #3 project—south of Cartagena and Barranquilla—will be put before the World Bank tomorrow. Thirty-five thousand hectares, a big undertaking and a demonstration of a modern way of developing land and food and people. I am very happy about all this, even without drinking some of the three bottles of aquavit Enrique brought as a gift.

During luncheon Penalosa described the complete change that has come over the Colombian Army in devising a method of dealing with the twenty-year-old "bandit violence" problem. Sounds like the frontiersmen's military answer to the British in the colonial wars: no uniforms, no large groups, and little equipment, such as tanks, which present day soldiers love so. The soldiers fight the bandits as if they themselves were bandits, and apparently it is working.

Maybe our military men ought to get "technical assistance" from Colombia.

The most remarkable item, I thought, was that the Army is helping people with their crops, their schools, their roads, their marketing. Perhaps our Vietnam efforts will one day catch up to those of our poor benighted Latin neighbors!

MARCH 24, 1966
NEW YORK

A call from Red Wagner [Chairman of TVA]. He has told John Macy at the White House that he wants John Oliver to be appointed to succeed Arnold Jones on the TVA Board. "You can tell John Macy," I said, "that the President couldn't do better than John Oliver."

Wagner was candid in saying that Frank Smith, a former Mississippi Congressman, has brought a strong political tinge to the TVA, strongly recommending some of his kin, and confusing the staff that has been brought up—I began it—to regard employment by TVA as something directors would not seek to influence. Director Jones has been a kind of negative and restraining force, while Smith has shown little talent for releasing the energies of a staff, a talent not too common anyway.

Red said that when President Kennedy had called him in to tell him he was being made Chairman he said, "Dave Lilienthal recommended you."

MARCH 25, 1966
PRINCETON

After my talk with Wagner about what he felt strongly was the grave importance of the right kind of appointment to the TVA Board, I talked to John Oliver this morning. John wants the appointment, would feel happier in the Tennessee Valley and in that kind of work, and if it is offered, would accept. I reminded him that D&R, thanks largely to his work, is now in the best condition it has ever been, so he would be leaving a successful enterprise; and also that if TVA really is in danger, certainly his loyalty to TVA far outweighs the admittedly tough time I will have for a while reorganizing the company because of his leaving.

MARCH 26, 1966
PRINCETON

Wednesday night I was Barney Tobey's guest, at his home, for his meeting of "the junto," a group of male friends of varied occupation (mostly businessmen) who have been meeting together for conversation for a good many years.

A most interesting discourse by a stocky, dynamic fellow, a Hungarian, Tom Forbath. He came to this country to study just before World War II and he is already a Vice President of American Cyanamid. He told of a four-day "school" he attended, along with five other top industrial executives, conducted by IBM. The purpose: to impart to these executives a better understanding of the theory and potential usefulness of computer programming.

We talked about the danger of atomic wastes—a bait to get me talking, I guessed, which I did, but with no particular enthusiasm. Then Forbath, a chemical engineer, said: "I don't think those dangers are as great as those of hunger, of vast shortages of food." It took no urging to get me going on this, my long-time preoccupation.

I grow more stimulated to do something really useful in this area the more I think about it. Dictated a letter to President Johnson on our thesis—"on-the-land assistance"—for his possible use in connection with Madame Gandhi's visit next week.

A few excerpts from my letter to the President:

"The purpose of this note is to convey to you my thought about the strengthening of the weakest link in the Indian effort to increase food production, obviously (next to peace) its gravest problem.

"The strengthening of food production is not a long-term and complex set of new technical means, though of course that too India needs.

But her food crisis needs alleviation next season, as well as in the next decade. I suggest that the most practical step is a selective but massive measure of assistance to the cultivators, or peasants, on the land where they are trying to feed their families, by the simplest methods of teaching, that is, to 'show how,' designed to increase productivity at the level of primitive agriculture on which most of the people of India depend, and do it now.

"India is a country in which a great deal of discussion, on a highly abstract plane, about agriculture (and other matters) goes on in the central and state ministries, but no one increases wheat or rice production sitting around tables in a ministry or in a planning commission. This takes place out on the land, if it takes place at all."

MARCH 29, 1966
WASHINGTON, D.C.

When it was my turn, last night, to be greeted by the President in the long line passing him and his guest, the dark-haired lady who is Prime Minister of India, he started right in: "Dave, that was a great memo." Turning to Madame Gandhi at his right, who smiled her recognition and warmth, he went on, leaning over her: "We were talking about you and what you said in that letter this afternoon."

Mrs. Johnson, in a glittering gown, said, "I like it when you write memos, because they excite the President so that I get to read them too."

As Helen and I came into the splendors of the East Room, I had gotten advance warning that this casual letter about so important a subject had not only reached the President (which was the most I had hoped for) but had stirred him. Bouncy Jack Valenti said the President "had it Xeroxed and sent all over the place; *must* reading, he said."

Then Secretary [of Agriculture Orville] Freeman pursued me into the corner of the Red Room: "Your idea made a big hit with the President; that's his kind of thinking. But you and I are about the only ones in this Government, beside the President, who go along with it." Then he went off on a criticism of AID ("they can't recruit the right kind of agricultural people"—true enough, God knows). And *then* out came the chief concern of a governmental bureau—*his* bureau. "Of course sending 1000 Americans out there right away—that's what the President is thinking—well, that might work, but the whole thing has to be kept in the Department of Agriculture."

I never felt more sure that staying out of government is the most effective place for me now. If I can come up with ideas that stir them up—or stir the public—but save myself the frustrating, consuming business of composing and calming the bureaucratic and jurisdictional vanities of this huge central government, I'll be serving both my country and myself better than being tossed back into that maelstrom.

Lyndon Johnson runs a White House formal state dinner the same way he runs the Government and his ranch: by being himself, the most informal and earthy of men. After the Kennedys, this is quite a change. As eager and constantly excited and charged as President Kennedy was, he never let anyone forget, so far as *my* observation goes, that he was head of state, successor to Great Figures, and the most powerful man in the world—hardly a man, an institution.

But Johnson is a human being all the time. Perhaps too human, too informal, for some tastes, though not for mine.

That hollering at me, across the Prime Minister of India: "Where y' stayin?" for example. And after most people were settled in their seats in the East Room, following the state dinner, to listen to Isaac Stern [the great violinist], the President of the U.S. stood up in front, peering through his glasses at the audience, and seeing some of the young people of the staff, and the Marine captains, standing, said, "They's some seats down here in front for you folks," and wouldn't take his seat until he was satisfied that the party was comfortably organized, stirring around in the front row as if he were taking care of his personal guests in his own home. And this is as genuine as can be.

And when he dances with the pretty young girls—he certainly has an eye for the tall, slender ones, which explains some of the bounce with which he attacks his fearsome job—he dances close, and vigorously, grinning and having a wonderful time—though by this time it was after midnight and his day probably began at 6 A.M.

Of course I don't really expect to be called in by the President to consult about my notion of a grass roots program for Indian agriculture. But the blowtorch has certainly been put to the men in government posts. They aren't too happy about this, some wish I would go away and get lost. The Washington habit is to hope that the President (this one, or any one) won't start anything new, leaving the "details" of getting something done to them. They are all so pressed, partly with speaking and TV-ing and partying, and partly fighting their jurisdictional battles.

4 P.M.
ABOARD "THE SHUTTLE," RETURNING TO NEW YORK

The affair last evening was full of little episodes that pleased me.

For one thing, Helen, I thought, had a good time. Her elbow neighbors at table were easy to visit with—more than one can always say about these affairs. Dr. J. George Harrar, head of the Rockefeller Foundation, and Robert Spivack, a diminutive, almost bird-like man with a great laugh. Helen looked quite regal, in her long pale blue gown with the wide golden belt.

The guests must have spent an hour mingling in the East Room before the ceremonial appearance of the loose-limbed President with the tiny dark head of state on his arm. So I saw and talked to many people.

At one point, I spotted Senator Bourke Hickenlooper [my "enemy" in AEC days] and without a moment's reluctance started off to greet him. He shook my hand, gave me a warm and friendly smile, and began an animated conversation, repeating every now and then how glad he was to see me. My emotions may have corresponded somewhat to his own, and accounted partly for all this cordiality: we were demonstrating the highest form of the politician's art, that however violently one "takes out" after an adversary, he doesn't permit himself a personal hate. Something like the old circuit riding lawyer's tradition, that he fight with bitter caustic words in court; then at the inn, drink the other fellow's health, as a mark of a civilized fighter.

Hick and I had certainly exchanged some nasty cracks about each other, and the score was about even.

The President paid court to Madame Gandhi, treating her, as Queen Victoria said Disraeli treated her, "like a woman," instead of the way Gladstone spoke to her, as a public meeting. Only the tip of Mrs. Gandhi's head was visible as Johnson leaned toward her, beside and a bit behind her, intently following her every word and intonation. I recall how his mind seemed to be far away when other heads of state have spoken, but last night he acted the part of the entranced listener. I say "acted" because he does play a different role all the time: the more or less avuncular way of kissing most of the ladies on the cheek, in a resounding way, when they come through the reception line, or after dancing with them. Indeed, I nominate him as our first kissing President. "On him it looks good." But imagine Coolidge or Wilson or Kennedy doing this.

At the dinner a pleasant visit with Bill Fulbright, who looks relaxed and well pleased with himself. "Witnesses today," he said, looking disgustedly into his highball, "really terrible. But some of them have been good. Ah've learned a lot about China, that's sure. I get hell about these hearings on Vietnam and China, but that can't be helped." He's having a wonderful time; after having held himself in about the dominance of the military in foreign policy matters for so long, it does him good to get it out into the open, before the world.

The columnists keep saying that because of Bill's questioning attitude about Vietnam the President has cut him off the visiting list at the White House. That would be mighty narrow; and not only is it not true, but I watched the President present him to Madame Gandhi, with the arm on his shoulder, the bending over him, the little pat that he couldn't do if he really had marked him off his personal list. And how stupid that would be, too.

Later, I heard Bill Fulbright's voice—an extraordinarily resonant voice it is, too—right behind me: "David, I would like to have you meet Isaac Stern." I turned around, looked at Bill, but saw nothing. Then, way down there, a hand, attached to one of the briefest men I have seen in a long time.

I have been playing this great artist's recordings for so long and with such rapture that I had a clear idea of how he *must* look. But not so: very short, square, rotund. A delightful, gentle, completely unarty personality, and so articulate, in a modest way, about things other than music. Later he played a series of great virtuoso selections, for the "command performance," played them with such a passion and intensity as could hardly be borne. When he finished each of these I found myself saying, "Ah," as if I had to relieve the tension this remarkable man and his fiddle created in that historic room.

I saw so many people I haven't seen in a long time: Stu Symington, he and his wife quite proud that their handsome son is now Chief of Protocol; Dean Rusk, looking well, walking around between tables, cultivating people in a manner I had never seen from him before—and a good thing, too. I chatted with him a few moments; he continues to have that almost bashful modesty and wryness that sets him off so distinctly from Dean Acheson. Acheson, whatever his self-doubts, always looked dignified and outwardly self-assured. He was too intelligent to be that sure, but he maintained that essential of a public servant, an outward demeanor of knowing just what he was doing—and in his case, knowing that his critics were "fuzzy" or mystics or generally incomprehensible.

At dinner sat next to Kay Graham. Remarkably frank woman, showing more than a little of her redoubtable mother's [Agnes Meyer] strength. A remarkable personality: to stand up to her powerful mother, and not be "spoiled" by her wise and successful father [Eugene]—*everything* he touched succeeded, though just why no one quite knew, he seemed so simple and gentle from the outside.

Kay *runs* the *Washington Post*, though she had had no experience in the newspaper business. She runs *Newsweek*—comes to New York at least once a week for that purpose. Both enterprises have prospered and become more and more influential.

Said Kay: "People come in to look at the female who runs a newspaper, a magazine, like looking at animals in the zoo. And the flunkying attention you get—how do you avoid having that ruin you? The only person around this Washington who hasn't been affected in that way is Bob McNamara. He told me he had to wait fifty minutes for the 7 o'clock shuttle from New York. I said, 'But, Bob, that's awful; we pay you to put your energies to work for us, you have no right to scatter them that way, with all those military planes around.' 'No,' he said, 'I tell the others they are not to use those planes when they aren't needed, when commercial planes are available, and that goes for me too.' "

We talked about what happens to people who have everything done for them in their "brief hour" of great power and she repeated what Tom Finletter said to her: " 'Kay, you have no idea how it was when I left.' What was it he left, Secretary of the Air Force?—'To have to pick up your own phone and say hello; not to have cars wherever you are.' "

"That is the kind of disconnection with reality McNamara is protecting himself from," I said.

This noon Aldewereld and three of his World Bank associates met with me at his office. A follow-up on my earlier talk about East Pakistan. Apparently my letter, analyzing the Bank's position and the report—the so-called Master Plan produced by the International Engineering Co.—had impressed him favorably. In the meantime he went to Dacca and found out how the Pakistanis feel.

They don't have any faith in the Master Plan, and agree with the Bank—and with my quick reaction—about it. So what next? This is what he wanted to sound me out about.

"We of the Bank had our differences with you about the Dez in Iran," he said, looking a bit sheepish, if so owlish a man can also look sheepish. (This was because we showed the fallacies of a Bank staff conclusion that the Dez Dam was inferior to small thermal plants.) "But everything about the agricultural work you have done out there in Iran is absolutely superior, the best thing of that kind we know of in the world."

Would we "without commitment" consider being active in the technical assistance to farmers of East Pakistan?

There will soon be a hundred million people in this one province! How will they be fed? The proposed development to answer this question, as well as to provide power and flood protection, is a ten to twenty-five year undertaking, costing at least $2 billion, one of the biggest food production undertakings in the world.

I quail at the idea of taking on such a responsibility, and overloading our little company with anything so huge and difficult. Besides, the Bengalis are known to be even more sensitive (if that is possible) than the Indians themselves, the kind of people who know "in their hearts" that they need help and need to change their methods, but must be handled with gloves.

If we are forced to decide—by having a proposal made to us, this time, instead of the other way around, as is usual—what will I say?

Tonight I am so tired I hesitate. I wonder, when so much more and better food can be raised elsewhere, why so much effort and money should be put into that most difficult place. Then a hundred million faces crowd my imagination and my "logic" takes a back-seat.

Lunched with Walter Lippmann at the Metropolitan. He doesn't look well at all; his eyes bloodshot and peering, rather protuberant, his color pasty. What he said about Latin America—that was what he wanted to "get your opinion" about—seemed to me only the rehashing of oft repeated fears ("Is there *time*; can something be done to improve conditions for the very poor before they revolt?") and a vague notion about opening up of new land.

APRIL 2, 1966
PRINCETON

Just as I reached the Council on Foreign Relations building on 68th Street Thursday, about 4 P.M., a sweet-faced young nun cried out, most excitedly, to three youngsters with her: "Here she comes, here she comes." The police car moved up, the door of a big black car opened, and a smiling woman stepped out, Indira Gandhi, and all of us, security guards and the lot, moved into the building. The most important woman in the world, yet how unostentatiously we do these things in this country!

I said to Madame Gandhi, "It just happened that this morning I was looking through a stack of photographs taken at the Prime Minister's House almost exactly fifteen years ago—in February, 1951—when my wife and I were your guests. One I found particularly moving: it was a picture of you in a field of wheat, with the great 'Residence,' mansion actually, immediately back of you, and a bearer in gay dress holding a basket of flowers."

She said: "Yes, I remember that that year we had a drought and we planted wheat in the garden area."

It was quite a lovely picture of a slender, graceful young woman, almost a girl; I used it in the Volume III pictures. But it made me realize with a kind of pang, too, what that lissome young woman had been through in these past fifteen years. Now she is no longer her father's daughter and constant companion, but the head of state of a nation of more than 450 million people.

Helen reminded me of a conversation she had with Mrs. Gandhi when we were guests in the Prime Minister's Residence. Helen's notes for February 22, 1951, simply say: "Mrs. Gandhi said to me it was difficult to be here, away from her own home and her husband a good deal of the time, but that her father had told her that he needed her and that she must stay with him."

Helen told me she remembers what a look of sadness and restrained emotion Mrs. Gandhi had when she said this. She not only gave up much of her personal life for her country in order to sustain her father, she set herself on a course that has given her the greatest active political experience of any woman, not excluding Queen Victoria, and this experience is only now in mid-stream.

It wasn't only the amber apple juice—in wine glasses—instead of martinis, that made the luncheon at Bishop Prince Taylor's "different" this noon.

The Bishop is a Mississippi black man, with what one *used* to call a "field hand" voice, and his wife, a Georgia Negro, has such a voice, too. To know that these two had moved from nameless cotton crossroads to an air-conditioned house in Princeton, *without being changed* in any essential, I thought was wonderful beyond words, made me proud of my country, and of the Methodist Church.

And to make the story even more curious, Bishop Taylor had a strong African flavor, unusual in a Southern Negro. He had been Methodist Bishop of Liberia, and his house was filled with mementos of African carving, jewels, a huge solid ivory ceremonial cane, with silver ornaments; his wife wore a great ivory and gold chain given her by the President of Liberia; their house servant was a handsome young Liberian, here to go through high school, then to return to help in agriculture in his country.

Still another Bishop and his wife, the Gerald Kennedys of Los Angeles, and the huge figure of the President of the Presbyterian Theological Seminary here, Dr. James McCord, and his slender wife. All told, this gave the luncheon a feeling, once familiar to me (though not recently), of being with preachers on their day off, and knowing that this will produce good yarns, just slightly derisive of preachers, not just to show that the tellers of these tales are good sports, but because being professional speakers, they *do* have good stories, and the sense of humor to go with it.

At times I get furious about a certain characteristic of contemporary American life. It is this: That concepts, ideas, premises that no longer have any real validity continue to be the basis of the thinking of accepted "leaders" (the Establishment) in diplomacy, in business, in the academic hierarchy, in religion, in notions about sex. The generals, we say with some superiority, are always fighting the last war. The same is even truer in other fields. Though the voice may be that of established reputation and authority, the *reality* is to be found in the voices from the generation just coming on.

This has, perhaps, been often true in history; but now it is outrageously true because change is coming along faster than the old sticks-in-the-mud and their outmoded ideas can be supplanted by the ideas that may make some sense in a new world.

APRIL 3, 1966
PRINCETON

Helen's 70th birthday. It is fifty years almost to the day that we had our first date at DePauw University—forced on us by a senior couple who thought each of us ought to go out more.

Helen is very well; I felt the urge to thank *someone* for all this good fortune, so suggested we go to the University Chapel service this morning.

APRIL 5, 1966
NEW YORK

I have a profoundly excited group around me these days. Bob Harkens dashed after me as I was leaving yesterday—wanted to see me about CVC. Seymour setting up a meeting to bring me up to date on their Inter-American Development Bank activities, before he and their "force" take off for several weeks in South America. The Peace Corps contract for Nigeria finished, the one on India to be ready in a few days, and good reports about all this coming in. I sense more spunk and *initiative* about the place (Anderson going off to Nairobi, Kenya, Ivory Coast, Iran, with no prodding, almost the contrary). Burnett with a new look in his eye. When I have men in and I tick off items I want to cover, the discussion is like musketry, one, two, three, and the meeting is over. This atmosphere speaks well for the satisfaction I get out of carrying my load in D&R.

A happy day when one can quite literally feel that people to whom you are responsible (and vice versa) are excited and creative about their work—and what a unique kind of work it is, like navigating waters never before crossed, where one must prepare his own charts and even invent his own compass.

Somehow we will turn up new men, one of whom can, given time, begin to shape up as my successor, or rather, the man who will carry D&R ahead when I'm not around. That time may be far off, or near, but the sense of mortality doesn't half depress me, as it did when I didn't feel the zest—or the responsibility—as much as I now do.

APRIL 8, 1966
NEW YORK

A long and evocative talk with Seymour: he and his boys are turning up ideas and even facts that have never occurred to others, that brighten the prospect for a giant utilization of the *great reserve of energy in the coal of the West.* Here public and private interest come close to coinciding, or being *made* to coincide, a goal of mine since TVA days.

The D&R engineering group has become a part of this task. When I dropped in on O'Brien, heading the engineering group, his face lighted up as I haven't seen it before, with excitement and deep interest.

Someday I feel the first *huge* electric plant in the Western mountains will be built, and these D&R men will have done the thinking that made it happen. That plant will send vast amounts of power westward to the coast, and eastward toward Minneapolis, too.

This concept I have been nurturing now for five or six years is one I believe is as great in sweep and consequences as Horace Greeley's equally "visionary" crusade for a railroad across the Rockies to the West Coast.

APRIL 10, 1966
PRINCETON

A hearty self-discovery that has marked recent years has worked a kind of miracle. I do get tired; "putting out," furiously, as I do, and with so many different things to do, naturally I get tired. Bored at times? God, yes. But remember, my boy, what you have learned, must have learned, after a long life: boredom is an "inside job." It is within you.

Enjoyment of life is within you, or it doesn't exist. What goes on outside you, if you haven't the capacity to enjoy, can turn anything to the ashes of boredom.

APRIL 12, 1966
NEW YORK

A turning point in the D&R story: I have just come from an hour of relaxed talk with André Meyer which confirms to the hilt the basic estimate I have of the man, his underlying character and motivations as a human being.

He told me that D&R has done such an outstanding job "as a public service" that if I want Lazard to reduce its ownership, or eliminate it by a redemption of shares, he is entirely ready to do this, "and it will not in any way change the warm friendship that exists toward you or our relations in any way."

If *I* had made an issue of the fact that Lazard gets one third of the earnings of a company whose earnings are the sole result of the efforts of its officers and employees, he might have been hurt or defensive. But by waiting it out, and having *him* suggest this as evidence of his faith in what we are doing, and in me personally, all such rancor is avoided.

He knows damn well he could sit tight, as an owner, and continue to take one third of the earnings, as well as the "glory" of a company which, as he says, "is doing very well and getting better all the time. In fact, if it were *not* doing well, if it were in trouble, if its prospects of growing and developing were not good, I wouldn't dream of changing things, of taking out the shares we have in; you know that." When I said: "You are really one of the most remarkable guys I have ever known, and as far from the conventional picture of a Wall Street banker as possible," all he said was, "I want to be fair. You decide what you, David, want to do and you can write the ticket."

This discussion came after I had reported to him the evidences of progress we are making. Then he said, "What you are doing is a service to the country, and indeed to the world. Maybe if a Wall Street banking house isn't getting some of the profits it would make a better picture for you. And as you know, making a profit out of your work has never been in my thoughts about D&R.

"When you began I was glad to try to help. As it turned out, you didn't really need help from a banker, but I was ready to give it then, and continue to. But now the company is well established; you don't need us; there's little we can do for you now. And you should be free, David, to handle the company in the way you want. It is a well run operation, and the people who are running it should have the benefits."

APRIL 14, 1966
NEW YORK

Jack Franklin came in this morning with a set of figures ("numbers" as the current jargon has it) that spells out concretely how the goal of making D&R a key-staff owned enterprise can be worked out. His basic assumption is that Lazard and Utah voluntarily reduce stock ownership from one third each, as now, to 5% each. This would make available some 6500 shares for purchase by people like Burnett, Anderson, and so on. I would retain the largest block, but I would expect the other key-staff members (if they wished) could in time together own as much as 40%.

APRIL 16, 1966
PRINCETON

"Oh, my dear Johnny, that's life."

The indulgently smiling, handsome George Woods, in the dark walnut-panelled recess of a room at the University Club, spoke to the intense, impatient John D. Rockefeller III.

John, head of the Population Council, presiding over a small meeting he had called to discuss "the next steps" on the international front to do something further about the "population crisis," had spoken almost in tortured tones about how, more and more, Prime Ministers and Health Ministers of some countries (Turkey had been discussed, and also India) "agreed, yes, they agree now that things need to be done, agree even on a program—but *action*, there they fall down, or act slowly."

John Rockefeller is the kind of public spirited very rich man that hardly exists at all in most other countries. There are many of his kind —few as rich or intense, true—in the U.S. Even the *idea*, the concept of private philanthropy represented by the Rockefeller name, is a rarity in Latin America and Asia.

I made one point that didn't set well, at first, with the experts *or* with John. It was simply this: that there was a strong tendency to consider population control as a technical matter, of contraceptives and their distribution and use. Actually, it is part of a broader issue, of people, where they are, where they are going, and how to motivate them toward improvement in their way of life. You must not see the future of life in Asia, for example, or Latin America, as residing in the uterus of females, or the "cure" in some kind of pill or "loop," however much needed and however ingenious.

Migration to the cities, for example, I suggested, is as much a part of the population problem as excess fertility.

APRIL 17, 1966
PRINCETON

"As I look back on what we did—twenty years ago now—I don't feel ashamed of it." Robert Oppenheimer, standing on the hillside of Olden Lane on the first day of spring—*such* a day of the magic of renewal—thus described his feeling about our Report on International Control of Atomic Energy. He continued, flapping his arms in an almost derisive way, "Proliferate, proliferate . . ." referring, of course, to what I regard as rather superficial talk directed to avoiding the spread of atomic weapons.

The report I had from Joe Volpe and others was a somber one:

Robert had developed a cancer of the troat, had been operated on, was receiving cobalt irradiation treatments. But his voice was stronger than usual, for he has always had a disappearing voice—and he seemed vigorous and almost gay.

APRIL 20, 1966
NEW YORK

A visit early this morning with Ervin Peterson, just back from completing the contractual arrangements for one of the most far-out responsibilities we have undertaken—the Peace Corps contracts for India and Nigeria.

Peterson has H. A. Morgan's sense of the dignity and importance of dealing with the land—the mystique of the earth as the beginning of all strength—with a modern understanding of the place of agriculture in the development process, which embraces industry and social and political progress as well. I am constantly looking for men like Peterson and Harkens and Anderson, who combine that understanding and feeling which working with the land gives men with an understanding of the way agriculture fits into the *whole picture* of modern development and modern living.

D&R will have responsibility in India to 1100 volunteers, scattered through the country, with nine to fifteen resident D&R employees and half a dozen offices; in Nigeria perhaps half that number. But the timing in terms of the acute awareness of the importance of increasing the world's food supply could hardly be better.

There seems to have been a turning of the tide in Persia, too. A letter about the new Dez agricultural program has a new tone. Ahmad Ahmadi, deputy in charge, writes that we may have a chance to carry forward the most important part of our task—the development of a world-famous demonstration of combining the work of training peasants with sophisticated and modern technical and management methods on the land.

Here is what Ahmadi said:

"The Dez Pilot Irrigation Project was to prove to the farmers and to the different organizations that by application of modern agricultural methods the farmers could improve their crop yields and consequently obtain higher income from their lands. *Fortunately with the assistance of the D&R we have been very successful in this program.* As a result of the experience gained in the Dez Pilot Irrigation Project (DPIP) we should establish a much more extensive type of agricultural extension in the Greater Dez Project. We hope to be able to establish this program with the assistance of your Anderson during his stay in Iran."

APRIL 23, 1966
PRINCETON

Led by a soft-spoken, warmly serious young woman, I was "presented" the day before yesterday to twenty-five or so Peace Corps staff members in Washington. It came over me—as I read the enthusiasm, the liveliness, the amateur spirit, as I used to say, in these faces—that this is the way TVA was in the early days.

After chatting with them—they included staff members concerned with both India and Nigeria—I went in to see the new Director, Jack Vaughn, whereupon we signed the India and Nigeria contracts between the Peace Corps and D&R, and a new chapter for both begins.

APRIL 24, 1966
PRINCETON

Wherever I have gone overseas in the underdeveloped countries, I would find contingents of American university technical people, sent there by the universities by grace of contracts with AID. And so often they seemed to us no more university people than I am, but recruited by the university to fulfill a contract with AID the university thought had advantages to them. There were of course some very able people, including faculty members, out to do as good a job as they could.

At a meeting of the EWA Board I warned about such strays—in Lagos and Ibadan, for example—who had no qualifications I could see for advising on agricultural matters in West Africa, enjoying the prestige of a university whose campus they had hardly walked upon, whose faculty they were never a member of.

Well, all of this has become a lively topic these past few days. Ironically, it tends to sully the good name (or sense) of a man I admire enormously, John Hannah of Michigan State. As part of their practice of contracting with AID on many subjects—chiefly agricultural —Michigan State also agreed to train men in civil police methods, for Vietnam, some years ago. A member of such a team told a story to a magazine, *Ramparts*, including a statement that five of the men in the Michigan State group were also CIA agents.

But this "scandal" has served a useful purpose, from my point of view. Dramatic and unfair as most of this charge may turn out to be—the CIA tag makes it news—it has raised in an unmistakable way the issue of whether universities are, in fact, the best way to staff foreign technical assistance enterprises.

APRIL 28, 1966
AT WASHINGTON AIRPORT, WAITING TO TAKE OFF FOR NEWARK

The morning session at the World Bank—Aldewereld, his deputy Hugh Ripman, the Egyptian Abdel El Emary (in charge of projects in Africa for the World Bank), Seymour, and Tom Mead were the group.

Before we all met, Aldewereld asked to see me privately, and once again talked about the East Pakistan picture. He spoke of two subjects. One concerned trying to find a basis of agreement between India and Pakistan about what is done on the two enormous rivers (together, probably the greatest in the world), the Ganges and the Brahmaputra, both of which originate in India (and Tibet), so that what is done on the lower reaches, in Pakistan, will depend upon agreement about the sources. Said he, "It's the Indus Basin all over again, where your great idea made a treaty possible."

The second thing he had in mind was to try to get agricultural results out of a project in Pakistan where a dam has long since been built but nothing by way of productivity has come out of it, to the disgust of the Paks, who say the "experts" from FAO et al. are "bums" (Aldewereld's word, perhaps theirs). "The Paks' Finance Minister was here the other day; he says the experts are no good, and they can do better themselves without this expensive help. But how can they?"

I share the skepticism of the Pak officials.

As I now feel about it, I hope we will never be asked to do this; a terrible place, East Pakistan, but one that wrings one's heart.

I have long since become accustomed to being "blamed" by the World Bank people for having "gotten us into" the Indus Basin negotiation, which was long and trying—but successful. Aldewereld's attitude today was quite different: grateful and admiring. "Except for two or three days when shots were fired (and war appeared imminent), the agreement between India and Pakistan was carried out without any interruption during their recent war. The canals even served a good purpose as tank traps!"

I spoke of Ghana, the purpose of our request to see Aldewereld. "I have always had serious reservations about the Volta River scheme," he said. "The engineering and construction are good, but the only economic justification would be very low cost power for a large load; Kaiser said they would build an aluminum plant if the rates were low enough. But the rates the people of Ghana have to pay are *twenty times* as great as the aluminum rate, and the people of the country won't accept or understand that, not for long."

APRIL 29, 1966
PRINCETON

Some excited comments to me by Aldewereld yesterday make a dire, strange postscript to the banking-dominated era of international economic development.

I can't get the sad, even foreboding, implications of this out of my mind.

"George Woods has asked me to go to Europe—West Germany, Sweden, France, and so on—leaving this afternoon," Aldewereld said. "I'll be making twenty speeches in twenty-two days, all on the same themes. One is the challenge of the growing gap between the affluent one third of the world and the two thirds that are in the poor and underdeveloped condition. This is a familiar theme.

"But the other may seem dull [it certainly isn't to me and it wasn't to him, though it does involve figures]. The fact is that the debt service, the interest, and the principal payments on development loans we made during these past twenty years of the World Bank are more than many, perhaps most, of the countries we have made the loans to can carry; their foreign exchange will almost entirely be required to repay and service these loans. This means that we simply made a major misjudgment—a mistake—when we assumed that conventional banking terms and conditions could be applied to such countries—India, Pakistan, countries in Africa. That's why we have opted for interest-free loans on a fifty year basis—'soft' loans in the future.

"But the problem of the drying up of resources for underdeveloped country investment because of the drain of their debts to us isn't the whole story. It is worse than that. I have written two speeches, the ones I will give on this trip."

Aldewereld's reference to the World Bank's *mistake* has stirred and amazed me. But he still doesn't fully get the point, though the growing emphasis on development versus lending since George Woods took over shows that he probably begins to see it. The *kind* of loans are *on the basis of projects*—they stick to that—which are "economically sound." But unless programs are financed that will generate economic health throughout a country rather than just in the *project* on which the loan is made, the whole house of cards becomes shaky and may tumble.

APRIL 30, 1966
EN ROUTE TO BOGOTÁ VIA AVIANCA

In a few hours Helen and I will be in a different world. Colombia, tomorrow, is having a national election. The bullet-headed, scholarly—

but tough—Lleras Restrepo is certain to be elected; the only question is how big a vote that incredible Rojas Pinilla, his opponent, will get and how much disorder there will be.

MAY 1, 1966
HOTEL TEQUENDAMA
BOGOTÁ, COLOMBIA

The view from this corner window on this May Day Sunday tells once more the kind of country Colombia is. The capital city, new skyscrapers on every hand, interlacing roadways through the Plaza before me, this fancy hotel.

Yet in a vacant lot less than a hundred yards away, a scrawny horse alternately grazing on the grass of the lot and biting an itch; a family set up to cook food which they are selling to the passersby; two women fanning the charcoal, the kids of the family being the salesmen. And now settling themselves on a piece of grass in the littered open space, a Sunday-dressed group having the lunch they bought from this impromptu restaurant.

A great ganglia of highway opposite this hotel, with people walking up and down, and hardly a car, walking in the middle of the street as they did in the little towns that are the mark of this country.

This being election day in Colombia, patrols of horsemen go by, two abreast, eight in a troop; helmeted soldiers, their guns at the ready, moving through the throngs; covered trucks decorated in wild red banners, with men leaning out, shouting and handing out pieces of paper.

It is May Day as well, so there will probably be a labor parade, perhaps a "demonstration" of students. No one expects violence or anything like a coup; but in 1948 no one did either, when General George Marshall was here and a bloody civil war broke out that lasted a long time and cost many lives.

One visual difference I note in Bogotá since I first came here in 1954: The crowd no longer seems to be on its way to a funeral, everyone dressed in black. Instead, a great deal of color, red ruanas, explosive pink dresses; there goes a bright green lady; children in gay colors. This must mean something. In any case, it makes for a happier scene, and somehow the faces seem less lugubrious, too. Not a scientific conclusion certainly, but I daresay as good an index as some of the statistics I have been reading this morning, or the gloomy forebodings of Lauchlin Currie of two years ago about the mounting debt and the inevitable disaster this would bring.

Lilienthal with former President Harry Truman.

Secretary McNamara, President Johnson, Dr. Walt Rostow, John McNaughton, and Lilienthal on "Air Force One" en route to the conference on Guam.

Lady Bird Johnson.

Clark M. Clifford in the Cabinet Room at the White House Conference on Policy in Vietnam.

Lilienthal reports to President Johnson and the Cabinet. Seated at the table facing the President are *(left to right)* Postmaster General Lawrence O'Brien; UN Ambassador Arthur Goldberg; Lilienthal; Secretary of Defense Robert McNamara; Secretary of Agriculture Orville Freeman.

Lilienthal and Secretary of Defense McNamara.

(Left to right) Dr. Carlos Lleras Restrepo, President of Colombia; Mrs. and Mr. Lilienthal; and U.S. Ambassador to Colombia Covey T. Oliver.

ilienthal and Averell Harriman at Iickam Field, returning from the onference on Guam.

J. Robert Oppenheimer. *(Ulli Steltzer)*

ilienthal and Peace Corps Director Jack Vaughn signing the contract for D&R raining of agricultural workers for India.

The wedding picture of Lilienthal's parents, September, 1897, Peoria, Illinois.

Johanna Lilienthal, Lilienthal's pa grandmother.

David E. Lilienthal, Jr. (pen name, David Ely).

Lilienthal's granddaugh Margaret Lilienthal.

Lilienthal on his horse, Mac.

Helen and David Lilienthal on the Vineyard. *(Alfred Eisenstaedt)*

Lilienthal and his brother, Ted.

The Lilienthals and Mr. and Mrs. John Oliver in Cuzco, Peru.

Visiting a pumping station of the Cauca Valley Corporation (CVC) in Colombia. *(Right to left)* Lillian Cordoba de Holguin; Helen Lilienthal; Elvira Garces de Hannaford; Lilienthal; Bernardo Garces Cordoba; Enrique Penalosa.

Examining new plantings in the Cauca Valley, Colombia.

The Shah of Iran.

Mehdi Samii, Governor of the Central Bank of Iran.

Lilienthal and Abol Hassan Ebtehaj, former head of the Plan Organization of Iran.

Villagers in Desht-i-Mishan, Iran, waiting their turn to see the D&R physician, Dr. F. G. L. Gremliza.

School children in front of a new school in the Dez Irrigation District, boys and girls together.

Market in the interior of the Ivory Coast.

Rice farmers in the Ivory Coast.

D&R resources inventory and tax improvement project in Nicaragua.

Lilienthal visiting a Montagnard village in the Central Highlands of South Vietnam.

Felipe Herrera, President of the Inter-American Development Bank.

Roger Baldwin and Helen Lilienthal.

Canal in the Delta of the Mekong River, Vietnam.

Ierman B. Wells, Chancellor of Indiana University and Chair-
ıan, Education and World Affairs.

ranklin A. Thomas, Executive Director of
ıe Bedford-Stuyvesant Restoration Corpo-
ation. *(Roy Stevens)*

General Edward S. Greenbaum and his wife, Dorothea, the sculptor.

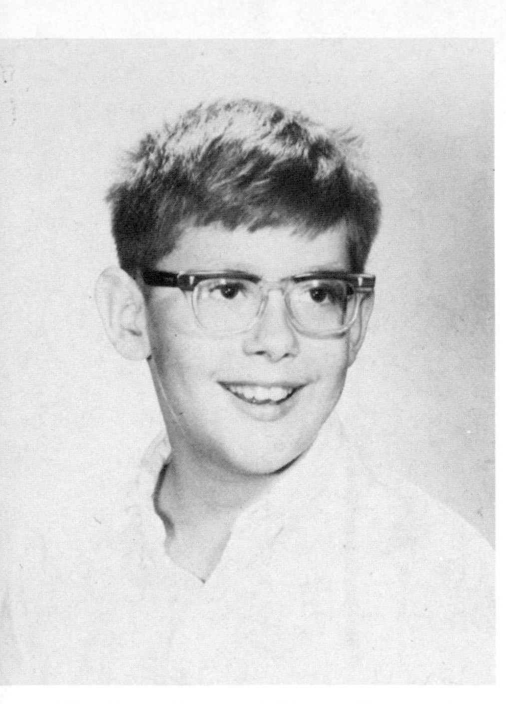

Allen Bromberger, Lilienthal's grandson.

Lilienthal and his fiancée, Helen Lamb, as college students.

Helen and David Lilienthal.

10 P.M.

The Sunday carnival is over, and so is the election. The streets are as empty as Main Street in Valparaiso [Indiana] would have been at 10 o'clock, in my boyhood, and those were the emptiest streets I can remember in my whole life.

Luncheon and much good conversation—not just talk—this noon at Enrique Penalosa's home. A most attractive house, with garden patios inside the house, and the outside garden, enclosed by a wall facing upon their bedroom, blazing bright through a great "picture" window.

One of the guests, Armando Samper, is a weathered looking man of perhaps forty-five, heavy glasses, a solemn expression, completely dedicated to the development of agricultural research and education on an inter-American basis. The headquarters for his work, strangely enough, is in Costa Rica. Also present was Ulysses Grant, head of the Rockefeller Foundation work in Colombia, who looks like a boxer (middleweight) who has recently retired: square jaw and head, square shoulders. And despite this appearance, one of the ablest, advanced technical men in agriculture in the Latin countries.

MAY 3, 1966
HOTEL DEL CARIBE
CARTAGENA, COLOMBIA

A great luminous pale yellow globe hanging suspended over the darkening sea, a fresh breeze, lights rimming the lagoon-like waters on the side away from the sea: a remarkable sight after a long day (beginning at 6 A.M.) of bump bumping over rocky roads, looking at parched land till my eyes near bugged out of my head—and hearing an exciting, fiercely intense story of how Enrique has set out to transform a great pie-shaped segment of the Atlantic province.

This morning we flew for nearly three hours in the Piper Aztec Enrique had chartered, going from Barranquilla almost to the Venezuelan border, then flying the length of the Cesar Valley, a half million hectare area now hardly able to raise one puny crop a year, but which he—and I hope D&R—will begin to study, looking toward a full-scale development in a half dozen years.

MAY 5, 1966
HOTEL NUTIBARA
MEDELLÍN, COLOMBIA

Last night we had dinner with one of the two chief industrialists of Colombia, Rodrigo Uribe. A nervy, cocky, tense man, quite short, a high narrow forehead, thick glasses, a movie kind of go-getter, the old-fashioned entrepreneur *except* that this one went to MIT (engineering). None of the "charm" that so many of the best Colombians have when they deal with strangers; rather a *driver* of the American school. In short, an Antioquian.

Not all of this trip was worth the time and effort; but there is no other way for me to get a feel for what we are doing, and a look into the future. I find ideas coming to me about *where* things are going when I *see* at first hand how they *were* and *are*. For example, some thoughts about the need to emphasize the *future* of Colombia's sprouting *cities*—or urban regions as they should be called, I suppose—come to me as I traipse around, covered with dust and soaked in sweat (it's been *hot* and humid).

On this trip there were long, long days, and very early departures. There were great changes of climate from the hot, humid, blistering temperatures of Barranquilla and Cartagena to the cool of Bogotá and of Medellín. There was constant flying, not infrequently at treetop level, with much circling over points we wanted to see, particularly the swamp areas in the Sinu Valley, where people are living a 14th century life. There were hours of driving on dusty, rocky, jarring roads in jeeps and cars designed before springs and shock absorbers were invented; walking over fields, looking at Sinu calves on an experimental farm; and talk, talk, talk about the transformation process Penalosa is driving through—we helping him with our action-oriented "experts" rather than just advice. Quite an intense trip this has been since we left Bogotá.

The way Helen took the undoubted rigors of this trip was a revelation to everyone who saw her. Not a surprise to me, for she is a good traveler, a fearless one (that was a mighty small plane to be flying in the fog and clouds of the Colombian mountains), uncomplaining and always interested in everything. So many people spoke to me about her, and particularly Enrique and Mrs. Penalosa, in the warmest terms of admiration and affection.

MAY 6, 1966
AT THE HOME OF ALEJANDRO GARCES
CALI, COLOMBIA

An early swim in an emerald pool, after a long night's sleep in a comfortable bed: I feel completely refreshed and ready for anything, after one of the most peripatetic and strenuous weeks in years and years.

Here in the quiet of the patio of Alejandro's house, how does this trip add up?

First, I feel a greater sense of hope and vitality and confidence than I have felt in Colombia for some years. I attribute this to the election of a strong and intelligent man, Carlos Lleras, last Sunday, by a wide margin. I am to talk with him tomorrow afternoon.

Not a New Deal so much as a New Dawn, an awakening to a hard and difficult but hopeful day.

Most impressive of all is the INCORA program, which has made an extraordinary beginning, from the projects in the flat, humid Atlantic coast, through the central plains to this southern valley.

The "land reform"—actually land development more than land *reform* in the conventional sense—is the emanation of two men: Carlos Lleras, who fathered the idea and pushed through the legislation, and Enrique Penalosa, who for four years has matched Colombian inertia and opposition with his own relentless energy and determination.

What appeals to me as much as anything about INCORA's programs—only a few of which I have seen this week—is that (1) they are geared for *action*, and (2) they deal with a *basic* and fundamental fact: that Colombia's future depends upon what she does, pronto, about her *land*. Increased productivity of the land will play a decisive part in meeting some of her most urgent as well as long-range difficulties—which include political instability—which really means a choice between a happier or a bitter people in the rural areas; more food; and products for export (pineapple, palm oil, beef); and improvement in Colombia's foreign exchange balance and therefore her ability to import the raw materials and machinery needed to keep her industries going and satisfy the demands of her people for things from abroad, some of them "luxuries" of the kind they insist upon.

MAY 8, 1966
BOGOTÁ

This intense and grossly peripatetic week covered almost the whole of Colombia. I wonder if anyone else has ever seen as much of this country, as closely and with such knowledgeable guidance and explicit motivation. As is so often the case in these travels-with-a-purpose, it is the array of people I encounter that makes the strongest impression on me.

10:30 A.M.
IN FLIGHT TO NEW YORK

The "array" of people includes men previously well known to me: Enrique Penalosa; Bernardo Garces; Virgilio Barco, former Minister of Agriculture; Manuel Carvajal (in some ways the most distinctive Colombian I have ever known).

Carlos Lleras Restrepo is the individual who stands out the most sharply in my mind. It is upon his slight shoulders (physically speaking) that the immediate future of Colombia—perhaps even Latin America—rests.

For a full hour yesterday afternoon I sat in his study, in a quiet street in Bogotá, while a young armed military policeman paced back and forth on the terrace right outside the window, protecting the man who a week ago was a "private" citizen (literally but not actually) and now is the man upon whom the hopes and future of twenty million Colombians depend.

The study itself gives a picture of the man, but definitely only a part of a picture. It is an oblong little room at the front of the small house. (The living room is still stacked with huge floral set pieces, congratulatory greetings, like a chapel the day after a big shot's funeral.) Three sides of the room filled to the ceiling with books in glass enclosed bookshelves. The books are mostly in English, many on economics and public finance; Albert Waterston's book on Planning was there. That he is a great reader, indeed a scholarly, academic "type," is the impression you would carry away not only because of the books, but even more because of the manner of the man himself.

I had visited him two years ago, but I had not remembered how short he is, barely to my shoulder. His voice is very soft, low, without great emphasis. A paunch is more or less hidden behind a voluminous blue double breasted jacket. You might be talking to a retired professor of philosophy, or even that familiar figure in Latin America, a "creative" writer or poet.

But his *knowing,* shrewd, twinkling—literally twinkling—eyes tell you right off that he is no withdrawn man.

I had been told of his relentless campaign, carried on at a time when violence was feared, going tirelessly to all parts of the country. But not with the oratorical flourishes of General Rojas Pinilla or the conventional and usual Latin political leader (Belaunde of Peru, for example).

He asked me, of course, my "impressions" about the things I had seen on this trip. I said the most intensely interesting of all, the most significant, was "Atlantico #3"—and went on to say why. This was an effort—with great prospects of success—of *combining* the goal of productivity with that of justice for the individual farmer, previously landless. Intensive agriculture using modern techniques can be made to produce remarkable agricultural results; but unless the individual farmer feels he has a stake in that function, justice is defeated, motivation dissipated, and resentment and disorder inevitable.

The road to productivity is justice—I used the term Latin Americans prefer, by which I would mean dealing with the people on the land as human beings rather than cogs in an agricultural machine, paid wages but having no rights of *ownership* in a particular piece of land. To combine these two has never been completely successfully accomplished. I put forward the view that Atlantico was well on the way—we thought—to achieving this pioneering goal, and if it did it would become one of the most famous undertakings in Latin America, perhaps in the entire agricultural, non-industrial world.

"It is something that cannot be explained by ordinary logic," I said, "that it is fair dealing and concern for the poor and struggling individual on the land that may be—I think it is—the key to productivity. God must have had a hand in fashioning this extraordinary 'contradiction'—as the conventional economist or industrialist would call it."

MAY 9, 1966
NEW YORK

Saturday afternoon Bob Harkens, Tom Day (our new Resident Representative in Colombia), and I met at the American Residence in Bogotá, the result of a request from the American Ambassador and his Acting AID Director, Francis Fisher.

I asked Bob to describe the facts about Atlantico #3. He did a superb job, overwhelming the group with his knowledge of the details without which these things are not really illuminating—conditions of soil, limitations about water, peculiar requirements of different kinds of crops, etc. He made the point about how this project reversed the usual—and unhappy—sequence in new agricultural projects. The usual sequence is that the civil engineers lay out a set of structures, diversion dams, sluices, canals, laterals, etc., and *then* walk away, saying to the agricultural experts and to the farmers, "Good luck, pal."

In this project, first our agricultural people established a cropping pattern applicable to each unit of this fairly large area, that is, what crops could be raised on a particular kind of soil with certain water availability, and what kind it was desirable to raise in terms of the need for crops for export, at a point close to good transportation for export, to wit, the city of Barranquilla nearby. *After* this and other agricultural and financial considerations had been worked out for each of these subunits, and a plan of organization for agricultural technical assistance developed with INCORA, then, *and only then*, were the engineers told to design a series of works, drainage canals, etc., to serve the agricultural production purposes set out in this way.

The Ambassador asked, "Where is there any prospect of leadership among the campesinos? Doesn't your whole project depend upon farmer leadership?"

Bob agreed, of course, that leadership was an essential ingredient.

But leadership is not something that you find as a precondition of going ahead with a program whose very *purpose* is to create leadership. You have to believe that the leadership will emerge when the circumstances of an opportunity to improve their lot become apparent to the farmers. This quality of leadership and initiative develops *out* of a job, rather than being something you "discover."

The President-elect came to dinner; he had a long and absorbing stand-up talk with Helen, who short as she is, towered over him like an Amazon. She said he talked eagerly in his soft voice about his plans for the future of Colombia and his great confidence in what could be done, and made some very generous remarks about her husband and his ideas.

MAY 10, 1966
NEW YORK

Whatever happened to that oath I swore after I left the AEC: "I will never again so live that an organization runs me"? How remote that seems right now. Not only runs me—dictates what I worry about, how I spend my time—but puts me into those ragging, rasping tests of strength and vanity of position between strong-willed people, which is surely the most trying part of an executive's life.

What occasions this comment, right after a happy, successful voyage to Colombia?

I got to the office early yesterday morning—perhaps 7:30—to find Leo Anderson, recently back from Iran, wanting to see me. Eyes puffed like toy balloons, tense as a rubber band. Had "a personal message for you and you alone" from Ansari, who had the previous day seen the Shah. Ansari was full of enthusiasm. The Shah wants the Khuzistan completely developed by the end of the new Plan period. Wants the World Bank to do a massive job of financing it. To persuade George Woods to do this is what Ansari asks if "Dave" will do.

But what about a contract for the Greater Dez?

Said Anderson, about getting a contract: if we got rid of all that nonsense about having administrative people around, and the personnel and accounting people who were just standing in the way of anything useful, he, Anderson, would get contract terms straightened out. And the lawyers, bah.

I appealed to Anderson on a personal basis, speaking of the great impact of a historic achievement, most of the credit for which belongs to him. Anderson agreed reluctantly to work with Burnett, provided Burnett understood that program matters were not his function; and Anderson recognized that legal and overall corporate policies were for Burnett.

This is part of the life of a manager: not just to order people, or flatter them, or unruffle their feathers, or soothe their hurt feelings; rather it is to so *define* a job that men find it possible and desirable to work together, calling upon their professional pride and craftsmanship, so they put the important *job to be done* ahead of other considerations. But the defining must be skillfully done, frankly stated, and firmly held to.

MAY 11, 1966
PRINCETON

Two great and colorful experiences today.

Early, a spot of molten gold darting in my rose garden: a female Baltimore oriole. And soon afterward, on a low branch, the gaudy black and orange of the male. Never have I been so close to these glorious birds; I was transfixed.

And then, at 11 A.M., before the dazzlingly white columns of the new Woodrow Wilson School, the orange cavalcade of Princeton Faculty marching two by two to a "special convocation" to dedicate the new building, with the President of the U.S. the speaker—and recipient of an honorary degree. (Goheen's recitation of *Latin*, to this Texas farm boy, seemed odd.)

The President was tanned and vigorous looking, his speech a great appeal for the dignity and importance of the public service. True, it was one of those compounds that emerge from speech writing teams representing several departments. There were a good many pickets outside with their "Stop the War in Vietnam" placards, but no incidents. One finally gets used to seeing state police on the roofs and in the windows overlooking the scene; and then considering how absurd all this is, in a way, when you *know* that Lyndon Johnson, afterward, is going to plunge into the middle of a crowd and shake hands on all sides, with no real protection.

It was a majestic ceremony in a country lacking much by way of pageantry.

MAY 14, 1966
PRINCETON

Spent most of the day sitting in my study at my kidney shaped desk or in the upstairs sitting room, fighting my way toward some manner of stating what I believe, what I have learned, what I think others should believe and know. I feel a desperate need to find out what it is in my thirty-five years of experience in getting things done that has worth and substance.

Anyone who enjoys developing ideas—enjoys even the distress that they *refuse* to come neatly and tidily—is a lucky man. *Thinking* is a pleasure, too.

A pleasure and a kind of torment. Justice Holmes had something to say about "original work": "No one can cut new paths in company. He does that alone." This was in Holmes' Commencement Speech at Brown, in 1897.

The following unorganized notes I include in this journal as part of the "sweating it out" process. These are the points I would like to make in the Fairless Lectures (not stated in any particular sequence):

THE MANAGERIAL WAY OF LIFE—
THE LIFE OF ACTION

I. The managerial function, the responsibility for getting things done, is undergoing a massive change. It is about this change that these lectures will deal.

II. What are these changes?

1. A dimly recognized awareness that abstractions, slogans, rhetoric, manifestos, will not give people the things they want; that what is needed is not more abstractionists, methodologists, theoreticians, scientists—but managers.
2. The management function is broadening, no longer a matter of a narrow skill but the broadest kind of understanding, a unifying force.
3. A recognition, still dimly seen, that the gap between the skills, the intuitions, and the responsibilities in the management of public and of private affairs, as previously known, is steadily narrowing. This will have profound effect on the roles both of government and of business.
4. A growing recognition that what people want and what they will get depend more upon the *ability* to get things done, i.e., upon a recognition of the decisive role of the managerial function.
5. The decisive function in the immediate future is that of the manager—using the term in the broadest sense.
6. Our concept of the managerial life is changing, will continue to change, as perhaps the most important single change in public thinking for the remaining third of this century. And the most important part of that change is that those who are entrusted with the powers of technology and science must, to succeed as managers, weigh the *consequences* of technology and science; to advance science without taking into account its consequences will no longer be acceptable.

7. The concept of the public manager as a kind of policeman, a guardian, will be replaced by an affirmative, creative, innovative function.
8. The intellectual excitement and satisfactions that lie in the life of the do-er will become more and more recognized.

III. A list of things that need *doing*—that people are demanding.

Has there ever been a time when there was greater eruption of demands, recognition of needs, the world over?

Most evident in two thirds of the world outside North America: Latin America, Asia, Africa.

1. This ferment of *wants* is a *fact*—the world over. But a heartening fact: the disheartening thing is when people have no interest, don't care. Examples of these wants:
2. More food
3. Land ownership
4. Jobs
5. Improved health
6. Population limitation

Not only in underdeveloped countries; in U.S. as well. Pollution of rivers, of air.

IV. *Goals* have been described by the poets, the revolutionists, the intellectuals.

The need now is not for goals, but a new dimension of do-ers, a new respect for the do-er function.

V. The intellectual satisfactions and demands of the managerial life as it is emerging.

It is the life of what *could be made to happen.*

VI. Examples—illustrations of needs for the do-er—out of my own observation.

1. The waters of America.
   "Policy" described by Theo. Roosevelt, M. L. Cooke.
   An example—TVA.
   But *action* crucial.
2. The land of South America.
   Atlantico Project as illustration—combining technology and justice, combining technology and motivation.
3. The Cities of America: The Great Rebuilding.
   Growing madly.
   Pittsburgh rebuilt.
   But takes more than reports.

VII. New perspective on life of action.

1. Those who *say*, who use words, have acquired an influence out of proportion to their function.
2. Sense of inferiority by those who *do.*

They, the do-ers, need to recognize it is they who change the setting of men's lives, and thereby their way of thinking and acting—not the wordy ones.

Have been scared off by cracks about "bathtub civilization."

The organizers of new diets, by freezing, canning, have had more influence than the intellectuals who describe the change, *after the fact*; the organizers of air transport have changed the intellectual life of mankind, its outlook; yet it is the wordsmiths with their books and phrases and their air of superiority who acquire a standing, that the do-ers don't have.

An abstract economist has no hesitation appearing before TV and expressing a judgment about how the war should be conducted—and he is listened to; an organizer of a soup business or a steel company may actually have better training for judgment—yet he isn't heard.

This will change. And what will change it is to realize that the underdeveloped and poor countries are *filled* with talkers, and short on do-ers. The respect for the do-er must increase.

Doing needs to be understood as a philosophy, a way of life. *To act is to live*, to give meaning to thought, to give meaning to reflection.

VIII. The ingredients of the management way of life.

1. Lippmann on art of politics.
2. Managerial life deals *not* solely with budgets, accounts, "market analysis," and statistics, but with some of the most subtle and intangible of values—in human relations; in judgment about alternatives.
3. The data processing computer picture has downgraded the creative qualities of management in the public mind.

IX. Don't yet understand that *to do to* is education.

Have been led to believe that education is the great need; and this is certainly true. But the prime educators are the do-ers, and the most important education is not that provided on the campus, or by thinkers, but in what used to be known as the "hard *school* of experience."

MAY 15, 1966
PRINCETON

Dean Brown, of the Princeton Faculty, told me, in a soft voice almost drowned out by the usual multiple decibels of sound at a large party, that he and a group of others were trying to get rid of some of the inflexibility in the training of engineers. "Why is it," he asked plaintively, "that young engineers—and most of their professors—seem so fearful about considering the consequences of engineering, the implications of it, and only feel secure when they are dealing with the—well, the *vocational* side of their profession?"

MAY 19, 1966
NEW YORK

To John and Jane Burnett's for a drink late yesterday afternoon; I invited myself so I could see the baby. And quite a baby for an intellectual-type mother to produce in a Greenwich Village "pad"—John's half-derisive word for their unusual apartment. A big, strapping boy, Anthony, friendly and looking very knowledgeable for a four-month-old character.

After two Scotches John spoke of his first days in D&R, spoke as if it were thirty years ago; actually it was mid-1960. What a different place it is now, particularly in the past two years. "I used to talk to Gene O'Brien about the puzzle: A company headed by two outstanding men, with only one client. And when—in the first days—something was said about getting more clients, or a particular prospect came up, you felt as if some great moral issue was involved, and the people we were discussing new work with were always in the wrong, we always in the right."

I got the impression that he was trying to say that the atmosphere at that time was, well, neurotic. And I would agree. I myself, after the first couple years, found Gordon's outlook so negative that I gradually lost interest.

We miss Gordon for his brilliant mind, but that quality he had which Marguerite Owen described long ago as "monk-like," of deliberately suppressed emotion, just doesn't live there any more.

MAY 22, 1966
PRINCETON

Up at 6 A.M., reading galley proofs of Volume III, of which I have about half from the printer.

A strange interlude: while living very much in the present I read, with the intensity galley reading demands, of events of far away and long ago, some quite moving: my picture of my last visit with the dying Dr. H. A. Morgan; my own father's desperate illness and his indomitable optimism; the beginning days with "business" when I didn't have the foggiest notion what it was all about.

And then a talk with Burnett about the commotion in Washington caused by my letter to the President about an agricultural program for India. Burnett reports a long phone conversation with Nick Farr of AID: my letter [of March 25th] got the President "all stirred up" and he, L.B.J., has been interpreting it as a call to arms. An intergovernmental committee, which Farr chairs, has been doing hardly anything else the past two weeks; it even sent for John Lewis of the India AID Mission.

Everyone is enthusiastic about the Peace Corps part of our idea; but the President, so Farr says, thinks "the Lilienthal plan is to send hundreds of American county agents to India; forget about fertilizers, insecticides, irrigation." Some*one* is interpreting that letter in that way, but certainly not me. I would guess it is Secretary Freeman, who has the money ($33 million in the Food for Peace program he administers) and who, acting as a Secretary of Agriculture always does, is "protecting" his "department" by putting them in the middle of the act, through county agents.

All morning reviewing the report we are making for our client Peabody Coal on a vast scheme for utilizing and "moving" Western coal—as electrical energy. Frank Spencer, an electrical engineer working on it, has enthusiasm and sureness about our conclusions—he said this with almost an apologetic tone, perhaps because enthusiasm doesn't seem quite consistent with being a precise, slide rule engineer. "But it will happen," he said, at the end of my recitation of points I thought should be changed or clarified.

"Then why doesn't the text show that enthusiasm?" I asked. "This can be one of the greatest events since the opening of the West, since the building of the Panama Canal, since the transcontinental railroad"—said I, throwing in everything majestic I could think of by way of analogy. "So let's make our client Peabody *feel* that they can be the means for great leadership, make themselves great economic heroes: the tone of this early part of the report should reflect this."

MAY 25, 1966
NEW YORK

Dean Rusk came through the door, into the huge reception, headed for the dining room and his evening stint. Flanking him, the perennial and ageless Jack McCloy and the "head table" contingent. Dean spotted me in all that throng, gave me what Damon Runyan called "a big hello," then went on to the Starlight Room—packed to the rafters. Biggest turnout I have ever seen in that ill-fated room.

I say "ill-fated" because some years ago a similar but not so large group of black ties heard John Foster Dulles, impelled to say something "new and bold," deliver his "massive retaliation" speech. That scared the pants off me—and half the world's chancelleries, I guess.

I thought to myself: I hope Dean doesn't feel impelled to get off some bold new line.

He resisted that impulse; indeed I don't think Dean needs to resist —he just isn't a public relations dominated Secretary.

Jack McCloy, in introducing Dean in his barking but witty style, said that Dean had the hardest job in the world, the most difficult position of any Secretary of State in our history, and then asked him: "But how is it you *look* so well?" Except for puffiness around his eyes (probably natural to him anyway), Rusk did look fine: sturdy, unperturbed, confident.

Dean's prepared speech on Vietnam was "the usual." But he said he would respond to questions. And here, where he could be extemporaneous, he was at his articulate best. His line concluding the last question (on Vietnam) was simplicity itself: "Either we get out of their way, and they move over us, or we meet them. We shall meet them."

Rusk has become a far warmer person, more *personally* outgiving, more confident and more given to reaching out for people than he used to be. This is my observation. Helen noticed this, as did I, at the White House dinner. This taking on of the warmth—which seems real, but real or not, is effective—of the good politician, but without cheapness, somehow seems to me to represent growth away from the highly intellectual and remote *public* stance of his predecessors, Stimson, Root, and certainly Acheson (men who were, I'm told, warm and outgiving in private relations—certainly Acheson was).

Rusk "orally" is one of the most articulate men I have ever heard. His sentences come out in a design, the phrases balance, he says what he means—the *first* time. But as a speaker, he lacks the fire to move or even hold an audience.

Met and visited with so many people out of my past—and present. A great many broadcasting figures, for this dinner was a kind of memorial to Ed Murrow. Ed's son, Casey, no longer the curly-headed little cherub I best remembered, was on the platform and was introduced. I was glad Janet couldn't be there, it being a male affair; it would have been hard even on her great composure. David Schoenbrun, now grown quite stout, but with the same eager, lively face and knowing eyes I remember when on our first trip to Paris in 1951 he had arranged a notable party for Helen and me with [Averell] Harriman, [Jean] Monnet, Eve Curie, and others.

All in all, a remarkable gathering, mostly of the already persuaded. The kids, the professors (for the most part), the dissidents, of course, weren't there—out in the picket lines outside the Waldorf, no doubt. So it was the faithful talking to the faithful: no one was unpersuaded by Dean's talk, certainly not I, but at the same time there would be no additions to the converted.

Before dinner, in a long "drinking" period, I visited with Hanson Baldwin. His comments about how military men were prevented from expressing their views under the McNamara regime were, I thought, quite fierce for so gentle a man. Partly the frustration of a newspaper man, but probably more than that. Does this apply, I asked, only to the junior officers? No, it goes right to the top. Professor [James] Billington of Princeton asked if Hanson had been able to talk to Russian military men. The answer was predictable; they are buttoned up in a way, I should say, that makes the Pentagon a kaffee klatsch by comparison.

Can't get out of my mind the picture of George Kennan, one of the most experienced and influential of all our foreign diplomats, coming into the Waldorf dining room last evening, late, when almost the last seat had been occupied. He looked awkward and self-conscious, in an ill-fitting dinner jacket. I stopped him as he was going by my table, which was way out in left field; we shook hands and he gave me that extraordinarily warm, boyish, shy smile, and then went on to a table at the edge of the ball park, among people who apparently didn't know what a very distinguished man was seated with them. Afterward I wondered, and still wonder, what must have gone through his mind as his former junior associate Rusk got a great ovation for policies and actions with which George had expressed such strong (and highly publicized) disagreement before the Fulbright Committee.

This, too, is democracy: when a man holds public office and temporarily has in his hands the power of the state, there is a nimbus about his head *or* that head is a free target for the most outrageous abuse (witness Rusk in the hands of Senators Morse and Fulbright). Then, when he no longer bears the mark of a people's designee, he can come into a great meeting, its purpose to discuss foreign policy of which he was an important designer, and he is just another dinner guest—as was George Kennan last night.

MAY 29, 1966
PRINCETON

At 4:00 yesterday afternoon, the all-day drizzle was continuing its dismal course; the prospects for our annual big garden party looked as glum as the sky.

At 5:00 the sun broke through; at 5:45 the guests—there were about fifty all told—began to arrive. Everyone seemed to have a good time, full of admiration for (*a*) the garden and (*b*) our standing with the Lord, which stopped the rain at just the right time. And at 7:00, when the guests had left—except those who stayed for a lap supper—the rain began again, in earnest, a hard thunderstorm and spring rain.

Alpheus Mason is the happiest, gayest historian I have ever known. So often they are on the solemn side; not he. He keeps peppering me with the kind of personal questions that I suppose portray the professional biographer. "Which of your two careers—business or writing—comes first with you?"

Before I could answer—or hedge—Bob Lively spoke up: "The one he is working on in the last hour." About right.

Some people's faces have written on them the kind of life they have lived, the strains and excitements they have been through, the things the world has taught them, the great sights—intellectual, emotional, physical—they have seen. Sometimes the facial evidences are like wound stripes; my face, particularly my crisscrossed forehead, shows that I have been somewhere.

Then there are others who have seen great visions and struggled with great ideas or trials and who show not a mark. John Wheeler, one of the greatest of the world's physicist pioneers, is certainly such a man with such a face, or so I thought as I looked at him in our garden yesterday. He is not only a quiet, soft-spoken, reserved man, but his face gives no evidence of what he is; seeing him without knowing what a great man he is, you would never guess that here is a man who has struggled with profound and, as it turns out, *literally* world-shaking concepts, and still does.

His wife, Janette, a bright-eyed, handsome, and very alive person, asked me if Helen and I still enjoyed foreign travel as much as we once did. Then she went on, in a characteristically overmodest way: "But with you, you see so many new things, things you are causing to happen. But when we go to a conference in some faraway country, all we see are physicists, and their pencils and their blackboards. That doesn't change no matter what country we are in."

Friday for some hours attended the Conference of the Committee of One Hundred set up to "review" the technical work and tentative conclusions of the Regional Plan Association. The purpose: to hear what the RPA has to offer as a "second Five Year Plan" for the New York Region.

I was expecting to have a dim view of what such an essentially technical group could come up with for so highly charged, complex, and unplannable (almost by definition) a picture as the New York Region (which includes parts of the great environs). But I saw that the facts and projections served a very useful function, even though neither the RPA nor any other single body, private or public, has the legal power to carry out such a plan.

Projecting for thirty-five years could be considered futile, a mere "exercise," when revolutionary changes are moving the very earth beneath our feet, unseen, not understood, and not even sensed. Not so.

I asked the group to tabulate the considerable number of levers of action that do exist. They *are* considerable. The important thing, I said, was to try to get something like agreement—and the facts to support the discussion prior to agreement—as to what the New York Region *wanted.* I said, "Be sure you yourself, as a technical group, and your Board, feel you know what you *want* to happen about these many problems; *then* and only then start to worry about the limited means to bring that 'want' into reality."

Met an extraordinarily intelligent and affable man, Amyas Ames, a member of the Committee, and an investment banker. The hours spent attending were worth it if for no other reason. Tall, fair, slender, with a keen sense of what is relevant and what is not, given to few words in a meeting, an excellent and relaxed conversationalist in the "breaks" between meetings.

One should never forget, in his near-despair about so complex an undertaking as making some sense and health out of New York City, that there are not only cheap, noisy, self-centered people, but a good many sturdy, public-spirited men of wisdom and experience ready to give time to these matters, people who, like Ames, carry on the patrician tradition of giving of themselves for civic or artistic ventures wholly unrelated to their private business concerns.

Among the younger (say, thirty-five-year-olds) in the staff there were some who look on me as a symbol of what they hope can be revived in America, and by this they mean—and say, with some eagerness—the achievements of TVA. "Can we ever recover that spirit?" one asked.

We *can recover* spirit, I would say (to myself, not to them), but it will be quite a different spirit, for another America and another set of dares that fortune throws at this vigorous and undefeated nation.

Just back from a visit next door with Robert and Kitty Oppenheimer, and Anne Marks, who was visiting them.

Robert wasting away. A terrible thing to see.

So beautiful a day it is, the dapple on the unbelievably green grass at Olden Manor in the dying sun.

Live every day fully, I kept saying to myself, as we walked back home, I feeling so desperately unhappy to see this—as it seems to me—imminent dissolution. For the first time Robert himself is "uncertain about the future," as he says, so white and—scared.

Kitty took me for a tour of the grounds. I asked her how Robert was getting along, and she bit her lip, her frail little body stiffened, a picture of a fighting woman. I leaned over and kissed her cheek, and she uttered such a moan, began to cry, caught herself, blaming me for making her weep. Then shook it off, looked at me with that little-girl look and asked me if she looked all right now, could we go back and join the others?

I have never admired the strength of a woman more. Robert is not only her husband, he is her past, the happy past and the tortured one, and he is her hero and now her great "problem."

I, who have known this man in the strength of his genius and the dash of his kind of arrogance, was saddened beyond words at this picture of deterioration, of a unique person being crushed by forces that pay no more attention to the magnificent sweep of his mind and imagination than they do to the most inarticulate peasant in the fields of Khuzistan.

Anne Marks more or less commutes between her house in Washington and Geneva, where she is a kind of public relations something or other for the U.S. Disarmament Agency. "I like what I am doing; it isn't getting anywhere, of course, but I guess I'm a political voyeur; I like to be where I can see what goes on. And it is fun to work with Adrian Fisher." Fisher is now the deputy to Bill Foster in the Disarmament discussions.

I looked a bit surprised at this comment; Butch Fisher has always seemed to me to have a puzzling, ineffective kind of brightness. Acheson told me more than once that he never could make out exactly what in the hell Butch was getting at.

"Of course, I know that most people can't make head or tail of what Butch says; but I seem to be tuned in on his wavelength. Anyway, he is fun to work with, and it doesn't really matter much whether he makes sense or not. We're getting nowhere; we're just a thorn in the side, to stick people now and then about arms.

"It's not a big agency—only about a hundred people, and only spends about ten million a year, so it doesn't matter too much. A good deal of research is nutty research [her words, delivered with her charming insouciance] but it does no harm."

MAY 30, 1966
PRINCETON

Memorial Day, and a beautiful one; sharp light on the garden, with its explosion of iris of a score of hues.

Beginning to read Lord Moran's *Diaries*, or rather his story of Churchill based upon his diaries kept while he went with Churchill as his physician.

Which prompts this thought about my own journal writing: so much of it is written on *top* of my stint of work, with such energies and time as I have left from my work; Lord Moran wasn't *working* while he wrote; only now and then would he have professional duties. His record shows that his diaries were his primary job, a literary exercise—and extremely well written they are, too—and received the cream of his energies instead of the remnant, as with me.

JUNE 2, 1966
NEW YORK

A restless up-and-down kind of night, distressed about the tensions between three D&R officers—Anderson, Burnett, and O'Brien. But a new and more affirmative perspective came out of last night's unease.

Let my distress stand as one more reminder that this is the *process*, this worrying, by which so often I have come through to something like clarity, even creative answers. And a sense that the world won't come to a complete stop if these men get into a row among themselves, or a row with Reza Ansari and company.

JUNE 3, 1966
NEW YORK

Yesterday afternoon's "departure session" with the "troika"—Anderson, O'Brien, and Burnett, heading for Khuzistan—was an answer to the question I so often ask myself: "Does experience count for anything much?"

I found the answer a strong affirmative yesterday.

Those long years of dealing with strong individuals went past the windows of my consciousness as I tried to guide—or lead—the conflict between these strong men into an accommodation that could be creative, that would substitute the needs of the job for the needs of their powerful drives for their own ideas and prestige.

Did I succeed? No, *I* didn't, but *they* did. Leo adjusted his own original, arbitrary insistence that the whole "authority" of the company be "delegated" to him. He accepted my suggestion that he let our people in Iran cry on his shoulder, if they needed it, but to pay no mind to their gripes, because he was going out there to create a new atmosphere, not to indulge in whining or scapegoating about the past.

But the most impressive part of yesterday's turnabout was the gracious and courageous way John Burnett accepted the alternative that Leo take the lead, and he, though now the Acting President, take a secondary, almost incidental role. That required manhood, and a devotion to the best interests—or best chances—of the future of D&R in a land where we have made a mark.

So how does "experience" justify itself? The answer is a cliché of management, but like so many bromides, it is true. Experience has taught me that the heart and life of management are people, *individuals*. With good human material, any kind of organizational scheme can be made to work. With individuals who aren't full-sized men, no organizational arabesque will work, however "sound" it is in the textbooks of management.

JUNE 4, 1966
PRINCETON

David and I lunched together yesterday. I spoke of my Fairless Lectures, how much it meant to me to make them *say* something, to become a minor distillation of what I see lies ahead in the Managerial Life. Would it be possible that he could give me a hand on this set of lectures? Suddenly he warmed up, became extraordinarily articulate, "communicating" in a rich and understanding way about the theme I had so briefly sketched: the way I go about the function I call managerial.

I heard him use the term "poetic" applied to my way of working; interpreting the *meaning of things* is the role of poetry, and that is what I do as a manager—this was the substance of his comment. And he went on to make clear why he used these words, this concept. He knows me, but it is far more than that: he has an understanding of life beyond that of anyone I have ever known, an understanding that combines a keen intelligence with a kind of intuitive sense of direction.

I asked him if in his writing of fiction he has some "theme" he is trying to express through his stories. "But it isn't in the stories that there is a theme," he said. "The stories are stories."

JUNE 6, 1966
NEW YORK

A phone call from Red Wagner. Wanted to thank me for my efforts to help solve TVA's Board problem; I shouldn't feel too badly that they hadn't succeeded, that Donald McBride had been appointed.

This morning McBride had told Red that when the Oklahoma delegation went in to see the President about McBride, the President said: "You know I have a committee here in the White House headed by John Macy that helps me find people for such an important job as the TVA Board. I told them there are three principles: the nominee shouldn't be too old; second, he shouldn't be too political; and third, he shouldn't be an engineer."

McBride is sixty-two; he has been active in politics practically all of his life; and he is an engineer.

So much for the President's criteria.

A visit from two Ghanaians, E. K. Quartey and E. A. K. Kalitsi.

Quartey, head of electricity supply in the country, is expected to be "Chief Executive," i.e., General Manager of the Volta River Authority; Kalitsi is a close friend of Tom Mead's. Tom's pride in the smiling Kalitsi, only in his early thirties, is paternal, and well it may be, for he was one of the young men Tom inspired and taught, and who became his Assistant District Commissioner, when Tom was in the British Colonial Service.

Kalitsi has charge, among other things, of the resettlement of the hundreds of villages and 80,000 villagers displaced by the reservoir of the Volta Dam.

Quartey is a dignified, formal man, with no touch of the revolutionary Nkrumah. And no recriminations about what has happened to their country since Nkrumah went off his rocker, if that indeed is what happened between the time we visited him in Accra in 1959‡ and a few years later, when as President he spent the country into bankruptcy and drove it into political tyranny.

In measured terms Quartey said he had been authorized by the National Liberation Council (which is presently "government" in Ghana) to invite us to send a group "to look about" and see what our company could do that hasn't already been done. If preparing reports were all we could do, I'd say the trip would be pretty futile.

I had inscribed a paperback copy of *TVA: Democracy on the March* for Mr. Kalitsi, at Tom Mead's request. I took a gentlemanly hint and presented Mr. Quartey with a copy. Looking at me solemnly over the top of his heavy-rimmed glasses, Quartey said, "I first read this book when

‡ *Journals*, Vol. IV, *The Road to Change*, pp. 326–331; 333–338.

I was a student in London in 1954." Sometimes all the trouble—and frustration—involved in writing is more than worth it. My pamphlet "The Road to Change," for example, still brings in letters requesting copies; last week a request from Colombia, for the Medical School of the Valle; and for 500 copies for an Appalachia region group.

JUNE 9, 1966
PRINCETON

When Helen Meyner invited us for dinner, with Governor Hughes and his wife as guests, I thought: This is part of putting the bee on Bob to run for the Senate against Clifford Case. And that certainly did turn out to be one of the items on the agenda last night; but only one, for it was a jolly, argumentative dinner party. The other guests included James McCord, head of the Princeton Theological Seminary, and his wife; Arthur Schlesinger, looking as well pleased with himself as he certainly has every right to, his book about Kennedy being a smash, and he in demand as a speaker all over the place; and my Law School classmate Wendell Davis and his forceful wife, Mary.

But easily the outstanding personalities were the Governor and his wife. At table I sat on her right; at first she seemed constrained in talking with me, but her natural ebullience and sense of fun soon was too much for such staidness, and when I began exchanging banter—about teenagers, about the absurd trials and tribulations of public life, and so on—and laughed as vigorously as she, we had a wonderful time and I saw that here was no ordinary woman. Her good humor and insouciance are so extraordinary that you might be talking to a sylph for all you notice her considerable size.

Hughes is a dead earnest man, looking much younger than I was prepared for, from his platform appearance. He had had a long and "terrible" day, he said, with the Legislature, a body that everyone supposed, after his decisive victory, would enact his program with great party discipline. No such thing, and for a time this frustration showed through. Then, after the ladies left the gents at the table, he set about the work he had cut out for himself: to try to get Bob Meyner, before witnesses as it were, to see that running for the Senate was just the thing he should do.

Bob likes an argument, and has the voice and manner and appetite for it. So they had at it back and forth, Hughes maintaining his solemn, slow manner, emphasizing his points with care. First he tried to dispose of Case as an opponent who was always vague about whatever he was talking about. "The people of New Jersey want a *voice*, the voice of a man they know is for the little man, is honest, and when he gets to Washington will say just what he thinks."

Bob wasn't impressed. Case, well, he could tend to that. But the issue in people's minds is the war in Vietnam. He made it very plain he thought Johnson had stepped into a deep hole on this one, that "as the boxes [of the dead] keep coming back" the people will become more and more determined to have an end to it; and how can a man run as a Democrat and not carry the burden of that Johnson policy?

Hughes didn't think so; he thought Bob didn't need to say a word about Vietnam. Bob was by no means convinced.

Arthur Schlesinger also enjoys an argument, likes to say provocative things and still measures everything in the Johnson Administration against what Kennedy did—which by Arthur's lights was always right.

Somehow the subject got around to automobile safety, about which Hughes knows a great deal, as an active watchdog of the state highway system. But Arthur waded in, with the same assurance he shows about almost everything: A remark of Henry Ford II that we let the industry work out the safety problem. Absurd; and to top it, Murphy, head of Campbell Soup, sounding off about those who try to tell the automobile industry their own business, the engineering of cars.

Arthur got off a provocative comment about businessmen: "Show me one issue on which businessmen have ever been right on a question of public policy, just one."

Arthur made a crack about these big business leaders just reading the speeches their paid ghost writers write for them. I said I had heard that there had been ghost writers in the White House, too. Arthur is too good a debater for me. He responded, a bit angrily, that the men for whom these speeches had been written had enough sense to know the difference between a good speech and a bum one.

He is certainly a man of extraordinary gifts, as historian and writer, and has a good sense of fun: this last was something I wasn't aware of until last evening.

The first cable from our three embattled emissaries to Khuzistan. Their reception "amiable," the discussion following the affirmative lines we had laid out in that memorable session in my office before the three left. What pleased me most was that the message was signed "Troika," the kidding name I had used to describe them as three men of equal standing.

JUNE 17, 1966
PRINCETON

Burnett, back from Iran, made an almost classic report to me and Walt Seymour. Clear, well organized. Sum total: the meetings with

Ansari, Ahmadi, and Shahmirzadi were with men who had *thought* about a future program for Greater Dez. This was matched by Leo Anderson's good, affirmative spirit about their ideas; result: real progress toward a definition of what they wanted done and what they expected of us, something that had been lost, somewhere, in the welter of vagueness or overprecise arguments about "contract terms."

Basically KWPA expects to acquire perhaps three fourths of the land of the Greater Dez area, then open it to peasants, *after* a cropping and water plan has been developed, regulating the use through their (KWPA) *ownership*. This goes a long way beyond what Penalosa is doing in Colombia, particularly in Atlantico. And it does represent innovation, which in the hands of men like Ansari can be expected not only to produce agricultural results, but to avoid replacing the dictatorship of landlords for the dictatorship of government functionaries. But I would like to know more about how much this scheme recognizes the "social justice" goal, which in the case of land means something like secure land tenure by the cultivators.

A load is shifting from my spirit by the report of a meeting in which the parties were not haggling, complaining about the inadequacies of our, or their, past performance, but were looking ahead to a venture of the greatest significance.

A curious and ironic story brought back by John Burnett.

Ansari to Burnett (during a three-hour talk, at the Governor's Palace reception Ansari gave for D&R employees):

"Couple of weeks ago a man by the name of George Sealy spoke to us about a big grain storage undertaking his company, Utah Construction, was negotiating with Iran. Said they were important owners of D&R.

"We think of D&R as Lilienthal, Oliver, Seymour, Burnett, and not big money like Utah Construction or a Wall Street banking house. That isn't the picture of D&R we trust and depend on."

Burnett, grinning, said he explained that we are, right now, in the process of turning D&R into an organization owned by its key staff.

The irony of this appealed to us. Here we thought that such big private companies as our "partners" gave a picture of D&R that would aid our development work; in Iranian eyes, it was just the reverse. Utah and Lazard as stockholders of D&R were a handicap to D&R!

The big event in the twisting, turning, and sometimes agonizing course of the writing of the Fairless Lectures is some written comments from David!

Here are a few excerpts from what he said:

"You refer to managing and manager 'in the broad sense of the term' without defining that term. Is not what you really are talking about Leadership? Leadership is your business, not management . . . unless you redefine management to mean leadership. . . . Management as a term does have a constrictive connotation, for it implies control without inspiration, whereas your life & meaning and what you seem to be reaching for in these notes has to do with the liberation of human energies, getting people excited, inspiring them to action, a process of prophecy and interpretation, of understanding and empathy, a creative function as art or music, an almost religious and poetic function . . . but *management* suggests virtually none of these elements.

"Really, management has not a very good ring to it nowadays. It implies a kind of expertise about human affairs which is at odds with your whole nature and purpose. This expertise in turn implies a condescension toward those lacking it. Leadership has the irrational elements of delight and faith, the capacity to be astounded by the achievements of liberated human energies.

"If you are talking about the heart & guts of your own beliefs and experiences, you cannot cram this into an ordinary Brooks Brothers suit. . . . If management is simply the art of getting things done, then I am not interested. You have more to say than that because you are not a manager."

This Fairless thing turns out to be far more than a series of lectures to an industrial institution: it is a re-examination of my insides.

Discovered last week that, while that is not why I write them, keeping these journals can have some value, for scholars, in the writing of current history.

A Professor of Geography at Yale, Aloys Michel, asked permission to include some quotes from one of my *Collier's* articles in a book he is writing about the Indus Basin.§

He spent most of a day in the conference room at the office, reading the full text. Much excited. Said he had found the exact place, in one of my journal entries, where the Indus proposal I had made had been changed from one of integrated development of the river, to a complex "partition" of the two countries that would prevent any hope of their later becoming politically joined together. His reaction confirmed once again that these day-by-day or current records have a validity that retrospective comments or "official" communiqués often lack.

As I read the galleys of this latest volume, however, I was dubious about the practice of hardly ever touching—or more than barely touching—the prose as it comes from the end of my pen. So often, particularly

§ *The Indus Rivers: A Study of the Effects of Partition*, Yale University Press, 1967.

when I am tired at the time of the writing, the sentences are wobbly, murky, awkward.

Yet if I write what might be considered "first drafts," and then do the amount of revising that is normal for my other writing (for other people's too), the *Journals* will lose the quality of spontaneity and will sometimes lose something of their credibility as firsthand evidence.

The worst thing about writing off the top of my head is that I thereby include a great deal of inconsequential and often pretty dull stuff, ruminations mostly. Much of the millions of words is written as speculation, a stream of consciousness having value only to me, *in the writing*, rather than value as a record of thinking that has some residual usefulness or importance.

So I have resolved that in any further publication of the *Journals* the rule of Volumes I and II ("don't tamper") will be modified; not to doctor, except where clarity or extreme bad taste may be involved, but *cut*. This leaves the complete and untouched original for the files at Firestone Library, unimpaired, but it doesn't inflict on readers of the *published* words great meaningless thickets to skip or push through, or arid or hopelessly tiresome stretches.

JUNE 22, 1966
NEW YORK

One of the favorite bromides about underdeveloped countries is that they must get their minds used to great change.

But suppose, in 1955, our American industrialists and managers had been told that in 1966:

There would be a vast communications company (COMSAT), *half public*, half private, avidly traded on the Stock Exchange.

Engineering design of automobiles would be the subject of Congressional investigation before TV cameras and of regulatory legislation.

Many major companies would be in partnership with foreign governments, many of them Socialist.

Prices for steel would be determined by a group of economists attached to the White House.

Or, in another sphere:

Contraceptive devices and medications would become a subject of public discussion anywhere—and become a major industry.

"Liberals" who have not had a really new idea since the New Deal are still legion, and many of them are teaching on our leading faculties, and lecturing the rest of us. Conservatives who haven't had a new idea since Eisenhower's Administration are still running important businesses and banks.

The changes through which we are living make both kinds of people emotionally useless and ill adapted.

Same thing is true of foreign policy; too many people are still thinking the same stock concepts of the early days of the Cold War, which is as far behind us as the Crimean War.

A bracing report from Leo Anderson and Gene O'Brien this morning, recounting their two weeks of detailed discussions with Ansari et al. The upshot: a program that had become stalled, with morale low in both KWPA *and* D&R, is certainly on the mend.

Will Leo's near-euphoria about what he accomplished be supported by the ensuing development? To make this work, the authority to act, to make decisions, must be clearly in Leo and O'Brien's hands. If John Oliver had undertaken these discussions, he would have had authority, but not the necessary understanding of the program itself, as distinguished from the contractual and fiscal and "personnel" aspects. The same is true of Burnett's time out there; the discussions inevitably turned too much on procedure, fiscal matters, overdue payments, "terms and conditions."

Whether having surrogates who are short on the procedural and administrative but strong on content will do any better still remains to be seen. But this approach is more in my line, more my way of going at things.

After a few months of this kissing and making up stage, someone will have to fight it out about budgets. I made it plain this morning that Anderson and O'Brien will have to carry this too; they have the whole ball of wax. They boggled a bit at this—I judge only from their almost alarmed look at this point. But this is the right way to do it. And they will have some things to learn out of it. Program people so often think they are "above" such grubby things as budgets. Well, they aren't, and can't be.

JUNE 28, 1966
PRINCETON

Sunday a garden party here for almost fifty Education and World Affairs people (Trustees, wives, staff). Since that time, waking and sleeping, immersed to the eyeballs with the first genuinely prickly discussions of policy in the several years' history of EWA, this sturdy kiwi, a well-heeled bird, but without wings or apparently (until this weekend) without the least inclination to fly. Just plod.

But *this* has been different. Two issues: (1) should we as a body deplore, warn against, oppose, moralize about, etc., the intrusion of "military intelligence" (that is a fancy term for CIA) into the virtuous groves of academe; and (2) should we provide some mechanism for a confrontation between the universities and academic community of the country on the one hand, and the Administration in Washington on the other, on the issue of American foreign policy, as evidenced chiefly by the war in Vietnam?

The CIA issue statement by the staff was a tough one, for me. After all, I had *begun* all this inquiry into the "covert" infiltration of ostensibly university or scholarly studies, when I had insisted we be told categorically that the EWA center in Hong Kong we were supporting was *not* just a cover for a military or political spying operation.

But the proposed draft was a sizzler. I thought it was an indictment of the universities, coupled with a plea of guilty as charged, with the plain inference that not only were there cases of using universities for covert intelligence activities, but that this was widespread and almost universal; that we should admit this but promise that it will stop.

One of our Trustees, whom I admire so enormously, John Hannah of Michigan State, read this statement with a fierce look on his face. He had been *battered* previously by the magazine *Ramparts* for permitting Michigan State faculty people to be a cover for activities in Vietnam—police training it was called. But the *Ramparts* "exposé" (of facts previously published elsewhere years ago!) coincided with a series of reports the *New York Times* had under way investigating the CIA. For a solid week, the *Times* front-paged *their* exposé of CIA, using the lurid charges of the *Ramparts* crowd to give their CIA essays the necessary zing that would justify first page handling.

John pretty well kept his composure during the discussion. He felt the statement it was proposed we issue *assumed* that CIA had "corrupted" the universities on a broad scale, and that the universities had almost welcomed all of this.

The text of the proposed statement indicates how the top staff of EWA (including not only Marvel but, I suppose, the imperturbable Herman Wells) felt about what was going on. Or what they *thought* was going on. They had talked to George Gant of the Ford Foundation, who had by no means quieted their apprehensions of the extent of the involvement of university people and institutions with CIA. (George later said he had *no way* of "giving assurance" that the thirty university contracts the Ford Foundation has for work in Asia and Southwest Asia were not also funded in ways unknown to him by the CIA or other intelligence organizations.)

This is an excerpt of the statement, proposed that the Trustees sign:

"We are deeply troubled by the growing suspicion and doubt surrounding the relationships of American universities and scholars with agencies of the military-intelligence community. . . .

"Unless determined steps are taken to clarify the roles and relationships of the military intelligence agencies vis-à-vis the academic community, however, we will indeed be in a situation where the right hand knows not what the left hand does. Worse still, the two hands will, in a fundamental sense, be in direct combat one with the other.

"To avoid further deterioration in this picture, we must reach out at once for a few simple guidelines.

"We therefore urgently recommend to the interested parties that the following four principles be adopted immediately as the basis of policy and performance:

> 1. Higher education's first responsibility is to maintain the university as the citadel of independent learning and the objective search for truth. . . .
>
> 2. The individual scholar holds the ultimate responsibility for preserving the high place which this country accords to scholarship and education. . . .
>
> 3. No agency of the federal government should be at liberty to compromise the integrity of universities, colleges and individual scholars. . . .
>
> 4. The power wielded by the military-intelligence agencies in relation to the academic community is largely one of money. This can be reduced simply for research, and especially for social science research overseas."

The discussion of this proposed statement was spirited. This morning, at a Board session, I expect we will decide to issue no statement *at all*,◖ this one or a modification and toning down.

The discussion of the second issue, the "alienation" between the academic community and Government, was equally spirited. What added spice and life was the presence of a group of "guests," Klaus Knorr, head of the Princeton International Center, Professor Billington, a terrific young fellow in the History Department (his inclusion was my suggestion, for I know what a fresh and saucy mind he has, and an extraordinary background of experience lecturing to Russian college students), Max Millikan of the MIT International Center (who was most influential in the Kennedy days—now so long ago—light-years ago!), and Adam Yarmolinsky, still in the Pentagon.

Difficult to exaggerate how widespread is the feeling against the Administration's policy in Vietnam. It is now expressed without hedging or "on-the-one-hand and on-the-other" among the better heeled or the intellectuals.

◖ No action was taken.

JUNE 29, 1966
NEW YORK

I take an inordinate pleasure in watching men work their way through complex problems, where no simple answer will satisfy them, being intelligent men, nor satisfy the demands of the problem. This clear conflict is between, on the one hand, the needs of the country, as assessed by the military, for "intelligence," i.e., information, and, on the other, of the needs of the institutions of higher learning, and scholars themselves, for a claim to integrity and candor.

A professional spy puts all that kind of conflicting loyalty problem behind him; but when a scholar, or a university, is engaged in clandestine activity for his country, he puts in jeopardy the scholar's expressed role of searching solely for the truth, causes uneasiness among his fellow scholars, and can put his university in a distorted, tortured light—witness the criticism of Michigan State arising out of its role in "training Vietnam's police."

The scholar in the physical sciences—the "scientist"—has been doing much talking in recent years—since the Manhattan Project particularly—about the need that the scientist-scholar be in a position of authority and power because of the transcendent importance of science in modern governing. Well, the universities and the scholars are beginning to learn that once you step out of the role of searcher for the truth and into the political arena where decisions must be made, icy logic and what *should* be (i.e., what is reasonable and rational) is definitely *not* the sole measure of human conduct.

6 P.M.

Footnote on the fluid society:

As I came into the elevator in the Roosevelt Hotel, a bell*boy*—as they used to be called, and were—hailed me with a wave: "Hi, Mr. Lilienthal; I played the Princeton course last Sunday, 18 holes."

When philosophers are kings, and bellboys play golf.

Max Millikan was a member of that Cambridge phalanx that did for Jack Kennedy, before he was President, something of what the Columbia brain trust troika of Moley, Berle, and Tugwell did for F.D.R. in 1932. Millikan's influence was probably even greater.

Although I had some acquaintance with Millikan, particularly at the time the foreign aid ideas were developing, this was the first time I saw him in action.

And I was amazed and saddened by what I saw. His manner was

the ivory tower, *abstract* muse-er, a pipe in his mouth all the while, stopping to light and relight it in the middle of a sentence while a dozen or more people were kept waiting for the next words, egregious manners of the kind that reveal the man used to dealing with a captive audience of "inferiors," i.e., students. He defended the idea that CIA could properly engage a university for "policy-oriented research." When I prodded him for what that meant specifically, his first illustration was a completely innocuous kind of study; I said, "Oh, come on, give us a marginal case, one about which there could be some question of its propriety." So he said: "A study of whether economic aid to a foreign country would affect its political stability."

This is the very kind of inquiry by U.S. university scholars working for CIA that, in my opinion, could lead to great resentment in that country, even if carried on very well. And Adam Yarmolinsky whispered to me: "Political and military stability—part of the same thing."

Policy-oriented research, in another country, by a U.S. university, about factors of "stability" seemed clearly the kind of thing that would lead to questions about left wing influence in that country, its political and military condition vis-à-vis the U.S. It is the sort of intelligence that the U.S. would want and need about Argentina, for example, prior to the military coup that ousted its President only yesterday; *but* it never seemed to cross Millikan's mind that CIA prying into this, under contract with a U.S. university, would have to be clandestine to be effective, and a clandestine task isn't appropriate for a university, risking the repute and involving the university in a kind of business that is outside its role as a teacher, and a searcher for knowledge in order to teach.

I spoke separately to Ed Mason, expressing my concern about Millikan's attitude that because the work needed to be done, and was "policy-oriented," there was no valid objection to a *university* doing it. Mason, a moderate fellow indeed, said he completely "disagreed with Max" about this, and Harvard didn't do it, though an individual scholar might be permitted to.

The star of Monday's show was Billington. His analysis of the pressure on Bob Kennedy to "keep the Kennedy mystique alive" was impressive and done with great humor and picturesque language.

"One of the reasons for the frustration and ill feeling about American foreign policy among the younger scholars in the universities," he said, was related to that mystique. "Kennedy becoming President was a declaration that the older people were out of the driver's seat, and a new young generation was now in charge. Then Kennedy gave way to a man without style or any of the attributes of Kennedy, and particularly none of his 'youth will be served' flavor. And they felt defeated and disgruntled, disregarding what Johnson did about every other issue except

Vietnam. The alienation of the intellectuals can't be understood without considering the age bracket of the younger men in the university."

University administrators these days are caught—even the sturdiest of them—in the loving but choking embrace of Federal funds.

The "dialogue" between the universities and scholars, and the Federal Government, had "deteriorated." That was the theme of much that was said, by the Trustees and by their invited guests, such as the shrewd, weather-beaten looking Klaus Knorr of the Princeton Center for International Studies.

In the final meeting, of the EWA Board alone, I said what was going on, as well as I could see, was not a "dialogue," or two monologues, as Frank Murphy or Billington had said. "What you are in," I said, "is a *negotiation*."

The academic world wants more recognition in foreign policy discussions and action, and their resistance about Vietnam, etc., is part of that process; "negotiation" to be effective, I thought, must be out in the public arena, not in more of the proposed meetings with the Secretary of State behind closed doors.

But Goheen (with general support from the academic leaders) shied away from this kind of line. No, a carefully prepared session with the Secretary and Walt Rostow was the right course. But I couldn't help thinking that part of the change from "fight talk" by university people when in these closed intramural meetings of EWA, and the notion of making *public issues* with the Government, was strategy. The financial budgets of even the most affluent universities—including Princeton—are now made up in the light of huge funds from the Federal Government. My view is that the proportion and amount of general university overhead being carried by the Federal Government has grown so large that it is not stretching it to say that the Presidents and administrative officers of the universities—Princeton, MIT, Michigan State, etc. —*are on the federal payroll.*

The universities are indeed in danger of losing their independence.

JUNE 30, 1966
NEW YORK

I had no "business" purpose in calling on André this late forenoon; I just wanted to greet him as one did any other good friend before a holiday absence.

"In a few weeks I will be sixty-eight years old. I'm working harder now than I ever have. It's perfectly silly." He said this looking steadily at me with a look of incredulity that he was calling himself silly. I know that feeling: one is considered a highly intelligent person, yet when it comes to the disposition of one's energies, "silly" is often the word for it.

"I have no time for anything, I have papers and papers to read. Can you believe it, *I haven't read a book* for I don't know how long." This seemed such a remarkable statement that he dwelt on it. And then he said something I'm not likely to forget:

"I work hard and my work takes all my time. But I don't always enjoy what I'm doing. You, what you do you enjoy, even those exhausting work trips. It all means something to you.

"But I don't know what to do about it"—this said rather sadly.

As usual, he took a few phone calls during our talk in the little office where I began with Lazard Frères fifteen years ago. I started to leave, but he pointed to the chair; I was to stay. Both of the calls had to do with "Jackie" and "Bobby." He volunteered, after the phone calls: "These Kennedys are difficult people to do things for. Bobby has such energy, is moving about constantly. The other evening we had dinner together on Third Avenue in a small restaurant. During the meal he left to go to put in an appearance at *three* dinner meetings; three times." Shook his head.

Well, with help from André, they are in good hands, and I am sure they know it. André has a background of world affairs quite unique: American based, but with an understanding and feeling for Europe matched by no other American in private or public life.

JULY 2, 1966
MARTHA'S VINEYARD

The auto trip to the Vineyard was a hard one. We reached our hilltop about 11 P.M. The rays of the full moon made a glorious silver altarpiece of the ocean to the south, a fairyland of grey and green of the woods all about us. The air was sweet and pure. What a haven this is. And today, in the bright sunlight, not another habitation to be seen; walking through the field, the twitter of young quail, the mother putting on the time-honored broken wing diversionary move.

JULY 7, 1966
MARTHA'S VINEYARD

Tuesday Eliot and Elizabeth Janeway and their younger son, Bill, just fresh from his first year at Pembroke College, Cambridge, in for a couple hours of animated conversation.

Bill is full of the relish of life, that wonderful feeling of the young that all things that are going on in the world are part of a great show put on especially for you. England today, says Bill, eyes aglow, is a story not of "economic crisis but economic disaster," a phrase he liked well enough to repeat later.

Eliot looked tired and worn, but his gift for the pungent phrase and his complete and life-long preoccupation with the "state of the economy" (particularly the international fiscal economy) makes anything he says more than worthwhile listening to, carefully. Which I did.

Seconded (and occasionally corrected!) by his eager, dark-eyed son, he drawled—his particular kind of ironic drawl—about "lack of international liquidity," which, of course, I simply don't understand. A private bank that can't meet its obligations because its resources can't be turned into cash—that I understand, and when that happens the bank is closed and the depositors get what is left. But when this happens to nations, you don't close the nations. There should be an international monetary conference, opines Eliot, but "that clown Fowler" [the Secretary of the Treasury] doesn't know what it is all about. So much for our one-time TVA lawyer, "Joe" Fowler.

All of which brought back my recent reading of Herbert Feis' book *Characters in Crisis*, the story of the attempted international monetary conference just as F.D.R. came into office in 1933.

I can well see how very bright men (Eliot and Bill are among the brightest) who live in the world of fiscal tides and currents, and the fiscal technology that has grown up over the centuries, should be chronically bearish. To one of my experience (and ignorance, really, about fiscal matters), I think about how many of the catastrophic things the economists predicted were inevitable just didn't happen, and didn't happen for reasons having little to do with the esoteric fiscal arts. Too many variables, human feelings, are involved in determining whether things go reasonably well or not, for me to take too seriously any strictly "economic" analysis. What a lot of money some of us have made in the past twenty years by our discounting or ignoring economists' predictions of dire disaster.

JULY 8, 1966
MARTHA'S VINEYARD

Birthday number sixty-seven. If this is the way it is being "elderly," I could use a lot more of same. The morning a benediction of light; walked the moors and the shore, very early, seeing not a soul, and feeling so lucky to be alive.

One reason one needs to be strong and healthy when he is the grandfather of screaming, bouncy, thundering-herd type boys (aged eight, ten, and eleven) is that it takes a hardy soul to stand them. *Sepa-*

rately, one by one (as when I had David 3d sailing today), they are wonderful; but mix even two together and it is physical pandemonium plus wild giggling.

JULY 13, 1966
MARTHA'S VINEYARD

A cable yesterday: Ansari has been made Minister of the Interior. Anderson seemed to think Ansari's appointment had a possible favorable interpretation for the Khuzistan program: that as Interior Minister he would be responsible for development by the provinces, the Ostands. This movement toward regional rather than national planning I ran into on my last visit to Iran. Anderson's interpretation may turn out to have some substance.

JULY 14, 1966
MARTHA'S VINEYARD

The Persians have given us a kick in the teeth, and no mistake. Cable from Sheridan giving the name of the new Managing Director of KWPA, Iraj Vahidi, a deputy of the Minister of Water and Power. So at the very time when we had reason to believe the Khuzistan was ready for a fresh initiative, we not only get a changed management, but one from a centralized Ministry antagonistic to the decentralization that Ansari and we have stood for.

Well, it isn't necessarily the end of the Khuzistan program. But the "new day" was a short one.

So far as D&R is concerned, we will be hit hard for a while if we have to withdraw, but that isn't too important. That this great regional program should fall into hands unsympathetic to regional decentralization would be a tragedy indeed.

The ups and downs of development: was there ever a more dramatic instance?

JULY 20, 1966
MARTHA'S VINEYARD

David and his entourage leave the Island in an hour, headed for Princeton, the *Raffaello*, Genoa and Florence. What an adventure.

Having felt sorry for myself (to myself) and a bit resentful the past couple days, with the place in a twirly-burly of grandchildren and me not getting that idealized *rest* that I "need," I said to Helen: "*You* certainly aren't a whiner." She looked surprised. "Well, I haven't anything to whine about." Said I: "Whiners don't need anything to whine about to whine."

JULY 21, 1966
MARTHA'S VINEYARD

Roger Baldwin came by on his annual "call." Roger continues to be puzzled about how I came to write these journal notes, all these years. "What is it; why did you keep this record of impressions and reflections?"

This rather stumped me, but I said: "I guess it is because I don't feel that an experience has been lived until I have written about it, and written down what it means to me; only then is it a complete experience."

Roger thought that one over and then continued the exploration.

"You are *aware* of the experience you have, and you're not content until you figure out what that means to you; and you try to understand who you are, and why things are as they are, in your observation of them. Now, that's a very useful thing, your recording these feelings, useful for others. But, Dave, do you think there are very many people who are like that, who reflect on things that happen to them? I don't think ten out of a hundred do."

I found this reassuring. This is a man of long experience of life.

JULY 23, 1966
MARTHA'S VINEYARD

Roger Baldwin has none of the sourness, the disillusion, or even the tired-tired outlook on life that comes—in one form or another—to most men and women who have lived through euphoria (as he certainly did, the perennial utopian and reformer) and disappointments (of which he has had more than his share, in both private and public matters).

I have often challenged him, and men like him, on their big "solutions," and their custom of chiding the world for not accepting these solutions: world government, racial equality overnight, etc. But we managers desperately need these feverishly impatient men (if they are as full of integrity as Roger) to spur us on.

I told him the story of the last several years in which the Princeton community fought over the issue of having two school systems (Borough *and* Township) or one; and Helen brought up her example of the eight years during which everyone has wanted a truck by-pass around Princeton, but always in someone else's neighborhood; so nothing has happened. My point: if you have such difficulty with simple things like these, how can we expect to solve the problems of China and world peace so quickly?

Roger rejoined in his great booming voice: "The big world problems are easier than those small ones because they are farther away."

JULY 26, 1966
WASHINGTON, D.C.

The idea that multinational aid has an acceptance that bilateral (i.e., U.S. to the aided country) does not is the chief argument against U.S. aid in the debates going on right now in the Senate. But if the time comes when there is only multinational, i.e., World Bank, aid, we will find that the growing resentment or skepticism of World Bank aid will break out into the open. No matter who provides the aid, it is going to be criticized like crazy.

JULY 27, 1966
WASHINGTON, D.C.

I never thought it would happen, but it has: Washington seems a provincial backwater! That is what a few years of living and working in a really metropolitan city will do to a country boy.

I sensed this yesterday, in lunching with Al Friendly, but it came out most strongly this morning reading a big, fat issue of the *Washington Post.* Local jokes, the gushy talk about the forthcoming wedding of the President's daughter, which sounded like LaPorte, Indiana. And the "crowded" streets and all the new glass buildings still have the flavor of a hick town. When I used to come here from the back country of the Tennessee Valley, it seemed boiling with big-city life.

New York is a place all its own; the word "city" doesn't fit; it is a form of activity, feverish, dirty, largely peopled by a different *kind* of people.

4:30 P.M.
ON THE CONGRESSIONAL LIMITED RETURNING TO NEW YORK

From 11 A.M. to 1 P.M. at the Peace Corps. A serious question about whether the Peace Corps, which began as a high adventure, may degenerate into a bureaucratic mediocrity.

What is remarkable is how strongly some of Jack Vaughn's staff feel and express themselves about the infirmities of his leadership. This is a far deeper reservation than his nitpicking quibble about whether D&R should be authorized to pay the men we find for our posts what we, who know them best, think they are worth (within the budget long since approved by the Peace Corps). Mrs. Diana MacArthur, of his top staff, quite aroused, made more sense about management than I have heard in a long time, directed against the "old-line ideas that now run this organization, ideas that don't fit when we are going into the kind of program we have contracted with D&R to develop and supervise."

The irony of a young woman talking about the old fogey ideas carried over from an earlier and crusading Peace Corps, when the whole enterprise is perhaps five years old!

JULY 30, 1966
PRINCETON

Have just come from a visit to the antiseptic little room in Princeton University's Firestone Library where, behind two sets of locks, the Lilienthal papers are at rest. It is connected to an air-conditioned work room. The guardian of the sacred portals is an attractive, dark-haired young lady. She had given up her Saturday afternoon to open the place up for me and Bob Lively. Another such room contains all that is mortal of Adlai E. Stevenson, i.e., his papers; next to him, Bernard Baruch in row upon row of neat rectangular cartons (plus some of the old boy's pet things in millionaire leather binding; just to set him off from the rest of us). In a dark and forbidding room, poor Jim Forrestal's "remains."

I was sure that next we would be shown the mummies of these gents, in glass-covered cartons.

And, talking in a whisper as I found myself doing, I couldn't help wondering what the hell I was doing walking about, apparently alive, while my three roommates were so thoroughly dead.

"Some technology problems," said Bob, looking over his glasses in a characteristic way. "If these files continue to be set upright this way, the carbon copies won't last very long; and in fifty years the paper itself of the originals will disintegrate." Fifty years from now who in the hell will care, I thought. But curators and librarians will, with all that investment of love and prestige and care, I suppose.

"In TVA," said Lively, "you gave a great deal of your time and energy to making TVA known, and it did become known, even worldwide. What you have been doing in D&R in the past ten years may well be the most significant of your several careers; I think so at least. While economic development in the less developed countries has been mostly failure and disappointment, you have at least two spectacular successes —in Colombia and Iran. And yet hardly anyone knows about these, or knows about D&R. You don't seem to assert yourself to make these things known. Why? Why the difference?"

I know the reasons—or rationalization—I give myself: we are operating in someone else's country, where I can't join issue with the critics and enemies of what we do; and it was the controversy about TVA in my own country that made my constant "interpretations" in the way of speeches and articles of news interest. Because D&R is a private company, formally at least, tooting our own horn too much seemed a bit out of line for me. Then, too, our philosophy was that we wanted our "clients" to have their confidence in *their own abilities* built up, and for us to claim too much worked against that. But I'm not sure such "explanations" fully explain why I opt for a "low profile" for D&R.

JULY 31, 1966
7 A.M.
PRINCETON

With Oliver, Burnett, and Seymour, I made an examination of what we need in the top management, branching off, inevitably, into an examination of one of our sorest spots, the absence of a complete understanding of what the management group (essentially Oliver, Burnett, and I) are doing, or not doing; in short, my gripe (and Burnett's) that the "program" divisions (technical) do not understand why they shouldn't run not only the technical side of what they do (and do damn well), but on the business side run their divisions as if each was a separate company in itself.

This is an old fallacy—or notion—among technical people. I found it in the early TVA days, and it took five years and great tumult to clarify the matter; it was also a source of friction in the early AEC. In fact, such headstrong free-wheeling personalities in AEC as Wally Zinn and Captain [Hyman] Rickover never did accept any restraints, and in Rickover's case, he played politics with Congress to get his way.

The discussion with Oliver and Burnett was almost a classic case in support of a managerial thesis of mine: that the organizational setup is a *consequence* of the kind of people, individuals, who make it up, a portrait of men, so that the question is not *where* in the organization do we fit this particular aggressive and able and stirring-up kind of man, but what would such a man do to the organization picture, its tone and direction.

Can the head, the leader of his company, perform his essential function unless he is also the kind who *digs into* "programs"? I don't see how. This, I think, is the prickly burr of doubt I can't get rid of about our top administration.

Perhaps it *is* enough to have a good "operator" as President. But the effect is inevitable: the program heads will run their shows without the kind of supervision and unified approach that makes a group of divisions into a single company.

I am searching for someone to join in this kind of outlook, and thus far I haven't found him. I'm too afraid of the risk of losing what we have to really go out for that (perhaps nonexistent) insatiable leader that I like to think I was in the early TVA days. The conditions are quite different, but the need for a fighting and not complacent head of this company to succeed me eats at me.

AUGUST 10, 1966
MARTHA'S VINEYARD

Even on a holiday I have had to keep my finger—and my ear—on D&R pretty constantly. The report on Latin American integration is something I have responsibility for, since it was my trip to San Cristobal that put us definitely into the stream of things about integration in Latin America. It has been a pioneering job of the greatest potential importance, provided we have ideas, and state them in a way that will be understood and arouse that essential ingredient, a kind of emotional response that says: "Yes, that's the way it is; yes, it can be done. Let's get at it."

Best of all is my solitary worship, early every morning: the walk to the calm and understated beauty of the moors on Cedar Tree Neck. I come back to my breakfast on the deck quite awed. The great upthrusting, everlasting boulders (the tide has been low these past mornings), the gleam of green algae at the shore where the water is trapped, the mist softening everything, the Sound, the wooded slope, a few little cabins at Miss Emma's (everyone still fast asleep) seeming so secure and cozy among the green, the beginning blush of red on the poison ivy leaves, the startled look of a tall plant with a bold yellow eye, just one eye itself. I stood back this morning; I drank all this in, with a sense of disbelief, almost, that it was all there for me, and for me alone. No wonder it seems like prayer, like worship.

AUGUST 11, 1966
MARTHA'S VINEYARD

Exuberant is the word for me on this blowy, foggy—and productive—day. It's my work that accounts for the elevation of spirits, that special kind of inner satisfaction that I get when the people I work with are fully responsive, and the work itself seems solid, pulling against the traces, hard and sustained, like a good team of Clydesdales.

AUGUST 16, 1966
MARTHA'S VINEYARD

The big D&R Latin American integration report arrived this forenoon. Today's review of it took four and a half hours, then a long phone conference with Seymour. Net result: (1) a good, strong, meaty report; and (2) I'm tired.

Penalosa cables agreement with my suggestion that we hold the Colombia-Venezuela integration meeting in Caracas.

AUGUST 17, 1966
MARTHA'S VINEYARD

After a restless night, and a hard working day yesterday, and the memory of so much of this summer spent ostensibly on holiday but actually with my work and problems, and the excitement and joy thereof all about me, I wonder: am I behaving sensibly not to have a real rest—just nothing, not even grandsons? Come October, with the hot breath of many things on me, where will the energy come from when there will be no chance for the recreation I could have here if I weren't such a pushover?

Has really *running* something again gotten into my blood so I think I'm indispensable? The honest response is I am afraid I do think I am just that to D&R, and that is a bad sign to take myself that seriously. Humorless, and bad administration.

And yet: to build this enterprise more soundly at the time when it shows white water along her lee rail as she does now, that is a sore temptation to press on more sail, bring in the main sheet, and plow ahead. These strategic times in the building of something you believe in *come when they come*, not when you feel rested.

The Logistics of Lilienthal—the title for what goes on so often in organizing me for movement; if logistics are the secret of military success, and mobility (as I believe) the heart of economic development, then getting me organized to move and be here and there, a complex business, is what makes me as effective (and, I guess, as happy) as I am.

The *flavor* of all this is an important part of what I do in this world. And if the flavor is exciting—and wearing—during an alleged "vacation," what must it be when the surroundings are the hurly-burly of New York City?

AUGUST 19, 1966
MARTHA'S VINEYARD

President Johnson made a big, expansive speech the other day celebrating the Alliance for Progress; much of it was given to "economic integration" of the Latin American continent. A strong U.S. pledge of support.

I ought to feel fine about this, since D&R's integration report is now (in draft form) in the Inter-American Development Bank's hands.

But will too much L.B.J. publicity help or hurt? If the White House, in the way it has these days, *must* take credit publicly for everything, does that help or hurt?

I feel that this integration movement will need two things: first, to keep the initiative and "authorship" *in Latin hands*, and second, plenty of financial support from the U.S. Both are needed, but if the White House's visibility is too great, then the *essential* ingredient of a Latin sense of *owning* this idea and running it for their benefit could be endangered, if not destroyed.

Whether the Johnson speech is going to have a good effect or a bad one I ought to learn before long. The exact *words* aren't so important as the effect on the minds of the Latin leaders. Some of them, i.e., Belaunde, will prefer to have "aid" come directly to them for their national projects. If integration means U.S. aid will be diminished for those national political and economic objectives, we may find this whole hopeful enterprise set back. And its chances are none too good at best.

Nancy and Sylvain's wunderkinder, Allen and Daniel, leave today for their new home in Newtonville; they have been here, in the guest house, for six weeks. Two more different human beings from the same litter I have never seen. Allen, skinny and tense, sputtering with energy so he is never quiet; Daniel, a charmer, husky with great shoulders and a dimpled grin that will make him a menace to womankind as time goes on. They "wrastle" constantly, sometimes in fun, sometimes in a fight.

I have had confirmed this summer that I have an addiction; not to LSD or heroin, but to Alexander Bell's gadget.

This growing necessity for having an earphone clapped to my head, this itch to dial and dial, is certainly *not* to be explained away—as I preferred to think—as a mark of my sense of obligation to my work.

I just *like* to keep in the middle of about the most interesting set of ideas and of action I have ever had anything to do with—and this covers a lot of ground.

The phone addiction may be my effort to assert power, since being "available" to the office (and more than available, ubiquitous, by phone), I know that I'll have my finger, or my whole sunburned ham, in everything that goes on, and with a kind of veto on everything. I, who prided himself, for a generation's time, on delegating with full confidence to associates, now turning into a Sewell Avery or a minor league L.B.J.? Horrible thought, but it could be.

AUGUST 25, 1966
KENNEDY AIRPORT, NEW YORK

My work is important; to me, certainly; and to others, many others, too.

But little by little I am coming to understand that there is something vastly more important. Living. The joy I got out of wind-moved leaves of a poplar tree in Central Park yesterday; the many colored heavy rowboats and the gaily dressed people on those boats; the baroque carvings on an arched wooden bridge across an arm of the lake; the formal angel statue and the fountain about it, the reddish color of the walk and the pavilion at this Bethesda spot, seen from the top of the heavy stone steps; the old Negro with steel spectacles and a hat high up on his head, waiting for his bus on upper Madison Avenue —a thousand and thousand things that are simple and unique—not "significant," not "important"; part of living.

If I could keep that sense warm and real within me, it would keep the blows and the pretensions and the exciting and the discouraging *things* in their place. All come second to the simple fact of living.

MARTHA'S VINEYARD

I gave "instructions" at the office that until I returned, on Labor Day, no more business, no more telephone conferences (which were the mark of this summer "vacation").

Wasn't home on this hill an hour until Helen handed me the phone with a resigned look: "The White House calling."

Someone named Komer: "Want to talk to you about Vietnam"—then he added hastily, and with a snigger, I thought, "the constructive side."

Then he went on, in a "selling" voice, to describe how much in the way of "physical assets" the U.S. had in South Vietnam—hundreds of millions. Morrison-Knudsen spent $105 million in one installation. The President wants to begin right away planning to put those assets to use after the war for the benefit of the people of that country.

He went on: "When the subject was brought up before the President the other day, he said, 'You get in touch with Dave Lilienthal, see if you can get him to go out there; we need the insights he would have.' " Said Komer, "The President said some very complimentary things about you. So now I'm calling you."

I asked many questions. What information was there—facts—about those assets, etc.? It seems Stanford Research Institute has been on a job for AID about Cam Ranh Bay, where the U.S. has built a huge port facility. I ought to see that before anything else. There was a report by Rand; "Doesn't amount to much," said Komer.

The upshot: I will see him on September 7th in Washington and see where things go from there. But anything we do should be a D&R assignment, not a personal one, I thought.

I could go out for a couple weeks as an individual; this is apparently what the President had in mind. But nothing much comes from that sort of thing; needs an organization effort, such as D&R could give it.

AUGUST 27, 1966
MARTHA'S VINEYARD

A letter from Henry Hough that Cedar Tree Neck would probably have to be sold, if Miss Emma could no longer run that establishment, or should die soon.

I had talked to Henry about the sad fate that would come to that beautiful point if "development" took over, the rock strewn shore, deep blue sea, companionable fresh pond, and comforting green moor. I wish I could own it, to preserve what it has given me (and anyone else? I never see anyone on that Neck). But that is absurd; it would require a big money investment, and we ourselves haven't that long to enjoy it. It means little to our children. So this is just dreaming.

Change does come: how many times I have written and talked about this, looking down my pretentious nose at those who resist change, or don't believe in it, or try to prevent it. So why should I think change can be averted on this island refuge, or our part of it? The Vineyard as a whole is changing, and the usual grumbling is going on. I don't feel like adding my voice to those others, unless I can give the time and energy to making the change less harmful than it has been in so many places.

11 P.M.

A silver flood fills the valley of green darkness, clear to the metallic band of light to the south, which is the sea; toward the Sound the trees caught in the moon's flood make dark blue shadows. The sounds are the sounds of approaching autumn, the cicadas, a deep rustle of wind that says that the summer is almost spent.

Is there such a thing as a moment of perfect happiness? It would be, I think, a very simple moment, even a very quiet one. Not like the exultation that comes at the moment of some kind of "victory" or profound passion. The texture of such a time of complete happiness would be delicate, gentle, an intimacy with things that are ordinary: wind-moved leaves against a pale blue summer sky. But inside, the sense of rightness, of closeness with all those things that make life rich, the quieter things that one can savor again and again, can look back on and say: That was a moment of perfect happiness. Such would be very rare. And wholly good.

AUGUST 29, 1966
MARTHA'S VINEYARD

Am I falling into an error of business (i.e., "activity") judgment I have observed and criticized in others, the "bigger and bigger volume" illusion?

D&R *is* getting more contracts, more gross revenue. The place, therefore, gives off a sense of going places in a business sense.

But how much does this mean, actually? We take on more people (added several professionals, good ones too, I gather) in agriculture, at Davis; we add to the burden of reporting, writing, conferences, decisions, at the top management level.

Each time we increase the number of our staff, instead of being able to delegate more, or "departmentalize," the load of responsibility increases for me, the threat of overhead forces us to take on more contracts, which in turn increases potential overhead drag (i.e., costs that can't be charged directly to a particular job); so we must increase the number of contracts to keep those people busy, and on and on the old merry-go-round whirls its futile way.

This pressure to get bigger reflects itself in the kind of judgment we exercise about the sort of work we do undertake. Won't we find ourselves taking on more and more of the short-term "survey" jobs, writing reports, sending out short-term "teams" of experts, becoming in effect a recruiting agency for experts? For these are the kinds of consulting jobs that are the easiest to get, the ones we are most often invited to submit proposals for.

And in the midst of my strictures on the need for *action*, not reports and investigations, aren't we in danger of becoming just another study and investigation and planning outfit, only bigger?

AUGUST 30, 1966
MARTHA'S VINEYARD

My personal "view ahead" is no more foggy than the view from our house this morning. "Is that a tree, that mound of grey? Is there something beyond that bank of fog, or is that the edge of all things, the rest swallowed up during a restless, tossing night?"

The cause of this kind of speculation: a long talk by phone with Walt Rostow at the White House, yesterday late afternoon. I called him after having had read to me by Miss Baron the full text of a letter to me "and a few selected institutions and firms," asking if we would be interested in taking responsibility for a "joint postwar development effort" in South Vietnam. In effect, an expansion of what Robert Komer had phoned me about last Thursday.

I called Walt Rostow, who now presides over foreign policy in the White House, to see if this assignment was of a priority of importance enough to justify my considering giving it a large part of my energy and time; i.e., should we submit my name as a principal participant, when D&R is being considered, along with other "consulting" outfits.

I referred to the call from Komer. When Walt made no response, I wondered if it could possibly be that he didn't know about the proposed planning enterprise.

"Know about it?" Walt replied. "I started it. Months ago."

And then on for fifteen minutes, when he broke into his discourse to say, "Excuse me, Dave, the President is calling; I'll call you back." Which he did five minutes later, and continued the exposition for another fifteen minutes, in his extraordinarily buoyant, highly articulate way.

"Yes, it is very important. Let me give you the picture as we see it today.

"We're now going through a long process out there, but you can see the balance shifting from chewing away at their military strength bit by bit to a whole set of constructive moves. On the military side, this means the classifying of areas, those that are in hand, those that are next."

A few words more of the military "progress," and then back to what I was interested in (though the two are obviously interdependent).

"A critical part is giving these people a sense that they not only have a future, but what shape it might have. This means a postwar plan; but it would have to be a particular kind [much vocal underlining of those last two words] of postwar plan. We're not thinking of the kind of economic planning that deals with the desired investment level, what the GNP should be and so on."

He went on: "If we get that *kind* of postwar plan we can begin to find ways to carry out aspects of an aid program while the fighting is still going on. The aid program now has been an import flooding aid program." (An interesting phrase, I thought; the newspaper and TV stories of black-market scandals involving aid material and gross inflation use far less abstract language than "import flooding"!)

"I regard this as having great *political* importance. More than that, it has short-range operational importance."

I suppose this last was an argument to persuade me that this wasn't just to be an economists' festival, about which nothing would be done for so long that then (the war over, happily) such a postwar plan would have little relevance.

"The President is for this; it has taken him some time to bring others in the Government around to seeing it, but he has. We're all in agreement."

I said it would be a big commitment on my energies. It would be important to know how much in the way of obstacles within the Government we would have to contend with.

"Yes," he said, "I realize you have limited resources. But I hope you will consider this seriously. You can count on it that the President and the White House would see that obstacles didn't arise, or would be removed. We want to keep this quite separate from current operational responsibilities both in Vietnam and in Washington."

I had a poor night for sleeping, with this in the back, or front, of my head.

Are we equipped for this? That is part of it.

The logistics are even worse than in Persia; this has always made that job trebly difficult and touchy, and recruiting always a headache.

The reasons for telling them next week that we do *not* want to be considered are many.

On the other side: this is a great challenge and a dare to anyone with my background and temperament. Vietnam is today a main issue, perhaps *the* main issue to which the country, perhaps the world, has given its chief attention. (Whether it deserves this I am not so sure.) Besides, this would be an experience in the Far East, where the future of the world is being shaped far more than in Europe or Africa. As the songs these days have it, "That is where the action is."

Am I so nearly finished for such strenuous jobs that I don't want to try another, to risk my reputation, which continues good, on so shaky a prospect? I must quit taking on huge new dares *sometime*. Is this the time?

SEPTEMBER 1, 1966
MARTHA'S VINEYARD

There *are* more important things in life than those that for so many years have absorbed me, have commanded almost all my energies —and my senses. How completely this career of work has driven me, making almost everything else secondary (or less), making this work-life the measure of everything, I hadn't realized, until the past few years.

Such ruminations flooded in on me in the hour or so I spent on the moors and the shore of Cedar Tree Neck in the very early morning, a couple hours ago.

A smoky, otherworldly blur over the dark green of the swelling moor, the smooth sheet of the little fresh water pond, and beyond it, such a turbulent growling and leaping surf as I haven't seen on the Sound since I can remember, great deep swells, the sky-reaching wave then gracefully turning and falling into a swirling sheet of white water, or exploding over the huge twin boulders that point toward the sky like breasts of some gargantuan woman. Just out of reach of the rushing salt water a green clump of vetch dotted with the lavender of its bloom, and nearby the glaucous leaves of some grey plant: the two worlds of the power of crazed water and the serenity and self-assurance of land-based life not five feet apart. The sights, the sounds, the joy of being *there* to see and feel and hear were ends in themselves, reason enough for being alive. This awareness, without purpose, the awareness being purpose enough, this I have missed for so many long years.

SEPTEMBER 2, 1966
MARTHA'S VINEYARD

Looking much less favorably on taking on the Vietnam assignment, requiring a big chunk of *my* time—perhaps a third of the working year.

To sum up: D&R needs to do a *far* better job on what we now do, so we shouldn't spread out and thin our efforts. Particularly mine.

The practical conclusion that appears to emerge is: let's not take on so difficult a job as the South Vietnam postwar planning task (if offered to us) and instead do a better job with what we already have.

A triumph! Not of good sense, and certainly not discretion, but a triumph over timidity and faintheartedness—and some fear.

In short, *Lili-put* and I sailed across the Sound to the entrance of Falmouth Harbor, on a day of considerable breeze and unusual wave conditions—great swells breaking in mid-Sound. (The wave conditions due to the edge effects of the hurricane off the Carolina coast.)

In midchannel it was wild, the wave pattern "contradictory," I guess is the term, and it was quite a problem keeping *Lili-put* from being hit hard on the beam.

But I made it over, *and back*, and was very happy. And now am insufferably cocky.

SEPTEMBER 5, 1966
NEW BEDFORD AIRPORT

Going through one of those crises of nerve, not of nerves. For in a few days I must decide whether I am willing to take on another "impossible" job, a snarled skein of political and managerial and economic and bureaucratic problems the like of which I haven't been confronted with before—has anyone?

The South Vietnam setting, in itself, makes this task tough, frustrating, and, because of the distances and the agonies of bloodshed, less amenable to reason and the guidance of precedent than anything I have ever tried.

Talking to Leona Baumgartner; she gave me a fight talk. Of course I should offer to take this Vietnam job. Had I ever run away from a "challenge"? Perhaps I could bring to the tangled and tired Vietnam story a fresh viewpoint. "And as for your health—if that thought has crossed your mind and made you hesitate, look at you; I have never seen you look better or stronger. And you know it."

SEPTEMBER 8, 1966
NEW YORK

An unappetizing job, with an absolute minimum of apparent prospects for doing something effective: that is the "morning after" feeling I have about the Vietnamese "postwar planning" proposal.

However willing AID may be to assure us that a minimum of the characteristic AID procedural constipation would mark this job, both their longstanding uninspired habits plus the real legal obstacles to their functioning as well as, say, a small town City Council Committee on garbage disposal, would make this a colossal bundle of frustrations.

Having said all this, if we are asked to undertake it, on something like our terms, I am sure we should try it. Sorely needs to be done; we can do it as well, probably better, than anyone else; patriotism more often than not is expressed by attempting impossible things.

The State Department Board of Consultants job on International Control of the Atom looked impossible. Nothing came of it, if the measure is that we "produced" an end to national rivalries in atomic weapons—a most modest goal indeed! And yet a good deal came of it; the hopes of the world *were* stirred, and not unreasonably, not fancifully; and, on a personal plane, it was an extraordinarily maturing experience for me.

We entered the West basement door of the White House at the appointed hour: 10 o'clock yesterday morning. We met Bob Komer, Rostow's assistant for Vietnamese affairs. A somewhat hyperthyroid fellow, very articulate, excited, full of remarks about the "bureaucrats," meaning AID, who are the source of funds for this operation, but an intense and devoted public servant withal, complete with the pipe which marks the present brains corps.

Oliver wanted to discuss the staffing problems we would have, getting people signed up on an assignment of this kind before anyone really knew what the approach or scope or conditions would be. Yes, they recognized that; they smiled on us indulgently, said the decisions would be made not by AID but "here."

SEPTEMBER 12, 1966
8 A.M.
BOGOTÁ, COLOMBIA

The plateau looked ever so green and prosperous as we flew in yesterday. To look at that fertile, verdant carpet below, with its elaborate barns, and the elegance of downtown Bogotá, you would never believe that this is an "underdeveloped" country. The enormous potential is here, human and material. What's wrong?

Enrique Penalosa met us at the plane, bounding with energy and smiles as usual.

He had invited a group of men to his home for dinner, to discuss the Venezuela-Colombia effort toward economic integration. Enrique is optimistic that something now can actually happen, after years of fencing. But Virgilio Barco, one of the guests, was less sanguine: "The Colombian delegation has too many representatives of the vested interests, who will be at the Caracas meeting to look out that nothing is done that will hurt their special interest. They won't understand the macroeconomic view." Lauchlin Currie, not given to lighthearted optimism about *anything* economic, seemed to agree.

This noon we go to the Palace for a luncheon for me given by the President; the discussion will be about the forthcoming meeting with Venezuela. I'm to meet Lauchlin Currie shortly, with a brilliant young MIT graduate, Rodrigo Botero,* the President's chief assistant, to see if we can work out, orally at least, an area in which we can make some headway, narrow though it may be at the start.

10:30 A.M.

Whatever have I let myself in for now?

Lauch Currie, looking brisk and happy and full of ideas, just here for an hour. He gave me an idea of how much they expect this "impartial Lilienthal, whom everyone trusts" can do to bring about a combining of economic forces between Colombia and Venezuela. Absurd. For an anti-economist, as I am, to be responsible for an economic study of the kind he visualizes should be terrifying or amusing—and I should take the first plane back. But I won't; the more fool I.

* In 1975, Rodrigo Botero became Colombian Minister of Finance.

5 P.M.

At a distance of perhaps fifty feet the diminutive Presidente Carlos Lleras Restrepo, reading quietly at a huge desk, made me think of the cartoon character The Little King. But what a contrast to the man who occupied that Presidential office the first time I saw it, twelve years ago: the military dictator General Gustavo Rojas Pinilla. *This* President has a brain, a very active, searching, alert brain. And eyes that twinkle with amusement.

With us at the meeting before lunch were an interesting sampling of Colombians. The President's secretary, the taut, tense, and extraordinarily handsome Rodrigo Botero. Edgar Gutierrez, big, curly headed, perhaps thirty-five, head of the Office of Planeacion. The wisp of a figure of Lauchlin Currie, once more an advisor of a President (he was most influential with F.D.R. as one of the famous "anonymous assistants") and upon whom this Colombian President is leaning more and more. Virgilio Barco, a solid and harassed man, persistently pursuing his goal of some important kind of economic cooperation between Colombia and Venezuela.

Barco's comments about why Venezuela is now probably receptive to the idea of working together with Colombia were very realistic: Venezuela has expanded its industrial capacity, enormously, but finds that without far greater markets than are now available to them, their costs are not competitive, and their food and manpower situation not as good as they once thought. Despite one and one half billion dollars of foreign exchange from their oil, annually, the country isn't doing well enough to continue to regard Colombia as its inferior economically.

The President was explicit. He wants D&R to enter into separate contracts, one with Colombia, one with Venezuela, to take charge of the studies to explore the possibilities of a kind of "mutual growth" (my phrase) that will also help to solve other kinds of problems—the migration of trained Colombians to Venezuela, for example, or the uneasiness that will come to Venezuela if Colombia continues to have so many people far poorer than the Venezuelans.

And now to read some e. e. cummings poems: to provide for me the lyricism without which I perish, surrounded as I am so much of the time with these sober, heavy thinkers.

SEPTEMBER 13, 1966
BOGOTÁ

Today I joined in lengthy discussion with two exceptional personalities, two of the best leaders with whom I have ever threshed out managerial questions. Both Colombians, citizens of an "underdeveloped country." What a laugh, for anyone to call a country "underdeveloped" which can produce two such men.

This morning, from 8:00 until 12:30 with Enrique Penalosa. A more lucid, sensible exposition of management philosophy and its application to a set of specific problems I have rarely heard. The issue: how to bring D&R's "collective judgment" to the aid of INCORA's nationwide agricultural reform and development program.

The second personality was Bernardo Garces. Though recently become Minister of Public Works, he continues to run my brain-child the Cauca Valley Corporation and doubtless will return there full time one of these days. We picked up our discussion about the need for a new ten-year look ahead at CVC.

"I told the CVC boys," said Bernardo, "that power was no more the chief function of a regional CVC; power supply now was a national matter. So it is the natural resources of the Cauca Valley that need a looking at, with a view to the best and earliest use of the land not now productive, or sufficiently productive. So the comprehensive survey you and I talked about is ripe."

After all these years in which CVC became synonymous for a successful and hectic attempt to keep up power supply, build dams and power plants, to have a man so supple of mind that he could say these things pleased me to my heeltaps.

SEPTEMBER 14, 1966
ON IBERIA AIRLINES, TAKING OFF FROM BOGOTÁ TO CARACAS

I have just had handed me by Lauchlin Currie a draft of "terms of reference" of a study D&R will be asked, at Caracas, to undertake on behalf of *both* Colombia and Venezuela. "The study," the draft begins, will be concerned, broadly speaking, with an exploration of the possible magnitude of a combined internal market of some 26 million people, and with ways and means of developing this market to the common benefit of the people of both countries; in pursuit of these broad objectives the study will place its main emphasis on how the combined effective demand may be increased and how this increased demand may be most economically met by a better utilization of resources . . . and so on.

Difficult as this is, it is not impossible for technical economists to make such a study. But will anything come of it if it is done as an exercise in economists' expertise? That is what concerns me most. And will I get bogged down by the superspecialists that economists more and more have become? And is it possible for D&R operating on an *indivisible subject* to operate with *two* employers, two sovereign and suspicious neighbors, even though (as is intended) we sign identical contracts with each?

SEPTEMBER 15, 1966
CARACAS, VENEZUELA

To face a group of gentle but tough-looking men, by the hour, and hear your name repeated again and again, and "resources and development" interspersed, and hardly understand one word! And to be picked out as the best hope of bringing together two neighboring nations, although an outsider. I wonder if quite this scenario has ever before been written for a *private person*?

This afternoon's meeting is with the industrial leaders of Venezuela, this incredibly rich country—rich with so many poor; the old story.

What greatly surprised and pleased me this morning was how little difference developed between the representatives of the two countries, or between the several representatives on each "side." The "terms of reference" the Colombians had prepared were discussed, point by point, and with only slight changes proposed, slight considering how deep into the life of these two countries we are expected to go in this study, assuming (as I do) that we will contract with them to carry on what may be a task of great scope and magnitude—and implications.

It is now 7 P.M., and we are still going. This morning the meeting was incisive, and decisions were made between the "missions" of the two countries quickly and with only very pointed discussion. This afternoon's meeting has reverted to the kind of Latin American style of discussion with which, alas, I'm familiar: much *talk*.

I find it deeply satisfying to note that the outwardly stolid Walt Seymour is so excited about these meetings and what may come of them. Riding over here this afternoon, he said, "We are not only seeing history; we are part of it." That's my kind of emotionalism, but that he feels it and says it gives some mark of how this has gripped us.

AT CORDIPLAN, IN THE "WHITE PALACE"

This morning a message that set everybody hastily putting on their coats (it had gotten to the shirtsleeves stage by that time): we were expected immediately at the President's office. And off we went, on foot.

Ushered into the usual splendor: much gilt on furniture, enormous portraits of Venezuelan heroes, and little brown men with automatic rifles. Seated, stiffly, on big chairs, after shaking hands solemnly with President Leoni.

Leoni was in the greatest possible contrast, in appearance and manner, with a President with whom he is so close in ideas, Carlos Lleras of Colombia. A big square man, great heavy glasses, a deep, deep voice. I was fascinated by the way his *fingers*, as he spoke, were constantly weaving. Except for those twining, almost serpentine fingers, he was most composed and rock-like. I heard myself referred to in his brief remarks; the rest was, I gather, the usual emanations of rhetoric about "dos paises."

Will they *ever* get through with the semantics around this table?

All of us Americans (including Currie, now formally a Colombian) say we have never seen a conference on so difficult a subject in which so much progress was made so smoothly. And not a particle of friction, or tension, or anything resembling hostility between these two groups.

SEPTEMBER 17, 1966
IN FLIGHT, PAN AM, CARACAS TO KENNEDY

Once again it was the men, the individuals new to me, with whom I worked, saw at close range, laughed and argued, that interested me the most. Not in the spirit of "the proper study of mankind," but something more specific. Part of the dynamics of change (change being my business) is to be understood and savored only by objective and yet warm comprehension of *particular individuals* who shape change. (For "change" substitute "development" perhaps, but I like the simple word better.)

What we *did* in the two days in Caracas, the outcome, is pioneering under very exceptional circumstances. Three gringos (Walt, Fred Moore, and I) sitting, initially, between two countries who have agreed on very few important things for a long time; then sitting *with* them, in an atmosphere of trust and cordiality and respect. And out of this unusual mark of confidence in us and the salutary effect of our presence at their international conference table came a series of agreements, which will be officially published today as the Acta de Caracas, signed by the authorized representatives of each country.

All this looks to an open-minded exploration of the possible benefits to both countries that could come from putting the "demand" and the resources of two very different countries together, piece by piece. At least I think it will be piece by piece, rather than in any dramatic joining together on a "global" basis. (How the Latins, in South America and Italy, love that word global, as an adjective.)

I was quite moved by the lean, intense, and very tired face and figure of Rodrigo Botero, the Colombian President's Secretary. He was exhausted by the long drain. But when I spoke to him, at the "cocktails" later, and reminded him of the unique opportunity he has not only to see the wheels of change, but to be part of them, he lighted up, his eyes glowing under a dark shock of unruly hair. I said, "The problem you have, as a man devoted to your family and to your intellectual interests, of making room for anything else beside the daily and nightly pressure of the President's Office, is one I know something about—indeed I knew about it at about your age [he is thirty-two]." This kind of recognition of him as an individual, not as a member of a mixed commission, appealed to him.

SEPTEMBER 22, 1966
NEW YORK

It is an up-in-the-clouds one day, an on-the-edge-of-the-precipice the next day, kind of enterprise, this D&R.

We hang by our fingernails because the long promised advance payment from Iran is still "promised"—two weeks more and we will be absolutely compelled to terminate our field forces of almost forty people or go broke trying to finance what they should be advancing funds for.

We have been through these financial cliffhangers before, God knows; but never before have we been anywhere nearly as close to eating into that reserve I insisted on almost eleven years ago. And at the very time when the substantive program in Iran seems definitely back on the track.

No amount of philosophizing about "that's the way it is when you are dealing with such a country" makes things seem any cheerier tonight.

By an ironic coincidence it was this afternoon late that I presided over a round table discussion at the Council on Foreign Relations to hear the Iranian Minister of Finance, Jamshid Amouzegar. A handsome, slender man in his middle forties, who has occupied four Cabinet posts —Labor, Health, Agriculture, and now Finance—he gave a demonstration of the Persian character: warm and friendly, unbelievably candid, defensively introspective about the sensitivity of the Persian because of the centuries of outside domination, extraordinarily lucid and almost terrifyingly intense. That he is aware that the "barter" deals the Shah has made with the Soviets lately are full of danger for Iran he made more clear by understatement than he may have realized. "But what alternative have we?" he kept saying; and answering his question: "The Americans and the British could provide help now at little cost to the West that could bring us through the difficult next few years."

Driving back from the Council with him, I spoke of the importance of Khuzistan, which underlines the point he made so emphatically and at length about the relative importance of agriculture in such a country, compared to more and more emphasis on industrialization. The Shah, he said, intends to continue to give this high priority to agriculture for "another twenty years."

"And it is important, too," said I, "because it gives a dignity to agriculture for young people, as a career, rather than crowding into the cities at a time when there aren't jobs for them there."

Miss Baron, amused by an editorial in the *New York Daily News* about "my" ideas about Latin American integration providing vitamins and "jet propellant" for Latin America, remarked today: "Any more jet propulsion from you and I will have to get a different job." I do drive hard; fact; but I also let up, and that, I hope, will keep me going, and happy, and therefore healthy.

SEPTEMBER 24, 1966
PRINCETON

A headline in this morning's *Times*: Litton Cancels Greek Contract.

Which brought to mind, of course, the long session in my office with Roy Ash, and his systems-minded John Rubel, months ago, when they tried to find out how *we* would go about the "transformation" of Greece.

For a long time now the aircraft and missiles people of the West Coast and the econometric zealots at MIT and Harvard have been obsessed with the idea that their systems analysis ideas could produce "models" that would make economic development "rational"—by their notions of what is rational. Lockheed and others came to AID with these notions.

Educated nonsense, I thought. Now comes this Litton "systems" debacle in Greece (after spending one doesn't know how much of Litton's and Greece's money and time). But also admissions of similar disillusion about simplistic worship of systems "models" by some World Bank economists; they are really quite sad; honest and candid, but sad, after all these years of being off the track.

To design a guided missile—which was Litton's staff's capability—techniques of systems analysis have been a great success. But men are not missiles; to guide missiles is one thing, *to guide men* takes not systems analysis, but human understanding, and these are quite different things.

Gradually our technical brethren are coming to realize that economic development is not just an exercise in systems analysis or econometrics; that what the technician euphemistically calls "political incompatibility" which makes his mathematical model of development a "dream" is really the *technician's* incompatibility with human institutions and emotions. Experience with human history and human institutions is the only way this incompatibility can be brought into harmony with the facts of life.

SEPTEMBER 29, 1966
WAITING AT PENN STATION, HEADING FOR PRINCETON

Our "advance" from Iran arrived just as I was starting for the train. What a relief. Two more days and Burnett would have been on his way to Iran to terminate thirty-five field people! That was a close one. Now to prevent its happening again when this money runs out in mid-November!

A call from Cardenas of the Inter-American Development Bank, speaking for "the President" (i.e., Herrera). The leading Lima newspaper, *La Prensa*, all heated up about something in our integration report; an all night session of the Peru Assembly: the IDB has an "aberration" that the waters of Lake Titicaca are of any concern to Chile. All this is the result of some incidental reference in our report that this lake's hydro and irrigation potential might be made the basis of a multinational undertaking for Peru, Chile, and Bolivia.

There will be many more irritated hackles raised before this integration report is fully absorbed in Latin America. It is getting a very wide distribution; the newspapers are carrying long stories and comment in Latin America, and the requests for copies are so numerous that IDB is printing 1000 more copies in English, added to the Spanish edition. In Buenos Aires, *La Prensa* opines, the report is expected to provide el fundamento for the meeting of the Western Hemisphere Presidents in early 1967.

So we have done something useful in formulating the issues and the prospects. Let's try to *make something happen*, is my prayer.

OCTOBER 1, 1966
PRINCETON

Yesterday my first gardening for weeks: digging up great juicy iris clumps, dividing them, slicing off the ends of the rhizomes with a butcher knife, replanting. The strange delights of working in the soil do not lessen with time.

Have been filled with an excited kind of indignation at what seems to me an unfairness toward President Johnson which one finds everywhere. Almost entirely over the war in Vietnam. I don't recall meeting or talking with anyone who doesn't express the strongest kind of criticism. That a war should be "popular" is nonsense, of course; but that a President's intimate personal characteristics and behavior should be so *contemptuously* assessed disturbs me. Part of this is the contrast with the attractive President he succeeded, his freshness, wit, and particularly his youthfulness. Wilson and F.D.R.'s personal qualities were much talked about and held against them; but I can't remember anything like this flood of antagonism for the way a man is put together.

OCTOBER 4, 1966
NEW YORK

Fed up to *here* with the Fairless Lectures—Humanist Art of Management—and D&R saving the world, I twisted Beatrice's arm, by phone, and demanded that she accompany me to the new Whitney Museum. Which she did, and for two hours, among those American pictures (from Copley to Pop-ley and all in between), I lived in another world—along with a huge mob of people, drawn to this extraordinary new concrete palace of the arts.

Almost twenty-five years ago, Beatrice took me to my first museum; introduced me to what art is all about; she had then and still has the best understanding of the *meaning* of painting and sculpture I have ever known. No prissy "lectures" to the art-heathen; no "art appreciation" condescension; just enough words of explanation to make the life of the artist, the *person* behind the painting, understandable.

4:30 P.M.
ABOARD EASTERN, WAITING TO TAKE OFF FOR NEW YORK

The Vietnamese Minister of Economy Thanh; the head of their National Bank, Hanh; and Ambassador to the U.S. Vu Van Thai are quite precious, highly sophisticated products. Can they possibly understand a rural population of rice growers? This is what ran through my mind as I looked at their delicate, citified faces, listened to their high-bred talk, their inordinate pleasure in having spent time with the President of the U.S. yesterday.

The assumption (spilled by one of Komer's aides, eager young Charles Cooper, but implicit with the rest of the group) is that D&R is the outfit that will head a field team for this post-hostilities project; that Lilienthal will accept responsibility for this operation.

This isn't as much of a compliment as it may sound: I would guess that most everyone else who could be considered has turned down the responsibility. If this is true we are in the position of winning a "competition" where all the competitors have said, "No, thanks just the same."

Can there be any doubt that this pinpoint on the globe—Vietnam—is brewing the deepest trouble for the whole of mankind? Vietnam is like an infection, a "culture" of some horrible disease, a cancer where the wildly growing cells multiply and multiply until the whole body is poisoned.

In the brisk, bright sun of the first fall day, walked back to the Hay Adams with Bob Nathan, who attended the Blair House meeting.

Bob had a dozen reasons why *I* should undertake this Vietnam business, and a dozen reasons why (I pressing him) *he* couldn't: his consulting company is already overloaded; he can't go out there himself; he has a wife and three children; he doesn't believe in Johnson (though in seeking and getting consulting contracts with AID for his firm he manages to see a good deal of Johnson); all of his Americans for Democratic Action liberal friends are shocked that he would get mixed up in anything to do with Vietnam, etc., etc.

I was shocked and angry at his refusal to get "involved" in an area in which he is professionally an outstanding man.

OCTOBER 7, 1966
NEW YORK

Dinner with Lauchlin Currie, an extraordinary man on every count. A bold *thinking* mind; and what a vast difference to Colombia that just this one 105-pound bright-eyed little man is there. What a good time he is having, thinking, writing, but most of all teaching young Colombians (and mid-career ones, too) some of the elements of his "version of economics"—this is the modest way he puts it, though of course, like most economists, he really believes his version is the right one.

As we had dinner he reminisced about his early days; utterly fascinating. Graduate of a small, remote Nova Scotia Catholic college, he went to London with no money. ("I lived during the week mostly on bread and milk so on Saturday night I could dress up and go dancing.") London at that time meant [Richard Henry] Tawney, Harold Laski, Bertrand Russell, great figures, "but most important to me was the whole atmosphere of London, the excitement, the whirling excitement of new ideas. I was almost made dizzy by it all."

Became a member of the Harvard faculty, then later head of the Foreign Economic Administration in Washington. The rest, I should say, is history: his closeness to F.D.R. he minimized, but I think the record is otherwise.

He said a perceptive thing about my journal writing. "Sometimes," he said, tentatively and gently, almost as a warning, "a journal takes over a man, becomes his reason for doing things so he can write about them. Has that happened to you?"

I don't know, actually. But since I do many other things than write these notes, the presumption surely must be that the journal helps me through the things I do, or attempt, most of which are in the field of action, rather than contemplation.

OCTOBER 7, 1966
AT PENN STATION WAITING TO LEAVE FOR PRINCETON

Brendan Gill has a rave review of the movie *Seconds* in the latest *New Yorker*, and he gives much of the "credit" to David Ely, his plot and novel. Praise from Brendan Gill is praise indeed.

Saw André Meyer at 3:30, for an hour.

I wanted to get his reaction to the proposition of my taking responsibility for a postwar planning effort in Vietnam. I recalled his very strong feeling, expressed to me first months and months ago, that the President had been badly advised; this country should have withdrawn; that when we couldn't withdraw, we should not have set down conditions to discussions, such as that we wouldn't include the Viet Cong in the peace conferences. Which *now* of course we freely grant.

But about the prospect that D&R be asked to do this important job being discussed with us: "Do it, by *all* means.

"I warn you," he said, with feeling, "against having more to do with the Vietnamese themselves than you can help to get the job done. It isn't that they aren't smart and able. But so many of them are just crooks. I know Saigon's reputation; I have known that city for fifty years. It is a sordid place. The French took everything they could out of Indochina, did whatever they did for their own benefit; some of the things were good, but most were just to fatten themselves. It is a country that could be made to produce food—things you know how to do."

McNamara has been talking with André recently; has asked to see him again when he returns from the trip to Vietnam on which McNamara leaves tomorrow. That André was pleased at this recognition was evident, and why not? But André intimated that even McNamara is ready to listen to those who press for a change in direction. That a new approach to Hanoi may be in the wind seems a likely surmise. If in fact the hostilities may be within a year of ending, then a postwar planning job isn't entirely a public gesture, at this stage.

André asked about Iran; he had heard how at the very last moment before we terminated our force, a payment had come in. I commented that the reason they gave was a "shortage of foreign exchange." He snorted. Said: "Swiss accounts." Then a pause, musing. "A few weeks ago the head of the Bank Melli was here visiting at Lazard, an excellent young man. Left to go to Paris. To buy more than a million dollars' worth of diamonds for the coronation—you know they are going to have a coronation soon. Yes, I know that they already have royal jewels by the bushels, but they aren't just right; have to spend a fortune on special diamonds."

He had that sad worn look one gets after a lifetime of seeing the way some powerful people behave.

André walked me out to the elevator. "How does the President himself feel about this work proposed for you in Vietnam?" I said I had been told by the men in the White House that he strongly favored the idea of an advance job on long-range planning for the rebuilding and strengthening of the country. But one of the White House group—a foreign service officer who has spent much time out there—said, "The trouble is that even those closest to the President are never sure whether to believe him or not."

As he put me in the elevator, André made a cryptic remark: "The President is better than he looks." I think André believes him, and I do myself, strongly in fact.

André had spoken with considerable pride, I thought, about how greatly pleased Herrera is with our IDB report. "I sat next to him at dinner the other evening and he was full of praise."

This is confirmed by a letter to me from Herrera, an extract from which I copy here.

"In my view the report has accomplished the following objectives: (*a*) through the presentation of the integration cause in such a concise and forceful way, public opinion in this country will realize the seriousness of the Latin American integration movement, and the need for not only technical and financial assistance but also for political and moral support; and (*b*) it conveys to the Latin American countries the idea that economic integration is a feasible objective, and that it can be achieved if we strive hard and engage all of our endeavors toward that end, especially if all the Latin American nations begin to think on a regional basis, with this common objective in mind.

" . . . Feel assured that the Bank is satisfied with the results of your cooperation and that of your staff and I am convinced that from our joint efforts good results will be achieved."

OCTOBER 13, 1966
NEW YORK

Stimulating days, indeed *over*stimulated times for me.

An intrepid—or foolhardy—man scales Everest to reach the highest point on the globe. But who ever heard of such a man setting out to reach those rarefied, ecstatic heights a *second* time?

In quite another way—but a comparable one—I find that having reached what for me is an emotional ascent to an altitude surely not everyone reaches does not mean that I am then content to put that kind of excitement aside by saying: "I have done it once; what point can there be in repeating it?"

These ascents (or sustained high altitude of excitement and emotional involvement) are what I am going through, and "enjoying it *thoroughly*," these latter days.

Not conducive to sleep at night, this sort of mountain climbing. But that can come later. It is the way I have worked on so many of these binges, these intellectual and emotional travels to what for me is an individual summit. Getting down, I should add, is sometimes accompanied not by "bends," but a letdown that can be uncomfortable, particularly for those around me. But what the hell. Everything, we used to say as kids, everything that goes up must come *down*. But think how awful if it never went up.

OCTOBER 15, 1966
PRINCETON

The last mile for Robert Oppenheimer—and it may be a very short one.

Yesterday I phoned to ask if I could drop in on one of my walks. Today he called me: Could I come by about 3 P.M.? A sunny day, of falling leaves, a harlequin pattern over this beautiful part of Princeton. We sat outside the white Bauhaus-type place to which they have moved, since the new Director of the Institute, Carl Kaysen, came to occupy Olden Manor.

Robert talked about his throat: it seemed to be well, they had a good summer, and then, a couple weeks ago, "It began again, badly. Said it was not operable, but I go in three times a week for radiation."

Kitty had all she could do to suppress her tears. We talked about Tony, their daughter. 'She is one of those young people who are unfortunate enough to want to do good," said Kitty, her great dark eyes looking right through me.

"I thought it was a mistake," said Robert, "for you to take the Chairmanship of the AEC after your part in that really important Board of Consultants—a great letdown. I was for you, of course, when I was asked, but for your own sake and that of the ideas you had about the atom, I had sober thoughts."

I spoke of his former secretary, wondering how she could enjoy the disarmament job. "I don't understand it," he said, "spending all that time and those years trying to make things appear good when they aren't good."

What does such a man think, confronted with death, a man with his head so full of ideas, so wise in so many directions, such great understanding of the way the invisible physical world moves and has its being—what goes through his mind, what goes on behind those eyes that were once so brilliantly blue, now rather bleary with pain and probably drugs?

What does he think of the inevitability he faces?

OCTOBER 16, 1966
PRINCETON

Spent an hour or so with an interesting Ghanaian, William Van Lare, who represents his country as Ambassador to Canada and at the UN. A friend of Tom Mead.

Much as he obviously likes and admires Tom (at one time District Commissioner in Ghana for the British Colonial Office), his comparison of the Americans he knew in Ghana, and the British, was all favorable to the Americans, and he wasn't careful to spare Tom's feelings. (Not that Tom seemed in the least sensitive about what "Willie" said.)

"The Americans would go out without a hat. All this business about having to wear a hat was just nonsense, they said. And they worked with their hands; they would get down there and work right alongside the Africans. The English overseer would wear his pith helmet and say: 'Do it this way; you there, do that.' The Americans would be down there *doing* it. Now, that made a great impression on us, a different way of operating entirely."

I was a bit puzzled at first about the bit about not wearing a hat. Now I see that this was part of the informality that appealed to the black people, particularly in the villages.

I asked him: "Why don't the Ghanaians themselves get more out of the electric power of the Volta, now that the power is there? There is barely a trace of it in Accra, and none at all in the villages." The Ghanaians "were told" that the cost of getting the power to the people in Accra was too great because the houses are not close enough together; and in the villages, they are much too far apart; too costly.

This provoked me; it was the same kind of nonsense that for so long kept electricity from the rural areas of the U.S., particularly in the Tennessee Valley, when TVA began thirty-five years ago. The fact is, I said to Van Lare, that the cost of services is likely to be as high or higher in a big congested city than in bringing power to the villagers.

OCTOBER 19, 1966
NEW YORK

The point of no return is close at hand in terms of that impossible yet fascinating job of national development for Vietnam. A phone call from Bob Komer yesterday noon: would I object greatly should the President decide that Manila is the place at which to say that "I have asked one of our distinguished Americans, Dave Lilienthal, to look into postwar planning for Vietnam," to announce this even before D&R had a contract, with all that fine print, to do the job?

It seems increasingly apparent to me that D&R—and I—will be selected for this tough, literally undo-able planning job with high visibility. The last chance to be cautious and noncommittal was yesterday in talking to Komer. But I didn't resort to cautiousness because three weeks of exploration convinces me that, somehow or other, we can do better than anyone else what needs to be done.

Helen came in to town with me Monday morning. That late afternoon we went to a movie house and saw *Seconds*, the film based on our son's book. The first part was very much in keeping with the serious and universal theme of middle age: the man who had "succeeded" in getting the things he wanted, or (as was implied in the novel) he was *taught* to want, and who found, at fifty, that they amounted to nothing.

The rest of the film dramatized in a spectacular and bizarre way, as did David's novel, the "successful" man's (and every man's and probably most women's) desire to have a second chance to find those satisfactions and excitements which he had thought he was going to find at the end of the rainbow of success—and hadn't.

To the annual dinner last night of the Planned Parenthood Federation. These public dinners are almost as tiresome—they last *so* long—when you sit in the dinner audience as when you are on the dais preparing to make a speech. But this one had one surprise, a source of great reassurance. Willard Wirtz, big, beefy, young, with a crew cut of grey-sprinkled hair, made an enormous impression on me. His speech (a response to the awarding of the Margaret Sanger Award to President Johnson) was a revelation. Graceful, philosophical, broad in its concept, delivered with the poise of an experienced speaker and a confident man, with a great voice.

I found this more than made up for listening for forty-five minutes to the singsong major speech about food by a man who had a lot of nerve advising the world on what to do to increase its food: Dr. Sen, the pallid-voiced Indian who heads FAO, the Food and Agriculture Organization. *Now* (after all these years) his organization is going to do something about the situation. And what does this consist of? A great big fat global planning job, and more wheat from the U.S., whose granaries are fast reaching a low level, thanks largely to the fact that India has done so damned little these fifteen years past to step up its own food production. I was furious, not at Sen, who is a sweet Anglicized Indian, but that FAO was just starting *now* on something it has been responsible for, and had botched, all these years.

At a few minutes after six this evening a subdued, almost deferential young man, looking tentative, came through the street door at the Century, and I could hear a soft, quiet voice inquire for Mr. Lilienthal.

I can't remember ever having my impression of a man change so much and so suddenly. As Senator Robert Kennedy told me of his plans for a new start for the black Bedford-Stuyvesant region of Brooklyn, I asked myself: Could this earnest young man possibly be the same fellow pictured by the press and TV as a cynical, ambitious, ruthless trickster dealing only with political issues that would "pay off"? And what about my own impressions as I watched him ruthlessly hammer the delegates on the floor of the Convention at Los Angeles in 1960, or strut cockily about at a White House dinner during his brother's reign?

As we sat at a round table in the half dark and wholly sedate Century lounge I was struck by what a difference there can be between the image of this man speaking to a huge TV audience and the man now concentrating on persuading a single individual, in this case me, to join in this humanitarian project he has begun. He has a fine resonant speaking voice in one-to-one conversation, deep, without the singsong or the Bahstan intonation of the TV Kennedy.

What brought this meeting about? A call from André; "Bobby," he said, "wants to discuss with you a big project he has in mind. I have agreed to be part of a group to work with him on it; he doesn't know you, and knows I do. Will you call him and discuss whether you can see him?"

I assumed from this account that it was André who had suggested that Kennedy get me interested in the Senator's "project"; when I said something of the kind to Kennedy, he grinned, looked at his two young staff men who were with us and said, almost shyly: "It was my idea to try to get you interested."

The "project" is at this point an idea, a new approach to the ugly, recalcitrant, intractable problem of the black ghetto in the great cities. Kennedy said, "Things are deteriorating, and the more money the Federal Government pours in, the more serious the problem becomes, because nothing basic is being done, except to put these people on a permanent dole."

His idea is more than an idea, since he has had the Pratt Institute and others in the area getting the basic facts about this section of Brooklyn. These he reeled off in an impressive way—how the people live, what they live on, etc. There are 400,000 Negroes in the Bedford-Stuyvesant area, but no political boss, as in Harlem, which he said makes the former area more feasible for study.

But the heart of his idea is to transform, to convert living, health, and educational conditions so the area may become a profitable and sound one for new manufacturing operations, providing jobs and training on the job, for people who at present are without the most meager education or qualifications for good jobs. Could Bedford-Stuyvesant be made a place where a business could be established with a chance of success? This is where he wants private business judgment, as well as mine, which embraces both private business and some knowledge of government and social questions.

I told him I would examine a report he handed me, and let him know in twenty-four hours or so whether I would be available.

The question I had put to André when he had called me was: Is this a political gambit? After listening to Kennedy I was fully persuaded that it was not political, certainly in the narrow partisan sense; of course, if he can spur things ahead and make the enterprise show progress, he will *obviously* benefit politically. But that's all to the good; that's the reward of hard work on a difficult and risky problem that calls for much thinking and work on his part and those he brings into it, which includes financing from the Ford Foundation and the advice of such men as Tom Watson of IBM, James Oates of Equitable Life Assurance, André, and others.

OCTOBER 20, 1966
NEW YORK

For a month or more, in the back of my mind has been the impasse between CED's economic advisors and the committee of members, of which I am Chairman, businessmen who have accepted the task of making a report on "business performance in America."

How can we bring some kind of shape to so amorphous a topic? It is surrounded by so *many* opinions. These include the most vexing ones held by a number of economists with a fixation on the "competition model" and "the market as the measure" of performance. Although these are the tenets that were taught for so long, neither of these articles of faith exists today as an explanation of most economic or political behavior of our society. So how can we base a report on the "performance of business institutions" on a "religion" that no longer bears much resemblance to the realities of life?

As I looked at the distinguished faces grouped around the huge baize-covered circular table at today's meeting I could sense a feeling of confusion and puzzlement.

By noon a pattern emerged for a possible basis for research and staff writing, and discussion by the committee. I could sense all around that we had made progress, with some expert help and professional optimism on the part of CED's bland but very perspicacious President, Al Neal.

OCTOBER 22, 1966
PRINCETON

An account of my hectic professional activities does not convey the full flavor of my life. Things go on all around us that give a much more representative picture of what it is to live and to think in October, 1966.

For example: the delivery man for our grocery, arriving with today's order, stops to chat a minute while I get out of my knee-muddy jeans—I had been doing heavy gardening. Someone had broken into his house out on the edge of Princeton, stole the thing that means the most to him, a brand new power saw; "they" knew he'd been away a week, that he had hidden the saw under a pile of his dirty work clothes; "they" found it and some other things, and tore the place up. Talked to the "plees"; since "these new laws" (meaning, I suppose, the Supreme Court decisions on the protection of suspects from questioning, etc.), the "plees" can't even search a man without a search warrant; one suspect had a razor strapped to his leg, another had a gun, but they couldn't frisk them, had to let them go. "These boys around Princeton know about this, they break into houses and steal things and know nothing cain't be done about it."

Yesterday Helen and I spent an hour talking with a representative of a burglar alarm company, and have decided to have this house wired, for protection. My concern is Helen's being here alone at nights; hers is that while we are away (and everyone knows we are away) for the whole summer, the place will be broken into and things smashed and slashed, the kind of vandalism cum robbery that is apparently growing even in this once quiet little university town as well as in the large cities.

So a burglar alarm on our home! The number of people installing them is growing, the agent said. Is this sort of thing closer to many people's thinking than, say, the war in Vietnam? *And* certainly the spectacular rise in the cost of food in the store is raising hackles. And why not?

OCTOBER 26, 1966
NEW YORK

Lunch at the Century with Harlan Hatcher, for the last fifteen years President of the University of Michigan (student population now 35,000!): A big man, a handsome head of grey hair and a knowing, composed face. Looks the way a Senator should look, as did Warren Harding—except that this man has brains.

I asked him what were the top-priority programs that, as president of a great university, he had to handle? All were areas, he said, that fifteen years ago would never have been in his domain: (1) labor relations; (2) research—now a major part of the university budget (it used to be a small fraction); (3) student activism.

President Hatcher told me about a group he had recently headed to study Latin American universities. He found student demonstrations and "activism" had produced a completely different kind of university than we have developed. Students decide which professors suit them, throw out rectors. "The next step," I suggested, "was that they would decide whether Juan, who got a B, should have had an A."

Except for the Berkeley uprising, Hatcher doesn't think student violence represents more than a handful of students. "But," he went on, half smiling, his broad countenance as unmarked as if he were thirty, not sixty (I suppose), "what would you do if a couple dozen students denied you access to your office by lying down in the halls or foyers and just staying there?" "Can't they be dismissed for misconduct?" I asked. "John Hannah, in our sister university, tried that," Hatcher replied. "He was faced immediately with a lawsuit challenging the university's right to dismiss; the prospect of a trial on that issue led John to give it up. And there are cases of private institutions—a Catholic college here in the New York area—that lost a suit on this issue. So dismissal isn't much of a protection. We'll just have to appeal to good sense and hope that events won't take the direction they did in Latin America, where the university as we see it has been pretty well destroyed.

OCTOBER 27, 1966
NEW YORK

A couple days ago I had a long and wide-ranging talk with Joe Barnes, now an editor with Simon & Schuster. He and Mike Cowles accompanied Willkie on the famous round-the-world trip, and doubtless had a great deal to do with the actual writing of Willkie's one book, *One World*. (How dated that book seems today; worse than "dated"—

eloquent in the effusion of a hope that had too little underpinning of reality. It was the underpinning of accomplishment, of reality, that must account for the continuing vitality of *Democracy on the March*, its ideas spawning so many things throughout the world; on this point I get added testaments almost every week.)

There is a new biography of Willkie by Ellsworth Barnard. I asked Joe what he thought of it, as a Willkie admirer (I might have said a *maker* of Willkie as a distinguished public figure).

A good scholarly book, one I should read. But not one commercial publishing house would touch it. "I turned it down myself, for Simon & Schuster. No other publisher would handle it."

Then he said what I thought was a puzzling thing: "The fact is that there just isn't a market for books about Willkie, even so good a one as this. There is no longer any interest in him. My own book didn't do well; a more poetic book—*One Life*—sold six hundred copies." He looked *very* sad.

OCTOBER 28, 1966
PRINCETON

"If I outlive you," said Helen, "in your coffin I'll put a shorthand notebook and some ballpoint pens, so you can write down your 'ideas.' Just as the Egyptians and the Etruscans put into the tombs of their dead the things the dead would need and want most in the afterlife."

I reminded her that the Etruscan tombs, for the men, had horses and nubile young women; how about that for me in addition to the notebooks? No comment.

This do-it-now guy did nothing today. That *is* news. Nothing but drink in the intoxicating crispness of the autumn air, the richness of the color of the trees. Our great Chinese ginkgo tree is like a golden temple of Siam. It towers just beyond the rose garden, which is having a panchromatic, lusty second spring. And as I stride down Battle Road, my heavy walking stick in hand, I look up into the canopy of a maple so yellow that the individual leaves fuse into a solid mass of blazing gold that moves the heart.

So you did "nothing" today? You lived, handsomely. Not just that old go-getter "recharging his batteries"—a utilitarian view of leisure, I *must* say—but doing nothing because it was fun doing nothing. And why do you call living pleasantly "nothing"?

NOVEMBER 1, 1966
NEW YORK

I didn't really need Dr. Atchley to tell me what a strong and healthy critter I am, at my annual physical examination routine, though of course it was pleasant to hear him murmur ("perfect") as he read the blood pressure gimmicks, or ran through the list of reports on his desk. For a guy who he described ten years ago as having "a monumental lack of self-confidence in his body"—and with less reason than anyone he knows—this is quite a change.

NOVEMBER 3, 1966
UNIVERSITY CLUB, CARNEGIE TECH
PITTSBURGH

If the response I got this afternoon from the large audience, six hundred mostly top flight businessmen, is an indication of what to expect from the "series" as a whole, then the year of organizing and writing and rewriting the Fairless Lectures was well worth it.

What I feared would be considered too vague or too idealistic was followed for forty minutes with as close attention from an audience as I have had in a long time. The questioning afterward, and a round table of the dinner guests—some forty-five men—showed that I had really said something new and fresh, something that *they* thought had substance, hardboiled though they are and naturally preoccupied with their own separate business concerns.

There were many comments on the content of the speech. The attentiveness with which it was followed made me sure that it achieved my purpose: to draw the outline of a new set of ideas before a sophisticated audience who live the life of management every day.

My idea that management is a humanistic, i.e., man-centered art, not a technical skill, seemed particularly to appeal to my listeners, who I am confident are themselves beginning to have a better perspective on this mathematical profile and systems analysis stuff when put forward as a kind of substitute for judgment.

But the comment that pleased me the most, in that kind of crowd, overheard in the hurly-burly of the subsequent reception, was this: "What he said made sense; but it was also almost poetry."

In spite of my grueling day both physically and psychologically, I have no awareness of fatigue. So I am not on my last legs yet.

But there are three old boys who sit in the lounge of this club where I'm staying who are. Retired professors perhaps. This is the conversation:

"You aren't going out to California, are you, all those brush fires. That smog will kill you off."

The second aimless putting-in-the-time old boy: "Good place to die, I guess."

"Naw, there's no good place to die."

"Not worse than being half dead, shuffling along like this." (Illustrating.)

Half dead. That is the reward of retirement, being half dead.

NOVEMBER 5, 1966
PRINCETON

What a delightful sensation to see the wise guy experts, with their pretensions to prediction, suffer an upset. And to watch the underdog shake himself and topple the "favorite." What a renewal of faith in the mysterious alchemy of the human spirit when aroused!

This I saw in a most spectacular setting this afternoon. It was "only" a big football game—Harvard against Princeton in a jammed Palmer Stadium—but it did my heart good. The only question the dopesters had, long before the opening whistle blew, was whether Princeton would lose by two or three touchdowns. And then, in some of the best football—on both sides—I have seen in many years, Princeton took the lead 18 to 14 in the closing minutes of the game, and kept it.

Went, as usual, with Frank and Virginia Glick. To sit next to Frank during a football game is like watching the galaxies with Harlow Shapley. Not a detail, not one fine point, not one error escapes him. And he relives the days—and happy ones they must have been—when he was down there on that field, captaining Princeton. We sat among members of his class of 1916, and these old boys were constantly leaning over to ask Frank what this or that could possibly mean, or more often to grin and say, "Do you remember that time when you put through three touchdowns in a row, whack, whack, whack?"

NOVEMBER 8, 1966
UNIVERSITY CLUB, CARNEGIE TECH
PITTSBURGH

The third lecture tonight was to an audience reduced in size but actually increased in understanding and interest—and prestige. (Roger Blough, Chairman of U.S. Steel, looking even more harried than usual, came, and we had a chat afterward.)

As I came into the hall I spotted a tiny, very attractive young lady, big dark eyes, pigtails, and I recognized her as Dorothea Greenbaum's sister's granddaughter. I reached practically to the floor to shake her hand, whereupon, quite fussed (and looking all the prettier for that), she fished out a letter she said was from General Greenbaum, began to read the part that told her about my lecturing, etc. Having done her duty, she started off (having, sensibly, no intention, as a freshman Fine Arts student, of going to so dull a business), gave a little wave, like the flap of a tiny doll's hand, and said cheerily, "Well . . . have a good lecture."

NOVEMBER 9, 1966
9:15 A.M.
EN ROUTE, TWA, PITTSBURGH TO NEW YORK

The three hard days at Carnegie are over. In closing the dinner meeting last night, Dr. Guyford Stever, the handsome, fresh, young, new President of Carnegie Tech, said what I most wanted to hear: that the ideas about the nature of management as a humanist art added an original dimension to the thinking of the managerial and technical people. He then added: "Mr. Lilienthal, you have made a big impact on us young fellows, and you *still* make an impact." It was the "still" that appealed to me.

Not the least of the pleasure of the trip was seeing young students, men and as attractive looking young women as I've seen on a campus in a long time. Best of all was taking a peek into the theatre of the Dramatics Department. A group of completely absorbed young people making up a set on the stage, others in the seats talking vividly about the stage and the dramatic art, which is what obsesses them. A happy sight, to see young people who are committed to something with their whole heart. But there was another, a bittersweet overtone.

This is the very place where my beloved cousin Bernard Szold first learned the craft that later became his life's work as director of the Little Theatre in Omaha and New Orleans and Pasadena. This, too, is where his sister, the dove-like Aline, spent happy years, and where she fell in love with Max Sholes, who also learned his craft in that building and on that stage.

New people, old memories revived, new experiences, new tests—what better can life hold?

NOVEMBER 10, 1966
7:30 A.M.
NEW YORK

The election results have the "Conservatives" happy and the Republicans coming out of the debris that buried them two years ago. Reagan in California is the only one who represents the kind of spiritual retrogression that happens to us quite often. The others—particularly Romney, Rockefeller, Case, Percy—are in the best tradition. But Reagan is a handsomer and defter lobbyist for the turn-back-the-clockers than we have had for some time.

NOVEMBER 12, 1966
HOTEL EL CONQUISTADOR
PUERTO RICO

He sat at his ease, surrounded by some of us of the Twentieth Century Fund, under the trees on a lovely and isolated beach, happy and full of his favorite dish, the politics of Puerto Rico: Don Luis, better known as Governor Muñoz Marín, builder of a modern region out of the destitute, disorganized, and volatile remains of years of Spanish colonial misrule. His entrancing wife, Inez, had invited the Twentieth Century gathering (almost the full attendance of Trustees and their wives—a highbrow junket, I'd say) for a swim and a luncheon on what I think they call Convento Beach. The water too warm for me, spoiled by the cold vigor of Vineyard Sound. But the whole expedition, including the two days in San Juan, were a good break, not just for me but for all the Trustees. Good for Helen, too; she enjoyed tramping about seeing houses in old San Juan, and was, as always, tireless.

NOVEMBER 13, 1966
SAN JUAN AIRPORT

The economic development of this Caribbean island in the past twenty years, and notably in the past ten, surely represents one of the greatest physical and social transformations in our hemisphere. Is the "formula" (or the format) transferable to other underdeveloped Latin American countries? At our Trustees' meeting last Thursday, Ted Moscoso, architect and manager of Puerto Rico's "Operation Bootstrap," made the case for an affirmative answer. Open the doors of the "rich" U.S. *market* to the Central American countries now in their seventh year of a Common Market, he said, and similar results could follow. Ted is a great promoter, in the best sense: enthusiasm, ideas, a kind of shining confidence. And later on, at the Muñoz' beach party, both the present Governor, Roberto Sanchez, and Luis himself made similar argument.

I questioned Muñoz closely about this point of view, stressing the differences between Central American–U.S. relations and U.S.–Puerto Rican relations. It was not the elimination of tariff barriers on agricultural products that he had in mind, but the products of Central America's industry that needed a favored access to the American market.

What has given industry in Puerto Rico such a boost, it seems to me, has been the attraction of tax exemption from *not only* Puerto Rican taxes (the least important), but the Federal corporate and personal income tax. Besides, since states of Puerto Rico are also states of the

U.S. (though Puerto Rico isn't a "state of the Union"), when jobs are scarce Puerto Ricans can, and do, come to the mainland in great numbers; this involves great cost and a social burden on New York City, Chicago, etc. Surely we wouldn't give states of Central America any such status, nor would we exempt American industries in Central America from U.S. taxes.

Apropos his "idea," and our D&R studies about integration in Latin America, Muñoz "warned" me about the State Department and its traditionally stingy "most favored nation" and general tariff views. He was particularly severe—though respectful—about Lincoln Gordon's views and his past writings on this subject. "Tell Sol Linowitz to be on his guard about the State Department," he said, referring to Linowitz' recent designation as representative to the Organization of American States.

FLYING OVER THE CARIBBEAN

I used to think of the great diversity of life as a great constellation of concentric circles, one within another.

Not so. Circles perhaps, but not touching, like the molecular nonstructure of glass, the molecules of which are placed at random. (This latter I learned in my fascinating morning at the Research Center of Pittsburgh Plate Glass, in Pittsburgh, last Monday.)

What is the occasion for this rumination about the pattern of life? Listening to a rapid fire of exciting talk about music—an intimate world as far apart from mine as if I had never heard a note or had not spent—as I did on the Vineyard one summer—an entire evening in the presence of a truly great conductor, Leonard Bernstein.

The conversation took place at a table at El Convento in San Juan. Mrs. Fred Dewhurst, newly married to that thin-voiced economist, once Director of the Twentieth Century Fund, was talking across me at the table to a lively teacher of piano in the San Juan Conservatory. They had worked together years before when she was the directing head of a music foundation responsible for the operation of Tanglewood and the Berkshire Music Festival.

Talk of Mahler, Casals, "Kuzzy," and "Lenny," musically, domestically, and personally, filled the conversational air. I was utterly fascinated by this intimate discussion of great artists; to me it might have been talk about Martians or astronauts.

The reverence in those women's voices when they reminisced about the last days of Koussevitzky! If it had been the disciple Paul or John, the aura of worship could not have been more visible. One anecdote followed another—all of this across me, as I sat completely invisible to these enraptured people. Said the sparkling little pianist: "Do you remember X, Kuzzy's valet? One time he was giving Kuzzy his rubdown at intermission and Kuzzy began to upbraid and storm at the poor fellow, who hauled back and said, 'Who do you think I am? Your or-kest-ra?' You know when Kuzzy was displeased with the orchestra how he would curse and yell at them. 'Who do you think I am,' said the rubber, 'your or-kest-ra?' "

NOVEMBER 14, 1966
NEW YORK

Lunch at the Fifth Avenue Club this noon with Jack Heinz. Still searching for a workable way to put agroindustry—or agrobusiness—effectively to work on a large scale on the stubborn problem of increasing food supply in some of the underdeveloped world.

John Burnett with us today, and he made a real "gutsy" contribution, to use the word Jack Heinz applied to John's perception of the practical problems.

To my surprise, and delight, John felt strongly that government, i.e., AID, could provide only an "atmosphere" that might be helpful in the countries where American private industry tried to apply the agrobusiness method of getting food up. The real drive would have to come from the prospect of profit (and risk of loss) rather than anything government could do. This same point applied, he thought, to D&R, now in the agrobusiness field, but only on a contract or cost plus fee basis.

My worry, expressed to Jack in Pittsburgh, was that to invite too many diverse interests—as originally proposed—would, as a starter, probably lead to one more conference, an exercise in generalities already known and accepted, another exhibition of the futility of the way this problem has been handled before, with the same cast of characters that have failed to make much headway on the problem in the past. I *think*—can't be sure at this stage—that Jack will try to steer things into an initial series of meetings by a small group that can be *guided toward action*. My strong preference is that as soon as possible in the process we head for a consortium of American business (including such a technical outfit as ours) covering food production, processing, seeds, machinery, and the other inputs, and then, *and only then*, have a great big conference with a capital "C," with *everybody* in. To start the other way, as originally proposed, will make it harder to get something specific going. And unless things get going, somehow, my interest in having a hand in further conferences or talkfests is damned small.

NOVEMBER 15, 1966
NEW YORK

When a person finds that he is repeating himself, following along the same path (however "successful"), he is probably going stale as a human being. The same thing applies to organizations.

I don't want this to happen to D&R. We are too young an organization, have too much enthusiasm for what we do, have too much opportunity for doing things differently, have too much experience in overcoming obstacles to allow ourselves to get into a rut.

I spent the lunch hour with Oliver and Burnett with this as a preliminary note, using the agrobusiness subject as the justification for this kind of fight talk with my two colleagues.

I sometimes forget how much I depend upon my ability to write shorthand, how much it increases my "output" and conserves my time and energies.

The volume of letters I write, for example. I rarely dictate, so Miss Baron can be transcribing my shorthand notes while I'm seeing people, or reading, or writing letters or memos. And of course these mountains of journals would not be possible without my being able to write shorthand. The journals have helped in clarifying my thoughts, in letting off steam, in making me more aware—because I write of them—of colors of nature, and sounds, and faces of people, more aware of the way people talk, both those I overhear and those with whom I must deal in my work.

Why should the journals increase my awareness, that is, why should it be that *writing* things, mostly for my own satisfaction, my own needs, makes me more *conscious* of so many things? Can it be that the impulse to write whets the perceptions?

I've been reading a painfully graphic account of leukemia in the current *Life*. Reading it brought back the profound sorrow—without self-pity—in the deep-set eyes of Mrs. Ken Galbraith. We had gone to the San Juan airport in the same car, she, Helen, and I. One of us referred to Robert Oppenheimer's dire illness; how sad that it was so often the most brilliant people who were struck down. Mrs. Galbraith said, softly, "We lost a son, seven years ago; he was such a bright and promising boy. There was nothing Ken and I could do but watch him go." Such pain as she spoke, but such formidable dignity and composure. As she looked intently at me, the drama of that waiting was reflected in her eyes. No matter how "prominent" or wealthy or brilliant one is, anguish can always be just around that black corner.

Two extraordinary letters from Bernardine within the week, both occasioned by what she calls "the book," i.e., the third volume of the *Journals*. What seemed most to impress her was "the beautiful way you developed your power of expression, your 'ear' in a way, and the fluency and poetry of many descriptions, your vivid attendance on nature . . . your sometimes wicked analysis of people and the honesty and insight you reveal."

This, from no mean writer herself (a professional writer for a long time indeed), but most impressively, coming from one who has known me since I was a kid, and who must still think of me as that earnest, sober youngster of fourteen back in the Gary days.

Some straight talk from Beatrice Tobey: "When you deprecate the importance of getting paid, and well paid, for your ideas, as you so often do, you deprecate your ideas and yourself. When you let people pick your brains because you like to think, and get satisfaction in being flattered by having your ideas respected and used, you make yourself almost foolish in the eyes of people. You are a professional, and you should behave like a professional."

NOVEMBER 16, 1966
NEW YORK

My luncheon "fight talk" appeal with Oliver and Burnett of yesterday started something specific. I got to the office at about 8 A.M.; fifteen minutes later Oliver appeared excitedly at my door. Thinking about what I had said had kept him up most of the night: about not just repeating ourselves; about a new "initiative" and particularly the agrobusiness concept on which Jack Heinz had consulted me.

We can get up a proposal for agrobusiness, John said, putting together a consortium of American business, with us organizing and providing much of the factual and technical guidance, that could take 20,000 hectares of Khuzistan and make it really produce, on a commercial basis. Even if nothing else happens, he added, wisely, it would improve our standing with the higher authorities in Iran, take us out of the mediocre workaday doldrums we are in, and give us and them an exciting new action program for Khuzistan.

Someone has to follow through on this; we can't just write a letter (which we will); someone must go out there and explain what we envisage, use some persuasion, get the Shah interested. Can't be fobbed off on some agricultural technical man. So John, knowing that I feel he delegates too much to others, grinned and said he would undertake to follow through.

NOVEMBER 17, 1966
AT A MEETING OF THE COMMITTEE FOR ECONOMIC DEVELOPMENT
NEW YORK

A couple hundred businessmen listening attentively to a discussion of "revolutions in education," with the speaker (Sterling McMurrin, former Commissioner of Education, now at Utah) at this moment talking in abstract philosophical language and ideas; listening carefully, those businessmen of a workaday world. Hard to believe, but here they are, and a heartening thing it is to see.

[My mind wandered; I thought of the cry of puzzled parents: "What have we done to our children? They show so little sense of dignity, consideration of others, of responsibility. What have we done to our children?" What a sad cry.

But isn't this part of the distortion between the generations in the shadowy land that the parent-child relationship makes almost impenetrable to the eye?]

A very cocksure young man, Patrick Suppes of Stanford, describes research work with elementary school children in teaching of arithmetic "via computer." To show that he is human, even if the computer isn't, he recites with delight that the computer is "instructed" to print, at the end of a test, "Goodbye." "Happy Halloween," etc. I'm aghast, I must say.

The *contact* between a good teacher and a child is gone in this "system," made "unnecessary."

NOVEMBER 18, 1966
PRINCETON

Carl Kaysen, succeeding Robert Oppenheimer as Director of the Institute for Advanced Study, eyes that are great dark caves, a sharp curved chin, massive shoulders, soft tentative voice, sitting on a sofa between peppery, question-prodding Jim Perkins, President of Cornell, on one side and sharp-eyed Bob Goheen, President of Princeton, on the other. This would have been quite a picture just as a picture, in the living room of Henry Chauncey's [of Educational Testing Service], where with twenty others we had a happy evening tonight. But Jim, with his tell-all look, and Bob, not missing a word, were asking Kaysen what he expected to do with the Institute under its new management and, in effect, why he had taken the job and what could be expected from him.

Kaysen, wisely, was pretty cagey. Partly he is trying to find out how to fill in the most difficult part of his concept of a fourth school at the Institute, supplementing mathematics, historical studies, and physics. But he knows, surely, that the test will be the quality of the appointments to the faculty of that prestigious and unique institution he makes in the coming months.

NOVEMBER 19, 1966
PRINCETON

A call from Henry Hough of the *Vineyard Gazette*. He has persuaded our neighbors, the John Daggetts, to accept a lower figure for their ancestral land, Cedar Tree Neck, to be sold to the Massachusetts Audubon Society. He needs additional money for a "down payment," and without hesitation, and with considerable satisfaction, I assured him we would take care of 25% of it. Henry has another 25%. Henry may have found a formula for saving in perpetuity some lovely spots on the Vineyard's North Shore. What an achievement that will be.

The solace to my soul that sweet moor has exerted over the years is something that can hardly be measured in money; to see it destroyed with a housing "development" would have changed my whole feeling about the Vineyard, I fear.

NOVEMBER 20, 1966
PRINCETON

To the politician I suppose the word is "power"; certainly that is a word beloved of the political theorist, the scholar of politics, and, of course, the commentator, all the way from Walter Lippmann to a tinny novelist like Allen Drury. But to the administrator and the manager the word—and concept—is "authority." For authority is *not* an abstraction, and it is by no means synonymous with "power." It carries with it responsibility and accountability.

These reflections have been riding around inside me since the spate of books and pieces "explaining" (and usually scorning) President Johnson, one of them a brilliantly written essay by Alfred Kazin in the current *New York Review of Books*—which by the by has emerged from a butcher-paper foundling of the New York newspaper strike of some years ago to become a voice of the pretensions, and passion to be articulate, of that variety of intellectual who regard bellyaching about everything, including each other, as the true mark of intellectual prowess.

NOVEMBER 22, 1966
SHERATON (COPLEY OF OTHER DAYS) PLAZA HOTEL
BOSTON

Came on the Merchants Limited for our Thanksgiving holiday. Walked around Copley Square. This was one place, thought I, that hadn't changed since Helen and I were in Boston, as an affianced couple. (*What* an odd and old-fashioned expression came out of my pen that time; it was old-fashioned even in 1922. But after you have been married to the same person forever, the time before you were married just seems an unreal denomination.)

Copley Square was then, and is still today, framed by a group of the most beautiful and impressive façades in America. Old South Church, with its Italian bell tower, facing Trinity Church across the Square, the Copley, her face recently cleaned, showing off the strength and chasteness of her proportions—on the outside; I'll certainly not vouch for the chastity inside.

A wave of sentimentality washed over me, induced by the familiarity of this place.

Imagine the letdown when, walking past the Public Library, Helen asked: "What place is this?" I would have been hurt, if I hadn't been so amused at the misplaced sentimentality of my own recollections.

Why, dammit, in that beautiful building are the Sargent murals of the Old Testament prophets! When I was still in Law School I bought a small copy of my favorite, Isaiah, and gave it to Helen, in 1923; it still hangs in her bedroom. "What place is this?" indeed.

NOVEMBER 24, 1966
NEW YORK

The *France* has just moved past my office window. What dignity and aloofness a great ship has against the setting of New York harbor at the confluence of the Hudson and East Rivers, with the Statue of Liberty looking benignly on it all. On this sunny late November day, there is a magic as well as a majesty about this body of water.

NOVEMBER 25, 1966
EDGARTOWN, MARTHA'S VINEYARD

This morning David and I spent an hour or two discussing the next volumes of the *Journals*. "This is not a story of economic development or foreign aid, these next volumes, nor of D&R. It is the development of a person, of you as it happens." This was his negative response to my question about including non-journal textual matter to make more comprehensive some of the events in the D&R story in Persia, for example.

NOVEMBER 29, 1966
NEW YORK

A call from Komer at the White House revived what I rather assumed had been the wilted enthusiasm about the Vietnam "postwar planning" undertaking.

The conversation between us went like this:

At the recent Manila Conference Komer discussed the subject of postwar economic aid with Prime Minister Ky, who he finds is an able fellow. Komer described what the State Department had in mind: that there be a Vietnam team chief and a U.S. Government team chief, and the possibility that D&R might be willing to be responsible for the U.S. team. Komer said Ky was enthusiastic about the idea and asked that it be checked out with the President and that he, Komer, come back with a proposed public statement to be made as promptly as possible. Komer said he did check it with President Johnson, who was in full agreement and directed that Komer get up a statement and that "we will announce it."

Komer said he has two cables which he wants to send off today, one a proposed statement from President Johnson and one a proposed parallel statement from Prime Minister Ky's office.

The proposed statement by the President read this way:

"Proposed statement from President Johnson:

"I am pleased to announce that in response to a request from Prime Minister Ky the Government of the U.S. will join with the Government of Vietnam in sponsoring a joint planning and study effort to lay the groundwork for the long-run development of the Vietnamese economy. It will be recalled that the Vietnamese Government stressed at the Manila Conference its plans for the building of an expanded postwar economy, including plans for the conversion of military installations when appropriate.

"Eugene Black, who recently returned from a personal tour of Southeast Asia, has reported to me that even in the midst of war, the foundation of future economic progress is being laid in Vietnam and that the outlook for the Vietnamese economy once peace returns is highly favorable. It is not too early to begin to address ourselves to the problems and opportunities of peace, and the exciting prospects of social and economic progress for the people of Vietnam which peace will bring. The planning effort which we are now launching together with the Government of Vietnam is an important step toward establishing the basis for the postwar economic development of Vietnam in partnership with the other friendly nations of Southeast Asia.

"Thus it gives me particular pleasure to announce that, with the concurrence of Prime Minister Ky, I have asked Mr. David Lilienthal to lead the non-governmental study and planning team. . . . Mr. Lilienthal has agreed to put together a team drawn from his Development and Resources Corporation and other U.S. sources with broad experience in developmental planning. He also expects to recruit several able Vietnamese planners to work as part of his team. It will operate under joint contract with the Agency for International Development and to the new GVN [Government of Vietnam] Ministry of Planning and Development. Mr. Lilienthal's experience and high qualifications are well known, and I am grateful that he has agreed to undertake this task."

I talked all this over with Oliver, Seymour, and Burnett. They were all for it. Komer on being called back said, "No problem; accepted." The cabled proposed statements go out tonight.

DECEMBER 1, 1966
NEW YORK

Thoughts on a recent Council on Foreign Relations meeting. Listening to a once giant figure, Paul Hoffman, I couldn't help reflecting how easy it is to slip into retrospection, or more precisely, "repeating one's self," replaying the record that *once* was fresh and full of meaning, but that with changed conditions becomes a record only.

In this vein I found myself recalling an old story, made famous by Alben Barkley, about an unappreciative former supporter in a Kentucky election. "Yes, Alben, you *did* all those things for me you say; but what have you done for me *lately*?" Well, one should ask himself—or *I* should ask myself: "What have you, Dave, done *lately* that is fresh, vigorous, relevant to *things as they are*? Well, speak up, son. What *have* you done lately?"

If the Vietnam statements that were cabled off night before last are approved by Ky, and issued, that job will certainly be something I can say I have *done* "lately," or tried damn hard to do, which amounts to the same thing in a world where only the tough and risky things measure the worth of the kind of person I believe I still am.

Lunched alone with André at 44 Wall Street at his invitation. When he speaks of the real estate ventures they are involved in, his face lights up, disclosing the inner satisfaction (despite his disclaimers) he gets out of big accomplishments—and they are big. How "important"? Well, who knows what is important, in private life particularly? Importance is made up of a lot of less-than-world-shaking acts.

The luncheon was pleasant, personal, very informal. "It is a good thing you didn't submit that book [my recent *Journals*] to me in advance; we would have had a long negotiation about it. Some of the things you said were much too flattering. Many people who read it have spoken to me about it. But I would have tried to get much of that out. Was it factually accurate? Well, it shows how memory is; many of the things that happened I didn't recall until I read of them. It was accurate all right; just embarrassing because of the praise."

But Mrs. Meyer "was deeply touched by the things you said about us." That comment gave me real satisfaction.

DECEMBER 4, 1966
PRINCETON

Two days of suspended animation, Friday and yesterday. When I "rest and recuperate" I seem to do it as intensively as when I plow ahead.

I don't like the idea that there are physical or nervous limitations to my doing anything I want to do. That's why it is so gracious of Nature that occasionally she makes me *not* want to do anything!

A talk by phone with Bernardine in Beverly Hills. Urged her to keep together the fabulous personal letters to her from scores of the literary lights of our generation: Glenway Westcott, Witter Bynner, Russell Davenport, and so on; they really should be published.

She was as full of bounce as ever, full of the social gatherings she always enlivens, glittering with names of her friends, such as Henry Miller and the (to me) dazzling Jennifer Jones.

DECEMBER 6, 1966
NEW YORK

At a few minutes before 9 this morning, jammed into a "Whisper Jet" shuttle, I saw Robert Kennedy come aboard, taking a seat near the door obviously reserved for him. At 7:15 tonight, back again in New York, I saw the same figure on TV, in a Senate Hearing on urban problems. (One of the other faces and voices on the screen came out of my earliest days as a young lawyer: A. Philip Randolph, a most distinguished personage, for whose Brotherhood of Sleeping Car Porters Donald Richberg and I were counsel in the early twenties.)

To Washington for a single conference, with the new Ambassador to the Organization of American States, Sol Linowitz.

The door of his office opened; in the background his slight figure, curly head tilted to one side like a listening bird, and out through the door came a stunning auburn-haired woman with a familiar brilliant smile. I greeted Nancy Kefauver, Estes' widow, with a big booming hello, and in my enthusiasm (and hers, matter of fact) bussed her on the cheek. She is an advisor on art for the offices of dignitaries in the Government; anything she does in replacing those pedestrian paintings in Sol's office (where Ellsworth Bunker, his predecessor, "resided") will be an improvement.

Sol is an unusual figure in the Washington hierarchy: a spectacularly successful businessman. In the process of "making" Xerox he amassed a substantial fortune. He isn't in a State Department post for the reason that, in the past, brought so many well-heeled businessmen the title of Ambassador, that is, through big cash contributions to the "party" (and usually little else). His "contribution" is brains and an engaging personality.

But his manner is that of a man who knows that he has a great need of ideas, that his business success alone doesn't make him qualified to represent his country. He even kids himself on this score. "In this job a month and they send me out to represent the U.S. of America," says he, looking at me as if to say, "How about that?"

When we had talked together, shortly after the announcement of his appointment, he asked me to come to Washington to help supply ideas and strategy about Latin American integration, having heard me in an EWA Board Meeting describing our Inter-American Development Bank report. His entire demeanor this noon was that of a man who really wanted every bit of insight from others he could gather. It takes a strong and essentially confident man to welcome ideas from others.

He has just come back from "the ranch" in Texas and Johnson's meeting at the border with the President of Mexico. Our President's endorsement of regional multinational developments, such as the joint dam across the Rio Grande, contained expressions that had a familiar ring. Sol confirmed what Seymour afterward put this way: "It is evident that there is more moving as a result of our report than we had known."

"What are the things you would most want to see happen?" was his closing question, after an hour and a half of spirited talk. "What can we in the State Department do, what 'whisper' can we make, that will help those things along?"

I thought getting D&R's proposed Colombia-Venezuela arrangement actually moving was perhaps the most important; that would be an example of integration in its broadest meaning: two countries actually digging into the facts and methods for something resembling economic union, something begun at their initiative, and in which many of the problems of economic integration throughout the continent would be examined and perhaps some of them tackled.

Sol asked me my views about the strong movement among the Latin American countries for the purchase from the U.S. of military equipment. When Sol tries to discourage this, the Latins rise up in wrath, to his surprise.

I pointed to a shocking article in *Business Week* about an Assistant Secretary of Defense whose job it is to persuade countries—including the Latin Americans—to buy military items made in the U.S.; the argument is that if they don't buy from us they will from someone else; besides, it helps our balance of payments—the same sordid kind of case armament makers—Merchants of Death—have always made about these transactions.

I asked Sol if some of the competitive impulse between these countries—Peru, Chile, etc.—in the purchase of armament wasn't stimulated by our own Government, and whether there might be anything in such a hypothetical scenario as this: a U.S. *official* telling the military crowd in Peru that Chile, he heard, was buying such and such jet fighter, which was much better than the ones that they, Peru, had. I don't find that kind of supposition fanciful at all. All in the name of promoting the business of the "industrial-military complex" that even President Eisenhower was able to see represented a danger.

After I had finished saying that this arms competition, between countries that had really *no* vital issues between them (absurd little territorial disputes at the most), could *cancel out* whatever gains they made, and our Alliance for Progress program made—cancel it out perhaps as much as the better known cause, increased population—Sol leaned over and said: "About this trade in arms, do you know, I think Secretary McNamara agrees with you."

Later as we walked down the corridor on our way to lunch Sol told me a story, roaring with delight at the punchline. It was good to hear hearty laughter in that stodgy, pasty-faced crowd.

The Ambassador goes off to Montevideo next Thursday, to a meeting of the Foreign Ministers of the Latin countries. He has a tough assignment and one that will stretch his seemingly boundless resourcefulness and stamina. But if he'll keep his sense of humor, even without any diplomatic experience, or public service experience, he will surely make it.

But all this detail about integration is peripheral, really. What *reveals the man* is what is important to me, as a former public servant and a student of men under strain and profound responsibility.

DECEMBER 8, 1966
ON A PENN TRAIN, FOR PRINCETON

New York City taxi drivers (it is well known) are a special breed, and the stories about them—what an anthology that would make. The other day the driver turned around and said: "I'm a cantor, that's my professional occupation; here's my card. 'Available for Bar Mitzvahs and Weddings.' " Whether being a cantor is his job and taxiing his moonlighting I didn't inquire.

The Minerals & Chemicals Philipp Board Meeting was an account of an extraordinary success story so far as financial results are concerned. But as I listened to the discussion I became once more aghast at the *little* things that grown and experienced and extravagantly paid men concern themselves with day after day. How much of it really matters, in a world beset with great problems to which most of these able men rarely put their minds, or even the smaller but impersonal problems of their communities?

The danger of being a snob about business and businessmen is one to be resisted. Because I have been lucky enough or farsighted enough to get involved with big things doesn't mean that "big" things aren't often made up of a multitude of relatively little components, no *one* of which is decisive.

DECEMBER 9, 1966
PRINCETON

Senator Kennedy: "Don't want to take up much of your time, but we plan a meeting Saturday in Brooklyn to announce the Bedford-Stuyvesant project we discussed with you. I wanted to be able to say that you would participate; is that all right?"

It was.

A call from Komer at the White House. The Prime Minister of Vietnam, according to an open cable from [U.S. Ambassador Henry Cabot] Lodge, was "enthusiastic; much impressed and gratified that so eminent a name would undertake this. He has already gotten rid of the General who was Minister of Planning for about two weeks; now he, the Prime Minister, would like to go back to the original plan of two 'teams,' one headed by a scholarly Vietnamese, the other headed by D.E.L.

"The President wants to announce this, in some way, next week early, probably with you coming to Washington for it." Would I go out there with Komer about mid-January? I said no; first we would want to send our reconnaissance group. Later, Oliver persuaded me that though the first trip would be "ceremonial and public relations" (*my* description), that doesn't mean it isn't important. So I called Komer back. He laughed. "Well," he said, "that saves the President twisting your arm."

DECEMBER 10, 1966
PRINCETON

I need to re-examine my energy priorities, in the light of the proposed Vietnam task.

I don't want us to do a jargonese, sloppy academic kind of job, a conventional report-writing technical economist performance. I am so tired and nauseated by the empty lingo of "experts"—and of half-baked journalists and columnists, too, for that matter—that never come up with any program for action, spelled out definitely; I would be heartsick if this job goes off in that direction.

One of my colleagues said I shouldn't be too concerned about the "risk to our reputation" in this Vietnam task, because no one has done one single successful thing in that whole "mess," so if we don't make a really affirmative contribution it will be no more than anyone expected in an "impossible situation."

I damn well don't like that kind of negative, almost cynical, attitude. I will simply have to ride herd on this task, and added to the other things for which I feel perhaps an excessive sense of personal responsibility, it will take a sense of proportion I don't often have to balance two impulses: to do a superior job that will make a difference out there, in the tired, disillusioned state of mind of the American public, and, on the other hand, not to take myself, and D&R, too solemnly, as if any one person or organization or "study" could basically change a fifteen-year-old tragedy all by itself. (That this undertaking will be financially costly, even perhaps disastrous for D&R as a business, is already clear.)

Returned half an hour ago from a visit with Robert Oppenheimer. Outwardly better—in color, voice, and substance—than a few weeks ago.

We spoke briefly of a young acquaintance who is in love with a much older man and intends to marry him though for many reasons it isn't likely to work. Robert said, "Love can be ugly and cruel . . . but how can one person convey that lesson of experience to another?" "One tries to make his experience useful to others who have not had it because they are young," I said. Robert broke in with a wry grin: "But experience isn't negotiable."

I spoke to him of the importance of his writing, perhaps brief essays, on the many things that draw upon his special and extraordinary spiritual insight (and, I might have added, great eloquence of language). I suggested essays, that is brief writings, rather than a long and systematic writing because the things he had to say were important *now* to a great many people. "A decade from now will have its particular needs," I said, "but it is today that I'm most concerned about."

He had thought of doing some writing—a kind of recounting of the story of science of this century—"but I am not quite up to it now, don't have the necessary gusto." As he walked me to the door, he spoke again of writing, in a suddenly vigorous tone of voice, "and it should indeed be now, today, not a decade hence. Perhaps in two or three months I'll be better." But I don't really believe he thinks so.

DECEMBER 11, 1966
PRINCETON

Dinner here last night: The Carl Kaysens, the Harry Smyths, Dr. James Watson, the famous biochemist (protein synthesis, virus research), and Ged† and Ellen Bentley. Very spirited and enjoyable evening, sparked by Mary Smyth, who was crackling with wit and, with her crown of auburn hair, quite handsome.

I have been increasingly uneasy about the U.S. providing highly enriched uranium—weapons grade—to any foreign countries other than Britain. A big shipment of enriched uranium from Oak Ridge to India was announced the other day, intended for a "peaceful" power reactor, it was said, and not for bombs or explosives. But that shipment of enriched uranium is the very kind useful for bombs.

I had written [AEC Chairman] Glenn Seaborg expressing my concern a long time ago (December 2, 1964); his answer: "If we don't, someone else will."

I asked for Harry Smyth's judgment, for his information is unsurpassed. He said he agreed with me, and as a member of the International Atomic Energy Agency in Vienna he had opposed such shipments to nations including West Germany. (He said he hadn't heard of any to India.) But the AEC didn't agree with him.

Senator Kennedy was on the first page of the *Times* this morning, announcing his Bedford-Stuyvesant project, to include a *Development and Services Corporation* of leading businessmen; I could hardly qualify, but in the press I found myself lumped with such indubitable "leading businessmen" as Douglas Dillon, William Paley, Thomas Watson, and André Meyer.

Will I ever get definite word from the White House? I continue to consider this only a half-certain decision, despite Komer's ebullience. Somehow the epidemic of unease about President Johnson has infected me, too, I notice; mildly, but definitely.

What is it about a man that full confidence in him can be undermined so quickly, from the height of heights less than two years ago (a landslide election) to the place where—as at our dinner party last night—the least anyone will do is to remain silent when his name is mentioned.

People *hated* F.D.R. aplenty, in the prewar period particularly, and Teddy Roosevelt too, I suppose. But contempt, distrust, and scorn—is this something new, reserved for President Johnson?

DECEMBER 12, 1966
NEW YORK

Two letters today from Iran, from Minister Rouhani, expressing real excitement about our agrobusiness approach to the Khuzistan

† Gerald E. Bentley, Murray Professor of English at Princeton University, and a distinguished Shakespearean, is a long-time friend.

plains, as embodied in a long (and in his words "eloquent") letter we wrote to him a couple weeks ago, the result of my conversations with Jack Heinz and John Oliver. I had proposed that we, D&R, develop an American *private* consortium, as a joint venture with the Iranians, to produce food, and process and market it.

Here are some substantial extracts from that letter of November 21, 1966:

"Your Excellency:

"It has been made clear to us by you, by KWPA, and by reported statements of His Majesty the Shahinshah, that emphasis in the Dez Irrigation Project should be placed upon the achievement of maximum productivity and that this involves the concept of commercial farms and the development of a modern agricultural industry.

"The physical resources of the North Khuzistan plains—the soil, water, and climate—make this an area with unusually great agricultural potential. The progress made in recent years by farmers in the [Dez] Pilot Project provides a vivid demonstration of what can be done there by *small* farmers when the right kind of assistance is given them. Large-scale agriculture could make still more productive use of these extraordinary resources. But clearly, steps taken in any move toward large-scale commercial agriculture must be harmonized with the concept and the framework of those principles of social and individual justice which His Majesty has repeatedly enunciated as the goals of his people. To reconcile these principles of social justice with the needs of maximum production is not impossible, but it will require planning and ingenuity. . . .

"One purpose of this letter is to ask whether you and KWPA would wish us [D&R] to start exploring with appropriate American (and perhaps European) agricultural and agro-industrial organizations, in as specific terms as possible at this time, their potential interest in participating and investing in agricultural production and processing enterprises in the area of the Greater Dez. . . . We are prepared . . . to take an early initiative in this matter.

". . . Some of the specifics . . . involved in promoting such external private investment . . . would include . . . the conditions and arrangements under which the use of land in the Dez area might be made available to private enterprises . . . regulations and controls which would apply to, and be of substantial interest to, this kind of private agricultural enterprise; inducements to investment which might be available to foreign, or mixed Iranian and foreign, enterprises of this kind.

" . . . The recently intensified world-wide concern about the vast and global food problem—and the mounting discussion in national capitals and among development financing agencies, of what to do about it—should make this agricultural opportunity in the Khuzistan especially interesting at this time—to those outside Iran as well as to Iranians, and to private firms as well as public agencies."

DECEMBER 14, 1966
NEW YORK

Just getting over (i.e., "pulling myself together from") a letdown from the White House on the Vietnam development project.

Called Komer yesterday: no word from him, as he had anticipated before the weekend, about a meeting with the President and an announcement about our engagement for Vietnam. Can he give me any light about where this stands?

"It is a story of frustration," he said. Other more critical issues are occupying the President's time during the week he is in Washington before he returns to the ranch. "Too many other bidders for his time."

Of *course* I understand that this is not necessarily a downgrading of the importance of what we are asked to do in Vietnam, involved as the President is with whether there should be a tax increase, the terrible military problems that lie on his head, the budget to go to Congress soon—and so on. Still, to have this thorny, messy undertaking announced with a brief mimeo handout to the White House Press Corps would prejudice its chances of achieving a new, affirmative, hopeful spirit to counteract, in part, the negative, tired feeling about that war.

A more hated war, in the mind of the general public, I can't recall in my lifetime.

The real motive—perhaps the only one—in accepting this tough assignment is that, because of my past work, I could help put people's minds on the future, on building for a future for the people of that country, and therefore even affect the prospects for some early solution.

Unless it is made to seem very important and challenging and consequential, we will have a devil of a time getting the kind of people to man the job that we need.

DECEMBER 15, 1966
NEW YORK

The news going along for days in a dull monotone of repetition. Bombings in Vietnam; will there or won't there be a tax increase; plodding statements of GOP leaders, leftover of the debacle of '64—and so on. No accounts of the drama of *human beings under strain.*

And then: Mrs. [Jacqueline] Kennedy strikes out at Cass Canfield and Gardner Cowles for going ahead and publishing a book she herself had wanted written by an author [William Manchester] she chose. Anguish shows in every line of her comment and the drastic action of seeking an injunction against a book that is already in type. The grounds: utter bad taste, "invasion of privacy," etc. What Cass and Evan Thomas must have been through, what that extraordinarily handsome woman must have suffered, struck in the face by the cruelness of life three years ago and now again. Drama so poignant that it seems hard to believe that the cast of characters are real people.

And in the same week Bill Moyers, the Texas boy genius, at L.B.J.'s right hand, resigning at a time when the President needs counsel, solace, personal assurance from those he can trust. What a painful thing for Johnson. What scenes there must have been. How important this changing of the inner palace guard will be, no one can be sure. It could be—contemporary historians may someday assert—it could be the beginning of the great downturn in the career of this forceful and imperious man. More than his career is at stake, God knows. Here is a highly charged President, sensitive as the devil and in the midst of near collapse of his influence, being watched by the whole Communist world as the clue to all *their* moves. How will they interpret Moyers' resignation—as a mere change in press secretaries, or as the rush to leave a sinking ship?

DECEMBER 16, 1966
PRINCETON

A phone call "from the White House" awaiting me when I got home about 5 P.M. yesterday. Bob Komer: "All set to make the announcement tomorrow, about 11 o'clock."

From a proposed meeting with the President and attendant fanfare, underlining how important this undertaking will be, things have dwindled down to the mere handing out of the President's and Ky's statements about the postwar planning project.

Several reactions from me. A feeling that the great enthusiasm of Rostow et al. last summer about the "operational value" of a postwar planning effort has dried up. And a feeling, too, that nothing the President could say would make any easier our job of recruiting exceptional staff and of doing an imaginative and inspiring (or spirit-lifting) job.

This hour is the very bottom of the pit of the President's influence in this country. Just why I should want his blessing at a Presidential press conference announcing his and Ky's program, I don't quite see, except out of blind loyalty. For this is a time when whatever he says by way of blessing (or cussing) is ignored, made fun of, rejected, and worst of all, not believed. A sad spectacle. I mustn't let it infect me. He *is* President and Commander, the only one we have, and he will be for two more years. As Komer, an enthusiastic fellow by nature, said on the phone yesterday evening: "We are just at the beginning, Dave. Anyway, there is no other place to go except up.

"Yesterday was a bad time," Komer continued, referring to Bill

Moyers' resignation. "Hit the Boss very hard; all of us. Bill is an extraordinarily intelligent man."

Scotty Reston's column today pounced on the Moyers resignation as another sign that this President is almost impossible to work with or for. Surely it can't be that bad, and the record shows that his Cabinet officers —among them truly distinguished, able men—have stayed. Perhaps stayed too long, would be Reston's comment. But Scotty and the critics of the President's personality can't have it both ways: that he is impossible to stay with *and* that too many men are staying too long.

The White House this morning handed out the announcement about our involvement in the Vietnam planning "exercise" (the current favorite jargon around the White House). It wasn't on the TV news programs at dinner time, and considering the muted note, the casual way it was handled, the colossal skepticism and boredom people have about any "peace"-oriented semantic acrobatics from President Johnson—considering all these things I would doubt if the statements find anything but a decent burial in Saturday morning's papers.

According to David, with whom I talked by phone today, for our whole Vietnam postwar planning venture to be forgotten, much less reported, would be great. He is pained "at the sponsorship" and sorry I let myself get pushed into "that mess." This isn't merely irritation because that "mess" just won't go away, which I think is the source of most people's apathy about Vietnam—and about Johnson for that matter. David has had an intense and eloquent conviction that our country should get out, should have gotten out long ago—no matter what. Said David: "What you are taking on isn't a challenging job; it is an impossible one."

DECEMBER 17, 1966
PRINCETON

The *Times* this morning had a front-page story of the Vietnam assignment, cum grim picture, and a good story, i.e., telling something about D&R and our other work.

So my fallible sense of what is news is wrong again.

At a cocktail party at the Bill Dixes' [Princeton Librarian], talked to one of the greatest of all American historians and archivists: Julian Boyd, architect of the monumental Jefferson Papers housed at Princeton. Boyd is a genuinely cultivated man, relaxed, affable, self-assured, and has a youthful, almost boyish appearance despite grey hair and distinction.

Speaking of the painful row involving Mrs. Kennedy and the publishing of material dealing with the murder of the President, Boyd said,

"The great mistake the Kennedys made—and it is always a mistake—is to try to *arrange* history."

He said to Helen that he admired "your husband's courage" in publishing those *Journals*. And he declared to me that as a historian he thought they were one of the great diaries of contemporary times. I continue to be surprised—and pleased—to hear how seriously these essentially *personal* records are being taken by sophisticated people.

All kinds of comments about "your new assignment." And of course: Are you going out to Saigon?

Of course, practically *everyone* has been to Saigon. It is the "in" thing to do these days. Strange; not too many years ago anyone who was going to Indochina would be something of a special person; now practically every Congressman and all sorts of characters make that junket. Well, in our case it won't be a junket, God knows. This is serious and tragic business.

DECEMBER 18, 1966
PRINCETON

A week from now this house will be filled with tissue paper, red ribbons, and the resounding shouts of two young boys "rastling"—or fighting. Nancy and Sylvain and the grandsons, Allen and Daniel, are expected next Saturday, for a week with us. Brace yourself; the boys are terrific, and full of life; but what a different household it is when they are here!

Didn't know, until reading the paper this morning, that my Princeton "walking companion," General Greenbaum, is counsel for Harper, and so is in the middle of this sad and perplexing controversy with the Kennedys.

As we two shuffled our way through the Institute woods he told me of the legal and intensely emotional and political aspects of the effort of Jacqueline and Robert Kennedy to prevent the publications, by Harper and by *Look* magazine, of the Manchester book.

The legal points, as Eddie described them, interest me as a one-time lawyer. For example: is Harper bound by the terms—and the alleged breach—of a contract between Manchester and the Kennedys, by which the writer promised not to publish his book without the express approval of the text by the Kennedys? And so on, with other interesting legal points, some of them doubtless novel.

But the issues are more than legal, for the controversy is charged with drama of a high order of intensity: a source of antagonism between President Johnson and Senator Kennedy; the anguish of the beautiful young widow; the heartache for Cass, personally and professionally close to the Kennedys for years, having published *Profiles in Courage* and his son married for a time to Jacqueline's sister.

The General was all wound up this morning. The old warhorse snorting with excitement, sensing the coming drama of the courtroom, the back and forth with opposition lawyers, the sense of responsibility he feels, the trust people put in him. His voice is a reedy one, and I have wondered at times what kind of impression his manner and sometimes thin voice would make in court. But this morning, as we stomped our way through the woods, now so familiar to us in these little tramps, I was sure that his great sincerity and intensity in such a matter would make him a formidable figure before any tribunal.

Eddie wanted to know all about the Vietnam undertaking. There really isn't much to say, with what little I know. I guess I surprised him when, he asking what the Big Boss had said, I told him I had never seen the President on this, not once in all the months this matter has been under discussion. I hope I hid the still slight resentment I feel that this is so, a resentment I confess tempered by the feeling that at this juncture in the President's plummeted fortunes in public opinion the less I seem to be "his" boy in any way, the better chance of succeeding in this terribly difficult and painful assignment.

That comment is a measure of how deep the antagonism and disillusion about L.B.J. have gone, in recent weeks. Much of it undeserved, but that is the hard fact.

Talked to Leo Anderson at some length this morning, he in Davis, California. Wanted the background on the proposal Bob Harkens, on our behalf, has made to Penalosa of Colombia. A very ambitious agricultural training center to service all of INCORA's project. The emphasis on a center for training, i.e., an operational emphasis, appeals to me. But the tab, a half million dollars, I feared would panic Penalosa and he might turn it down without letting us discuss an idea *I* have.

My thought is to bring the Rockefeller and Ford Foundations into this, as a natural outgrowth of their agricultural work, not in the research sense, developing new seeds, etc., but to devise innovative methods for getting the results of new knowledge *to farmers and agricultural workers*, Colombians brought to the center for this purpose. A far cry from the conventional land grant college "extension" service concept.

DECEMBER 19, 1966
NEW YORK

Sol Descartes was for years the great, tall, Spanish-looking motor that drove the Puerto Rico power program from one achievement to another. The bright eye of an expert rifleman, a sharpshooter, the commanding figure of a conquistador, he was one of that group of spirited young men brought together by Muñoz Marín, who lifted Puerto Rico from a Caribbean slum to an almost-modern state.

When he came in to see me today, the alertness was still there but his disenchantment with Muñoz was evident.

I had asked Sol rather pointedly why the agricultural side of the island was way back yonder, while industrially, and in tourism, and in terms of urban development so much progress had been made. He admitted that agriculture has lagged. Sugar is actually losing money. "Yes, you're right, there are nearby markets for truck crops. The reason behind the present situation is not that there aren't some very bright young men in the agriculture department, no. It's all politics, my friend."

I have had the impression that the steam and vigor and perhaps even much of the idealism has gone out of the "great experiment." Sol's discourse, if true, would confirm it.

Puerto Rico is too young for this to happen; it needs what TVA has had in recent years, in part at least, what I once called a "second spring." The agricultural development of the island, to keep pace, and to follow upon the success, in industry, of Operation Bootstrap, could bring the whole island along.

Why don't they call on D&R for help? We know agriculture, we could bring good firms to Puerto Rico.

"Of everyone else they are suspicious," Descartes said, "but they would trust you. Why don't you speak to Muñoz, have them invite you to tell them what could be done?"

David arrived about 6:30 P.M., looking like a writer, his curly hair cut European style. He laughs at this; says he has to satisfy people that "I look the part of the business I am in." We had a good meal at Mercurio's, sitting at my favorite corner table. David is full of enthusiasm, is to see his publisher tomorrow about promotion for his new book, *The Tour*. And his enthusiasm for his old man seems to me at a new high.

He is not resigned to my taking on the "impossible" Vietnam job, but I sense he half admires my absurd willingness to do so. I thought I detected some feeling that conceivably my luck and sense of timing may pull me—and Vietnam—through this one. Bringing the theme of the Fairless Lectures to bear on the problem of Vietnam's economic future may erase some of the slick White House slogans, focus the emphasis on human beings, on the people out there, as a point of departure for thinking and planning and projecting. Perhaps this kind of a new concept could help.

DECEMBER 20, 1966
NEW YORK

I have fallen heir to, or I suppose I should say I have created, fashioned, a special and perhaps unique way of using myself. Several times today I thought: the issues, the intellectual content, the to-and-fro of the ideas you deal with, the decisions you must make—they are actually on the broad scale and amplitude of a man in high public office. Yet consider the freedom you have that a public servant does not have: to pick your associates, to select the problems you choose to wrestle with. Here you act as a free and independent man, unencumbered by the several constraints of bureaucracy: intellectual, financial, organizational.

As an example: this morning for a couple hours, Seymour and our new Chief Economist, Fred Moore, an ex-RAND man, churned and chewed and analyzed what we thought should be investment policies for the "economic integration of Latin America."

The discussion had the ease and informality of good conversation, though the ideas we tossed around were serious business, very serious, both for our enterprise and for the hemisphere to the south. For example, the considerations that would impel investment in a steel or chemical plant in a particular country, in a place and under conditions where there is a market big enough to make the product competitive both with world prices and in the overall Latin American market. And so on: figuring out those components of what Moore called, felicitously, "the raw material of industrial policy."

Part of the reason such closely reasoned discussion seems so stimulating and enjoyable is that this is not an academic excursion. I share the *responsibility* of making recommendations on matters that will affect, for good or ill, for agreement or disagreement, the minds and decisions of many individuals—businessmen, economists, public officials, and the ordinary man on the street—in many parts of a continent of 200 million people.

This is the kind of thinking that harassed public officials like Secretary Linc Gordon or Ambassador Linowitz give themselves over to; but unhappily they are oppressed with the manifold pressures of seeing officials (some among them pretty empty-headed ones) from twenty-two nations of Latin America. So they don't really get the time for, nor can they enjoy, the relaxed comradeship of the kind of discussion we had in my office, looking out at the charcoal-tinted glowering harbor, a snow coming on.

Felipe Herrera [head of the Inter-American Development Bank] came to our office at about 2:45. Looked fresh, unperturbed, eager, and enthusiastic about the agreement he has been able to secure among five of the six nations of the Plata Basin for the next step in a study of the development of that huge Parana River complex.

Bob Lively's comment about the recent escalation of my efforts for Vietnam, Latin America, etc.:

"You remind me of Henry Adams. Everything you do is getting ready for the next thing you do."

DECEMBER 26, 1966
PRINCETON

For the past several days it has been low tide: energies seemingly depleted, worries about the state of D&R hard to fend off, abnormally long hours of sleep during the day and the night. A general feeling of unease.

But since noon, when I took young Allen out for what I called a "Lewis and Clark expedition" in Marquand Park, through the drifted snow, I can feel the tide is coming in. By tomorrow, when I return to the office for a lively set of decisions, I'll be myself again.

A review in yesterday's *Times* of Dos Passos' book *The Best Times*. (Those were the times of his youth, and of Hemingway's.)

At the end of the review, this about Dos Passos—and the rest of us, perhaps, who belong to his generation:

"He [Dos Passos] could be great friends with Hemingway because they shared excitement over the rich immediacy of youthful experience."

And then this tragic closing sentence, a warning perhaps:

"They shared also the inability to build up something to replace youth, and to realize that this lack might hold greater and ultimately more devastating results than any they ever faced in war."

I don't honestly believe I have been unable to build up something to replace the excitement of TVA and AEC. I definitely have done so, though I went through a kind of lower-case hell to achieve it. But there are shoals still ahead, new adjustments yet to make, before I can say with assurance that I continue to hold to something that has the "rich immediacy" of those earlier days.

DECEMBER 27, 1966
NEW YORK

In a somber mood. There is coming over me a sobering sense of how desperate is the challenge I have accepted, in taking on, with ardor and inexplicable confidence, the Vietnam development enterprise.

Not that I haven't thought much about what it is I expect to be able to do that will shorten the agony, open the door to new light for the Vietnamese and for the now profoundly anxious American people. No, what makes for the somber mood are the many expressions of high expectations from so many friends. "Somehow Dave will make a difference." That kind of thing. The most moving was a kind of love letter to me from the Tennessee Valley, an editorial in the *Decatur Daily*, as personal and direct as a friendly, compassionate clap on the shoulder. Letters out of the long ago past such as the one from John Cady, now a distinguished historian and authority on Southeast Asia, whom I last saw when he and I were on the football squad at DePauw. Father Ford tonight at dinner at the Century, his eager face alight, saying words that made me realize how people somehow expect one more miracle out of this sometimes tired carcass, for they insist that TVA and Persia and CVC and the Acheson-Lilienthal plan were "miracles" in their way.

DECEMBER 28, 1966
NEW YORK

I had plans for next week, and they did *not* include going to South America and back. But this morning a cable from Botero: Venezuela and Colombia holding a "final" discussion of your proposal for study of economic union; desirable that you be here January 3 and 4.

Long and intense discussion with Bill Warne, replaced by Governor Reagan as head of the huge California state water resources program. My decision: we should offer him a post for a year, perhaps to develop into something permanent if that is the way it goes on both sides. Warne obviously excited and interested in this remarkable outfit, but uncertain about how he would fit in a "business" situation. To return to public service would be comfortable, he would know what he could do. "Can I make the adjustment?"

Dashed uptown to the CED office for an hour or more with "Pete" Collado, Executive Vice President of Standard of New Jersey (he is Chairman of the Research and Policy Committee of CED), Fred Borch, President of General Electric (shades of Gerard Swope and Owen Young!), and Al Neal, President of CED.

The meeting was occasioned by my trying to get off the ground the "business performance" policy study and statement which I chair.

I summed up the two points I thought we should follow: take plenty of time to have the intellectual community—the experts they have engaged—develop a series of hypotheses about ways of measuring and evaluating the performance of big business units; and try to get some interim reports before that time dealing with achievements, or deficiencies of performance, in particular and specific areas where the public interest and corporate goals should be parallel. I concluded by saying that I would agree to "stay with it" despite the furious increase in the demands on my own time, e.g., the Vietnam business.

Was struck with how defensive and almost resigned these top drawer big business tycoons were. Particularly Collado, with his greatly respected State Department background and long years as recognized *spokesman* for the progressive business community, via CED.

Collado was shaken by the antibusiness influence of the intellectuals and "academics." "And it will get worse, too," said he, shaking his great head and looking defeatedly at the floor. He thinks that fighting the government makes no sense and told the mutual investment trust boys who are spoiling for a fight against the SEC's recent criticism not to waste their time.

Prodding and curious—and full of disbelief at this apparent loss of nerve (or conviction) among the business community—I said: "But do you ascribe all this influence to a group of professors with a captive audience in the universities?" This brought a rise out of them: "But that's exactly it. They [the professors et al.] are the ones who are teaching the coming generation who will decide the course of the country."

I didn't suggest that doing a better job to promote, through private corporate action, the public goals business leaders rhetoricize about so eloquently (through ghost writers, usually) would be better than one more round of a public relations job.

The impressive thing was how resigned and overwhelmed by their critics these powerful men seemed to be.

DECEMBER 30, 1966
PRINCETON

Warne has accepted a post in D&R. Hard for me to put into words what a powerful lift this gave me when the word came from our office in Sacramento. No man in America has done a more exacting and successful job in the water resources field than he, heading California's billion dollar program, and before that a pioneering tour of duty as head of Point Four in Iran. When he returns to Iran for D&R, with his forceful personality, it should shore up that Khuzistan program in a way that lackluster but good technical people could never do. This should mean that our days in and usefulness for Iran, instead of being numbered and limited, are beginning a new chapter, truly a "second spring."

A man with force and sophistication in the ways of large organizations. What a tonic this will be! So sure am I of this that I am underwriting his salary for the year though I recognize this is wrong in principle—my way of betting that we will not suffer a loss from this addition to our overhead at a time when we are very much in an earnings decline, a decline that the Vietnam work will accelerate.

Sol Linowitz' phone call—fully a half hour long—was the other big event of an exciting day.

I am confident that this fresh, attractive man from the "outside world" will be able to change the whole spirit of United States relations with Latin America. The new Ambassador to the OAS will give some of the traditional State Department pussyfooters and milquetoasts a bad time—particularly since he has the President's ear and attention.

Linowitz was impressed with the news that we had taken on the Vietnam job; but he was anything but enthusiastic. It is difficult for him to see how anything heartening could come out of that tragic country.

And a call just in from Burnett. Oliver, Seymour, and Volpe have agreed, as has AID, to a contract covering the first four and a half months of our Vietnam work.

DECEMBER 31, 1966
PRINCETON

Year's end. Calendar year, that is.

Year's beginning, too, with a vengeance. The year ends, and 1967 begins, with a commitment to try to breathe something affirmative and hopeful into the increasingly ugly, bloody, and well-nigh hopeless Vietnam impasse. The biggest "event" of 1966, the unfolding story (beginning last summer) of our being pushed and shoved perhaps insanely into that responsibility.

This was a year much occupied by two "professional" events outside my main business, D&R. First, the hours and hours going over the MS of Volume III of the *Journals* and its subsequent appearance and excellent reception by the reviewers. And second, the satisfactions and agonies and absurdly long hours trying to write my three Carnegie lectures, which turned out to be much more than that: a real attempt to state my life's philosophy about getting things done, a new concept of management.

On the more personal side, there was great satisfaction in the peace of our home in Princeton, however impatient I was at times that it was too "peaceful" and bland, the delight in seeing David become more and more an established and recognized writer of high rank (the film not the least kind of recognition), his qualities of judgment more and more evident along with his creative abilities as an artist; and Nancy in a new setting, Sylvain more sure of himself as a scholar and an individual at MIT.

A great deal of reading; good health; and above all, a sense of still being able to give an account of myself.

Good year.

IV

1967

Trip to Colombia—Washington and preparation for Vietnam undertaking—Trip to Hawaii, Thailand, and Vietnam—Report to President Johnson—Conference at Guam—University of Illinois Commencement—State dinner at White House for Shah of Iran—Trip to Vietnam—Report to President Johnson and the Cabinet—Trip to French Polynesia en route to Australia

NEW YEAR'S DAY, 1967
NOON
FLYING OVER THE CARIBBEAN, HEADING FOR BOGOTÁ

If this new year itself begins as resplendently as this New Year's *Day*, it will be indeed a glory. What I saw was literally the dawn of a new year.

I left Princeton in the dark of night. Half an hour later a dawn sun cascaded light over the whole of the east, while in the little farm houses and the barns were the early lights, people beginning to get the coffee on, the cows fed. As we crossed Staten Island, heading for Kennedy Airport, Manhattan's peaks glowed a soft warm pink. How soft and supple the arcs of the great Verrazano bridge, as we crossed it, then doubled back, getting a second view of what must surely be one of the great works of American art. And under the bridge, steaming majestically, slowly, the liner *United States*.

I am still somewhat surprised to find myself on this trip to Bogotá. (This was a week set aside for quite different things.) Prospects are excellent for our achieving agreement between Colombia and Venezuela, the first instance in contemporary Latin American history of a coming together of two proud countries. I find it difficult to believe they would be sending for me unless there were an assumption that our proposal makes sense, in its basic purpose and in the strategy of the work program we've outlined.

A lengthy talk yesterday afternoon with David, by phone, about Volume IV of the *Journals*, now in preparation for the printer. In the first two volumes we considered that we were dealing with a document of some historical importance concerned with two significant American public enterprises, TVA and AEC. Therefore I was most reluctant to cut or revise any part of what I wrote *at the time*. This was also true of parts of Volume III.

Not so with this volume. We will cut liberally without feeling we are "compromising the integrity" of a historical document, for it is not that. And we can take some account of some of the more serious criticism and reviews. They have been almost entirely favorable, but here and there they do provide clues that may make this volume somewhat faster paced without damaging the whole narrative.

David insists, however, that the initial concept that the *Journals* are a "personal narrative" should be retained. I agree. It was his concept, not mine, though I became a convert after a period of doubt.

JANUARY 3, 1967
HOTEL TEQUENDAMA
BOGOTÁ, COLOMBIA

This altitude (almost 9000 feet) slows me down, as the day progresses.

This morning an hour and a half with Bernardo Garces in his golf course size office in the Ministerio de Obras Públicas. Bernardo's office and surroundings change, but not Bernardo. The same ironic grin, the perpetual cigar puffed vigorously, the same little chuckle as he recites even the most dramatic of events.

The recent descent upon Colombia by the "mission" from the International Monetary Fund was dramatic enough for any taste. They insisted to President Lleras Restrepo, in office less than four months, that he must enter into an agreement with the IMF to devalue the peso from 13 to 20 to the U.S. dollar. The President, Bernardo said, recognized the technical symmetry of their reasons for so drastic a step, but IMF seemed quite unaware that if he took this step the Government would fall and the country be in far greater trouble than it is as a result of the almost complete cessation of buying of coffee, the country's chief source of foreign exchange.

After each member of his Cabinet, at a late evening session, expressed the view that devaluation of such kind would be disastrous, the rotund little President explained the theoretical reasons *favoring* devaluation and then added: "*But* it will be put into effect by someone else, not by me. I will go to the Congress, state the demand of the IMF that unless devaluation is proceeded with, no further international lending will be made—and ask Congress to appoint my successor." Quite a man.

CVC is about to appoint—or perhaps by today has named—Henry Eder, son of the tragically murdered Harold Eder‡, as the Managing Director of CVC to succeed Bernardo. As good a choice as possible. A new thrust into the agricultural field, along the lines we proposed almost a year ago, is greatly needed to give CVC the beginning of a new era in its life; without a permanent head this wasn't likely to happen.

Monday afternoon Enrique Penalosa spent a couple hours with me. Each time I see him he seems a stronger man, more sure of himself. This was notably the case when he spoke of the foreign exchange crisis in which Colombia now finds itself. When he speaks of President Lleras Restrepo he must get out of his chair, his arms wide in a gesture of acute enthusiasm. Never has the President's prestige and support from the country been so great: he told organized labor they must keep wages from rising and told business they must not increase prices; he got a "100% increase" in the gasoline tax through the Congress without any backfire, and had the funds put into a revolving fund for the use of the highways. It was considered a great achievement.

But how Colombia is going to repair the damage of the drop in coffee prices he didn't say, except (as Bernardo explained in greater detail during our talk this morning) by some effort to get the coffee-consuming countries (the U.S., France, and West Germany) to set up a coffee compact under which quotas and prices will be fixed. Said Bernardo: "It isn't so important *what* coffee prices are—45 cents or 60 cents. What is important is that we *know* for some time ahead what the prices will be so we can plan on it."

I asked Penalosa what he thought about the proposal our Bob Harkens had made for an agricultural operational center, to service the needs of all the INCORA projects. He didn't meet this head on, which means he has grave doubts. "I agree that we need such a center staffed by overseas technical people. But I don't agree with Harkens' *approach*."

He feels that the great need is—as I would say in TVA—to begin from where we are and fears that this center, as Bob has conceived of it and would run it, "would wait until all the tests have been made, wait

‡ Harold Eder was murdered in March, 1965. See pp. 123–125.

for several years to be sure that the cattle program or the production program was just exactly right, technically." He said, "Well, we can't wait. It would be fine to increase production of these cultivators by 80%, say, but what I want is to begin *now* to increase their output by even 10%. That would be better than 80% five or ten years from now."

"Do you mean the program is too perfectionist?" I asked. Well, he recognizes that Colombia needs many of these improved techniques, but needs help for the ordinary farmer now even more.

I sympathized immediately with this reaction. I have had the same kind of problem with technical people of all kinds, and particularly agricultural ones. But I also saw that Penalosa was trying to have it both ways: he wants the best techniques and intensified agriculture; but he doesn't want to wait while that is coming about. Most of these small farmers, he thinks, wouldn't be able to put to use the techniques that this center would be developing and demonstrating.

JANUARY 4, 1967
BOGOTÁ

Is integration disintegrating? We—Seymour, Moore, and I—sit around waiting to hear from the "mixed" Colombia-Venezuela commission, who requested my urgent presence down here for "final discussion" of our proposal. And we are getting a bit tired waiting. Are issues we thought were settled months ago now subjects of serious debate?

But empty waiting for someone else's conclusions, or even their availability, is part of the life of many people. However, I don't take kindly to it, as a matter of temperament, and I have for years been spared that kind of test of patience, if patience is the correct term.

"Patience is its own reward"; that is the axiom. Well, I say to hell with it. Besides, waiting conflicts with my lifelong habit of recoiling from wasting time.

An absurd concept, that, that time can ever be "wasted." It is spent, and how fruitfully or pleasantly or emptily depends upon how much of an artist of living one is.

3:45 P.M.

A good solid kick in the teeth is what we got at eleven this morning. With a most polite and dignified lack of courtesy.

At 11 we were ushered into a huge room in the Palace by Rodrigo Botero, the President's economic secretary. At the head of a great oval table the beetle-browed Dr. Hurtado, head of Planning for Venezuela; flanking him, Currie, Botero, and the others of the joint commission on integration.

Botero began: "Our Venezuela associates must return to Caracas at once, for the dedication of a bridge, so this meeting with you cannot last for more than an hour. Therefore there will be no opportunity to go into the details of the conclusion we have all reached about your proposal. We will communicate our views in a couple of weeks by a brief letter."

No reference made to the fact that we had been explicitly asked to fly 6000 miles "to discuss" the proposed program, one we had prepared at their request and within guidelines they had worked out at Caracas. This meant four days of my time and that of two seniors of our company taken away from other things, and at considerable expense to us, for an hour meeting which we are told was not for discussion, but to be told that we would later get a *written* communication.

Botero explained: "There has been a communications gap. The program your proposal describes is not at all what we had in mind. What we wanted was a statement of the philosophy that supports the idea of integration between these two countries; you do not propose a conceptual framework, but rather a comprehensive and exhaustive collection of facts to support integration. But suppose, as a political issue, we conclude that instead of integration of our countries we should build a barbed wire between them? What we wanted was a statement of the concept underlying integration, not the facts that support it, or that would show benefits to each country were integration actually effected.

"I once had a professor who said, about statistics, that you should not collect statistics, or garbage, unless you knew before collecting it what you would do with those statistics or garbage. The statistics you propose to collect—about public health, for example—how can anyone know that any of this is relevant to *action* by the two countries?"

Up to this point what he said on behalf of the joint commission could be construed as a criticism of the extremely wide range of the investigation which Seymour and Moore had written into the proposal, a three year program to cost one and a half million dollars. This is something we—particularly John Oliver and I—had raised questions about back home, but the answer we got was that to do a good, effective technical job required this scale of effort.

This part of the criticism I took very well. So I said to Botero that if their negative reaction meant that they wished, initially, to have a philosophical conceptual statement of the benefits that might accrue in general terms from making each country have available the markets afforded by the other, there was this difficulty: if such a philosophical concept is simply "more of the familiar rhetoric about the virtues of integration" it would be no more persuasive, in practical terms for the guidance of the countries, than the rhetoric already existing on the subject, of which there has been a great deal. The countries would not need our professional services for such a statement of philosophy; the brief "communication" he promised to send us would probably state the concept, and that would be that, no need for our services.

But I could not see how such a statement of concept could be very meaningful, except as more rhetoric, unless there are a number of examples of how integration, *in particular cases*, might be beneficial.

Botero, translating this to Hurtado, didn't like it too well—partly, I expect, because he saw, as an able economist, that dealing in vacua with such a subject would not constitute any real contribution.

After some hurried translation back and forth, we had our final answer. No, the commissioners would not want to get into facts. Their later written "communication" to us would make that clear. (At this he seemed abashed, and his face colored; the other men around the table, his associates, looked embarrassed. I thought to myself: Why in hell don't they apologize for having had us spend the weeks we have spent on this subject, or say one word of apology for having had us come all this way and be told that there would be no discussion, except for an hour in which they would say they had changed their mind about the whole business?)

And so, without a word of thanks for the time and effort we had expended, we were dismissed, very coolly, our hosts' manners outwardly intact. Currie, looking worn down with what must have been a long session before we met with them, shook my hand rather sorrowfully, said he was "sorry this has been so negative," and out we went.

I thought to myself: They are beginning to see that if D&R does the job we proposed, or even a first-phase portion of it, we will be presenting a *set of facts* and opportunities about both countries that will stir up more *political* issues and unease than they want to face.

The fact is, they just don't want to discuss the subject with us—or face the issues between their countries. That is their privilege. But it is our privilege to have no part in a meaningless charade. And to remember this example of discourtesy to friends and professionals.

As a professional group preparing an analysis of the pluses and minuses of integration, we must do so from the viewpoint of the countries which we serve in this professional capacity.

But are the *interests of my own country* served by progress toward Latin American integration? Should we urge Linowitz and the President to encourage integration without considering whether, if it is achieved, this *helps or hurts* U.S. interests?

I made a strong case that the most we would expect if integration by the Latin countries succeeded, through their own efforts, would be a strong bloc organized against the United States, in an economic and, therefore, in a political sense.

With the U.S. already the world's Number One Patsy, should we, through our *own* initiative and efforts, help countries of Latin America to combine in a way that would help their people, as we believe, but would make things harder for the people of the United States?

I don't believe the answer is an unqualified No. But a good many people, even intense internationalists, are beginning to think this way—partly for rational reasons; partly for emotional ones. When such pioneer internationalists as Walter Lippmann, George Kennan, and Senator Fulbright find their earlier internationalist convictions reversed or modified by the way policies of *helping everyone,* regardless, have actually worked, it is time to re-examine. And this is what must be going on in many homes and schools and street corners these days.

It may be that Botero et al. are simply saying: You propose far too much at a first bite. Here I would tend to agree. But if we have in fact—as I believe—had a strong kick in the teeth, then we of D&R should turn to something more likely to be productive. And be more skeptical the next time.

JANUARY 5, 1967
7:45 A.M.
BOGOTÁ

Seymour, Moore, and I had something of a postmortem late yesterday afternoon. Did we understand what they wanted or did we plunk for the kind of elaborate and *perfectionist* professional study that our technical people wanted to make to satisfy a sense of style and high standards of competence?

I left it this way: Let's face up to the fact that we failed, in that the proposal, in its purpose of persuasion, failed so far that the Commission would not even discuss how it could be amended to meet their desires.

Moore, a talented economist, and a high-spirited, confident, and aggressive man, seemed to listen, for the first time, to the notion that presenting a proposal calls for a sense of tactics and of savvy as well as economic professional skills.

I put this whole integration business between Colombia and Venezuela behind me. Let's learn from it though, if we can. And the same goes for the failure of our elaborate proposal for an expensive agricultural operational center of INCORA. These failures may give us some insight into the effect, on a struggling country like this, of *counsels of technical perfection.*

11 A.M.
ABOARD BRANIFF

Bernardo, calling me at the hotel this morning: "How did the integration meeting go?"

"Well, Bernardo, I was nonplused. We were told that we had misunderstood what the countries wanted. They wanted a conceptual framework, not an investigation into the facts about integration."

"That," said Bernardo, "would be just more oratory. We've had plenty of that. If they mean business, they *must* have some facts to work on. I can't speak for Venezuela, of course, but Colombia means business. I am nonplused, too."

The meeting with Enrique Penalosa at breakfast in my hotel room was *most* satisfactory.

What is the "approach" that Enrique has in mind?

He wants the focus of agricultural work to be changed from the "usual" style of research to getting help, often of a simple kind, out to the farmers who need it. This is not the way the Rockefeller Foundation functions, nor many of the agricultural graduates of our own universities.

"What I want [how emphatic that man can be, his whole body put into these sentences] is not to increase the yields for the fellow who already has high yields. What I want, what the country needs, is that the little farmer's yield be increased, not seven times, but, say, from one to one and a half. To do that we don't want more research, more papers written by Colombian or foreign research people, but men who will go out from this center to show the little farmer on his own land how he can make these modest but important improvements in his output."

Of course, all this fits into my experience. That is what our TVA "assistant county agents" did, making the *individual farm* the "research" center rather than the fancy experiment stations.

Before the alcoholic prelude to my Braniff luncheon overwhelms me, let me recount one concrete illustration of what was an extraordinary exposition of practical monetary economics from two knowledgeable operators (not just theoreticians), Garces and Penalosa, at the special passenger lounge at the airport:

"A devaluation by fiat, of the peso, from 13 to 20 to the dollar, as insisted upon to the President by the International Monetary Fund, would, among many other things, increase *internal* price inflation, the very thing the pigheaded Chairman, head of the Fund's experts, expected devaluation to accomplish.

"The purpose of devaluation, these experts say—with only their European background, Italy, Britain—is to make our exports competitive in the *world* markets. But making the peso worth only 20 rather than 13 to the dollar means that prices rise throughout Colombia.

"But here is the poignant and most credible illustration—even the woman in the village who has eggs to sell says: Ah, yes, the peso is worth less, so eggs are more expensive. Nothing to do with the cost of producing the eggs."

I very much liked this homely illustration of how devaluation actually defeats its purpose, by increasing prices that have nothing to do with increased costs. And eats up the whole advantage of the devaluation, to bring costs more in line with the stated value of the peso.

I asked them: Should the U.S. President encourage a conference this spring of the other Western Hemisphere Presidents? I doubt it. What say you?

They answered that if the discussion is about agricultural progress and education—which is what Linc Gordon's agenda seems to emphasize—the answer, we think, should be No. The U.S. will be offering more free advice to the Latin countries; they have had a lot of that.

But if Johnson is ready to tackle the present unfairness to Latin America of *low prices for their raw materials*, which is what most interests the Latin American Presidents and countries, then, Yes. But we doubt if the U.S. is prepared to meet that *specifically*. If not—we wonder what advantage there is to anyone in one more grand potpourri of generalities.

NEW YORK

It is a crazy kind of life I lead. Me with a quiet, handsome home and me in this tiny hotel room, with a TV going lickety-split through the thin wall; and eating alone amid convivial (and probably boring) couples. More stupid than anything, going full tilt this way: to South America on Monday and back on Thursday, and a lot of wear and tear in between.

I made a New Year's resolution to shed much of this kind of behavior. But I knew even as I made the resolution that once I get over the reaction to this quick trip I'll be back at it as hard as ever. Damned fool.

JANUARY 7, 1967
PRINCETON

Fred Friendly, looking as big—and pleased with himself—as a pro football tackle, at the Oppenheimer lunch table, putting away huge quantities of "the best goose liver in the world—that's why I come to the Oppenheimers'." Robert, at the head of the table, looking so subdued, his eyes strained. "The guests have stayed too long," whispered Kitty.

Friendly said, "I stole words from you, David. I was going to write you about it; now I can tell you. I looked over the statement about use of a satellite paid for by the people, for an educational TV channel, and I said to Bundy: 'Mac, it's too cold.' So we stole your phrase from your TVA book: 'a people's dividend.' And that phrase is what warmed it up and was the phrase that was quoted everywhere."

I had wanted to talk to Robert about doing some informal essays for the *Atlantic Monthly*; had a letter from the editor with a suggestion for "A Dialogue between Robert Oppenheimer and David Lilienthal." But there was no chance to discuss this at luncheon and I knew I must leave very shortly; plodding home through the snow, swinging my heavy stick, I felt even more grey than the overcast skies. For as he got my coat (he always insists on holding it for me!) Robert said: "I don't feel very gay; the doctor gave us bad news yesterday." And Kitty, acting the perfect hostess, amusing us with a story of an experiment she—as a biologist—had "invented" years ago, having to do with some esoteric fungus, took me outside as I left—and broke down.

Impending death is no new story; but this is one that seems so wasteful and cruel. But Robert, in my presence at least, looks at it with those eyes of the doomed, that seem to look inward, rigid, caught up in the final reality.

JANUARY 10, 1967
NEW YORK

Lunch with Jack Heinz alone, yesterday noon. Just back from skiing, looking twenty years younger than I (though he is actually approaching sixty). Perhaps because he doesn't take things so damned solemnly as I do. But it is more than that. He doesn't joust with windmills either, as I fear I do.

As we talked about Khuzistan as a place for agrobusiness, it was demonstrated once more how poorly equipped D&R is with people who have any real sense of business. And since I respect the business way of thinking in its place (and a big place it is), I thought to myself that we have so few who could really dig into the key question about food production by a big commercial group, which is this: what will the *customer* prefer, or even will there be customers?

The theoretical people now are having a big time remarking on how the Soviet system is moving toward a "market view" of their economy (and there soon will be articles in *Foreign Affairs* about this from their stable of professors, I'm sure). But such matters as food habits and the ways in which people are willing to spend their money—the heart of the "market economy" precept as applied to food—will seem too prosaic.

Actually, how the townspeople of Andimeshk in provincial Iran are willing to spend the money they now are earning, after so long a time without money, seems to me much more interesting to the imagination and far more useful than anthropological studies. Will they spend money for canned food? Will they prefer motor bikes or Japanese toys to supermarket products to eat?

JANUARY 11, 1967
WASHINGTON

The first "Vietnam day"; or putting it another way: the first day of my New Life, Vietnamese Style.

Began the morning, along with Oliver and Moore, meeting with the fragile, alert, cricket-quick little Vietnam Ambassador to the U.S., Vu Van Thai, at their Embassy. The Ambassador's last day in this post, so he spoke "candidly," as he put it, in his brittle little voice. Learned a lot from this hour or so about the disdain these elite French—in Vietnamese guise—feel about the upstart generals who, as they feel, took over their country and are "The Government."

From there we went on to a series of "briefings." In a big room, lined with AID thinkers, the "Vietnam Situation Room" (that's the official designation for this map-infested, "secure" room), we heard a lecture about the "political" picture of Vietnam; it could have been given to a course at any university so far as anything either secret or very perceptive is concerned. But I fixed my eye on the tortoise-shelled young man who gave the spiel, as if every word was a startling new insight. I had time for a question: do I understand that the Viet Cong is a *political* party? Yes he said; it has an ideology, a discipline, a program. I suppose I must say it is a political party; one that uses methods of violence, but with a very considerable following. In fact, it has more of the marks of a political party than the twenty-five groups called parties who support the military government.

The best of the several sessions today, excepting that with the hot-rod, impatient, and strong Presidential Assistant, Komer, was with Ambassador Leonard Unger, a Deputy Assistant Secretary for the Far East. Handsome, the very picture of an intelligent foreign service professional, he made a lot of sense and was quite candid. "One of the sources of the rebel Viet Cong strength is this: that they have given land to peasants, who know that if the military government prevails that land will be given *back* to the landlords from whom it was taken by the Viet Cong."

Are the Viet Cong members an able group? "Yes," says the Ambassador (formerly to Laos, I believe), "yes, they are. In fact, Ambassador Harriman says they are the ablest people in Vietnam."

Komer wants a report that will be purely and solely a ten-year look ahead *at what could be*. That may be what we shall be forced to undertake.

"I want your private group to compete with the bureaucrats of AID and of State, here and in Saigon," he said. "You will be very discouraged at times. The best way to keep from being too discouraged is to separate yourself from those who are running this AID welfare program—as it must be—and put together the elements of what a real *development* should be, when the war is over."

Over the phone this morning Komer said in his bouncy way: "We have won the war. They won't tell you this, but that's the fact. The war itself is over."

That isn't what the President said in his State of the Union address last night, and I doubt that Komer means it literally. What he means, I would think, is that the question of whether we will have a military hold on the country is decided. That isn't the whole story by a long shot, but if it is 75% true, then he is correct when he says: "We will be screaming our heads off for your development plan in six months."

Not likely, I think, but possible. Something is in the wind.

JANUARY 12, 1967
11 P.M.
WASHINGTON

A whirling nightmare, a Fellini impressionist film, and a stirring summons to probably the strangest, most demanding task I have ever laid my hand—and head—to. That's the total impression I get from the remorseless "briefing" on Vietnam at the hands of a series of highly charged experts and "specialists" ranging from police ("public safety") to rice culture, from land reform to health, all day long, with "high level" meetings with the Secretary of State and the head of AID. What a day—and what a job that looms ahead.

I can't believe all of this is happening to me; that in less than a week I'll be heading westward to the East, on the beginning of what for me will be a test and an adventure, but that has a serious, desperate core of meaning far greater than an incredible extension of my own experience into a world that I still don't believe exists—the extraordinarily complex military, economic, social, ethnic, and *above all moral issue* we call the Vietnam "situation."

I recall the sense of awe and disbelief I had when the secret facts about atomic weapons were first revealed to me, the first days of the State Department Board of Consultants—now twenty years ago. Something of the same opening of a world I don't believe but know is real grows on me as I hear the story of Vietnam unfolding, and realize that before long I will be flying over that country, coming closer and closer to one of the most perplexing, devisive, ugly, cruel, and yet potentially educational experiences in contemporary American history.

JANUARY 13, 1967
WASHINGTON AIRPORT

Clark Clifford has the manner of a gentleman of the old school plus a command of the expression of ideas and an eloquence that I have rarely heard excelled—and in the three quarters of an hour I had with him just before dashing out here, he surpassed himself.

At first, we reminisced a bit about our experiences together in the Truman Administration.§ "There was a mutual respect and confidence in that Administration that I have not seen equalled since," Clifford mused. "In the Kennedy Administration, contrary perhaps to the accepted idea—there was nothing resembling this—crosscurrents were rife. And the same is true of the present Administration. You and I were fortunate to serve in that Truman atmosphere."

I explained the Vietnam assignment. Clifford responded with one of his usual right-on-target questions: "Is it a report you are to prepare or are you to carry out a program?"

I'm afraid I didn't give him a very clear picture of just what our efforts were directed toward but stressed my belief that we should make an effort to draw a picture of what South Vietnam's future *might* be, as the hostilities drew to an end, and afterward. "The essential, the decisive fact, the fact that will provide all of us, Vietnamese and U.S. alike, with the drive and motivation to give this everything we have," I said, "is this: it is continuously stated to us that the President and his top officials believe this is an important, and vital, task, and not just a cosmetic layer to cover the ugly side of military operations, nor a purely academic 'exercise' in economic planning."

He sat back in his chair and put his hands together in a pyramid before him. Glancing around his elegant law office (he still calls his firm Clifford and Miller, although his friend Miller was with him only a year or so and then died), it occurred to me that it had the serenity of the office of a Dean of Philosophy.

"Now I would like to make two or three comments."

Which he did, for perhaps a half hour, smoothly and quietly, with

§ See *Journals*, Vol. II, *The Atomic Energy Years.*

a sense of conviction when he said "this President believes . . ." You would not doubt that not only was this true, but that probably this tall, wavy-haired, relaxed man had himself formulated for Johnson the things which Johnson believed, had made him aware of those beliefs, or even persuaded him of the very form and pitch of his beliefs about one of the most desperate issues a President or a country has faced for a long, long time.

"It isn't winning the war, it isn't the military operations that are closest to the President's mind. It isn't even South Vietnam. It is a pattern for a kind of life that the people of all Southeast Asia can begin to enjoy that is at issue. So what the President wants is to make a *demonstration*, a demonstration in South Vietnam into which North Vietnam can be persuaded—later, and after difficult problems—can be persuaded to participate because they see it is good for them. And also because South Vietnam has many of the things that North Vietnam lacks and needs, and vice versa, both economically and politically.

"In the Cabinet Room I now sit in the same chair that I sat in when I was Special Counsel during President Truman's day. And in that seat I hear this same refrain of the Truman days; it is that same broad humanitarian issue. This is the issue that is more important now than Europe or the Soviet Union."

(This emboldens me to introduce early on the concept of a "future picture" of Vietnam, North and South, and of Eastern Asia, and not just "that little strip along the China Sea." "I guess more precisely the Bay of Tonkin," Clark added.)

"The President is prepared to stake *everything* on this vision of what we can help bring about in Southeast Asia," he said. "Everything. The military operations, yes, they have to be gone through, and for as long as necessary. And every time an American boy dies out there it is another dagger thrust into the President's heart—that's not well known, but I assure you it is true.

"David, you have had big and difficult jobs, complex ones, ones that took stamina and imagination, and they were vastly important to your country. Let me say to you that nothing you have ever undertaken and accomplished, nothing whatever, compares in importance to your present involvement in Southeast Asia."

Clifford went on to touch on a number of incidental points: "Withdrawal—that sounds easy, but the carnage that would follow would be awful beyond imagining. The so-called Gavin-Kennan enclave idea completely misses the reason for our being there. They say: 'We will hold this piece of land and you can have the rest.' What a tragic failure to see how much turns on making a demonstration to all the countries of Southeast Asia of what our intentions are. There never before has been a country that has used military force that didn't do it for a return.

We want nothing but that these people, with our help, have the chance of living out their destiny. European countries—indeed many other countries—can't possibly understand that, can't believe it. But they will."

As I got up to go he asked if I had taken all the health precautions: "The White House saw that I had yellow fever shots and the rest; but I contracted hepatitis while I was out there for quite a stay [curious how completely quietly he works; I didn't know he had ever been in Vietnam]. That was ten months ago and I'm not completely over it yet. Be sure you get gamma globulin shots. Now write that down in your notebook.

"And later on, when you get farther along, come in and tell me about it."

JANUARY 14, 1967
PRINCETON

Secretary of State Rusk is reached only after one is escorted through an elegant, brightly lighted tunnel lined with the painted portraits of his predecessors, then through a kind of golden grille into an anteroom the size of a nine-hole golf course; and *then*, beckoned on, in thick silence, by an awestricken-appearing lady of uncertain years, while the portals open. Then: there *he* is, standing silhouetted, looking down at a paper on his desk, and the warm, casual, friendly voice, "Hello, David," breaks the splendid mortuary spell—and it's just a round-faced, smiling Georgia boy. No change in Rusk; just the setting.

I've entered that place a good many times, years ago, in the days of General Marshall and then Acheson, another "Dean," and never felt the awe squirting all over me. So it was probably the state of my emotions rather than the surroundings that produced this effect on me of opening an Egyptian underground burial place of kings that had been sealed for millennia.

I looked carefully for the signs of wear and tear that show in Secretary Rusk's TV appearances lately, and even worse in his still pictures in the press. But though he had been on a very early TV show that morning (so he told me; the *Today* show on NBC), he was not only relaxed and unhurried, but he showed no marks of the extreme fatigue I had been told (by the know-it-all columnists) to expect.

I explained that I only wanted to have five minutes with him this time, as I was just beginning to learn something about the commitment we had made about Vietnam's economic future. But he motioned me to a seat, put his heavy-rimmed glasses on and off (and into his vest pocket) quite frequently, but otherwise seemed to want to leave his "official" role and just visit.

I hadn't known whether he had even heard of the kind of job to which I was expected to turn my energies and those of my company. Actually he did know; he expressed appreciation almost profusely for so outwardly composed and professional a diplomat, and spent almost a half hour talking about it.

"You will not find a ravaged country, nothing like France when it was a battlefield, nothing like that. The people go about their work and lives except when the bullets whistle or the terrorists explode grenades. But the countryside and Saigon aren't desolated. Once the present violence and fighting wanes—and that may come sooner than one might think—the country will be ready to pick up and move on to a substantial future, with none of its plant, its roads, its agriculture badly damaged."

He referred to an intelligence dispatch he had just read that morning: captured documents indicating the Viet Cong plan for keeping opposition going sporadically, a kind of plan for an orderly retreat—though retreat wasn't the word he used. A program for harassment rather than moving ahead.

"We're not going to be driven out; they understand that now. This means that in your work you can plan things that go ahead from wherever there is some measure of security."

I broke in: "In getting the feel of development we of D&R are a group of activists, and we do best when we can see things, real things, rather than only figures that are often not reliable anyway."

"You can go practically anywhere in the country, though not on the ground—that's a bit dangerous. But in a small plane or helicopter, which will take you almost anywhere. And probably will. Have to be in touch with the field commanders about this, but you will get to see things. For example, the installations at Cam Ranh Bay; they will make your jaw drop open." He grinned that knowing farmer's grin that is quite affecting.

"A great many things can be done that will have an immediate impact, too. And much of this kind of development has been done—for example, garbage collection, never done well before, now is. Water supply in the country. And so on."

I got up to take my leave; he was still talking and responsive, though I knew there was an important meeting with the President and McNamara next on his schedule. At the door, a quiet, almost shy expression of "our appreciation."

JANUARY 16, 1967
NEW YORK

Whatever frustrations and angst and puzzlement we encounter on the road of the Vietnam "mission," one thing today made clear: I am once more—as in the case of control of atomic weapons—to be precipitated into the middle of an issue of the greatest magnitude and importance.

In a three hour session with the distinguished Trustees of the EWA Board, and through a lengthy luncheon meeting with the top staff of the *New York Times*, it was the Vietnam war that was at the very center of discussion, of the perplexity, an issue not only military, political, and economic in nature but—as are all issues on a grand scale—ethical as well. Perhaps most important of all, an *ethical* issue.

JANUARY 17, 1967
NEW YORK

No amount of set grins, stiff upper lips, or ruddy sanguinity can change a shaky *cash* position. I still can't quite get over to my civil service minded senior associates that a "fine" balance sheet, made up, as ours now is, of one third of a million dollars' worth of "assets" in the form of solid accounts receivable, will not save us from the inability to pay our current obligations of salary, rent, etc., *unless* those receivables are of the kind that promptly produce *cash*. You can't meet a payroll with a beautiful balance sheet of that kind.

JANUARY 18, 1967
NEW YORK

An hour and a half session on the Vietnam assignment, with Oliver, Seymour, Moore, Mead, and Burnett.

Made it the opportunity to describe the conceptual framework that has apparently been buzzing around in my head, without my being consciously and systematically aware that I was thinking about it. It seemed to be well received, and in any case, accepted as an earnest of my commitment to take responsibility for this job and see it through, certainly during the next six to twelve months, as a top personal priority, at great financial cost to D&R.

This started last summer as a "postwar planning" concept. Built into that phrase were a set of assumptions, only a few of which, perhaps none of which, were any longer valid.

The "postwar planning" assumed, whether it was expressed or not, that this tragedy in Vietnam was like any other war: Yesterday there was war, today there is a ceremony on the deck of the battleship *Missouri* or at Versailles or in the woods in Germany—and tomorrow there is "peace." There was a postwar assumption that Vietnam had been flattened, and had to be rebuilt, as were Japan and Germany. There was an assumption that when the "war is won," the military pull out, the boys come home, America dusts its hands and says that is that, or leaves an occupation force, or mounts a Marshall Plan.

There was a further assumption last summer—only a few months ago—that this Vietnam war is a confrontation between the dirty Communists bent upon world domination and aggression against their little neighbors, and the strong arm of the U.S. military, something very closely comparable to the military confrontation in which the North Koreans were kept out of South Korea by a clash of armies; that the Viet Cong are synonymous not simply with guerrillas but with hard core Communists who "have to be exterminated" and that Hanoi is an "enemy," that North Vietnam could not possibly be considered as any kind of associate in the "postwar" period.

My own hunch is that virtually *none* of these hard edge, black and white concepts stand up to the *facts* as they have unfolded (as distinguished from the rhetoric on the subject).

First of all we need to avoid getting into the same grooves of thinking that we heard rattled off in many of our Washington briefing sessions (I especially exempt discussion with Ambassador Unger, who is thinking in more realistic terms) and to work toward a program and studies and action that fit the special circumstances of this Vietnam war.

It will not be easy to avoid being sucked in by the clichés of the tired, harassed, and utterly dedicated and able men in the AID Mission in Washington and in Saigon, in the State Department, and in the Defense establishment. But if we are worth our salt, we will somehow not only insist on our being independent, a "private contractor" as they say, but we will behave that way in our thinking processes.

One illustration of how my thoughts are running was my suggestion to my associates this morning that we should think of our team and group and company as drawing upon non-Americans and non-Vietnamese, to give it a genuine *Asian* as well as multinational character. For example, drawing upon one or two able Japanese planners and developers, or Cambodians skilled in rice culture, perhaps a Filipino, certainly a Korean. And also to preserve our flexibility and to increase our stature as a new and unhackneyed voice in this babble of clichés and outworn notions. To think hard right now about the economic and physical relationship between South Vietnam and North Vietnam, though they are now at war, looking ahead to peace in eighteen months or ten years. It does not matter, in terms of thinking, which of these time spans turns out to be the better guess.

I want to be sure—and this is what I talked about this morning—that the matrix of this undertaking be far removed from the original AID and White House concept: just a bunch of economists doing a highly professional job of economic planning. Economists will play an essential role, but the orchestration should not be determined by economists or even by the so-called science of economics. It is up to us to give some real content to the rhetoric that says this is not only a military operation, this war, and asserts that the troubles in Vietnam in which we are involved have a predominantly political significance.

Rhetoric alone does not take one very far; it is D&R's job to lay out some *specifics* that show that we understand what is meant when we say that this is *basically a political, a human problem.*

I qualified much of this by a comment to Fred Moore. We may find within six to nine months a need to be professionally well equipped to deal with some of the short-range but potentially disastrous crises that are clearly in the province of a sophisticated economist. One example of this is the consequences of the importation into Vietnam at the rate of a billion dollars a year of goods from the outside, in a country that has never imported even a significant fraction of that amount. This produces immediate pressures of an inflationary and of an ethical character that can't be ignored. They can't be put aside by D&R, as planners, with the disdain of the abstractionist or the legalistic view that "our contract" is to prepare a long-range, long-term plan for the country.

JANUARY 19, 1967
WAITING, WAITING, FOR TWA TO TAKE OFF FOR SAN FRANCISCO
KENNEDY AIRPORT, NEW YORK

When I finished talking to my colleagues yesterday about our Vietnam undertaking I felt a tremendous amount of satisfaction.

There is nothing more gratifying than that feeling of acceptance from one's co-workers. It is part of the great satisfaction that comes when one asserts leadership not by his corporate title or the number of stars on his shoulders, but by the force of his ideas and the capacity to move the minds and spirits of his close associates, the men upon whose enthusiasm and understanding he must rely to accomplish what is close to his heart.

Going back to last Monday and the "publisher's luncheon" at the *Times*.

When "Punch" Sulzberger—young Arthur—came bouncing out of his 14th floor office to greet me I had two simultaneous reactions: missing his father, the familiar, warm, one-sided grin, the love of irony and even of puns that were so much a part of this remarkable and lovable man; and incredulity that one so young could show such assurance, the assurance of both his father and mother. But they—Arthur and Iphigene—had earned that assurance by immersion in the veneration and stern standards that surrounded Adolph Ochs, the Founder.

Young Arthur, "publisher and president" alone, carries the "authority" and presence of the young prince; at the luncheon table, later, surrounded by the older men who carry the flag daily, the aura of his name diminishes. Which is to his credit. He has inherited a great task and responsibility, and has carried himself very well; but like his father before him (who also inherited, but in a somewhat different way), it will take time until he, too, is recognized in his own right. And his father *did* become "head" by the force of his ability and insight and courage in the crunch.

There was a further sharp reaction ahead of me, a surprise. For seated at the lunch table was a silent man, shattered by illness, his very heavy glasses (postcataract, I suppose) and the pale parchment of his skin disguising what was once one of the most cheerful and social of men, Arthur Hays Sulzberger. He motioned me to his right, shook my hand. But there was no conversation. I was told by young Arthur that before the luncheon was over he would probably want to leave, he usually did; and so it turned out; late in the lunch he was moved into a wheelchair and left.

Arthur's and my friendship began long ago; I was saddened beyond words. But so it goes. And in the meantime his redoubtable wife, Iphigene, has just returned from a trip to Africa. Her energy and good spirits seem inexhaustible; there is much of that in Punch.

The man at the large oval luncheon table who impressed me most, because he was new to me, was a blond, sun-tanned, young-appearing man, the Executive Vice President, Harding Bancroft. It was he who identified what I am most hopeful about regarding the Vietnam enterprise on which I am now setting out, by using the perceptive words: the significant thing could be "the psychological impact."

Clifton Daniel, now Managing Editor, pale and fragile looking, said: "Before we get to Vietnam I would like to ask about how you are doing in Iran: I wrote a piece about it, it must be ten years ago."

This was a welcome question; so I got off a few sentences about how much of a transformation there had been since his interview with Gordon Clapp and me at 50 Broadway so long ago. And it gave me a chance to talk about the commercial farming prospect, now very much in my mind—and presumably in the Iranians'.

Clifton is very sharp: "But doesn't that require large mechanized farming units? And what about the land reform program; that isn't in the same pattern, is it?" To which I agreed, for such a flat and sparsely populated area as the Khuzistan plains.

"It *is* a revolution—moving from 'breaking up' of landlord holdings to a commercial kind of farming, particularly if our concept of agrobusiness by an American consortium can be worked out. You are correct; it is a hundred and eighty degrees from the land reform idea of a few years ago. The Shah has shown, I think, the indispensable quality of a good ruler: flexibility confronted with the facts. And without large-scale farming but with protection for the peasant cultivators you may get kudos for social justice but you won't get food. And more food is what everyone agrees these countries and their people must have."

Markel led the questioning about our Vietnam "mission." Now and then across the table, in ironic tones I heard "bombing," "napalm." But there was no belligerence that I was "lending myself" to a propaganda move to underwrite, with a respected "liberal" and humane name, the Johnson Administration reign of terror in Vietnam. They may have *thought* so; they certainly were too polite to say so to me.

I did talk about what I *thought* we, as a private company, could do to bring some affirmative building notes to this extraordinarily complex—and painful—chapter in our national history.

"Are you going to include *North Vietnam* in your studies, in your concept? Are you going to North Vietnam?" No. "Have you *asked* permission to go?" This was in part the excitement they feel about the coup of the *Times*' Harrison Salisbury's remarkable series of pieces from Hanoi.

"Not now, of course. Not the first go-around. But I am *free*, and so is my company, to do what we think makes sense. We are truly independent."

Markel: "But suppose you are pressed by the Government; how about your 'independence' then?"

If we find we aren't independent, they will just have to get someone else, I said.

JANUARY 20, 1967
SAN FRANCISCO, ABOUT TO TAKE OFF FOR HAWAII

We should be capable, we of our now invigorated D&R group, to devise an integrated organizational approach to development. One that will *not* involve a group of agriculturalists plus an overlay of engineers, the whole stifled in a morass of economist-type analysis and jargon and subject to "review" by a central management group.

One group of technical people added to another and another simply does not make up the distinctive *common intelligence* I am so desperately seeking. Nor does having a single report writer, putting all this stuff together, signify that there is an overall unified intelligence at work. One person will have to shape this common intelligence approach from the beginning, and keep a hand on it continuously. To wait until the separate contributions have been written, the separate, specialist viewpoints hardened, won't do. The kind of thinking I have in mind must permeate the thinking of the separate specialists.

My influence in TVA was of this kind, though I didn't think of it as a "problem" but rather as the way TVA went about its job. I wrote about instances of this in *TVA: Democracy on the March*: how a unified way of looking at things affected the *separate* kinds of expertise.

JANUARY 26, 1967
KAUAI, HAWAII

The shining splendor of this night is an enchantment. Encircling mountains loom against the lustrous sable of the night, white phosphorescence streaks the surf below, and, outshining even the stars, a full moon. I walked down the steep hill to the lookout far below, and thought to myself: This Hawaiian picture postcard is just too corny to be taken seriously.

JANUARY 27, 1967
KAUAI

A helicopter flight this morning as beautiful and inspiring as anything I have ever experienced in the air. Up to the narrow rim of a great ridged canyon, then over the top and suddenly, down below, perpendicular green columns, dropping away three or four thousand feet, with threads of waterfalls like silver chains dangling from the mountain's top.

FEBRUARY 3, 1967
KAUAI

The impulse to write in my journal shorthand book has been weaker during the two weeks Helen and I have been here than for a long time. This has been partly, of course, because this is not an intellectually stimulating place; and it was chosen for that reason. But emotional stimulus is back of much of the necessity to write things down. And this has *not* been absent during these two weeks: the beauty of the surroundings and the joy I get out of vigorous physical activity—swimming two or three times a day, walking up the steep hill that leads from the shore, and yesterday clambering up the Kalelulu Trail, a formidable climb along the face of a cliff overlooking the sea.

And during the past week my work has excited me, too. Thoughts of the Vietnam "challenge"; the prospect that at long last I, "river rat" that I am, shall be involved in the great Mekong River Basin—a multinational river if ever there was one. Most of all by the way things are opening up on the D&R organizational picture: these things have occupied me more than they should have on a "vacation."

I have been on the phone with New York almost every day, sometimes more than once, for the past several days. (This morning twice before breakfast!) And at outrageous expense. But D&R is at a turning point, and my support, interest, and ideas seemed worth transmitting at the time when leverage was important, which was now.

Most of this concerns the too long delayed tightening up of the agricultural side of the business, specifically the incorporating of D&R's agricultural center at Davis (which had developed into somewhat of a splinter group) into a D&R "Western Office" based in Sacramento. Headed by Warne, with a water engineer attached to him, the new office would unify the corporate functions, including agriculture, water resources, engineering, and general management.

Warne, thus far, seems to be satisfying my hunch that here is a strong man. If he can build a water resources business around him, as part of a functionally *unified* organization, we shall indeed have made headway.

If we can inject a stronger talent for close, careful financial planning and management, the outlook for D&R in another ten years looks good indeed. But in *ten* years I will be over seventy-seven! Better make it *five*.

FEBRUARY 4, 1967
KAUAI

The vacation, the "winter break," is at an end. This noon we leave the beauty of those green shoulders that, towering above the sea, embrace the profound blue of sky and sea. Here in this synthetic tropical setting I came as close to stopping all mental activity as is possible for me.

Now I am about to return to the kind of world without which I don't believe I could live—or more than exist—the world of tough problems, ranging from small-scale personnel jockeying within the company to grave issues of statecraft such as those I'll be tangling with next in Bangkok and then in Vietnam.

During this holiday I read a good deal, from Byron to Claude Bowers' teenage diaries. (The term "teenage" hadn't yet been invented in the late nineties.) Young Claude's self-examination and self-discovery in those remarkable and ebullient high school journals of his stirred up nostalgia and memories of my own youth. His high school days in Indianapolis predated my own in Indiana (he graduated in 1898, I in 1916), but we shared the same passion for "self-improvement"—Helen's way of putting a tag of identification on Bowers' time as a youth, and my own teenage youth. Bowers' intensity about "oratory," his recital of oratorical contests, probably held in the same church (Pilgrim Methodist, in Indianapolis) as my own when I won the Indiana college oratorical contest, his references to Beveridge, to DePauw, to the careful, self-conscious way he studied "gestures" (as I did in my time as an "orator") —this made delightful reading, but led to a mood of self-examination as well.

Now on to what could be a *test* of everything I have been through in these past forty years or more, a test of stamina, patience, good sense, and of keeping my intense desire for "doing something about it" within workable bounds, without losing the capacity to see farther than many men do.

FEBRUARY 5, 1967
ABOARD PAN AM #1, HEADED FOR TOYKO

As I boarded Pam Am #1 in Honolulu, a public address voice informed me that I was en route to "Tokyo, Hong Kong, Bangkok—and around the world."

And so here I am over the Pacific (and will be looking at its blue expanse for nearly ten hours)—destination Japan. As I head toward a venture that will have its share of puzzles, frustrations, and disappointments, I have one unwavering resolve: I will do my very best. This means strict professionalism: No bleeding like an amateur at every setback, no expecting perfection, no fits of personal oversensitivity. Too much depends upon the way we carry out this grave responsibility, for millions of people in Asia, and particularly for my divided and agonized country, to behave other than as a pro should.

It is strange to think of Helen with her Matson Line cruisemates settling down for the five days' slow crossing of the Pacific to the American mainland while I head toward the Orient. We have rarely traveled separately this way in all our years together.

As I relax in my seat, my mind turns back to my conversation last night with H. M. "Robbie" Robinson, who spent nine months in Khuzistan on the D&R Haft Tapeh sugar project as Manager, although at the time he was a general Vice President of C. Brewer and Company, Ltd.

After an excellent dinner at the Outrigger Club, we returned to the Robinsons' and installed ourselves on the terrace. Comfortably settled in a big chair, Robbie was not at all reluctant to talk about C. Brewer's disastrous experience in Puerto Rico.

It all began when, some five or six years ago, Brewer, among the ablest people in sugar production and refining, bought out a Puerto Rican company's several mills. It ended when Brewer announced a week or so ago that they were "abandoning" their operation in Puerto Rico because it had been suffering large losses and they didn't feel they could operate successfully on that island.

Why on earth did Brewer buy those plants? They had sent some Brewer men to look things over; they came back with a good report. After they took over the properties Brewer found "the plants were in terrible shape, the two varieties of sugar being raised were terrible, just awful." And that was just the beginning of their discoveries.

The men wouldn't work. Their supervisors would falsify the record of how many men were working. Brewer had twenty-three different contracts with labor unions. "Think of that; having to negotiate contracts with twenty-three different union officials. And when you would complain about terms and conditions we found that the head of the sugar unions was also Puerto Rico's Secretary of Labor.

"It took several times as many men to cut cane as in Hawaii. We paid the men in Hawaii $5 an hour, but it took five men in Puerto Rico to do the same amount of work as one man in Hawaii.

"The sugar industry has been a whipping boy in Puerto Rico for a long time. There was a time when it deserved to be severely criticized, no doubt about it. The present dominant political party came into power, and stayed there, because of their fight against the sugar industry, and though the industry has changed, the feeling against it hasn't."

Rex Tugwell, when he was Governor of Puerto Rico, got a law passed limiting the amount of land that any holder could own to five hundred acres. He also set up a Land Authority to buy large acreages with the plan of dividing them into five-hundred-acre plantations to be owned and operated by independent growers. "But no one wanted to buy the land," Robbie explained, "so most of it is still owned by the public Land Authority. In fact, the Authority is still the largest grower of cane on the island; they supply most of the cane Brewer ground in its mills, and that's the case with the other privately owned mills. But the Land Authority doesn't want to own plants—too many problems with the unions, too much political agony in it."

At a time when we in America are talking so boldly about increasing food supply in "underdeveloped countries," and gearing American public policy to that goal, here we see a demonstrable failure. Not in India, but in a part of the U.S. family. And a part of the U.S. pictured widely by liberals as a great democratic triumph of development (and in industry and tourism and social stability certainly it is).

Robinson, as a Brewer man, obviously is not disinterested. But the fact is indisputable: conditions in Puerto Rico are so bad for raising cane that this noted and self-proud international food-raising firm had to write off its research expenditures, and concluded that it is better to abandon its plants rather than operate them.

Brewer's abandoning of Puerto Rico is a tough fact, one hard to explain away if things in Puerto Rico are as good as represented by the uncritical Puerto Rico worshippers in the U.S.—among whom I am *not*.

A report I have just read about Vietnam's agriculture, by a cool official American investigator, uses Puerto Rico as a prime example of how Vietnam should organize itself "at the village level." Well, I wonder.

So many of my friends and well-wishers say what a "distinction" it is to be asked by the President of the U.S. and the Prime Minister of Vietnam (both world figures in a world-shaking struggle) to help design a future for that country, even while war and violence continue to rage. But more of them say, "Poor Dave," and even those who don't actually say it quite evidently feel sorry for my getting into such a "mess."

What I'm about to say, before the work actually begins, may be "famous last words"; that is, after wrestling with this task for two weeks or two months or two years, I may have to swallow my present long-range viewpoint. But anyway, here it is:

First of all, the issue isn't limited to the ugly war in South Vietnam. The issue I'm bound to face, in charting a future for that little country, is the shape of things to come in Eastern Asia, indeed in all that vast part of the world that borders on the Pacific seas.

This future will require *several decades* completely to unfold. But I firmly believe the coming *new balance of history* lies in those lands of the Pacific.

That this is true is as difficult to see in our present-day agonies in Vietnam—the cost in lives and treasure, the corruption, disorganization, all the things that so disturb all of us—as it would have been difficult to see the real importance of the war of 1776 when the puny upstart American colonies defied and defeated the British (with the "intervention" in *that* civil war, it should be remembered, of the French).

A new world balance of thinking, of influence, of trade, of civilization began with the emergence of the American continent three hundred years ago. But the significance of the emergence of Southeast Asia is even more difficult to see and comprehend, for Asia for many centuries was powerful and mature, and then died away; until almost yesterday Japan was literally closed to the modern world.

Now, for David Lilienthal, by a freakish set of acccidents, to have a ringside seat, and some influence on the beginnings of this Asian emergence, not as a scholar or writer but as a participant with extraordinary freedom to speak and even to act on the beginnings of this emergence, this new balance, and public recognition of it, is surely a stroke of infinite good fortune for a guy who has always relished great experiences, however tough. (Phil LaFollette said to me, apropos my appointment to TVA in 1933: "It will never amount to anything but Roosevelt rhetoric." Again, "Poor Dave." A close friend of Felix Frankfurter said to me about my appointment to AEC: "Avoid it; this is Nemesis.")

How I will handle the opportunity is the only question. If I let it obsess me, if I get delusions that my hand alone (or that of my D&R team) will be decisive, then I'm just plain crazy, and will squander myself, and for that misfortune will have no one but myself to blame. But I am firmly resolved not to let that obsession overwhelm me—though at times I'll lose heart, and have heartaches and exhaustion and setbacks and vile feelings of impatience.

There is a square Rotarian expression that "a problem is opportunity in working clothes." This "problem" of America and Vietnam, of the Pacific, is a problem—and therefore a great opportunity.

FEBRUARY 7, 1967
TOKYO INTERNATIONAL AIRPORT, WAITING FOR PAN AM #1 TO BANGKOK

It was sixteen years ago that we were in Tokyo. MacArthur was our host, and this country was his to govern in a regal way.◖

I wonder if any place on earth has changed as much, visibly and in spirit, in so brief a time? I'm still stunned by what I have seen. (Thanks to Felix Posen, in charge of the Philipp Brothers Far East Office, and particularly his wife, I did a great deal of my special brand of "sight-seeing," which tells me most about a people and a country.)

I suggested to the Posens that what I would find most illuminating would be my old standby for observation, the shops and markets. And in the interest of time, why not a "middle class" department store? What a revelation *this* was. Such a variety of goods I have rarely seen. And people. The *children*, so many and so handsome. And their mothers so patient, never raising their voices.

But the chief impression of Tokyo—so recently devastated—was one of the unbelievable *vitality* in this city. The people are small (made me feel, all afternoon, like a giant), but how full of life. I won't find much analogy to these people, I'm afraid, in Vietnam or perhaps *any-place* else in Southeast Asia.

FEBRUARY 9, 1967
HOTEL ORIENTAL
BANGKOK, THAILAND

A blue funk has always been part of my beginning a new chapter. I began to wonder whether this time I wouldn't have a period of being

◖ Visit with MacArthur in Tokyo. See *Journals*, Vol. III, *The Venturesome Years*, pp. 117–127.

just plain skeered and vaguely depressed. Well, last night I certainly had it, a reaction perhaps to that burst of brave and grandiloquent words I wrote in shorthand on the plane a couple of days ago.

I had the usual and natural feeling in the early hours this morning: why in the hell should you subject yourself to the separation by 10,000 miles from what is familiar and precious to you back home? Tackling new and mixed-up problems, dealing with still another set of mediocrities. The fear that this particular glass of water or that dish of food won't be free of illness is something I try to put away, but subconsciously it does affect one's spirits.

The trip from Tokyo, begun at 6:30 P.M., took most of the night; I arrived here in the early morning hours and couldn't sleep when I did get a bed. (Partly, of course, this was the metabolic "clock," partly the excitement of the fascinating and noisy river traffic just outside my hotel window.)

Then we went to the U.S. Embassy, had a visit with Lee St. Lawrence, now here as representative of AID for this whole region; discussed the Mekong Basin Coordinating Committee's work, heard him and an associate repeat what I have been told before, that Gene Black had said "you need a man of the stature of Lilienthal" to get an overall appraisal of the work, etc.

And made it plain—however briefly put—that I had not even a remote interest in any such function. Certainly it would be a great mistake to give any impression that we want to be put into some kind of umpire role in this highly scattered effort. "Scatteration," that is the word that fits an effort to develop a basin with so many unrelated consultants, engineers, and Mother's Helpers from so many countries. Fantastic managerial concept, or lack of it.

Doesn't mean that a good deal of excellent work may not have been done, in separate compartments, and after spending ten years and over a hundred million dollars. But I can't see any cohesion, any way to judge what comes first, what the effect of one set of studies or projects has on the whole fabric.

I am told that this kind of *international pork barrel* approach is the only way to get things rolling in the Mekong River development. Maybe so, but it is wasteful of time and money—and technical integrity as well.

Hart Schaaf, "Executive Agent" of the United Nations Mekong Coordinating Committee, is a driving man, passionate about the Mekong River almost to the point of frenzy at times. A small man in stature, the kind that sometimes makes up for his physical size by an aggressive manner and attitude. When we came into his big office today he had three of his Asian senior staff with him, although for an hour none of them got a word in, edgewise or otherwise. And yet I am sure Lee St.

Lawrence is right when he says that if it were not for this dominating personality, with the eyes of a missionary out to save souls by the very ardor of his words and convictions, "nothing would have happened on the Mekong."

A great deal *has* happened, though it has taken a tremendous amount of money (115 million dollars so far) and it has been ten years since the program was launched with the "Speck" Wheeler report in 1957.*

But it has been a typical "project by project" approach, with investigations going on on every subject under the sun. It has been an undertaking dominated by parochial and conventional engineering thinking. No matter how hard I tried to get Schaaf to talk about what the *entire* undertaking concept was, he was off and running on this site and that —in short, so far the Mekong development is simply dams or proposed dams.

In other words, it is nothing remotely resembling the comprehensive unified report TVA published in 1936 or the D&R Khuzistan Unified Development Report, of March, 1959, with its comprehensive picture of the development of an entire region: sites of fourteen dams set out, it is true, but a *concept of overall development* sketched with considerable sureness. And in both cases, TVA and D&R–Khuzistan, the beginning of actual work didn't await the preparation of the unified report, and far less money was expended for preliminary investigations and feasibility studies than has already been spent, I believe, on the Mekong.

The Mekong Committee has one problem we in TVA and Iran's Khuzistan didn't have: the river flows through four countries, and the organization itself is a United Nations one. The policy of the UN is to let any of its nation members who will contribute funds have its nationals do a piece of the work, indeed to encourage this. This produces a crazy managerial patchwork of scattered and unrelated studies, depending upon the interest or capabilities or financial contributions of the many countries in the UN.

For the first time ran into strong statements of concern about Japan. The Japanese are so able, have so much money and technical competence, that all other things being equal in a free race they would soon dominate this whole South Asian area economically, as they once tried to dominate it by military means. They are prepared to invest huge sums, and they have it to invest, in Southeast Asia.

The memory of the Japanese in the war hasn't softened as much here as it has in the U.S. No wonder. There are too many graves of tor-

* General Raymond A. Wheeler, formerly Chief of the U.S. Corps of Engineers.

tured prisoners to remind these people what they were subjected to twenty-five years ago.

I am astounded by the amount of building activity in Bangkok. Much of it is recent, and much of it takes the form of very large and elaborate hotels. We lunched at one this noon: the Siam International. And there are ten more almost as large and all constructed within the past several years. This city has become not only a tourist attraction in a big way, but the locus of countless international seminars, conferences, etc. And then we have a very large contingent of troops here, in the north. The best guess is 35,000. The amounts of money poured into this country by way of "military assistance" must be huge. The war next door is tragedy compounded for the Vietnamese people and our American soldiers, but it has been a chief spur to prosperity and growth in this country.

9:30 P.M.

Have just read, at a sitting, Arthur Schlesinger's latest book, *The Bitter Heritage*. This brilliantly written book is a good introduction to the next step in my initiation into American policies in the Far East. For it will help keep me from an uncritical acceptance of many things I ought constantly to question. *What* a blasting he gives much of our policy and action in Vietnam! Arthur can at times irritate me—and many others—by his manner on the platform. But there is little of this in this powerful polemic, and there is less of the ordinary run-of-the-mine pundit's assumption that he knows far more than anyone else. And, by crediting those who don't agree with him with patriotic motives and with as great a revulsion as his own against the bloodshed, he opens some minds at least (mine, for example) to an understanding of the kind of commitments we have made, and therefore to the importance of continual critical assessment of our present course.

What struck me, as I put down this brief book, was how vulnerable the United States' role in Vietnam is, or certainly can be made to appear, and therefore how readily critics can "get away" with the proposal of a middle course that contains one concealed booby trap after another and leads to difficulties as great as those resulting from following our present course.

FEBRUARY 10, 1967
BANGKOK

Just back from a "tour" by water, through the canals that are the arteries—and the veins—of this remarkable city, capital of the only country in Southeast Asia that never lost its independence. (Thai, I am told, means Free.) It was the usual tourist bit, in part, but as a way of seeing how people live, and particularly how they *make* their living, it is anything but the "looking through the bars of the zoo, at the strange people" sort of thing that makes me so prickly about going on sightseeing expeditions.

Helen and I did much the same trip almost ten years ago.† The temples are the same—though somewhat more crumbly and dusty. And the families living on boats, the little children waving merrily, the produce being sold by "floating" merchants, usually very determined-looking women, very skilled with the paddle—this is much the same. The biggest difference is the appearance of the noisy motorized gondola (or whatever is the appropriate word for these slender little boats).

A very thin, diminutive elderly man, a shock of white hair standing on end: this was my Harvard Law School Siamese classmate, Lekhyananda, come to pay a call on me.

When I last saw him he was a stocky young man with a bristling bush of dark hair and the happiest, biggest smile in the Law School. Rumor had it that he was some kind of Siamese prince. Actually, so he told me, he came back and became successively a judge, a member of a cabinet, a senator.

What moved me most about our little visit was when Lekhyananda ceremoniously unrolled a tight scroll that he had brought with him. It proved to be a faded picture, perhaps three feet long, of our *entering* class in the fall of 1920, standing before Langdell Hall. I found myself choked up a bit to see the ironic grin of my study companion and boxing partner, Hank Dorrance of the wavy hair; Jim Nicely, looking so self-assured and grave; Mal Sharp, dark-eyed, fierce, solemn; Jerry Smith looking like a caricature of Jerry Smith, his tie slipped down, his jaw dropped—and David Lilienthal, a quizzical grin, a full head of hair—looking startlingly like his son at twenty, which was then my age.

"We all looked so innocent," said my white-haired classmate. Yes, I thought to myself, innocent; and I know so well that *one* of that group is still innocent, more vulnerable even than in those starry eyed days. Among that group of young men from all over the country lined up to look into the camera came Chief Justices of State Supreme Courts, wealthy lawyers, at least one head of a huge corporation. Have they really become so much less vulnerable, so much less innocent than those youthful, cocky, anxious, and *personally* terribly ambitious young faces of that faded, carefully saved scroll my Siamese classmate brought with

† The previous visits to Bangkok are described in the *Journals*, Vol. III, *The Venturesome Years*, pp. 61–64.

him and unrolled for me, to revive those days now forty-seven years past?

FEBRUARY 11, 1967
BANGKOK

A dinner for me at Lee St. Lawrence's elegant house.

His wife, Ann, is very English; I often have difficulty in understanding her quick, tripping speech. But she is a remarkable hostess, whether in the midst of that long-remembered blinding sandstorm in ugly Ahwaz, or here in a lovely tasteful house with plenty of good servants.

I sat at table with the American Ambassador to Thailand, Graham Martin,‡ and next to him, U Nyun, a Burmese, Director of the Economic Commission for Asia and the Far East, ECAFE in the alphabet jargon.

Martin is a very soft-spoken man, I would say western North Carolina or Virgina, in his tone and manner; perhaps fifty-two or three. His appearance and manner are not those of the stereotype Foreign Service officer, but what he says certainly is. That is, he gives quiet little lectures supporting everything the State Department has said about the Vietnam war and rolls out figures about the truly remarkable economic and political success of Thailand. Predictable, I suppose, for a man who spends much of his time trying to impress or persuade visitors about our Government's bitterly criticized conduct in Vietnam.

During the course of the evening, Martin showed another characteristic quite common among foreign service career Ambassadors by implying that he was a kind of Peck's Bad Boy with "the Department," who said things "to Washington" that they didn't like to hear. "If I keep this up I'll probably be fired, but I will." This was sincerely said, but it was also for the benefit of the local market present.

This professional disagreement with the "home office" is not only standard procedure for an Ambassador vis-à-vis Washington (I recall Ken Galbraith's scorn with his "Assistant Secretary" in Washington when Ken was in India) but the same belligerence is found in almost any organization—the field versus "those fellows" at the main headquarters.

U Nyun is of the melodious, gentle, even-tempered variety. Persistent, I'm sure; but he hides this behind a bland, supple exterior. Whereas, as another guest, Howard Parsons, whom I had met when he was an AID Director in Iran, remarked last night, the Persians are hard-edged, "harsh," given to battles out in the open, the Southeast Asian

‡ U.S. Ambassador to Vietnam at the time of the fall of South Vietnam in 1975.

is outwardly soft, "though when it comes to getting rid of a competitor they know how to do it in their own way."

A Thai guest last night, however, showed that a Southeast Asian can be as vigorous, dynamic, and even as loud as anyone else. This was Dr. Boonrod Binson, head of the Thai National Energy Authority and a member, representing Thailand, of the Mekong Committee. Whether his demeanor stems from the fact that he is a graduate of MIT and Harvard and, therefore, exposed to the Western aggressive spirit, or whether there is that much difference between Southeast Asians, I wouldn't know. But he had a ringing voice, vigorous gestures, and a booming, infectious laugh.

Stepping into the elevator, I trod on a bare heel, that of a stocky, bushy haired Thai boy. He grinned his pardon; a great flash of teeth, merry eyes; yes, I was excused. Then I notice: his legs, his arms, his face are black with coal dust; he had been bringing in coal for the kitchen. As we rode up I noticed him turn to the big mirror in the back of the elevator, look at himself approvingly, then give his black pompadour a pat. That kind of personal self-esteem can be called amusing vanity in so "dirty" a boy, or can be thought of as the saving grace of self-respect.

If I'm going to survive in this Vietnam setting, much less make any substantial mark on it, I'm going to have to become far more skeptical than I normally am, far less gullible, far less willing to take what people say at face value.

But naturally "trusting" I really am. And I do *not* consider that a useful trait, just a temperamental weakness. After some pretty tough experiences in public life I simply had to become more cautious and cagey—and I suppose insecure within myself. I didn't like myself, either, with *those* characteristics. It made me stuffy, even made me minor-sickness prone. I got over that occupational suspiciousness and caginess about ten years ago, and have been much happier, more relaxed, and more effective since.

On this Vietnam job I will have to reacquire some measure of caution, will have to take what people say with considerable salt, and guard my own tongue against saying all I think, or "thinking out loud," a practice that makes life much pleasanter because it is such a good way to think one's way through a problem. But, as I noticed last night, one is quoted, usually out of context, quoted about broad or half-deliberated statements.

At dinner, Tom Mead remarked about how many people in America, without having given the matter study, have a firm opinion about what's wrong with our way of dealing with the problem of Vietnam, and even have strong conclusions about military strategy. "In all this certitude and sureness you never hear anyone," he said with a one-sided grin, "who is puzzled."

If what I am heading into in Vietnam is indeed a moral question, a question for the heart to answer, as I think my son David believes, as do his daughter Pam and all the other Davids and Pams, then am I not better equipped for the task than if it were chiefly a question of intelligence or knowledge, where I am definitely weakest? For on tough questions requiring a certain kind of blind courage, or mulish stubbornness, or independence, or integrity—whatever one calls it—I have shown at times that I am at my best.

FEBRUARY 12, 1967
BANGKOK

"Conductor: Miss Surang Tongvivat"; so reads the typed slip of paper of the "Excursion Schedule for Mr. Lilianthal, February 12, 1967."

Well, the "conductor" turned out to be a shy, soft faced, youngish Thai, in a purple dress of the now worldwide brevity, highest-heeled shoes, and carrying a leather handbag. A delightful lady, described by her employer, Dr. Boonrod Binson, as his secretary, and extremely knowledgeable about many things, as we put questions to her in the ride to Smudsakorn.

Smudsakorn is a small city north of Bangkok. Intensely interesting: the market, the wharves, the streets (quite wide and modern), a great fishing center. A prosperous, well-fed, apparently happy lot, the farm people and the townspeople.

I noticed quite a number of girls and young women in the most violent-colored and positively tightest stretch pants I have ever seen; and in the same block an old woman in the ancient Siamese getup made familiar in *The King and I*—a kind of droop-drape not unlike the Indian males' absurd dhoti. I asked the "conductor" whether there was any one kind of prescribed dress for women, whether Western dress such as she wore or some national costume. Said she, in a pleasing low voice and with great good sense: "We dress in whatever pleases us."

Toward noon we visited the reputed ancient capital: Nakorn Pathom, far to the west, reached by wide recently paved roads. An imposing palace ground, and a huge pagoda, one hundred twenty feet high or more, known as Phra Pathom Chedi. It was a gay sight on this last day of the Chinese New Year, celebrated in Thailand as a holiday. Our modern little escort removed her shoes; so did we; then she put flowers and a joss stick before the huge gold figure of Buddha, sank to her knees and bowed low, along with children and older women. No men, I noticed; she explained that men and women may not worship together.

Altogether a pleasant diversion.

When I got back, a message that two men, with a plane, had arrived, were preparing to brief us on our Saigon expedition, and that we take off at noon tomorrow. One of the men told Tom: "When it comes to postwar planning, the Vietnamese are very much excited, and twenty-five young men have volunteered to try to help us. We have had permanent quarters for our group assigned, and office space along with the Vietnam parallel group."

FEBRUARY 13, 1967
BANGKOK

This is the last morning I'll awaken to the sound of the boat motors on the Chao Phraya River outside my window.

Trying to sort out my thoughts about what I should say (it should be as little as possible) when the meetings begin in Saigon, and what I should try to accomplish in this initial visit. While I'll want to see as much of Vietnam as I can, this will be as much by way of expressing my viewpoint ("This is your country; if development is to take place *you* will do it; what are *your* ideas?") as anything else. They may take my words as empty rhetoric, inundated as they are with eager experts (I understand there are now 1200 AID people here!), or they may find that I really mean this, and trust me.

What I have so often said comes back to me: we have overestimated what we of the West have to give the underdeveloped countries.

It appears that there is an AID project to teach the Thais boat-building and vegetable growing! I wish everyone could see the skill and cunning the Thais show in the boats one sees abuilding along the Chao Phraya River near Bangkok, the beautiful "housekeeping" of their boat yards and lumber mills, and the glory of their vegetable truck farms. Teach them indeed. They build and operate boats best suited to these particular waters; successful adjustment to one's environment is something no bright-eyed character from the outside can foist upon a people.

Yesterday I asked Dr. Binson about the "long-tailed" outboard motors; why the very long tails, reaching far back of the boats? And who had come up with the idea of adapting this diesel fueled little motor to a circular sawlike instrument for cutting rice, etc.? Very ingenious and economical, I could see. This was invented by a Thai, he said, trained at MIT originally. Johnson Motors would never have thought of this because the motor and shaft are specifically adapted to local conditions. So even on many technical matters it is *we* who have a lot to learn.

As regards Saigon, I'm concerned that Fred Moore and the Vietnamese economists will get mired in planning and broad statistical "exercises," when what I want is to focus on a *few* things it will be possible to get going. This is in contrast with the "strategy for development" concept—which to my mind piles too many things on the plate, covering practically every aspect of life.

I am also uneasy about the evidences of making things too luxurious for the American Government employees in Saigon, including me.

This is a "contract" Beechcraft. It is taking me to Saigon and the "official" beginning of a puzzling venture. Instead of flying the direct route from Bangkok, across Cambodia, we must make a detour along the coast. Cambodia won't permit anyone going across their territory except for the commercial lines who have "negotiated" permission. "All of the *towns* are safe," says one of the alert young Americans sent to bring me up. "Now, *that* town," pointing on the map, "that has a good Chinese restaurant." So far on this flight I have listened mostly to talk about good places to eat, about where the girls are "better," about the "accommodations" at our quarters.

We pass over a big island. "That is now Vietnamese," say my informants. "The tip is strongly VC." "That cement plant off there was built by the French; of course they are gone now. You'll see some smoke coming up near those little islands; they're always bombing them."

"There are three bomb flashes now—see them? This is a fishing area, where we're trying to get a refrigeration plant going. The area is *very* insecure, however; the town has already been taken."

Now I am looking down on as tortured a country as I have ever seen, yet it looks so green and peaceful—and unreal.

My first taste of aerial bombing "in anger" brings me back to reality. As we approach Saigon I see a puff of black smoke along a rim of trees, about four miles away according to one of my companions. Then a jet fighter-bomber darts off out of sight, as another, coming from the opposite direction, swoops way low, followed by a second puff of smoke on the ground. These two wasps make several such passes, then disappear into the blue.

Seen from my aerial vantage point, these maneuvers have all the reality of the Navy's target bombing over Nomans, off the Vineyard. But as we draw closer, we began to see the craters, the many holes in the highway along a great canal.

I am now in my suite in the "VIP" quarters, an old former French colonial kind of residence.

We were told again and again that we must reach Saigon at precisely 4 o'clock, as Ambassador Lodge had made a very special point about meeting me. As we came down the runway I could see a military band and troops lined up beside a platform. I *knew* this couldn't be for me, all these soldiers, etc., but my companions weren't sure.

I got off and was greeted by Donald MacDonald, the tall, tense, handsome man who heads the AID Mission, and beside him, his eyes gleaming with eagerness, one of the shortest and most diminutive, but sharp-looking of men, "Professor" Vu Quoc Thuc, who is the Prime Minister's representative and head of the Vietnam side of this postwar planning undertaking.

I learned that the Army was there to greet the Prime Minister of South Korea.

I have never seen more bemedaled chests and solemn looking characters. If the fierce opéra bouffe mien these officers displayed had been equalled by their feats upon the field of battle, there would have been no need for hundreds of thousands of American soldiers to clop clop over the dreary mountains of Korea, many of them to remain in graves.

FEBRUARY 14, 1967
81 NGUYEN DINH CHIEU, SAIGON

The above is simply the Vietnamese for the address of this spacious guest house. I am learning to recognize Vietnamese place names and the names of a considerable number of men I am being taken to meet, so far all government people. They seem to be a monosyllabic people as to names.

I insisted the very first thing this morning, before I had even called on the American Embassy, that we ask Professor Thuc to come to see us, since his office as head of the Vietnamese team of long-term planners, counterpart to D&R, wasn't ready.

What a bubbly and likable man. We spent perhaps two hours getting acquainted with each other's approach to this job. I did my best to extemporize on the validity of projecting future productivity for the country, and preparing for the kind of problems that will have to be faced, whenever the war subsides, as well as tackling the many problems and opportunities that are with them now. In some areas that are "secure" the war is already over for those people—the An Giang area in the Delta region, for example.

Thuc was pretty candid about some of the concerns he has as a private citizen doing a public job. He recognizes the importance of continuity and is concerned that frequent changes in government officers and even agencies might stop or interrupt our work. How can this be anticipated and avoided? He thinks the only chance is to keep his side of the work out of immediate politics by not being attached to an existing Ministry. Is this possible? He will try. At the moment he is reporting directly to Ky, the Prime Minister, rather than a Ministry, though we will be seeing Minister after Minister, as we did today and will tomorrow.

None of this seems insuperable, *provided* the U.S. makes sufficiently "credible" long-term commitments to support the development of this country. It was for this reason that later, at a meeting at the home of "super Minister" Truong Thai Ton, alert and game in spite of a dreadful case of hepatitis, Thuc asked how long a period ahead I thought a long-term plan should be projected—five years? When I said not less than ten years, he tried to get me to raise it to twenty.

And Thuc wants us to commit ourselves to help train the eager young Vietnamese who are volunteering to join in the work, because unless there are men trained to carry out the plans as they have been formulated by us and by his group, there can be no effective action.

During our talk Thuc voiced a fear about the kind of long range planning we both feel is so important. "If people see an organization growing up covering all the development of the country won't they fear it will be a kind of supergovernment?" he queried. That is the other side of the coin.

At about six a tall, slender, very handsome, grey-haired man came to the guest house door: it was Ambassador Henry Cabot Lodge, quite alone. I answered the door, and we sat down for a ten minute gab. Wanted to say how glad he was I was undertaking this task, how it might even help to win the war by raising people's hopes about the future, etc. He wanted to tender me a formal dinner invitation, an evening with the chief Vietnamese Government people, etc. When I told him I wouldn't be here for long on this trip, to my relief (and doubtless his too) he agreed to skip that for this trip.

We drove around the "downtown" part of Saigon this afternoon. Very French appearing, jam packed with people and bicycles and motor bikes. Not many American soldiers, though later in the day there would be plenty, crowding the innumerable bars. The women, mostly young-looking, all slender, long hair down their backs, in a kind of costume I haven't seen anywhere else: long silk pajama-type pants, with a panel, freely flowing, fore and aft. When they are riding a bike this billows out like a parachute. In the crowds they look very attractive indeed, like little colored birds moving among otherwise drab surroundings.

Lawrence Crain, who has our goings and comings in charge, pointed out this and that place that had been blown up, mostly billets of American troops. And Viet soldiers and military police *everywhere*; practically every block a high sandbagged little fortress. Last night, not long after our arrival, the Viet Cong shot a mortar shell into the city, and you could hear our cannons booming, gently rattling my windows. (Later I learned that twelve men had been killed, mostly American soldiers, in the very heart of Saigon.)

How very quickly one takes such things in stride. No wonder wars last so damn long, when, it would seem, men should be so terrified they would be ready to quit right off.

Quite a setting for "long term planning"!!

FEBRUARY 15, 1967
NOON
SAIGON

We have just come from a meeting with the Prime Minister, Air Vice Marshal Ky, at the "Palace."

The Palace is one of the most beautiful public buildings I have ever seen; indeed, I think the most beautiful. Not because of its grandeur, though there is something of that. But the design is that of an open space through which air and light flow almost as if visible. Instead of marble (as in Tehran, for example) there is a happy combination of all kinds of materials—here the deep dark brown wood of the twin stairways leading up to the Prime Minister's office; there a wall of small matched blocks of limestone. The feeling of being in a beautiful park. And only two sentries in special uniforms, standing at attention with short bayonets attached, in contrast to the flocks of guards and little fortresses of sandbags spread all around this city.

Prime Minister Nguyen Cao Ky, in a shiny silk suit of a kind of lizard green-gold, sox with yellow stripes, immaculate, dandyish, and extremely young-looking, actually only thirty-seven.

He said some very sensible things. Not a single word about the war; no appeal for support, nothing defensive in his attitude. I would say that here is a man who laughs at the way he must spend his time with "visiting Congressmen" and journalists, who speaks with mock unhappiness about how many different interests he must satisfy but who has felt the intoxication of a kind of power which few men can resist.

If I hadn't known that he is a professional soldier, the choice of a junta of generals, I would say that he is a candidate for the Presidency if and when there is an election. Eisenhower isn't the first nor will he be the last military man who finds the rewards outweigh the grief of public office.

"When President Johnson suggested starting now in the preparation of a program for after the war, I said OK, fine. We get offers of 'help' from all kinds of countries: Japan, Korea, many countries, all free. But I want to find out first what our country needs; then if we can use this help, that's fine, but it must fit into some kind of scheme, or plan."

I commented about how much time having too many advisors could take, the toll on officials that conferring with those bearing gifts of aid can take in terms of leaving no time to figure out *what* was needed, and *how* it would advance the needs of the country. To this there was assent from the Vietnamese contingent seated across from the sofa on which Ky and I sat, separated from us by one of the most beautiful rugs I have ever seen, Chinese, severe and yet gay in a canary yellow, a spot of beauty in the grandeur of this huge room, and in keeping with the *outdoor* feeling of the Palace.

At times during our meeting Ky would look at the floor, either thinking or waiting for me to speak. Usually these pauses were used to formulate an idea which he then expressed in colloquial American: "My idea about this is . . ." But during our half hour together he didn't once mention the war, the need to win it "first" before thinking about "afterward."

I had been warned by Professor Thuc that there was concern that my presence here to discuss what should be done at war's end might have a bad effect upon the Vietnamese troops, fearful that the Americans were preparing some kind of "deal" to end the hostilities suddenly, behind their backs, as it were. No hint of this at all in anything Ky said or implied.

He said he wants results that can be seen, results that improve the life of people, so the ordinary "paz-ant" can see that the future is going to be better for him. The standard talk of any political figure.

The only note that disturbed me was his obvious concern that something should show for our efforts *soon*, very soon, something definite.

Well, this was a good spur to us not to be too academic and leisurely, and I was glad he made the point. When *I* make it, it sounds to some technical people like the denial of our whole thesis, since long-term planning deals by definition with a future time and long-term objectives need to be analyzed and prepared for. While agreeing completely with this, I think the *practical* approach is to devise intermediate steps for use on an interim basis.

Ky spoke a good deal about education, about training. He searched for the word "vocational," obviously less given to training lawyers or even engineers at a high level than mechanics and farmers. I spoke of the analogy of Abraham Lincoln's establishment of the land grant colleges toward the end of the Civil War; of the fact that education until then had not been adapted to the *needs* of a developing country. These colleges, unlike the colleges of the Eastern seaboard, situated in the Middle West chiefly, were designed to train men in the "practical arts," agricultural and mechanical. Something like this, I suggested, was needed here. Ky listened intently, fixing me with his dark, shrewd eyes.

When this almost foppish man, considered a demon in many parts of the world, said, "I set Professor Thuc's team up to be outside the Government because governments and officials change, but development must be continuous," I felt I was talking to a knowledgeable man.

8:30 P.M.

Meetings with five different Ministers in five different fields all in one afternoon, topped off with an intense and disturbing hour with the chief AID official for development, Bob Culbertson. Up the stairs of a public building with the usual dirty corners, the shabbiness, into the presence of a series of bright, attractive, and generally *very* young Vietnamese Ministers—or Commissioners, as some were called—in charge of transport and communications, public works including power, and so on down the line.

I must say I got tired hearing my own voice go on about our expectations and desire to cooperate, and the questions that brought forth a torrent of great explanations. Those who accompanied me looked even more bushed than I felt at the end of this day-long stint.

Moore and I were agreed on an important proposition: we have never seen so many uniformly attractive women as we saw on the streets of Saigon. A kind of grace, a brightness of eye, the charming costume so modest and yet so utterly feminine. Not "female" to mean blatantly "sexy" in the U.S. of A., but feminine. Along every street, in the open half-plaza, crowded and noisy, these fluttering birds—butterflies?—with the incredibly tiny waists, the silken long brilliantly white "pants" with the dark panels fluttering fore and aft, half concealing and half not the long silken legs. This is quite, well, dramatic in effect.

And the dark, night-dark, hair and darting black eyes, with none of the contrived shyness of the women recently emancipated—such as in Morocco, say—but looking out from their perch on the postilion, or the driver's seat, of a motor bike as boldly as you please, anything but coquettishly. These aren't the more or less professional Vietnamese geishas or "hostesses"—of which I doubt not there are many; but that would be later, at night, in the bars perhaps. No, these are the new generation of young women working in the shops and offices.

FEBRUARY 16, 1967
SAIGON

There is an excitement about this country, and this place, and my suddenly finding myself in the very midst of still another great happening makes sleep difficult.

The obvious respect, the even rather awkward business of being greeted like a "historical character" may be part of it. All up and down the line this *expectation.* "This fellow spreads excitement wherever he goes" is, to be honest, the atmosphere of all these encounters.

I got this in a big way this afternoon in a group of labor advisors in the AID Mission, headed by a huge, tough, but extraordinarily intelligent organized-labor graduate of the new school (articulate, passionate, youthful, impatient), Emil Lindahl. Pent up feeling that the labor organizations in this country, unexpectedly (to me) large and mature, were not being used to help organize many of the things needing to be done.

My insistence that we dig into Vietnam's labor organizations, which led to this meeting, is a clue to the value I put on the labor background of my early career. And we are expecting later to meet labor leaders among the agricultural and fishing fields (tenant farmer and fishing industry worker representatives).

In a setting of very short, sophisticated, French-educated, and sometimes precious-looking young Ministers, this Scandinavian type, Lindahl—looking like an ex-New York Jet pro footballer—was a great tonic; and his associates, who had the facts but also the same thoughtful and driving attitude, were a reminder of home—but home years ago when the labor movement and labor leaders were younger and more positive, less cautious, less like "personnel directors."

Why the hell doesn't AID make more use of men from U.S. organized labor for purposes of general organization and welfare and "getting things done"? This lack nearly drives me crazy. I went for this fellow Lindahl head over heels. Such a man has difficulty in being heard and even greater difficulty in being understood by the harassed and "public administration" types that come out of years of being AID career executives.

This could be a new world in the making we are in the midst of, and nothing could better demonstrate this than the kind of inference in everything this man and his assistants said (but chiefly Lindahl, articulate, booming, straining at the restraints of the administrative leash). He stressed the fact that it is only in a wartime situation that attitudes can be changed, that instead of waiting until more nearly "normal" times to get things done, this is the very moment to act. This was the underlying philosophy of much of the best of the earlier American labor movement, but alas, that was in another and in some ways a better day.

One picture: riding through the terribly crowded bustle of downtown Saigon, a civilian jeep goes by. Sitting on top of the rear is a serious-looking young man, in civilian dress, scrutinizing the crowd with a concentrated air, carrying a big carbine across his knees—"riding shotgun," said I to my colleagues. The rules are that anyone can carry arms—and if anything symbolized the wild and woolly but *building* U.S. West, that character with his carbine across his knees in the middle of an apparently law abiding city crowd was it. Adventurers are attracted to Saigon, says one of the AID men who accompany us to look out for us. Here was a whiff of our own early West which I never saw—outside of the movies—but that I revere. The rough, tough, self-seeking, non-intellectual guy who doesn't sit around Greenwich Village or Berkeley and moan about "alienation," but goes where the trouble and action are—even in the "static" Far East.

10:30 P.M.

Just back from a ripsnorting night on the town: Saigon, the legendary den of iniquity.

But our version was just plain dull. We sat up late at a table on the sidewalk café of the Continental Hotel (there is a curfew for Americans at 11) without seeing anything remotely riotous. A handful of freshly washed young men in plaid shirts and slacks—quite obviously GI's wandering around, out of uniform and back from the "front" (maybe a desk in an Air Force base *or* the jungle fighting).

Along these streets one "bar" after another. I suppose this is where the helling goes on. Buying tea (called whiskey) for a Vietnamese girl and making conversation, as sober-sides Tom Mead says, with a "stranger" must have its appeal to the lonely womanless man, and what they do afterward, and where, I suppose is about as old a story as there is. But the picture of roistering, furniture-smashing, yelling soldiery and the female camp follower—this either doesn't exist or we missed it. Looked like a dull Saturday night in one of the Hoosier towns I know so well, say Kokomo or Wanatah.

So much for deviltry. More of this goes on on East 56th Street than in all of Saigon, by my witness.

But while we were taking our ease at the café the sky was bright with flashes from the bombing.

Tran Quoc Buu is an old-time labor leader. Looking as Chairman Mao must have looked at fifty, even wearing everywhere that high-buttoned coat one sees in the pictures, he presided over and practically dominated a meeting I requested with the leaders of the trade unions—the Tenant Farmers Union, the Fishermens Union, and the Plantation Workers Union—held in the offices of the confederation of unions late this afternoon.

Said the bulbous and loquacious Buu: "We have had some delegations of Americans who wished to discuss military and political matters. This is the first time any delegation of Americans showed an interest in economic matters and matters of social justice involving the poor people of this country. And we appreciate this opportunity."

That there should be *any* unions in such a country, after all the turmoil, surprised me. I didn't get a direct answer to my questions: Are you representative of the poor working people you talk about? And are your unions free and independent (meaning independent of the government or of the Communists)?

This morning, by contrast, we visited two associations of Vietnamese businessmen. At the second, the Confederation of Industries, there were perhaps twenty men gathered around the table. Very interesting faces, and their answers to our questions and the foci of their own interest were far more sophisticated and modern than I would have thought possible.

The labor men were still fighting the French, i.e., their memories of what they had had to put up with came to the front, partly to justify what little progress they have made in organizing the workers. The businessmen complained less about the French and admitted that much of their industry still has strong French ownership.

There is one thing the French did and did well: they laid out a magnificent city. Even as run down as it has become, the avenues, the concept of Saigon, is one of grandeur and space.

The town may *look* peaceful, but the 11 o'clock news tells the story of fighting within a few miles of where I am tonight—and in the Delta, where we are going by helicopter in a couple days. The radio broadcaster for the Armed Forces Radio says: "Twelve helicopters were brought down in the last twenty-four hours, most of these in the Delta."

FEBRUARY 17, 1967
NOON
SAIGON

We were seated in a circle in the huge office of the Governor of the National Bank, Nguyen Huu Hanh, discussing the monetary and fiscal problems pressing so hard upon them here. The dire consequences of inflation, etc. Suddenly the wooden sun shutters, twelve feet high, I would guess, rattled furiously. A few seconds later there was a low, muffled thud and again the shutters and now the tall windows shook and rattled.

Artillery and bombs only a few miles away are the accompaniments to the most sophisticated discussions of monetary issues. And no one—now not even I, after only a few days—seems to pay much attention to the sounds of bombing.

Hanh I met first at a Blair House dinner in Washington only a few months ago. He is a round-faced beaming man, hardly five feet tall, I would guess, speaking colloquial American perfectly. But when he spoke of the impracticality of grandiose plans, most of which would have to be carried out by government for the time being, and how the government administration "gets worse day by day," a great anxiety changed the bland roundness of his face to one of great intensity.

"The French when they ran this country did not train anyone for responsible posts; and when a man would be trained well, in Paris, when he returned there was nothing but routine work for him. So thirty thousand Vietnamese, for various reasons of course, stayed in France. And they simply will not come back, neither the skilled workman nor the engineer. There they have better living conditions; many have married French women!"

But, I insisted, what about the younger Vietnamese now in France, when they find that important jobs and opportunities await them back home, the war being over?

By this time both of us were on the edge of our seats, leaning forward. (I liked that sense of passion about this subject of "after the war"—liked it on both our parts.)

"Yes, perhaps it would be possible that one thousand might return."

That would be enough possibly to start the flow, was my comment.

Then I referred to the "reverse migration" which we saw happen in Persia, when able younger Persians saw that there *were* opportunities—and a measure of freedom—for them in their country. When *that* happens, when the younger men begin to come back, this is a mark of confidence that means a kind of turning point. Could it be made to happen—even a beginning of it—in Vietnam? No answer.

Very early this morning we went to the office of the General Manager of the American construction consortium called RMK (Raymond International and Morrison-Knudsen International). Stalwart-looking man of perhaps fifty-five by the name of Lilly. The office is in a rabbit warren of a building, filled with Americans running to and fro, many young women, clerical and secretarial people. Didn't project the tough construction company image I am so familiar with. Nor did Lilly: more the public relations, house-broken man for the front office, for "contacts."

But once we got him off his prepared spiel (they must see thousands of inquiring and idly curious visitors, poor fellows), he responded to some questions in a way that was distinctly relevant to our D&R job.

For example, what about the thousands of Vietnamese peasants brought from their villages to work on construction, men who not only didn't know the words for "saw" or "nail" but had never ever *seen* these objects, much less the huge machines RMK used in their big earth-moving jobs?

RMK found the Vietnam peasant made a good workman. He worked hard, ten hours a day, six days a week. He was open minded, liked to learn, and while illiterate, could understand directions by pictures or being shown. But best of all, Lilly said, he was an "aggressive" worker. While I suppose this could become a problem at times, it certainly is a great asset, and so at odds with the journalistic picture of the Asian as "submissive and passive."

Lunched at the Embassy with Ambassador Lodge; his guests a Dr. Stark, a plastic surgeon of New York who comes out each year, at his own expense, to work in the hospital of "reconstructive surgery," and his pleasant, interesting wife, both perhaps about forty-five; the new Economic Counselor, Calhoun; Donald MacDonald, head of the AID Mission; and arriving quite late, Mary McCarthy, the brilliant, hard-boiled, cynical novelist.

I was placed at one end of the long table, where conversation with Miss McCarthy was not easy, so the only clear impression I have is of her appearance. Straggly hair, white patterned stockings, and an extraordinary visage: the profile very masculine, by which I mean not only *not* feminine in quality, but also the bone structure strong and hard. She was obviously giving the patrician Ambassador a hard time.

Spent an hour discussing the press corps here in Saigon with the head of the U.S. Information Office, Bob Collinge, a sharp bird-like man who certainly has his hands full. A press corps of almost five hundred, of which about one hundred are Vietnamese. Most of the U.S. correspondents are very young, some of them on their very first assignment! Even the men on the big newspapers (with only a few exceptions) are young and inexperienced.

After weighing the pros and cons of the usefulness to our work of attending one of the daily press briefings (there is a 5 o'clock military briefing seven days a week) I decided the pros had it, and will appear before this press meeting next Tuesday.

9:15 P.M.

A "reception" for me at the big house of Donald MacDonald. A long day and a long two and a half hour stint standing up shaking hands and visiting with people.

The impressive thing about the reception was the outpouring of Vietnamese, headed by my new "partner," Professor Thuc. It was more than evident that the AID people rarely see these Vietnamese and *that* at least is something I have contributed, if I do nothing more.

A letter today with that long-familiar handwriting; the envelope said "mailed at sea." But it had been written February 6 while Helen was just barely beginning her return, and what I had so much wanted was word from her that she had arrived safely in Princeton; even sent a cable asking whether she was all right. We write each other so infrequently now, who for *years* wrote every solitary day; the telephone is so much more personal and easier. I was particularly touched by the simple way she thanked me for "giving" her a fine vacation (and it *was* a good one) and an endearing last paragraph. I had almost forgotten how much it means to be reminded of how close we are, despite years and the changes in some of the outward family things that make two people depend so much upon each other: young children, a career to make, crises to face—the lot.

FEBRUARY 18, 1967
5:45 A.M.
SAIGON

In a few minutes I reach for some coffee, bestir my colleagues and we head for the flying and helicoptering that goes with seeing the prodigious things that America "hath wrought" in the port of Cam Ranh Bay.

I am—as a friend has remarked more than once—"a ham." I put out. It's fair to say that a new face and figure, as I am here, in a tired setting, is always a dash of cold water. The question: Can the people I can get together keep up this enthusiasm, or will they too, like so many of the AID Americans out here, just go round and round, sorry for themselves "way off here," let down? How long will it last, the shot in the arm I am able to give a jaded critter?

FEBRUARY 19, 1967
SAIGON

Bob Komer, whose phone call months ago was the first link in the chain of circumstances that led me to Vietnam, came by to see me late yesterday afternoon. The exuberance he projected by telephone last summer seemed a thing of the past. The reason: "the pacification program" (what a God-awful piece of semantics, that) *still* isn't going well.

I told Komer some of the cause for a certain enthusiasm I feel, ignoring the dark spots for the moment (e.g., yesterday the visit to the vast Cam Ranh Bay port city—built with American funds and technology—was itself a horror; the thesis repeated ad nauseam in Washington that it can be made a major industrial city is absurd).

I included Ky in the catalogue of Vietnamese we had seen. (All of my visits incidentally had been arranged by Professor Thuc or some other Vietnamese, for I am deliberately careful to keep the U.S. Embassy out of our arrangements as much as I can.)

Bob reacted with the kind of special intensity that is his trademark. "You have already seen Ky? When—the day after you arrived? How did this happen?"

I said Thuc and Minister Ton must have arranged it.

"That's the best thing I have heard since I've been here. You mean Lodge didn't take you in; it was Ky wanted to see you for a half hour? We have been getting this stuff about how Americans wanted to force economic development down their throats. Why, that's wonderful."

The military establishment at Cam Ranh has probably been seen by more American visitors than any other single thing in this country, about which now there is so much desire to say: "Oh, yes, I visited Vietnam," usually meaning Saigon. A less likely place than Cam Ranh for the much touted future industrial development I would have difficulty in imagining: a sandy peninsula, close to a range of utterly beautiful mountains, but no immediate hinterland. They had built a small shanty hamlet on most inhospitable sand, in sullen rows, and here they moved some five hundred refugees from the north. The men, and probably most of the women, were working (at prodigious wages for them, no doubt) on the military construction, so the hamlet was left to the children, scores of them, all small, who followed us about. No begging, but also no smiles despite our tentative overtures. These hapless people were second-round refugees, having moved out of North Vietnam.

A disturbing and worrying letter—a long one—from Oliver. He had committed the company to take a lease on some expensive space in Sacramento, unless there was a "veto" from me. I cabled Burnett to hold up on this until I could call him from Honolulu.

A substantial addition to our overhead to house a department of agriculture that has been running losses for months, and a new department of water resources that has yet not a dime of income, and the prospect that this new office will not bring in *cash* income of any substance: quite a jolt. The office space is fancy, in a brand-new building, at a high cost. This is put up to me on a last-minute basis—the old pistol to the head tactic: "The space will be rented to someone else if we don't act *at once*."

None of this would have disturbed me quite so much if there had been in Oliver's letter a single word about a program, a financial projection, some figures, some kind of estimate.

Why on earth *begin* a new function, at this critical juncture in our affairs—taking on this patriotic but financially unrewarding Vietnam task—and at the same time loading D&R with the *best* space in Sacramento, with great emphasis in the accompanying letter of just how beautiful the layout is, with the bureaucratic preoccupation with a "corner" office for A, and an "executive office" for B, etc.—all this baffled and distressed me.

I recalled that I began my work as a founding director of TVA in a little, ugly office, and my country Valley visitors, and later "distinguished visitors" from abroad, did not mind the crudity of my surroundings. As TVA grew I stayed in that office for almost fourteen years. I don't like the attitude of mind that puts such emphasis on these expensive accouterments.

A few minutes ago an AP man called to ask me if I had heard of Robert Oppenheimer's death, and to request a comment.

A note to Kitty; perhaps I should record parts of it here:

"My dear Kitty: The AP has just called with word of Robert's death. . . . Out here, where violent death is an hourly occurrence, and the rumble of bombs commonplace, the death of so sweet and noble a man can't be reconciled with the beauty of a world he graced. How *much* it meant to me, those Saturday afternoon little visits. What a game and strong man; it is only the strong who can be as gentle and sensitive. . . ."

Seven straight days of hard, intense concentration on new things, new problems, new faces, new sounds. And travel. And a special feeling in the air, when one hears the grumble of bombs or sees their flash at night, and sees sandbags and automatic rifles *everywhere*, and soldiers and the smell of war in the midst of a strange Eastern setting.

And tomorrow at dawn begins still another long day, by "chopper" into the Delta, into villages and flying low over canals and rice paddies, and again meeting many people and hearing new facts, or alleged facts, as people try so hard to get you to see things their way.

Not the least source of satisfaction comes from being with two professionals, men I can be so proud of, Moore and Mead. Absolutely first rate, and companionable.

FEBRUARY 20, 1967
6 P.M.
SAIGON

The day began twelve hours ago. But a glorious day it has been. I don't remember when I have been so impressed, so overwhelmed, by the possibilities of a region as I have today, flying for six hours at low altitudes over the delta provinces southwest from Saigon, the grand, awe-inspiring mouths of one of the world's great rivers winding its several ways through the richest kind of land. An area that has an abundance of water, stretched out below us, canals spreading in all directions like the arms of a great and benevolent spider; the green of palms, coconut and banana, orchards; vegetable squares luscious even at 1000 feet; villages nestled along the streams, and almost a dozen good-size towns, two or three considerable ones, modern, sophisticated, and seemingly prosperous.

Now and then one of the men accompanying us, either Vietnamese or AID, would point his finger earthward and say: "Full of VC." But except for such references (including a remark, "I had a friend killed down there," by an AID man name of London), the picture the press and TV had given me of this country being wracked and devastated by war left me mystified.

The real story of Vietnam hasn't been told: it is now a developing country in every sense, physically and emotionally. Confidence that there is a future, and that that future is good, was evidenced *everywhere* during our visits to the little villages and the big towns and cities, as it is, in fact, here in this bustling, clamorous Saigon.

The picture of a submissive, slow, lethargic, inscrutable Oriental land torn by war is almost completely belied by what one sees of the *people*. But on the other hand there is the large number of soldiers, of sandbags, of war planes, and the detailed radio accounts of what the cub reporters out here call "battles," though even in our Civil War or in World War II these would have simply been called skirmishes.

Finally a letter from New York, dated the 13th, giving me news that Helen had in fact reached home.

FEBRUARY 21, 1967
SAIGON

The dinner for Komer given at the huge French-colonial-type palace home of National Bank Governor Hanh last night was a glimpse of the upper crust in a social setting. All of the men—nine or ten (except five Americans)—were "Ministers" whom we had "conferred" with in their offices. There they reflected the atmosphere of the shabby offices so characteristic of many bureaucracies in the "developing" countries, particularly those trying to live with the remnants of colonial administration. But at this affair they were quite different men. The very youthful Minister of Communications, Truong Van Thuan, emerged as a Parisian playboy in manner; the long, slender fingers of the sad, ascetic-looking young Minister of Commerce, Nguyen Kien Thien An, laced and unlaced, reached for a cigarette, etc., as if he were at a salon in Paris; the jovial, round-faced Governor, our host, had lost the profound look of anxiety he wore throughout our hour with him at his cathedral of banking the other day, and was beaming, joking noisily with the robust Komer—partly in French—about their troubles, rather than moping about them—the very picture of an American tycoon relaxing, doing his negotiating thrust by way of hearty, masculine wisecracks or derogatory comments intended to be amusing and not to be taken any other way.

I had my first (probably not the last) completely Vietnamese dinner. Komer, peering sharply through his glasses, his head tilted forward in his characteristic way, assured me, across the beautiful table, that the Governor was a famous connoisseur of both Vietnamese and Chinese food, and that I was eating a meal that couldn't be equalled anywhere. The irony of this display of ostentation didn't escape me, but it *was* a remarkable meal. Except for a soup, I had never had anything like these "courses." One of them was a kind of sausage, hot with spice, each guest himself wrapping the pungent cylinder in bits of lettuce *and* peppermint leaves, then dipping it in the special favorite sauce of this country, nuoc mam, which I can't compare in flavor with anything I know, but which is used as the Chinese use soy sauce—or we Worcestershire sauce; made of fish, allowed to decay, more or less, in salt, smelling to high heaven as it is made—and eaten.

We had a series of tiny glasses of a white rice wine, and the Deputy Prime Minister, Nguyen Luu Vien, across the table from Governor Hanh, kept raising his glass and inviting the whole table to drink with a phrase that must be the equivalent of bottoms up. This ritual gathered momentum after a while, and "keeping up" was not only a matter of courtesy but a kind of duty. Most of the quiet appearing gents became quite aroused and boisterous during this little ceremony, pointing to an empty glass as if this were a form of competition. Surprisingly no one got anything resembling drunk.

FEBRUARY 22, 1967
8 A.M.
SAIGON

Toward the end of a restless night of off-and-on sleep (overstimulated and perhaps overtired), about 4 o'clock I heard the bong bong of bombing: the B-52s bringing in their cargo on the morning milk route run and plopping them a few miles from Saigon.

Which reminded me of a most remarkable exposé of military obtuseness, related by a senior Foreign Service Officer.

At about 11 yesterday we were passed through sandbags and a series of guards to the office of Deputy Ambassador William G. Porter. (The buildings all around had been destroyed by Viet Cong blasts not too long ago, but are now rebuilt and ready for another explosion whenever the VC think it worth the effort.)

At first impression Porter is almost a scholarly appearing man. Glasses, medium tall, pale, piercing, quizzical eyes, greying sandy hair, his dress careful and well groomed. (Definitely no striped pants.)

Omitting the usual opening palaver, he tilted back in his chair in the middle of his office and cut loose. He sounded as if he had just come from a battle—of ideas—with the military leadership here, for he sailed into the whole concept of how such a war *should* be fought—a flood of vigorous, unsparing, and even sarcastic criticism of the American military establishment.

How this extraordinarily candid salvo was set off, to complete strangers, is significant in itself.

I made some comment about the unwisdom of sending Vietnamese young people, in large numbers, to the U.S., as compared with the method of training them, as Professor Thuc proposes to do, here in Vietnam, where they can confront Vietnam's problems in terms of their own national habits and "institutions."

Suddenly he rar'd back. "You are dead right. And this is the trouble with the way the Vietnamese Army has been losing out to the guerrillas, and the terrible waste of our great big force here, that has proved so ineffectual against the kind of guerrilla war that they are so good at.

"We organized and trained the Vietnamese Army, as far back as 1954, organized them by American standards of how an army should be organized and should fight. And that just has nothing to do with fighting this kind of war; and what makes it worse, the Communists are preparing to probe in the same way into Burma and Thailand, to stir up trouble wherever they can, using the same methods as the VC here. And we keep on throwing great bombs at them at enormous expense and with little effect. They hide out and we hit nothing most of the time. Every dawn you can hear the bombs drop near Saigon from the B-52s. The cost is fantastic, but they just *dump* the bombs and fly back, and consider that is doing a job. It isn't.

"When I say this to Bob McNamara, it makes him mad as hell. But it is true, and I'll continue to say it.

"For example, the way the Vietnamese military have been trained, by American methods, if there is a choice between defending a post or defending a village, the Vietnamese, following American training, defend the post. That just suits the guerrilla; they move in on the village and pay no attention to the post."

Quite recently Porter was brought in from Algeria, where he saw years of French efforts to stem guerrilla fighting, and he is full of that sad analogy of conventional French military methods; "and the American military is pretty much the same; we seem not to pay any attention to what happened in North Africa or to learn anything from it."

With things in Vietnam going so badly, it was apparently decided to try a new tack; presumably by the President's order Porter was put in charge of *all* non-military activities in the field, grouped under what is called the Office of Civil Affairs, I believe. That is, all AID technical and development people outside Saigon are assigned to Porter's OCA. A drastic step. This includes the so-called revolutionary development program, the latest verbal gimmick in what was previously the village pacification program; now a new phrase for this has been invented which the Vietnamese like better: New Life program.

So Porter's views about economic development are quite important to our work.

I was fascinated by the almost indiscreet way he spoke. There was no hint even that he wouldn't say this same thing from the housetops if he felt like it, no hint that this was "confidential," on the contrary.

But the time was passing, and I had our particular non-military responsibility to consider. So to bring the discussion back to matters which directly concerned my work, I said, "Mr. Ambassador, this is very interesting. But may I ask whether the Government of the U.S. takes *seriously* the economic long-term assignment we are here about?"

The chair tilted, and abruptly; he looked at me for the first time as if I were a person rather than a means of getting off a considerable head of steam.

"I can't speak for the Government as a whole; I guess the President has already done that in requesting that you do this difficult job. But personally, in terms of my own responsibilities here, *I* take it very seriously. If we are to move in a political direction, what you propose, with your great prestige, will fit into the concept of giving the people a greater stake in their own country."

Supposing that he had satisfied me, as indeed he had, Porter went on, most interestingly, considering who he is (that is, the lever with the greatest political force here), to discuss the general situation as he saw it.

"We caught the VC off balance; they never thought we would bring a large force of men into this country. That was at the start. Then they adjusted to this, and though there are occasional engagements in which they pit large units against ours—there was one yesterday in the north—

they have gone back to their guerrilla methods. The Army will hardly recognize the Special Forces units *we* have, the Rangers, fighters using guerrilla methods themselves.

"So we are in an impasse. The only way that impasse can be resolved is by dealings between Vietnamese, those we are supporting and those we are fighting. That's the only hope of an accommodation, and sooner or later there will have to be an accommodation between Vietnamese. They may go on sporadically fighting each other for quite a while, but it will be Vietnamese against Vietnamese."

What all of this means I'm too ignorant to get. But it certainly doesn't sound like the kind of thing that is being said publicly these days from the White House or the State Department.

I found all this bracing: a man who had the courage—and the background—to risk his career by a tough line. And he struck me as a tough man indeed.

2:30 P.M.

A roomful of newspapermen preparing to devour their solitary victim is nothing entirely new to me. But the "press conference" (the word "conference" seems peculiarly inappropriate) I attended at 5 o'clock yesterday afternoon was the weirdest, most amateur, unprofessional, and sadistic in my experience, perhaps in the experience of anyone now practicing the role of either victim or aggressor.

I was asked to mount steps to something like a stage, with TV lights suddenly turned on me. The newsmen listened to my low-key opening remarks closely, with apparent curiosity. I explained what the joint long-term development program was all about, how it originated, emphasizing that D&R was private, not part of the U.S. Government, etc. Then came perhaps ten or fifteen minutes of questioning, none of it cynical, some of it quite perceptive. For example: "Does the history of the TVA have any usefulness as an analogy, by way of technique, to Vietnam's development?"

The American press corps here, except for a few top metropolitan papers, appears to be made up of the least experienced newsmen, recently out of journalism school, "cubs" as we used to call them, some of them very young-looking.

How this happens, except as an economy measure, I can't figure out. This is a very important place to cover, and to send someone who at home would be lucky to be assigned to the traffic violation courts I can only explain by the large number here from quite small papers not ordinarily sending out "foreign correspondents."

But this amateur quality is not what made this press meeting so awful; it was the "daily military briefing" that preceded my appearance.

A literally battered-faced Lieutenant Colonel came through a curtain at the corner of the "stage," arranged his notes before him on his lectern, referred to the mimeoed release that had been distributed, and began to run through recent combat actions, which were illustrated on a magic lantern screen.

His commentary included estimates of "Communists killed" in each engagement. He called this a "body count." *All* of the questioning, in the most you-are-a-liar tone, resembled a young assistant county attorney's cross-examination in a chicken-stealing case. "But you say that is an AVN [Army of Vietnam, I suppose] count. What was the count of the U.S. advisor?" If this varied by one "body" there would be several minutes of cross-examination on the reason for this discrepancy, conducted in rasping, smart-alecky voices.

I was absolutely appalled, not just by the grisliness of the whole business—calling dead men "body count"—but that these men of the press corps had such a distorted concept of the interpretative function and responsibilities of a free press that a full forty minutes would be devoted to this effort to trap this man. Later the same routine was repeated with an Air Force briefing officer, over a minor numerical discrepancy.

Afterward, Jon Randal, a *New York Times* correspondent, a veteran correspondent in Algeria and here for some five and a half months, came up to speak to me; he came back to the guest house and we talked for more than an hour.

These five o'clocks are called the "Five O'clock Follies," Randal explained. He seemed to share the feeling I expressed that some of the questioning seemed sadistic, an excuse for novice newsmen to vent their frustrations or unwillingness to try to dig out the real news as they would back home. He was scornful of their trying to trap the briefing officers in some minor discrepancy, as if the soldier in the field's first responsibility was to be a good body-number accountant.

Randal was ashamed of the performance; said we had hit a pretty bad exhibition by some of the lesser correspondents. "But you can understand it, in a way," said Randal, "because we all believe our Government is and has been lying to us."

I could fully understand and sympathize with that.

Randal took many notes during our talk and seemed genuinely interested in whatever I said that seemed hopeful. Spoke of how dispiriting and corroding it was to be "only a correspondent" in so futile a business as this war seemed to him to be. "And it is *not* going well," this with a shake of his head.

I arrived somewhat early at the command offices for my meeting with General [William C.] Westmoreland, the four-star commander of the

American Forces (called the U.S. Military Advisory Command, I think; the "advisory" has become pretty largely historical!).

I had to prove my right to get through the barricade-and-sandbag fortress; this command center is, unwisely I am sure, right smack in the middle of the busiest part of Saigon. A mortar was aimed at it the night we arrived, and until it is removed to a better place, it will be quite a target.

General Westmoreland is a big square-shouldered man, with deep-set eyes and a brow of noble proportions. He came bolting out of a door as we got to the top of the stairs, and invited me into his office—a very small one, with a few mementos (one looking like an elaborate foreign decoration), but all in all not "military" except for a carbine on the floor beside him. He wore no battle ribbons, had his paratrooper star and air pilot star, but that was all, on his short-sleeved plain shirt.

Some of what he said about the "Communn-ists," as he pronounced it, was probably part of the speech he must be called upon to give to many a visitor. "The analogy I've worked out is that of termites, silently boring into a building that looks all right from the outside but is weakened; and then a bully comes along with a crowbar and hits that weakened structure and it all caves in." Well, the termites are the guerrillas, and the bully is the armed forces of the North Vietnamese in large units, battalions, even regiments and divisions.

He spoke with the eloquence of a graphic mind about the kind of war this is; agreed with my comment that there is no precedent for it in military history, for Vietnam, after French domination and then the termites, is no longer a "real nation-state" and it will take many years before it becomes one.

Westmoreland then described the problem he has with the echelons of Vietnam Army below the very top corps commanders. "Today, for example, we launched a big operation, and we didn't dare give word of it to any except the topmost level of the Vietnam Army, lest the information be compromised. That has happened too many times to take further chances."

I said the position of the American Army under his command, presumably parallel with the Vietnam Army (they fearful of foreign domination, after the French), presented a management problem of unique difficulty quite aside from the military aspect. "We have to deal with the Vietnam Army with great tact, make them feel they are participating in the decisions. There is no unity of command—on paper—but in fact we are running this war. Have to."

All of these things said with composure, without any of the ferocity of a lesser man: simply an operating problem for a professional soldier.

But when he talked about how the peasants particularly had been bilked and sucked dry for generations by the French, by the Chinese merchants, by the Communists, he showed a kind of compassion that was unmistakable.

"To these peasants nothing about government is good, and so to blow up a railroad—government owned—or a road, built by the government so they can get at the peasant and tax him or run him, that's fair game. The VC have built up this hatred of anything about the government.

"They say there are two wars, the military war and the 'other war.' [This is the official line.] But I don't believe that. There is only one war, but it has several faces. The military face. And making things better for the peasants particularly. And that is why what you are undertaking to do is so important: it will make the peasant feel that someone is concerned about him. And if this can be done not by government but by his own organizations in his own village or hamlet, your work will have a lot to do with the winning of the war."

I told him we were intensely impressed with the richness of the delta of the Mekong; wanted to consider, soon, some action projects in the countryside. But in many places we were told there is "lack of security."

Suppose, I said, we find some such opportunities; can I come to him to see if military operations can be adapted or directed in such a way as to make that particular economic development in the Delta reasonably "secure"? He looked very stern and thoughtful; then said: "I want to review your plans; you can see me any time about them. And we can probably see that military measures of protection can be taken in conjunction with your development plans."

After forty-five minutes of conversation I was all set to leave, but the General continued talking excitedly, his deep-set eyes aglow. An attractive man by any standard. None of the "charm" of Ike in the early fifties, but a different kind of military-politician type, much more rough hewn. If he can bring off this war, he will be a public figure, whether he likes it or not.

After more than an hour I finally got up, and thanked him. Knowing what happens in the Pentagon, where a major is practically an office boy to a four-star general, I was impressed when he said: "I'll escort you to the door," and stepping ahead of me, went down the narrow circular stairway to the ground floor. The officers in the anteroom scrambled to their feet, he paying them no mind, and he took me out to my car, in the driveway, assuring me again that he wanted to see me from time to time as our work progressed.

FEBRUARY 23, 1967
4:45 A.M.
SAIGON

The thunder of the big guns is particularly heavy this morning, shaking the air now for a full ten minutes. I assume they are the 155 mm artillery guns, judging by the regular pattern of the boom. The dawn comes up sounding like summer thunder, but it is really that "dumping" of explosives Ambassador Porter tossed off as making so little real sense.

9 A.M.

Last evening I had dinner alone here at the guest house (now the "D&R residence in Vietnam"). Kind of a relief from the constant chit chatter. Then about 9:30 the most thoughtful professional in the broadcasting business came in to see me, Charles Collingwood. Charles is as handsome as ever, with his regular features, wavy brown hair, and an extraordinarily pleasing voice to which one has become accustomed through years of hearing it on the airwaves. I hadn't realized that Collingwood had spent a great deal of time since 1960 in Vietnam. And not just fleeting sorties; this present trip, for example, has been a matter of months. Explaining this, he says, "My colleagues in New York think this is noble of me." (That big, winning grin of his, which he almost never shows while broadcasting, no matter what the subject matter.) "Well, it isn't noble; I just am in love with this country, absolutely fascinated by it, by everything about it. And I warn you, David, it will get to you too, I'll bet on that.

"This is not a revolutionary people; there is no revolution going on here, even in what are called the 'areas that are not secure'; this is nothing like Algeria; nothing at all like Cyprus, where I spent a good deal of time; nothing at all like Palestine, where two million people were just too much for 100,000 British soldiers."

"Then you wouldn't call this Viet Cong business a civil war?" was the natural question for me to ask.

He said no. "Take this example," he went on, "from one of many experiences I have had—this happened the day of your press conference, just the day before yesterday."

Then he described an airfield and an American Army brigade headquarters he had visited in the north central part of the country. A highway goes right through the airfield camp, in which are gathered several hundred civilian employees—cooks, clean-up women, repairmen, etc. He asked the Commanding Officer: what about security? Do you have a security check on all these people; what about the cars and trucks that come down the road and through your reservation?

No, they don't have a security check; they close the road at night, with a couple strands of barbed wire. Now and then a mortar is lobbed in; they found a mortar emplacement nearby, and dug it out. Booby traps show up now and then, and some of their men have been hurt. But it is nothing more than the usual amount of trouble from, say, bad traffic accidents. Anyway, they don't consider this an insecure place.

"Well," said Charles, "in Algeria or Cyprus that just couldn't happen. The whole population, the entire population was in revolt, and no amount of troops can survive when that happens. But these are not that kind of people, there is no universal revolt or universal popular uprising against the government or against the Americans. Besides, these people aren't 'natural assassins,' like the Arabs can be, or the Cypriots or the Mafia. The VC love the mechanics of destruction and violence, a conspiracy comes natural to them. They like to devise booby traps, or leave a plastic bomb and then run like hell. But they aren't given to sticking a knife into a man, or shooting him at close range. And they have great courage; those VC who climbed up on the tanks today, so the tanks were forced to shoot at each other—that takes resolve and courage."

Whether all of this adds up to an "answer" to the oft heard argument that this is a civil war and therefore we Americans shouldn't be moving in on it, I am not clear. But Collingwood is an experienced man whose words I do not take lightly.

NOON

A morning visit with Donald MacDonald and Robert Culbertson, his Associate Director for development of USAID (this is one word out here). Even MacDonald's Scottish ancestry couldn't prevent him showing his emotion about what a "tonic" it was to have Development & Resources' presence, "and particularly yourself, with your record and prestige." Culbertson chimed in that the effect on the "young intellectuals" was the most impressive.

Then I went over to the Embassy office for a brief goodbye visit with Lodge. I gave him my general impression about the people of this country as I had observed them—this is a standard reaction, I could see, but how much he shares my high opinion of the Vietnamese people I can't be sure.

But the chief burden of what I said was about the AID Mission. I know this group is always vulnerable, and I have myself said some very derogatory (and deserved) things about some of the missions. But while there are surely mediocrities and "drones" (Lodge's expression),

I also found some individual talents of extraordinarily high caliber. The chief shortcoming, I thought, was the customary one in the Washington Government, and in many business organizations: specialization that has created walls between what should be interrelated fields and prevents dealing with a problem as a unity. Since this aspect of management has concerned me a long time, I thought Development & Resources could contribute something helpful in this area.

6:35 P.M.
ABOARD AN AIR FORCE "TANKER" HEADED NONSTOP TO HONOLULU
MY FIRST TIME ON A MILITARY PLANE SINCE AEC DAYS

This plane is loaded with brains, young and eager, as well as two more or less older crocks, Komer in the seat opposite, and yours truly. Much going over of papers, exchanging of views, and general milling about.

We left in a flurry of "protocol" appearances at the airport by some of the best men in the American Establishment—the two Ambassadors, MacDonald—and my already "old" and now ebullient "friend" Professor Thuc.

The stewards, male and U.S. Air Force, but with *jackets* and company manners, have just laid the white tablecloths and asked, "How would you like your steak, *sir*?"

There is something about this group of men on this office-in-a plane streaking across the Pacific that recalls the spirit of the early New Deal and is somehow in keeping with the other-worldly character of this whole adventure.

"VIP" GUEST COTTAGE AT HICKAM AIR FORCE BASE, HAWAII

It is Thursday, still February 23, 1967, 4:45 (this being earlier than we left Saigon). This loss of a day is always a mystery.

Because Komer is a "Presidential assistant" we were received with much ceremony when our big transport rolled in at 11:30. This is the center of the entire Pacific Command. Two of the bright young men in our entourage, Charles Cooper and Richard Holbrooke, just gave the senior officers here a "briefing" about Vietnam. Vietnam is actually the responsibility of this Command; General Westmoreland in the "chain of command" is "under" Admiral U.S.G. Sharp, the head of the Pacific Forces. But about all the officers here do is keep up with the "cable traffic," to use the lingo of my alert youthful friends. What it all *means* is beyond them. And these high officers are hungry for "company"; they sit out here with nothing much to do but read cables.

I find it refreshing to be among such cocky, merry, horsing-around young fellows, full of ideas, brash enough to make cracks about anything, and completely absorbed and devoted to the Vietnam story.

That devotion is tested by more than words. This afternoon a young man limping on a cane came to our guest house to see Holbrooke. They sat talking seriously, Holbrooke, curly-headed, very young (twenty-five!), slumped back in his chair. Both had served in the provinces of Vietnam. His visitor, perhaps thirty, had been injured by a land mine. "I was lucky," said Holbrooke; "they shot up a plane I was in but nothing much happened." Yesterday, Bernard Fall, a newsman and photographer, was killed by a road mine. It is not all done behind desks, this work, and I must be prepared for things to happen to some of the men for whom I shall be personally responsible.

After I had been assigned a cottage, these young fellows gravitated toward me. One of them was frank about it: he said I represent a kind of high mark of public service, of my time. Holbrooke, a former aide to General and Ambassador Maxwell Taylor and then to Lodge, in Saigon, said in a break-the-ice manner (he had looked at me until then as if I were some sort of mirage), "When I was about twelve or so my mother bought me a set of Ed Murrow's records, the *I Hear It Now* ones, and I played your 'This I Do Believe' over and over again."

Thanks to their attitude, instead of feeling like an ancient has-been, I nourished the thought that perhaps I had the advantage of more *continuity* than most men they met, and so meant more to these young and brilliant fellows than if I didn't reach back into what must seem to them a period as remote as the *Federalist Papers*.

In talking to New York I was told that Jon Randal had done a piece appearing in today's *New York Times* that was quite favorable, stressing the air of confidence my presence in Vietnam had given there. If that *is* what he wrote, as I hope, it would be absurd to deny that all the signs indicate that this is in fact the case; to follow up on this with deeds is quite another matter, but just to change the air of cynicism and weariness of this whole profoundly tragic business would be *some* contribution.

FEBRUARY 25, 1967
PRINCETON

Back home, Vietnam already seems so far away that unless I write some addenda items now they will never get recorded, or will be noted down so far after the fact that some of their flavor will be lost.

My earlier feeling about the basic character of our problem in Vietnam has been reinforced and confirmed by this exposure to the realities during our whirlwind expedition. Unless we establish a close *mutuality with the Vietnamese*, our "economic studies" will be just another study;

the establishment of an emotional rapport is not just something desirable, but a condition precedent to getting on with our work and being useful to these people.

During our afternoon meeting of Thursday last, I emphasized, in a ten minute exposition to Moore and Mead, both solemn as owls as I spoke, that the main criterion in the selection of individuals of our field team, including the next group, is that they should in every case be men who comprehend—are capable of comprehending—that *stimulating the Vietnamese people* is the heart of the job; that we can never, never do that ourselves, but must rely upon the collective and individual judgment of knowledgeable Vietnamese. While they will not always agree among themselves, they will, however, *sense*—must be made to feel—that we want to know and be guided by the desires, aspirations, and particularly the distinctive temperament and history of the Vietnamese people, that we are not there to Americanize through the device of providing "technical aid" or "planning techniques."

This will not be easy, for *they* have an overly high regard for our American technical capabilities, and they will be inclined—most of them—to look at "planning" as a wholly technical exercise. It is *nothing of the sort*; of that I am sure.

In some areas technical competence is uppermost, perhaps. Fiscal and monetary constraints within which long-term development must operate, for example. Hydrology, among many other of the physical sciences, for another.

But the essential ingredient that can give life and acceptability to our "technical" competence is something *every* member of our group must have constantly in mind—and those who can't manage it should be sent home: that an understanding of these people and a willingness and eagerness to turn to the Vietnamese for that understanding is basic to the work we have undertaken.

FEBRUARY 26, 1967
PRINCETON

Yesterday was a day given over to remembrance of Robert Oppenheimer, from the gathering for a buffet luncheon at Olden Manor, through a long memorial service at Alexander Hall, to a reception in the library of the Institute.

So many faces out of Robert's life that were also part of mine: General Leslie Groves, tanned, genial, not unaware of his re-emergence in the vast current press accounts of his great achievement, the Manhattan District; Jack McCloy, a noble head on a more and more rotund body, the man whom everyone wants to put on every committee and board; Carl Kaysen with his cavernous eyes, most impressive as the new leader of the Institute; George Kennan, cool and restrained, but delivering a magnificent statement about Robert before this big audience in the Romanesque surroundings of Alexander Hall, a candid eulogy, shining with integrity, not omitting Robert's years of "eating his heart out" in Princeton after he was no longer permitted to help his country; merry little "Rab" (I. I. Rabi), his hair now white but still looking like the bright boy on the block; Arthur Schlesinger with his built-in owlish expression; the handsome Bob and Helen Meyner, Bob being greeted by the cops with deference as "Governor"; Hans Bethe, perhaps the greatest of them all, with his puffs of white hair and his too-good-to-be-true Dutch accent. And Tony Oppenheimer, a most affecting picture, tall, strong-looking, no longer the child racing her sorrel mare across the Common.

People need some mark such as these gatherings to comprehend the fact of death, to close the chapter, to reflect on what a man meant, and to reflect on the inevitability and the *rightness* of an end.

FEBRUARY 27, 1967
WASHINGTON

During the day yesterday I read through David's new book, *The Tour.* The writing I found as good, indeed better than, say, Evelyn Waugh or Graham Greene at their best, and it resembled those masters of irony or satire.

But from the middle of the book on I looked for some escape hatch, some tiny note of affirmation, some relief from the anger and violence, hatred and frustration, and found hardly a one. No one loved anything or anybody—plenty of sex though little sensuality and no tenderness, no hint that human beings can *give* of themselves, whether as man to woman or in other relationships.

Well, a story is first of all a story: that is the refuge to which the fiction writer can retreat. No such easy out for a man like myself.

But there was a more personal reaction in my heart. Looking at the world in the sanguine and uncritical and optimistic way that I do, by temperament, I felt a stranger to one who could, through a whole full-length story, picture a group of people and a situation so lacking in hope and tenderness and basic human integrity. I go too far toward a romantic, unreal world, no doubt. But isn't it closer to the truth about us poor mortals and the world we live in?

David called to tell us that he had decided to move his family to Italy (Florence) next summer. I am genuinely happy that he has established himself in a profession where he can live where he wants to live, and move about as it pleases him.

And miracle of miracles: I looked out of the window of my room, the sunshine bright on the snow, and there, in a great patch of winter's green, was a big fat belligerent robin, whacking away defiantly at the frozen ground. I hold that picture in my mind. I think of it rather than the thought that at noon today I am to "report" to President Johnson across Lafayette Park about our trip to Vietnam.

FEBRUARY 28, 1967
NEW YORK

The hour and a half with President Johnson—from 12:45 until 2:15 or so—resembled nothing I have ever been exposed to in many sessions at the White House. The President's whirlwind manner I had seen before; still I wasn't prepared at all for the tumultuous, almost visible emanations of vitality, exuberance, a sense of power; the flow of anecdotes going back (in *detail*) to his administration of the National Youth Administration in Texas a generation ago; descriptions of his military concept about future bombing in North Vietnam; purple passages about *my* public career—on and on, engaging, sometimes terrifying, a flow of ideas, words, emotions, facial expressions that would tax an accomplished actor: "the man in charge." It was as prodigious an exhibition of energy and the pulling out of all the stops as ever I have seen, or expect to see.

MARCH 2, 1967
PRINCETON

It was a unique hour and a half in the White House, where I have in past years spent a good many hours with two other masters of the craft of statesmanship. But nothing was ever remotely like the outbursts of energy, the art of showmanship, the personal warmth and intimacy, the dizzying gyrations from a very serious issue to an anecdote out of the past, the apparent squandering of time and then the shrewd use of an extraordinary phrase or a glowering gesture.

I would like to keep my own personal reaction to what was said out of this recital, saving that perhaps for later on, and with the advantage of a two-day interval of reflection and scattered note-making, first describe the setting and the *facts*. As if one can reduce to "facts" the picture of so protean a personality in the midst of his wield of great power—and notably military power, during a war.

Komer's and my appointment was for 11:30. We were put in the Cabinet Room, and we sat and sat. About noon a puffy-eyed, most impersonal clerk said, "Mr. Watson wants to move you closer to his office." Watson is the current Appointments Secretary, a mysterious figure I never did see, but clearly unlike F.D.R.'s jovial wraith, Marvin McIntyre, and his robust successor, Pa Watson, whose booming voice I can still hear as he laughed at his own stories—thus keeping impatient Congressmen from fussing too much when he explained: "The Boss is running late today."

This Boss was indeed running late. We could hear his voice exchanging rumbling sounds through the door with his departing visitors: the remnants of the White House press corps, for the President had suddenly called a press conference, an important one, as the next day's transcript in the *Times* made clear, mostly about the latest Vietnam military steps—laying mines in North Vietnamese rivers, and the VC's mortar attack on the U.S. Marine base at Danang.

Then the door was opened, and I saw the huge bulk of the President, and heard his yell: "Hi, Dave."

He led us not to the Oval Room but into a tiny, very much upholstered darkish room, pushed me into a seat at the end of an uncomfortable sofa, lowered his big hulk into a chair, leaned forward with his elbows on his knees, took me in through the top of his glasses and started in: "When I was learnin' typing, we had a sentence that said, 'Now is the time for all good men to come to the aid of your country,' and that's what I asked you to do, and that's what you are a-doin'."

Without a pause, looking down at his hands: "When you were in a peck of trouble with old Senator McKellar, some of us in the House would get together and work for you—Maury Maverick, Helen Douglas, and so on. Now I need *you*, and I'm asking you to leave that polluted air of New York and try to help folks again the way you did in the TVA, and makes no difference that their skin is brown, they need your help."

While this was being said the light in this tiny room changed to a fierce white, and a young man in big dark tortoise shell glasses moved up right next to us, and I could hear the click of a camera. This picture-taking kept up for perhaps the first ten minutes of our talk. There will be a photographic record of this President's every move filling the files, judging from what I saw of this ubiquitous young man, who with his camera followed us around for the next hour. The President was constantly "on stage," leaning forward or gesturing—and then the lights went down to normal intensity.

The President now settled back in a kind of half-contour-type chair, pulled a whole sheaf of folded papers out of the inside of his coat, peered at one after another until he found what he was looking for, unfolded it, cleared his throat, and went on:

"This morning I got a cable from Lodge, and I read it just a while back to the joint leadership" (of the Congress, I assumed).

So he read the cable at length. Lodge had talked with Ky. Ky told the Ambassador that if a civilian government is elected this year he, Ky, head of the Vietnam armed forces, would support it *even* if the military doesn't agree with the results of the election.

"Now," said the President, looking at me sternly, his head tilted forward so he peered over his glasses, "that is sig-*nif*-icant."

At about this juncture Bob Komer, his pipe clenched between tightened jaws, fiddled with a memo he had prepared summarizing what he had found about the "other war." He hadn't yet had a chance to say a word. The President had said something about the press not reporting anything but the fighting; but then he, the President, had told them almost nothing about anything else.

Komer leaned forward and said, "You scooped us this morning, Mr. President, with that press conference." The President twisted around, yelled to someone back of him: "Get George Christian [his Press Secretary]." Christian, a meek, smooth, and scared-looking man, came in almost as if by magic. "Are they still out there? Get them together, in my office. And the TV and photographers, too."

Then the President rar'd back, and looking at me as if this were a private little tête-à-tête, went on: "There are six power plants that supply Hanoi. Four of them are right in Hanoi. Couldn't take them out without killing a lot of civilians. But two are way out. We could take them out without killing anyone—maybe an operator. I have drawn a circle around those plants and will have to decide what to do."

Leaning over toward me, in that confidential air he added: "If I send a bomber in to get those outer plants and a couple of MIGs get after him, the flier may want to get out of that place and jettison his bombs and they might kill a lot of people—and [grinning] it would be just our luck if he was a Texas boy that I appointed to the Academy."

The President went on and on about military matters, making me ill at ease, since it was nothing I knew anything about and certainly not part of my job. But he was really talking to himself, a man with a great burden of responsibility and power relieving himself by talking, excitedly, about how we need "to keep putting the pressure on."

An anguished look, as he got up—Christian must have said that they were ready for us in the Oval Office—and the President said: "We have got to get this thing straightened out. It is ruining everything—NATO, everything." (I wrote this phrase down exactly, along with other reminder notes, a half hour later, while on the shuttle back to New York. It was poignant and made me realize that, however exuberantly he talked about the way things were going in Vietnam, inside he was an agonized man—or so I felt at the time.)

The President now marched us into the Oval Office and pointed to a corner of a sofa (with those damned cushions that I had to haul out from behind me; how I hate being part of the upholstery of a place to sit!). He sat in a straight chair, which he pulled up to my elbow. Bob Komer on my right, still clinging to his pipe and still wondering, no doubt, whether he was going to get the important chance to tell his version of the progress his "pacification" program is making.

The still photographers and movie cameramen came piling in, one man held a strong light over his head and switched it on, while a White House attaché held a watch in his hand, the cameras clicked and whirred, and the man with the watch intoned: thirty seconds; forty-five seconds —and then punched his watch and out went the lights.

While this was going on, the President would lean across to me, point to something on a paper—it was a typed transcript of his earlier press conference, I guess—and gesticulate for the cameras.

The photographers were swished out, and in came the press corps, crowding back of a long sofa, facing "we three" at perhaps six feet distance, the sofa being a kind of thus-far-and-no-farther mark.

The President led off, the press looking bored—how many press conferences in an hour can you have? But what he said, while it was extravagant and unpersuasive praise of me (e.g., "the name Lilienthal is still magic in this country to a lot of people"), did lay the background: He had convinced me to "take this on," though he was not very clear about what was involved.

"What Dave is doing is more important than anything Westmoreland can do." (This said while tilting his chair back and looking fiercely at me. What an array of facial and vocal gestures this remarkable man has!)

"Now, I have asked Dave to tell you what he has recommended"—and then he got up and I could see him walking over to a desk at the far side of the Oval Office, reading some papers on the desk with his nose practically on the desk itself. But soon he was back, at my left in the straight chair.

I hadn't "recommended" anything, of course; indeed I had hardly had a chance to say anything to him, except that I was surprised and greatly encouraged by what I found. So I talked about the people instead, saying they were "hard-working bastards," in the affectionate way one uses that term (and fearing later that someone would pick that up and I would have a foot-in-mouth headline to live down!).

While we were waiting for the press to file in, the President was looking at what I supposed was his recent press conference transcript, but without looking up or stopping his reading he took hold of my left arm and said almost to himself—what I suppose is a formula he uses with all visitors—"Dave, what three things would you do if you were President, and what three things would you stop doing? As if you were God."

That stumped me; I started to stutter out something, and then realized he didn't expect nor would he hear a reply.

I noted in the *Times* report of the prior conference that the reporter had spoken of the high mood of the President, his leafing "excitedly" through papers before him; that his moods were quite different from his TV personality (which I find is usually pretty much of a monochrome).

Finally someone said, "Thank you, Mr. President," and the newsmen started out. We moved toward the main door of the office, then the President stopped. Two White House men—one of them I thought was Robert Kintner—were standing by. "Want you to get this man before the TV cameras; *Today* show. Let the country hear him philosophize; do us all good."

And then he dug down again into that big stack of papers in the inside breast pocket of his blue suit, and went through them until he found what he wanted.

"Listen to this," and he read aloud every word of a three-page, single-spaced letter, we standing there on one foot and then the other, he not looking up from the reading. Someone in this letter to him was reporting on the gross unfairness of the press, describing the Five O'clock Follies—the daily briefings in Saigon which had so shocked me.

"You ask me what I would recommend, Mr. President," the letter said (in substance). "I would recommend a short stop of the bombing, and if Hanoi resumed sending in supplies, etc., or didn't respond about peace talks, then you would be in the clear: you could intensify the bombing, etc."

No comment from the President about this subject, nor about the reference to "peaceniks" (the letter-writer's phrase). It was an intemperate letter, in a way, and the President's reading of it (I assumed he had read it more than once, it looked dog-eared) must have meant that it appealed to him. It certainly didn't appeal to me, in tone or in content; but the President simply folded it up, put it back among the other papers in his pocket, turned to me, and said: "Give this a sense of urgency." Then he told a *long* anecdote (we were all still standing there at the door) about how when he was National Youth Administrator in Texas thirty-odd years ago he wanted only "can do" people around; how he told men across the state they were to be in Austin on a certain date, which meant driving all night; "pack one pocket [he slapped his side pocket] with aspirin and the other with Ex-Lax—no exercise—and get going or you'll not have a job."

My personal reaction to this picture of the President in action is a very mixed one. L.B.J.'s words, informal and unguarded with me, probably do not fully represent the caution with which I hope he approaches these matters. But it was disquieting.

On the other hand, what he said about the extreme importance of the constructive side of the Vietnam venture assigned to us was genuine and came out of his long background of belief and action for people who need help.

This is the tragic ambivalence not only of this war, but of most global matters. Our world is a poor place in which to find easy answers.

MARCH 4, 1967
PRINCETON

I came back from Vietnam with a great head of steam, an overwhelming enthusiasm about the capacities of the people. Particularly the "peasants," their versatility and willingness to work hard, their quickness to learn, and so on.

Then I began to wonder. Is this just Lilienthal's congenital optimism, his notorious ability to see what he wants to see? Could I perhaps be a poor observer, in spite of my years of experience? And back and forth.

Then last night I got full confirmation of my findings, from a worldly wise source. Ray Male, a scrawny, delightful, witty gnome of a man, a guest for supper and the evening, reported the same conclusions as mine. But with these differences: he has spent months in Vietnam, in the field, in strikes, in work force crises. He has a special background for judging the "labor force," teachability and responsiveness, as State Labor Commissioner of New Jersey. He has that special access to what goes on in people's minds and in their conduct because he has run for elected office, and was Mayor of a small city, i.e., Princeton.

He is a man who loves life and comprehends people, as individuals, unlike the analytical students or the overintellectualized economists, anthropologists, etc., who think of people as an abstract subject for the writing of papers and learned articles.

And he was brimming full of anecdotes, pictures of what he has seen, which confirm these sanguine estimates of mine, though based on longer experience in Vietnam, and, I think, closer recent experience with working people.

I did throw out one "instance": how quick these yesterday's peasants are in repairing a piece of machinery, with a few absurd tools, setting up shop on a street corner of Saigon. Male would add other such examples, and he has a talent for bringing these people right into our living room.

This was Vietnam night at 88 Battle Road. The other guests included Richard Holbrooke and his tall, handsome wife and a sad-faced South Carolinian, John T. McAlister, a Ph.D. in International Studies. Scholarly and at times incomprehensible because the jargon of the social sciences is so abstract and special. It throws me. Suddenly, without any introduction, McAlister started telling of a "voyage" he took up the Mekong River, from near Saigon, as a young Navy Ensign, shoving a fleet of Landing Craft (LCM) up the river, threading them through the uncharted stream and then over the falls to Cambodia. The mission: to deliver these clumsy craft to the "Cambodian Navy." He spoke in his slightly drawling southern speech, the scholar was submerged for a half hour by an earthy country boy's tale of an outlandish adventure.

Bill Marvel and I had had no opportunity since my return to talk about the great buzz of things he, Herman Wells, and Education and World Affairs (EWA) have been in the middle of since we left for Hawaii in mid-January, and particularly their busyness in Washington at the very top of the Government.

The morsel that interested me most was a meeting, called by McGeorge Bundy, of all the major foundations (George Harrar of Rockefeller, Case of Sloan, etc.) to discuss with EWA the noisome mess—so the public must think, at least—arising from the "revelation" that the CIA (public synonym for cloak and dagger and clandestine spooking) was subsidizing just about every organization except possibly the Epworth League—and doing much of it through a maze of "fronts," small tax-exempt foundations, mostly, and some not so small. In view of the danger that the Ford Foundation is in, from such revelations about the use or misuse of foundations as covers for intelligence efforts, Bundy is trying, constructively, to explore some way whereby the activities "exposed" could be publicly supported by some agency other than the CIA, asking EWA to consider acting as a kind of negotiator among the foundations and the Government.

My misgivings about CIA financing—and perhaps use—of outwardly charitable or educational institutions go back a long way. They stem from that conversation almost three years ago in the library of the Council on Foreign Relations about the fact that the African-American Institute was having a harder time raising money now that CIA support had been withdrawn. From then on I pestered EWA for out and out categorical denials about our EWA Hong Kong Center and other activities.

And, so Bill says, the biggest revelation is yet to come: that the Asia Foundation, with branches throughout that continent, is the biggest recipient of CIA funds.

Why CIA covertly supports the National Student Society, for example, rather than having them openly backed if such support is justified (and doubtless it is, in many instances), isn't hard to see. CIA, and anything in the Defense Department, can get money easily and doesn't really have to account for it. It is the easy way, and that appeals to a certain kind of bureaucrat who doesn't relish having to go before Congressional committees to explain himself and be abused. It *may* be easier that way, *until* the storm breaks—and apparently it is breaking all over the place. A bad situation.

Bill reported an episode that is somewhat amusing of his visit in Washington. Secretary John Gardner, Doug Cater, and the EWA officers were having luncheon in the Fish Room at the White House the Monday I was with the President. They were discussing the International Education Bill, on which EWA has been helping.

Shortly after I left the President's office, the President went to the Fish Room, pulled up a chair, and was expected to stay for five minutes. Instead he talked to the EWA contingent at length, mostly, according to Bill, about Vietnam, still apparently steamed up about what I had said to him and at the press conference. "Your name came up at least five times though it had nothing to do with the International Education Bill. And then he pulled out a three-page typed letter from his inside pocket and read the entire thing to us; it was a strong attack on the press treatment of the Vietnam situation, and was particularly strong about the press corps in Saigon."

This, of course, was *the very same letter* that the President had read every word of to me and Bob Komer just a few minutes before. What a curiously strong feeling he has about the press, and what a strange squandering of the time of a man whose time and energies are about all that protect all of us.

MARCH 17, 1967
PRINCETON

Last weekend, under a warm and caressing sun of first spring, I drew away the light cover of salt hay from our beloved garden. As always, I'm impatient. This morning the whole world, garden and all, is covered with a deep snow, and a wild blizzard is in charge, the swirling snow filling the air, erasing the false spring.

But inside of me it is spring. And that despite a television gesture from Eric Sevareid last evening. His comment: President Johnson, at a time when half the population is twenty-eight or younger, the day of the young, is turning to old men of experience. This apropos the naming of Ellsworth Bunker, the seventy-three-year-old newlywed, to the toughest job in the diplomatic service, to Saigon. And then Eric went through the list of other "elderly" on whom Johnson is relying. But though I was included it almost made me seem a juvenile: Harriman at seventy-five, Acheson seventy-three, Jack McCloy at seventy-one. Still, to be "officially" described as "elderly" was amusing.

A phone call from David at dinner time. Wanted to make sure I knew how strongly, deeply, he felt against my taking responsibility for this economic development task in Vietnam. I had become part of the "war machine"; the American course of action in Vietnam is wholly "evil"; "those people" (meaning the President, Secretary of State, etc.) were doing a thing that was "evil and morally wrong."

The occasion for this statement, given in a voice that was completely under control but full of emotion, was the word that I was going to Guam with the Presidential party.

David made the point that when I first spoke to him about the possibility of undertaking the Vietnam project I had "resisted," seemed most reluctant, and he had assumed this meant that I didn't approve of the Administration, but was looking for a way out of a commitment it would be hard to "resist"; that I was concerned, as he was, that even though it was "postwar planning" I would be "used" as propaganda to "ameliorate" the ugly image of the Vietnam military operation.

He just wanted to be sure that I knew to what extent he was opposed to the whole business, so much so that he felt great sorrow that his father should have anything to do with it and with "those people." However my role was described, he said, I have allowed myself to be made part of the entire apparatus, because to some people my participation, in whatever role, would give a better appearance to this immoral business than it might otherwise have.

I didn't attempt to argue the merits; the emotional tone was too high to attempt this in any sustained way, particularly over the phone. But I had to declare how I feel about washing my hands of an issue, "standing aloof" when the going is tough, rather than trying to assert such influence as I can to make an admittedly bad situation better (and is any violence or warfare or terrorism or bloodshed ever good?).

As Helen and I talked this over afterward she reminded me of how in the past I had not stayed out of ugly issues in order to keep my own record pure and unsullied. When I first went to the Tennessee Valley I confronted a wicked political dynasty, men such as Ed Crump and Senator McKellar; in Mississippi, John Rankin and That Man Bilbo; in Alabama, Bibbs Graves. I had a choice: to do my work or to stand aloof so no one could say I had dirtied my hands by being seen on the same platform or at the same meeting or luncheon with such low fellows. I had enough self-assurance, enough confidence in my own integrity, to go ahead. I tried to change the things I abhorred because I had faith in the rank and file people, those most immediately affected by TVA. And the people of the Valley as time went on sided with me and with TVA against the elected leaders of the Valley, and they elected new young men of the first quality—men like Lister Hill, Estes Kefauver, Albert Gore, John Sparkman—to replace the ones I had found in the saddle.

And in Persia I had at first to deal with the worst kind of landlord and knew that I was surrounded by some corrupt officials. I could have washed my hands of the whole thing, rather than be seen in public with "those people." But Khuzistan became a changed place, and a generation of young leaders of a far better stripe has grown up. My own reputation wasn't damaged, and the peaceful revolution now under way in that country might not have occurred if I had refused to *risk* my good name, to risk my being used as a cover for what I had as much repugnance for as anyone could have.

I sorrow that this has happened between David and me. But I admire his manliness in speaking out about his feelings, in the strongest kind of condemnation of what I am doing, and therefore of me. I feel a continuing warmth for him, despite what I feel is an unrealistic view, for I love this man, and love can stand almost any strain.

MARCH 19, 1967
5 A.M. (EST)
ABOARD "AIR FORCE ONE," THE PRESIDENT'S PLANE

The President came aboard looking ten feet tall as he shook my hand, greeted me, went into his "quarters," and asked: "What time do we take off? Midnight?" He was told 11:30, and soon we were on our way.

My very comfortable berth is way forward; I have just gotten up for a drink. Spread out before the pilots, with their many-colored Xmas tree panel lights, is San Francisco. But we will go on for another five hours to Hickam Field for an hour's refueling and then on to Guam: about nineteen hours of straight flying.

Practically everybody in the Government is on this plane. Aft, it looks like the New York shuttle, five abreast, on a Monday morning.

9 A.M. (EST)

A good night's sleep, in "bed" eight hours. After refueling at dawn at Hickam Field, on to Guam. We have been flying virtually continuously now fifteen and a half hours, still another four and a half to go.

I squirm a bit when I think that the "fate" (to use fancy rhetoric, but hardly overstated) of millions will depend pretty largely on the brains and emotional clarity of the occupants of "Air Force One," a group of experienced, well-intentioned men, some driven by that terrific inner compulsion called ambition, some by a sense of craftsmanship, but all of us clearly inadequate to the *needs for an accommodation* in that agonized little country that has become the focus of the world's fears.

What a lot of people it takes to man such an expedition as this. In the President's quarters, the Secretaries of State and Defense, with their secretaries. Back here, the Rostows, Komers, Gauds—the professional administrators. And the technicians manning a complete system by which messages keep pouring in, printed on two Telex kind of machines, telephones, etc. Two flight crews. Typewriters clacking back of me, operated by two secretaries typing the many revisions of public statements, which probably the President will disregard!

The agenda for the conference on Guam, so I'm told, calls for a statement on "postwar planning and development." I suggested that Professor Thuc lead off, and I will probably pull the heavier oar. I have warned everyone around me in this cabin that I don't believe in making public predictions at this point; they come home to roost, if made long before you can show some results. But if I am in fact called upon, it will be a good opportunity to emphasize the joint, cooperative character of the economic planning undertaking between Vietnam and the U.S., to express the hope to Premier Ky that Professor Thuc gets ample support from the professional economists, agriculturists, and engineers, and to draw some kind of line between long-term and immediate development ideas.

The past few hours I have been reading the big volume of briefing papers rather carefully. It is the old story: one man must create some definite policy or concrete action out of the *chaos* of many "statements of facts" or presentations about "options" (i.e., not taking a definite line of action). How much attention the President—or the Secretary of State, for that matter—will pay to this stack of papers is a question. He must trust his hunch about the way what he says will affect the profound doubts of the American people (which are more than considerable), and how those same words will be taken in Peking and Moscow.

Rostow comes steaming out of the President's quarters (having first put on his shoes, pulled up his tie, smoothed down his hair). "Now, this is what the President has to have prepared for him." I assume this is something to be said as he gets off the plane and greets the Vietnamese—if I'm correct that they will be there when we arrive.

I find it hard to throw myself into the spirit of the occasion. Let the professional staffers enjoy this all they please; I have had enough of it for a lifetime. Too much of a façade for my present sense of perspective and independence.

It is 9:15 in the morning of Monday! I feel I have lived through a day, and here there is to be a working lunch, a 3 to 5 P.M. meeting with Chairman Thieu and Prime Minister Ky, then a whole series of "discussions," by Westmoreland, Komer, and Thuc and me. And then a dinner, I suppose.

I have just come from a session in the President's big conference room on this aircraft—and what a performance he put on. A tough football coach between the halves, with his boys not doing so well, giving them the devil and then the praise. What a dynamo this man from Texas is.

How sensitive he is to how the press has been playing up the ugly side, to the way the mothers back in Johnson City, Texas, react when Secretary McNamara walks out of a Congressional hearing and says that "pacification" may take ten years or more ("My boy has to be out there for ten years; let's throw that Johnson out").

The setting: a kidney-shaped desk, the huge President in a heavily padded high-backed swivel chair, the fourteen or so of us sitting around him, he in a grey heavily embroidered shirt with the tails on the outside: Texas or Philippine? There never was a Filipino as big as this huge figure using a hog caller voice quite different from the solemn, almost quiet tones of some of the recent TV speeches.

"There'll be eighty newsmen there. Most of them are leftist and pacifist, and they get paid by the column inch. So you fellows give them just one opening and they will turn this meeting, that's intended to be constructive, into a war council. They are writing stories that what we are going to decide here is what other targets we should select. I have got more targets right now than I can use.

"At the Honolulu conference at the very end Peter Lisagor [*Chicago Daily News*] asked Ky a question about whether the Viet Cong would be included in any government that was coming and Ky let loose with that terrible belligerent statement—and bang, there went the whole conference down the drain.

"Just the other day the Secretary of State and Bob [McNamara] and I in my press conference made three different statements that didn't jibe at all, and only the good Lord saved us from getting hell beat out of us.

"So this time I'm saying *nothing* except these written statements that you are preparing for me, and no one is to answer questions from the press except Secretary Rusk and Secretary McNamara; no one, hear?"

Here he spun his chair around, leaned over, and looked hard at me. "No, except Dave Lilienthal—and he can talk all he pleases about the future, the great things that can come, like he did in that press conference in my office that was badly covered. Dave, you give them some of that philosophy, that good TVA philosophy like your letter to me. As much as you want."

Rostow (now Director of the National Security Council and very tense) said to me that the *New York Times* had requested an opportunity to interview me with Professor Thuc, and that the President had approved the idea. I said this would be all right, if I was kept entirely out of any discussion of "pacification"—which I don't care for at all, either as to the methods or the semantics. I got the President's permission, staying afterward to do so, that the Press Secretary omit my name completely from anything to do with that subject.

"The three greatest battles of this war," said the President in a tremendous voice, clear above the roar of the jet engines (hours and hours of them and they still are wearing on one): "The first big battle in this war was the election for members of the Constituent Assembly; the second was the adoption of a Constitution, just yesterday; and the third will be the election of a President, and I hope that third can be mighty soon."

I broke in to say that the village council elections, scheduled for early April, should provide a dramatic picture for correspondents and TV cameras if they really are interested in a picture of an "emerging democracy." The President talked about that some, but seems to feel that the preoccupation with combat stories and pictures, as well as a desire to irritate the Administration, is so strong in this press and TV corps that they may just scrap anything that looks "constructive."

The new Director of the CIA, [Richard] "Slim" Helms, said he thought he had a couple rabbits up his hat in ways to provide protection against the VC in some of the villages. Helms is a shrewd-looking man, but as far from the "professional" intelligence operator of the movies as one can imagine.

I was asked to confer with Thuc and see if I could get him to speak at the big conference "for only two or three minutes." Sometimes the Vietnamese get started and it is hard for them to stop. Just how I am to accomplish this abbreviation wasn't explained, but on the occasions when Thuc and I have spoken together, he struck me as very brief and telling, in his modest way. So we'll see. But this doesn't square with the President's desire that I spread joy—perhaps I can manage it, but two or three minutes isn't going to go far.

When the President asked me to draw a picture of the wonderful things that *could* be done, I interjected that we had to be careful about predictions. I had in mind the predictions about how long the war would last, how we were winning, etc., that have led to widespread disbelief (because they were successively proved wrong). The President, raising his eyebrows and wheeling around at me, commented: "Of course, you have to be judicious about it."

You can't fight a war, and an ugly and unusual kind of war, and still make it look good. But the President is dead right that since our purpose is not conquest but peace and then U.S. withdrawal, the constructive, beneficial things we are doing deserve a hearing.

But I haven't a definite idea right now what I can say, except to express confidence and the kind of hope that is taken more seriously from me, with my background, than from some of the other anxious faces around that airborne council table.

MARCH 20, 1967
NIMITZ HILL, GUAM

Around a great oval table a remarkable and a fateful meeting: the President and his group, opposite General Thieu, the young-looking Chief of State, and Prime Minister Ky, looking tiny in the presence of the great hulk of a Texan across the table.

The President was at his very best. He dutifully read the statements dished out for him by that mass of helpers as the plane crossed the Pacific, read them in a very low and uninflected voice, *showing no interest* or spark. Then he went into his own act, and it was evident that the Vietnamese understood just what he was saying, in a relaxed way, kidding himself, making fun of his predicament with the American voting public, soothingly calling on the Vietnamese leaders, without saying so directly, to reconcile their differences with the Viet Cong ("bring them into your fold"). "And if anyone can find a way to negotiate with Hanoi, it won't be U Thant or the Pope or Kosygin or some of my Senators; it will be you folks."

He was great, and everyone there felt it.

That the President understands the limitations of military action, and that the Vietnamese across the oval table partly grasp it, wasn't made at all clear in later news reports. But as the President leaned across the broad table I saw a political leader—a seasoned "politician"—at his best, because he was functioning as a persuader; not a teacher with superior knowledge, not a military ally, but talking as one politician to another.

"Of the great 'military victories' that must be won," he said, "you have just brought to us here one of the most important, in this completed Constitution agreed upon almost unanimously last night in Saigon. A Constitution that was agreed upon because of compromises, because you understand the importance of unity. As a matter of fact [he added ruefully] you have done a better job on unity than *I* have, back home. Another victory will be the election of a President—and you have moved that election up to August, though this early a date makes for problems for you. And then another military victory will be when you elect a legislative body."

A picture flashed into my mind of the achievement of the Articles of Confederation by the colonists, the war against Britain still on, the product of compromise and the need for unity.

After the Chief of State, General Thieu, had read a long statement, Prime Minister Ky read a document directed as much or more to his fellow Vietnamese as to us. Then after the head of the Vietnamese Army spoke in a dull way about nothing new, the President looked around at me, seated in the second row behind the principals, motioning me to take a seat at the table, Rusk on my left, Bunker on my right.

Then Professor Thuc spoke, glowingly, of the effect of my visit a few weeks ago in dispelling "uncertainty" about the future of development and how closely alike he and I saw these problems, how political questions needed to have the setting of the facts which we would uncover but which were not yet known. And how the two groups expected to go about their problems, how much "enthusiasm" there was among all kinds of people "since Dr. Lilienthal came to Vietnam."

Professor Thuc made me out a kind of Billy Graham; before I came there was uncertainty and even fear of the consequences of a postwar planning effort; but my visit changed all that, so he said, in a winning way.

The President's face wore that special half-grin of satisfaction and amusement that is so typically his. "I hope some of Mr. Lilienthal's enthusiasm can wear off on some people in the U.S.," he said, and then asked me to say something.

I said we were at the very beginning, so there was not much to add to what Thuc had said. But I wanted to emphasize that I thought it basic that the two development groups "live in the same suit of clothes—in fact that is about what we are doing, occupying the same building and set of offices. But I do want to add a word about the prospects for development. The Vietnamese are extraordinary people. Development depends mostly upon the spirit of people and not upon elaborate reports." Then I said how little cowed I found them. "I have found more fear and timidity at my club in New York than I found in some of the villages that had been exposed to the ravages of attack by the Viet Cong." All of this received in complete silence around the board.

I didn't have a statement to read, as almost everyone else did, and I had junked such notes as I made. But it went well. Bunker, Lodge, Harriman et al. spoke to me afterward about it as a "moving statement."

Bunker's quiet "I want to see you in New York if possible" pleased me immensely. I think he sees the importance of not jamming things down the Vietnamese throats (though I doubt if this *could* be done) better than some of the more military minded or bureaucratic minded people on the U.S. side of that table.

MARCH 21, 1967
4 A.M.
GUAM

Guam has been on the edge of a typhoon these past several days. The wind blows like mad on this hill overlooking, at a distance, the great harbor and the limitless Pacific, blows so hard and noisily that sleep isn't easy.

5 A.M.

Out of this extraordinary experience so many pictures. For example: The President half-submerged in a low divan, in his quarters, as we awaited dinner, his mountainous bulk turned halfway so he almost hid the tiny Prime Minister Ky, and on Ky's other side the also not inconsiderable bulk of the Secretary of State. Ky listening and looking like anything but the masterful and cool character who "received" me in that beautiful Palace in Saigon three weeks or so ago.

The occasion for this high-powered huddle (with McNamara hovering attendance) was a paragraph or so in Ky's prepared remarks to the joint meeting yesterday afternoon. "How long," Ky had asked, would the North Vietnamese and the Viet Cong be permitted the "sanctuary" of Laos, into which to retreat and reform and infiltrate into South Vietnam? How long until our B-52s will hit them in that sanctuary of Laos, which is helping to destroy the lives of Vietnamese and American fighting men? And so on. Ky released his entire speech to this "confidential" conference to the press. How that must have made the President boil, after the way he had emphasized, as we speeded 600 miles an hour toward our Guam rendezvous, that we wanted not to make this a war council, as the papers already describe it around the world, but to stress the protection of the peasants, the so-called (and *badly* called, in my opinion) pacification program.

Hence the two outsize statesmen trying to explain to the diminutive man between them how inflammatory his statement had been. Ky's whole body, in that low sofa, was less than the size of the President's shoulders; his eyes cast downward like a boy being scolded.

Many pictures.

A strange place, Guam, to select for a peaceful goals conference. This is the main base for the B-52, the greatest bomber in history; it is from here, on a huge field we shall see today, that these aerial monsters start with their store of bombs to pound North Vietnam. And Guam is as well the home of a fleet of Polaris submarines that patrol the China coast. A modern citadel, extending American power as Singapore once extended the Asian power of the British Empire.

5:30 P.M.
LEAVING GUAM ABOARD "AIR FORCE ONE"

All this splendid professionalism about this war, the apparent impersonality of secret military expositions about future target and estimated "gains" and casualties, the look of agony on the face of the President, the harassed and puzzled look on the no longer springy Secretary McNamara, the sight of the great vulture-like B-52s with their droopy aluminum wings, the jaunty soldier-like bearing and burning eyes of General Westmoreland—add it all up (and more that I have heard and seen these several days) and I find myself sad, sad, sad. Unutterably sad.

It has been a unique drama that I have been "privileged" to see. These leaders—Johnson and his advisors—are compassionate and greatly skilled and thoroughly human individuals. They bear no remote resemblance to the war lovers, not the remotest. And the shadow of public "misunderstanding" and criticism, in the U.S. where it counts, and around the world where it hurts, is constantly hovering over men who have at their disposal greater destructive power than men have ever had, and greater resources of every kind. As McNamara said to me this noon, "We have poured more bomb loads onto North Vietnam than in the whole of World War II and yet we have no sign that it has shaken their will to resist, none."

This comment by the brilliant civilian head of our great military establishment brings to mind the picture of the briefing session that went on all morning, this one attended only by Americans. The vast oval table, the charts, the maps, the Colonels and Generals, the President slouched in his great high-back swivel chair. Rusk imperturbable, McNamara (the only man in shirtsleeves, his shirt open at the neck) completely silent, asking not one question, making not one comment as the Air Force officers went through their paces, pointers in hand. This North Vietnamese "target" and that pointed out. The President's invariable question as to each proposed target: what is the cost, in men, in civilians, in American planes?

But the most memorable picture was that of Westmoreland. A man with a face and manner so far removed from that of a killer, the face almost of a professor of political science, or, come to think of it, a grandfatherly Eisenhower. Standing before the huge map, discussing the technical deployment in a matter-of-fact professional voice. In answer to a question—or did he volunteer it?—came the statement: "As things now stand it may take ten years." The look on the President's face! (I was seated to his right, where I could see him in profile.) Ten years, my God! I admired Westmoreland's candor; it didn't sound to me like a "sales" argument, the kind that one has come to expect at appropriation time before Congressional committees, but the honest judgment of an open-faced South Carolina country boy who "made it" at West Point, and through internal Army politics, to the most important military command since the Korean War. Ten years. I imagined I could read the President's mind: think of the mothers of eight-year-old kids; could they possibly face up to that? And should the bombing be greatly increased, as the soldiers recommended, to avoid that impossible ten-year agony?

Seated across the aisle from me, alone, is a grey figure of eminence, Averell Harriman. He comes on this long and tiring trip, moving more slowly than of yore, perhaps, but what I notice particularly is the sad, almost Newfoundland dog look in his eyes. He too is puzzled—and yet he has dealt with Stalin, Molotov, Mossadeqh—all the hard nuts to crack through the years. He sits there poring over position papers—of which we have had so many, signifying not nothing, but (I fear) little.

President Johnson's colloquy, or exposition, to the Vietnam leadership yesterday afternoon—how I wish that could be made a public record complete with his expressions. What a superb example it was of a man reaching out—from an utterly different background and assumptions—to make other men understand *his* problem, which is that of a powerful man who could level Hanoi and Peking overnight, and yet is constrained by that watchdog of democracy, American public opinion.

Ambassador Porter wasn't included in this gathering, though Lodge and his successor, Bunker, and Locke, Porter's successor, were. Why? There may be a simple explanation; perhaps someone had to be left to care for the store. But I wonder if Porter's intelligent dissent and criticism of the military policy and posture—which I recorded some few weeks ago—may have been the reason. A stronger and more independent man I have never met in the Foreign Service. It would be a great pity if his independent criticism of the military (and Rusk's) position was a bit too much for them. Not one word of praise for him from the President during the whole business of showering encomiums on Lodge (who performed brilliantly today in explaining the Vietnam political situation), and on Bunker and Locke.

History may tell. I noticed that Komer, given new duties and prestige, and duties for the "pacification" program, was quite sour about the loss of Porter. Good sign.

The burden of a brilliant and surprisingly forceful statement to the conference this noon by Cabot Lodge was this: what Vietnam needs—and doesn't have—are modern politicians.

Lodge didn't say "statesmen"; and this was to his credit, and the credit of good sense and vast experience. Politicians. And he held out no hope that enough of this breed could be raised between now and the fall elections in Vietnam, although Ky *was* displaying some of the characteristics: long *patient* efforts to keep the military from dividing among themselves; studied efforts to understand Johnson's political problems in his country.

The President's physician sits in the row just ahead of me. One of the young women who travel in the President's quarters has just asked for sleeping pills for him. Even the great and mighty and apparently inexhaustible have to let down somehow.

We barely stopped in Honolulu—forty minutes—and with a tail wind of fifty miles we should be in Washington by six—only three hours hence. I have had precious little sleep—did stretch out in my clothes for a couple hours. But Ellsworth Bunker, six years my senior and able to take over the most difficult assignment of his career, sat up reading all night and looks fresh as fresh.

A big flurry in the seats just ahead of me. Rusk, with that half-smile, just as imperturbable in his grey rumpled pajamas as in a rumpled dinner jacket (he is anything but a sleek, dapper man, that one, and this I like), pushed his heavy glasses down over his nose and started writing on a pad; McNamara, just out of a bunk, looking serious but perky; Walt Rostow, the bouncy ebullient member of the cast, running back and forth from the "Communications Center."

Helms, with whom I had been visiting, explained the to-do. The President early in February had written a personal letter to Ho Chi Minh proposing negotiation; the "flying ticker" has just reported that he publicly released the President's letter and is now replying: stop bombing; get out of Vietnam; etc. So when the President gets to Andrews Field he will make a statement.

The President appeared in the doorway, filling this end of the plane with his enormous *presence.* Gave me a quiet good morning, and with a half-grin, as if the Ho Chi Minh letter release fits his book, said, "I *have* asked for negotiation; it gets nowhere because of Hanoi."

Last evening a long long "listen" to Averell Harriman, who seemed in a talking mood. "No," he said, "I have never encountered as complex a puzzle as this one." I could see in his somber mien what I thought were pictures of his other difficult "negotiations" with difficult statesmen.

Helms is a slender, youthful man, one who outwardly doesn't take himself as solemnly as some of his predecessors did (e.g., Allen Dulles). Good hard sense. But he did look somber when I spoke of how many Americans feel an unwarranted sense of guilt about their country and downgrade its capabilities. A cloud went over his face as he cited a further comment of Westmoreland's yesterday: "If the VC doesn't crumble and if we don't pound Hanoi harder, the war could last indefinitely."

Toward the end of the afternoon the President asked six or eight of us to come into his apartment: the Secretaries, Bunker, Helms, Rostow, Harriman, John McNaughton [Assistant Secretary of Defense, later Secretary of the Navy]. They moved aside a half-circular partition, put up a movie screen, and showed a Chinese film, in high propaganda style, about the preparations for and the explosion of the first two Chinese nuclear weapons. In color, with plenty of good cheer, scenes of happy dancing Chinese girls and wildly enthusiastic boys. But what astounded me were the close-ups of the highly sophisticated measurement devices. No primitive society could produce those. If it is the Russians who provided them to the Chinese, they must now view this picture of the terrifying mushroom cloud with something less than calm.

As we filed out, Dean Rusk smiled wanly at me and repeated what he had said the other day in his office—now against this spectacular background of Chinese "glory": "Too bad we never got your Acheson-Lilienthal control plan accepted." The understatement of all time, I'd say.

10 P.M.
AT THE HAY ADAMS, WASHINGTON

All that efficiency, all those brains, the elaborate Secret Service and White House staff: and damn if they didn't lose my suitcase! Periodic calls from the White House since I got here at 7:30: "We are tracing it; we think maybe General Maxwell Taylor's driver took it by mistake," etc. I find this more hilarious than exasperating, though I may not think so by morning. And they couldn't find my beat-up hat, as we were all getting ourselves ready to walk down the ramp behind the President. The reason: Ave Harriman was wearing it, down over his ears, too! And thus in the midst of great events little things happen that display the "powerful" as damned human.

How the Captain brought "Air Force One" down at Andrews Field is more than I can guess, for we saw the runway lights only five seconds before we touched down. The fog was so dense that the chopper into which the President and some of us were put for the last leg of the voyage got lost (operates by contact, I assume). Finally found the river, then passed within spitting distance of the Washington Monument and eased us onto the White House lawn.

Nicholas Katzenbach, now Under Secretary of State, greeted the President at the chopper. A man with as lively and alert a face as ever I have seen. He was pleased as punch about the disclosure that Ho Chi Minh had rejected the President's secret letter of February 8th, proposing negotiation. "That takes care of the credibility-gap talk," said he.

How sensitive they are in the Administration to that charge. This will set the critics back, for the President's letter to Ho Chi Minh was written at the time when the President was being charged with lying and bad faith in saying that he wanted negotiation.

MARCH 26, 1967
PRINCETON

Crocuses spreading their golden trumpets through the snow, melting at last under a belated spring sun.

The newspaper reports of the Guam conference were so thin and even contemptuous ("tired men," "nothing happened," "Ky steals the show," etc.) that I was shocked, for how else than through the press does the American public learn about anything except the military operations; and these they see day after day: the first war fought in the living rooms of an entire population.

My puny attempt to give some perspective on the historic significance of that meeting was pretty much a flop. NBC sent Bill Ryan and a crew out here Thursday afternoon. I spoke my piece, but when it was shown yesterday it had been so abbreviated and edited that I didn't think much came through.

One pertinent question Ryan put to me, and my response, does, however, seem worthy of inclusion here:

"Q. How viable a country can South Vietnam become without North Vietnam?"

"A. The South needs the North and the North needs the South in an economic sense. The North has aggressive people, they have industries, some of them have been injured, but these are repairable. The South has great sources of food, which the North does not have. These two countries need each other and, when countries need each other that much, first you begin to trade and then perhaps some kind of political rapprochement appears. . . . All Southeast Asia in a way is a unit. We're really thinking about the emerging of a new society in Southeast Asia, and that takes time."

Perhaps only the President can say the things I want said and get any kind of hearing.

MARCH 27, 1967
NEW YORK

I received a long and eloquent letter from David, dated March 24th, from Edgartown, spelling out his reasons for so strongly opposing my accepting the Vietnam postwar economic development role.

I concluded not to reply to the letter, thinking this would only increase the tension between us.

[Helen, wholly on her own initiative, drafted a letter; she too concluded not to send it; her remarkable letter has been preserved but will not be part of the published *Journals*.]

MARCH 30, 1967
NEW YORK

Reading the classic book on the National Liberation Front§ by Douglas Pike, who lived in Vietnam for six years. Two things struck me:

"If there was an essence of the NLF indoctrination effort . . . if there was one emotion the leadership found of greater utility than all others combined, if there was one personality trait that differentiated the Vietnamese of the two camps, indeed if one were obliged to write the history of the NLF in a single word, it would be *hate*. . . .

"Apparently the effort by the NLF was an attempt to copy the Chinese, who deliberately, efficiently and effectively had put hate to work. Lucian Pye noted that 'no other political culture places as much stress upon the emotion of hate as does the Chinese.'"

And the scholarly Pike, in his (August, 1966) Preface, concludes:

"My heart goes out to the Vietnamese people—who have been sold out again and again, whose long history could be written in terms of betrayal and who, based on this long and bitter experience, can only expect that *eventually America too will sell them out* [my italics]. If America betrays the Vietnamese people by abandoning them, she betrays her own heritage."

Why in hell should I or anyone else feel so defensive about our protection of the Vietnamese people? Yet that is what one gets on all sides these days, and some able people have been brainwashed to accept as noble a picture of America abandoning people who have had to fight a doctrine of "hate," a doctrine that Hitler and Stalin found so useful—for a time.

§ *Viet Cong: The Organization and Techniques of the National Liberation Front of South Vietnam*, Cambridge, Mass., MIT Press, 1966.

MARCH 31, 1967
8:30 A.M.
NEW YORK

A sense of being fully alive, overwhelming moments of well-being, an acute awareness of how delicious are the little things around one—how sad I am for those who, moping and whining about what an "alienated" and horrid country this is, miss all of that.

Our first "report" from the five men D&R now has in Vietnam. A long document, a kind of shopping list of questions and possibilities, but an excellent first approximation of a comprehensive job.

4:15 P.M.
ON THE PENNSYLVANIA TO PRINCETON

Luncheon conference with Ellsworth Bunker at the Century.

Tall, outwardly reserved man, looking about sixty, erect, bending slightly forward as he walks. The "cool" gives way to a warm smile. Now it is "Dave"—Mister doesn't last long with me.

Took him in to shake hands with Charles Collingwood and grinning, chunky Ted White, the writer, both of whom will see him in Saigon this spring.

Collingwood asked Bunker: "I visited in Washington yesterday with Bob Komer; is he on your organization chart?" "Everyone is on my organization chart," said Bunker. People will find that Bunker is no Lodge, and not given to dividing authority; easily the strongest man in the Foreign Service, perhaps in the whole government except for the President.

After the soup I spoke to Bunker of "my idea": fitting our development planning into the most important fact about Vietnam, as I saw it: the establishing of the beginnings of a *political framework.* The great hope—perhaps the only solid one, I thought—was that the dissident Vietnamese people join in the task of nation-building, that the creation of a new government, after elections this October, provided for a better course than any form of military action (pacification, "clearing and holding," etc.). But if all the newly elected government has to offer the dissidents is political rhetoric, however noble or true (habeas corpus, freedom of speech, freedom of the press, etc.), that would mean very little *to the people in the villages.*

What the new government, the legislature, the new politicians must offer are concrete things that mean something in people's everyday lives. And *they*, the new political leaders at *all* levels, must be given credit for the concrete program of development which will put flesh on the bones of the Constitution's terms: farm-to-market roads, a program for regional development in the Delta, the forest areas, etc.

I was delighted to see that Bunker concurred. "You are so right," he said, his cool grey eyes glowing. "Sukarno told me, in Indonesia: ◖ the romance of revolution—that is where the future lies. And look at Sukarno now." He grinned with the satisfaction he must feel to have worked out that sticky and "impossible" situation.

"I am assuming," I said, "that one of the lines of effort you will follow, with your experience in getting people together, will be making it worthwhile for those outside the family in South Vietnam to return to the fold, even perhaps the hard core Viet Cong, but certainly those not fully committed. The elections should help, I would guess. But they must be followed, it seems to me, by something substantial—a development program."

"You are dead right," Bunker replied. "There isn't time to win the country over by military measures and 'pacification' alone; unless the President has made real progress within a year he will have a very tough time in the election. But what about the time element? Can you come up with ideas, specific places where development can be done by the time the new government has been elected this fall?"

I said I thought we could. Our technical people will want to work things out to the third decimal point before proposing anything, but I have found that my hunches—after a lot of experience—are better than the three-decimal technical studies, which can come afterward to confirm the hunches. He laughed: "That is the way it was with me in thirty-four years of private business."

But I will have trouble with my staff people just the same. There is an instinct to be negative, automatically, at first. Bothers me, that *habit* of seeing the difficulties before seeing the plus side of a new idea.

Bunker leaned over the table, looked at me quizzically, and then said: "You know, Dave, you have had the most fascinating career of any man alive. When I get through with this job, I'm going to come to you for a job."

APRIL 5, 1967
NEW YORK

Attended my first meeting of the directors of Development and Services Corporation, formed to renovate the Bedford-Stuyvesant region. Much mouthing of commonplaces (the eager young staff gathered on the edges) until a great straight-standing black man, with a brilliant

◖ Bunker had been U.S. Ambassador in Indonesia.

yellow-striped necktie, entered that room in J. H. Whitney's office—Frank Thomas, the first Negro Deputy Police Commissioner of New York. What an impressive, balanced, articulate man, giving out such a sense of power and wisdom. Made me and the rest of us directors look puny.

APRIL 7, 1967
NEW YORK

A visit with Paul Carroll, in charge of our job of developing the almost unpopulated spaces of the Southwest Ivory Coast. A compact man, very short but powerful-seeming, a genuine scientist in the field of tropical soils, but with the *presence* of a man of action—which he is, going off into the bush as he does. No complaints about living conditions for himself and his family. And he feels the soils he found, while leached and thin, as are most all West African soils, can be made, by special techniques, capable of holding nutrients and thereby made better than most in that region.

APRIL 12, 1967
NEW YORK

This noon I was Chairman of a special "panel" at a big luncheon meeting, part of a conference on world food problems sponsored by Jack Heinz. This was the shindig Heinz and I talked about at length in Pittsburgh early last November, and in my office since. I had intended to talk for five minutes at least about the new turn of events in Iran toward commercial agriculture—"agrobusiness"—which could give the Khuzistan program a shot in the arm and be a new and exciting turning point in our relations with Persia, but the other participants spoke with such deadly seriousness that it was up to me to make my points with stories. Funny how people remember my speeches over the years not because of the serious points but because of the stories—usually about the Tennessee Valley.

APRIL 14, 1967
PRINCETON

Yesterday, in Punta del Este, nineteen Presidents of Latin American countries adopted a lengthy resolution, a kind of charter of immediate and long-range goals.

In that historic rhetoric (thus far it is only rhetoric, and unhappily it may well never be more than that) are the marks of a thinking process and a recording of that thinking, in which I had a part, as did D&R and some of my associates.

This arose out of the long story of Felipe Herrera's discussions with us about economic integration, culminating in the report we prepared for the Inter-American Development Bank, released last September.

Chapter 2 of the "charter" Plan of Action at Punta del Este is headed "Multinational Action for Infrastructure Projects." Part of that chapter comes directly out of our report, and therefore reflects our thinking:

"We will lay the physical foundations for Latin-American economic integration through multinational projects.

"The undersigned Presidents affirm that economic integration demands a major sustained effort to build a land transportation network and to improve transportation systems of all kinds so as to open the way for the movement of both people and goods throughout the continent; to establish an adequate and efficient telecommunications system; to install interconnected power systems and to develop jointly international river basins, frontier regions, and economic areas which include the territory of two or more countries."

So it turns out I was *wrong* in thinking that the very holding of such a "summit" as that of the Presidents at Punta del Este would do more harm than it possibly could do good—from the viewpoint of the U.S. The meeting did considerable good: the endorsement at the political plateau (if not "summit"!) of the propositions such as the one I have quoted gave our report on multinational physical projects a nudge forward.

I was *wrong*, too, in fearing that the Presidential meeting would be devoted chiefly to unattainable demands by the Latins upon the U.S. Except for the Ecuadorian President (whose passionate oratory was about the only one that conforms to the usual pattern of baiting the Yankee), the tone throughout was moderate. And Johnson's performance came through as splendid: dignified, not taking the limelight and turning this into a Big Brother political show.

And finally, I was *wrong* in thinking that illusions would be nourished that economic integration was something easy. Which would have been damaging.

APRIL 16, 1967
PRINCETON

Dinner last night at Eric Goldman's, the American historian, until recently the "intellectual in residence" at the White House. He left the Capital quite disillusioned and I would gather that the disillusionment was on both sides, since Administration liaison with the intellectual community (one of his chief functions, supposedly) could hardly have been worse. The reasons for this intense disaffection are complex, and not ones that Goldman or anyone else could remedy by any technique of having a university man in the White House.

Goldman is hard at work on a book; I assume it will follow the current vogue and rip Johnson apart, which will undoubtedly insure it wide notice. But what might such a book do that could be constructive? After all, Johnson *is* President, and may be for another five years—though about this latter increasing doubts are expressed as the Vietnam war hangs on and promises to continue to hang on.

One guest was Eugene Wigner, the great Nobel Laureate in physics, one of the half dozen greatest figures in science of a half generation ago.

He seemed to be genuinely pleased by a chance to talk with me, and I soon found why. (Not that, in his bright-eyed way, he is not a very friendly kind of man—and *so* European, more precisely, so Hungarian, with his winning half bow as he meets people, his fascinated naïveté about ordinary, earthy human affairs.)

The reason—so I thought—Wigner grabbed hold of me and talked to me so intensely was that he is looking for converts to his present passionate, although almost unknown, campaign for a large-scale shelter program against atomic attack. When I said I thought such a program might upset or turn backward the gradual improvement in U.S. relations with the Soviet Union, he peered incredulously over his glasses and asked: "Don't you believe in protecting human life? Don't you favor an anti-missile missile program?"

That a huge effort, upsetting everything in American life, to build shelters throughout the country would be taken as an indication that we were preparing for the probability of *ourselves* attacking the Soviets—that point had been made by others, but he simply could not understand it.

I suppose he has written reams about such a program; I suppose the learned journals are full of it, with fierce debates between those—like [Linus] Pauling, I suppose, and [Edward] Teller—who are still reliving the time of the glorification of the atom when they were in the limelight along with anyone else who "helped bring on the atomic age." This phrase is the medal they wear, though it has less luster than of yore.

Nothing in theoretical physics qualifies a man to have an opinion about the effect on the prospects for peace of a gigantic shelter program.

I asked Wigner about the young physicists and progress in theoretical physics. Oh, the young men are wonderful, he said, the quizzical troubled look leaving his narrow face. He beamed. The famous quiet Wigner charm was irresistible. And then a shadow passed over his expressive eyes. "But the great days of physics are gone; they are gone and will never come again."

Why? "Not enough time to think, too many machines—the big atom smasher, $200 million in one machine; too much Federal Government money. Too many publications, too much to keep up with."

He referred to the lectures I gave here in Princeton some time ago—the Stafford Little Lectures. At the time he hadn't agreed with some of the things I said, particularly my reservations and skepticism about atomic power—for example, the doubts I expressed about the huge "breeder" program. Frederic de Hoffmann of General Dynamics was in to see him the other day; he and others doubt the value of pushing that breeder program; it is going too fast. There is more uranium in the world than was thought possible some time ago.

De Hoffmann's opinion I didn't consider too objective; probably the reputed shambles of General Dynamics' program, which he started and runs, has something to do with his point of view. But it is the first clue I have had that the roars of anger at my strictures—and particularly my satirical remarks about atomic power—in those lectures may be giving way to something like serious attention to facing the problems and solving them.

It troubles me to see how lightly and casually the increasing hazards of so many of these atomic power plants are taken. Especially when the recent Apollo space program's troubles turned on simple human carelessness, not some major scientific miscalculation.

When something like that happens, if it involves a large reactor located in a densely populated area, it will be little satisfaction for me to say: I tried to warn you. But perhaps my groans about hazards have had some effect—as a gadfly if nothing more. I notice that the Reactor Safeguards Review Board of the AEC, examining the safety conditions of the new huge TVA atomic plant, said some cautionary words, and one member wasn't satisfied with the design; there were references in their report (an "in-house" document, too) to the acknowledged emergency coolant failures anticipated even in a successful operation.

I feel as sad about the brutality and agony of the war in Vietnam as I have about any war I know about. I am depressed by the oversimplification of some of the critics, their lack of any substantial ideas that have the slightest chance of reducing violence or bringing the war to an end. These emotions are particularly strong in me at this moment because yesterday was the day of great peace demonstrations in New York and San Francisco.

In a carefully worded letter to the *New York Times* earlier this month, I set out my views about the political program within Vietnam that just might have a chance of bringing that accommodation among the Vietnamese people that no amount of either warfare or "peace" demonstration can bring.

This is what the letter, dated April 4, 1967, and addressed to Arthur Ochs Sulzberger, President and Publisher, said:

"During my recent visit to the countryside in Vietnam, and in the meetings at Guam, I thought I saw unmistakable signs of a beginning, at least, of what seems to me the very essence of the democratic process, which is the accommodation and reconciliation of conflicting human interests and opinions.

"So I was greatly heartened by the theme of the lead editorial in the *Times* of Sunday, the 2nd, and even more by the extensive news coverage of such things as the promulgation of the new Constitution and the holding of village council elections.

"I thought the editorial and the news coverage showed historical perspective, and a recognition of the heart of the problem faced by the people of Vietnam, that is a beginning on the road to finding their own way to an accommodation among themselves.

"The success of long-term comprehensive economic development—the task recently assigned, jointly, to a Vietnam non-governmental group and to Development and Resources Corporation—depends upon an indigenous political framework and indigenous initiative that, even during the terrible violence of war, are beginning to be seen at Vietnam.

"It is so easy for perfectionists . . . to belittle these beginnings, as your editorial did not; it is so easy for perfectionists to downgrade these efforts by anticipating the almost certain occasional setbacks in this process.

"For all the intellectual distinction among some of the perfectionists, they forget the lessons of our American story; for example, that the Articles of Confederation were seen at the time as a poor beginning. But wiser men, who rarely are perfectionists, encourage beginnings rather than sneer at them and downgrade them and, therefore, discourage them. The *Times* editorial does not at all underwrite these beginnings. But it does encourage those men of Vietnam and of America who are, I honestly believe, trying to devise, in the midst of this awful war, political and economic acts that may wither the roots of violence."

APRIL 19, 1967
NEW YORK

Very disappointed with the quality of some of the work our company has been producing recently. The Greater Dez Irrigation feasibility report is not only pedestrian in tone, it is lacking in perception about the vital points. The "pilot plant" (50,000 acres in the Khuzistan) is *not* like a chemical plant *pilot*, a test prior to scaling up. *It is itself a beginning of the process of development*, a beginning so important that when the 250,000 acres now under study are put into cultivation many of the things not in existence for the "pilot" operation should, by then, be going concerns, such as agricultural credit, health and sanitation organizations, organization of machinery depots and maintenance, etc.

But the crowning disappointment in the D&R staff report was the calculation of "benefits," part of that old worn out mechanistic concept of a ratio between cost and "benefit" in monetary terms. The basic assumption about rate of return on the projected investment in facilities (canals, etc.) was a twenty year period of development of the land; that twenty year period was selected because of the experience on the pilot area, yet almost in the same breath it was clear that the 250,000 acre development would be bound to be *quite superior* in performance to the smaller one. Yet the writers of the report blandly proceeded to stick to the twenty year basis, which resulted in a return far lower than justified by the results learned and achieved as a consequence of the initial pilot operation.

APRIL 22, 1967
PRINCETON

Just called Dorothea Greenbaum: "Tell your husband that he has a great future ahead of him as a lawyer. I predict he will keep coming up in his profession." She shrieked with laughter. "He's not here; I haven't seen him for a couple days, but I'll tell him. And come to dinner next Saturday."

All of this banter occasioned by the sensational story that fills this morning's *Times*: Stalin's daughter, Mrs. Svetlana Alliluyeva, arriving in New York yesterday. This morning (with page after page of the *Times* giving the details) it appears that Eddie, my Sunday morning walking companion, and our neighbor George Kennan, arranged for her coming to this city from Geneva.

That Eddie! Ten days ago he was seventy-seven years old. Yet he has been nursing the *Times* along through a trying near-strike, has just completed the wearying battle over the Manchester book about the Kennedys, on Harper's behalf, and in between carries on a social and business life that would exhaust any ordinary mortal!

It is great to see a man, at any age, able to carry such a load and do so gracefully.

From about nine o'clock this morning until two this afternoon, Dr. Richard G. Hewlett, "official historian" of AEC, and his associate, Dr. Francis Duncan, quizzed me about the three years during which "I was an atom." They sat at my semicircular desk, turning over a stack of cards with questions on them, following one query with another. I was surprised that my recollection *seemed* to be as good as it was about events and policy of more than fifteen years ago. I say "seemed," for I notice that I usually answered directly and explicitly—and then would often add, "but the documents of the time may show it wasn't the way I remember it." My questioners didn't seem to think so.

I told them how John Palfrey, a former AEC Commissioner, reviewing Volume II of my *Journals*, ended on a note that puzzled me. He said my alleged "disillusionment" with the peaceful atom was due—as I recall his *New York Times* review—to a *personal* wound, the rough handling I had during the Congressional hearings.

Both men agreed that I had expressed doubts about the peaceful atom very early in the AEC, and cited examples from statements I made while AEC Chairman: "Atomic civilian power is *not* just around the corner, not around two corners," etc. And as to my strong reservation about safety and the dangers of radioactive waste materials—fission products of long life—from an atomic power reactor, they recalled my initiative in establishing the Reactor Safeguard Committee; my opposition to locating the materials testing reactor at Argonne, near Chicago, and insisting that it be way out in the desert of Idaho at Arco; and the stir I made about the dangers of locating the Knolls Atomic Lab at Schenectady.

APRIL 23, 1967
PRINCETON

When I read criticism of the war—and the *Times* Letters to the Editor column and the articles are full of it, of course—I find myself re-examining my own beliefs, and my own involvement in Vietnam.

What the position of the most objective and thoughtful of these critics comes to is essentially: this is "none of our business," this conflict between Vietnamese, North and South. Yet isn't it part of our American faith to have a *world* conscience? Otherwise couldn't we say the same thing about hunger in India—none of our business? Fighting between India and Pakistan? None of our business?

Some of the critics come down to this point—that all these things *are* part of our business as human beings and as Americans, but not *as far* as we have gone in Vietnam. They refer particularly, of course, to military operations.

My involvement in Vietnam is of another kind. How can I say: I'll not have anything whatever to do with Vietnam's *future development* because I find the *war* wrong or distasteful or badly handled or misguided? How can I wash my hands of a constructive activity; how can I write myself out of having some influence *from the inside*, just because accepting support from the Johnson Administration, even in the most non-military activity, is equated by some with a sanctioning of the war?

I have been reading Harold Macmillan's memoirs—his account of the appeasement of Hitler by Chamberlain. *There* was arrogance for you; not Hitler's; his was more than arrogance. But Chamberlain's conviction was that Britain could "negotiate" a settlement *for the Czechs.* And did. Shoved it down the Czechs' throat. That's arrogance for you. Surely we are not going to do the same thing for the two warring elements of Vietnam, North and South?

APRIL 24, 1967
6:30 P.M.
WASHINGTON, D.C.

Bill Fulbright came out of a Committee hearing to keep his appointment with me. He opened a briefcase alongside his desk, took out a small bottle, tipped it up and took a swig, and gave me a wink. "It's not liquor; it's cough medicine"—as it was. This was the only merry moment in the hour I had with him.

"Dave," he said, with a slight croak of fatigue and hoarseness, "Dave, I'm so de-e-pressed by this whole war that it's no good talking to me; it might be contagious and I don't want to make you depressed about what you have to do."

And he did seem terribly discouraged and down. "I think," he said sadly, "that right after Tet [when there was a cease-fire for several days] the President decided there was nothing to do but win a military victory, make the VC collapse and surrender. And here is Westmoreland in New York talking to the Associated Press editors, and then to a joint session of Congress, and the papers say there's to be a further escalation—bombing the airfields. And we are being prepared—the way the President does these things—for a demand for another lot of troops. They sent a young intelligence officer up to see me today, and he sat there and said we would have to have another 75,000 troops. And if Johnson doesn't get a victory he will probably lose the election and we may get a nut like Nixon, God forbid, or some new face like Percy no one knows anything about and people will therefore figure he will be better than Johnson, or Romney, who is a silly man, no depth at all. I just don't talk about this any more; what's the use?"

And, with a sigh, "I fear the die is cast."

I agreed. Whatever the mistakes or miscalculations made by Johnson and Kennedy and Eisenhower that had brought things to where they are, this *is* where we are, and we have to go on from here.

What was my company supposed to be doing? Reconstruction after the war, he supposed. "If Hanoi collapses, and the Russians and Chinese don't come in, I suppose we will have to occupy the country—it will be a colony of the U.S. and what you are doing will have to be done, I guess.

"But I doubt if they will surrender. The harder people are hit, when they are defending their own country, the harder they will fight. After all, they think we are trying to take their homeland from them. I suppose we can blast them back into the Stone Age, as someone has said, and maybe that's all there is left for us to do. Then you will have the job of building the country back, as our colony."

I said we had defeated Germany and then built it back and gotten out; and after flattening and occupying Japan, we had returned it to the people. And look at both countries. So wasn't our record of helping the former enemy but not hanging on pretty good?

He hedged the issue, except to say that those were sophisticated countries, whereas Vietnam "is a primitive country."

Fulbright's sorrow is *so* deep over what he believes is a defeat of all our principles. "Just because we are bigger and stronger, why should we go way off there and flatten this country? And surely Vietnam is no threat to the life of this nation"—this said with a wry and most unhappy grimace.

Finally, almost as a measure of his long friendship for me, the Senator asked me to tell him what our group can do while a war is going on. I explained that the chance of accomplishing something constructive was "a hundred to one" (though actually it is closer to ten to one, as I see it), but that I didn't see how I could refuse *to try*, despite the difficulties. "No, of course not. You are like a soldier who has to do what his country needs done, or try to."

During our conversation, Senator Fulbright commented that as a country we have become schizophrenic. I would put it differently—and I think I may try my hand at this theme for my University of Illinois Commencement address.

As a topic: *On Living a Double Life.*

Meaning that on almost every question or issue the graduates will find that there are two ways of looking at things—and that far from being a kind of "sick" attitude (i.e., schizophrenic), this approach is so much better than the fanatic's or the cynic's. The duality of life runs through everything.

And so it is about the war. We hate the bloodshed, the violence of fighting the North Vietnamese and the Viet Cong. That is a creditable feeling. We just aren't people who worship war for its own sake, as the fanatical little group around Hitler did. On the other hand, we don't like to see a people pushed around and butchered, and want to help prevent it. Call it schizophrenic or call it the duality, the double life of a compassionate people.

I left Bill Fulbright, full of profound admiration for his unshaken belief in principle. I found him, more than ever, a thoughtful man, tortured by the—well, the duality of life. Our talk so depressed me, however, that I wondered, momentarily at least, how I had let myself get into this tough spot.

But only momentarily. I don't want to commit myself only to things that are simple, one-sided, where the road is clear ahead, where "development" has no ethical problems, puzzles, implications.

I want to live in the world as it is, and be a participant, actively, taking the risk that I may, as the events turn out, be on the "wrong" side, on the unpopular side, on the "unsuccessful" side. Self-righteous as it may sound, I believe in taking risks if it is for a worthwhile purpose.

APRIL 25, 1967
9:30 P.M.
THE SHERATON PARK
WASHINGTON

For an hour I have been sitting on the steps leading down to the hotel's big assembly hall, a hall packed full—perhaps two thousand earnest brains—of physicists. The spring meeting of the American Physical Society.

The talks were about Oppenheimer. And quite moving.

One speaker reviewing "the Los Alamos days" recreated the atmosphere of that spirited group spurred on to adventures of the mind rarely equalled in scientific history. Mused the speaker: "How often it has been true that it is only struggles, often brutal struggles, that give rise to great advances in our knowledge of the world. No one can predict whether these breakthroughs are good or bad until many years have passed."

And so it will probably be about the ugly war in Vietnam. In the perspective of history those things that so profoundly disturb sensitive and warm-hearted people—Fulbright, David, Jr.—*and Sr.*!—may turn out to be the beginnings of a great new chapter of human life.

APRIL 26, 1967
PRINCETON

All morning on the phone—in my pajamas. The garb gives me the illusion that I am "resting." But hardly more than an illusion.

My two hour meeting, at the Vietnam Embassy, with Vu Van Thai was that part of a strenuous two days that left the deepest mark on me. I say this not because I learned anything *specific* of great consequence. It was because here is one of the architects of the present-day Vietnam, who in his person represents that piece of recent history out of which has emerged an agonizing division in American life.

Vu Van Thai, bright-eyed, handsome in the special way that these alert people are, has withdrawn himself from formal political participation in Vietnam affairs.

Thai expressed his undisguised concern about the continuation of the military group in charge of his country. How can there be a proper election this fall if Ky and Thieu are in charge of the government? This suspicion or competition between the civilians and the military persists despite the real achievement of the Constitutional Assembly in producing a Constitution and the even greater achievement of Ky and the Generals in agreeing to provisions that would narrow their power and invade their philosophy and personal prerogatives. So the enthusiastic comments I made about what the Vietnamese brought to the meeting at Guam and handed to our President weren't an overstatement, were perhaps an understatement. Thai made it clear that this "unity" was in the face of large residual fears among the Vietnamese of their own leadership—because it is dominated by their Generals.

So Thai wants it both ways too, just like so many of us Americans: wants a strong government, yet is fearful of the men who give it most of its strength *at present*, i.e., Ky, Thieu, and company.

Thai is deeply troubled by a dilemma. On the one hand he is sure that more and more American military power is needed, and will doubtless be supplied. If that isn't done the Communists will be able to continue the war indefinitely, and perhaps even subdue the South Vietnamese.

But, says Thai, looking at me sidewise, carefully watching my reaction: *But* increasing the American military more and more makes this an American war, until the Communists will finally be able to make this out as a war *by the U.S.* against the Vietnamese *people*. Here Thai leaned forward and looked strained and terribly intense. In a voice free of its usual tinge of singsong monotone, he continued: "*That* is *their* Communist strategy; that is why they continue to hold out. That is in fact the Communists' worldwide 'strategy.' "

A telling point. And one that gave me a pause before I asked:

"Are the Vietnamese people of the kind of mentality and temperament so they *can* forgive their enemies, forget the past, and work together?"

Here a long, dramatic pause.

Yes, Thai thought so. "In 1945," he explained, "I was one of those who met at Fontainebleau to decide what course we Vietnamese should take now that the Japanese were defeated. The French proposed that they should resume the role in Indochina that they had before the Japanese conquered us. But the spirit of nationalism was running high among our people. Ho Chi Minh was Chairman of the meeting. Some of us at the conference table were against the Communists, some, of course, were Communists. All agreed that if the French returned, following the Japanese defeat and removal, that we would fight the French. Ho Chi Minh went around that table and asked each one of us in turn. We, Communists and anti-Communists, all agreed we would oppose the French.

"So there *are* times when—answering your question—Communists and non-Communists who are Vietnamese can agree, and once did agree. Perhaps it could happen again."

Yesterday I called on Sol Linowitz at the State Department. I was enthusiastic about how he and his associates had made the Punta del Este conference produce something worthwhile.

I can see that Sol's wisdom had a good deal to do with the relative success of the venture. He said, "I advised against L.B.J. bringing a big promise of money. Perhaps it was just as well that the Senate wouldn't give him the authority he asked.

"The President on the way down on the plane was very low in his mind about the prospects. Even after 'a couple bourbons' he kept saying, 'Look what a mess you fellows got me into; nothing good will come out of this.' "

But when he got to Punta del Este he "gave them all the Johnson treatment" and it worked. "They *liked* him, liked his big man informality, liked the way he would slap them on the thigh as he told stories. He was at his best, and that is as good as there is.

"And your report, the Multinational Investment report, helped—you saw how the Plan for Action took over part of it wholesale."

Sol insists that it is "a crime" that I'm not down here all the time, "in the Government." I shied like crazy. I hope he quiets down along this line. I don't want to have my arm twisted about a permanent affiliation with the Government again. The Vietnam assignment is about as close as I will ever get!

Bob Komer, that tireless public servant, and I met for an hour or so Tuesday with Rutherford Poats, nominated as Deputy Administrator for AID, and Don MacDonald, the Saigon AID Chief. We focussed mostly on discussions about the next step, a preliminary report and outline of future work which we of D&R hope to have ready by about May 20th. All this went well enough.

At lunch, in the White House staff mess, Komer said: "We have had an aid program in Vietnam for about twelve years. It is sad to think how very little, how very, very little, there is to show for it today." MacDonald, looking glum, shook his handsome head, looking down at the table, then said: "Very little to show for it."

3 P.M.

Have just sat, in a kind of awe, before the TV in our living room, listening to Mrs. Svetlana Alliluyeva, the daughter of Joseph Stalin, in what was called a "press conference"—but was more a period of revelation.

A most magnificent response to those of my fellow Americans who habitually pour scorn on their country, finding nothing but bitter words and even obscenities to describe their native land.

General Greenbaum has performed a real national service by working out the entrance to this country of a remarkable new voice, a universal voice. And my waning respect for the intellectual was checked—for this woman, who considers herself a writer (not synonymous with being an "intellectual"?), put into simple, modest words, without a touch of grandiloquence or overstatement, what is in my own heart about this country.

APRIL 30, 1967
PRINCETON

At General and Dorothea Greenbaum's for dinner last evening. Of course we were all keen to have Eddie "open the curtain" (as he himself put it) about the extraordinary series of events leading to the arrival in the United States of Mrs. Alliluyeva.

The General is a veteran of human affairs, and is as unlikely as any man I know to be euphoric or undercritical. But he certainly went clear overboard about "this wonderful girl." Not only because she handled herself so magnificently in last week's press conference—a historic tour de force by any standard—but because of her qualities of great warmth and directness.

He told some things about her departure from Moscow to go to India; of the way the Russian Embassy in Delhi treated her. It was a significant slant on the stultifying effect of the bureaucratic habits of the Russians in all areas.

The warmth of the American heart when it sees a "real person" (Eddie's phrase, and a good one) is legendary; but Mrs. Alliluyeva has brought out that national warmth and naturalness, so often disguised by our feverishness and excess vitality.

MAY 4, 1967
NEW YORK

"In the fullness of my heart" . . . an ancient form of expression (is it Biblical? surely), but how wonderfully expressive of those too rare moments so beautifully and fitly expressed by that phrase.

And so it was: having dinner, quite alone, in the noisy chatter and cave-like light of the Roosevelt's Roast Beef Room—of all places. And yet, that surge of well-being, of thankfulness. That despite a very full day on top of a week of constant pressure—pressure of time, pressure of responsibility, of "problems." But also a time of reawakening.

Met Khodadad Farmanfarmaian at the Plaza, walked with him for most of an hour talking about Iran, about Khuzistan, about his hero (and mine) Ebtehaj, until the time came for his appearance before a round table at the Council on Foreign Relations, where I presided.

He said my letter to Mehdi Samii about the next step in agricultural development of the Khuzistan created much excitement; Samii read it to Khodadad aloud, apparently setting off a chain reaction through the Government.

I told Khodadad we were having the usual trouble, with new contract formulae being proposed, one after another, taking time and energy and patience. And the money always late, so we were constantly on the brink of cancelling because we simply couldn't finance the Iranian Government even for a month.

"Oh, that is terrible. But by this time, surely, you know the *weakness* of my country, the morass of the bureaucracy." I sensed that he was telling me: you shouldn't lose heart *now*, now when your important concept for food production is so well and enthusiastically received, and about to become reality.

Just the same, if we don't get our overdue advance in a couple weeks or so, we'll just *have* to give notice of cancellation.

And have to trim down our organization by more than half, overnight.

But somehow these "brinks" have been surmounted. Probably this one will be, too.

Khodadad made a big hit with his talk to the Council's round table. Iran had no deep fear about the Russians and was encouraging increasing trade with them. Such a contrast with only a few years ago when I thought the Shah appeared nervous and distraught about "Soviet subversion."

Then Khodadad made a major and perceptive proposal: the sending to the U.S. of 100,000 Persian youths (*not* to Harvard or Yale) to learn the English language and live with Americans and find out how generous and kind they really are, the farmers in Kansas, etc. And have Congress enact a law providing for a special kind of visa which would make it mandatory that these two-year visitors *must* return to Persia.

He spoke extremely eloquently about the great importance of the English language in paving the way for an understanding of American democracy. The rest of his presentation was also clear-headed and well received: it was the outline of the Iranian success story of the past few years. And quite a story it is, as I can appreciate better than most because I saw where the story began ten or twelve years ago.

MAY 9, 1967
NEW YORK

Zero Mostel, walking along 43rd Street; a geometrically square man (like a Steinberg drawing); rakish beret from which crinkly grey hair tried to escape, chewing gum vigorously, a half leer, half satisfied grin, pushing along on a cane that looked far too slender for his massive physique.

He is now a figure of the comic stage, after *Fiddler on the Roof* and now a successful TV show, *Zero Hour*. How circumstances change. Years ago (how many?) I went to the funny, tiny theatre in the Barbizon Plaza to watch him put on some way-out tableau or other. He had been blackballed for his "political views" (left, of course) and that was about the only place he could perform.

A great thing about this wonderful country. We do have our rashes, a kind of illness of the emotions about Reds—or whatever—but usually they give way, after a time, to more rational impulses.

MAY 10, 1967
NEW YORK

A good report from Tom Mead about Vietnam.

Tom is really functioning; this is *his* kind of job, brings out all his liking for people—and theirs for him—and his wide experience dealing with "villagers."

And Thuc shows evidence of democratic statesmanship. Has written letters explaining what the "joint group" is all about to 1000 recently *elected* village leaders. And feels it imperative that the joint group have something specific to recommend to the "new government" expected to be installed in August or September.

MAY 11, 1967
NEW YORK

A very moving letter yesterday from Senator Fulbright which included a treasured sentence, and one to try to live up to: "I only wish there were more people like you who knew how to deal with people as well as with ideologies."

MAY 12, 1967
NEW YORK

Bunker's first move has been to put *all* programs under Westmoreland. Does this mean that the "military" will decide on non-military priorities, such as those of development and "welfare"? I can hardly believe this. What then does placing the entire "pacification" effort in Vietnam (or "revolutionary development," or you name it) directly under the Commanding General of the American forces mean?

In terms of the "pacification" program the meaning seems fairly clear: this is, after all, a paramilitary function, and the kind of divided responsibility that has obtained—depending upon "cooperation" rather than line authority—strictly speaking wasn't "administratively sound." But something can be administratively sound and be carried on "efficiently," yet with the wrong motivations. So you move more "efficiently"—along the wrong course.

But does putting Komer in as a deputy of General Westmoreland, in charge of all civilian activities but still the military command's deputy, change the relation of the AID program out there, and therefore perhaps put our work also under the military aegis? That is a murky question, and one that perhaps only time and testing will clarify.

MAY 16, 1967
NEW YORK

"The Institute woods," Sunday morning, were dripping with doughty little migrating warblers, and that special genus, the dead-in-earnest, binocular-festooned, conscientious bird watchers. And all about a gay carpet of spring beauties, violets and other assorted blooms looking out upon a tardy, very tardy spring.

Eddie Greenbaum and I, resuming our habit of a Sunday morning walk, saw all this; or I did. The General was deep in thought about a decision he must make the following day about the publication of a piece of writing by his world famous client, Svetlana Alliluyeva. A very moving thing, according to Eddie, and of high literary quality. It will appear in the *Atlantic Monthly* in a couple of weeks, and will doubtless arouse great interest.

The General's problem, as her advisor: should he permit the text to be sent out to the press generally (by *Atlantic Monthly*, I suppose) or should he permit only a more limited distribution. What did I think?

Not having seen the prose didn't cause me to say, "Well—I don't know." I thought I *did* know; to give this piece wide publicity would damage the picture the country now has of this remarkable woman, would start her transformation into a political propagandist, whereas her great role, thus far, has been that she spoke from her heart as an individual, as a woman, to the hearts of others.

So I said, "The seat of politics is the human heart"; the most potent "prime mover" in the world is not political or ideological or economic ideas or dogma, or "logic" or "dialectics." Beyond all such movers is the purity of human emotion, a precious quality and the most pervasive force in the world. And the rarest gift a person can possibly have is *to be able to communicate that emotion* to others. To do so he or she must not adopt the methods of ballyhoo or the public relations artist.

If General Greenbaum, the sagest of advisors, wants to preserve this distinctive quality Mrs. Alliluyeva injected into the American scene with her press conference and TV hour so recently, he must avoid appearing to press her ideas or personality through the "media." That would be committing the unforgivable crime and a "violation of good taste" (as a friend has called it) known as generating too much publicity. How much is too much? Ah, well, that is where judgment comes in. But my advice would be to be most conservative about where and how her ideas and spirit are distributed.

The ugliness of violence, the bitterness and hatred that we see in our living rooms and day after day in the press—that isn't *all* that is going on. The most important things are positive, of that I have complete confidence.

An item of evidence: this morning the announcement that after years of patient (and impatient) discussions at Geneva, fifty nations have agreed to reduce tariffs and therefore speed the movement of goods between nations. "The Kennedy Round" it has been called: actually it began in the very beginning of F.D.R.'s first term, with that gloriously stubborn Tennessee mountaineer Cordell Hull.

Thirty years later, years of unsensational patient persistent effort, this news. This may be far more important to the hungry, more important to the peace of the world than all the words of argument that keep pouring out these days about such current issues as Vietnam.

Violence and rioting and shooting and propaganda: but somewhere in the world this morning quiet men are patiently working at ideas that in perhaps another ten or another thirty years will move the world along.

9 P.M.

Dropped by the Harper offices; Cass Canfield came *striding* out of his little office, greeted me with the happiest smile, and we settled down at his desk. Probably the least showy office in the world of a conquering publisher, head of a 150-year-old house which has just pulled off two historic coups.

The happy look wasn't for me; it was what happens to a man who has outperformed the field at seventy years of age. And in such contrast to the mask of a professionally taciturn man that I have so often seen him wear—and it has caused me to wonder what there is about this austere-looking, pipe-puffing man that has enabled him to stir the imagination and loyalty of so many impressionable, sensitive, talkative people—me included, come to think of it.

Hammered hard this afternoon to get the theme of our forthcoming interim Vietnam report to AID in shape. Expect it to be ready to submit early next week. A remarkable group of men working on it: Seymour, as steady as a rock; Fred Moore, a talent developing into new realms of imagination; and Tom Mead, looking so alive and full of conviction.

By Friday night we will have most of the rough places in the interim report pretty well smoothed out. "Report" isn't quite the word: a picture of the work there *is* to do before we can come up, step by step, with what we think *can* and *should* be done, in the near future, and the long run, to make Vietnam a going concern again for the Vietnamese people.

MAY 18, 1967
NEW YORK

The corporation to help the "re-hab" (the planners' jargon) of the Bedford-Stuyvesant Negro slum in Brooklyn was born yesterday late afternoon in the most elegant maternity quarters in history, without a doubt: the 35th floor of the brand new and very arty CBS Building on 52nd Street. The "delivery room" was rich with floor-to-ceiling walnut paneling; two fabulous French paintings hung on the walls, glowing symbols of economic power in the center of the world's economic power.

As I was escorted to the conference room, what seemed a quarter mile or so from the elevator down corridors that flashed huge abstract paintings at each adit, I said to the cute young lady who was my guide that I never saw a more appropriate place to talk about getting rid of slums, as CBS had certainly eliminated them on the 35th floor.

The meeting itself lasted more than two hours and accomplished a great deal. An executive officer was named, a building purchased in Bedford-Stuyvesant, and there was much discussion of "Olympic sized swimming pools and multiple basketball courts," to give the young people something to do this summer besides riot.

I arrived on time, and so did William Paley, our host, and André, and we circulated among the dozen or more staff people. Since tax-exempt foundations (Ford, Astor, etc.) are footing the organizing costs, I was a bit confused by the talk about Bedford-Stuyvesant as a "demonstration of what free enterprise can do," the talk that usually accompanies discussions of this new kind of attempt on the intractable Negro-in-the-city problem.

Shortly after we began Senator Robert Kennedy came in, moving with a kind of panther glide, looking quite handsome in spite of the fact that his tie wasn't fully pulled up, his suit was rumpled, his sox were droopy. He listened with an intentness that was almost painful, occasionally rubbing his eyes with fatigue, his knees drawn up against the edge of the table; from time to time he doodled (as I did), but he never let his mind wander nor did he relax for a second.

After an hour or so he explained that he had come from Washington on the 4 o'clock shuttle and would have to go back for an evening engagement. As he shook hands with me, thanking me for being there, he murmured—about his returning to the Capital the same afternoon—"I'm a yo-yo."

MAY 21, 1967
PRINCETON

Just back from forty-five minutes with President Goheen. He had read most of the Fairless Lectures and found the identification of management and humanism particularly appealing. Said he: "Philosophers today seem more occupied with improving their professional techniques than with making the insights and sensitivities of philosophy relevant to today's problems. Perhaps this is because they don't feel their role is welcomed."

I said that the funds I envisioned making available to Princeton in conjunction with the gift of my papers and journals were not large by the standards of some of Princeton's largest donors, but would provide seed money that might be used to interest foundations which haven't recently done much in the circle of the humanities as applied to current human affairs.

"The amount of money isn't the most important thing with us," Goheen assured me. "It is the knowledge that we will have the benefit of your ideas and experience that counts most."

MAY 25, 1967
NEW YORK

Yesterday's preliminary D&R staff "report" on the economic rebuilding of Vietnam made a strong impression. I was quite proud. Among the half dozen in the offices of the President's Vietnam Assistant, Ambassador Bill Leonhart (whose great eyebrows arch like the antlers of a solemn and determined buck deer), and in the dozen men gathered about Poats, there was real respect for this necessarily hurried job. It lays out the outlines of what can be done and the philosophy underlying the difficult task: to draw a picture of the future of a country in the midst of a savage and still undecided war.

Lunched, quite elegantly, with Felipe Herrera. I burst out with a plea (which I called "a modest proposal") to let the world know what a majestic empire is the La Plata River basin, affecting several countries of South America. Until people know widely that there is such a noble river, the piddling efforts to organize to "study" it will stall. The kind of step that is needed is to describe in an organized and dramatic way D&R's vast experience in river valley development and our ability to get things done. As long as the picture of this great basin is left to the slow and tortured bureaucracy of the Inter-American Development Bank, nothing much will happen.

The needs and aspirations of these vast countries situated in the basin are as far ahead of the capacity of their political and social institutions and the people responsible for moving them along as the first trip to the moon is ahead of the present-day navigation and transportation capabilities of South America.

How do I sustain my faith against this massive passivity?

MAY 26, 1967
NEW YORK

Up at 6 A.M., a walk through the November chill of this crazy month of May to the NBC studios, to go on the *Today* news show, said to have the most numerous audience in the world.

Hugh Downs, who conducts the interviews (*and* the commercials), operates, deliberately, on a very low key. This means there is no "tension" in the conversation with him; I felt it made me *too* relaxed, which is a drawback—I didn't feel I came through with the kind of conviction that this subject calls for, "this" being Vietnam, of course. But some of my more critical listeners telephoned that they didn't agree: that the main points *were* made effectively.

Here are some excerpts from the *Today* show interview:

Hugh Downs explained our company's assignment in Vietnam: "to formulate a long-range plan for the economy of South Vietnam." He then asked me what I thought of the prospects for "accomplishing the stability of the economy in South Vietnam."

LILIENTHAL: Well, I think they're very good. All wars are tough and bloody and ugly. This one is no exception. But the war rather overshadows the real prospects of this country. A good deal of this depends on your point of view. [In the 35 years] I've been working in the field of development in our country and other countries, the place I begin is to see what kind of people there are.

Ideologies come and go and these packages of ideologies—Communist, anti-Communist, escalation, non-escalation—these phrases that we fall into have very little to do with the prospects of a country. What really counts is what kind of people they are. And these are remarkable people by almost any standard.

DOWNS: Are they the kind of people that can assimilate the standards that may be necessary to build an economic picture that you're trying to build?

LILIENTHAL: Well, they may not assimilate our standards, and in a way I hope they don't because they have a culture that's much older than ours. . . . But they are a people who in their past have learned somehow, after conflict, to agree. . . .

And what's more significant even than that, it seems to me, is the way we've been able to work with a private Vietnamese group, who are also engaged with my American colleagues in this long-term look at their country. . . . They respond with ideas of their own. For example, their students: ordinarily students are the center of protest and frustration. The joys of being different. Forty of these students asked to participate in this planning development work. . . . These are young people who are now in the university. They go out two by two [into the villages]. . . . They want to build their country; when you've got that kind of spirit, then the long-term prospects are good.

DOWNS: Two things I want to ask you about: to what extent would the project be undermined by the Viet Cong and the terror that they impose . . .

LILIENTHAL: . . . Where the Viet Cong are assassinating people . . . that makes this kind of work quite impossible. . . . [But] a great many of these people are looking for something better than a continuation of warfare, whether it's conflict with the Viet Cong—their own people, these are Vietnamese . . . or conflict with the North Vietnamese, who are also Vietnamese. . . . They want to get back to their fields. They want a chance to live the life that pleases them. . . .

My guess is that if what we're doing works . . . this will do a great deal more than military methods to unite the country and perhaps even to help unite all of Southeast Asia. . . .

DOWNS: Now, you said something in your book here, *Management: A Humanist Art*, in connection with the development of underdeveloped countries. You said money alone certainly won't suffice. What else is needed besides money to—you pour money into a country—what else should one do to insure that it will work?

LILIENTHAL: [The usual Western foreign aid thinking about development is] that technology, techniques are [what are] needed most. This happens not to be my own experience or view. I think what you need most of all [is] some way of stirring the desire of the people. Giving them the chance to be let alone, . . . to work out their destiny in their own way, in their own village, in their own province or in their own country; and somehow releasing the great latent talents of people.

This, I think, is the function of a manager—I use the word "manager" in a broad, broad sense, it's a form of leadership; but this, I think, is needed more than, even than capital, a great deal more than capital; because with capital alone or technology alone you don't get results that you can have where leadership is spurred and excited so that people see a chance to do something for them selves: then you really have development.

And one of my greatest criticisms of our 25 years of [Western] effort in overseas development is that we have downgraded the capacity of people in these underdeveloped countries to do things for themselves; and have thought that because we have technology that we are going to solve [their] problems. Well, we haven't; and I don't think we shall. . . .

Large amounts of capital are not nearly as important as giving people a faith in themselves and showing that we care about them; that we work with their own planners, their own economists, their own engineers, their own village chiefs—this, I think, will do more to restore a feeling of confidence and of forward movement than anything that [our technology or] capital can do.

DOWNS: Has that been a sin of ours in the past, of trying to Americanize everybody because I know we believe—and probably with good reason—that we have the best way of life in the world; but the necessity to impose it on everyone just as it is might be looked at askance by people who don't care to be Americanized. I can understand that. It's part of your plan to avoid that pitfall, I take it?

LILIENTHAL: Yes. We've, I think, managed to avoid it in other places in the world where we've worked. In Persia, the Iranians are running their own show that we began [in 1956] at their request; in Colombia these things [we helped start are now] being done in the Colombian way [by Colombians]; and I think in Vietnam it ought to be done in the Vietnam way. . . .

This is not too easy because many technical people somehow don't see any limitations to their capacities because they know that technically they're usually superior to other people.

But technology is by no means the answer in the development of the world. By no means. You get some pretty horrible civilizations out of people who are [merely] technocrats; and I myself want no part of it.

MAY 28, 1967
PRINCETON

A day of glory. If one had but *one* such gift of nature in a lifetime, it would be marked on one's calendar with the reverence with which a pious Catholic must record a miraculous Vision. The early morning cool and fragrant; noon, the sun's warmth a *personal*, intimate communication from the source of all life and energy; the midday with a breeze rustling the fresh green leaves. And our beloved garden bursting with bloom after two weeks of raw cold and ugly skies. Sitting beneath the ancient, redoubtable apple tree, the world is indeed good.

Just this moment the carillon at the Princeton graduate school begins to fill the soft spring air. What an idyllic afternoon.

Remember *that* the next time a wave of fatigue or discouragement hits you, remember that for you the low places are few, your strength is really great, however tried it may be.

MAY 30, 1967
PRINCETON

Beatrice and Barney Tobey with us on this unbelievably beautiful spring day. We sat in the sunny garden talking with gusto while we had our pre-lunch drinks and ate fried chicken, basking in our guests' admiration of our garden (which deserved admiring, for it was almost at its peak today). Then walked through the Institute woods, which the city-bound Tobeys seemed to enjoy greatly. When we climbed up the slope of the Institute I got rid of my shoes and flaming red sox and my bare feet felt the grass—and restored my soul completely.

Barney was relaxed as I haven't seen him in a long time; we reminisced about their trip to Norris to visit us twenty-five years ago; Beatrice was full of fun and vivacity—her usual self. And all in all, a right happy day.

Reading an introduction to a translation of *Anna Karenina*, I learned from the editors that Tolstoi kept a diary continuously throughout most of his life (as did Benjamin Franklin).

But, said the editor, Tolstoi for his lifetime kept *two* diaries: one for others, and one for himself alone. What a second diary, for my eyes alone, I could write! It would have a livelier audience, I daresay.

JUNE 1, 1967
PRINCETON

Egypt's Nasser's revival of the Arab feud against Israel has almost shoved the war in Vietnam off the front pages.

Which has one ironic aspect: The people who were marching, protesting, denouncing war, proclaiming peace, scorning the U.S. for bombing, and so on, have had to make one of the fastest turnabouts in recorded history. Now many of the very loudest cursers against "intervention" in Southeast Asia are demanding of that ogre, L.B.J., that he send warships and planes, *at once*, to destroy the Egyptians. No nonsense *this week* about acting only in concert with other nations; no, sir.

Writes the gifted historian Barbara Tuchman, in a passionate letter to the *Times* the other day: If the U.S. doesn't act, right now, unilaterally, to kill the Arabs, our moral foundations are gone.

And the *Times* editorial writers have had to do a big flip. Killing Arabs is different than bombing North Vietnamese because we get our oil from the Middle East, they say!

Art Buchwald, the nutty humorist, is the only pundit capable of handling this flip—and he did it in a funny way tonight. "But I thought, Mr. Dunkleberry, that you are a dove, not a hawk." "I'm a dove that has lost its temper."

JUNE 2, 1967
PRINCETON

Yesterday a construction company executive dropped in briefly at the office. A very attractive straightforward able young businessman. But when I asked him how their proposal for building millions of dollars' worth of wheat silo storage capacity in Iran was coming along, his face fell almost to the floor. Very discouraged.

And what was the matter? "Well," he said, "it is a darn shame. One third of the wheat they raise is destroyed after it is harvested, by spoilage, by rats. The country needs at least a million tons of storage and it has about 125,000 tons. We had some very competent American firms lined up with us on transportation, handling distribution, and the lot. We got some Senators to lobby on our behalf with the Department of Agriculture about getting PL-480 funds as part of the deal and we took in as a partner an Iranian who said he had the right political 'connections.' But politics has killed the deal." This last said in a tone of outrage.

I said to him: "The second law of thermodynamics, that for every action there is an equal reaction, applies in public affairs, too. You decided to take a political figure into your enterprise, and to lobby among Senators about a business proposition. You should not be too surprised that some of the Ministers, seeing that Iranian politics had been injected into this, would inject some of their politics into it, too."

He took this like a man. "Yes, I suppose that is right, but we thought we really had no choice. The strength of D&R's position has always been," he said in the most guileless way, "that you never went at things that way and this is why your company got along in Iran so well."

The title of this little vignette might be Innocents Abroad. But some of the big, international companies so often think they can beat the game in offbeat ways. And I guess they frequently do.

The Khuzistan story is hotting up again. This time it may take a long step forward, with me getting a renewed interest in that program, now sadly diluted, or it is conceivable that it will take a decisive turn and we be thrown on our ear.

The occasion for this bittersweet observation is this: The Minister of Water and Power, Rouhani, and the new Managing Director of KWPA, Vahidi, are touring the Tennessee Valley, escorted by John Oliver. John called today to say that the Tennessee Valley was giving them a big show, that Rouhani did a long interview for the *Chattanooga Times* which pointed to the benefits Persia had had from the Tennessee Valley concept and from the Tennessee Valley alumni in D&R.

Further, a cable in from Khodadad Farmanfarmaian saying that Mehdi Samii, Governor of the Central Bank, expects to see me in a few days. My inference from this message is that we will try to solve the real obstacle to D&R's doing a good job at this turning point in Khuzistan history, namely, the sticky business of getting funds to keep our part of the work going on the advance-funds basis on which we began, and therefore to avoid the traumatic experience every few weeks of preparing to cancel and bring our field forces home.

As I have often noted, it is this highly unsatisfactory deterioration on the financing side that more than any other single thing has drained me of much of my personal enthusiasm and buoyancy about that program. It isn't that I don't understand that a rapidly developing country always is short of funds, even an oil-rich country. My gripe is that if the Khuzistan program truly enjoys the very top priority that the Iranian leaders, and particularly the Shah, give to it, then there are administrative measures within the competence of so skilled bankers as Samii and Farmanfarmaian for seeing to it that the flow of funds, within a budget, is not subject to these debilitating delays and these last minute episodes that we have been having every few months now for several years.

The press and TV continue to be full of the so-called Middle East crisis. The pictures presented are of a confrontation between Israel, fearful for its life, and Egypt and the other adjoining Arab states, threatening to redress the injustice that rankles with them over the establishment of the State of Israel and the plight of Palestinians, the so-called refugees. Another face of the picture is, as the pundits and commentators would put it, the "confrontation" between Moscow, which supports the Arab position, and the United States, which is committed to the continued existence of the State of Israel. And in the thumping of the drums and the rumble of war there is the ominous effect of all of this excitement, and possible hostilities, upon European and American supplies of oil from the Middle East.

In this picture Iran is in what seems to me a strangely anomalous position.

Iran is a Muslim country, as are, of course, the members of the

United Arab Republic. But the enmity between President Nasser and Iran is of long standing. This is due, in part at least, to the Persians' ill-concealed low opinion of Iranian Arabs, who live mostly in the Khuzistan region—a form of ethnic snobbery that is deep-seated and historic. To this antagonism has been added the fact that although a Muslim country, Persia has maintained a lively commercial relationship with Israel, buying her products, engaging Israeli technical assistance groups, and on the other side of the equation, selling Israel much, if not most, of its supply of petroleum.

A good deal of the Shah's insistence on military aid from the U.S. was his conviction that he had to protect the Khuzistan oil fields, the source of most of its foreign exchange (and the West's fuel), from the threat of Nasser, either directly from Egypt or through stirring up the Iraqis across the Shatt-al-Arab, or some of the Kurdish tribes. The Shah's decision to build a big oil export installation on an island in the Persian Gulf and to expand the port of Bandar Shahpur, rather than to depend almost entirely on the port of Khorramshahr—these acts were induced by fear (a not unjustified fear in my opinion) that Khorramshahr was vulnerable to interference through acts of violence or sabotage or by claims of the Iraqis that would interfere with the use of the port of Khorramshahr for oil export. Persia's windpipe was too vulnerable, and the combined antagonisms of Nasser and the Iraqis a source of very real anxiety on the part of the King and his Cabinet.

And here the disillusion on the part of the Persians with the position of the U.S. in the last few years becomes clearer. The Shah put a good deal of pressure on President Kennedy for more military assistance, and got a most limited response. I remember leaving the White House after a state dinner for the Shah and having Kennedy walk me out to the portico asking—but not waiting for my comment—"Do you think that the Iranians really need more military equipment or is this just to strengthen the Shah internally and mollify his army officers?" I didn't see then, as everyone surely does now, Nasser's belligerence toward Israel, and so I had real doubts, within my limited knowledge, about why Iran should spend so much money on its military.

The point of these recollections is that I assumed that Iran's chief justification for an extensive military and naval establishment would be fear of Persia's northern neighbor, the Soviet Union. This may turn out to have been a complete miscalculation on my part. Also, and what is more important, a miscalculation on the part of our State Department and our Government.

For though Iran vs. Egypt has not been mentioned, so far as I have noticed, in the tumult of these last days, it just could be that this enmity on the part of an almost destitute country, Egypt, for an oil-rich country, Iran, may become a major factor in this complicated situation.

The supreme irony of this infinitely complex international ballet of death is the change of policy in recent years of Iran toward Russia.

Iran, denied by the United States all it felt it needed in the way of military assistance as well as major financial assistance, turned to Russia and to other Communist countries of Eastern Europe. And when it turned, it turned almost full circle. Long-existing and profound suspicions and antagonisms between these two countries were transformed almost overnight.

Iran entered into a major contract for the Russians to build a big steel complex in Iran, to be paid for in gas and perhaps petroleum from the Khuzistan, transported by pipeline into Russia. This also involved the sending of Russian technicians to Persia and presumably the sending of Iranian steel plant trainees to Russia. The Shah has made extensive barter arrangements, using not only petroleum and gas but other products, hides, leather, etc., in deals with other Communist countries, such as Rumania and Bulgaria.

George Kennan, Walter Lippmann, Arthur Schlesinger, Ken Galbraith, and Bill Fulbright have been pounding at Dean Rusk apropos Vietnam chiefly, making him out an old fogey because he does not know that "the Cold War is over," that the Russians have become tame and would not harm a Western fly, that continuing to talk about the Communists as if this were twenty years ago is a lot of dangerous nonsense, etc. But there are some of us who remember earlier periods when the Russian leopard was represented as having changed its spots, the period of the sweet songs of that naïve character Ambassador Joe Davies, and later the illusions of the "Spirit of Camp David," under Eisenhower.

The answer to whether Russia is really a changed creature will turn on the way in which it makes use of the eruption of Egypt against Israel, which may well lead to a direct confrontation with the U.S. (though not by any means necessarily beyond peaceful resolution).

How extraordinarily interwoven are the strands of foreign policy. (Which simply means how interwoven are the strands of human destiny.)

The establishment of the State of Israel by the labyrinthine paths of history may lead to an explosion or near-explosion between the two greatest powers in the world today.

I would never have dreamed when we made our first trip to the Khuzistan a little over eleven years ago that the Persian Gulf which borders that region might be the locale for a contest of power that in a way extends from Vietnam to the State Department in Washington to the Kremlin in Moscow.

JUNE 4, 1967
PRINCETON

Our spring garden party yesterday, with glowingly beautiful weather and perhaps forty friends, quite evidently enjoying each other's company. But the star was the garden. The look in people's eyes as they stepped into the garden was even more eloquent approval than the rather extravagant comments.

And this morning, very early (before six), I made my rounds, and I must say I have never seen a palette of color to match the irises in that early light. And the mixture we have managed to effect: the dots of coral bell on their slender rising stems, the pastel cloud effect of the mountain columbine, and as background, the mounds of rhododendron, scarlet predominating, the later pink touching off the solid banks of red.

A garden is indeed a lovely thing, and a joy.

It even eases or overlays for a time the persistent pain that hardly leaves me over the strange rupture with David. Helen sent off a note last midweek, wishing them (for both of us) a good voyage and a happy year in Italy. How often I listen for a hoped-for phone call, and how I steel myself, should it come, not to "fold."

JUNE 5, 1967
NEW YORK

Lunch with that remarkable Iranian leader Mehdi Samii, at the Century. Very deliberate of speech, extraordinarily reserved and collected in his manner.

He did not think it was "within the possibility" that Iran would "change its policy of economic relations with Isri-al"; the Israelis are building a dam for Iran near Shiraz, in Fars; they have many technical things going together. "No," he said thoughtfully, "I do not think it is possible. Of course, we issued a statement of sympathy for the other Muslim states—that was inevitable." He seemed not a little concerned about the questions the Shah might have to answer before a group of Congressmen he is to see next week, particularly about Iran's arms assistance from Russia.

The headlines of the afternoon papers blaze out the tragic news: Israel and Egypt are at war.

But soon, no doubt, we have to get used to dispatches about fighting in *that* part of the world, as sooner or later we got somewhat "used" to the bloody story from Vietnam.

JUNE 7, 1967
PRINCETON

The Oriental poppies in the west garden carve a vivid gash, made the more startlingly sensuous by the clump of giraffe-tall Siberian iris, deep deep blue, and beside them, bearded iris, white and yellow. What a gaudy artist a gardener can be—for I planned this effect last autumn.

The Israeli forces seem to have overwhelmed the Egyptians and Jordanians almost overnight. Now what?

Oil is very much involved. A number of Arab oil states say they will not ship, or doubtless permit, the export of oil to countries supporting Israel—which is a large part of their market. But some of them, Kuwait, Saudi Arabia, etc., after *saying* the right thing politically, are unlikely to forgo their Cadillacs and the luxuries of Paris for the sake of standing with Nasser.

And how will all this affect Iran? The first item in that puzzle: a telegram from the Social Secretary of the White House: the state dinner for the Shah and the Empress cancelled, the Shah returning to Iran forthwith.

JUNE 9, 1967
NEW YORK

The news of the Israeli-Egyptian war is at the center of things today, of course. And preparing myself for a meeting tomorrow with KWPA's Vahidi, the Khuzistan's Managing Director, I keep wondering again how this humiliation of a Muslim nation and the resulting turmoil in the Middle East will affect our Khuzistan work.

Iran's position is strange. The Shah is close to Hussein of Jordan, one of the more sensible Arab leaders, who also resisted Nasser. Then Hussein collapsed the other day, and today his kingdom is prostrate. And Iraq, provoked by Nasser against Iran—how will it behave now that its area leader has suffered such a great defeat?

And will it be possible now for Israeli moderates and Arab moderates (if there be any of *either*) to plan joint economic development projects?

JUNE 10, 1967
PRINCETON

That David should leave next week for Italy without my talking with him, the bitterness that he might well feel, the grimness of this whole rupture if neither of us took the initiative: I wrestled with this through the night.

I have just phoned him. How good his voice sounded to me. How I kept mine steady and casual, despite a racing pulse, I don't know. "Of course," he said, they wanted to see us. I suggested New York on my return from Washington next Wednesday.

JUNE 11, 1967
PRINCETON

The overwhelming military victory of the Israeli forces, particularly in Jordan, revived in my mind the specific program we helped formulate years ago for a "TVA on the Jordan." But that was to be essentially a State of Israel effort, for which they had the technical competence, the outside financing, and the determination to put through. And despite Jordanian-Arab opposition, a small part of the effort to put Jordan water to use has been realized.

Both the military victory over the combined forces of the Arabs of Egypt, Jordan, and Syria, and Israeli economic development are heartening things. But I must confess that I fear the consequences of dominance and superiority of the Israelis in both military and economic fields. The Arabs are the people who should be the center of our concern now.

What has been attempted before for the Arabs, by the outside world, has been compassionate. But it has been a "welfare" task: the settling of these hapless Palestinian refugees. Three of my friends have tried their hand at this: Jack Blandford, Gordon Clapp, and Joe Johnson. To no avail. Gordon tried to get attention on a constructive note, the development of the tiny Litani River. But none of these efforts made any progress. Partly, I think, because they were explicitly directed to the "refugee problem," a dismal way to lift people's spirits and their energies. Partly because the Arab leaders—and followers—still believed that Israel as a state could be overthrown.

If Israel now can be accepted as a reality, and with instances—like the Khuzistan—to point to what can be done to increase productivity and health, a joint Arab cum Israeli development effort has, perhaps, the best chance.

I plan to send a check to the United Jewish Appeal Emergency Fund. But I wish there were also some way of expressing, in a tangible fashion, the feeling I have for the Arabs, as presently humiliated human beings who should also be helped, however difficult it may be to persuade them now that help from American sources can be accepted.

But the greatest help would be a vision, presented by men who have a record of doing more than welfare work or drawing "plans," of a Mideast *development* program, on a twenty-five-year basis, for the benefit of both Arabs and Jews.

How else? Must we go through another decade or more of bitterness, or can all this energy be put to better use?

Iraj Vahidi, Reza Ansari's successor as KWPA Managing Director, is, as the girls in the office couldn't fail to notice, "tall, dark, and handsome," with wavy hair, huge Persian eyes, and a distinguished presence. I spent half the day with him and Burnett and O'Brien last Friday. My chief purpose was to provide some kind of emotional lift or philosophical perspective on his pioneering job, otherwise the discussions of engineering overhead, etc., become bogged down and fussy with penny pinching kind of detail.

Vahidi was visibly moved and excited by the picture I drew of the kind of responsibility and opportunity he has, he and he alone. At one point his eyes became moist. At my suggestion, he cancelled his departure "for Paris" when I said he was needed, and his King would know that he was needed, in the World Bank meeting scheduled for Monday.

How much this evident emotional response to the historic importance of his Khuzistan job will mean, in concrete terms, remains, as the pundits always say, "to be seen." I found I was greatly impressed with this young-looking man (actually, he says he is 40). And I was once more convinced that long-range perspective is essential for shorter-range decision-making.

JUNE 12, 1967
WASHINGTON

The Lilienthal Grand Prize for the Worst Architectural Taste (Bizarre division) was awarded, by me, this evening, to an apartment block in the western corner of M Street and Thomas Circle. A human being designed this concoction, human hands built it. But what is the story behind this hunk of ugliness? There it is: a green ice cream cone, complete with curving iron tongues bedecking story after odd-shaped story. It stopped me in my tracks, I who have seen the horrors of wooden apartment houses in Cambridge and other manmade monstrosities.

Minister Rouhani really turned on the charm when he and Vahidi arrived at Aldewereld's [World Bank] office this noon. A warm smile, the clasping of my hand between his two hands, murmurs about "the honor," etc. But there is far more to this square, baldish man than charm; he made a great impression on the non-impressionable banker, Aldewereld, with the Minister's concept of a big overall plan for Iran, his earnest manner, his sense of putting things together—not just a scattered project or two, but the overall aspirations of his country.

Aldewereld spoke in the highest terms about what D&R is providing Iran in the Khuzistan; this he said first to me, when we were alone, and then repeated it in spades to the two Iranian visitors and to his own deputies.

Almost overnight the Bank under the new Presidency of George Woods has become the discoverer and advocate of the importance of agriculture. Looking at the record of the previous ten years, and particularly the thumbs down attitude regarding our agricultural pilot project in Khuzistan in the early crucial days, this is a bit ironic; but the important thing is the stated policy *now.* And Aldewereld sees that "broad plans" aren't so important as the more earthy business of teaching good agricultural practices *to the farmers*, not by "agricultural economists" but by practical farmers in the field.

I should hail this—to myself at least—as a long-sought victory, but I no longer get much satisfaction out of this kind of "I long ago told you so." Besides I have been wrong myself often enough to know that the important thing is that things do come right at last.

JUNE 13, 1967
WASHINGTON

A great new idea in international development—or a mere paper gimmick—announced this morning: Litton Industries International Development Corporation. This is sequel to their several false starts in Greece. They will undertake to raise capital in the "international capital markets" and develop programs and carry them out. And be paid costs plus 11% of costs.

Why do we in D&R continue to follow so conventional a line as the one we are discussing, this morning, with the Iranians? What D&R is paid for our work is a small percentage of the costs of ordinary engineering work, plus a small lump sum to promote agrobusiness development in the Dez irrigation project.

The answer to this question is not simply that we don't have the resources that fat Litton has had to work with on such an undertaking as theirs in Greece for—it must be two years. And D&R has so far undertaken to generate internally all its working capital—virtually a fiscal impossibility. Yet we have done it. True, being undercapitalized as we always have been is a disadvantage compared to almost any other conventional private business, but the main difference compared to other firms is in *basic outlook.* We don't believe in going into a country and taking on indefinitely the responsibility that the country's young leaders should carry.

And it is the rise of these young men that Aldewereld thought was the most hopeful part of what is occurring in Iran. I certainly agree.

Our way of going at things does have a conventional engineering approach—*now.* That is partly because through our well-designed training program we have brought the younger Iranians along to a point where they don't really need Litton *or* D&R to do their entrepreneuring for them.

Hasn't the moment come for me to give more and more time to ideas about the *meaning* of acts, the requirements of leadership? This is more my métier, my chief interest, than economic development of physical resources and the raising of capital for that development.

You have done your share of pioneering in *that* area. Now to try something *really* difficult. And not the ivory tower kind of "just talking" —pretentiously called "dialogue"—extensively reported again this morning in the *Times*.

10:30 P.M.

Met for an hour with Ambassador Bill Leonhart, in the Executive Offices. A greater contrast with his predecessor, Bob Komer, as Special Assistant to the President on Vietnam it would be quite out of the question to imagine. A subtle, carefully organized mind, measured tones, no gestures, a man of intellectual perception, whereas Bob was sharp, driving, given to reaching for the simple and direct. I like them both, and find both very good men to work with, to expound one's ideas to, and to get a response from, Bob's being put, usually, in sulphuric, unqualified, and almost explosive terms, Leonhart expository, contained, but very, very clear.

He said he thought my *Today* interview was very good, agreed with the philosophy, had sent excerpts to the President for his reading. Then I turned the talk to current problems centered around my determination that we keep the *joint* relation with the Vietnam group headed by Thuc a reality, not, as in so many of these "counterpart" arrangements with AID, a façade, a ploy to avoid making trouble for the American group.

JUNE 14, 1967
3:30 P.M.
WASHINGTON AIRPORT

Before 9 A.M. I was at James Grant's office at State. He has just been named "in charge" of Vietnam. He got in shortly afterward, and though he is an old hand at the ups, downs, and fogginess so common among "foreign aid" agencies, I thought he looked more than a little "shook" by the prospect before him.

His questions about our assignment were the kind you expect from a seasoned public administrator: "What will I tell a Congressman who wants to know what we expect Lilienthal will deliver to us at the end of eight months?"

It will not take much time for a man with Grant's perception to understand that we aren't "delivering" anything, and wouldn't "deliver" it anyway to AID, but to the Vietnamese. Even our basic idea of *joint* development is a good deal to expect him to grasp right off.

A hard-looking fellow, who shook his head as we were leaving: "The chance of doing something . . . whew, I don't know."

Well, that's the way I felt at first, and at odd moments still do.

Met Interior Secretary [Stewart] Udall for the first time. A big fellow, who looks on me, I'm sure, as a relict of another era, the New Deal days. It was a good era, but I don't suppose he can believe I've done anything "since the thirties"—his phrase. But he has all the right words, the right motivation, and probably a good deal of administrative ability, too. On the whole, though, he gives out an aura of a run-of-the-mine politico, more so than any other man in a Cabinet of otherwise *superior* men—John Gardner, Robert McNamara, Dean Rusk, "Joe" Fowler, Lawrence O'Brien, et al.

JUNE 15, 1967
8:30 P.M.
NEW YORK

David arrived at 5:30, looking so big and handsome—and grey. It was a painful hour and a half. At 7 he stood up, looking so stooped and sad, and as he got to the door, threw that great arm around me, held me very tight against his rough bearded face, and whispered, "Dad—I'm so sorry." His eyes filled with tears as we parted.

I sat down almost at once and wrote him a note: "You are a real man. I respect and love you more than ever; not just as a father, but you can *count on me* as a steadfast friend."

As David said, "Now we are moving to Italy. It is a watershed of my life."

What a heavy burden of sorrow is lifted from my heart. David and I, David and his mother, if not reunited, certainly no longer without communication.

Alienation of parents and mature children is an experience we—Helen and I—share these days with so many others, no less painful and puzzling for that fact.

JUNE 17, 1967
5:30 P.M.
O'HARE AIRPORT, CHICAGO

The Assembly Hall at the University of Illinois Commencement was a completely new experience for me as a speaker. From the outside the double mushroom looked like a huge flying saucer, the space ship of the cartoons, out of which the little gremlins emerge. But inside it is a giant bowl, with the 16,000 people banked high about the speaker on all sides, rising almost to the zenith. What a sight.

I had an extraordinary emotional reaction as this great audience rose to sing "America," and I looked out over the throng of young people. Truth is, I gulped and almost wept. It *is* moving: a son of immigrants, "greenhorns," born in tiny Morton, Illinois, standing in the Illinois plains and being introduced to this audience in extravagant terms.

JUNE 21, 1967
NEW YORK

The stock phrase is: "New York has everything." And indeed it does: noise, clatter, pushing, and clawing. But also *such* a richness and diversity.

Thus, tonight, I saw Shakespeare under the sky, in Central Park, and enjoyed it—and citified or no, a homey kind of audience along with the play—as much as almost any performance of Shakespeare I have ever heard. It was "A Comedy of Errors," played broadly and slapstick and merry. The bowl was filled; no admission charge; a highly professional cast.

That, too, is New York.

Talking in my office this morning—on my initiative—with Dr. Emanuel Neumann, the scholarly Zionist leader. We discussed the war between Israel and the Arab nations, of course; but my interest was in seeing whether some of the ideas of joint economic development between Israel and Jordan and Syria could not be revived, the concept behind the TVA on the Jordan studies—and later project—years ago.

While I was listening to this quiet-spoken, kindly man, Miss Baron brought in a letter from the Chairman of the Senate Foreign Relations Committee. Quite a good bit of timing, I thought, as I read the letter, and then handed it to Dr. Neumann.

This is what Bill Fulbright wrote:

"Thank you so much for your letter reminding me of the 'TVA on the Jordan.' I know this is one of the best things that might be done to help heal the wounds that opened again in this area. If we can get over this immediate crisis and they can begin to talk in a more restrained manner, this project ought to be brought forward again.

"The speeches this morning by the Russians and the Arabs were so inflammatory I am afraid it is premature to talk of such programs, but surely they will calm down after a bit. I certainly hope so!"

JUNE 22, 1967
NEW YORK

The word from Vietnam makes me shudder; almost an entire American Infantry company destroyed in battle in the Mekong Delta. More than 11,000 Americans killed thus far. Is there something basically wrong with our military leadership? We have overwhelming, uncontested control of the air, unprecedented mobility and fire power, and we're fighting a people with no great military tradition. Yet it is difficult to see that we're making any military progress toward our goal of peace.

And if the military picture grows worse, our diplomatic bag of ideas and initiatives seems equally empty. I share with many of my fellow Americans some of their desperation—no, utter confusion about this inconclusive war.

JUNE 23, 1967
PRINCETON

The zest, the fun of meeting new people, casually, at random, unexpectedly, their personalities falling within my line of vision, continues to be a delight. And relishing the experience afterward is part of the pleasure. I see my world expanding: that is what it adds up to.

For instance, on the plane trip back from Urbana last weekend, my seatmate was a strapping, alert young fellow, deeply absorbed in a paperback. It was dog-eared, and he was studying it rather than just reading. It turned out to be a manual prepared by the Marine Corps; and he had just come from training camp with his brand new commission as a Second Lieutenant of Infantry. He told me that after his leave (he was in civilian dress) he was headed for Vietnam.

The manual, which he said I could look at, had a lot about "civil action programs" for Marines. And, of course, many pages and diagrams about booby traps, malaria, small arms, and so forth.

The light in this young fellow's eyes as he talked about "what I'll find when I get out there" was that of a fellow heading for an adventure in which he was *eager* to prove himself. A Second Lieutenant of an Infantry combat platoon has definitely the most dangerous post of any, but nothing in his manner gave any indication of this.

He had just come from his girl's graduation exercises. Yes, a lot of people talked to him about how wrong the Vietnam war was, and he didn't argue much with them. Said he felt it was the only thing this country could do, and why get into a big argument about it? A less resigned man I never saw. Felt pretty proud of him, and a lot of other young men who behave much the same way. Studying his job, proud of his commission, ready to do the job.

Another in the cavalcade of personalities: a youngish Iranian. A kind of alumnus of D&R's Khuzistan Development Service, he is now in charge of the Haft Tapeh sugar complex, which D&R initiated. His name: Nader Hakimi. A graduate of MIT; high forehead; full of zeal and excitement about new managerial techniques. His eyes literally burned as he told me how he would like to see modern methods applied to the further development of Khuzistan. He has pretty well mastered the sugar operation, so I'm told; he is restless to see more done elsewhere in Iran, and particularly the still unrealized potential in Khuzistan.

With my unlimited faith in human potential, his success does not surprise me. But who would have predicted *among Iranians* that such enterprise and excitement about getting things done actually existed, say, fifteen years ago?

JUNE 26, 1967
PRINCETON

Last night to a dinner and post-dinner meeting with the Trustees of EWA, the so-called "annual retreat."

I have rarely heard such a dismal view of the present and future of American universities overseas. To describe the consequences on American university influence in the developing countries of the "exposures" of CIA covert financing of all kinds of educational and other American private organizations, the mildest term used was "disastrous."

But *why* this mounting evidence of antagonism to all educational activities by the universities of the U.S. in providing technical aid to developing countries?

I said that what we Americans offer to these countries needs reexamination, critically. Is it really so good that we can blame all of the lack of "receptiveness" on the developing countries; how much of the blame should attach to us?

We of D&R are determined to avoid the taint of trying to Americanize the long-term development program for Vietnam through the device of a joint planning group. But the device isn't as important as the spirit. And it is this spirit of respect for what the developing countries have, in people, ideas, and history, that may—just *may*—account for the better success D&R seems to have over some other enterprises, most universities included.

JUNE 27, 1967
NEW YORK

It is rarely considered wise or effective to make a *direct* assault on a public issue charged with heavy emotional content. Such an issue is the "alienation" from the American involvement in Vietnam of the academic community—the faculties of the universities and colleges.

Some months ago EWA made an earnest and fruitless effort to close this breach by the direct confrontation route, a discussion of *why* the alienation—but much of it in the abstract. This included a long session by Herman Wells and William Marvel with President Johnson and Secretaries Rusk and McNamara.

I pushed for an alternate approach, my favorite route, that of a concrete flank attack. It is that EWA sound out the universities—or a representative sample—on this specific issue: that members of their faculties be asked if they would participate in applying the intellectual resources of their institutions *to studies of Vietnam.*

The EWA staff was impressed (or so I thought) by this idea; they came up with an affirmative proposition on the limited step I had in mind, and to this added the idea of an American-Vietnamese Foundation to further long-range development and reconstruction of Vietnam.

This was the subject of the long and rather exciting discussions around the square table at the Princeton Inn, at meetings Sunday night and Monday morning.

It was also the subject of a weekend discussion with about fifty faculty members from all over the country, which the Trustees did not attend.

To my surprise—and delight—the usual dogmatic and almost hysterical emotionalism about the Vietnam war wasn't present. None of the kind of violent and even abusive noes that we got from certain university people we asked to consider joining D&R for our work in Vietnam.

I took this opportunity to restate my own philosophy: build on the foundations you have; start from where you are. And I told the group that there was reason to be hopeful, considering what that country and those people have been through. "How would you feel," I asked, "if half a million Vietnamese soldiers were planted right here, in New Jersey? With the American Army in their country, that is a kind of parallel of what faces the Vietnamese."

JUNE 28, 1967
ONE WHITEHALL, NEW YORK

At eye level, close enough so I can see their every movement, the steelworker stiffs are beginning the day's work, raising to the sky the octagonal frame of the new Seamen's building. These are sturdy men, these steelworkers. And while I wish that the space off toward the outer harbor had been left uncluttered, for the sake of my own view from this office, it is an inspiring sight, seeing men build, watching construction American-style, so technically skillful, so swift, so bare of the crude, inhumane backbreaking way of building in so many countries I have seen.

JUNE 29, 1967
NEW YORK

Noon today I fly to the Vineyard. I leave New York for several weeks with mixed feelings. I'll miss it all, for despite all the incredible noise and clamor, and the tensions and worries that D&R creates, this is a good life. (Actually, many of the worries and most of the tension *I* create, deliberately; that is a more accurate statement!)

Yesterday morning I began early: reached the office at 7:30. A New York footnote: the Roosevelt Hotel's breakfast room was full of foreign visitors, a group tour of French. Middle-class commercial people, I would guess. A couple days before it was a German tour. This is Europe returning the American group tour. Something comforting about this: that Europe is so far recovered from war and the rest, that middle-class people can make the expensive grand tour of America; then they can go home with the same sense of superiority about those strange ways of the Americans that American tour groups carry home after a hectic tour of the Continent.

Quick going over of progress, or lack of it, about recruitment for Vietnam, which so far has been an almost total zero. But Moore is working hard at it. It doesn't help recruiting to find the papers full of the news that an AID staff man has probably been executed by the Viet Cong, after two and a half years as a prisoner. (He was kidnapped on a road in the suburbs of Saigon itself!)

A charming and warm letter from the First Lady. I had written her about the *Today* program and sent a transcript; this is what she wrote in response:

"There should be no doubt in anyone's mind who saw and heard this program that America's intentions and obligations to help the South Vietnamese people against Communist aggression are more far reaching than in just military assistance. It is so exciting, constructive, and I dare to use the word 'hopeful'—and so little understood.

"One of the most interesting encounters with a foreign head of State

I have had was to listen to the Shah of Iran at dinner one night discuss the power development and river control projects in his country and the part you were playing in it. I really felt I was listening to something enormously important that could affect a whole level of living. I longed to hear you describe it from your viewpoint. I was keenly disappointed when the Shah had to cancel his visit—I had looked forward to hearing the current chapter in that great venture from the two of you."

JULY 2, 1967
MARTHA'S VINEYARD

A phone call last night from General Greenbaum. Had I read a letter in the *Times* of yesterday (by an Abraham D. Levitt), "For a TVA on Jordan"?

What did I think of the idea; would it make sense as a way of getting something constructive done, "right now"?

He went on: Iphigene Sulzberger had spoken to him about it; did it seem like a good thing to try to persuade the UN to do something definite, now, about this idea?

I gave the General some of the background; the visit to TVA and to me of Dr. Emanuel Neumann and his colleagues as far back as 1942; that the report on a Jordan Valley development, prepared by a former TVA engineer, Jim Hayes, with help from others in the TVA organization of that time, was a sound technical idea; that it had been rejected, in effect, by the Jordanians, so the Israelis went ahead with "their side" of the Jordan; that I thought the idea represented a constructive way to advance Arab-Israeli peaceful coexistence, and an end to the hopeless and degrading business of treating the "Arab refugees" as a permanent welfare problem, rather than offering them an opportunity for productive work on their land.

According to the General, Mrs. Sulzberger thinks this is the time to move on this idea, while the issues between Arabs and Jews are at the center of things at the UN. I said the very day it was evident that the Israelis had won the war I had phoned Dr. Neumann, then told the General of Neumann's visit to my office a few days later. I also cited Fulbright's rather enthusiastic response to my suggested revival of a Jordan TVA as well as his feeling that until there was an abatement of the fury of the Arabs toward Israel and the inflammatory anti-American words of Kosygin at the UN nothing much could be done.*

* *Journals*, Vol. I, *The TVA Years*, contains several references in March, 1943 (pp. 555, 579, 594–595), to a visit I had in Washington with the British scientist Chaim Weizmann, one of the founders of the State of Israel, and a prophetic statement by him.

To "communicate" in a warm, human way is *not* synonymous with two people's abilities to discuss ideas, *objective* ideas. The true communication is not on matters that are impersonal, in the strictly intellectual realm of sheer ideas, however stimulating and often delightful this can be.

To be able truly to communicate there must be a capacity and an ability and a willingness, even an eagerness to deal with personal relations, in the realm of emotions.

JULY 3, 1967
MARTHA'S VINEYARD

The fog softly moves up our hilltop, solid, opaque, surrounding us and finally blotting out all else. This little house is the only reality, this and the sad moaning of the Nobska foghorn, away off, are all that exist. A very special, unique feeling, not so much of losing the world, as the world losing itself.

A good lazy day today; a furious squall hurling angry rain in great torrents upon the windows and against the drumhead of our roof. Helen off shopping, me here alone, before a wood fire (for it was quite cool) reading Blake's big, fat *Disraeli* (with relish, and occasional incredulity) and dreaming about pleasant things, enjoying the isolation.

The *Disraeli* is a long and at times a dull book. But distinctly relevant, because of the light it sheds on the realities of parliamentary functioning. For the parliamentary life is just another expression of the effort to harmonize power in the hands of elected men with the strong tidal forces with which power must deal when the foundation of that power is not wholly the power of force.

Apparently a casual suggestion of mine, at a Bedford-Stuyvesant Board Meeting some weeks ago, made a real dent in Senator Kennedy's thinking. My point was that to get new business to locate in slum areas (and thereby provide employment) would require more than swimming pools and parks ("amenities" I called them). It would require a real *business incentive*; the quick way would be by tax advantages and incentives, advantages not existing in other locations. After the meeting André phoned me to say that Kennedy had called him to say that I had come up with a good idea. But probably they were just being polite, I had thought.

Today's *Times* front-page column-one story tells of Kennedy's national plan for slum improvement combining private enterprise and government help; "at the heart of the plan" is a set of "industrial incentives"—using the tax route, as I had suggested.

Providing incentives through tax forbearance and advantage is something that has been used a long time—but not for creating jobs (i.e., new business) in the slums. This is a familiar, almost classic illustration that *adaptation* of ideas rather than their creation is one of the important skills of the innovator.

JULY 7, 1967
MARTHA'S VINEYARD

An amusing aside about the Vineyard, its fogs, and the many well-known figures who come up here in summer, from the *Gazette* for July 4th:

"Toasts were exchanged by President Lyndon B. Johnson and King Bhumibol Adulyadej of Thailand in the state dining room at the White House on the evening of June 27.

" 'We feel a very special bond of kinship with Your Majesty,' the President said, 'because you were born among us. I have heard that during your early years you used to go from Cambridge to an Island off the Massachusetts coast known as Martha's Vineyard.

" 'Some members of my cabinet—some members of my staff—have been known to disappear into the fogs of the Vineyard for long stretches of time. Some of them even claim that the fog obscures not only land and sea, but the sound of the White House telephone. We are delighted that you were able to find your way back from that isolated and mysterious place.' "

JULY 8, 1967
MARTHA'S VINEYARD

The past two days were certainly not vacation; but though "work," work of the pleasantest kind under the pleasantest surroundings.

Stephen Shepard of *Business Week*, accompanied by the knowledgeable, beaming Warren Fugitt of D&R's staff, stepped off the plane Thursday, and from then on I went through the longest sustained "interview" period I can remember.

Shepard's interviewing line and the theme of the piece became quickly evident: How can a private company perform essentially public services and do so at a profit? This would be a *Business Week* angle, apparently.

Shepard is a tall, slender young fellow (perhaps thirty) with intense dark eyes that bore right through you when he is probing. He didn't let me "get away" with my customary general themes, such as my basic propositions about what D&R is all about. By pressing me for "for instances" and illustrations he did me a great service, making me test (and fortify) my convictions.

He asked me to sum up my basic notion about "development"

overseas. I said, "Development will be done by the people directly concerned or it won't be done"—or words to that effect. The corollary fundamental proposition of D&R (and my own long experience) is that people almost everywhere, in the underdeveloped regions and countries, *are* capable of developing their resources and themselves; but this means that the "outside helpers" must have *faith* and confidence in those people, and they must show it. The almost exact reverse has been what has caused development to sag so.

Now much of this sounds like "help people to help themselves"—an old cliché. But neither private business development overseas nor that sponsored and supported by public agencies of the U.S. or the World Bank have shown a sustained conviction that the people in underdeveloped countries have the potential capacities my experience has shown that they have.

So this is one of the distinctive things about the D&R way of going at its work.

How all of this will come out when the story appears in mid-August I certainly wouldn't predict. That Shepard is thoughtful, well-prepared, I have no doubt. But long experience has taught me never to be surprised if what would seem to be a good job of discussion with a writer is received in stony indifference by the public to which it is to be directed, or that the story itself is entirely different from the one you hoped for and had reason to believe your comments would produce.

But we had a good time together, in the course of the talks under the hot and welcome sun here on our deck, and in the lively conversation over meals in which Helen joined—and was lively and interesting in what she said and how she said it.

About the last question Steve put to me he asked as if he was afraid he was "invading privacy." "What about your *own* plans; you don't sound as if you are preparing to retire." "No, I'm not," I said. "My colleagues will have to carry me out of my Chairman's chair the way they carried out old Sewell Avery of Montgomery Ward."

Brave talk; but almost the way I felt. And feel, this day, which is my sixty-eighth birthday.

JULY 10, 1967
MARTHA'S VINEYARD

The Greenbaums came to lunch, here, yesterday. Eddie and I spent almost three hours talking about the way to reactivate the Jordan Valley as a step (a short one, no doubt) toward better conditions in the Middle East between Israelis and Arabs.

Eddie on a slow walk through the Institute woods or at a social gathering in his home looks genial, composed, and is full of banter.

But when he is burrowing into a question new to him he is every inch the wise trial lawyer, in manner and in the kind of question and comment that issues from him. Eddie's eyes turn on you when he doesn't "understand"—or says he doesn't, which may be two different things. "Say that again: I don't understand," and he leans toward you, his eyes almost hooded. Or I strike fire with an idea and his face looks somber, the poker face of the trial lawyer who has got the answer he wants from the witness, on a question he has spent half the night devising.

The subject of the Jordan Valley development is remote from what he already knows. But being a good "family" lawyer (and a good journalist—after all, he has long been a trusted advisor to the *Times*), he soon dug out of me all he *needs* to know, which is usually less than the "expert" knows, but more than enough to get at the heart of the question.

JULY 14, 1967
MARTHA'S VINEYARD

The weather distinctly did *not* continue good. But Gerald Bentley and I set off in Erford Burt's 27-foot Bristol just the same. And by the time we set foot on the Vineyard again, two days later, we had *lived* in fog of a thickness, an opaqueness that was spectacular, no other word for it. And most of the time dead calm, glassy water, "oily" as Erford called it.

To Hadley's harbor, a beautiful landlocked enclosed small body off Buzzards Bay, then on to Cuttyhunk for the night. By motor almost the entire way: an indignity for us who wanted to *sail*; but it turned out to be a juicy kind of experience. Erford insisted that he had never seen heavier fog; at times we could see the gunwale of our boat, but only barely the water alongside the bow! How he navigated by dead reckoning (never missing a buoy) was a great performance. Following a line of lobster pot buoys—he knew they would be along a shelf.

The night at Cuttyhunk, with the dark outlines of other boats all about, every shape and sound distorted, was eerie, otherworldly, and delightful.

Heading back Erford decided (unwisely, he thought a time or two, I could see by the anxiety on his face) to head for the Vineyard through Canapitsit Channel. No visibility at all; the sky and the sea were *one*, no horizon, no nothing. And then he found the two buoys that mark the channel: perhaps seventy-five yards between them, and on both sides of that narrow opening ugly black rocks and a reef over which a hungry surf pounded, a swirl of angry white water.

But all in all, with the spice of danger and the chance for Erford to show us what real piloting is like, it was a good warm experience, perhaps better than the straight sailing we had been counting on since the day months ago when I invited Ged up for a cruise.

Today a letter from David, from Florence. They have established themselves in what he describes as a house well adapted to their needs, including the needs of a big shaggy and beloved dog, and the special needs of a writer. Now if he can settle in and turn loose that magnificent talent of his he may indeed, in his words, find that he "is at a watershed in my life."

JULY 17, 1967
MARTHA'S VINEYARD

Ged Bentley (so patrician with his gleaming white hair) is such an interested man, interested in everything, so full of zest, so remote from the conventional picture of the "scholar" that I enjoyed the week, disappointing as was the sailing (or non-sailing). And his wife Ellen so full of life, so happy in the discovery that there is no statute of limitations on love (each having lost well-beloved spouses only a few years ago).

Actually, I enjoy the fog, *except* when I want to sail. And last night, for two solid hours we four watched in silence and utter enchantment while the western sky, from our hilltop, displayed a sunset that varied from the splendor of broad bands of gold to an angry and embattled steely blue, to a floating billowing pink. How lucky we felt to be quiet witnesses to Nature in such a gorgeously expansive mood.

General Greenbaum just phoned to ask what I thought of Cyrus Sulzberger's "second piece" on the editorial page of yesterday's *Times*, disclosing more about Eisenhower's plan for the development of the Middle East. (The "associate" who prepared it turned out to be Lewis Strauss.) I hadn't seen the *Times*. Eddie explained that it called for development of the region "from the Euphrates to the Nile," the drive to be provided by three great atomic power plants—to desalinize sea water, I assumed. "The reservations you expressed the other day," said Greenbaum, "before you saw this article, apply to this: it is grandiose and not likely therefore to produce anything tangible, soon at least."

Utter quiet, except for an arrow of silver sound, a bob-o-link. The air still, the waters of the Sound a counterpane of grey-blue silence, of nothingness, of peace. The term "still life" comes to mind, the familiar paintings of dead fish or game or fruit; still, yes, but not "life."

Looking out from this our soundless refuge on Indian Hill off to the motionless Sound, and then to the south the great sea itself, I am struck with a thought, a question, quite unlike my perpetually restless self.

The question: How would it be to be as empty of desire as the view from this hill on this motionless noon? How would it be to feel genuinely relieved—as some men are—that there is nothing one really wants, no compulsion to do or feel or strive for anything: just to sit and wait for the tide to come in, and then go out again, without any intervention of one's own? A strange and foreign idea for me, ordinarily; but I can, at this moment, get some glimpse of how such a desire-less world might be.

JULY 19, 1967
MARTHA'S VINEYARD

To do constructive "building" kinds of things in the midst of destruction, cruelty, and hatred—*that* is a real test of one's manhood, the strength of his spirit, his faith that tomorrow can be better than today.

This kind of rumination skims across my half-consciousness as a vague way of describing the "fix"—or opportunity—we of D&R (and I in particular) are in, in our Vietnam task.

This is borne in upon me as I realize how chilled and even horrified I am by the abandoned brutality of the war out there. Is it possible—this thought occurs to more than one person, I happen to know—that a man of Dave Lilienthal's sensibilities and his record as a humane person can approve what goes on in that ugly war? And if he doesn't approve, if in fact he is revolted by this story of man's inhumanity to man, how can he of all people bring himself to take even a remote responsibility for furthering the objectives of the conflict, even though not directly part of the killing—and being killed?

But isn't the ability to do *even a few* humane and constructive things in the very midst of horror and bestiality a role we must all play, unless we withdraw, tidily drawing our skirts about us, to avoid being splattered by the mud of living?

Vietnam does seem specially barbarous to all of us outraged by what we read, or see on the TV screen.

But think of what went on only a few nights ago in the warfare in the streets of Newark. A "good cause" (equality of opportunity for Negroes) besmirched by bloodshed and cowardly killing—a fire chief shot down in the street, answering a "false alarm"; hundreds of unjustly treated black people destroying and looting the shops of white innocents (though who is innocent where men are unjustly treated?). Is a green National Guardsman, with fixed bayonet, ordered to prevent further violence with his gun, or is the compassionate Governor Hughes himself to be condemned for the use of violence in trying to stop rioting?

Consider the acts of violence and of inhumanity toward Jordanians in the area recently conquered by the Israeli armed forces. The pictures of those hapless Arabs, their children about them, their few possessions on their backs, being driven out of their homes by fear. The violence and injustices toward the Jews by the Arabs, the ghastly lives of the people displaced by the Jews, the Arab refugees—do these ugly things mean that at the risk of the kind of criticism one gets in working in Vietnam I, for example, should have "nothing to do" with trying to find some way—such as a Jordan Valley development—that will provide hope for some constructive answer, that will bring something like justice and hope for both Israelis and Arabs?

Still giving much thought to the prospect of using the potentials of "economic cooperation" in Dr. Walter C. Lowdermilk's concept for the Jordan Valley as an emerging pattern for the relations between the now victorious Israelis and the defeated and distraught Jordanians in that part of their country which has been conquered in the recent war. And trying to think of a proper way by which the Shah might be appealed to by me to mediate between the Israelis (who are and have been on good terms with Persia) and Jordan's King Hussein, the Shah's personal friend, the Shah being the most statesmanlike ruler able to approach both sides with a proposal for economic coexistence.

JULY 20, 1967
MARTHA'S VINEYARD

What a wave of sorrow swept over me as the little Sony radio told me the incredible news: John McNaughton, his wife and eleven-year-old son all killed in an airplane collision. My mind reverted to a picture—in "Air Force One" waiting to take off for Guam last March—a very tall, sober man, standing in the plane's aisle with his pretty wife, kidding each other about what their children were "doing" at a teenage party, while she came out to see him off on the long flight. Our conversation about DePauw, where they were students together and where they became engaged, as Helen and I had years before. John and I rooming together in the same Navy residence on Guam; my admiration for his skeptical mind, something McNamara badly needed, I thought, in so close an aide. His promotion to become Secretary of the Navy less than a month ago. And then, a senseless, meaningless event, a Cessna colliding with their commercial plane, and the bright promise of a great future and a happy life gone in a few seconds.

Life is *now*, this day, this hour, this very moment. The future: a big "perhaps."

JULY 21, 1967
MARTHA'S VINEYARD

So lovely was the fog this morning that I stuffed myself into my new Norwegian foul weather gear—huge jacket and voluminous pants—and in this brilliant yellow garb, topped with my beat-up porkpie felt hat with its cocky drake-tail curl, headed for rocky shore of the Sound.

The outward scene—the tide was exceptionally low—had something of the timelessness and monumental patience of Nature. But the man in yellow standing atop a cliff looking out over this serene picture was anything but serene inside himself.

A long phone conversation yesterday afternoon chiefly about efforts to shore up our lagging "resident team" in Vietnam. The two men we can get now are young; sending them out *before* the older, more seasoned men we are trying to get I know is contrary to the best administrative practice.

But trying to get these younger men has a positive virtue: the job is one that requires younger men. Partly because it is a physically rugged place to work. More than that, the Vietnamese "group" with whom we work are mainly young and unseasoned men. It is not too bad to have some of their American fellow workers also young and relatively unseasoned professionally.

JULY 22, 1967
FLYING TO WASHINGTON FROM BOSTON

This morning, muggy and overcast, just right for digging a four-foot hole into which to put the post I had picked for our new "private road" sign and attaching to it the new sign I painted yesterday. How I enjoy physical labor—such as digging that hole through the sand and loam with a long-handled shovel—so the sweat fairly pours and my shirt is soaked. How ghastly it will be when I can no longer do vigorous physical activity.

JULY 23, 1967
WASHINGTON

Talked with Bob Komer by phone this morning: he came back from Saigon with McNamara ten days or so ago, but will return to continue to try to put more energy into the pacification program. Says Bob: "McNamara, summing up the picture out there, did me a great favor by saying that the one program that isn't going well is pacification. That means that *any* improvement I can make is to my credit.

"I'm certainly learning the difference between what it means to be the operating man, in the field, and the policy maker or analyst, sitting in an office in Washington."

Komer remarked vividly on the "great change in McNamara"—whom he admires greatly—since they were in Vietnam together last October. Then the Secretary was so discouraged that his mind was on some way to "stabilize" the military situation, because otherwise the war would go on indefinitely; now by contrast he sees the military situation *turning*. But McNamara, one recalls, has been bitten so many times in the past by projections made for him by the intellectuals he surrounds himself with, the policy and the systems *analysts* who made predictions that were not sustained by events, and he has been beaten up so furiously by that series of wrong guesses.

A long visit with Marguerite Owen,† in her elegant and beautiful new apartment, and then luncheon in Georgetown. She has definitely retired from TVA.

She showed great insight into the self-righteous and "arrogant" attitude of some of the "liberal crowd" about Vietnam and almost everything relating to "Daddy Bird," the President. Went to a meeting, she said, as a guest, of the Americans for Democratic Action, now presided over by Ken Galbraith. "I could hardly stand it. I said to them: 'Your job is to *persuade* people that your opposition to the war is the right policy. But what do you do? You call the war "immoral and evil" and attack the integrity of the people who think otherwise. Now that's no way to persuade anyone, to dismiss their views as immoral, and try to let it go at that! How can anyone discuss a policy when you deny that they have integrity? How arrogant can you be?' "

Carl Sandburg dead: columns of obituary. Who says we Americans don't honor poets?

Seeing Carl's picture on the front pages—that wonderful boyish grin, even at eighty—reminded me of the last visit I had with him, here in Washington. Eating at the Occidental with Helen and David, Ed Murrow, Eric Sevareid, and Carl at a table nearby. We joined forces. Carl had his big guitar, and without need of urging from Ed (who loved the man, and never looked happier than when watching and listening to him), Carl began to sing ballads. Then he proposed we all go to someone's quarters and spend the night hearing him sing. We didn't go, unfortunately.

† Former head of the Washington office of the Tennessee Valley Authority.

JULY 27, 1967
NEW YORK

Much to reflect on, too, about those four days in Washington.

For the first time, I found Washington a beautiful city. And this despite—or because of—the crowds of papas and mamas and their (mostly) bored, but handsome, young ones, trooping through *their* city, from all over America's hinterland.

This time I had a more understanding way of looking at these thousands of my fellow countrymen arriving by great sightseeing buses. As one who for years came to Washington *to work*, the crowds always seemed to me "outsiders." This time I saw the people—the "tourists"—as the very reason and the glory that makes those great public structures and memorials look and be different than those in any other place in the world.

Monday my meetings about our work in Vietnam heartened me greatly. Particularly with Jim Grant.

He had just returned—with the McNamara party—from his first look at the tough job he has undertaken. Stern and muscular personality as he is, with a strong public "organization man" background, his frank enthusiasm for the thesis of *joint* development I have been trying to develop was generous and moving.

"What you have already been able to do in discovering and stimulating *non-governmental* vitality, in individuals and organizations—farmers, labor leaders, students, the universities, and so on—may be the decisive factor," he said.

"But in the end," I replied, "the Vietnamese *themselves* will have to work out a new nation, *between themselves*. And if with our work we can strengthen the non-governmental citizen forces, so that there is a *place* for them in the new nation, these non-governmental forces will have a stronger place in the adjustment *between* Vietnamese—including, of course, the Viet Cong—that must take place if this struggle is to end and a new chapter begin."

The wave of violence that is sweeping the country is a shaking thing to observe, even at a distance. (Not so distant: stores of Fifth Avenue were smashed and robbed last night only a block away from this hotel, the Roosevelt.)

The people who found great satisfaction in stirring up hatred "in a good cause," and the stupid people who think that police and guns can solve anything, have had their day. The result is a wave of terror such as I cannot remember. The President speaks tonight in about an hour. But what speeches will do now is hard to see.

JULY 30, 1967
PRINCETON

Two hours of talk about the Middle East at the edge of Joe Johnson's aquamarine pool, with the wise General Greenbaum serving the function of a great lawyer: to ply the "experts" with questions, with doubts to be resolved, to act as a kind of human radar beam that keeps the thought vehicle heading for the target.

And that "target": some concrete, practical, though limited steps toward progress in the highly emotional and extraordinarily complex Middle East crisis.

A big order indeed. But since it is apparent that our State Department has no very impressive ideas to date (judging from Joe's report of his meeting there Thursday), the General thinks the expertness in political matters that Joe has to an extraordinary degree, and the professional experience that I and D&R have, might together produce some ideas.

We began, of course, with the vast desalination program proposed recently by the British Zionist De Rothschild, and a similar one a few days later by Lewis Strauss, endorsed by General Eisenhower. I said I thought the very act of presenting such a major very-long-range idea was constructive. But—and it was a big "but"—what immediate steps can be taken? What can be done in another ten years is one thing; what can be *started* now, what can be done between now and the first of the year, is what interests me most.

In the short range, I thought a beginning needed to be made, modest in scale, that would demonstrate the Israeli and American desire to be helpful to Jordan in that area Israel now holds by conquest, the so-called West Ghor. This is an area in which Jordanians live and have become the immediate responsibility of Israel, their military and civil authorities administering that territory. What goes on in that West Bank area agriculturally; could Israel and the U.S. speed up that agricultural development, or remove obstacles to it? The West Ghor canal, for example: is it being held up; could it be expedited, as a modest token of good will which might be acceptable to the victors in the war, and yet not compromise the rights or the dignity of the Jordanians? Would such a demonstration of technical and financial assistance in that limited but critical area begin the long process of some kind of rapprochement?

What about asking D&R to examine the possibilities of intensive water and land development of the Euphrates and the Tigris rivers, flowing through Syria and Iraq? The purpose of this suggestion was to avoid efforts that, while they might bring Jordan and Israel closer together (at first in a modest way), would antagonize other adjacent Arab countries and perhaps again make the mistake of emphasizing the "Arab refugee" issue, which in the past has been an impossible political stumbling block.

Joe gave us copy of an excellent memorandum by a Mrs. Georgiana Stevens. While it pays more attention to desalination than I think warranted right now, it supplies some additional critical information: for example, that the head of the Israeli Army is General Dayan, who is also head of the Israeli *water* program! And Israel is therefore in possession today of most of the critical areas "commanding" the Jordan waters.

JULY 31, 1967
NEW YORK

Months ago—in February or March—Bill Warne mentioned that he had an idea about desalting of water for municipal and industrial use, based on his experience in California; he had spoken of it to the Shah, in Tehran, had left with him a memorandum on the subject. At the time I paid little attention to his recital, since the costs were far too high for agricultural use.

But almost overnight desalination may have taken on a *relevance* in a crisis area, the Israeli-Arab struggle. Today I listened to Bill's ideas with the closest attention, and tried to make them fit into the crazy quilt that resulted from the Middle East Israeli-Arab war.

Bill's recital about how D&R might go about desalination *in Iran* along the arid Persian Gulf, appeared to me to remove one of the main impossibilities about the De Rothschild-Strauss proposal. For Bill's idea about desalting in Iran is that the energy needed would come from Iran's natural gas or oil, eliminating the alarming hazard of the De Rothschild-Strauss plan, that of using, as fuel, the large quantities of fissionable materials in atomic power reactors (practically atomic weapon material), put right in the middle of that already explosive situation. And if one used gas now being flared, i.e., burned as a waste, the cost of the fuel for the desalting process (a chief cost) would be cut down almost to zero, bringing the cost of the water within somewhat closer reach even for agricultural use.

The joint Soviet-Iran development of the river that is the border between Russia and Iran‡ has proceeded reasonably well. One could use that success as an analogy for the ideas I hope we can develop of a cooperative development between Israel and Jordan, perhaps other countries. This is the short, short run idea I described to Johnson and Greenbaum yesterday. The long-range plan, of desalination, would also require cooperation, hard to achieve at best, but perhaps better achieved if it is known that other nations—Russia and Persia—once so antagonistic, had managed to benefit on both sides of their boundary by such an

‡ The Moghan Irrigation Project on the Aras River.

arrangement. The Arab-Israeli picture is much more difficult than that between Russia and Persia, for they have had two recent wars. But while more difficult, the *need* to do something constructive is much greater between Israel and the Arab nations.

AUGUST 1, 1967
NEW YORK

"Saw Bob Lovett this afternoon," said Dr. Dana Atchley as we sat down to a drink late yesterday. "Never saw him so discouraged. That *awful* war, wholesale crime—riots are no word for it. Bob felt that the country was falling apart at the seams. Anyway, that's the way it seems to me, too."

This from my philosophical physician, who used to buck me up with his profound perspective on life!

No doubt it *is* a period of trouble. But certainly not as profoundly dark and shadowed as other valleys through which men have walked, and come out to the sunlight.

A long chain of young men parading, with picket signs, before the Army recruiting and induction center a block away, as I came to our building [at One Whitehall Street]: "Peace"—and so on; other reminders of heartaches: the roster of dead seamen, on that technological triumph the aircraft carrier *Forrestal*, limping through the seas after a disaster. Outbursts of violence in the streets of Milwaukee last night, adding that "civilized" once Socialist-led city to the already long list of far less cultivated places that have seen disturbances this summer. De Gaulle supported in France with his invitation to the people of Canada to break up that country and plunge her into strife, for no apparent reason except separatist doctrine.

Yes, there is plenty of conflict in today's news, and yesterday's, and probably tomorrow's. But I'm too moved by the conviction that only in times of trouble and conflict do creative solutions appear to let these and similar events weigh my heart down.

AUGUST 5, 1967
MARTHA'S VINEYARD

The war in Vietnam is not going well. The President's asking for more troops and a tax increase to meet the added costs of the war seems to confirm the impression.

When Abraham Lincoln was confronted with defeats or stalemates —and draft riots when more troops were called up—he began shopping around for a new commanding general. But President Johnson prefers, apparently, to accept the advice that he gets from Bob McNamara and General Westmoreland that all is going well.

What happened when the British lost their great battleships during World War II? Churchill continued to support the leadership of the Admiralty. Actually, Churchill (the "Naval Person") *was* the Admiralty. Perhaps that is why President Johnson doesn't do something drastic about the conduct of the war—i.e., he, Johnson, feels he is directing it.

AUGUST 10, 1967
MARTHA'S VINEYARD

Long talk by phone with John Rockefeller III, who called me this morning.

Wanted my counsel about what could be done to get more action into the population control program, worldwide. Much progress has been made: certainly the subject is now more candidly and widely and favorably discussed. But *results* are quite disproportionate to the great needs. He asked: Is there some analogy to overcome this *action inertia* that occurs to you, out of your atomic energy experience, perhaps, where a huge organized effort was mobilized to get something done quickly, by giving it a high priority?

Of course, such huge technical enterprises are quite different in most respects. But, I suggested, they may be apposite in the central idea, namely that it was the *priority* of intense feeling, high importance, etc., that made such great progress possible in those fields.

The action lag on population control is, I think, simply one more manifestation (or symptom?) of a general, universal, and large contemporary disability, a lack of skill, or concern, or appetite for *doing.*

Consider the number of conferences, papers, research projects, scholarship grants, foundation grants, speeches, think-tankism—and so on—on the issues of "policy." Then compare all this—and the prestige and emphasis associated with "policy" talk-talk—with what is given to *how* to get some things going. The contrast may be enlightening.

AUGUST 11, 1967
MARTHA'S VINEYARD

The Vietnam tragedy deepens steadily. The news pours in of the almost farcical deterioration of any semblance of a representative "election." I know, and have known since Guam, that the *national* election was bound to be *far* from the neat plebiscite our theories would expect it to be.

I know how unreasonable it is to expect a miracle of democracy the first time these people have that chance, and in the midst of a war. But when the crude facts are made so plain, by the collapse in the past couple days of what we, in this experienced democracy, would call a "campaign," it is a pain almost beyond bearing.

Ky has been a strange figure. What he is saying is "these ignorant peasants" can't possibly know how to choose between the many candidates, not in a few weeks, not in a few years. No matter how much of a campaign. Yet the chilling, negative effect of what he says is so casual and flip.

If the "election" turns out (as seems almost certain) to yield a vast majority for the military candidates, then it is discredited by those who want to discredit it before the election is ever held. And who can say that there is any better alternative—who, on the merits, can say that? But to discredit the election in this way will make anything we of the Joint Development Group do most difficult. Perhaps impossible. If the election is a palpable fraud (like a ballot-stuffing election in Memphis was under Boss Ed Crump), then we of D&R shall simply have to withdraw; we can't do the constructive professional things that are expected of us.

I don't expect a fraud, i.e., a deliberate vote-stealing kind of election. Just an election that will not convince anyone that a legitimate government of the public has been elected. It may well *not* even be true, but it *is* what is likely to be believed, the world over.

If we Americans were being pushed hard by enemy forces—as we were so often and so perilously in the early period of World War II—one could say: No matter what, we will all push together and endure and prevail. As we were, and did.

But we say—most people do—this is not *our* war, but "theirs." And if "they" don't stand up and fight—and *vote* honestly—then what is there at stake for us?

AUGUST 14, 1967
MARTHA'S VINEYARD

Saturday the *Business Week* issue with the Shepard article§ about D&R arrived and was read with gratification. The sight of my craggy, very much lined, and quizzical face filling the cover was something of a shock. But the piece itself I thought was a tour de force of catching the spirit and motivation of what we are trying to do.

A dozen quail go by, led by a haughty, fierce cock; looked at through the glasses, his curved beak and zebra stripes make his head look like an eagle's. And the hens scurry when he makes for them, though, hen-like, they don't seem to do more than give the appearance of scurrying: "hard to get" is perhaps the phrase. But the whole flock is so lovely in the high grass all about our house, in the complete silence of this hilltop.

§ "Selling Self-help at a Profit," *Business Week*, August 12, 1967.

Silent now, but half an hour ago the air was filled with the concussion of bombing—Navy target practice on Nomans Island. The same incongruous effect as the sound of bombing was each early morning in Saigon.

My memory carries me back to the long afternoon of briefing at Guam, the President slouched way down in his huge chair, the military chiefs around him, an air officer describing the targets "available," the President asking what would be the "cost" (i.e., in planes lost and civilian casualties) of hitting those targets. And in the past ten days or so, the order has been given to strike those very targets, including the bridges to China across the Red River.

Has the President concluded that there is only one way: a rout of the North Vietnamese army and economy, and that otherwise this country faces a debacle? Any form of American "caving in," described in whatever proud public relations words, would mean just that. And is "limited war" suited any longer to the literally unlimited commitment we now have?

Never mind now how we got into our present posture, unwisely and tragically or no. The North Vietnamese and their partners the Chinese and Russians, have got us pushed into a corner—or we have gotten ourselves into a corner—from which only the taking of long risks and the use of great military power can extricate us. And this whether the Vietnamese *want* us to fight for them or not: in theory that is *still* the test (as Senator Kennedy reminded the country the other day). But at this point is it any longer the test?

Suppose ten days before the Normandy landing the French had advised us that they no longer wanted us to "liberate" them—not a preposterous position for the French at that!—would we have called our armies back? Of course not. However the horror of World War II *began*, what it finally became was the United States against Germany.

How does the Vietnam war, right now, differ markedly?

AUGUST 21, 1967
NEW YORK

A half hour or so with McGeorge Bundy this afternoon. Where did the story start that this is a cold, "arrogant," austere man? He was anything but that in our talk. His eyes are extraordinarily alive and warm, at times almost twinkling through his glasses, at others showing the disdain and disappointment we both feel about the "deterioration" (my term) in the Israeli-Arab picture since Joe Johnson talked to him about my ideas, now some three weeks ago.

He agreed that the grandiose atomic desalting schemes are as badly conceived as I myself think they are. "John McCone, Lewis Strauss, Jim Ramey, and Alvin Weinberg of the AEC have all been at me to push a billion dollar desalting scheme," he explained. "Quite aside from anything else, the idea of putting that much atomic weapons material out there is frightening and wrong . . . but the President, you know, he hates to see Eisenhower steal his own line: making the desert bloom and that sort of thing. But so far the President hasn't taken a position."

Told Bundy I thought our efforts to prevent the "proliferation" of atomic weapons—i.e., their spread to other countries—were negated by what we are already doing all over the world, exporting enough atomic weapons material to make a very large stockpile. I had protested to [AEC Chairman] Seaborg but got nowhere.

"Seaborg on this subject has a deaf ear. No one on the present Commission sees that at all," Bundy said. "*We* are the proliferators—you're exactly right. And it would be a public service—in view of your background and public prestige—if you were to say so publicly."

I explained how we proposed going about a desalting program on the Persian Gulf, modest in size, related to the flared gas, not holding out golden promises of cheap irrigation water for general purposes.

As I left I said I would like to talk to him someday about our Vietnam assignment. "How do you find the Vietnamese who are working with you?" he asked. When I replied that I thought they were extraordinarily competent, particularly the younger men, his face lighted up. His final words: "That's the key; that's the key," and surely it is.

AUGUST 22, 1967
NEW YORK

The Ivory Coast President, Felix Houphouet-Boigny, a diminutive fellow, neither young nor old in appearance, and his wife, a most handsome woman, quite young certainly, gave us a warm welcome last night. He hung—or pinned—decorations on "Soapy" Williams and four others of us.

This is all very touching somehow: this little country, a product of French colonialism, adopting the trappings of American style in the most elegant of the Waldorf's ceremonial rooms.

Governor Williams begins to look like one of the discards of politics, the unhappy look partly disguised by his ebullient playboy manner. When I asked him about his state of Michigan (meaning the terrible scandal of the Detroit riots) he was vague and wanted to change the subject. All the genuinely felt "loving care" and partisanship he exhibited, as Governor, for the black population of Detroit, all the money spent, the wise things done by him and his successor, all the to-do about his becoming the American representative *in Africa* of the American black population he had "understood" so well—what did it amount to when the test came in his own state? I couldn't help having this probably ungenerous personal reaction. And the New Haven riots the other day, in the "model city" to which Ed Logue and other able, dedicated people gave so much of themselves. Everyone is puzzled, I most of all.

AUGUST 23, 1967
WASHINGTON

I have had my share of the wear and tear of public service and of the equally searing vexations and worries of the kind of public service in a private role that has been my choice of a life in the past eleven years.

But at last night's State dinner for the Shah at the White House I was paid in full, and more. Paid by a unique kind of recognition from *two* heads of state. To pretend that it didn't warm a heart that has had more than its share of kudos as well as often empty honors would be absurd.

When the hour came (after the dessert) for the President to offer the usual pro forma "toast" to his visiting guest, the Shah, he read (and well) from a script before him. But it wasn't the standard brief set of generalities about the "friendship that has marked the relations of our two countries and I therefore ask you to drink a toast."

His words were an extended statement of the achievements for progress of the Shah's regime in recent years: the figures on land reform, growth of democratic institutions, the building of the natural resources of the country. Then he left his text, and looking at me across the room (I was at a little table with the Shah, the First Lady, Secretary Rusk, and six others), spoke of his pride that this "distinguished American, David Lilienthal, is with us tonight," who "has done such great things for his own country, and now is doing such great things for Iran."

The President's speech was serious; the lessons to be drawn from Iran he applied—without saying so precisely—to the troubled state in the Middle East. But it had a touch of humor: "We miss his beautiful and charming Queen tonight. But she is preparing for a coronation. The Shah has shown his great sense of timing in that coronation, to be held in October. *He* is going to be crowned while *his* polls are *up*." (A wry reference, of course, to the fact that the President's polls, so high six weeks ago, are at their very lowest today.)

The podium was installed before the Shah; he rose and without the semblance of a note began a ten, perhaps fifteen, minute speech. A little of it was the usual general rhetoric customary with these reciprocal toasts. Since I sat just across the table from him I could study his face—and what a handsome face it is. He stated as well as a man could what he is doing and has done; that it is just a start; that it is going too slowly.

And then he turned to look directly at me.

"A mark of the *spirit* of your country toward mine and one of the greatest contributions your great country has made to my government and my people has been that of this very distinguished citizen, who has wrought such wonders in your country, David Lilienthal.

"Years ago he told me things about my country, even detailed facts about its potentialities, that I myself didn't know." This with a quiet grin. "And the plan he proposed and has been carrying out confirmed all his predictions. What he has done to instill faith in my people—and in me—in what Iran can do for itself is one of the great gifts of this great land to my people. And more is to come. We are now on the way to increasing the production of food utilizing the experience of America. You in America have shown the way. We hope to utilize that experience."

After the dinner there was a good deal of "gathering around," people a little goggle-eyed (as I was) by my being singled out in this way. After years of trying to learn how to "take" flattering remarks by making some self-deprecatory wisecrack—I now just thank people, and let it go at that. But the comment "I guess you were the guest of honor" was a bit much, and I must have looked as nonplussed as I felt.

The "entertainment"—an American cowboy ballet by Agnes de Mille—over, there was the usual festive gathering in the foyer for coffee and dancing. But the President's usual gaiety and high spirits had seeped out of him. He greeted a few friends, and then moved off and left for the family quarters. I have rarely seen anything so sad as the droop of his shoulders, the set of his back as he walked through a door and left.

It has been a very, very tough go, these past few weeks particularly, even the past couple of days, as two American fliers were shot down on Chinese soil, and all the second-guessers (as well as the many honest doubters in Congress) have poured out their criticism of the war in language that they wouldn't have dared utter six weeks ago.

Standing in the foyer, listening to the music and wanting to start for my hotel, I saw Mrs. Johnson. She turned from the people she was talking with, headed for me, gave me a look, and went on past and through a door to a room off the foyer. I was disappointed, but thought perhaps she, like the President, had had enough of the evening.

Later on, I saw her bearing down on me. She took me by the arm and said, "I wanted to talk to you, and when I got out of the room found you had abandoned me; I was pretty deflated." I explained that I didn't realize she had intended me to follow her.

She led me to a little settee in one of the lovely rooms that lead from the foyer, asked me to sit beside her, turned her extraordinarily alive face toward me, put her hand under her chin, and looking intently, said:

"I don't know anyone, not anyone, who has had such a fascinating life as you have had."

Lady Bird is such an utterly genuine person that I didn't know what to say except to agree that I had had an extremely interesting life, and it still was. And we went on from there.

I told her what a remarkable man the Shah was, that in the past few years he had openly confronted and prevailed over elements in Iran that when I first went out there tried to dominate him: the Mullahs, the *local* religious leaders, the great landlords; the ancients in the Senate, the Mossadeqh people, the younger disillusioned people. And now his position was secure and his country was making the spectacular progress in all directions recounted in the President's speech at the dinner.

She looked very anxious: "*How* did he do this, how?"

By having a definite program, was my opinion. Five or six years ago he laid down the things he wanted to achieve, and managed to make this plain to many of the people. And then he got behind the Khuzistan program—about which many, indeed most, Iranian leaders had been skeptical at first, though the Shah from the beginning gave it—and me—unfailing support—and soon there was *evidence* that people could see of what that program could mean to them. And his philosophy: pride in Iran's ancient history and culture, but the determination that Iran be modern—these things struck home, and eventually persuaded even the intellectuals.

Our conversation must have lasted ten or fifteen minutes, while in the adjoining space the music was going full tilt.

Out of the corner of my eye I saw a portrait of Mrs. Roosevelt. That portrait, of an older woman, seemed bemused and tolerant, not the crusader. But as great a woman as Eleanor Roosevelt *became*, there was a time, when she lived in that great House, when she was much, much less well organized, focussed, and realistic than this dark-haired intense young woman with the strong Southern accent, sitting there beside me. (I say "young" because she seemed just that: her vitality, stamina, the sense of her being involved keenly in everything that went on around her, and around her husband's work.)

I said some hopeful things about what I found among some of the Vietnamese, particularly the younger ones, and my hope that we could make things move even during the war. But their spirits needed a lift; this was crucial. "It would be great if you would have a visit among the villagers, and among some of the young people we have met," I said. "You have a way of showing your heartfelt interest in others; this they need badly." She considered this a moment. I could almost see her storing away my words, perhaps to take up with that huge hulk of a man, back now bowed, hair much whiter even than when we travelled together to Guam.

"The President," I went on with Mrs. Johnson, "has a great talent for teaching what democracy means. I heard him at the great oval table at Guam, preaching that doctrine of 'getting together' to Thieu and Ky—and it was a classic, a positive classic, so moving and so right, and it produced results.

"If only there had been a tape recording of that talk. The words weren't so important as the fervor, the intonations, the dramatic effect."

"Yes, it is too bad there wasn't a tape recording." She paused, her dark eyes sad. "If we go down . . . " A nervous laugh. "If we go down in history there may not be any record of these things, but only the formal speeches. And the President is at his best in a small group, fifteen or twenty people. On TV none of that warmth and strong feeling comes through."

In spite of a memorable evening, all in all I found the atmosphere at the White House—including this morning in the few minutes with Rostow—pretty whipped. Except for Dean Rusk. He seemed utterly composed, almost puckish, as he talked to the jewel-laden lady next to him at dinner. Rusk, of all of them, seems to believe everything will come out all right.

In Walt Rostow's outer office this morning, I saw McGeorge Bundy bent over a sheet of paper, busy revising. He informed me that he had just reported our conversation "to the Boss," who thought, too, that "it would be a public service if you spoke out against the grandiose big atomic desalting idea." Maybe, but I doubt it.

A productive visit with Walt, who seems less frantic (understandably) than when I saw him on the Guam trip. I left him with the impression I wanted: that we were working hard to bring something good out of the misery in Vietnam, knowing full well how slender were the chances and how stony the road.

Went on to spend half an hour with Dean Rusk this afternoon. I summarized my thoughts to the Secretary about the West Bank of the Jordan as a possible place to start some direct dealings between the Israelis and the Jordanians. I assumed, however, that the prospects were not at all bright now; that the Israelis gave every appearance of planning to continue to occupy the West Bank indefinitely.

"You can't assume that," Rusk said; "there are signs that something between occupation and a returned Jordan sovereignty may be negotiable. In which case your ideas of an intensive development of the West Bank might be possible. But the Israelis will certainly not want to have that area occupied entirely by Arabs; it would change the whole character of Israel in a relatively few years."

He seems to like the idea of a regional program of some kind. I also spoke of the possibilities of extremely cheap water for irrigation out of the Tigris-Euphrates, as part of what I called a Mideast Water Pool. And the use of Iran's flared gas for desalting appealed to Rusk.

"That gas could be transported by pipeline a long way, couldn't it, perhaps all the way to Jordan?"

AUGUST 24, 1967
FLYING TO THE VINEYARD, VIA NEW YORK

On a scale of 100, last night's jamboree for the Shah and twenty-five "business" men, at Governor Harriman's, would certainly rank at least 80.

The Shah looked drawn and thin, after a full schedule of serious discussions in Washington which he must bear almost alone. But the Shah is an army in himself; he really needs no staff support. And he appears to be tireless. After a dinner, an excellent speech by Averell, the Shah's strong exposition of his country's "hopes and possibilities," statements by others (including one by me), and two hours of visiting with individuals, he left about 11:30, restored, jaunty as ever, his eyes warm in greeting people, his earlier signs of fatigue overcome by the convictions and sense of success that shows in everything he does. And I wonder if some of the sense of new confidence and ease he shows these past few years isn't due to his marriage.

The Shah's talk was directed principally to the businessmen Governor Harriman had brought together. He emphasized the "revolution" he had put into effect ("in one big effort—it couldn't be done gradually"), getting rid of a "feudal" system of land owernship (his phrase), ridding the country of the exploitation of one man by another ("that is gone now in Iran and the people know it"), by laws such as those providing that the workers in the factories are entitled to 20% of the profits.

Then he got around to development of agriculture. He quoted me as saying that there are "a million hectares of good land." He wants, he said, to introduce to his country modern American methods of raising of food and its processing. To that end every kind of protection can be assured to foreign investors. "Investors isn't quite the word," he continued. "It isn't so much capital we will need as technical know-how, managerial know-how, in which your country excels. And we are not so blind or proud that we don't know that we are not as advanced in these respects as this country. We welcome your participation. You can be assured of fair treatment; there is no chance of loss because of government policies or political instability."

Stewart Udall made a disappointing speech, one right out of his barrel, full of platform rhetoric about "land and water and resources as the foundation of a nation," etc. In Iran he had found these concerns were foremost in the Shah's mind. Ickes, when he was Secretary, for all his consummate vanity and irritability, would never have made such a flag-waving conservation lecture to that kind of action-minded group.

My disappointment was multiplied when Udall and I talked, afterward, about desalting. "That big desalting scheme of Strauss'—fellows like Clint Anderson and Scoop Jackson and Mike Mansfield don't want to see the Republicans steal our issue; we've got to do something to stop that." I was shocked: was he willing to put forward some headline-snatching scheme that would die when the facts became better known (and Udall surely knows how far off the beam are the Strauss atomic desalting figures) just to keep "the Republicans" from having an issue?

Governor Harriman called on me to say a few words. I said, "I can't add anything to the rhetoric, with all of which I agree based on my eleven years' work in Iran." Then I talked some specifics about the agrobusiness ambitions of the Shah, and D&R's assignment in it.

There had been a good deal said about petrochemical plants, steel mills, pump manufacturing factories. "An *industrial* operation looks pretty much the same wherever you see it," I said. "In fact, you walk into a petrochemical plant in *any* country and except for the identity of the operators, you couldn't know what country you are in.

"But that isn't true of agricultural production, of farming. Farming is the most complex of all production tasks, if well done. You can train a man right out of the rice paddies of Vietnam to run a tractor or repair a motor bike. This I have seen. But to make a good intensive irrigation farmer takes time.

"It is *people* who raise food; not fertilizer or insecticides or machines. And that is where you have to begin—at least that is where we began ten years ago in Khuzistan. And these Iranian peasants—that's a word I had to learn; I myself would call them 'cultivators' [the Shah smiled gently at this crack]—did learn well. Once their diet and health were improved, their initial physical weakness gave way to vigor.

"And as for the 'profit motivation'—you don't need to lecture these cultivators about the principles of free enterprise. The tiller of the soil practically invented the profit motive.

"But because the land and water resources of the Khuzistan are so remarkably favorable doesn't in itself ensure that American businessmen, responsible to stockholders for what they do with the company's assets and manpower, will automatically develop agricultural production and processing in Iran. So the Shah has assigned to D&R some responsibility to help American business become interested in this opportunity, and to give some of the detailed answers to detailed questions that they will have."

I described the agreement—as Warne understands it—to have a D&R man in Tehran to interpret Khuzistan to American agrobusiness, and an Iranian in our Sacramento office to observe agrobusiness in California and elsewhere and carry that story back to Iran with him.

AUGUST 31, 1967
MARTHA'S VINEYARD

One of the worst examples of how far a few critics have flipped their lid is a full-page ad in the *Vineyard Gazette*. A highly personal attack on the now Under Secretary of State, Nicholas Katzenbach, who summers at Chilmark on the Vineyard.

John Oakes, Editor of the editorial page of the *New York Times*, was at "Topside" (our Vineyard house) last Saturday for cocktails. A soft-voiced, conciliatory man in manner, a man of convictions but with an inquiring mind, I've always thought, and still do. I said I was disturbed by the tactics some opposed to the Vietnam war were indulging in, and cited the full-page ad. He colored, ducked his head, shook it sadly, I thought. "Yes, I agree about that ad," he said. "The man who initiated it, and mostly wrote it, and paid for it, at the end wouldn't sign it himself, saying it would put him in a cross fire."

Thinking hard about our forthcoming report and joint recommendations to the Vietnamese Government to be elected Sunday. Then tried my hand, in a casual way, at a letter to Tom Mead and Fred Moore, on the front line in Saigon. The letter goes like this:

"What is the essential and basic function of the economic, engineering, agronomic, and administrative talents D&R (and the Vietnamese partner-group) brings to this [postwar development] task? Is it to provide the technical and managerial guidance and proposals by which to strengthen what South Vietnam now has in the way of its social structure, in short to point the way to a more 'productive' Vietnam, if the Vietnamese choose to follow the way suggested or recommended?

"Or—are we looking toward much more than that, and is much more than that expected of us? . . . Isn't it our duty to our convictions to consider what we recommended—however technical the terms and the corpus of our report or ideas—to be the means of basic changes in the direction of . . . 'social justice,' or to use a more colloquial expression, 'to give the little fellow a better break' as a consequence of and as the inspiration of our economic and technical studies, analysis, and recommendations?

"I think the answer is a sturdy Yes, that is our duty and our underlying function."

SEPTEMBER 1, 1967
MARTHA'S VINEYARD

Wind northeast and very cool: the first sense of autumn. The little pyramids of sumac, the glow of goldenrod in our meadow, the dark glowering sky, unlimited visibility, the Elizabeth Islands *and* the ocean plain as plain; they all say: we *told* you summer wouldn't last forever. And I'm glad about that: this has been a long, long stint, this summer.

But yesterday I sailed again, in a very gutsy, strong breeze. Snapped the clew outhaul, leaving me with a wildly flapping main, just before I was preparing to come into and *among* the close-packed fleet in the inner harbor. Quite active, there for a while it was.

Finishing *War and Peace* the other night—for the third or fourth time, over the years—I came on a description of Nikolai's theory of farming, written a hundred years ago. "He laughed at theoretical treatises on estate management, did not care for . . . so costly grain, and as a general thing did not confine himself to one department of agriculture alone; he always kept before his eye the welfare of the *estate* [D.E.L.: "integrated and unified development"] and not one particular part of it."

Then: "The chief thing to his mind was not the nitrogen in the soil or the oxygen in the air, nor manure or special ploughs, but the principal agent by which nitrogen, oxygen, manure and plough were made effective—the peasant labourer . . . it was the peasant who especially attracted his attention: the peasant seemed to him not merely a tool but also an end in himself . . . he studied the peasants attentively, trying to understand what they were after, what they considered good and bad, and only made a pretense of supervising and giving orders while in reality learning from them their methods. . . .

"And it was only when he had gained an insight into the peasants' tastes and aspiration, had learnt to talk their language, that he began boldly giving them orders—in other words, fulfilling toward them the duties expected of him. And Nikolai's management produced the most brilliant results."◖

SEPTEMBER 2, 1967
MARTHA'S VINEYARD

"A Vineyard day," at last, the first of the summer. The waters of the Sound this morning were profoundly dark, dark and steely, rimmed by the whitish scallops of the Elizabeth Island cliffs. And by turning one's head slightly, there, spread high somehow *above* the horizon, the

◖ Tolstoi, *War and Peace*, Penguin edition, p. 1358.

band of azure blue that is the great ocean. And that glint this northern air gives everything it touches, when the special kind of atmosphere reaches us from the Polar region. Each leaf is a distinct and separate object, seeming to give out light.

SEPTEMBER 4, 1967
OUR 44TH WEDDING ANNIVERSARY
MARTHA'S VINEYARD

I don't *at all* feel that the turbulent world of today has forsaken the values I held dear when I was younger, those I believed in and fought for during my middle years.

Per contra, much of the turmoil and conflict and even the physical violence that is so characteristic of this time is a mark of the very struggle that in my younger radical years I also fought for and at times paid a rather high price to try to maintain.

The time may come when, being a *really* old one, I may sadly shake my bowed head, and mutter about how the world has abandoned most of the solid "values" of the past. It may come, but not while my blood vessels are as resilient as they are now, at sixty-eight plus.

SEPTEMBER 7, 1967
NEW YORK

This morning the *New York Times* published a fair-minded report about the Vietnamese. The Congressional delegation of twenty watchers who visited Vietnam at election time was quoted as expressing the kind of admiration for those remarkable people that I have expressed in recent weeks. Said they hardly recognized the country, so different—and better—was it than the press and TV reports they had been exposed to.

A long letter to Cabot Lodge, commenting on a highly theoretical report prepared by his son George last June asserting the need for a new *political* structure in Vietnam as a precondition of any economic gains. But the basic assumption, I fear, is that the U.S. can reconstitute this political structure, as we did in Japan as an occupying power. (Not that that lasted very long after MacArthur and our army left.)

Only the Vietnamese—South and North—can remake the political structure of their country, and it seems to me there is a fair chance they can and will do it.

SEPTEMBER 18, 1967
NEW YORK

The *Business Week* cover story has evoked the most extraordinarily varied mail. Several of the do-good type from the ministerial area: an assistant pastor in Oklahoma City (three intense pages) and a Catholic "seminarian"; any number from hard-boiled people who read the "philosophy" of D&R as what they have been looking for, straight from the shoulder, that sort of thing. Some esoteric ones from these people who call themselves systems analysts, or words to that effect, filled with the kind of weird convoluted reasoning, abstract as a zero, and meaningless to me; some from men who are running some kind of smallish business who want to have a "part of more significant things in the world."

How can it be that these varied responses, from all the often *conflicting* points of the compass, are in full and enthusiastic agreement with the very same set of ideas in the identical article?

SEPTEMBER 20, 1967
NEW YORK

Just back from a great day in Washington.

Leonhart of the White House detail, at lunch, not at all sure about the Vietnamese election yet. But apparently sure—as I am—of one thing: that my slogan "Vietnamese solutions for Vietnamese problems" is better than any battle cry so far. Pretty dour about the military "posture."

Later in the day five of us D&R-ers met with Jim Grant and his wise, soft-spoken deputy Roy Wehrle, for more than two hours. Jim Grant looked worn and harassed, having just received word of the resignation of the heads of the Volunteer Agency in Vietnam, with a biting public letter about AID—and the war, of course. Grant will have more of this, as our country becomes increasingly divided and bitter about the war, from wanting it "stopped" (as if it is all that easy), to wanting stepped-up bombing.

But Grant has made an emotional commitment: with each passing month the end of military opposition grows closer, thus the need for a long-term program is increasingly imperative. I don't agree about his timetable ("at the most," he says, "eighteen months"), but do agree that our work is central to the *present* as well as the future.

SEPTEMBER 21, 1967
NEW YORK

Lunched, alone, with General Sarnoff in his baronial quarters atop Rockefeller Plaza.

Greatly disturbed and unhappy about the state of the world; his highly dramatic sense of gloom is nothing new for him, though he says that never in his life has he felt that the world was in worse condition: American democracy "disintegrating"; mobocracy taking over; "collective bargaining is finished, finished, and nothing left but that the government fix wages, and that means fix prices . . . the young people entirely out of hand." The works. I argued back, that there are things we can't now see, any of us, all we can be sure about are the negative aspects.

Oddly enough, what has upset him and caused him to "suffer"—his word—most is a book called *The Wisdom of Sarnoff and the World of RCA*, by Leon Gutterman. Apparently the book portrays him as if he were next to God, so as to subject him, he fears, to ridicule. He has apparently spent most of this summer trying to make everyone aware that he repudiates the book, which was published *without* his approval.

"After all," he said darkly, "one slip can destroy the good or the standing that a man has built up during a lifetime."

Extraordinary the things men worry about.

SEPTEMBER 23, 1967
PRINCETON

Dean Rusk's eighteen-year-old daughter marries a young Negro in a big fashionable wedding. The daughter of the man—a Georgian—who ranks next to the President. May this not be an event as important, in its cultural significance, as anything that has happened, more important than Thurgood Marshall's becoming a Justice of the Supreme Court?

The new Board of Directors of D&R has its initial meeting, around the table being the new owners, the men who do the work, the staff. A great sense of controlled excitement and even emotion. For me, an important event, though the decision itself was made almost a year ago.

We talked around the table about the prospect of putting D&R into the urban field, to try to provide *ideas* of a managerial sort to cope with perhaps the most urgently felt need of the country: what to do about the urban mess, how best to begin to turn the vitality urbanism represents into a great opportunity to build a new kind of urban society.

Lunch yesterday noon at the august banking house of Lehman Brothers as the guest of a partner, Paul Davies, a skinny, sharp little man, until recently head and leader of Food Machinery Corporation. Also present, my cousin Jim Szold, with that deceptively sleepy look of his—he is bright as a new tack—and a wryness that is his form of humor. Also, tough as nails General Lucius Clay, a recent partner, the hero of the Berlin Airlift. Piercing eyes, a hawklike visage, a great record as a military administrator rather than as a combat General. I asked him how he had felt in crossing the bridge between public service in the military, and being a banker. He wasn't sure his associates at Lehman would admit that he *was* a banker. But the big difference had been this:

that in investment banking each partner was on his own with his problem; there was none of the dealing with an organization, selecting of personnel, none of the activities of a manager.

This stirred memories for me, for without quite realizing it, it was this difference—and lack of savor to which I had become accustomed in the managerial life—that had made me feel so lost when I first took my place in that tiny little room at Lazard Freres' investment bank almost fifteen years ago.

SEPTEMBER 24, 1967
PRINCETON

Dinner with our Princeton neighbors, Bob and Helen Meyner.

Helen's parents were among the guests, the William Stevensons—very distinctive people. He is tall, handsome, with his erect figure and sense of assurance, she still a classic and much admired "beauty." Helen's enthusiasm for her mother, and pride in her father's career, so evident at dinner, was such a happy contrast with the current fad among offspring to "disinherit" everything their parents have stood for. For eighteen years President of Oberlin, and, so his daughter assured me, he "made the place human." Then Ambassador to the Philippines.

After dinner, Dick Hughes, Governor of New Jersey, and his remarkable wife, as big of heart and stamina as she is big of person, came sailing in—as I had hoped.

Hughes has an outward humility and lack of pompousness rare in those who have reached the pinnacle of Governorship of a major state. In a lemon yellow sports jacket, he looked like a backfield football coach.

He talked to me, with more conviction than I expected, of his recent trip to Vietnam, as one of the "observers" of the election. In measured language—for he is a deliberate kind of man, though there must be a good deal of passion underneath—he spoke of the press corps out there, who are constantly looking for ways of discrediting the U.S. and the Vietnamese. But the press corps is beginning to be "divided right down the middle" because the *New York Times*, which dominates the scene because of money and numbers, has made the others leery of them.

I spoke warmly about what Hughes was doing to solve New Jersey's problems, particularly in education and urban development. He replied, "Yes, but I'm not an administrator. When I get back from a trip there's that lot of papers and correspondence two feet high. My secretary says: 'Governor, how about first answering this mail that is a year old!'" (At this a boyish grin.) "Now, Bob [Meyner] scribbles something on a letter or paper that comes in and someone else disposes of it. I have to do it all myself!"

What amused me about this—though I said nothing—was that the most crucial and rare administrative talent is the one he has: his ability to pick excellent people and induce them to serve the state: Paul Ylvisaker, Clarence Dillon, and so on. Being an administrator isn't just being able to "delegate" jobs.

SEPTEMBER 27, 1967
NEW YORK

Yesterday an extraordinary personal letter from Tom Mead. How well he understands the respect due the talents and desires of the people with whom and *for* whom one works, in those countries that are *rising*. It is not just the countries that are rising—rising *again*, in the case of the ancient lands—but the *people* as well, individuals who are trying to assert themselves against heartbreaking odds.

Never such a case of this very tragedy as Vietnam. For the Americans called upon to help save them from a *native tyranny* (within South Vietnam or from the North) are beginning to find the "superior" Americans coming more and more to resemble *in attitude* the very colonialists that after so long and at such a cost were ousted.

The clamor and the agonizing about the Vietnam war have risen to new heights these past few days. Even Senator Case, not the most daring or positive of men under any circumstances, but cautious and judicious, has fired a salvo at the President as if the war could be undone, the 12,000 young Marines brought back to life, if it turned out that his legal argument about the meaning of the Tonkin Gulf Resolution could be established by a series of debaters' points. Morton of Kentucky has pricked up his never very great daring, to admit that he was wrong and the President has been brainwashed by the military-industrial complex. And the full-page ads, the resolutions, the petitions signed by thousands asking that we "negotiate now"—with whom? when what they *must* mean is give up the whole sad business as a bloody mistake, and let Ho Chi Minh take over the Vietnamese.

OCTOBER 9, 1967
NEW YORK

The intensity and warmth of this man Ebtehaj haven't diminished a whit in the ten years and more that I have known him, thought I as he came bouncing across the reading room at the Century, where we met at 3 P.M. today.

After some brief reminiscing (neither of us likes to spend much time looking *backward*), he spoke of all I might do for the further fruition of the Khuzistan, now that Iranian annual oil revenues are in excess of three quarters of a billion dollars (ten years ago barely $100 million).

"When the Shah returned from his trip to Washington," Ebtehaj said, "he had a meeting at the Summer Palace of the Prime Minister and the other Ministers and also Asfia. He said how enormously impressed he was to find what standing Mr. Lilienthal had in America." And then proceeded to give directions about the priority to be given Khuzistan and particularly the agrobusiness idea.

It hurts Ebtehaj, that is evident, that those in power whom he feels had vilified him should now recognize that what he said about Khuzistan was true: that it was Iran's greatest asset. "If I were asked to help with the Khuzistan I would make myself available on that program, *not* [he shook his head vigorously, in that emphatic way he has] within the Government, but without regard to position. I would be willing to swallow my pride. In fact, I sent the Shah a cable of congratulation recently, and got a gracious reply. The question of my assistance is being discussed actively. But it all turns on whether you, Mr. Lilienthal, would be prepared to give Iran again the service you can give it."

I said that if D&R were to continue to be regarded as just "another contractor," as we had been in recent months, then they should *not* count on me. The result of the present course will be a scattering of what should be a coordinated and unified program, great waste, and poor results. But if we return to the earlier style of program, great progress could be made. Khuzistan could be what he had predicted it would be, a place unique in the world.

"Rouhani sees things differently now; at first he was antagonistic —you are right about that. But no longer."

You don't fight life; you love life too much for that. And what you find that isn't good you try to control and do something about.

OCTOBER 10, 1967
NEW YORK

All morning—and until nearly 2 P.M.—getting a view of a deteriorated (not "underdeveloped") region of a great city. Across the Williamsburg Bridge, through a deep blue haze that softened the whole cityscape: the peaks of Manhattan covered and lost to sight, the dramatic bridges like something in a Japanese print. And the Bedford-Stuyvesant area a labyrinth of the old, the battered; and now new hope for what has for so long been a forgotten part of American city life, swept out of sight while most of us admired the new glass cubicles of Park Avenue or the Fifties.

I had not come here as a do-gooder or "social worker" peering at the black poor, the scene of riots and a revolt most of us thought would never happen—either here in New York or across the country. My purpose was to see the first glimmerings of new life.

I made the trip as a Director of the Bedford-Stuyvesant Development and Services Corporation. What made it memorable was that my guides were men who have set out to *do* something about it. Frank Thomas, one of New York's most distinguished black citizens, and the brilliant young Executive Director of Bedford-Stuyvesant D and S, Eli Jacobs. Jacobs is slightly stooped, with the look of a Talmudic scholar, tired and worn with his first job as a do-er, extraordinarily quick to see what it takes to achieve a transformation. And that is a skill most of the highfalutin technical "planners" don't possess. The "formula," the beginning of wisdom, is simple: you must begin with the people themselves in this battered community, have *them* tell the technical people (e.g., the architects) what *they want*. This takes infinite patience, much talk, putting up with foolishness, chatter, and discord on the part of all concerned. But most of all it takes *faith* that people can be aroused and given confidence in their ability to do something about the way they live.

What enchanted me was that much of what we saw in the way of early progress was not the bulldozer clearing out areas that were no longer habitable, nor model superblocks (though the beginnings of this we saw, too), nor abandoned factory buildings being made over for community purposes. What gave me such excitement was that the people on Thomas and Jacobs' staff so clearly understood that grass roots principles apply in the transformation of the black ghetto precisely as they would in the Anglo-Saxon Tennessee Valley—and in those remote places overseas where I have tried to give those principles and methods vitality.

Thomas, with that quiet smile of his, said a large private concern, sincerely interested in the developing of the area, began their talk with him by saying: "Give me ten blocks" for renovation. But to Thomas and his people that was like saying: "We'll decide for the people in those ten blocks how the place should be done over" (a method which would have been sure to backfire).

Instead the D and S people find one obvious leader (or a group) in a block and have him (them) get together the people of the immediate neighborhood and begin the patience-wearing process of talking things out together down to the last detail.

This is what creates an urban community; not the architects and builders and planners, the technical people, but building a solid foundation among the people directly concerned. Even, I thought to myself, in Vietnam.

Another example of the D and S hardheaded approach to bringing about change involved garbage collection! This is a problem of the very highest priority in Bedford-Stuyvesant—next only to schools, and ahead of more jobs—according to Thomas.

Having the front of the houses and tenements littered with garbage, uncollected, spilling out of the cans, or just dumped: that produced the most severe complaint, particularly among the women of the area. And of course uncollected garbage means rats, and bad morale, and health hazards.

Thomas gave me the details I wanted to hear about how he attacked the problem of uncollected garbage by showing me some streets that were neat as a pin. "You have to be willing to make fifty phone calls a day, beat against the City Commissioner, find out that much of the Sanitation Department's equipment is so old that it is in the repair shops most of the time, do something about parked cars on the streets that make the Sanitation Department trucks give up trying to get the garbage collected. Why, just having two garbage cans instead of one helps at once, and is much cheaper than more frequent collections. That sort of down-to-earth thing that rhetoricians and abstract planners and such don't go for—not romantic or dramatic enough."

Garbage: *there* is an urban symbol to replace some of the simple rural things we in TVA did, in the early days, to change the very climate of people's feelings, to give them a feeling that something concrete and visible was being *done*.

OCTOBER 13, 1967
PRINCETON

Have just read the transcript of Dean Rusk's historic press conference statement of yesterday. I don't know when I have been more moved. This is the way a *man* behaves: strong, composed, clear, articulate, brave and, to me, persuasive.

But the divisions about Vietnam are now so deep that one wonders what effect this or *any form of words* can make on those who made up their mind long ago and appear immovable. Some of their motivation is definitely pure—but not of this world. They don't believe in bloodshed or intrigue or violence or hatred, and they act as if the Communists, historically veterans in the use of hate and violence, don't believe in those ugly things either.

But the "critics" are not all just the pure. There are also the softies. Years ago the groundwork was laid for internationalism in American contemporary life. But when the *price* of that leadership is demanded, the designers of internationalism back away from it. "Soft on Communism" used to be the smear term of the McCarthy era. But now the cry is that we are too tough on the Communists, up to the point where Ho Chi Minh is believed before they will believe our own President.

Be nice to Ho—stop the bombing—and he will be nice to us. How unrealistic can you be?

With my skepticism about professional planners, and planning dissociated from doing, it was somewhat ironic that the professional planners should have thrown me such a big bouquet this week. And out of a past now quite remote—the early and decisive days of TVA, when I first found out that planning-for-its-own-sake was not for the likes of me.

The citation to TVA, received this midweek, on the 50th anniversary of the American Institute of Planners, reads:

"TVA is a symbol of the best in American governmental traditions. Countless numbers of persons from the world over have made pilgrimages to see the achievements made in the Valley and to learn about this experiment in decentralizing the administration of Federal functions, vested in one public authority. But the brilliance of an idea in government is not sufficient to insure success. It took a deep sense of commitment to the idea, a vision of the possibilities, and creative leadership personified in David E. Lilienthal, to make this a splendid and viable experiment in resource management. From the vigorous and creative leadership of Lilienthal and his contemporaries and of a distinguished line of successors has emerged a tradition of innovation. Indeed, innovation pervades wherever TVA has linked up programs in flood control, navigation, power, land use, reforestation, and human well-being."

And the citation goes on to embrace the philosophy of *decentralization* I built into TVA, by stubborn persistence, and wrote about as the theme of *TVA: Democracy on the March*:

"Especially noteworthy is the creative way in which planning and development have been interwoven into one indivisible process of resource use. TVA put the principle of integrated planning and development into practice twenty years before it came to be widely recognized and put to use elsewhere. Notable, too, is the successful meshing of TVA's developmental planning with the work of established units of government. By consistently pursuing a policy of working through the states, the counties, and the municipalities, TVA has been a unifying influence, a basis of cohesion, and a source of strength to planning and development efforts in this region over the years."

OCTOBER 15, 1967
NEW YORK

At 7 P.M. saw Helen and Nancy through the SAS gate at Kennedy Airport; next stop Copenhagen. This is the first trip across the ocean for Nancy, the first time she has left her children for more than a day or so. And for Helen it was something new, too. She has set off on many a long trip, but almost always before, I have been along. And for me it was different, too: this time I am the one left behind.

Came back from the airport by helicopter, a dazzling view of the greatest of all cities. All that and an almost full moon, too. Over the mountainous buildings in mid-Manhattan, and swooping toward what seemed a tiny patch of light no bigger than a card table: the landing pad atop the Pan Am building. It seemed pure chance that we would land on that tiny rectangle.

Six months ago I would have said that the President's position couldn't be worse in the country, about that miserable war. I was wrong: it has hit a new low and the end not in sight. When will the upturn come—or will it? *Or should it?*

OCTOBER 17, 1967
NEW YORK

Began the day's work at my desk over twelve hours ago; went straight through from 7:30 in the morning; it was 7:30 at night when I left the office at One Whitehall. The harbor lights looked like a field of lightning bugs in early June; the lighted torch of the Statue of Liberty out there seemed much too theatrical, more like some gadget one sees in a certain kind of living room.

OCTOBER 19, 1967
NEW YORK

Just walked down Park Avenue in the crisp first touch of almost-winter, the walls of the canyon blazing with lights. Attended a dinner meeting at the Council on Foreign Relations. The honored guest, as windy as the thirty miles breeze on the Avenue: Lee Kuan Yew, Prime Minister of the independent (almost!) Republic of Singapore; the guests included Governor [Thomas] Dewey, who has the most remarkably fine speaking voice I have ever heard.

Lee's appearance is quite unusual for a Malaysian. A big man, broad shoulders, a huge head, anything but the picture of a man from the Far East. The cunning of a man who has had to use his wits (as well as a ready wit) to stay on the good side of the British naval brass for all these years, and yet win the confidence of his fellow Malaysians. His speech is more than fluent, and bears the mark of his Cambridge University training.

He stood by his statement—when closely and quietly cross-questioned by Governor Dewey—that if we do not win in Vietnam (or if we lose) the whole of Asia will be *lost to Chinese power*, as far west as India and Iran.

OCTOBER 22, 1967
PRINCETON

"*No one* has any right to as many of the greatly good things of life as are mine."

These are the words that went through my head as I swung my ash walking stick, striding across the luminous green of the Institute grounds. The colors of early autumn, the vivid air, the sense of almost volcanic well-being, after a day spent in doing nothing but being an animal recharging his batteries, snoozing like a cat, full of no-caring, the tough chore of last week's beating ideas and heads together, the even more exacting job ahead in Vietnam, where I will be in a fortnight—all this blotted out by the joy of being very much alive.

Let me count the ways, said the poet. Well, let me count the ways that make the life that began at sixty (not forty, *that* certainly not) a source of mostly undeserved and eager joy.

Not the least to be grateful for, in that counting, are those things I must have angst about. For my "worries"—the chief ones—are *worth* worrying about. They are among the most important things going on in the world today.

A cable: Helen and Nancy safe and happy. That's a relief to know.

OCTOBER 25, 1967
NEW YORK

To Washington and back yesterday: a very early departure, after a punk night of sleep, thanks to my next-room neighbors and their affection for the late late late TV show, blasting off. New York hotel life, for the hard-working, is not a rest haven.

Chief purpose of the trip, with Seymour, was to visit with Jim Grant and Wehrle of AID. The subject: where our groups found ourselves, after these months of work, and the last week's drive to put the pieces together.

Grant spoke most intensely about making greatly increased production of *rice* the theme, the symbol, a political as well as an economic symbol of our undertaking. Someone has told him—the Department of Agriculture perhaps—that with guaranteed higher prices to the farmer (now decided upon), and new seeds, fertilizers, techniques, etc., rice production could be multiplied several times in a short time. He was quite eloquent about this, using the analogy of Turkey and wheat production. Walt demurred: not until water was put under control upstream (in Cambodia, particularly) could you have *double* cropping of rice, and until that time such increases were not possible.

I reserved judgment about this; I have seen so many things called "impossible" by technical people and then found there was a way they hadn't thought of. But Jim's face fell a foot. I said something about the need to be skeptical about technical negative judgments. We must find a way that will not involve the years and years of delay and vast expenditures of controlling the Mekong in other upstream countries. Are our people right about this? I know the reasons they assign: the low water flow produces a saline intrusion; only limited irrigation for a second crop is possible, etc. But I'm still not completely convinced.

But banking so heavily, as Grant hopes we will, on rice, rice, rice, bothers me. He is influenced, doubtless, by the fact that rice can produce foreign earnings, and Vietnam must get on its own in some way; finding industrial products as "import substitutions" doesn't appeal to him as being large enough or prompt enough. These are valid reasons. But should we, i.e., D&R, press them upon the Vietnamese? I wonder. If the long-term future of their country is not rice—though in the short term this may be true—should we *fasten* this on them, as the planters fastened cotton onto our own U.S. South, producing affluence and foreign earnings for a time, but dooming the South to the use of low grade and ignorant labor and a corrupt social order? I am going to reserve judgment about this rice phobia, though I suppose Secretary Freeman and probably the President (who likes quick, simple solutions) have already committed themselves.

But they can't commit me.

That's the strength of our position, as private citizens in a public policy setting.

An exciting session this afternoon, being part of what I described to my younger associates as what could be the beginning of a new chapter in the D&R idea: the birth of new and fresh ideas and outlook about *urban* development within the U.S.

The factual framework is a particular and specific opportunity: Oakland County, Michigan. The head of the Planning Commission of that county, George Skrubb, wants to consider what we could do to help guide its future development.

What a great way to live: to throw one's heart into the agony of Vietnam, trying to find *something* constructive and workable in that heartbreaking ordeal, and still have the energy and spirit to start something entirely new in our own country.

OCTOBER 28, 1967
SATURDAY NOON
PRINCETON

Burnett, hoarse as a frog, reported yesterday on his and Wood Tate's visit to Oakland County. Good solid progress. The prognosis is that the men who decide things in that county (the elected ones and the Business Advisory Council, which includes some labor union people) will in a few weeks want us to go ahead.

I find this promising beginning in a new field, urban development, has a decided *personal* emotional meaning for me: that my days of innovation aren't over, not yet anyway.

Here is something I only dared enunciate publicly a year ago (in the Fairless Lectures). The competing sources of wisdom in this field have been at it a long time. Yet we may have a chance to plow a fresh furrow. And the place, a still relatively undeveloped county in the Midwest (i.e., underdeveloped in an urban *illness* sense) may be an ideal place to start.

My months of griping and close surveillance of D&R finances cost me a good deal in peace of mind. And some of my colleagues probably could have cut me into little pieces at times for my not behaving like a "chairman of the board" but more like a financial vice president.

Whatever the reason, the first quarter's earnings are at the highest level for a long time. More in September than in the whole of last year. This doesn't mean that the rest of the year will be all that good; it does mean that we can and should invest or risk some money in new people, superior people, not just the conventional and uninspired ones who might be "available."

The press, the journalists, and the columnists continue to amaze and sometimes amuse me, about Vietnam. So often, like most of the rest of us confused and troubled mortals, they *talk* so big, so dogmatically, they know everything that's wrong, "deploring" and nothing more.

Richard Rovere of *New Yorker* magazine, a brilliant writer, with time to think, is an example of this national puzzlement. After spewing unhappiness over several pages about how dismal everything is, how many mistakes have been made, what a liar and lunkhead President Johnson is, he finished his article saying, almost literally: "Talk is cheap. I don't know what should be done, haven't the foggiest. I don't like this war and wish we could withdraw [which earlier he had recommended strongly] but I know we can't."

The other night in Princeton, walked up Witherspoon Street. A big group of burly Princeton students sitting in a lighted store, studying, some of them sitting on the floor for lack of space, two with football jerseys with the big numbers. They were stuffing the contents of their laundry bags into laundromat washing machines, or sitting quietly, book and notebook before them, waiting for the clothes to be ready to haul out. How American! What Italian or Latino male would be caught dead even carrying a package? These boys do this naturally. And what would anyone have thought of a football hero of my day doing his own laundry, and in public!!

OCTOBER 29, 1967
PRINCETON

One hears tales from anguished parents of a chilling warfare between them and their children in their teens. Defiance, even expressions of hatred of their parents, renunciation of everything about their parents—and on and on. These are well-to-do parents from "good" homes. And the stories one reads of the more extreme youngsters, once called beats, now hippies, range all the way from drugs and sex-for-sex's-sake, utterly without affection or taste, to violence and murder.

Now, there must be many families who don't have to go through this battle of the generations, many of them. But the evidence seems to be that though these kids are bright as can be, the word "revolt" is not used metaphorically.

I heard such a story about a sixteen-year-old girl, whose mother always had a special talent with young children. She was utterly baffled and defeated by this youngster's behavior, and saddened by the open hatred toward her.

What I wonder about when I hear such stories is this: is this war between the generations so much more extreme at this time that it is really a difference in kind rather than *degree* from the "normal" and immemorial gap between parents and children?

NOVEMBER 3, 1967
HOTEL OKURA
TOKYO

Why, oh, why, doesn't the U.S. of A. *lose* a war now and then? Economically, it is hard to see how this *thoroughly* beaten country, Japan, could be better off if it had *won* the war. Third greatest industrial nation, tycoons and their lovely women in their embroidered cocoons all over the place. True, the Okura is—well, the Waldorf or the Plaza, in

U.S. terms. But the whole place reeks of a Japanese—not an Oriental—version of America under superaffluence.

Luncheon this noon in a Chinese restaurant in the hotel. A sumptuous Japanese family party going on. The *generations* all mixed together; this impressed me as exceptional. When the party was over the guests came out, led by the patriarch, *followed* by his womenfolk. The old boy, surrounded by helping hands, holding him up, was crinkled and bowed double, looking like a week-old okra pod; the older Japanese ladies are like elderly turkeys whose feet hurt and who have had their tail feathers docked.

NOVEMBER 4, 1967
5:45 A.M.
TOKYO

Dawn over Tokyo. The city absolutely motionless. That great ball of fire, the sun, looks like the spot of red on the Japanese flag.

So many of the tired clichés are truer than the profound new flashes of insight or rhetoric.

Tired cliché number one, for example. "The technology of communication and transport has made the world smaller." But it is only when you know you can pick up that tan instrument over there on the bedside table and in a minute talk to New York that the cliché becomes a profound thought.

But the truism overproves itself. Genuine communication between people isn't a matter of overcoming distances or even the barriers of language. The difficulty we all have of being sensitive to what is in another person's heart and mind isn't materially minimized—nor added to—by the fact that the other human being is eight feet away rather than 8000 miles away.

10:15 A.M.

I have just seen Fuji for the first time, high above the solid cloud bank which almost always obscures it from the ground. A noble sight. And the hours I spent in the *domestic* part of the Tokyo airport were entrancing. The Japanese people are just as restless and forever on the move as we are at home, but, of course, much more interesting to my eye.

We overflew Manila; the typhoon made the captain decide not to try to land. And in the midst of a beautiful tropical rain, we landed in Saigon.

NOVEMBER 5, 1967
5:00 A.M.
209 HIEN VUONG, SAIGON

Up and down during the night after a long day's flight yesterday.

What I find here is so cockeyed: an American presence that is overwhelming, that appears to be—and believes itself to be—the ones who make decisions, allocate resources, fight a war, reorganize a government and an economy—and yet I feel that we are kidding ourselves: the Vietnamese are the decisive force here. In principle, I feel passionately that they *should* be—though few Americans around here really think so or talk that way.

Well, this is part of the "just before the battle, Mother" funk I usually experience. Not that I have any doubt that D&R's work is on the right track. Nor do I doubt that we are able to present a set of ideas and programs for action that can make sense.

But will anything come of it? How far a spread will there be between what I see *can* be begun and what these people will be willing or able to get approved and begun?

Saigon *is* noise—*incredible* unceasing noise—and great incessant wave upon wave of motor bikes, mounted by diminutive people dashing through the air, barely touching the streets.

9 P.M.

Spent the morning with Professor Thuc, my co-chairman. For the first hour he talked enthusiastically, without a break, about the prospects for the Joint Group's work being well received, his earlier diffidence replaced by strong confidence. We ended the morning with a definite schedule he will try to bring about: seeing the President, the Prime Minister, formally presenting the initial report, etc.

What we propose to do is full of booby traps. I am a private citizen, and my company is non-governmental; but what we say will be taken as an implied commitment of the U.S. Government—no amount of disavowal will change that.

Good ideas came out of the talk—ideas about how to bring Cambodia and Vietnam into some kind of relationship through my favorite *non*-diplomatic device, a river in this case, the Mekong.

Urged that President Thieu make a State of the Nation address devoted to economic development—using our report as the basis.

NOVEMBER 8, 1967
SAIGON

What changes do I notice since I was here nine months ago?

Among the Americans I have talked with—Ambassador Bunker, Komer, MacDonald, et al.—a more sober, somber feeling. Even Komer is far less ebullient—I was about to say less cocksure. Among the Vietnamese—and I have already talked with a good many of those we work with—I sense a greater self-assurance. Saigon has changed noticeably: the bustle, the streets more crowded with the Hondas, the men, women, and children on bikes, in makeshift buses.

Myself, I feel strangely enough *less* confident, much more inclined to ask direct provocative questions about finding an accommodation with the Viet Cong, who must have *something* that fits this country. I have great uneasiness within me at the obvious signs of people having much more money than they have ever had, war prosperity and war profiteering at American expense. And an even stronger feeling that there are far too many Americans here. What I said in the States about de-Americanizing Vietnam I feel to be doubly true since I have been here. I said it yesterday to Ambassador Bunker—with his strong, fervent agreement; said it to a luncheon meeting of the senior members of the Thuc group with which we are working (to their obvious approval).

Whether my glumness and critical frame of mind are mostly due to lack of decent rest, or because the war looks interminable—I don't know.

At a dinner last night given for Jim Grant by Don MacDonald, I bristled (but said nothing) because an American rice expert, an AID man from East Pakistan, glowingly described the seed of the new rice strain (called IR-8—with the Madison Avenue advertising man's slogan Miracle Rice) as the complete answer to Vietnam's rice production problems. How narrow these one-shot "experts" can be.

Ellsworth Bunker seemed more composed than ever yesterday morning when I saw him at the Embassy (it was he who invited the meeting). In his quiet way, his eyes boring into you, he listened while I said that I had been told when I took this assignment that the Vietnamese rated economic development a high priority goal, as did the U.S., but I wasn't at all sure that the new government felt that way about it, in which case I would want to reconsider my commitment.

He gave me verbal assurance: he was certain President Thieu (whom he found an impressive man) would understand how important our aims were. Then Bunker launched into a ten-minute story

I am sure he recites to all American visitors: "We are making progress—not spectacular but slow and sure. The Vietnamese have recently won victories in the field," and so on, the same old song about the military progress we have made.

I found this preoccupation with how the war goes a natural and understandable confirmation of my concern that no one is really *seriously* considering that long-term economic development has much of an importance at this stage.

As I went on to express concern that the number of Americans in AID continues to increase, almost doubling over last year, Bunker broke in, troubled and as near exasperation as I suppose he ever appears: "Counting American contractors and AID, there are 9500 Americans here. Take a look at the AID organization chart. It is an unbelievable mishmash. There are so many of us that the administration of our own organization takes up most of the effort—AID is taking in its own laundry without much time for anything besides running the organization we have created. So I'm completely with you on your approach."

At our second meeting, later in the day, he said, "I'm afraid I have to go back to Washington this week. The White House wants me. The President is nervous. He is an impatient man, as you know. He was that way about the Dominican matter;* used to telephone me at least once a day about what was happening. I finally told him not to fret himself that way; that it would come out all right. But he wants something dramatic to happen. I don't see what it could be.

"As a matter of fact, I wish we would stop talking about negotiation all the time. Just say we have expressed a willingness to negotiate, and leave it at that. Ho Chi Minh must think we are desperate if we keep saying that over and over again."

The conversation then turned to the development of the Mekong Delta, so high on the list of our recommendations. To get the full benefits of rice production, water control in high flood times is necessary, and that requires a reservoir of considerable size at Stung Treng *in Cambodia.* But Cambodia has been at odds with Vietnam ever since the end of French rule in Vietnam, has no official relations with the U.S., and is providing sanctuary for Viet Cong and North Vietnamese military forces.

The reservoir's controlled water would benefit rice production in Cambodia as it would benefit the lower Mekong. Thuc, quite eager and enthusiastic—and an experienced man in dealing with Cambodia—believes he could begin talks with certain Cambodian leaders that

* Bunker was the President's representative to the Dominican Republic at the time the U.S. landed Marines.

might lead to agreement about a damsite, division of its cost and benefits, etc.

I pointed out to Bunker that this use of physical, technical, and functional matters to effect political ends was the theme of my proposal for the division of the waters of the Indus between India and Pakistan.† He nodded, recalling how that had improved relations between Pakistan and India. He expressed no reservation about Thuc approaching Cambodia, should the Vietnamese Government have no objection. Something important could conceivably come of this; Mead and I will be discussing it further with John Wood, a representative of the UN Development Fund, which has responsibility for the Mekong River Committee, headed by Hart Schaaf.

Toward the end of our visit Bunker showed signs of discouragement—he who I thought as never having a doubt or low moment. But no man alive can confront this "trap" in Vietnam and not occasionally have a low moment—perhaps more than occasionally (speaking for myself).

Looking at me rather sadly, he said, "I have a brother-in-law who is quite a fellow: interested in business, in art, other things. I have a letter from him telling me how bad things are going with American public opinion. He ended his letter [at this Bunker smiled quizzically] by saying: 'Ellsworth, come home.' "

We are indeed a torn country about this little sliver of real estate. Our Joint Group report seems but a weak reed with which to mount an assault on so formidable a world issue! But at least we are trying.

NOVEMBER 10, 1967
9 A.M.
SAIGON

We had some thirty or more of Thuc's group, chiefly the "students," in for a visit last evening. Among them six young ladies, very attractive in their gay colored long fore-and-aft paneled dresses. And so diminutive!

Why the apparent enthusiasm of these younger people for the "postwar planning group" I can't quite figure. Part of it certainly is Thuc. He was surrounded by a dozen young men, hanging on his every word. They obviously find him a magnetic teacher.

I asked Thuc where some of these younger people came from. One tiny young lady in gleaming green came originally from an agricultural village in the Delta. Another was brought from North Vietnam by her family years before—perhaps 1954. Said Thuc: "I myself was born in

† See *Journals*, Vol. III, *The Venturesome Years*, p. 199 (footnote).

Hanoi, you know, educated there. The other day, when I heard that the area near Haiphong was bombed, I thought that probably my home had been destroyed." He registered no emotion as he spoke; just looked at me with those eyes that never seem to blink.

God, how I wish we could have let these people settle their differences *among themselves*. Hardly a profound thought, but responsive to my growing feeling that however bitter all of this is, the Vietnamese, North and South, seem to have a more objective (or resigned?) way of looking at their war than we Americans.

For example, a paper by three of the young students of our group on Vegetable Marketing. They cite, in the most matter-of-fact way, how trucks bringing vegetables from the production area near Dalat to market in Saigon are stopped by the Viet Cong, who make the truckers pay a tax that seems to be regularized. The students regarded this as one of the "costs" of getting vegetables to market. And in the same matter-of-fact way they refer to the "Tea Money," which they sometimes call bribes, that the truck drivers must pay to the Vietnam Army checkpoint guards; the bribe is in lieu of the guard's ransacking their loads of vegetables, "looking for concealed weapons." Just another cost of operation.

The emotional fervor and hatred just wasn't there. Perhaps it *is* in fact. But the tone was "this is the way it is."

12:30 P.M.

A visit with Charles Cooper, now head of AID's Economic Division. A huge young man who has grown more, in understanding, in a given period, than any economist I know. His handsome face bears the marks of having bumped into hard political realities here in Vietnam and he is more prone than many economists to come to grips with what you *do* about things. When I proposed certain specific ways of getting the Vietnamese to face up to those economic realities in terms of their obvious emotional needs—saving face, the desire for "independence" of the Americans, etc.—he instantly picked up on my ideas. The same with encouraging the accordance of more revenue and responsibility to village councils. When Moore and Mead countered this suggestion with an analysis of how small in piasters is the local land tax the villages recently have been authorized to collect, Cooper, the pragmatist, retorted: "But it's a beginning; let's encourage that and improve on it."

Quite impromptu, I made a proposal which, an hour later (as I write these notes), still seems to have merit.

My line of reasoning and the proposal went like this:

1. Our Joint Group's report shied away from the prickly political issues of increased taxes on city dwellers, the increasingly affluent

middle and top group. To come right out with a demand attributable to the U.S. that the well-to-do be more equitably taxed would produce political problems so great that Thieu, Loc, et al. would probably not be willing or able to face them.

Yet to turn aside from such taxation of the well-heeled ignores the resentment in the U.S. of the extraordinary support we are giving to the Vietnamese economy, by the vast commercial import program (almost a billion a year, or more) plus American expenditures for the military here. This creates a festering political problem in the U.S.—and I sympathize with those who emphasize the issue.

2. But suppose, through the Joint Group, a Five Year Plan for *economic independence for Vietnam* were proposed. Proposed as part of the emphasis on economic development, which is the theme, of course, of the Joint Group's first report.

Let's stop talking *only* about economic development. This ignores the cost (by way of taxation and reform, e.g., reform of the Customs service, the Government services, etc.).

Let's couple with economic development *independence from the Americans*, on a graduated basis. So much increase in independence, i.e., *self-support*, in the first year, so much in the second, until in X years, say five, Vietnam is treated by the U.S. the same way as any developing country, with program loans but *not* operating support.

I think this may have something in it. It appeals to a sense of national pride, and to a Vietnamese political objective. It appeals to America's desire not to have this burden upon it, forever. And yet doesn't imply a sudden breaking off of necessary support, support which right now if withdrawn would bring complete economic and political collapse to Vietnam.

NOVEMBER 11, 1967
3 A.M.
SAIGON

The slim, youthful Major General [Forsythe] came into the broad expanse of living room of Ambassador Komer's residence looking despite his field uniform more like a college professor than a soldier in from the wars. Komer appeared in due course and said, "We are winning the war; I keep telling people that." I replied, with what was obviously a skeptical frown, that according to the reports we have been getting for so long, we have been winning the war all along, but the American public is getting tired of these predictions. A long explanation followed of how different this war is from other wars, made up of many pieces, etc., etc., ad nauseam.

I had *hoped* Komer would come out here and re-examine critically the reports that have obviously led the President to place more and more hope on a sudden military victory, the collapse of the VC and the North Vietnamese.

But the time spent with him only impressed me that he, too, has been taken in by the glamour and the "play soldier" attitude of the professional soldier.

Not one question, not one word all evening about economic development or the work I was talked into doing.

When Komer, accompanied by some elegantly attired lady, departed "for the Marine Corps ball," a formal affair with tuxedo, long dresses, and dress uniforms of blue, I was really depressed.

Seeing the dark cloud that must have settled on my somewhat transparent features, the college professor-appearing Major General said: "But how do I explain what we are trying to do out here to my eighty-four-year-old mother? She has two sons who are professional soldiers, and she is proud of us. Proud or not, she keeps asking me to explain what it is we think we are doing. And I try. But she shakes her head and says: 'But tell me, *why* are you out there?' and I guess lots of people are like that."

A low moment indeed.

NOVEMBER 12, 1967
DALAT, VIETNAM

War? Absurd. What a delightful, serene spot, a very old-fashioned hotel with sixteen-foot ceilings, and a view of the low mountains that could be the foothills of Switzerland. And quiet, the first time since I arrived in Vietnam that my ears and head have not been pounded with the hellish noise of trucks and Hondas.

Our companions are two of the older Vietnamese members of the Joint Group, Dr. Nguyen Truong and Mr. Vu Quoc Kha. I kept questioning them, as we walked the hills—two miles—from the military airport to this hotel, trying to learn more from them about the VC—a weird story, a kind of Capone-gang-with-a-political-mission. Now we are going out to look more closely at the extraordinary vegetable-growing lands that abound in these gentle hills.

I asked the brisk crew-cut AID man who drove us about Dalat what industry (besides vegetable growing) there was in this city. "Right now, house construction; a good many high Vietnamese Army officers are building fine houses here," and he pointed out some of them, still building, elegant big places on the slopes.

Ugh. What odious things there are about this country, that has cursed not only the Vietnamese people, but even more, my own countrymen.

This was a city built by the French as their place of recreation and display. The climate much of the year, as today, is delightful, and the green hills soft and lovely to the eye. While the French were here, so I was told, they would not permit any Vietnamese, except as servants.

Touches of the American "presence" one sees here and there. God help us if we begin to act like colonial overlords, too. It just could happen. I'm resolved that our Joint Group, and D&R particularly, do what it can—and it can do a good bit—to inhibit the colonial habit of domination, the "I know better than thee what is best for thee" latent in all human beings, I fear.

NOVEMBER 13, 1967
DALAT

Long talk this morning with Dr. Nguyen Truong and Mr. Vu Quoc Kha. The subject: a new and fresh attitude on one of the most evil and barbarous consequences of this long war: the two million or more displaced people. One of the first steps I suggested was to stop calling them "refugees" and substitute something like "relocation" or "resettlement" or "colonization."

The problem is enormous, heart-rending, and politically dangerous for Vietnam and within the U.S. But it also has an economic development aspect, and so it falls directly within the purview of the Joint Group's long-term development obligations. At a time when manpower is short for production, agricultural or otherwise, here are hundreds of thousands of people who are sitting around, unhappy, without employment.

This valley of Dalat! Almost literally, a garden spot. Such a cornucopia of green! One evidence of how lavish is this dark red soil, and how skillful are these hard-working people, is the town's market, from which we have just come.

Such noble vegetables I have never seen! And in almost unlimited variety, from strawberries in great mounds to avocados, plump, firm, glossy; carrots as long as one's forearm; cauliflowers the size of cabbages; lettuce tender and luscious. Displayed so attractively; and the market so clean and orderly. Well fed people, well dressed.

The U.S. military pump primer is certainly evident. Will this generate enough energy to perpetuate this obvious prosperity? And in how many other places less favored by nature can this affluence be duplicated?

NOVEMBER 14, 1967
SAIGON

The door of the gaunt and hideous living room at the D&R residence popped open, about 11 o'clock, and through it came a burst of energy and excitement: Professor Thuc, eyes flashing, all his usual formality gone—and looking as if he had been driving, driving the whole weekend long. He must have done just that, for with a voice full of pride and nervous tension he handed me the Joint Group report, *in Vietnamese*. Holding it up in triumph, he said, "One hundred forty pages; imposing, don't you think?"

If ever I saw the *reverse* of the "enigmatic inscrutable Asian," Thuc is it. And when he says he will arrange this, or that, ranging all the way from a meeting with the most powerful man in the Cabinet, his friend Minister of Economics Ton, or a big press conference and ceremonies with the new President, Thieu, I now feel I can count on it, that this is just what will happen.

Thuc explained that he had written a complete new preface and introductory part, putting aside what we had prepared to explain the "philosophy" of the work. I liked that. It may resemble what we had prepared, perhaps closely, but *his* writing it makes it genuinely a *Vietnamese* state paper.

There is one problem of course. Since the part that Thuc wrote or rewrote is in Vietnamese, which I can't read, and of which we have no English translation, I recognize some risk in being asked to sign a report—as Thuc asked me to—the exact language of which I haven't seen. But what the hell! I'm swallowing, on this worrisome job, a great many worse risks than that.

A long letter this morning from the Western Australian Minister of Industry, Charles Court, forwarded from New York. Seems to be quite serious about having me come to Australia to assess the possibility of a regional program for that huge area—a *million* square miles!

Can I possibly add this to what I have already committed myself to, including a trip to Iran, finishing the fourth volume of the *Journals*—and having some life outside my work? But my friends in the company would feel let down if I said: Vietnam is enough!

So I cabled that we were strongly interested; the only question was when we could come.

I'll have nightmares forever of rivers and torrents of motorcycles roaring past in an endless ribbon of motion and sound, mounted by dark-haired beauties and by families of five, two little ones behind with the wife, one across the saddle bow. Until midnight this goes on and on.

It will be my dying memory of Saigon, erstwhile Pearl of the Orient.

NOVEMBER 15, 1967
8:00 A.M.
SAIGON

The radio announcer warns against standing in groups while waiting for a bus. "Two is a crowd, three is a target." And the sullen bong bong sounds and the flashes in the sky last night and early this morning remind you: this is war.

8:30 A.M.

Yesterday afternoon a meeting with Minister of Economics Ton, whom I had briefly met on my previous trip to Saigon, a holdover from the Government under Ky. Professor Thuc proudly displayed and formally presented the Joint Group's "report."

Ton is an interesting man. Essentially a career civil servant, hence accustomed to leaving decision-making to a "higher authority," usually the foreign power that occupies the country. A compact and handsome man, seemingly not more than forty or forty-five. His face is bland and composed, but I noticed that he was constantly pressing his index finger against the edge of his thumb until both were almost raw.

He was frankness itself. "I am afraid to be Minister of Economy; the economic problems we have are very great," he said with a disarming and handsome smile. "I said to President Thieu and to Prime Minister Loc, 'Why should I be sacrificed; I held this job for more than a year. It should be someone else's turn to be sacrificed.' But they insisted; said I was the only man on whom Thieu and Ky, who do not agree on many things, and the new Prime Minister could agree. So . . . [a sad, deprecating smile] so I accepted and here I am."

Thuc explained the content of the report, emphasizing not only the Mekong Delta but the "refugee problem." We discussed how the presence of two million displaced people could be an opportunity for economic development as well as a "welfare" problem. Mead's favorite theme on this subject is, instead of using generalities, to identify one place where land could be made available that would support the population as farmers.

"But," said Minister Ton, "many of these people may be better qualified for some kind of industrial job; they may not want to farm in a strange place among people of a different background. The people of one part of our country don't usually like to live with the people of another, such as the Delta people among the central highlanders, or central coastal people."

This kind of thinking doesn't daunt Mead. "Let's try and see, on a small scale initially," he says, quite sensibly. We were reminded, however, that when former President Ngo Dinh Diem tried a resettlement program, he had to move many people "at the point of a gun."

Ton explained that "Prime Minister Loc had wanted to receive you before this time. But he had no office; he still doesn't have an office; the Prime Minister has an important job but no office." This seemed to him both a joke—at least he laughed nervously—and also a kind of indignity.

The explanation: Prime Minister Ky had his office and staff in Independence Palace, and I suppose has no intention of moving out. So we are to see the new Prime Minister in some kind of rest house for dignitaries.

This isn't opéra bouffe; too many real lives are being lost and too much real suffering going on to make this a musical play about the mythical country of Ruritania. But it does have its moments!

Dinner last night in Cholon, Saigon's Chinese section. Quantities—too much by far—of interesting and strange Chinese food. John Bennett, an able "show me" man from the Washington AID office with us, puffing vigorously on his pipe, and looking out on the Vietnamese scene with more perspective of time than anyone I know. He has been in and out since 1962, even before, during the Diem regime. "There was 48% unemployment in Saigon then; now there is overemployment," but he doesn't view this as a mark of health, necessarily, since in the meantime we have poured money and goods into this country, and they have not yet done much to carry the burden they are now—thanks to the U.S.—so much better able to bear. And this is precisely my greatest concern.

My impromptu views about phasing out American super-foreign-aid expressed on November 10th to Chuck Cooper of AID were transmitted to Washington today; I received a copy.

According to the summary of my views, I have been stressing the need for the Vietnamese to take greater responsibility for their own economy. "This is the nub of his thinking and the direction he wishes to give the Joint Group's work. . . .

"Lilienthal is pressing his theme of planning for gradually increasing Vietnamese economic independence. This idea may be a most productive and appealing one, and although this week's joint report will be only another early step in the planning process, the effort seems to be moving well."

8:30 P.M.

To have David Lilienthal, with all that overblown reputation—away from home—advance upon you with a big fat report on your very first day in office as Prime Minister: this was obviously an ordeal that "Lawyer Loc" understandably confronted at five this afternoon with something less than complete aplomb.

We were brought into a large drawing room in a building along the waterfront used to house visiting dignitaries (Loc's "temporary" office), so the poor man didn't even have the moral support of such accouterments as a flag in a standard back of him—a prop we in the States resort to to fortify the vanity and self-confidence of the lowliest deputy under secretary.

He looked pale and slick, dark hair plastered back severely. We spoke through the intermediary of Thuc, who was even more bright eyed and bushy tailed than usual.

After exchanging the usual polite greetings typical of these extraordinarily well-mannered people, Loc asked whether I thought there was anything proposed in the report that was not practical and could not be carried out. I said no, though the war would make some things much more difficult. A massive understatement, that.

I went on to say that as a private American citizen I understood that a commitment to economic development was a top priority of the Government over which he presided (I doubt if he will in fact "preside" over much of anything) and that this news would be greeted with great satisfaction by Americans generally.

The Prime Minister commented that it was a remarkable matter of timing that he began his duties of office with a complete proposed program before him, instead of having to wait months to have one prepared. We D&R characters, and Thuc, smirked with self-satisfaction as if we were indeed responsible for the apparent split-second timing of the report, the fact that it was ready at the very first moment of a new government's life. And indeed it *did* hit the time target beautifully, a fact that wasn't lost on the Prime Minister, or on the AID people either.

At dinner tonight, our boys were feeling very cocky, and I must say I'm proud of their pride.

One of our guests from the Embassy said, apropos our Joint Group arrangement, "Yes; RAND has an operation out here and they *too* make use of some Vietnamese in their organization."

Said I: "We don't make use of Vietnamese; they make use of us."

NOVEMBER 16, 1967
MIDNIGHT
SAIGON

A big ceremony at the Palace, with all the publicity "fixings." The President, Vice President (Ky), the Prime Minister, Minister of the

Economy, United States Ambassador Locke (looking quite bored), and Tom and Fred; plus eager little Professor Thuc presenting the fat report to the President, before the cameras. Standing at Thieu's left hand, I read a brief statement of response.

Speeches in Vietnamese. The President gave the report a big send-off and whispered to me, "There will be an official communiqué, but I haven't seen it." The ceremony sounded like "business." But will anything *actually happen*? That depends partly on us, partly on the gods, mostly on the intelligent men in that room.

The evening's crowded press conference was certainly not one of my best performances by a long shot. But it is over; I hate to run away from ordeals.

As we left I told Barry Zorthian, the solemn, utterly dedicated U.S. press officer in Saigon, how I admired his sticking, through almost four years, with the job of dealing with such a huge and rapacious press corps: more than five hundred American correspondents alone. He pulled off his heavy tortoise shell glasses and said sadly, "But it's been a failure. We have failed to communicate what this is all about to the American public. They have lost confidence almost completely."

Perhaps true, but surely not his fault. Wherever the blame lies—most would put it at the feet of President Johnson, I suppose—the *fact* is that the country is more divided and snarling than even six months ago. Call it what you will: "failure of communication" or a failure to persuade, or the consequence of frustration or a tragic mistake of several Presidents and Congresses *and* editorial writers in getting involved as we are. In any event, it is too late to think much about the reasons why. The *fact* is that the American mind is profoundly troubled. The pressure of the press to make things look bad—and therefore newsworthy—plays a part. But there is something far deeper than that in this sorry business.

NOVEMBER 17, 1967
SAIGON

At the Guam Conference, Thieu, then "Head of State" of the War Cabinet, sat impassive of face and manner directly across from our anything but passive President. It was Ky who was the aggressive and vocal one, who was in the press and photographic limelight.

Yesterday, when Thieu came through the great double glass doors into the beautiful ceremony rooms (set off by two gigantic elephant tusks mounted in a beautiful wooden carved pedestal), he still seemed to be the most impassive person in the room. Compact, squarely built, he wore a constant half-smile. Ky, seated at his right, didn't look as if he enjoyed the business of being Number Two, but he remains a much more dramatic figure than Thieu.

After the photographing, Thuc came center and presented the bound report to the President. Thuc had explained to me on the way to the Palace that he had spent more than an hour with Thieu yesterday, describing the report, and that the President had shown "astonishing" interest in and curiosity about the document. "Very encouraged," said Thuc. (Thuc seems to be learning fast how to switch horses, for he was once closer to Ky and Ton than to the new President, Thieu.)

After Thuc's brief summary of the report, delivered in English with a solemnity appropriate to the fact that this was the first act of the new Government and Cabinet, he asked that I make some comment. A couple hours before I had pounded something out on a typewriter. So I read it, in a loud voice.

Here are excerpts from my text, as I read it:

"This Report is in every essential a Vietnamese report prepared largely by Vietnamese and solely concerned with the future of Vietnam —beginning now, while the war is still on.

"But the report is more than just one more survey or report. It is a call to action. It is the first of a series of steps in the most comprehensive effort ever taken by a nation, still fighting for its very existence, to draw a map of its own economic future.

"To my mind, the distinctive fact about this initial Report is that it grows out of the soil of Vietnam, the product of Vietnamese intelligence, Vietnamese understanding of your conditions and aspirations as a people, and designed to be carried forward into action, step by careful step, by the Vietnamese people, with whatever technical and financial help from the outside as may be appropriate, feasible, and desired by the Vietnamese people.

"Especially I want to emphasize how large, indeed how critical, a part of the task has been the contribution made by the many younger Vietnamese—some of them graduate students—whom Professor Thuc has brought together. For it is these young men and young women, alert, earnest, hard-working, who will learn the tasks of future leadership in the process of this comprehensive program of planning for and carrying out the economic development of their own country."

With his unchanging half-smile, President Thieu made a rather lengthy extemporaneous response, in Vietnamese, though he speaks excellent English. A meek little man, standing before me in the half-circle, translated after each sentence or so, in a voice not audible across the room. "The report truly represents the aspirations of the Vietnamese people. . . ." Turning to face me: "We wish to thank President Johnson for making your distinguished service available." And so on.

As we sat drinking—the President and I had whiskey and soda, most of the other Vietnamese sticking to their favorite orange cola (ugh)—big, handsome, Ambassador Locke tried to relieve the solemnity of the occasion. "Those are beautiful elephant tusks," he said.

The President seemed grateful for this chance for some small talk. He explained happily: these tusks did not come from one elephant; in fact, usually one tusk is quite different from another in the same animal—and so on. But the sharp points of those gleaming spears fascinated me, and I kept thinking how symbolic, in a way, they were in that beautiful room. These white curves pointing upward were the visible two horns of a tragic dilemma; and how appropriate, for that is just where the U.S. is impaled—on *both* horns: sticking it out, or withdrawing—*both* bad.

Late yesterday afternoon, shortly before the ceremony, an excited call: Marshal Ky wishes to see you—and a car came to pick me up, with Thuc.

Ky is often described as a "colorful" personality. He lived up to this reputation in the hour we spent with him. He was dressed in a tightly fitted glossy black jacket and pipestem trousers, semi-military, with a pale lilac silk scarf, Ascot-style, about his neck. Why I thought of a slender serpent-like Mussolini I don't know; the black dress, I suppose. A heavy mustache, dark hair severely groomed.

Ky listened *intently* while Thuc summarized our report, as his subsequent comments showed. He could not resist peppering his remarks, however, in true politician's style, with asides like, "I already *knew* that; that's what I told President Johnson," or "That is already part of our program."

Thuc opened up about interesting Cambodia in cooperating in the building of a dam within Cambodia that would control waters in the Mekong Delta. He went on to describe the background of Cambodia's grudge against Vietnam. It arose out of an agreement with Cambodia which Thuc had helped work out, when Indochina was broken up. At that time Vietnam promised, so he said, to pay Cambodia a very large sum as part of the liquidation of the intercountry relationship under the French. But Thuc had inserted as a condition that the payment would be made to Cambodia if and when the French paid Vietnam what was owing it—which France never did. Hence Cambodia distrusted Vietnam.

2 P.M.

The newspaper headlines—both the English and the Vietnamese—gave a big splash to my speech of yesterday. The phrase "a call to action" made an appeal. Please God it may prove to be more than just another emotional response and another round of empty rhetoric.

10:30 P.M.

The fact that the President and the Vice President made such a big thing of the report yesterday is the big news in the Vietnamese press, so Thuc tells me tonight, his eyes wide with astonishment. And tonight Professor Nguyen Quoc Cuong told us that my statement and the report's emphasis on economic development will be felt by the Viet Cong; he assured Moore that the Viet Cong will find it necessary to come out now with an anti-Lilienthal competing economic development program.

This noon Henry Kernan (our scholarly and reserved forestry consultant) came back beaming from a visit with the new Minister of Agriculture, Ton That Trinh. "The first thing Trinh did his first day in office was to sack three out of four men of the Department because they were not qualified as forest or wood products men. Imagine!"

And Chuck Cooper, the AID Economic Counselor, wishing me bon voyage, looked as pleased as punch tonight. "You got more publicity about the economic situation than this country has had since devaluation. You ought to feel you did an awful lot in the time you fellows have been on this job."

NOVEMBER 18, 1967
8:30 A.M.
SAIGON

More heartened this day than I would have felt possible, after the near-despair I felt during the early days of this trip, and for weeks and weeks before. Surely there is something good here, something that is destined to right itself in spite of backsets and disappointments and even betrayals and lies and cheapness and shallowness—this latter almost the worst of all.

And you are lucky among men. The way they listened to you, talked to you, those very young, eager Ministers (how absurd to call such gentle, earnest, open-eyed young men "Minister"). They believe you have some kind of touch that can help.

Can I indeed help *build* where before there was only blind, negative destruction? This morning—how long the sense of it will last I can't say—but this morning I feel I can, and must, and shall.

4 P.M.

"The Viet Cong official radio is filled with word of our report, and makes much of the fact that the very first act of the new Government was to receive Mr. Lilienthal in a formal ceremony, and to *endorse* the program of economic development. The Viet Cong make much of Mr. Lilienthal's description of our Joint Group's report as 'a call to *action.*' "

These are Thuc's words, delivered soberly, almost somberly, only a couple hours ago at our residence.

The occasion was a meeting of seven intellectuals and professors, Thuc's Vietnamese colleagues, and an equal number of D&R's.

And then, very quietly indeed, Thuc continued: "Before the presentation of our report our work has gone unnoticed, almost as if it were secret. But not now. The way it has been received makes this group highly visible. It has had a great psychological impact, with the publicity the Vietnamese press has given us."

The seven members of his group heard this recital motionlessly. I wondered what was coming.

"We will now be a target of the Viet Cong," he concluded. "We must take steps for our security."

I was incredulous. "Not here; not here in the middle of the city of Saigon," I said.

"*Especially* in Saigon," said Thuc, looking at me solemnly but without raising his voice or making a single one of his characteristic hand gestures.

He went on. "I now live in the suburbs, about ten miles away. I shall give up my home, and move into the city at once. This is the advice I have received, and it is based on what we know about Viet Cong plans. Our Joint Group's present office, in a villa, is highly vulnerable; we must seek to get office space for the Joint Group on the upper floors of an office building, and while this is being done post plainclothes police outside our present office and your own villa.

"And now I suggest we go on with the agenda for our meeting concerning the research and development work for the coming months."

I made sure that each of the Vietnamese was asked for comment. Dr. Nguyen Cao Hach, Thuc's senior associate, presented a different view than we had posited, and this was accepted; Vo Guan Han proposed a "seminar" on village government; Thuc suggested that we invite to such a round table some of the most respected village council chiefs and other civilian leaders from the rural areas—and so on.

The high spot of this afternoon's Joint Group meeting was when Thuc told us, quietly and firmly, what he had already *done* to implement the Group's effectiveness.

"Among the newly elected Senators are several men whom I know well who are technicians—economists, engineers, and so on. I am in touch with a few who are my personal friends, asking them to join our Joint Group."

I welcomed this line of approach because it showed some faith in the educational value of the legislative process.

6 P.M.

For a solid half hour I stood at a street intersection a block or so away and watched what I daresay is a unique cavalcade. The *variety* of people, vehicles, dress is almost infinite, and I was utterly fascinated. Papa driving furiously a speeding motorcycle, mama behind, two *babies* sandwiched between them. Great burly Army Sergeants banging a huge U.S. Army truck slam bang through the streets. An MP jeep patrol suddenly turning loose its siren and going hell bent, as a helicopter zeros in on some kind of trouble a few blocks ahead. Pedicabs, the human motive power, usually in a pith helmet (why? no one else wears them), sitting high up, like the mahout driver of a small elephant, two patrician mandarin ladies taking their ease in the chair before him, or a slicked-up young American soldier taking it all in, as I was; something royal and dated about the elegance (somewhat shabby, it's true) of being propelled through the streets by a servant's leg power.

My last night in Vietnam this trip. What happened to the half-resolution I made a week ago: "No more trips out here"? I can hardly wait for some good solid reason to get back.

NOVEMBER 19, 1967
FLYING TO TOKYO

The brilliantly scalloped coastline of Southern Vietnam now left behind. And, momentarily, Vietnam is left behind, too: its tragedy, its human warmth, and the appeal its people have to me.

As we said goodbye at the airport, Professor Thuc confided: "Last night I slept the night through for the first time in two weeks: everything I hoped and planned for had been accomplished, and I slept, at last."

NOVEMBER 20, 1967
FLYING TO NEW YORK

Fred Moore and I spent an hour this morning at the American Embassy in Tokyo with the counsellor for economic affairs, Minister Laurence Vass, and the Second Secretary, Robert Fritts.

My purpose: to spur Japanese industry's interest in Vietnam. And one influential base would be this Embassy. I intended to keep Vass and his associates well and candidly informed about what the Joint Group is doing, what our specific ideas are.

The Japanese industrialists, within the past several months particularly, have moved rapidly toward *investment* overseas, something new for them, Vass said. But what is most relevant for us is whether they would be willing not simply to *sell* equipment (an old story with them, of course) but to provide management on a continuing basis.

Fred Moore was *very* effective: cited specific examples of things we are considering recommending by way of industrial activities which the Japanese might be interested in competing for (a urea fertilizer plant, a pulp mill, etc.). I mentioned the importance of finding employment opportunities for Vietnamese; one such possibility would be the assembly in Vietnam of presently imported Japanese motor bikes, the ubiquitous crawling creatures that foul the air and pound the ears in Saigon, but which do promote mobility.

The political relations between Japan and the U.S. are an important factor in my thinking. Said Vass: "Sato [the Prime Minister], while in Washington, made the strongest statement supporting the U.S. position by any Asian power not actually a military ally of the U.S. in Vietnam. The Japanese have moved from opposition to half-neutrality and now almost to full support. So what we are talking about here, if followed up, could be quite important."

Economic development programs aren't just economics or "planning"; they are a part of statecraft. Certainly the case of Japan vis-à-vis Southeast Asia is a good, perhaps the best example.

So, in my passion for "experiences" and widening my understanding of the world, Japan is added to the list, in an oblique way—or perhaps not so oblique after all.

To the money exchange desk at the hotel in Tokyo: a crude handwritten little sign: "No exchange except $US." In this way, and many others, no doubt, the word of the British devaluation of the pound has gone clanging around the world.

DECEMBER 1, 1967
PRINCETON

Long talk by phone today with Professor James MacGregor Burns of Williams College, calling from the White House. Burns is hard at work on his second volume about F.D.R.: *The War Years*. He said some pleasant things about the *Journals*: "Some of the vignettes are very telling. But mostly I enjoyed the way you made the diaries *personal*."

This comment was appreciated, coming from so distinguished a historian. Glad to have one judgment, and a respected one, that it is the "mix" of personal and serious that gives the reading of the *Journals* —as it did and does the writing of them—a kind of validity and immediacy, as if they came from a living human being rather than a sage or a writer of treatises.

DECEMBER 3, 1967
PRINCETON

"The press" (which simply means men who write for newspapers) is having a field day of speculation over the resignation of Robert McNamara as Secretary of Defense.

What I find most ironic, though, is how sympathetic everyone is, now that he is out, for the exhausting ordeal a public servant goes through, and this one in particular. These cries of pity come even from Senators, the very men who have been making his life miserable for years in the one-sided contest between the man on the dais in the Senate hearing room and the hapless witness.

That McNamara is a complex and a sensitive man even a limited knowledge of him makes plain. His recent doubts about the course of the war were clear to me from my observation of him at that fateful meeting at Guam and in particular through his comments in a brief talk with me.

Assuming he felt our course needed a drastic change—which is only partly "speculation" on my part, based upon Guam—then why did he stay on so long, why did he give the orders that he gave? Could it be the same impulse I feel—on a much lower scale of importance, to be sure—that one can't just disapprove; he must stay close enough to a nasty business to be able to exercise some influence, however limited. To say: It is a mess; I disagree, so I'll not have anything to do with it—that is something I find difficult to do. It is because in one sphere—economic development—I may be able to have some influence that I pull up my sox when I get disappointed and my heart aches (as it does so often these days) and stick with it. Stick with it until I get pushed out.

I have returned to an America more focussed than ever on the war in Vietnam: the boiling emotions of the Anti-War, or Peace, groups; the unhappiness and acute distress and antagonism against President Johnson; the endless editorials and harangues, and the quieter but profound doubts. All now seem to consider the Vietnam war as the sole "peace" issue, a shift from efforts to bring about peace in the world as *an all-embracing goal*, down to the narrow issue of Vietnam.

A secondary refrain in our national thinking is that Communism is no longer a monolithic force; "look at Tito," and therefore "the cold war is over"; to concern ourselves about the threat of Communism should no longer be part of American foreign policy.

Yet under our very eyes the development of more and more devastating atomic weapons grows at a terrible pace. Grows in the Soviet

Union, grows in the U.S. Gilpatric's article in today's *New York Times* and Scoop Jackson's atom-rattling on the floor of the Senate last week bring this home.

Gilpatric finds no evidence that the atomic arms race is slackening, as the euphoria that greeted the test ban treaty led many to believe. The only way, he says, to slow up this race is for one side or the other to offer to slow up his efforts, hoping for reciprocation. And since at the moment the U.S. has a superiority in these weapons, so Gilpatric asserts, we are the ones who should take the initiative.

When the ban on testing atomic weapons was announced and agreed upon, I described it, in a letter to the *Herald Tribune*, as an important "public health" measure, but nothing more. The notion that this was really a step toward disarmament, in itself, seemed to me—then in a distinct minority—to be an illusion.

Now Scoop Jackson describes, with obvious relish, in his Senate speech last week, the great progress in weaponeering that is being accomplished by *underground* testing.

The only effect of the test ban, it now appears, is to make somewhat less convenient to the scientists the development of more and more ferocious weapons. The race goes on underground at an accelerated pace.

If these young people who storm the citadels and sign petitions—and the older ones, too—would only realize it, withdrawal or a settlement in Vietnam, as highly desirable as this would be, would in no way touch on the sorest of issues affecting peace, the atomic arms race between the two nations who, we are told, are in the midst of a détente! Détente indeed!

DECEMBER 6, 1967
7:40 A.M.
ON THE SHUTTLE FOR WASHINGTON

Add to the bumper-to-bumper way of life the early morning air shuttle. At 7:30 A.M., a *line* of nearly one hundred businesslike looking businessmen marching to get on an 8 o'clock plane. Me among them.

3 P.M.
ON THE SHUTTLE BACK TO NEW YORK

What was to have been a half hour with the President—if I was lucky and he not too "far behind"—turned into a half hour in the President's office, with the news cameras brought in for pictures; a walk with him to his movie-taking room while he made a speech for the cameras about farmers (and did it very well); talk on the way back, with him reading letters and memos poked at him by aides, every few feet; an invitation for me to talk (which I did for ten minutes) to the Cabinet, which had gathered awaiting him (he sat me at the Cabinet table immediately opposite him, with McNamara and Ambassador Goldberg flanking me); and then *another* press conference with the full White House press corps in George Christian's office.

DECEMBER 7, 1967
NEW YORK

What impressed me most about the five hours in Washington yesterday—a day full of one surprise after another?

The first thing, of course, is the President. His sheer bulk and vitality. Big in his ability to absorb a multitude of ideas, issues, and decisions, great and ephemeral—all the kaleidoscopic interstices of problems that make up the duties of by far the most complex and demanding task that any man's mind, spirit, and physique have ever had to bear.

When I first was shown into the Oval Office he was absorbed, completely, looking down at the floor; with him a staff member. He saw me, gave that big open-air, countryman smile that the TV cameras somehow never quite register, grabbed my hand in his enormous one, led me to his padded rocking chair, signaled me to a sofa at his right, tilted back in the rocker. He sat closer to his visitor than F.D.R. or Truman—or probably the more reserved Jack Kennedy—would find comfortable. He opened up, twirling his rimless glasses. "And what did you find out there; tell me." And after a brief moment when I assumed he was thinking about something else—he does change subjects and pace a hundred times a day, I daresay—he listened, hard and fully absorbed.

I said our main hope in preparing and presenting this long-range development report to the new government was to get them to "*thinking* hard and specifically about their economic problems and future, and what it would take to move ahead, but beginning now, toward less and less Vietnamese economic dependence on the United States."

"Tell me, Dave," he interjected, "what do you want the President of the U.S. to do to help in that very thing?" The question is the kind of "putting you at your ease" gambit that probably grows out of a lifetime of dealing with "constituents." But it is a good way to sharpen up what is so often a wandering discourse.

I responded that I hoped he could get the word through Ambassador Bunker—who agrees completely with our aim, about attention to economic development—to the new government and particularly the President and Vice President.

Then in came the score of photographers, at a signal. L.B.J. looked straight ahead, went on talking about his hopes that "we can divert the resources that are now going into destruction to the very things Dave here has been talking about, building the country and helping its people."

When the White House pressman told the photographers that "time was up" and switched off the big light, the President went on: "We get pictured as being butchers who love killing people. And I get pictures of me in the press with a whole battery of generals. I want you to come with me—I have a filming to do right now, about farming—and then go with me to the Cabinet, which will be meeting in a few minutes, and have some pictures taken that won't be just about the military side of this war. And tell them in ten minutes what you have told me."

The way he said "this war," his voice sounded weary of that whole mess, as well indeed he might be, and as I am.

The President carries his Chief Magistracy wherever he goes and at every moment he is in the White House. I found this envelopment of the man by his great office almost awe inspiring, as if one were visiting with an institution, not a man.

As the President entered the Cabinet room, the men at the table and around the wall rose. I looked around for a place to sit. The President motioned to a high-backed chair directly across from his seat, which is in the middle of the oval Cabinet table, the chair usually occupied by the Vice President, who was absent. (Except for Dean Rusk, he was the only absentee.) Some of the familiar faces around the table grinned at me—surprised at my being there—and I settled down.

Johnson's capacity to be many men, for many interests, all focussed on communicating and stirring others, was shown in the close interest he took in an outstanding presentation made by John Macy, his chief advisor on personnel management, during the Cabinet meeting.

Macy described his efforts, as head of the U.S. Civil Service Commission, to improve the day-to-day working of the whole Federal establishment. This the President followed closely, as did Secretary John Gardner and Ambassador Goldberg. (Helms, head of CIA, made a detailed classified report on the recent Soviet military budget, which has been considerably increased.)

The President asked Macy about the housekeeping side of government, earthy questions, gave directions to the Cabinet to give him a report on how *their* departments were performing on these detailed subjects, subjects far, far away from major policy about Vietnam or protecting the dollar—the grand issues that ordinary Presidents are supposed to be exclusively concerned with and interested in.

Johnson, unlike Kennedy, had a real feel for the unglamorous, nonnewsworthy side of running a huge government.

And most of all I was impressed by the President's very evident good health and vigor. He looked rested, of good color, never irritable.

This is very reassuring. When that political campaign opens in earnest, the country, I would predict, will see a man who can perform prodigious feats of running for President and running the government.

The Postmaster General, Lawrence O'Brien, was called on by the President and for ten minutes summarized the status of legislation. While he was talking the President leaned over, reached out toward me, and tossed me a folded note, signed, in tiny letters at the bottom: L.B.J. This is what I read:

"Dave—I'll call on you for ten min. when he and his team conclude 10 min. from now. You may want to jot down an outline for you to follow."

So, though the "outline" would be something I wouldn't follow, it was up to me to scribble some shorthand on the pad before me. And of course I didn't use the notes, since I had in mind what I wanted to say.

Which was not too coherent, but I hope conveyed the spirit of confidence and enthusiasm that I feel about the Vietnamese *people* themselves, and how some of the new young Cabinet members—technocrats—reminded me of the young men of the early New Deal, who were in their early thirties, too.

As an illustration of the caliber of these men of the Joint Group, and how they felt more than free to differ with our American group, I took the example of Thuc's quite on his own revising and expanding our Joint Report. I thought it significant: that they did not feel blanketed and overwhelmed by Americans.

Why did the President make so much of my visit? "All you hear in the papers is about how bloodthirsty we are, nothing but killing and blood—not a word about the kind of thing *you* are doing and stand for. Bobby Kennedy was on three TV shows last week. I want the country to hear the whole story, the constructive things, the building things. You tell Sarnoff," he said, "and Stanton to get you on one of these panel shows and tell the country what you told me and told the Cabinet."

DECEMBER 10, 1967
PRINCETON

The most impressive part of the goings on at the White House last Wednesday, as I have here written, was the President. The second strongest impression was made on me by that most talked about man in the Cabinet these days, Secretary McNamara.

Sitting at his side at the Cabinet table, I was appalled by his gaunt, worn appearance. The bones seemed to protrude from his face; his eyes were hollow. Here is a gallant "intellectual" who has stood up to whatever he thought his terrifying job demanded—or rather, to what *he* demanded of himself.

The wear and tear was evident and visible: seven years of outrageously long, vacationless days, weeks, and months, fighting the problems of establishing some order and managerial discipline in the Defense Department.

But that is by no means the whole story. This is not a man who can shrug off lightly the killing of American soldiers or the killing of any human beings, even "the enemy."

His intense and uncomplaining loyalty to the job, and to the President, are both impressive and touching. After seeing the warm communication, without words, between him and the President across that Cabinet table, I simply do not believe a word of the wise-guy speculations (which fill the press and magazines these days) attributing his resignation to a rift of war policy with the military brass or with the President. The President is a driver, but a compassionate man who must have seen that this gallant man should not be forced to drive himself over the precipice of a breakdown.

The cases are utterly different, and yet have a resemblance: Forrestal, driven by the job of trying to run the Pentagon, having it overcome him, and jumping to his death. *This* man would not even contemplate that kind of exit. But it must have occurred to him, and to his family, that the human system can stand only so much. And the World Bank Presidency, which would not stay open for long, would provide a change toward equally difficult but far less emotionally wearing tasks, and it would be more fulfilling for a man who must enjoy constructive things, after this bath of blood and controversy.

McNamara writes with his left hand; he made a number of notes on tiny, torn scraps of paper, which he stuffed from time to time into the outer breast pocket of his jacket.

From the viewpoint of my work and that of D&R, McNamara's taking charge of the World Bank could be a plus. His predecessors and their senior officers had the *banking* expertise about development; here is a man who has a managerial outlook and experience to bring to the task. The banking approach to development has fallen short; it is time that it be replaced, and for that to happen requires a man at the Bank's head who understands more than finance and lending operations.

DECEMBER 13, 1967
NEW YORK

Have just talked by phone to Perth, in the westernmost corner of Australia; Minister Charles Court's voice was clear, strong, and with that toughness of timbre that one thinks of in those latter-day pioneers.

I don't take casually this business of talking halfway round the world. It moves me—the very idea. A cable, yes, that I can understand.

But hearing the voice of a man is very close to being in his presence, and this man spoke from almost 15,000 miles away!

He said, "Things are going so fast out here that a study in depth [for a regional plan for the State of Western Australia] might be too late if we wait too long. Could you reach Perth sooner than January 22nd? I know the problems of schedule you must have." I assured him I would be in Australia early in the year.

DECEMBER 16, 1967
PRINCETON

A busy, intense, and happy week this has been. I function best under the pressure of self-imposed deadlines and the joy—not too romantic a word—I get from having around me people who exude excitement and zest and confidence that things can be done, not just talked about.

Burnett, just back from a trip to South America: very early in the morning (it must have been 7:30), we perched in my office while he raced through his adventures in Colombia, Chile, and Brazil, all in less than a week.

John brought back a heartening story from the Cauca Valley. The nub: to move away from the preoccupation with production of electricity.

The new Managing Director, Henry Eder, is not just an heir to his predecessor, Bernardo Garces: he intends to write a new chapter, and one along the general lines we proposed: a new look at the water and land resources.

It would be great if after almost fifteen years my child, the now sturdy CVC, would again become an important part of my work, and D&R's work.

Tuesday I had a good visit with Mehdi Samii, the soft-spoken, tactful, and keen-witted Governor of the Iranian Central Bank.

Samii looked so relieved that the Coronation went off so well—and it was one of the most successful ceremonial events in recent history. He was at the center of this, because as head of the Central Bank he is custodian of the fabulous Crown Jewels. He arranged in Paris for the design and fabrication of the two crowns, jeweled robes, and so on—a task that must have taken all the tact and quiet decisional powers he has.

I spoke of the luscious color photographs in the French magazine *Match*, and particularly that of the young Crown Prince, marching along by himself in the ceremonial. "The little boy, the Prince, completely stole the show, stole it completely," he said, throwing back his head with laughter—and pride. To the Persians royalty is even more important a part of their national and racial pride than it is to the English.

DECEMBER 17, 1967
PRINCETON

On Wednesday (the 13th) spent some time with McGeorge Bundy at his office in the new Ford Foundation building on East 43rd Street. A pretentious and expensive oddball building, reminding me of something in a World's Fair exhibit. A great enclosure, a well, ten stories deep, with the offices surrounding it, and at the bottom of the "well," trees and shrubs. Whoever designed it, it certainly wasn't Bundy's style.

As a man of many talents combined with simplicity of speech, Bundy impresses me more each time I see him or talk to him on the phone.

The purpose of my visit was to report on my visit to Vietnam about long-term economic development—about the priority assigned to economic matters, in fact. I mentioned the visit with the President and the Cabinet.

"The President asked me to do some writing or to do some TV panel things," I said, "because almost everything people hear about is the killing—and not the constructive things. So I did talk to the White House press group. The President is burned up about how little the press carries about anything except military operations."

McGeorge looked more quizzical (if possible) than usual. "Yes, he replied, "the President naturally wants you to see the press and be on TV. But the press made up its mind, while I was still in the White House, that anything that comes out of officials or people who are close to the President, like yourself, just *isn't copy* any more. And I made up my mind that it was a waste of time to get these things into the newspapers." He grinned in a kind of sheepish way. "The President doesn't agree with that; he thinks that is just the New England in me."

I said I had heard Dean Acheson on Channel 13 the other night, and he took an even stronger view: don't spend all that time explaining and trying to persuade people who simply aren't listening. He feels you should go ahead and *do* your job; the results are the only things that count. President Truman believed that and behaved on that principle, and he wishes President Johnson would do the same.

Said Bundy: "It's easy enough for Dean to say that, but there is very little comfort in that advice to the man on the griddle.

"Dean, by the way, is busy as can be these days writing his memoirs. Yes, I know, he said this he would never, never do; almost made it a religious issue, something immoral about 'telling all.' Every once in a while his work on these memoirs is interrupted because he has to write an angry footnote answering something George Kennan has said in *his* memoirs."

DECEMBER 18, 1967
NEW YORK

On my desk this morning a letter from the President:

December 14, 1967

DEAR DAVID:

You have given your President and your nation many proud moments. To them we now add your report to the Cabinet last week.

It was impressive and hopeful testimony to the faith we all place in your leadership and vision. Every Cabinet Member, together with the admiring people of America and South Vietnam, will always be grateful for the faith in freedom and peace you have so eloquently confirmed for us. . . .

God bless you and bring you all success.

Sincerely,
LYNDON B. JOHNSON

DECEMBER 20, 1967
NEW YORK

I wrote to the President today, responding to his letter about my Cabinet report. Since my reply reflects on the "price" and "compensations" of public service, I'm quoting from it here:

"Most of my adult life has been spent as a public servant; 19 consecutive years. Even now, as head of what is ostensibly a private business, almost all of what we do is essentially public service.

"One who has spent most of his life as a public servant knows good and well that his compensation must be chiefly the inner satisfaction of working for something he believes in.

"Once one really understands this—as I came to understand it when I was still in my early thirties—he is ready to pay the personal cost of public service: the kicking around, the facile self-righteous digs, the wearing load of work, the impugning of motives, and all the rest.

"Your letter to me is the kind of affirmative recognition that usually comes to a public servant in controversial fields only after he is dead, if ever. . . ."

DECEMBER 22, 1967
PRINCETON

A pre-holiday clean-up day at the office, working at a "high trot." Dictated a very long letter to Professor Thuc, setting out my philosophy about the *primary* place of the Vietnamese in a design for development.

This letter stated better than I ever have what profoundly motivates me about development *in someone else's country*, whether Vietnam or Persia.

In the case of Vietnam the implications of the kind of thinking underlying my views go much further than economic development: the *Vietnamese leadership must themselves reach a settlement with the Viet Cong*; the notion that we Americans, the outsiders *and* the defenders, should "negotiate" the terms of that settlement, as many of our American intellectuals and political noisemakers insist in page after page of petitions and rhetoric, is just plain wrong. Chamberlain "negotiated" directly with Hitler about someone else's freedom. But we must not.

DECEMBER 24, 1967
INTERNATIONAL AIRPORT, LOS ANGELES

With any luck—or rather, with the usual Luck of the Lilienthals—Helen and I shall see the rising sun in Tahiti tomorrow morning. With all our traveling to way-out places, the South Pacific Islands I never thought I'd see. Though, as an afterthought, I remember that at one time I was responsible for sending a good many men off for the Marshalls (secretly) for the atomic tests at Eniwetok.

Lunch with Bernardine [Szold Fritz] in her lovely and so utterly tasteful house in Beverly Hills. She has all of her old-time good looks—it's hard to believe she is any older than she was ten years ago or even twenty. She keeps up that conversational glow that has been part of her ever since I can remember—more than fifty years ago.

DECEMBER 28, 1967
TAHITI, FRENCH POLYNESIA

Our two days in Papeete were lazy, blessed with fierce sun and marked by vast spaces of profound sleep and spirited swims in a mountain-stream-fed pool.

Tahiti has long been a synonym for escape. Escape to the simpler life, escape from the complexities of modern life. Gauguin and his dark-skinned, naked Polynesian women, the green lush growth where one can live without working, without the pressure of time, without the bustle, the social conventions. Tahiti for a long time has been the refuge, in fantasy, of many men (only a *male* fantasy, I think).

There is certainly loveliness and grace in the women, and sturdiness and smiles among men, in the villages we saw yesterday, and among the hotel personnel. And a perfection of sea and sand and color of water and sense of remoteness. The debate about whether "natural man" is all that natural or happy can be left for others: this is a restful, beautiful place.

Dinner last night with one of my favorite among the newer breed of elected public servants, Senator Joe Clark of Pennsylvania. With him his new wife, Iris, a handsome figure of a woman whose intelligence and humor were evident almost at first glance. Also Tom Hamilton, President of the University of Hawaii.

The last time I had a real visit with Clark was when he was the new Mayor of Philadelphia. A member of the Philadelphia "establishment," by birth and prestige, he went into the hurly-burly of the politics of one of the toughest and most conservative of American cities, and (though a Democrat) licked a Republican machine with the essential help of Republicans, and began transforming that city both politically and physically. All the more impressive because it is perhaps the most stick-in-the-mud of the major cities of the country.

Senator Clark is on his way to Vietnam. As a member of the Committee on Foreign Relations, he has been outspoken in his skepticism and opposition to the war. When I expressed admiration for Bill Fulbright, and some sadness that the course of the Johnson Administration has so terribly depressed Fulbright's spirits and outlook on the state of the world, Clark nodded. "I follow Bill's leadership, and I share his sadness about the way things have gone, in that war, and in America. I, too, think we ought to get out of Vietnam, but I have *no idea* how we can do it."

Which comes pretty close to what most people think. Perhaps *I* put more emphasis, however, on the responsibility to follow up the statement "we must get out" with more emphasis on *how we get out* and what happens in that country, economically and socially, when and if we do.

Senator Clark looks on the date of President Kennedy's assassination as a watershed date in contemporary history; from that time on the moral climate of America, as well as the good sense of our policies, took a sharp drop downward. And of course the "style" of L.B.J., the Texan, is so remote from the standards of this devoted and patrician public servant—and of his wife—that it is difficult for him to temper his distaste.

DECEMBER 31, 1967
BORA BORA, FRENCH POLYNESIA

Year's end. As I head into 1968 and my Australian adventure, this seems a good time, here on this remote Pacific island, to take stock of the kind of year it has been.

It was one of the best of recent years. Clearly.

My work took on a greater *traction* than in any single period since I founded D&R. I saw more of the design of the unique kind of work and of organization than ever before.

But professionally, 1967 was also marked by very low periods as well.

On the personal side there were times of anguish, but the year swung to a close with greater personal satisfaction than I have ever had in my whole life, of a kind I never believed existed, for me certainly.

The fact that life can shift from low to high in a matter of weeks is a vivid demonstration of its miraculous fluidity and resilience.

It has been above all a year of strength. Strength in work. Strength in facing up to the struggles and conflicts of an entrepreneurial way of life. And most of all, strength in understanding myself and in my relationships with those I love.

INDEX

(Prepared by Helen M. Lilienthal)

Abram, Morris, 176
Acheson, Dean, 20, 121, 126, 128, 167, 226, 251, 353, 409, 432
Adams, Brooks, 88
Adams, Henry, 87–88, 93, 96
Adulyadej, Bhumibol (King of Thailand), 467
Afghanistan, 2, 95
Africa, 10, 176. *See* Ghana, Nigeria, Republic of the Ivory Coast
African-American Institute, 38, 408
Agriculture, 93–94, 189–190, 490, 501–502. *See also* Agrobusiness, Cauca Valley Authority, Dominican Republic, Colombia: INCORA; India, Iran
Agrobusiness, 312, 313, 314, 325–326, 348–349, 426, 439, 488–489
Ahmadi, Ahmad, 33, 33n, 234
AID (Agency for International Development), 61; L. on, 192–193; Freeman on, 223; Heinz on, 312. *See* Vietnam, Manila Conference, Guam Conference. *See also* Africa, Colombia, Dominican Republic, Iran, Afghanitan, Pakistan, Thailand, Peace Corps, Peru, Ivory Coast, India: Council on Administrative Science
Aiken, George D., 43
Aldewereld, S., 227, 236, 256–257; on World Bank, 237
Algeria, 185
Allen, John, 94
Alliance for Progress, 20, 164, 279
Alliluyeva, Svetlana, 431, 438, 441
Aly, Bower, 35
America, L. on, 88, 122, 213
American Arbitration Association, 148
American Assembly Conference, 157
American Association of Retired Persons, 63
American Booksellers Association, 63
Americans for Democratic Action, 296, 474
American Institute of Planners, 499
American Physical Society, 435
Ames, Amyas, 254
Amini, Ali, 29
Amouzegar, Jamshid, 292, 293
Amrine, Mike, 70
An, Nguyen Kien Thien, 389
Anderson, Clinton, 488
Anderson, Esther, 107
Anderson, Leo, 95, 145, 168, 210, 214, 230, 234, 331; and Iran, 244, 256–257, 261, 264, 272; and India
Ansari, Abdol Reza, 29, 31, 32, 92, 111, 116, 118, 130, 131, 244; Governor General of Khuzistan, 52–53; Minister of Interior, 272; on L., 52
Appalachia region, 25
Arab-Israeli war, *see* Middle East
Arnstein, Margaret B., 162, 162n.

Arthur D. Little, Inc., 89, 90
Ash, Roy, 147, 169, 293
Asfia, Safi, 125, 126
Asia, Southeast, 121, 352–353, 364, 500. *See* Vietnam: issues at stake
Asia Foundation, 404
Atchley, Dana, 21, 51–52, 68, 69, 478; on L., 80, 306–307
Atlantic Monthly, 348, 441
Atomic energy, 4, 66, 66n, 276; Board of Consultants, 22, 22n, 148, 233, 299; L. on, 350–351; Acheson-Lilienthal Plan, 335; A-bomb, 173; H-bomb, 22, 22n; underground testing, 526; atomic testing ban, L. on, 526; arms race, 525–526; "breeder" program, 429; nuclear power plants, 2–3, 5, 134; hazards, 37–38, 38n, 429, 432, 477; atomic wastes, 90, 222; desalination plants, 46, 477, 481–482, 486, 488; shelter program, 482; proliferation of atomic weapons material, 325, 482

Bacon, Francis (quoted), 51
Baldwin, Hanson, 252
Baldwin, Roger, 156–157, 156n, 273
Bancroft, Harding, 358
Barco-Vargas, Virgilio, 46, 241, 287, 288
Barkley, Alben, 319
Barnard College, 216–217
Barnard, Ellsworth, 306
Barnes, Joseph, 305–306
Barnett, Vincent M., 142
Baron, Mildred, 69, 282, 293, 313
Baruch, Bernard, 275
Baumgartner, Leona, 61, 155
Baumgartner, William J., 65
Beaverbrook, Lord, 41–42
Bechtel Corporation, 92
Bedford-Stuyvesant, 325, 425–426, 443–444, 466–467, 496–498. *See* Robert Kennedy
Belaunde-Terry, Fernando (President of Peru), 72, 73, 74, 98, 149, 150, 151, 152, 188, 194, 195, 242, 279
Bell, Daniel, 16
Bell, David, 9, 193–194, 195
Bellow, Saul (quoted), 150–151
Benavides, M., 150–151
Ben-Gurion, David, 90
Bennett, John, 516
Bentley, Ellen, 325, 470
Bentley, Gerald E., 325, 325n, 467, 470
Benton, Rita, 65
Benton, Thomas Hart, 65
Benton, William, 8
Berger, Clarence, 89
Berkner, Lloyd, 161, 161n
Berle, Adolf A., Jr., 87, 152, 176, 267
Bernstein, Leonard, 311
Bernstein, Marver, 171
Betancourt, Romulo, 39
Bethe, Hans, 401
Bhabha, Homi, 190
Billington, James H., 252, 266, 268, 269, 470
Binson, Boonrod, 371
Black, Eugene R., 366
Blough, Roger, 150, 308
Bock, Edwin A., 135
Bolivar, Simon, 45, 46, 163
Borch, Fred J., 335
Boston, 89–90, 316–317
Botero, Rodrigo, 287, 287n, 288, 291–292, 335, 342, 343, 344, 345
Bowater Paper Company, 18
Bowers, Claude, 361
Bowles, Chester, 100
Bowles, Dorothy, 101
Boyd, Julian, 329–330
Brademas, John, 218
Bradley, William, 17, 17n
Brandeis, Louis D., 86, 87
Brandeis University, 89
Brazil, 167–168, 189, 200, 531
Bromberger, Allen (grandson), 271, 279, 330, 334
Bromberger, Daniel (grandson), 271, 279, 330
Bromberger, Nancy (Lilienthal) (daughter), 80, 80n, 279, 330, 337–338, 499–500
Bromberger, Sylvain (son-in-law), 279, 330, 338
Brooklyn Museum, 164
Brown, James Douglas, 249
Buchwald, Art, 449
Bundy, McGeorge, 348, 408, 481–482, 486, 532
Bunker, Ellsworth, 320, 409, 424–425, 425n, 441, 507–509
Burnett, John G., 7, 95, 230, 249, 250, 276, 294, 346, 351; and Iran, 83, 130, 189, 244, 256–257, 260–261, 264, 456; and Vietnam, 319, 337, 355–356. *See* agrobusiness, Oakland County
Burns, James MacGregor, 524
Burt, Erford, 469
Business and businessmen, 19, 19n, 160–161, 166–167, 172, 313, 335–336, 488
Business Week, 321, 467, 480, 480n, 491–492

Buu, Tran Quoc, 382
Bynner, Witter, 320

Cady, John, 335
Cairns, Huntington, 161
Cambodia, 502, 508–509, 520
Canada, 2, 13, 140
Canfield, Cass, 1, 327, 328, 442–443
Cardenas, José, 179
Carnegie Endowment for International Peace, 308, 309
Carnegie Institute of Technology, 307, 308, 309. *See also* Fairless Lectures
Carroll, Paul, 426
Carvajal, Manuel, 241
Case, Clifford P., 259, 260, 309
Case, Everett, 408, 495
Cater, Douglass, 152, 215, 409
Cauca Valley Authority (CVC), 74, 75, 289, 335, 341, 531; reputation of, 72; and World Bank, 123
C. Brewer & Co., 362–364
Central Intelligence Agency (CIA), 39, 235, 408
Chadwick, Sir James, 89
Chamberlain, Neville, 433, 534
Change, Hope, and the Bomb, 35, 44n, 189
Chattanooga Times (Tenn.), 450
Chauncey, Henry, 315
Chenery, Hollis, 61, 61n
Cherne, Leo, 207, 207n
Chicago Tribune, 139, 140, 141
Childs, Marquis, 150
Chile, 120
China, *see* People's Republic of China
Christian, George, 404, 527
Churchill, Sir Winston, 41–42, 256, 479
Clapp, Gordon R., 29, 90; and D&R, 16, 167; and Iran, 26, 44, 358; and Dominican Republic, 132, 133, 163, 163n, 198
Clark, Iris, 535
Clark, Joseph, 535
Clark, Tom, 206
Clay, Lucius, 206, 493–494
Clifford, Clark, 350–353
Coal (in Western U.S.), 3, 18, 18n, 82–83, 94, 134, 190–191, 321
Coffee House Club, 5, 16
Collado, Emilio C., 335, 336
Collier's magazine, 262
Collinge, Robert, 384
Collingwood, Charles, 396–397, 424
Colombia, 11, 129, 221, 239, 240, 241, 341; L. trips to: *1964,* 11–14, 44–46; *1966,* 237–244, 287–289; *1967,* 340–346; Bogotá, 13, 238–239; Buenaventura, 11, 11n, 72; Cali, 14; Cucuta, 44–46, 45n; INCORA (Instituto Colombiano de la Reforma Agraria), 12, 12n, 13, 210–211, 241, 243, 289, 331, 341–342; Atlantico #3, 221, 242–243, 261, 345, 346; and World Bank, 13, 14, 123, 221, 236. *See also* Latin America; Inter-American Development Bank: integration report; Cauca Valley Authority
Colorado School of Mines, Research Foundation, 94, 191
Columbia University, 86n
Committee for Economic Development (CED), 153, 165, 171–172, 303, 304, 335–336
Committee for Improvement of Executive Management in the Federal Government, 8–9
Committee of One Hundred, Conference of, 254
Connally, Tom, 123
Consolidated Edison, 2–3, 5, 5n
Coolidge, Calvin, 225
Cooper, Charles, 295, 398, 510, 521
Copeland, Elise (niece), 19
Corcoran, Thomas E., 154, 179–180
Corson, John J., 8
Costa Rica, 239
Council on Foreign Relations, 38–39, 168–169, 228, 292, 319, 439, 500
Court, Charles, 514, 530–531
Cowan, Louis G., 60
Cowles, Gardner, 305, 327
Crain, Lawrence, 376
Cronkite, Walter, 92
Crump, Ed, 410
Cuba, 20
Culbertson, Robert, 379, 397
Cuong, Nguyen Quoc, 521
Curie, Eve, 252
Currie, Lauchlin, 238, 287, 288, 289, 291, 296–297, 342, 344

Daggett, Emma, 277, 281
Daggett, John, 316
Daniel, Clifton, 358
Davenport, Russell, 320
Davies, Joseph, 452
Davies, Paul, 493
Davis, John W., 23
Davis, Mary, 259
Davis, Wendell, 259
Day, Thomas, 243
Dayan, Moshe, 477

Decatur Daily (Ala.), 335
De Gaulle, Charles, 478
de Hoffmann, Frederic, 429
Denver Post, 62, 94
DePauw University, 139, 140, 192, 335, 472
De Rothschild, 476, 477
Descartes, Sol, 331–332
Developing countries, 57, 129, 130–131, 199, 263, 500; planning, 9, 34, 216, 378–379, 446–447, 448, 462, 490, 490n; technical assistance, 74, 235. *See* Tennessee Valley Authority; Development and Resources Corporation: purposes, principles, methods of work. *See also* Middle East; Jordan Valley Development; Indus Basin Plan; Mekong Basin; Iran: Khuzistan; Colombia: INCORA, Atlantico #3; Bedford-Stuyvesant; managers and management; population control; agrobusiness; integrated development; food
Development and Resources Corporation (D&R) 51, 79, 82–83, 230, 231–232, 261, 430–431; creation of, 78; purposes of, 15–16, 152–153, 166–167; principles of, 131, 449, 457, 468; philosophy of, 275–276; methods of work, 74, 333, 458, 483; management, 84, 115, 203–204, 276, 493; finances, 292, 294, 386–387, 439, 457, 503; *comments on*: L., 147, 150, 152–153, 282, 313, 430–431; David Lilienthal, Jr., 85–86; Grant, 475; Hettinger, 15; Lively, 275; Burnett, 249–250; Davis Agricultural Center, 190, 209, 210, 211, 214, 361, 386–387, 489; *overseas projects*: Colombia: INCORA, Atlantico #3; CVC, Inter-American Development Bank: Integration report; India; Iran; Guinea; Republic of the Ivory Coast; Vietnam; *U.S. projects*: Bedford-Stuyvesant, coal, Oakland County. *See also* water, Lazard Frères, André Meyer, Utah Construction and Mining Co.
Dewey, Thomas E., 500
Dewhurst, Frederic, 311
Dewhurst, Mrs. Frederic, 311–312
Diawara, Mohamed, 126
Diem, Ngo Dinh, 516
Dillon, Clarence, 206, 207, 495
Dillon, Douglas, 206, 325
Disraeli, Benjamin, 466
Dix, William, 239
Dominican Republic, 126, 129, 132, 200, 508, 508n; and D&R, 132–133, 163, 192–193, 193n.
Dorrance, Henry, 369
Dos Passos, John, 334
Douglas, Helen Gahagan, 206, 403
Downs, Hugh, 445–447
Drucker, Peter, 152
Drummond, Roscoe, 207, 207n
Drury, Allen, 316
Dulles, Allen, 39
Dulles, John Foster, 39, 39n, 251
Duncan, Francis, 431

Ebtehaj, Abolhassan, 17, 17n, 25–26, 113, 114, 439, 495–496
Eccles, Marriner, 85, 85n, 135–136, 138, 180, 185
Ecker, Frederick H., 11
Eden, Sir Anthony, 197
Eder, Harold, 123–124, 341, 341n; Garces on, 124; L. on, 124–125
Eder, Henry, 341, 341n, 531
Education and World Affairs (EWA), 81, 141–142, 187, 218, 235, 321, 408–409, 462, 463; CIA issue, 264–269, 266n
Egypt, *see* Middle East
Einstein, Albert, 71
Eisenhower, Dwight D., 60, 377; administration of, 126, 433; and Middle East, 476, 481
Eisenhower, Milton, 60
Electric energy, 3, 4, 18, 66, 66n, 82, 83, 133–134, 169, 191–192, 300. *See also* coal, atomic energy: nuclear power plants
El Emary, Abdel, 236
Elias, Nathaniel, 56
Elias, Leona, *see* Baumgartner, Leona
Elizabeth II, Queen of England, 114, 198–199, 198n
Ely, David, *see* Lilienthal, David E., Jr
Engelhard, Charles W., 160, 178–179
Ensminger, Douglas, 103, 107, 145, 216
Evans, Llewellyn, 145–146
Export-Import Bank, 95

Fairless Lectures, Benjamin, 165, 208, 246–248, 257, 295, 338; theme, 307; given, 307, 308, 503; David L., Jr., on, 261–262; Goheen on, 444. *See also* *Management: A Humanist Art*
Fall, Bernard, 399
Farmanfarmaian, Khodadad, 29, 439–440
Farmer, James, 176
Farr, Walter G., Jr., 85, 250
Feinsinger, Nathan, 183

Feis, Herbert, 271
Fermi Award, 22, 22n
Finletter, Thomas, 227
Firfer, Alexander, 192
Fisher, Adrian, 255
Fisher, Francis, 243
Flom, Joseph, 69–70, 84
Food, 1, 10, 19, 189–190, 209, 210, 220, 222, 227–228, 301–302. *See* agrobusiness, Colombia, India
Forbath, Thomas, 222
Ford, Father George, 335
Ford Foundation, 39, 145, 265, 303, 331, 408
Foreign Affairs, 348
Forrestal, James, 59, 64, 275, 530
Forsythe, George I., 511
Fortas, Abe, 150
Fosdick, Raymond, 193
Fowler, Henry H., 271, 459
France, 10, 89; in Vietnam, 185, 297, 382, 383, 513
Franco, Romulo, 151–152
Frankfurter, Felix, 68, 92
Franklin, John, 78, 136, 232
Freedom House, 121–122, 204–207
Freeman, Orville, 223, 250
Friendly, Alfred, 41
Friendly, Fred, 347–348
Friendly, Jean, 41
Fritts, Robert, 523
Fritz, Bernardine Szold (cousin), 314, 320
Fugitt, Warren, 467
Fulbright, J. William, 49, 212, 226, 252, 534; on Dominican Republic, 132, 133, 142–143; on Southeast Asia, 163; on China, 112, 225; on Vietnam, 112, 433–435; on Jordan Valley, 460; on L., 434, 440.
Future Farmers of America, 64–65

Galbraith, Catherine, 313
Galbraith, J. Kenneth, 7, 34, 136, 313, 370, 474
Gandhi, Indira, Prime Minister of India, 215, 216, 222, 223, 225, 228–229
Gant, George, 265
Garces, Alejandro, 240
Garces, Bernardo, 72, 73, 123–124, 129, 241, 289, 340–341, 346, 347
Gardner, John, 409, 459, 528
Gaud, William S., 412
Gavin, Paul, 212, 352
Geraghty, James, 220
Germany, 353, 434; West Germany, 325
Ghana, 236, 258, 300
Ghirshman, Roman, 28–29
Gill, Brendan, 297
Gilpatric, Roswell, 173, 526
Glennan, Keith, 142
Glick, Frank, 308
Glick, Virginia Kirkus, 308
Goheen, Margaret, 37
Goheen, Robert F., 37, 37n, 81, 142, 245, 269; on L.'s papers, 315
Goldberg, Arthur, 150, 205, 527, 528
Goldman, Eric, 427–428
Goldman, Robert, 214
Goldwater, Barry, 53, 68
Gordon, Lincoln, 311, 333, 347
Gore, Albert, 410
Gould, Leslie, 97
Grant, James, 458–459, 475, 492, 501–502, 507
Grant, Ulysses S., 239
Graves, Bibb, 410
Greece, 26–27, 159, 206, 457
Greeley, Horace, 231
Greenbaum, Dorothea, 23, 308
Greenbaum, Edward S., 17, 23, 71, 308, 330–331, 431, 438, 441, 442; and Jordan Valley, 465, 468–469; and Middle East, 470, 476
Greene, Nathan, 29, 54; death, 64; L. on, 68, 70
Greene, Rosalinda, 54
Gremliza, F. G. L., 31, 31n, 167
Groves, Leslie R., 400
Gaudeloupe, French West Indies, L. trip to, 75
Guam, 417, 419
Guam Conference, 411–421; Americans and Vietnamese participating; topics discussed; postwar economic development, 412, 414, 416; Vietnamese elections, 414, 415, 419–420; Chinese film on China's nuclear weapons, 421; Johnson on U.S. reports and reporters, 413; L. on, 422; L. on Johnson, 415, 417; L. on conference, 411, 412
Guaranty Trust, 23
Guatemala, 200
Guinea, 10, 18
Gunther, Jane, 134–135
Gunther, John, 134–135
Gutterman, Leon, 493
Guttierez, Edgar, 288

Hach, Nguyen Cao, 522
Hakimi, Nader, 462
Hamilton, Edith, 91
Hamilton, Thomas, 535

Han, Vo Xuan, 522
Hanh, Nguyen Huu, 295, 384–385, 388–389
Hanna, Bert, 66
Hannah, John, 80, 142, 235, 265, 305
Harkens, Robert, 210–211, 230, 234, 243, 331, 341–342
Harper & Row, 330
Harrar, J. George, 225, 408
Harriman, Averell, 252, 409, 487
Harvard University, 93, 94; Harvard Corporation, 21
Harvey Aluminum Co., 18
Harza, 141
Hastie, William H., 162, 162n
Hatcher, Harlan, 305
Hawaii, L. trip to: 360–364; Kauai, 360–362; Honolulu, 362–364, 398–399
Hayes, James, 465
Heflin, Van, 8
Hefner, Hugh M., 127
Heinz, Henry John, 11, 312, 314, 348–349, 426
Heller, Francis, 65
Helms, Richard M., 420–421, 528
Hemingway, Ernest, 46, 334
Herrera, Filipe, 10, 163, 164. *See* Inter-American Development Bank: integration report; on D&R report, 298
Hersey, John, 91
Hettinger, Albert, 15–16, 137–138
Hewlett, Richard G., 431–432
Hickenlooper, Bourke B., 37, 225
Hill, Lister, 410
Hitler, Adolf, 433, 534
Ho Chi Minh, 420, 422, 436–437, 495, 498, 508
Hoffman, Paul, 319
Holbrooke, Richard, 398, 399, 407
Holmes, Julius, 28, 28n
Holmes, Oliver Wendell, Jr., 23, 246
Honduras, 200
Hough, Henry Beetle, 281, 316
Houghton, Amory, 150
Houphouet-Boigny, Felix, President, Republic of the Ivory Coast, 482
Houser, John, 198, 199, 200, 201
Hoyt, E. Palmer, 62, 66
Hudson Institute, 189
Huff, Clay, 167
Hughes, Elizabeth, 259
Hughes, Richard, 259, 260, 471, 494–495
Hull, Cordell, 442
Humphrey, Hubert H., 177–178
Humphrey, John, 2
Huntley, Chet, 186–187
Hurtado, Dr. Hector, 342, 344
Hussein, Ibn Talal, King of Jordan, 472
Hutchinson, Edmond, 80
Ickes, Harold, 53
Illinois, 204
India, 2, 7, 24, 85, 99–100, 100n, 104, 120; L. trip to, *1965*, 100–109; New Delhi, 100–101, 108; Punjab, 104–106; and AID, 85; Council on Administrative Science, 99–109; agriculture, 104–106, 107; irrigation, 103–104, 108–109; bureaucrats, 102–103, 108; D&R analysis, 106; D&R proposal, 109; L. on, 109; food, 100, 101–102, 209, 215, 222–223, 302; and Iraq, 120–121; L. letter to President Johnson on, 222–223, 250; and Pakistan, 159–160. *See* Indus Basin Plan, Peace Corps, Planned Parenthood, population control, developing countries
Indiana, 139
Indiana University, 81, 139
Indus Basin Plan, 236, 262, 262n, 509, 509n
Institute for Advanced Study, 17, 173, 315, 400–401
Integrated development, 32–33, 74, 93–94, 144–145, 179, 339, 359–360, 430–431, 446–447, 462, 467–468. *See* D&R, TVA, Colombia, Iran, Vietnam, develing countries, Middle East
Inter-American Development Bank, 168; D&R contract, 179, 188; integration report, 277, 321; comments on, 294; Colombia-Venezuela economic integration, 10, 46; meeting in Caracas, 289–292; meeting in Bogotá, 342–344; D&R proposal rejected, 343, 345, 346; L. on, 344–345. *See* Latin America, Punta del Este, Herrera
International Monetary Fund (IMF), 340–341, 347
Iran: coronation, 531; food, 19, 449; agriculture, 487; L. trips to, *1964*: 27–33; *1965*: 110–118; Plan Organization, 26, 43, 114; Ministry of Water and Power, 83, 92–93, 115–116, 119, 120, 125–126, 141; and AID, 36; and U.S. 27, 120; and World Bank, 36, 49, 226, 244, 456–457; and Russia, 43, 439, 477, 477n (*see also* Middle East, Oil); Khuzistan region, 16, 27, 30–31, 110, 111–112, 113, 326, 335, 411, 488; before D&R, 44, 110, 113–114; importance of, 32–33, 43, 48, 121, 126; prosperity of, 27–28, 111–112, 293; Greater Dez Pilot Irrigation Project, 234, 244, 261, 264; L. on, 430–431, 496; Khuzistan Water and Power Authority (KWPA), establishment of, 76, 144–145; autonomy of, 32–33,

Iran (*cont'd*)
116; under Ministry of Water and Power, 52, 53, 111, 272; L. on, 189; Pahlavi Dam, 27–28, 112, 120. *See* Shah Reza Pahlavi, interest in. *See also* agrobusiness
Iraq, 48, 120–121. *See* Middle East
Israel, *see* Middle East
Ivory Coast, *see* Republic of the Ivory Coast

Jackson, Henry, 488, 526
Jacobi, Susan, 308–309
Jacobs, Beth, 1, 2
Jacobs, Eli, 497
Jacobs, Lenworth, 1–2
Jamaica, L. trip to, 1964, 1–20; 199
Janeway, Eliot, 58, 270–271
Janeway, Elizabeth, 58, 270
Janeway, William, 270–271
Japan, 367–368, 491, 504, 506, 523–524; L. trip to, 1967, 504–505, 523–524; Tokyo, 365, 505
Jenkins, Walter, 66, 67
Johnson, Claudia (Lady Bird), 40, 171, 223, 464, 484–486; on President Johnson, 486
Johnson, Joseph E., 38–39, 38n, 89, 143, 195–196; on Middle East, 476–477
Johnson, Mrs. Joseph E., 143
Johnson, Lyndon B., President, 20, 47–48, 57, 150, 212, 258, 402–406, 467; 1964 campaign, 58, 62, 66; elected, 69; at White House State functions, 40, 223–227; 483–486; and India, 215; L. letter on, 222–223, 250; and Dominican Republic, 126, 163, 508, 508n; and Latin America, 194, 195 (*see* Punta del Este, Alliance for Progress); and Vietnam: war in, 404, 433, 478–479, 481; economic reconstruction of, L. report to, 521–529 (*see* Guam Conference, Manila Conference; *see also* Vietnam: U.S. sentiment against war; and Asia, Southeast, 352). *Speeches*: 121, 121n, 205, 245, 278; honorary degree, 245; on Shah of Iran, 47, 48, 483; on L., 404, 483, 533. *Comments on Johnson:* Monroney, 41; Friendly, 41; Hoyt, 62; Hettinger, 138; Meyer, 260; Fulbright, 49, 123, 132; Clifford, 353; Sevareid, 409; Bundy, 532; L., 155, 294–295, 327, 328, 402, 486
Johnson, U. Alexis, 162
Jones, Arnold R., 221
Jordan, *see* Middle East
Jordan Valley Development, 450, 460, 465, 465n, 472. *See* atomic energy: desalination plants
Journals, 14, 74, 339; contents of, 91, 262–263; method of work, 4, 157, 213; use by scholars, 262; teaching material, 135; *comments on*: Szold, 84; Mason, 87; Schlesinger, 196; Meyer, 319; Fritz, 314; Macy, 155; Burns, 524; Boyd, 330; David E., Lilienthal, Jr., 317

Kahn, Herman, 189
Kaiser Engineering Co., 236
Kalitsi, E. A. K., 258
Kampmeier, Roland A., 191
Katzenbach, Nicholas, 422, 489
Kaysen, Carl, 315, 324–325, 400
Kazin, Alfred, 316
Kefauver, Estes, 320, 410
Kefauver, Nancy, 320
Kelce, Merl C., 191
Kennan, George, 130, 207–208, 252, 345, 352, 400; on labor unions, 129–130; and "cold war," 208; L. on, 128–129
Kennedy, Gerald H., 229
Kennedy, Jacqueline, 270, 327–328, 329
Kennedy, John Fitzgerald, 23, 60, 294, 330; as President, 25, 126, 206, 221, 268, 433, 528; *comments on*: Clark, 535; Clifford, 351; Robert Kennedy, 23
Kennedy, Robert, 23, 206, 268, 270, 320, 481, 529; and Bedford-Stuyvesant, 302–303, 323, 325, 444, 466–467
Kernan, Henry, 521
Kerr, Clark, 44, 44n
Keynes, John Maynard, 136
Keyser, P. V., Jr., 18–19
Kha, Vu Quoc, 512, 513
Khera, S. S., 159–160
Khrushchev, Nikita, 67
Kipling, Rudyard, 104
Klein, Howard, 63
Knight, Douglas, 218
Knorr, Klaus, 266, 269
Komer, Robert: on L.'s Vietnam assignment, 280, 283, 301, 317, 319; and D&R report, 340, 350; on AID program, 437; under Westmoreland, 441, 458; in Saigon, 385–386, 388–389, 398, 507, 511–512; on pacification progress, 473–474
Korea, 375

Korsmeyer, F. B., 19
Kosygin, Aleksei, 465
Ky, Nguyen Cao, Prime Minister of South Vietnam, 233, 319, 376, 377, 378–379, 386, 480, 516, 517; on civilian government, 403; Joint Group report, 520; on postwar planning, *see* Manila Conference, Guam Conference

Labor Unions, 13, 182–184, 300; L. on, 130, 182–183
LaFollette, Isabel, 156
LaFollette, Philip, 156, 364
LaFollette, Robert M., Sr., 66
Land grant colleges, 217
Laos, 47
Latin America, 20, 39–40, 81, 134–135, 178, 188, 194, 195, 219, 293, 305; Airlie House Conference, 164–165; Common Market, 310; trade in arms, 319–320; Conference with U.S., 347; *comments on*: Johnson, 195; L., 189; Gunther, 134–135; Lippmann, 194. *See* Herrera, Alliance for Progress, Inter-American Development Bank, Punta Del Este, Organization of American States, developing countries, Colombia
Lazard Frères & Co., 4, 18, 18n, 83, 150, 231–232, 494
Lazarus, Emma, 3
Lee Kuan Yew, 500
Lehman Brothers, 493
Lekhyananda, Sudha, 369
Leonhart, William, 444, 458, 492
Leoni, Raul, 290–291
Lerner, Alan Jay, 8
Lewis, John P., 85, 100, 106, 109, 250
Levitt, Abraham, 465
Lilienthal, David E., Sr., overseas development work (*see* Development and Resources Corp.); overseas trips, *1964*: Jamaica, Iran, Colombia, Peru; *1965*: India, Iran, Peru; *1966*: St. Vincent, Colombia, Venezuela; *1967*: Hawaii, Vietnam, Thailand, Guam, Japan (*for other activities see* Education and World Affairs, Planned Parenthood, Population Council, Committee for Economic Development, Bedford-Stuyvesant, Twentieth Century Fund, Rockefeller Public Service Awards, Conference of Committee of One Hundred; *see also* AID, atomic energy, Indus Basin Plan, Jordan Valley, Mekong Basin, TVA, World Bank, Minerals & Chemicals Philipp Corp.); *honors*: University of California, Indiana University, University of Illinois; *decorations*: Ivory Coast, Peru; *health*, 67–68, 79, 108, 307; *recreations*: gardening, 21–22, 121, 294; sailing, 52, 490; walking, 79, 80, 306, 501; music, 61; introspection, 10–11, 14, 21, 23–24, 134, 147–148, 299; impatience, 71, 127, 143, 299; work, 284; method of work, 86–87; optimism, 88–89, 132; convictions, 410–411; *reflections on*: living, 280; emotional pain, 30; change, 24, 26, 35; discontent, 57; timidity, 144; duality of life, 434–435; planners, 35–36, 499; technologists, 447; systems analysis, 93, 94, 99, 293–294, 315; the bureaucratic mind, 101–102, 144–145; public servants, 5–6, 9, 87; decision-making, 101–102; the reality of statecraft, 130–131; economists, 86–87, 131, 171–172, 271; social scientists, 164–165; jargon, 175; intellectuals, 126–127; abstract thinkers, 129; innovators, 145–146; the entrepreneurial spirit, 61, 202–203, 470 (*see also* business and businessmen, managers and management, young people, developing countries); *books*: *see TVA: Democracy on the March; This I Do Believe; Change, Hope, and the Bomb; Journals*, vols. I, II, III, IV, V; *talks to groups*: Coffee House Club, University of Kansas; *speeches*: Newark (political), Hillman Lectures; Benjamin Fairless Lectures; Brandeis University; Herald Tribune Book and Author Luncheon, Planned Parenthood; *article*: "300,000,000 Americans Would Be Wrong" (*New York Times*); *TV appearances*: 422, 445–447.
Lilienthal, David E., Jr. (son), 62, 85–86, 87, 95–96, 257, 272, 332, 337, 372; move to Italy, 459, 470; and *Journals*, 4, 340; as author (David Ely), 58, 85, 156, 165–166, 297, 301, 401; on L., 257; and Vietnam, 329, 409–410, 423; on D&R, 85–86; L., on, 411, 423
Lilienthal, David E., III (grandson), 48–49, 62, 146, 154, 272
Lilienthal, Helen M. (wife), 28, 29, 57, 88, 225, 229, 230, 240, 244, 272, 306, 310, 362, 385, 500; on L., 410–411
Lilienthal, Leo (father), 250
Lilienthal, Margaret (daughter-in-law), 55–56, 58, 62

Lilienthal, Margaret L. (granddaughter), 62
Lilienthal, Nancy (daughter), *see* Bromberger, Nancy
Lilienthal, Pamela (granddaughter), 170, 372
Lilienthal, Theodore (brother), 19–20
Lincoln, Abraham, 478
Lindahl, Emil, 380–381
Lindsay, John V., 182, 183, 190, 192, 206
Linowitz, Sol M., 196, 311, 320–321, 333, 337
Lippmann, Walter, 68–69, 179, 188, 194, 228, 316, 345
Lisagor, Peter, 413
Littlefield, Edmund, 3, 18, 133–134, 192
Litton Industries, 147, 159, 293; Litton Industries International Development Corp., 457, 459
Lively, Robert, 253, 275; on L., 334
Lleras, Alberto, 12, 12n, 20, 334
Lleras-Restrepo, Carlos, 12–13, 220, 221, 237–238, 241, 242; *comments on*: A. Lleras, 12; Penalosa, 341
Loc, Nguyen Van, 510, 515, 516, 517
Locke, Eugene M., 518
Lodge, George, 491
Lodge, Henry Cabot, 323, 376, 384, 397, 399, 403, 491. *See also* Guam Conference
Loeb, Robert A., 162, 162n
Look magazine, 330
Lovett, Robert, 478
Lowdermilk, Walter, 472
Luce, Gertrude, 158

MacArthur, Diana, 235, 274–275
MacArthur, Douglas, 365, 365n, 491
MacDonald Donald, 376, 384, 385, 397, 398, 437, 507
MacLeish, Archibald, 217
Macmillan, Harold, 433
McAlister, John T., 407–408
McBride, Donald, 258
McCarthy, Joseph, 59, 163, 498
McCarthy, Mary, 384
McCloy, John, 251, 400, 409
McCone, John, 481
McCord, James, 229, 259
McCormick, Ann O'Hare, 157
McCormick, Robert, 139, 140, 141
McCullough, Frank, 141–142
McElroy, Neil, 8
McIntyre, Marvin, 402–403
McKellar, Kenneth M., 403, 410
McMahon, Edward G., 90
McMurrin, Sterling, 315
McNamara, Robert S., 41, 212, 227, 252, 390, 459; *see* Guam Conference; and Vietnam, 142, 297, 478, 572; resignation, 525; Komer on, 474; L. on, 529–530
McNaughton, John, 472
Macy, John W., 154–155, 221, 258, 528
Male, Raymond F., 407
Mali, 10
Management: A Humanist Art, 446
Managers and management, 41, 211, 244–245, 262, 276, 316. *See* notes on "The Managerial Way of Life," 246–248. *See also* Fairless Lectures; *Management: A Humanist Art*
Manila Conference, 318–319
Mann, Thomas, 20
Mansfield, Michael J., 488
Mansour, Hassan Ali, 29, 52–53, 130, 131
Markel, Lester, 358
Marks, Anne, 255–256, 299–300
Marshall, George C., 36, 238, 353
Marshall, Thurgood, 205
Martha's Vineyard (Mass.), 56, 153–154, 156, 277, 281, 316, 466, 470, 480–481, 490–491
Martin, Graham, 370, 370n
Martin, William McChesney, 136, 138
Marvel, William W., 196, 218, 265, 408–409
Mason, Alpheus, 87, 87n, 253
Mason, Edward, 218, 268
Massachusetts Institute of Technology (MIT), 46, 93, 94; Revelle Commission, 93
Maverick, Maury, 403
Maxwell, Donald, 139–141
Maxwell, Marjorie, 140
Maxwell, Philip, 141
Mead, Thomas, and Africa, 18, 71, 126, 236, 258, 300; and Vietnam, 353–356, 371–372, 373, 399, 489, 509, 510; interim report, 443; L. on, 287, 440, 495
Mehta, Ashok, 103, 106
Mekong Basin, 362, 366; L. on UN Mekong Basin Coordinating Committee, 366, 367, 367n, 509, 515
Metropolitan Museum of Art, 122
Mexico, 321
Meyer, Agnes, 226
Meyer, André, 79, 85, 97–98, 184–186, 269–270, 319; and D&R, 4, 78, 82, 147, 150, 185, 231–232; and Vietnam, 185, 297; and Iran, 297–298; and Bedford-Stuyvesant, 302–303; L. on, 184, 185, 186

Meyer, Bella, 319
Meyner, Helen, 89, 186, 259, 401 494
Meyner, Robert B., 37, 42, 185, 187, 259, 260, 401, 494
Michel, Aloys, 262
Michigan State University, 81, 235, 265, 305
Middle East, 157, 450–452, 476, 477–478; Arab-Israeli war, 448, 453, 454, 455, 472, 486; American sentiment, 448, 449. *See* atomic energy: desalination plants
Miller, Edward G., 20
Miller, Paul Duryea, 89–90
Millikan, Max, 267–268
Minerals & Chemicals Philipp Corp. (M&CP), 160–161, 178–179, 185, 232–233
Mitchell, James, 162
Mohr, Charles, 2
Moley, Raymond, 267
Molotov, Vyacheslav, 419
Moncloa, Manuel, 129
Monnet, Jean, 174, 252
Monroney, A. S., 40–41
Monroney, Ellen, 40–41
Montaigne (quoted), 51–52
Moore, Frederick T., and Latin America, 291, 333, 342, 343, 345, 374, 379, 399; and Vietnam, 349, 355–356, 357; interim report, 443; and Japan, 523, 524; L. on, 387
Moosa, Pierre, 10
Morehouse, Edward W., 94
Morgan, Harcourt A., 234, 250; Atchley on, 69
Morgan, Harold Van, 181–182
Morris, Newbold, 89
Morrison-Knudsen, 383–384
Morse, Wayne, 195, 252
Morton, Thruston, 495
Moscoso, Teodoro, 132, 310
Moses, Robert, 36
Mossadeqh, Mohammed, 157, 419, 485
Mostel, Zero, 440
Motley, Constance B., 206
Moyers, Bill, 328, 329
Mullins, T. C., 190–191
Muñoz, Inez, 310
Muñoz-Marín, Luis, 310, 311, 332
Murphy, Franklin D., 42, 269
Murphy, Robert, 162
Murrow, Charles, 251
Murrow, Edward R., 29, 59, 60, 399, 474; death, 122, 125, 186–187, 251
Murrow, Janet, 59, 122, 251
Museum of Modern Art, 51
Nakhai, Hassein Ghods, 114
Nasser, Gamal Abdel, 448
Nathan, Robert, 296
National Broadcasting System (NBC) 422, 445–447
National Security Council, 47, 48
National University Extension Association, 35
Neal, Alfred, 153, 171–172, 335
Nehru, Jawaharlal, 38, 38n, 100, 160, 228–229
Neumann, Emanuel, 460, 465
New Jersey Meadow Lands Commission, 92
New York City, 23, 38, 50, 51, 67, 69, 93, 96, 148; transit strike, 169, 170, 182–184, 219, 460
New York Daily News, 293
New York Herald Tribune, 71–72, 98
New York Review of Books, 316
New York Times, 10, 19, 23, 293, 357–359; news, 2, 25, 51, 171, 208, 268, 325, 328; *Magazine*, 166, 166n, editorial, 449; and Vietnam, 429, 491, 503
New Yorker, 121, 220, 299, 503
Newsweek, 226
Nicely, James M., 23, 369
Nigeria, 235. *See* Peace Corps
Nixon, Richard M., 435
Nizer, Louis, 8
Norris-LaGuardia Act, 182
Noyes, David, 64

Oakes, John B., 36–37, 489
Oakland County (Mich.), 502
Oates, James, 303
O'Brien, Eugene, 231, 249, 257, 264, 456
O'Brien, Lawrence, 459, 529
Ochs, Adolph, 357
Oil, 43, 157, 454
Oliver, Covey T., 243
Oliver, John, 29, 147, 174, 209, 222, 276, 313, 386, 450; and Latin America, 133, 149, 343; and Vietnam, 318, 323, 337; and Iran, 44, 49, 52, 92, 125, 126, 141, 189, 261, 264; and TVA, 221, 314
Ontario Hydro Commission, 43
Oppenheimer, J. Robert, 37, 89, 169, 173–174, 176, 315, 348, 438; Fermi Award, 22, 22n; and atomic energy, 22, 22n, 174, 233; health, 234, 255, 299, 313, 323; death, 387; memorial service, 400–401; on L., 299

Oppenheimer, Katherine (Kitty), 22, 130, 254, 299, 348
Oppenheimer, Katherine (Tony), 299, 401
Organization of American States (OAS), 132, 311, 320
Outlook, 101, 101n
Overseas Consultants, Inc., 95
Owen, Marguerite, 474

Paar, Jack, 23
Pacific Gas & Electric Co., 134
Pahlavi, Farah, Empress of Iran, 40, 42, 483
Pahlavi, Mohammed Reza, Shah of Iran, 34, 52–53, 114–115, 483; attempted assassination of, 118; program for Iran, 485–487; in Washington, D.C., 40, 43, 483, 484; in Los Angeles, 42–43; trip to Khuzistan, 28–30; interest in Khuzistan, 28, 43, 83, 244, 496; on importance of, 43; audiences with L., 31, 42–43, 116–121; on Arab-Israeli war, 472 (*see* Middle East); on L., 44, 484; *comments on Shah*: L., 485; Mrs. Johnson, 465; President Johnson, 47, 48, 483
Pahlavi, Reza, Crown Prince of Iran, 531
Pakistan, 93–94, 159, 160, 507; and World Bank, 16, 227, 236
Paley, William S., 59, 443
Palfrey, John, 432
Parsons, Howard, 370–371
Pastoriza, Tomas, 129, 163
Paton, Alan, 176
Pauling, Linus C., 428
Peace Corps, 214, 217, 230, 234, 235, 250, 274–275
Penalosa, Enrique, 13, 13n, 220–221, 239, 240, 241, 261, 277, 287, 289; and INCORA, 331, 341–342; on Colombia, 346–347; on Lleras-Restrepo, 341. *See* Colombia: INCORA, Atlantico #3, Latin America, Inter-American Development Bank: Colombia-Venezuela economic development
People's Republic of China, 212. *See* Asia, Southeast
Pepper, Claude, 206
Percy, Charles H., 309, 345
Perkins, James A., 40, 315
Perry, Ralph Barton, 65
Persia, *see* Iran
Peru, L. trips to: *1964*, 72–75; *1965*, 149–152; Cuzco, 88; Lima, 151; Piura region, 73–75, 129, 149, 151–152, 287; L. on, 73–74, 74n, 98, 150–151; and World Bank, 74; and AID, 74. *See also* "Diarist's Note," 75
Pestana, Carlos, 72
Peterson, Ervin, 214, 234
Philipp Brothers, 184, 365
Pike, Douglas, 423, 423n; L. on, 423
Planned Parenthood, 7, 50, 166, 166n, 301–302. *See* population control
Playboy magazine, 127, 165
Plumb Plan, 183
Poats, Rutherford M., 437, 449
Population control, 1–2, 54–55, 220, 333, 479
Population Council, 233
Porter, William G., 390–392, 396, 419
Posen, Felix, 365
Pratt Institute, 303
La Prensa, 294
Presbyterian Hospital, Harkness Pavilion, 67–68, 69
Princeton (N.J.), 273, 304, 504
Princeton Press, 35
Princeton University, 81, 219, 245, 329; L. papers and *Journals* given to, 275–276; Woodrow Wilson School, 171; Princeton Fellows in Public Affairs, 5; Rockefeller Public Service Awards, 161–162
Prud'homme, Hector, 26
Pryce-Jones, Alan, 46
Puerto Rico, 310–311, 332, 362–364
Punta del Este, 426–427, 437

Quartey, E. K., 258–259
Quill, Michael, 182, 183, 184

Rabi, Isidor, 189, 401
Racial issues, 54, 55–56, 57–58, 60, 155, 471, 482–483
Radio Corporation of America (RCA), 185
Ramey, James, 481
Ramparts magazine, 235, 265
Rand Corporation, 280, 517
Randal, Jon, 393, 399
Randolph, A. Philip, 320
Rankin, John, 410
Rao, K. L., 100, 102–103, 105, 107, 108, 109
Rao, V. K. R. V., 103–104
Rau, Lady Rama, 7
Reagan, Ronald, 309, 335
Regional Plan Association, 254

Republic of the Ivory Coast, 78, 126, 426; and AID, 70, 71, 77, 82
Republican Convention (1964), 53–54
Reston, James, 329
Revelle, Roger, 93
Richberg, Donald R., 183, 183n, 320
Rickover, Hyman G., 276
Ridgway, Matthew, 206, 212
Ripman, Hugh, 236
Road to Change, 86, 86n, 259
Robert R. Nathan Associates, 95, 191
Robinson, H. M., 362–363
Rockefeller, Blanchette, 178
Rockefeller, John D., 3rd, 178, 220, 233, 479
Rockefeller, Nelson, 53, 309
Rockefeller Foundation, 178, 220, 233, 419
Rockefeller Public Service Awards, 160–161, 177
Rogers, Harold, 158
Rojas Pinilla, Gustavo, 238, 242, 288
Rome, 98–99
Romney, George, 309, 435
Roosevelt, Eleanor, 187, 485
Roosevelt, Franklin Delano Sr., 187, 295, 325
Roosevelt, Franklin D., Jr., 25
Roosevelt, Theodore, 325
Rossi, Renato, 98
Rostow, Walter, 46, 194–195, 269, 282–284, 328. *See* Gaum Conference
Rouhani, H. E. Mansur, 53, 92, 115, 116, 119, 126, 325–326; at TVA, 430; and World Bank, 456–457
Rovere, Richard, 503
Rubel, John, 159, 293
Rusk, Dean, 20, 212, 226, 250–251, 252, 459, 493, 520; on Vietnam, 353–354, 498; on Middle East, 486–487. *See* Gaum Conference
Russell, Richard Brevard, 49
Russia, 173, 175, 348; spaceship, 65. *See* Middle East, oil
Ryan, William Fitts, 216

Sachs, Daniel, 169–170
St. Lawrence, Anne, 370
St. Lawrence, Lee, 130–131, 366, 370–371
St. Vincent, British West Indies, L. trip to, *1966*, 196–204, 198–199, 198n, 199–200. *See* Young Island, John Houser
Salisbury, Harrison E., 359
Saller, Raphael, 70, 71, 120
Samii, Mehdi, 29, 36, 298, 439, 453, 531
Samper, Armando, 239
Samuels, Ernest, 87
Sanchez, Roberto, 310
Sandburg, Carl, 474
Sarnoff, David, 59, 185, 492–493, 529
Sato, Eisaku, 524
Schaaf, Hart, 366–367, 509
Schlesinger, Arthur, Jr., 176, 195–196, 259, 260, 368, 401
Schoenbrun, David, 251–252
Schreiner, Olive, 146
Seaborg, Glenn T., 325, 482
Sealy, George, 261
Seconds, 296, 301
Seeger, Pete, 62–63
Sen, Dr. Binay Ranjan, 301
Sevareid, Eric, 409, 474
Seymour, Walton, 18, 236, 260, 261, 276; and coal, 94, 191, 231; and Latin America, 179, 230, 277, 290, 291, 333, 342–343; and Vietnam, 319, 337, 355, 356, 501, 502; interim report, 443
Shahn, Ben, 62
Shahmirzadi, Hassan, 261
Sharp, Malcolm, 369
Shepard, Stephen, 467–468
Sheridan, Roger, 272
Sholes, Aline Szold (cousin), 309
Sholes, Max, 309
Shriner Convention, 54
Skrubb, George, 502
Slocum, Josiah, 152
Smith, Frank, 221
Smith, Jeremiah, 369
Smyth, Henry de Wolfe, 37, 325
Smyth, Mary, 325
Socony Mobil, 19
SOFINA (Société Financière de Transports et d'Enterprises Industrielles), 83
Somaliland, 200
Southeast Asia, *see* Asia, Southeast
Southern California Edison, 134
Spain, 138
Sparkman, John, 49, 410
Spence, Derick, 1
Spence, Kitty, 1
Spencer, Frank, 250
Spitzer, Lyman, 7
Spivack, Robert, 225
Sporn, Philip, 97, 138–139
Stafford Little Lectures, 429
Stanford Research Institute, 280
Stanton, Frank, 59, 329
Steelman, John, 216
Stern, Isaac, 224, 226

Stevens, Georgiana, 477
Stevenson, Adlai, 60, 150, 187, 205, 275; death, 149
Stevenson, Eleanor, 494
Stevenson, William E., 494
Stever, Guyford, 309
Stimson, Henry, 251
Stock Market, 136–137
Stone & Webster, 18
Straus, Donald B., 50, 54–55, 148, 168
Straus, Anna Lord, 162, 162n
Strauss, Lewis L., 476, 477, 481, 488
Subramaniam, Chidambara, 102, 103, 106, 108, 109
Sukarno, 425
Sulzberger, Arthur Hays, 357, 358
Sulzberger, Arthur Ochs, 357, 358
Sulzberger, Cyrus, 208, 470
Sulzberger, Iphigene, 357, 358, 465
Suppes, Patrick, 315
Sweeney, John, 25, 25n
Swidler, Joseph, 155, 191, 192
Symington, Stuart, 225
Syracuse University, Maxwell School of Citizenship, 135
Szold, Bernard (cousin), 309
Szold, James Harold (cousin), 84, 84n, 493

Taft, Robert, 90
Tahiti, L. trip to, 1967, 534–536
Tate, Wood, 503
Taylor, Maxwell D., 399
Taylor, Prince A., 229
Teller, Edward, 22, 428
Tennessee, 410
Tennessee Gas Transmission, 84
Tennessee Valley Authority (TVA), 25, 72, 180, 222, 258, 276, 300, 335; purpose of, 19, 19n; principles of, 131, 149; method of work, 72, 74, 149, 367; flexibility of, 10; reputation of, 72, 75, 195, 254, 275, 465; citation by American Institute of Planners, 499
Thacker, Maneklal Sankalchand, 106, 108
Thai, Vu Van, 295, 349–350, 435–437
Thailand, L. trip to, 1967, 365–374; Bangkok, 368, 369, 369n; Smudsakorn, 372; and AID, 373
Thieu, Nguyen Van, 506–507, 511, 514, 515, 518, 519. *See* Guam Conference
This I Do Believe, 399
Thomas, Evan, 328
Thomas, Frank, 426, 497, 498
Thoreau, Henry David (quoted), 61
Thornton, Tex, 159
Thuan, Truong Van, 389
Thuc, Vu Quoc, 375, 376, 379, 385, 390, 398, 508–509, 510, 523; and joint report, 506, 514; presentation of report to Vietnamese officials, 515, 517, 518, 519. *See* Guam Conference, Vietnam: Joint Reconstruction Program for Economic Development
Time magazine, 98
Tobey, Barney, 122, 222, 448
Tobey, Beatrice (cousin), 24, 122–123, 164, 215, 295, 448; on L., 314
Tobey, David (cousin), 122, 158, 184
Tobey, Nancy (cousin), 123, 158
Tolstoi, Leo (quoted), 490, 490n
Ton, Truong Thai, 376, 386, 514, 516
Tongvivat, Surang, 372
Tonkin Gulf Resolution, 495
The Tour, 401
Trinh, Ton That, 521
Truman, Harry S., 63–64, 126, 206, 209, 351, 352, 532; on L., 64, 216
Truong, Nguyen, 512, 513
Tuchman, Barbara, 449
Tugwell, Rexford G., 267, 363
Turkey, 206, 501
Turner, Howard, 196
TVA: Democracy On the March, 19n, 25n, 87, 258, 306, 348, 499
Twentieth Century Fund, 34, 176, 310–311

Udall, Stewart L., 459, 487, 488
Udin, Ann, 63
Ulam, Stanislaw, 22
Unger, Leonard, 349–350
United Arab Republic, *see* Middle East
United Nations, 2; FAO, 44, 95, 114, 236, 301–302. *See* Mekong Basin: Coordinating Committee
United States of America, L., on, 345; Space Agency, 9; Information Service, 59; antiballistic missiles, 172, 172n, 174; Disarmament Agency, 255–256, 299–300; *see* atomic energy, CIA
Universities, 265–266, 268–269, 305, 462–463
University of California, 81, 190
University of California, Los Angeles, 34, 42, 44
University of Illinois, 459–460
University of Kansas, 65
University of Michigan, 305
University of Texas, 171

U Nyun, 370
Utah Construction and Mining Company, 3, 4, 18, 83, 232, 261
Uribe, Rodrigo, 239–240

Vahidi, Iraj, 272, 450, 456
Valenti, Jack, 47, 223
Vandenberg, Arthur, 133
Van Doren, Irita, 71–72
Van Lare, William, 300
Vass, Lawrence, 523, 524
Vaughn, Jack, 165, 235, 274
Venezuela, L. trip to, *1966*, 289–291. *See* Latin America, Inter-American Development Bank
Vien, Nguyen Luu, 389
Vietnam, 2, 48; L. trips to, *1967*, 374–398; 506–523 (*see* Guam Conference, Japan, Southeast Asia, President Johnson, Fulbright, Clifford, Rusk, Collingwood, Porter); *situation in*: 354, 374, 506, 510; refugee problem, 515, 516; *political situation*: 349, 479–480, 494; Ky on, 403; L. on, 424–425, 429–430; Thai on, 436; Saigon, 330, 376–377, 381, 382, 506, 514, 515, 523; Dalat, 512, 513; Cam Ranh Bay, 280, 385, 386; *Mekong Delta Basin*: 508–509 (*see* Mekong Basin), agriculture, 501–502, 507, 513; labor, 384, 407; labor unions, 380, 382; businessmen, 382; economy, 510, 511; L. on interdependence of North and South Vietnam, 422, 507; pacification program, 386, 391, 412, 441, Komer and MacDonald on, 437; U.S. military position, 390–391; progress of war, 141–142, 350, 391–392, 403, 461, 478, 508, L. on, 481; Viet Cong, 349, 350, 391, 521, Thuc on, 522; feeling in U.S. about war, 180, 205, 245, 266, 448, 475, 478, 489, 495, 498, 503, 518, 525; American press corp in Vietnam, 392, 393, 444; U.S. civilian personnel, 373, 385, 492; *Joint Reconstruction Program for Economic Development*: U.S. plans, 283–284, 318; U.S. assumptions, 355–356; L. on, 356; issues at stake, 212, 364 (*see* Southeast Asia); L. asked by President Johnson to go to Vietnam on fact-finding trip, 280–281; L. on, 282–283, 285–286, 295–296, 301 (*see* Manila Conference); L. accepts assignment for D&R, 319; *comments on*: Meyer, 299; Ky, 323; announcement of L.'s assignment, 325, 327, 328, 329; Aid-D&R contract, 337; L. on his involvement, 284, 319, 323–324, 337, 350–351, 371, 432–433, 471; role of D&R, 283–286, 350, 354, 356–357, 399–400, 489; role of L., 359, 391; importance of, 351, 352, 397, 507; staffing, 464, 473; D&R work, 350, 359, 424; interim report to AID, 443, 444; President Johnson asks L. to head U.S. group, 403; Ky on, 379; Thuc on, 375–376; Vietnamese in group, 376, 446, 482, 509–510, 522, 529; problems, 376; *Joint Report*: content of, 489, 510–511; presented to Ton, 515–516; to Loc, 516–517; to Thieu, 518; to Ky, 520; to President Johnson, 526, 527–529; Cooper on, 516; L. on, 519, 529; press on, 520–521; North Vietnam radio on, 521, 522
Vineyard Gazette, 467, 489
Vision, 214
Volpe, Joseph, Jr., 216, 233, 237
Voorduin, William L., 120

Wagner, Aubrey J., 221, 222, 258
Wallace, George, 54
Wallace, Henry, 171
Warne, William, 335, 336, 361, 477, 488
Warren, Earl, 205
Washington, D.C., 10, 274, 475
Washington Post (D.C.), 41, 226, 294
Washington University, 51–52
Water, *see* India, Iran, Jordan Valley Development. *See also* atomic energy: desalination plants, Indus Basin, Mekong Delta, Middle East
Waterston, Albert, 242
Watson, Edwin M., 402
Watson, James, 234
Watson, Thomas J., Jr., 303
Watson, Thomas J., Sr., 303
Watson, William M., 402
Webb, James E., 8
Webster, Bethuel M., 145–146
Wehrle, Roy, 482, 501
Weinberg, Alvin, 481
Weizmann, Chaim, 465n
Wells, Herman, 81, 142, 218, 265, 408
Westmoreland, William C., 393–395, 398, 433, 475: *See also* Guam Conference
Wheeler, Janette, 253
Wheeler, John A., 253
Wheeler, Raymond A., 367, 367n
White, J. G., 95
White, Theodore, 424

Whitney, J. H., 426
Whitney Museum, 295
Wiesner, Jerome, 59, 173
Wigner, Eugene Paul, 428
Wilkins, Roy, 176
Williams, Mennen, 482
Willkie, Wendell L., 71–72, 305, 306
Wilson, Woodrow, 295
Wirtz, Willard, 301
Wood, John, 509
Woods, George, 209–210, 233, 237, 244, 257
World Bank, 189, 209, 216, 236, 237; Aldewereld on, 237. *See* Colombia, Iran, Pakistan
Wylie, Alexander, 123
Wyzanski, Charles, 21

Yarmolinsky, Adam, 266
Ylvisaker, Paul, 495
Yntema, Theodore, 153
Young Island, 196, 197, 198, 200, 201
Young people, 35, 64–65, 81, 127, 213, 215, 315, 504

Zinn, Walter, 272
Zorthian, Barry, 518